D1357197

EX LIBRIS

educated

TARA WESTOVER

HUTCHINSON
LONDON

Leabharlanna Poibli Chathair Bhaile Átha Cliath·
Dublin City Public Libraries

5 7 9 10 8 6

Hutchinson
20 Vauxhall Bridge Road
London SW1V 2SA

Hutchinson is part of the Penguin Random House group of companies
whose addresses can be found at global.penguinrandomhouse.com

Penguin
Random House
UK

Copyright © Tara Westover 2018

Tara Westover has asserted her right under the
Copyright, Designs and Patents Act, 1988,
to be identified as the author of this work.

This book is a work of non-fiction based on the experiences and recollections
of the author. In some cases the names of people and other identifying details
have been changed to protect the privacy of others. The author has stated to
the publishers that, except in such minor respects, not affecting the substantial
accuracy of the work, the contents of this book are true.

First published in the USA by Random House in 2018
First published in the United Kingdom by Hutchinson in 2018

www.penguin.co.uk

A CIP catalogue record for this book is available from the British Library.

ISBN 9781786330512 (hardback)
ISBN 9781786330529 (trade paperback)

Typeset in 10.5/14.5 pt Sabon LT Std by Jouve (UK), Milton Keynes
Printed and bound in Great Britain by Clays Ltd, St Ives plc

Penguin Random House is committed to a sustainable future for our
business, our readers and our planet. This book is made from Forest
Stewardship Council® certified paper.

For Tyler

The past is beautiful because one never realises an emotion at the time. It expands later, & thus we don't have complete emotions about the present, only about the past.

—Virginia Woolf

I believe finally that education must be conceived as a continuing reconstruction of experience; that the process and the goal of education are one and the same thing.

— John Dewey

Contents

Author's Note   xi

Prologue   1

PART ONE

Choose The Good   7

The Midwife   18

Cream Shoes   30

Apache Women   39

Honest Dirt   50

Shield and Buckler   65

The Lord Will Provide   80

Tiny Harlots   90

Perfect in His Generations   99

Shield of Feathers   108

Instinct   115

Fish Eyes   122

Silence in the Churches   131

My Feet No Longer Touch Earth   142

No More a Child   154

Disloyal Man, Disobedient Heaven   166

PART TWO

To Keep It Holy   179

Blood and Feathers   187

In the Beginning   195

Recitals of the Fathers   203

Skullcap   212

What We Whispered and What We Screamed   217

I'm from Idaho   230

A Knight, Errant   240

The Work of Sulphur   250

Waiting for Moving Water   258

If I Were a Woman   263

Pygmalion   271

Graduation   282

PART THREE

Hand of the Almighty   295

Tragedy Then Farce   306

A Brawling Woman in a Wide House   316

Sorcery of Physics   322

The Substance of Things   328

West of the Sun   335

Four Long Arms, Whirling   342

Gambling for Redemption   352

Family   361

Watching the Buffalo   367

Educated   375

Acknowledgments   379

Author's Note

This story is not about Mormonism. Neither is it about any other form of religious belief. In it there are many types of people, some believers, some not; some kind, some not. The author disputes any correlation, positive or negative, between the two.

The following names, listed in alphabetical order, are pseudonyms: Aaron, Audrey, Benjamin, Emily, Erin, Faye, Gene, Jessica, Judy, Robert, Robin, Sadie, Shannon, Shawn, Susan, Vanessa.

Prologue

I'm standing on the red railway car that sits abandoned next to the barn. The wind soars, whipping my hair across my face and pushing a chill down the open neck of my shirt. The gales are strong this close to the mountain, as if the peak itself is exhaling. Down below, the valley is peaceful, undisturbed. Meanwhile our farm dances: the heavy conifer trees sway slowly, while the sagebrush and thistles quiver, bowing before every puff and pocket of air. Behind me a gentle hill slopes upward and stitches itself to the mountain base. If I look up, I can see the dark form of the Indian Princess.

The hill is paved with wild wheat. If the conifers and sagebrush are soloists, the wheat field is a corps de ballet, each stem following all the rest in bursts of movement, a million ballerinas bending, one after the other, as great gales dent their golden heads. The shape of that dent lasts only a moment, and is as close as anyone gets to seeing wind.

Turning toward our house on the hillside, I see movements of a different kind, tall shadows stiffly pushing through the currents. My brothers are awake, testing the weather. I imagine my mother at the stove, hovering over bran pancakes. I picture my father hunched by the back door, lacing his steel-toed boots and threading his callused hands into welding gloves. On the highway below, the school bus rolls past without stopping.

I am only seven, but I understand that it is this fact, more than any other, that makes my family different: we don't go to school.

Dad worries that the Government will force us to go but it can't, because it doesn't know about us. Four of my parents' seven children don't have birth certificates. We have no medical records because we were born at home and have never seen a doctor or nurse.[1] We have no school records because we've never set foot in a classroom. When I am nine, I will be issued a Delayed Certificate of Birth, but at this moment, according to the state of Idaho and the federal government, I do not exist.

Of course I *did* exist. I had grown up preparing for the Days of Abomination, watching for the sun to darken, for the moon to drip as if with blood. I spent my summers bottling peaches and my winters rotating supplies. When the World of Men failed, my family would continue on, unaffected.

I had been educated in the rhythms of the mountain, rhythms in which change was never fundamental, only cyclical. The same sun appeared each morning, swept over the valley and dropped behind the peak. The snows that fell in winter always melted in the spring. Our lives were a cycle—the cycle of the day, the cycle of the seasons—circles of perpetual change that, when complete, meant nothing had changed at all. I believed my family was a part of this immortal pattern, that we were, in some sense, eternal. But eternity belonged only to the mountain.

There's a story my father used to tell about the peak. She was a grand old thing, a cathedral of a mountain. The range had other mountains, taller, more imposing, but Buck's Peak was the most finely crafted. Its base spanned a mile, its dark form swelling out of the earth and rising into a flawless spire. From a distance, you could see the impression of a woman's body on the mountain face: her legs formed of huge ravines, her hair a spray of pines fanning over the northern ridge. Her stance was commanding, one leg thrust forward in a powerful movement, more stride than step.

My father called her the Indian Princess. She emerged each year when the snows began to melt, facing south, watching the buffalo return to the valley. Dad said the nomadic Indians had watched for her appearance as a sign of spring, a signal the mountain was thawing, winter was over, and it was time to come home.

All my father's stories were about our mountain, our valley, our jagged little patch of Idaho. He never told me what to do if I left the mountain, if I crossed oceans and continents and found myself in strange terrain, where I could no longer search the horizon for the Princess. He never told me how I'd know when it was time to come home.

PART ONE

PART ONE

I

Choose the Good

My strongest memory is not a memory. It's something I imagined, then came to remember as if it had happened. The memory was formed when I was five, just before I turned six, from a story my father told in such detail that I and my brothers and sister had each conjured our own cinematic version, with gunfire and shouts. Mine had crickets. That's the sound I hear as my family huddles in the kitchen, lights off, hiding from the Feds who've surrounded the house. A woman reaches for a glass of water and her silhouette is lighted by the moon. A shot echoes like the lash of a whip and she falls. In my memory it's always Mother who falls, and she has a baby in her arms.

The baby doesn't make sense—I'm the youngest of my mother's seven children—but like I said, none of this happened.

A year after my father told us that story, we gathered one evening to hear him read aloud from Isaiah, a prophecy about Immanuel. He sat on our mustard-colored sofa, a large Bible open in his lap. Mother was next to him. The rest of us were strewn across the shaggy brown carpet.

"Butter and honey shall he eat," Dad droned, low and

7

monotone, weary from a long day hauling scrap. "That he may know to refuse the evil, and choose the good."

There was a heavy pause. We sat quietly.

My father was not a tall man but he was able to command a room. He had a presence about him, the solemnity of an oracle. His hands were thick and leathery—the hands of a man who'd been hard at work all his life—and they grasped the Bible firmly.

He read the passage aloud a second time, then a third, then a fourth. With each repetition the pitch of his voice climbed higher. His eyes, which moments before had been swollen with fatigue, were now wide and alert. There was a divine doctrine here, he said. He would inquire of the Lord.

The next morning Dad purged our fridge of milk, yogurt and cheese, and that evening when he came home, his truck was loaded with fifty gallons of honey.

"Isaiah doesn't say which is evil, butter or honey," Dad said, grinning as my brothers lugged the white tubs to the basement. "But if you ask, the Lord will tell you!"

When Dad read the verse to his mother, she laughed in his face. "I got some pennies in my purse," she said. "You better take them. They'll be all the sense you got."

Grandma had a thin, angular face and an endless store of faux Indian jewelry, all silver and turquoise, which hung in clumps from her spindly neck and fingers. Because she lived down the hill from us, near the highway, we called her Grandma-down-the-hill. This was to distinguish her from our mother's mother, who we called Grandma-over-in-town because she lived fifteen miles south, in the only town in the county, which had a single stoplight and a grocery store.

Dad and his mother got along like two cats with their tails tied together. They could talk for a week and not agree about anything, but they were tethered by their devotion to the mountain. My father's family had been living at the base of

8

Buck's Peak for half a century. Grandma's daughters had married and moved away, but my father stayed, building a shabby yellow house, which he would never quite finish, just up the hill from his mother's, at the base of the mountain, and plunking a junkyard—one of several—next to her manicured lawn.

They argued daily, about the mess from the junkyard but more often about us kids. Grandma thought we should be in school and not, as she put it, "roaming the mountain like savages." Dad said public school was a ploy by the Government to lead children away from God. "I may as well surrender my kids to the devil himself," he said, "as send them down the road to that school."

God told Dad to share the revelation with the people who lived and farmed in the shadow of Buck's Peak. On Sundays, nearly everyone gathered at the church, a hickory-colored chapel just off the highway with the small, restrained steeple common to Mormon churches. Dad cornered fathers as they left their pews. He started with his cousin Jim, who listened good-naturedly while Dad waved his Bible and explained the sinfulness of milk. Jim grinned, then clapped Dad on the shoulder and said no righteous God would deprive a man of homemade strawberry ice cream on a hot summer afternoon. Jim's wife tugged on his arm. As he slid past us I caught a whiff of manure. Then I remembered: the big dairy farm a mile north of Buck's Peak, that was Jim's.

After Dad took up preaching against milk, Grandma jammed her fridge full of it. She and Grandpa only drank skim but pretty soon it was all there—two percent, whole, even chocolate. She seemed to believe this was an important line to hold.

Breakfast became a test of loyalty. Every morning, my family sat around a large table of reworked red oak and ate either seven-grain cereal, with honey and molasses, or seven-grain pancakes, also with honey and molasses. Because there were nine of us, the pancakes were never cooked all the way through. I didn't mind the cereal if I could soak it in milk, letting the cream gather up the grist and seep into the pellets, but since the revelation we'd been having it with water. It was like eating a bowl of mud.

It wasn't long before I began to think of all that milk spoiling in Grandma's fridge. Then I got into the habit of skipping breakfast each morning and going straight to the barn. I'd slop the pigs and fill the trough for the cows and horses, then I'd hop over the corral fence, loop around the barn and step through Grandma's side door.

On one such morning, as I sat at the counter watching Grandma pour a bowl of cornflakes, she said, "How would you like to go to school?"

"I wouldn't like it," I said.

"How do you know," she barked. "You ain't never tried it."

She poured the milk and handed me the bowl, then she perched at the bar, directly across from me, and watched as I shoveled spoonfuls into my mouth.

"We're leaving tomorrow for Arizona," she told me, but I already knew. She and Grandpa always went to Arizona when the weather began to turn. Grandpa said he was too old for Idaho winters; the cold put an ache in his bones. "Get yourself up real early," Grandma said, "around five, and we'll take you with us. Put you in school."

I shifted on my stool. I tried to imagine school but couldn't. Instead I pictured Sunday school, which I attended each week and which I hated. A boy named Aaron had told all the girls that I couldn't read because I didn't go to school, and now none of them would talk to me.

"Dad said I can go?" I said.

"No," Grandma said. "But we'll be long gone by the time he realizes you're missing." She set my bowl in the sink and gazed out the window.

Grandma was a force of nature—impatient, aggressive, self-possessed. To look at her was to take a step back. She dyed her hair black and this intensified her already severe features, especially her eyebrows, which she smeared on each morning in thick, inky arches. She drew them too large and this made her face seem stretched. They were also drawn too high and draped the rest of her features into an expression of boredom, almost sarcasm.

"You should be in school," she said.

"Won't Dad just make you bring me back?" I said.

"Your dad can't make me do a damned thing." Grandma stood, squaring herself. "If he wants you, he'll have to come get you." She hesitated, and for a moment looked ashamed. "I talked to him yesterday. He won't be able to fetch you back for a long while. He's behind on that shed he's building in town. He can't pack up and drive to Arizona, not while the weather holds and he and the boys can work long days."

Grandma's scheme was well plotted. Dad always worked from sunup until sundown in the weeks before the first snow, trying to stockpile enough money from hauling scrap and building barns to outlast the winter, when jobs were scarce. Even if his mother ran off with his youngest child, he wouldn't be able to stop working, not until the forklift was encased in ice.

"I'll need to feed the animals before we go," I said. "He'll notice I'm gone for sure if the cows break through the fence looking for water."

I didn't sleep that night. I sat on the kitchen floor and watched the hours tick by. One A.M. Two. Three.

At four I stood and put my boots by the back door. They were caked in manure, and I was sure Grandma wouldn't let them into her car. I pictured them on her porch, abandoned, while I ran off shoeless to Arizona.

I imagined what would happen when my family discovered

I was missing. My brother Richard and I often spent whole days on the mountain, so it was likely no one would notice until sundown, when Richard came home for dinner and I didn't. I pictured my brothers pushing out the door to search for me. They'd try the junkyard first, hefting iron slabs in case some stray sheet of metal had shifted and pinned me. Then they'd move outward, sweeping the farm, crawling up trees and into the barn attic. Finally, they'd turn to the mountain.

It would be past dusk by then—that moment just before night sets in, when the landscape is visible only as darkness and lighter darkness, and you feel the world around you more than you see it. I imagined my brothers spreading over the mountain, searching the black forests. No one would talk; everyone's thoughts would be the same. Things could go horribly wrong on the mountain. Cliffs appeared suddenly. Feral horses, belonging to my grandfather, ran wild over thick banks of water hemlock, and there were more than a few rattlesnakes. We'd done this search before when a calf went missing from the barn. In the valley you'd find an injured animal; on the mountain, a dead one.

I imagined Mother standing by the back door, her eyes sweeping the dark ridge, when my father came home to tell her they hadn't found me. My sister, Audrey, would suggest that someone ask Grandma, and Mother would say Grandma had left that morning for Arizona. Those words would hang in the air for a moment, then everyone would know where I'd gone. I imagined my father's face, his dark eyes shrinking, his mouth clamping into a frown as he turned to my mother. "You think she chose to go?"

Low and sorrowful, his voice echoed. Then it was drowned out by sounds from another conjured remembrance—crickets, then gunfire, then silence.

The event was a famous one, I would later learn—like Wounded Knee or Waco—but when my father first told us the story, it felt like no one in the world knew about it except us.

It began near the end of canning season, which other kids probably called "summer." My family always spent the warm months bottling fruit for storage, which Dad said we'd need in the Days of Abomination. One evening, Dad was uneasy when he came in from the junkyard. He paced the kitchen during dinner, hardly touching a bite. We had to get everything in order, he said. There was little time.

We spent the next day boiling and skinning peaches. By sundown we'd filled dozens of Mason jars, which were set out in perfect rows, still warm from the pressure cooker. Dad surveyed our work, counting the jars and muttering to himself, then he turned to Mother and said, "It's not enough."

That night Dad called a family meeting, and we gathered around the kitchen table, because it was wide and long, and could seat all of us. We had a right to know what we were up against, he said. He was standing at the head of the table; the rest of us perched on benches, studying the thick planks of red oak.

"There's a family not far from here," Dad said. "They're freedom fighters. They wouldn't let the Government brainwash their kids in them public schools, so the Feds came after them." Dad exhaled, long and slow. "The Feds surrounded the family's cabin, kept them locked in there for weeks, and when a hungry child, a little boy, snuck out to go hunting, the Feds shot him dead."

I scanned my brothers. I'd never seen fear on Luke's face before.

"They're still in the cabin," Dad said. "They keep the lights off, and they crawl on the floor, away from the doors and windows. I don't know how much food they got. Might be they'll starve before the Feds give up."

No one spoke. Eventually Luke, who was twelve, asked if

we could help. "No," Dad said. "Nobody can. They're trapped in their own home. But they got their guns, you can bet that's why the Feds ain't charged in." He paused to sit, folding himself onto the low bench in slow, stiff movements. He looked old to my eyes, worn out. "We can't help them, but we can help ourselves. When the Feds come to Buck's Peak, we'll be ready."

That night, Dad dragged a pile of old army bags up from the basement. He said they were our "head for the hills" bags. We spent that night packing them with supplies—herbal medicines, water purifiers, flint and steel. Dad had bought several boxes of military MREs—Meals Ready-to-Eat—and we put as many as we could fit into our packs, imagining the moment when, having fled the house and hiding ourselves in the wild plum trees near the creek, we'd eat them. Some of my brothers stowed guns in their packs but I had only a small knife, and even so my pack was as big as me by the time we'd finished. I asked Luke to hoist it onto a shelf in my closet, but Dad told me to keep it low, where I could fetch it quick, so I slept with it in my bed.

I practiced slipping the bag onto my back and running with it—I didn't want to be left behind. I imagined our escape, a midnight flight to the safety of the Princess. The mountain, I understood, was our ally. To those who knew her she could be kind, but to intruders she was pure treachery, and this would give us an advantage. Then again, if we were going to take cover on the mountain when the Feds came, I didn't understand why we were canning all these peaches. We couldn't haul a thousand heavy Mason jars up the peak. Or did we need the peaches so we could bunker down in the house, like the Weavers, and fight it out?

Fighting it out seemed likely, especially a few days later when Dad came home with more than a dozen military-surplus rifles, mostly SKSs, their thin silver bayonets folded neatly under their barrels. The guns arrived in narrow tin boxes and were packed in Cosmoline, a brownish substance the consistency of lard that had to be stripped away. After they'd been cleaned, my brother Tyler chose one and set it on a sheet of black plastic, which he folded over the rifle, sealing it with yards of silvery duct tape. Hoisting the bundle onto his shoulder, he carried it down the hill and dropped it next to the red railroad car. Then he began to dig. When the hole was wide and deep, he dropped the rifle into it, and I watched him cover it with dirt, his muscles swelling from the exertion, his jaw clenched.

Soon after, Dad bought a machine to manufacture bullets from spent cartridges. Now we could last longer in a stand-off, he said. I thought of my "head for the hills" bag, waiting in my bed, and of the rifle hidden near the railcar, and began to worry about the bullet-making machine. It was bulky and bolted to an iron workstation in the basement. If we were taken by surprise, I figured we wouldn't have time to fetch it. I wondered if we should bury it, too, with the rifle.

We kept on bottling peaches. I don't remember how many days passed or how many jars we'd added to our stores before Dad told us more of the story.

"Randy Weaver's been shot," Dad said, his voice thin and erratic. "He left the cabin to fetch his son's body, and the Feds shot him." I'd never seen my father cry, but now tears were dripping in a steady stream from his nose. He didn't wipe them, just let them spill onto his shirt. "His wife heard the shot and ran to the window, holding their baby. Then came the second shot."

Mother was sitting with her arms folded, one hand across her chest, the other clamped over her mouth. I stared at our speckled linoleum while Dad told us how the baby had been lifted from its mother's arms, its face smeared with her blood.

Until that moment, some part of me had *wanted* the Feds

15

to come, had craved the adventure. Now I felt real fear. I pictured my brothers crouching in the dark, their sweaty hands slipping down their rifles. I pictured Mother, tired and parched, drawing back away from the window. I pictured myself lying flat on the floor, still and silent, listening to the sharp chirp of crickets in the field. Then I saw Mother stand and reach for the kitchen tap. A white flash, the roar of gunfire, and she fell. I leapt to catch the baby.

Dad never told us the end of the story. We didn't have a TV or radio, so perhaps he never learned how it ended himself. The last thing I remember him saying about it was, "Next time, it could be us."

Those words would stay with me. I would hear their echo in the chirp of crickets, in the squish of peaches dropping into a glass jar, in the metallic *chink* of an SKS being cleaned. I would hear them every morning when I passed the railroad car and paused over the chickweed and bull thistle growing where Tyler had buried the rifle. Long after Dad had forgotten about the revelation in Isaiah, and Mother was again hefting plastic jugs of "Western Family 2%" into the fridge, I would remember the Weavers.

It was almost five a.m.

I returned to my room, my head full of crickets and gunfire. In the lower bunk, Audrey was snoring, a low, contented hum that invited me to do the same. Instead I climbed up to my bed, crossed my legs and looked out the window. Five passed. Then six. At seven, Grandma appeared and I watched her pace up and down her patio, turning every few moments to gaze up the hill at our house. Then she and Grandpa stepped into their car and pulled onto the highway.

When the car was gone, I got out of bed and ate a bowl of bran with water. Outside I was greeted by Luke's goat, Kamikaze, who nibbled my shirt as I walked to the barn. I passed the go-kart Richard was building from an old lawn mower. I slopped the pigs, filled the trough and moved Grandpa's horses to a new pasture.

After I'd finished I climbed the railway car and looked out over the valley. It was easy to pretend the car was moving, speeding away, that any moment the valley might disappear behind me. I'd spent hours playing that fantasy through in my head but today the reel wouldn't take. I turned west, away from the fields, and faced the peak.

The Princess was always brightest in spring, just after the conifers emerged from the snow, their deep green needles seeming almost black against the tawny browns of soil and bark. It was autumn now. I could still see her but she was fading: the reds and yellows of a dying summer obscured her dark form. Soon it would snow. In the valley that first snow would melt but on the mountain it would linger, burying the Princess until spring, when she would reappear, watchful.

2

The Midwife

"Do you have calendula?" the midwife said. "I also need lobelia and witch hazel."

She was sitting at the kitchen counter, watching Mother rummage through our birch wood cabinets. An electric scale sat on the counter between them, and occasionally Mother would use it to weigh dried leaves. It was spring. There was a morning chill despite the bright sunlight.

"I made a fresh batch of calendula last week," Mother said. "Tara, run and fetch it."

I retrieved the tincture, and my mother packed it in a plastic grocery bag with the dried herbs. "Anything else?" Mother laughed. The pitch was high, nervous. The midwife intimidated her, and when intimidated my mother took on a weightless quality, whisking about every time the midwife made one of her slow, solid movements.

The midwife surveyed her list. "That will do."

She was a short, plump woman in her late forties, with eleven children and a russet-colored wart on her chin. She had the longest hair I'd ever seen, a cascade the color of field mice that fell to her knees when she took it out of its tight bun. Her features were heavy, her voice thick with authority. She had no license, no certificates. She was a mid-wife entirely by the power of her own say-so, which was more than enough.

Mother was to be her assistant. I remember watching them that first day, comparing them. Mother with her rose-petal skin and her hair curled into soft waves that bounced about her shoulders. Her eyelids shimmered. Mother did her makeup every morning, but if she didn't have time she'd apologize all day, as if by not doing it, she had inconvenienced everyone.

The midwife looked as though she hadn't given a thought to her appearance in a decade, and the way she carried herself made you feel foolish for having noticed.

The midwife nodded goodbye, her arms full of Mother's herbs.

The next time the midwife came she brought her daughter Maria, who stood next to her mother, imitating her movements, with a baby wedged against her wiry nine-year-old frame. I stared hopefully at her. Besides Audrey, I hadn't met many other girls like me, who didn't go to school. I edged closer, trying to draw her attention, but she was wholly absorbed in listening to her mother, who was explaining how cramp bark and motherwort should be administered to treat post-birth contractions. Maria's head bobbed in agreement; her eyes never left her mother's face.

I trudged down the hall to my room, alone, but when I turned to shut the door she was standing in it, still toting the baby on her hip. He was a meaty box of flesh, and her torso bent sharply at the waist to offset his bulk.

"Are you going?" she said.

I didn't understand the question.

"I always go," she said. "Have you seen a baby get born?"

"No."

"I have, lots of times. Do you know what it means when a baby comes breech?"

"No." I said it like an apology.

The first time Mother assisted with a birth she was gone for two days. Then she wafted through the back door, so pale she seemed translucent, and drifted to the couch, where she stayed, trembling. "It was awful," she whispered. "Even Judy said she was scared." Mother closed her eyes. "She didn't *look* scared."

Mother rested for several minutes, until she regained some color, then she told the story. The labor had been long, grueling, and when the baby finally came the mother had torn, and badly. There was blood everywhere. The hemorrhage wouldn't stop. That's when Mother realized the umbilical cord had wrapped around the baby's throat. He was purple, so still Mother thought he was dead. As Mother recounted these details, the blood drained from her face until she sat, pale as an egg, her arms wrapped around herself.

Audrey made chamomile tea and we put our mother to bed. When Dad came home that night, Mother told him the same story. "I can't do it," she said. "Judy can, but I can't." Dad put an arm on her shoulder. "This is a calling from the Lord," he said. "And sometimes the Lord asks for hard things."

Mother didn't want to be a midwife. Midwifery had been Dad's idea, one of his schemes for self-reliance. There was nothing he hated more than our being dependent on the Government. Dad said one day we would be completely off the grid. As soon as he could get the money together, he planned to build a pipeline to bring water down from the mountain, and after that he'd install solar panels all over the farm. That way we'd have water and electricity in the End of Days, when everyone else was drinking from puddles and living in darkness. Mother was an herbalist so she could tend our health, and if she learned to midwife she would be able to deliver the grandchildren when they came along.

The midwife came to visit Mother a few days after the first birth. She brought Maria, who again followed me to my room. "It's too bad your mother got a bad one her first time," she said, smiling. "The next one will be easier."

A few weeks later, this prediction was tested. It was midnight. Because we didn't have a phone, the midwife called Grandma-down-the-hill, who walked up the hill, tired and ornery, and barked that it was time for Mother to go "play doctor." She stayed only minutes but woke the whole house. "Why you people can't just go to a hospital like everyone else is beyond me," she shouted, slamming the door on her way out.

Mother retrieved her overnight bag and the tackle box she'd filled with dark bottles of tincture, then she walked slowly out the door. I was anxious and slept badly, but when Mother came home the next morning, hair deranged and dark circles under her eyes, her lips were parted in a wide smile. "It was a girl," she said. Then she went to bed and slept all day.

Months passed in this way, Mother leaving the house at all hours and coming home, trembling, relieved to her core that it was over. By the time the leaves started to fall she'd helped with a dozen births. By the end of winter, several dozen. In the spring she told my father she'd had enough, that she could deliver a baby if she had to, if it was the End of the World. Now she could stop.

Dad's face sank when she said this. He reminded her that this was God's will, that it would bless our family. "You need to be a midwife," he said. "You need to deliver a baby on your own."

Mother shook her head. "I can't," she said. "Besides, who would hire me when they could hire Judy?"

She'd jinxed herself, thrown her gauntlet before God. Soon after, Maria told me her father had a new job in Wyoming. "Mom says your mother should take over," Maria said. A thrilling image took shape in my imagination, of me in Maria's role, the midwife's daughter, confident, knowledgeable. But when I turned to look at my mother standing next to me, the image turned to vapor.

Midwifery was not illegal in the state of Idaho, but it had not yet been sanctioned. This meant that if a delivery went wrong, a midwife might face charges for practicing medicine without a license; if things went very wrong, she could face criminal charges for manslaughter, even prison time. Few women would take such a risk, so midwives were scarce: on the day Judy left for Wyoming, Mother became the only midwife for a hundred miles.

Women with swollen bellies began coming to the house and begging Mother to deliver their babies. Mother crumpled at the thought. One woman sat on the edge of our faded yellow sofa, her eyes cast downward, as she explained that her husband was out of work and they didn't have money for a hospital. Mother sat quietly, eyes focused, lips tight, her whole expression momentarily solid. Then the expression dissolved and she said, in her small voice, "I'm not a midwife, just an assistant."

The woman returned several times, perching on our sofa again and again, describing the uncomplicated births of her other children. Whenever Dad saw the woman's car from the junkyard, he'd often come into the house, quietly, through the back door, on the pretense of getting water; then he'd stand in the kitchen taking slow, silent sips, his ear bent toward the living room. Each time the woman left Dad could hardly contain his excitement, so that finally, succumbing to either the woman's desperation or to Dad's elation, or to both, Mother gave way.

The birth went smoothly. Then the woman had a friend who was also pregnant, and Mother delivered her baby as well. Then that woman had a friend. Mother took on an assistant.

Before long she was delivering so many babies that Audrey and I spent our days driving around the valley with her, watching her conduct prenatal exams and prescribe herbs. She became our teacher in a way that, because we rarely held school at home, she'd never been before. She explained every remedy and palliative. If So-and-so's blood pressure was high, she should be given hawthorn to stabilize the collagen and dilate the coronary blood vessels. If Mrs. Someone-or-other was having premature contractions, she needed a bath in ginger to increase the supply of oxygen to the uterus.

Midwifing changed my mother. She was a grown woman with seven children, but this was the first time in her life that she was, without question or caveat, the one in charge. Sometimes, in the days after a birth, I detected in her something of Judy's heavy presence, in a forceful turn of her head, or the imperious arch of an eyebrow. She stopped wearing makeup, then she stopped apologizing for not wearing it.

Mother charged about five hundred dollars for a delivery, and this was another way midwifing changed her: suddenly she had money. Dad didn't believe that women should work, but I suppose he thought it was all right for Mother to be paid for midwifing, because it undermined the Government. Also, we needed the money. Dad worked harder than any man I knew, but scrapping and building barns and hay sheds didn't bring in much, and it helped that Mother could buy groceries with the envelopes of small bills she kept in her purse. Sometimes, if we'd spent the whole day flying about the valley, delivering herbs and doing prenatal exams, Mother would use that money to take me and Audrey out to eat. Grandma-over-in-town had given me a journal, pink with a caramel-colored teddy bear on the cover, and in it I recorded the first time Mother took us to a restaurant, which I described as "real fancy with menus and everything." According to the entry, my meal came to $3.30.

Mother also used the money to improve herself as a midwife. She bought an oxygen tank in case a baby came out and couldn't breathe, and she took a suturing class so she could stitch the women who tore. Judy had always sent women to the hospital for stitches, but Mother was determined to learn. *Self-reliance,* I imagine her thinking.

With the rest of the money, Mother put in a phone line.[2] One day a white van appeared, and a handful of men in dark overalls began climbing over the utility poles by the highway. Dad burst through the back door demanding to know what the hell was going on. "I thought you *wanted* a phone," Mother said, her eyes so full of surprise they were irreproachable. She went on, talking fast. "You said there could be trouble if someone goes into labor and Grandma isn't home to take the call. I thought, He's right, we need a phone! Silly me! Did I misunderstand?"

Dad stood there for several seconds, his mouth open. Of course a midwife needs a phone, he said. Then he went back to the junkyard and that's all that was ever said about it. We hadn't had a telephone for as long as I could remember, but the next day there it was, resting in a lime-green cradle, its glossy finish looking out of place next to the murky jars of cohosh and skullcap.

Luke was fifteen when he asked Mother if he could have a birth certificate. He wanted to enroll in Driver's Ed because Tony, our oldest brother, was making good money driving rigs hauling gravel, which he could do because he had a license. Shawn and Tyler, the next oldest after Tony, had birth certificates; it was only the youngest four—Luke, Audrey, Richard and me—who didn't.

Mother began to file the paperwork. I don't know if she talked it over with Dad first. If she did, I can't explain what changed his mind—why suddenly a ten-year policy of not

24

registering with the Government ended without a struggle—but I think maybe it was that telephone. It was almost as if my father had come to accept that if he were really going to do battle with the Government, he would have to take certain risks. Mother's being a midwife would subvert the Medical Establishment, but in order to be a midwife she needed a phone. Perhaps the same logic was extended to Luke: Luke would need income to support a family, to buy supplies and prepare for the End of Days, so he needed a birth certificate. The other possibility is that Mother didn't ask Dad. Perhaps she just decided, on her own, and he accepted her decision. Perhaps even he—charismatic gale of a man that he was—was temporarily swept aside by the force of her.

Once she had begun the paperwork for Luke, Mother decided she might as well get birth certificates for all of us. It was harder than she expected. She tore the house apart looking for documents to prove we were her children. She found nothing. In my case, no one was sure when I'd been born. Mother remembered one date, Dad another, and Grandma-down-the-hill, who went to town and swore an affidavit that I was her granddaughter, gave a third date.

Mother called the church headquarters in Salt Lake City. A clerk there found a certificate from my christening, when I was a baby, and another from my baptism, which, as with all Mormon children, had occurred when I was eight. Mother requested copies. They arrived in the mail a few days later. "For Pete's sake!" Mother said when she opened the envelope. Each document gave a different birth date, and neither matched the one Grandma had put on the affidavit.

That week Mother was on the phone for hours every day. With the receiver wedged against her shoulder, the cord stretched across the kitchen, she cooked, cleaned, and strained tinctures of goldenseal and blessed thistle, while having the same conversation over and over.

"Obviously I should have registered her when she was born, but I didn't. So here we are."

Voices murmured on the other end of the line.

"I've already *told* you—*and* your subordinate, *and* your subordinate's subordinate, and *fifty* other people this week—she doesn't *have* school or medical records. She doesn't have them! They weren't lost. I can't ask for copies. They don't exist!"

"Her birthday? Let's say the twenty-seventh."

"No, I'm not sure."

"No, I don't have documentation."

"Yes, I'll hold."

The voices always put Mother on hold when she admitted that she didn't know my birthday, passing her up the line to their superiors, as if not knowing what day I was born delegitimized the entire notion of my having an identity. You can't be a person without a birthday, they seemed to say. I didn't understand why not. Until Mother decided to get my birth certificate, not knowing my birthday had never seemed strange. I knew I'd been born near the end of September, and each year I picked a day, one that didn't fall on a Sunday because it's no fun spending your birthday in church. Sometimes I wished Mother would give me the phone so I could explain. "I have a birthday, same as you," I wanted to tell the voices. "It just changes. Don't you wish you could change your birthday?"

Eventually, Mother persuaded Grandma-down-the-hill to swear a new affidavit claiming I'd been born on the twenty-seventh, even though Grandma still believed it was the twenty-ninth, and the state of Idaho issued a Delayed Certificate of Birth. I remember the day it came in the mail. It felt oddly dispossessing, being handed this first legal proof of my personhood: until that moment, it had never occurred to me that proof was required.

In the end, I got my birth certificate long before Luke got

his. When Mother had told the voices on the phone that she thought I'd been born sometime in the last week of September, they'd been silent. But when she told them she wasn't exactly sure whether Luke had been born in May or June, that set the voices positively buzzing.

That fall, when I was nine, I went with Mother on a birth. I'd been asking to go for months, reminding her that Maria had seen a dozen births by the time she was my age. "I'm not a nursing mother," she said. "I have no reason to take you. Besides, you wouldn't like it."

Eventually, Mother was hired by a woman who had several small children. It was arranged; I would tend them during the birth.

The call came in the middle of the night. The mechanical ring drilled its way down the hall, and I held my breath, hoping it wasn't a wrong number. A minute later Mother was at my bedside. "It's time," she said, and together we ran to the car.

For ten miles Mother rehearsed with me what I was to say if the worst happened and the Feds came. Under no circumstances was I to tell them that my mother was a midwife. If they asked why we were there, I was to say nothing. Mother called it "the art of shutting up." "You just keep saying you were asleep and you didn't see anything and you don't know anything and you can't remember why we're here," she said. "Don't give them any more rope to hang me with than they already have."

Mother fell into silence. I studied her as she drove. Her face was illuminated by the lights in the dashboard, and it appeared ghostly white set against the utter blackness of country roads. Fear was etched into her features, in the bunching of her forehead and the tightening of her lips. Alone with just me, she put aside the persona she displayed for others. She was her old self again, fragile, breathy.

I heard soft whispers and realized they were coming from her. She was chanting what-ifs to herself. What if something went wrong? What if there was a medical history they hadn't told her about, some complication? Or what if it was something ordinary, a common crisis, and she panicked, froze, failed to stop the hemorrhage in time? In a few minutes we would be there, and she would have two lives in her small, trembling hands. Until that moment, I'd never understood the risk she was taking. "People die in hospitals," she whispered, her fingers clenching the wheel, wraithlike. "Sometimes God calls them home, and there's nothing anyone can do. But if it happens to a midwife—" She turned, speaking directly to me. "All it takes is one mistake, and you'll be visiting me in prison."

We arrived and Mother transformed. She issued a string of commands, to the father, to the mother, and to me. I almost forgot to do what she asked, I couldn't take my eyes off her. I realize now that that night I was seeing her for the first time, the secret strength of her.

She barked orders and we moved wordlessly to follow them. The baby was born without complications. It was mythic and romantic, being an intimate witness to this turn in life's cycle, but Mother had been right, I didn't like it. It was long and exhausting, and smelled of groin sweat.

I didn't ask to go on the next birth. Mother returned home pale and shaking. Her voice quivered as she told me and my sister the story: how the unborn baby's heart rate had dropped dangerously low, to a mere tremor; how she'd called an ambulance, then decided they couldn't wait and taken the mother in her own car. She'd driven at such speed that by the time she made it to the hospital, she'd acquired a police escort. In the ER, she'd tried to give the doctors the information they needed without seeming too knowledgeable, without making them suspect that she was an unlicensed midwife.

An emergency cesarean was performed. The mother and baby remained in the hospital for several days, and by the time they were released Mother had stopped trembling. In fact, she seemed exhilarated and had begun to tell the story differently, relishing the moment she'd been pulled over by the policeman, who was surprised to find a moaning woman, obviously in labor, in the backseat. "I slipped into the scatterbrained-woman routine," she told me and Audrey, her voice growing louder, catching hold. "Men like to think they're saving some brain-dead woman who's got herself into a scrape. All I had to do was step aside and let *him* play the hero!"

The most dangerous moment for Mother had come minutes later, in the hospital, after the woman had been wheeled away. A doctor stopped Mother and asked why she'd been at the birth in the first place. She smiled at the memory. "I asked him the dumbest questions I could think of." She put on a high, coquettish voice very unlike her own. "Oh! Was that the baby's head? Aren't babies supposed to come out feet-first?" The doctor was persuaded that she couldn't possibly be a midwife.

There were no herbalists in Wyoming as good as Mother, so a few months after the incident at the hospital, Judy came to Buck's Peak to restock. The two women chatted in the kitchen, Judy perched on a barstool, Mother leaning across the counter, her head resting lazily in her hand. I took the list of herbs to the storeroom. Maria, lugging a different baby, followed. I pulled dried leaves and clouded liquids from the shelves, all the while gushing about Mother's exploits, finishing with the confrontation in the hospital. Maria had her own stories about dodging Feds, but when she began to tell one I interrupted her.

"Judy is a fine midwife," I said, my chest rising. "But when it comes to doctors and cops, *nobody* plays stupid like my mother."

3
Cream Shoes

My mother, Faye, was a mailman's daughter. She grew up in town, in a yellow house with a white picket fence lined with purple irises. Her mother was a seamstress, the best in the valley some said, so as a young woman Faye wore beautiful clothes, all perfectly tailored, from velvet jackets and polyester trousers to woolen pantsuits and gabardine dresses. She attended church and participated in school and community activities. Her life had an air of intense order, normalcy, and unassailable respectability.

That air of respectability was carefully concocted by her mother. My grandmother, LaRue, had come of age in the 1950s, in the decade of idealistic fever that burned after World War II. LaRue's father was an alcoholic in a time before the language of addiction and empathy had been invented, when alcoholics weren't called alcoholics, they were called drunks. She was from the "wrong kind" of family but embedded in a pious Mormon community that, like many communities, visited the crimes of the parents on the children. She was deemed unmarriageable by the respectable men in town. When she met and married my grandfather—a good-natured young man just out of the navy—she dedicated herself to constructing the perfect family, or at least the appearance of it. This would, she believed, shield her daughters from the social contempt that had so wounded her.

One result of this was the white picket fence and the closet of handmade clothes. Another was that her eldest daughter married a severe young man with jet-black hair and an appetite for unconventionality.

That is to say, my mother responded willfully to the respectability heaped upon her. Grandma wanted to give her daughter the gift she herself had never had, the gift of coming from a *good* family. But Faye didn't want it. My mother was not a social revolutionary—even at the peak of her rebellion she preserved her Mormon faith, with its devotion to marriage and motherhood—but the social upheavals of the 1970s did seem to have at least one effect on her: she didn't want the white picket fence and gabardine dresses.

My mother told me dozens of stories of her childhood, of Grandma fretting about her oldest daughter's social standing, about whether her piqué dress was the proper cut, or her velvet slacks the correct shade of blue. These stories nearly always ended with my father swooping in and trading out the velvet for blue jeans. One telling in particular has stayed with me. I am seven or eight and am in my room dressing for church. I have taken a damp rag to my face, hands and feet, scrubbing only the skin that will be visible. Mother watches me pass a cotton dress over my head, which I have chosen for its long sleeves so I won't have to wash my arms, and a jealousy lights her eyes.

"If you were Grandma's daughter," she says, "we'd have been up at the crack of dawn preening your hair. Then the rest of the morning would be spent agonizing over which shoes, the white or the cream, would give the right impression."

Mother's face twists into an ugly smile. She's grasping for humor but the memory is jaundiced. "Even after we finally chose the cream, we'd be late, because at the last minute

Grandma would panic and drive to Cousin Donna's to borrow *her* cream shoes, which had a lower heel."

Mother stares out the window. She has retreated into herself.

"White or cream?" I say. "Aren't they the same color?" I owned only one pair of church shoes. They were black, or at least they'd been black when they belonged to my sister.

With the dress on, I turn to the mirror and sand away the crusty dirt around my neckline, thinking how lucky Mother is to have escaped a world in which there was an important difference between white and cream, and where such questions might consume a perfectly good morning, a morning that might otherwise be spent plundering Dad's junkyard with Luke's goat.

My father, Gene, was one of those young men who somehow manage to seem both solemn and mischievous. His physical appearance was striking—ebony hair, a strict, angular face, nose like an arrow pointing toward fierce, deep-set eyes. His lips were often pressed together in a jocular grin, as if all the world were his to laugh at.

Although I passed my childhood on the same mountain that my father had passed his, slopping pigs in the same iron trough, I know very little about his boyhood. He never talked about it, so all I have to go on are hints from my mother, who told me that, in his younger years, Grandpa-down-the-hill had been violent, with a hair-trigger temper. Mother's use of the words "had been" always struck me as funny. We all knew better than to cross Grandpa. He had a short fuse, that was just fact and anybody in the valley could have told you as much. He was weatherworn inside and out, as taut and rugged as the horses he ran wild on the mountain.

Dad's mother worked for the Farm Bureau in town. As an adult, Dad would develop fierce opinions about women working, radical even for our rural Mormon community. "A woman's place is in the home," he would say every time he saw a married woman working in town. Now I'm older, I sometimes wonder if Dad's fervor had more to do with his own mother than with doctrine. I wonder if he just wished that *she* had been home, so he wouldn't have been left for all those long hours with Grandpa's temper.

Running the farm consumed Dad's childhood. I doubt he expected to go to college. Still, the way Mother tells it, back then Dad was bursting with energy, laughter and panache. He drove a baby-blue Volkswagen Beetle, wore outlandish suits cut from colorful fabrics, and showcased a thick, fashionable mustache.

They met in town. Faye was waitressing at the bowling alley one Friday night when Gene wandered in with a pack of his friends. She'd never seen him before, so she knew immediately that he wasn't from town and must have come from the mountains surrounding the valley. Farm life had made Gene different from other young men: he was serious for his age, more physically impressive and independent-minded.

There's a sense of sovereignty that comes from life on a mountain, a perception of privacy and isolation, even of dominion. In that vast space you can sail unaccompanied for hours, afloat on pine and brush and rock. It's a tranquility born of sheer immensity; it calms with its very magnitude, which renders the merely human of no consequence. Gene was formed by this alpine hypnosis, this hushing of human drama.

In the valley, Faye tried to stop her ears against the constant gossip of a small town, whose opinions pushed in through the windows and crept under the doors. Mother often described herself as a pleaser: she said she couldn't stop herself from speculating what people wanted her to be, and from contorting herself, compulsively, unwillingly, into whatever it was. Living in her respectable house in the center of town, crowded by four other houses, each so near anyone could peer through the windows and whisper a judgment, Faye felt trapped.

I've often imagined the moment when Gene took Faye to the top of Buck's Peak and she was, for the first time, unable to see the faces or hear the voices of the people in the town below. They were far away. Dwarfed by the mountain, hushed by the wind.

They were engaged soon after.

Mother used to tell a story from the time before she was married. She had been close to her brother Lynn, so she took him to meet the man she hoped would be her husband. It was summer, dusk, and Dad's cousins were roughhousing the way they did after a harvest. Lynn arrived and, seeing a room of bowlegged ruffians shouting at each other, fists clenched, swiping at the air, thought he was witnessing a brawl straight out of a John Wayne film. He wanted to call the police.

"I told him to listen," Mother would say, tears in her eyes from laughing. She always told this story the same way, and it was such a favorite that if she departed in any way from the usual script, we'd tell it for her. "I told him to pay attention to the actual words they were shouting. Everyone *sounded* mad as hornets, but really they were having a lovely conversation. You had to listen to *what* they were saying, not *how* they were saying it. I told him, That's just how Westovers talk!"

By the time she'd finished we were usually on the floor. We'd cackle until our ribs hurt, imagining our prim, professorial uncle meeting Dad's unruly crew. Lynn found the scene so distasteful he never went back, and in my whole life I never saw him on the mountain. Served him right, we thought, for his meddling, for trying to draw Mother back into that world of gabardine dresses and cream shoes. We understood that the dissolution of Mother's family was the inauguration of ours. The two could not exist together. Only one could have her.

Mother never told us that her family had opposed the engagement but we knew. There were traces the decades hadn't erased. My father seldom set foot in Grandma-over-in-town's house, and when he did he was sullen and stared at the door. As a child I scarcely knew my aunts, uncles or cousins on my mother's side. We rarely visited them—I didn't even know where most of them lived—and it was even rarer for them to visit the mountain. The exception was my aunt Angie, my mother's youngest sister, who lived in town and insisted on seeing my mother.

What I know about the engagement has come to me in bits and pieces, mostly from the stories Mother told. I know she had the ring before Dad served a mission—which was expected of all faithful Mormon men—and spent two years proselytizing in Florida. Lynn took advantage of this absence to introduce his sister to every marriageable man he could find this side of the Rockies, but none could make her forget the stern farm boy who ruled over his own mountain.

Gene returned from Florida and they were married.

LaRue sewed the wedding dress.

I've only seen a single photograph from the wedding. It's of my parents posing in front of a gossamer curtain of pale ivory. Mother is wearing a traditional dress of beaded silk and venetian lace, with a neckline that sits above her collarbone. An embroidered veil covers her head. My father wears a cream suit with wide black lapels. They are both intoxicated with happiness, Mother with a relaxed smile, Dad with a grin so large it pokes out from under the corners of his mustache.

It is difficult for me to believe that the untroubled young man in that photograph is my father. Fearful and anxious, he comes into focus for me as a weary middle-aged man stockpiling food and ammunition.

I don't know when the man in that photograph became the man I know as my father. Perhaps there was no single moment. Dad married when he was twenty-one, had his first son, my brother Tony, at twenty-two. When he was twenty-four, Dad asked Mother if they could hire an herbalist to midwife my brother Shawn. She agreed. Was that the first hint, or was it just Gene being Gene, eccentric and unconventional, trying to shock his disapproving in-laws? After all, when Tyler was born twenty months later, the birth took place in a hospital. When Dad was twenty-seven, Luke was born, at home, delivered by a midwife. Dad decided not to file for a birth certificate, a decision he repeated with Audrey, Richard and me. A few years later, around the time he turned thirty, Dad pulled my brothers out of school. I don't remember it, because it was before I was born, but I wonder if perhaps that was a turning point. In the four years that followed, Dad got rid of the telephone and chose not to renew his license to drive. He stopped registering and insuring the family car. Then he began to hoard food.

This last part sounds like my father, but it is not the father my older brothers remember. Dad had just turned forty when the Feds laid siege to the Weavers, an event that confirmed his worst fears. After that he was at war, even if the war was only in his head. Perhaps that is why Tony looks at that photo and sees his father, and I see a stranger.

Fourteen years after the incident with the Weavers, I would sit in a university classroom and listen to a professor of psychology describe something called bipolar disorder. Until that moment I had never heard of mental illness. I knew people could go crazy—they'd wear dead cats on their heads or fall in love with a turnip—but the notion that a person could be functional, lucid, persuasive, and something could still be wrong, had never occurred to me.

The professor recited facts in a dull, earthy voice: the average age of onset is twenty-five; there may be no symptoms before then.

The irony was that if Dad was bipolar—or had any of a dozen disorders that might explain his behavior—the same paranoia that was a symptom of the illness would prevent its ever being diagnosed and treated. No one would ever know.

Grandma-over-in-town died three years ago, age eighty-six.

I didn't know her well.

All those years I was passing in and out of her kitchen, and she never told me what it had been like for her, watching her daughter shut herself away, walled in by phantoms and paranoias.

When I picture her now I conjure a single image, as if my memory is a slide projector and the tray is stuck. She's sitting on a cushioned bench. Her hair pushes out of her head in tight curls, and her lips are pulled into a polite smile, which is welded in place. Her eyes are pleasant but unoccupied, as if she's observing a staged drama.

That smile haunts me. It was constant, the only eternal thing, inscrutable, detached, dispassionate. Now that I'm older and I've taken the trouble to get to know her, mostly through my aunts and uncles, I know she was none of those things.

I attended the memorial. It was open casket and I found myself searching her face. The embalmers hadn't gotten her lips right—the gracious smile she'd worn like an iron mask had been stripped away. It was the first time I'd seen her without it and that's when it finally occurred to me: that Grandma was the only person who might have understood what was happening to me. How the paranoia and funda-mentalism were carving up my life, how they were taking from me the people I cared about and leaving only degrees and certificates—an air of respectability—in their place. What was happening now had happened before. This was the se-cond severing of mother and daughter. The tape was playing in a loop.

4

Apache Women

No one saw the car leave the road. My brother Tyler, who was seventeen, fell asleep at the wheel. It was six in the morning and he'd been driving in silence for most of the night, piloting our station wagon through Arizona, Nevada and Utah. We were in Cornish, a farming town twenty miles south of Buck's Peak, when the station wagon drifted over the center line into the other lane, then left the highway. The car jumped a ditch, smashed through two utility poles of thick cedar, and was finally brought to a stop only when it collided with a row-crop tractor.

The trip had been Mother's idea.

A few months earlier, when crisp leaves had begun slipping to the ground, signaling the end of summer, Dad had been in high spirits. His feet tapped show tunes at breakfast, and during dinner he often pointed at the mountain, his eyes shining, and described where he would lay the pipes to bring water down to the house. Dad promised that when the first snow fell, he'd build the biggest snowball in the state of Idaho. What he'd do, he said, was hike to the mountain base and gather a small, insignificant ball of snow, then roll it down the hillside, watching it triple in size each time it raced over a hillock or down a ravine. By the time it reached the house, which was atop the last hill before the valley, it'd be big as Grandpa's barn and people on the highway would stare up at it, amazed. We just needed the right snow. Thick, sticky flakes. After every snowfall, we brought handfuls to him and watched him rub the flakes between his fingers. That snow was too fine. This, too wet. After Christmas, he said. That's when you get the *real* snow.

But after Christmas Dad seemed to deflate, to collapse in on himself. He stopped talking about the snowball, then he stopped talking altogether. A darkness gathered in his eyes until it filled them. He walked with his arms limp, shoulders slumping, as if something had hold of him and was dragging him to the earth.

By January Dad couldn't get out of bed. He lay flat on his back, staring blankly at the stucco ceiling with its intricate pattern of ridges and veins. He didn't blink when I brought his dinner plate each night. I'm not sure he knew I was there.

That's when Mother announced we were going to Arizona. She said Dad was like a sunflower—he'd die in the snow—and that come February he needed to be taken away and planted in the sun. So we piled into the station wagon and drove for twelve hours, winding through canyons and speeding over dark freeways, until we arrived at the mobile home in the parched Arizona desert where my grandparents were waiting out the winter.

We arrived a few hours after sunrise. Dad made it as far as Grandma's porch, where he stayed for the rest of the day, a knitted pillow under his head, a callused hand on his stomach. He kept that posture for two days, eyes open, not saying a word, still as a bush in that dry, windless heat.

On the third day he seemed to come back into himself, to become aware of the goings-on around him, to listen to our mealtime chatter rather than staring, unresponsive, at the carpet. After dinner that night, Grandma played her phone messages, which were mostly neighbors and friends saying hello. Then a woman's voice came through the speaker to remind Grandma of her doctor's appointment the following day. That message had a dramatic effect on Dad.

At first Dad asked Grandma questions: what was the appointment for, who was it with, why would she see a doctor when Mother could give her tinctures.

Dad had always believed passionately in Mother's herbs, but that night felt different, like something inside him was shifting, a new creed taking hold. Herbalism, he said, was a spiritual doctrine that separated the wheat from the tares, the faithful from the faithless. Then he used a word I'd never heard before: Illuminati. It sounded exotic, powerful, whatever it was. Grandma, he said, was an unknowing agent of the Illuminati.

God couldn't abide faithlessness, Dad said. That's why the most hateful sinners were those who wouldn't make up their minds, who used herbs and medication both, who came to Mother on Wednesday and saw their doctor on Friday—or, as Dad put it, "Who worship at the altar of God one day and offer a sacrifice to Satan the next." These people were like the ancient Israelites because they'd been given a true religion but hankered after false idols.

"Doctors and pills," Dad said, nearly shouting. "That's their god, and they whore after it."

Mother was staring at her food. At the word "whore" she stood, threw Dad an angry look, then walked into her room and slammed the door. Mother didn't always agree with Dad. When Dad wasn't around, I'd heard her say things that he—or at least this new incarnation of him—would have called sacrilege, things like, "Herbs are supplements. For something serious, you should go to a doctor."

Dad took no notice of Mother's empty chair. "Those

doctors aren't trying to save you," he told Grandma. "They're trying to *kill* you."

When I think of that dinner, the scene comes back to me clearly. I'm sitting at the table. Dad is talking, his voice urgent. Grandma sits across from me, chewing her asparagus again and again in her crooked jaw, the way a goat might, sipping from her ice water, giving no indication that she's heard a word Dad has said, except for the occasional vexed glare she throws the clock when it tells her it's still too early for bed. "You're a knowing participant in the plans of Satan," Dad says.

This scene played every day, sometimes several times a day, for the rest of the trip. All followed a similar script. Dad, his fervor kindled, would drone for an hour or more, reciting the same lines over and over, fueled by some internal passion that burned long after the rest of us had been lectured into a cold stupor.

Grandma had a memorable way of laughing at the end of these sermons. It was a sort of sigh, a long, drawn-out leaking of breath, that finished with her eyes rolling upward in a lazy imitation of exasperation, as if she wanted to throw her hands in the air but was too tired to complete the gesture. Then she'd smile—not a soothing smile for someone else but a smile for herself, of baffled amusement, a smile that to me always seemed to say, *Ain't nothin' funnier than real life, I tell you what.*

It was a scorching afternoon, so hot you couldn't walk barefoot on the pavement, when Grandma took me and Richard for a drive through the desert, having wrestled us into seatbelts, which we'd never worn before. We drove until the road began to incline, then kept driving as the asphalt turned to dust beneath our tires, and still we kept going, Grandma weaving higher and higher into the bleached hills, coming to a stop only when the dirt road ended and a hiking trail began. Then we walked. Grandma was winded after a few minutes, so she sat on a flat red stone and pointed to a sandstone rock formation in the distance, formed of crumbling spires, each a little ruin, and told us to hike to it. Once there, we were to hunt for nuggets of black rock.

"They're called Apache tears," she said. She reached into her pocket and pulled out a small black stone, dirty and jagged, covered in veins of gray and white like cracked glass. "And this is how they look after they've been polished a bit." From her other pocket she withdrew a second stone, which was inky black and so smooth it felt soft.

Richard identified both as obsidian. "These are volcanic rock," he said in his best encyclopedic voice. "But this isn't." He kicked a washed-out stone and waved at the formation. "This is sediment." Richard had a talent for scientific trivia. Usually I ignored his lecturing but today I was gripped by it, and by this strange, thirsty terrain. We hiked around the formation for an hour, returning to Grandma with our shirtfronts sagging with stones. Grandma was pleased; she could sell them. She put them in the trunk, and as we made our way back to the trailer, she told us the legend of the Apache tears.

According to Grandma, a hundred years ago a tribe of Apaches had fought the U.S. Cavalry on those faded rocks. The tribe was outnumbered: the battle lost, the war over. All that was left to do was wait to die. Soon after the battle began, the warriors became trapped on a ledge. Unwilling to suffer a humiliating defeat, cut down one by one as they tried to break through the cavalry, they mounted their horses and charged off the face of the mountain. When the Apache women found their broken bodies on the rocks below, they cried huge, desperate tears, which turned to stone when they touched the earth.

Grandma never told us what happened to the women. The

Apaches were at war but had no warriors, so perhaps she thought the ending too bleak to say aloud. The word "slaughter" came to mind, because slaughter is the word for it, for a battle when one side mounts no defense. It's the word we used on the farm. We slaughtered chickens, we didn't fight them. A slaughter was the likely outcome of the warriors' bravery. They died as heroes, their wives as slaves.

As we drove to the trailer, the sun dipping in the sky, its last rays reaching across the highway, I thought about the Apache women. Like the sandstone altar on which they had died, the shape of their lives had been determined years before—before the horses began their gallop, their sorrel bodies arching for that final collision. Long before the warriors' leap it was decided how the women would live and how they would die. By the warriors, by the women themselves. Decided. Choices, numberless as grains of sand, had layered and compressed, coalescing into sediment, then into rock, until all was set in stone.

I had never before left the mountain and I ached for it, for the sight of the Princess etched in pine across the massif. I found myself glancing at the vacant Arizona sky, hoping to see her black form swelling out of the earth, laying claim to her half of the heavens. But she was not there. More than the sight of her, I missed her caresses—the wind she sent through canyons and ravines to sweep through my hair every morning. In Arizona, there was no wind. There was just one heat-stricken hour after another.

I spent my days wandering from one side of the trailer to the other, then out the back door, across the patio, over to the hammock, then around to the front porch, where I'd step over Dad's semiconscious form and back inside again. It was a great relief when, on the sixth day, Grandpa's four-wheeler broke down and Tyler and Luke took it apart to find the

44

trouble. I sat on a large barrel of blue plastic, watching them, wondering when we could go home. When Dad would stop talking about the Illuminati. When Mother would stop leaving the room whenever Dad entered it.

That night after dinner, Dad said it was time to go. "Get your stuff," he said. "We're hitting the road in a half hour." It was early evening, which Grandma said was a ridiculous time to begin a twelve-hour drive. Mother said we should wait until morning, but Dad wanted to get home so he and the boys could scrap the next morning. "I can't afford to lose any more work days," he said.

Mother's eyes darkened with worry, but she said nothing.

I awoke when the car hit the first utility pole. I'd been asleep on the floor under my sister's feet, a blanket over my head. I tried to sit up but the car was shaking, lunging—it felt like it was coming apart—and Audrey fell on top of me. I couldn't see what was happening but I could feel and hear it. Another loud *thud,* a lurch, my mother screaming, "Tyler!" from the front seat, and a final violent jolt before everything stopped and silence set in.

Several seconds passed in which nothing happened.

Then I heard Audrey's voice. She was calling our names one by one. Then she said, "Everyone's here except Tara!"

I tried to shout but my face was wedged under the seat, my cheek pressed to the floor. I struggled under Audrey's weight as she shouted my name. Finally, I arched my back and pushed her off, then stuck my head out of the blanket and said, "Here."

I looked around. Tyler had twisted his upper body so that he was practically climbing into the backseat, his eyes bulging as he took in every cut, every bruise, every pair of wide eyes. I could see his face but it didn't look like his face. Blood gushed from his mouth and down his shirt. I closed my eyes, trying to forget the twisted angles of his bloodstained teeth. When I opened them again, it was to check everyone else. Richard was holding his head, a hand over each ear like he was trying to block out a noise. Audrey's nose was strangely hooked and blood was streaming from it down her arm. Luke was shaking but I couldn't see any blood. I had a gash on my forearm from where the seat's frame had caught hold of me.

"Everyone all right?" My father's voice. There was a general mumble.

"There are power lines on the car," Dad said. "Nobody gets out till they've shut them off." His door opened, and for a moment I thought he'd been electrocuted, but then I saw he'd pitched himself far enough so that his body had never touched the car and the ground at the same time. I remember peering at him through my shattered window as he circled the car, his red cap pushed back so the brim reached upward, licking the air. He looked strangely boyish.

He circled the car then stopped, crouching low, bringing his head level with the passenger seat. "Are you okay?" he said. Then he said it again. The third time he said it, his voice quivered.

I leaned over the seat to see who he was talking to, and only then realized how serious the accident had been. The front half of the car had been compressed, the engine arched, curving back over itself, like a fold in solid rock.

There was a glare on the windshield from the morning sun. I saw crisscrossing patterns of fissures and cracks. The sight was familiar. I'd seen hundreds of shattered windshields in the junkyard, each one unique, with its particular spray of gossamer extruding from the point of impact, a chronicle of the collision. The cracks on our windshield told their own story. Their epicenter was a small ring with fissures circling outward. The ring was directly in front of the passenger seat.

"You okay?" Dad pleaded. "Honey, can you hear me?"

Mother was in the passenger seat. Her body faced away from the window. I couldn't see her face, but there was something terrifying in the way she slumped against her seat.

"Can you hear me?" Dad said. He repeated this several times. Eventually, in a movement so small it was almost imperceptible, I saw the tip of Mother's ponytail dip as she nodded.

Dad stood, looking at the active power lines, looking at the earth, looking at Mother. Looking helpless. "Do you think—should I call an ambulance?"

I *think* I heard him say that. And if he did, which surely he must have, Mother must have whispered a reply, or maybe she wasn't able to whisper anything, I don't know. I've always imagined that she asked to be taken home.

I was told later that the farmer whose tractor we'd hit rushed from his house. He'd called the police, which we knew would bring trouble because the car wasn't insured, and none of us had been wearing seatbelts. It took perhaps twenty minutes after the farmer informed Utah Power of the accident for them to switch off the deadly current pulsing through the lines. Then Dad lifted Mother from the station wagon and I saw her face—her eyes, hidden under dark circles the size of plums, and the swelling distorting her soft features, stretching some, compressing others.

I don't know how we got home, or when, but I remember that the mountain face glowed orange in the morning light. Once inside, I watched Tyler spit streams of crimson down the bathroom sink. His front teeth had smashed into the steering wheel and been displaced, so that they jutted backward toward the roof of his mouth.

Mother was laid on the sofa. She mumbled that the light hurt her eyes. We closed the blinds. She wanted to be in the basement, where there were no windows, so Dad carried her downstairs and I didn't see her for several hours, not until that evening, when I used a dull flashlight to bring her dinner. When I saw her, I didn't know her. Both eyes were a deep purple, so deep they looked black, and so swollen I couldn't tell whether they were open or closed. She called me Audrey, even after I corrected her twice. "Thank you, Audrey, but just dark and quiet, that's fine. Dark. Quiet. Thank you. Come check on me again, Audrey, in a little while."

Mother didn't come out of the basement for a week. Every day the swelling worsened, the black bruises turned blacker. Every night I was sure her face was as marked as it was possible for a face to be, but every morning it was somehow darker, more tumid. After a week, when the sun went down, we turned off the lights and Mother came upstairs. She looked as if she had two objects strapped to her forehead, large as apples, black as olives.

There was never any more talk of a hospital. The moment for such a decision had passed, and to return to it would be to return to all the fury and fear of the accident itself. Dad said doctors couldn't do anything for her anyhow. She was in God's hands.

In the coming months, Mother called me by many names. When she called me Audrey I didn't worry, but it was troubling when we had conversations in which she referred to me as Luke or Tony, and in the family it has always been agreed, even by Mother herself, that she's never been quite the same since the accident. We kids called her Raccoon Eyes. We thought it was a great joke, once the black rings had been around for a few weeks, long enough for us to get used to them and make them the subject of jokes. We had no idea it was a medical term. Raccoon eyes. A sign of serious brain injury.

Tyler's guilt was all-consuming. He blamed himself for the accident, then kept on blaming himself for every decision that was made thereafter, every repercussion, every reverberation that clanged down through the years. He laid claim to that moment and all its consequences, as if time itself had commenced the instant our station wagon left the road, and there was no history, no context, no agency of any kind until he began it, at the age of seventeen, by falling asleep at the wheel. Even now, when Mother forgets any detail, however trivial, that look comes into his eyes—the one he had in the moments after the collision, when blood poured from his own mouth as he took in the scene, raking his eyes over what he imagined to be the work of his hands and his hands only.

Me, I never blamed anyone for the accident, least of all Tyler. It was just one of those things. A decade later my understanding would shift, part of my heavy swing into adulthood, and after that the accident would always make me think of the Apache women, and of all the decisions that go into making a life—the choices people make, together and on their own, that combine to produce any single event. Grains of sand, incalculable, pressing into sediment, then rock.

5

Honest Dirt

The mountain thawed and the Princess appeared on its face, her head brushing the sky. It was Sunday, a month after the accident, and everyone had gathered in the living room. Dad had begun to expound a scripture when Tyler cleared his throat and said he was leaving.

"I'm g-g-going to c-college," he said, his face rigid. A vein in his neck bulged as he forced the words out, appearing and disappearing every few seconds, a great, struggling snake.

Everyone looked at Dad. His expression was folded, impassive. The silence was worse than shouting.

Tyler would be the third of my brothers to leave home. My oldest brother, Tony, drove rigs, hauling gravel or scrap, trying to scrape together enough money to marry the girl down the road. Shawn, the next oldest, had quarreled with Dad a few months before and taken off. I hadn't seen him since, though Mother got a hurried call every few weeks telling her he was fine, that he was welding or driving rigs. If Tyler left too, Dad wouldn't have a crew, and without a crew he couldn't build barns or hay sheds. He would have to fall back on scrapping.

"What's college?" I said.

"College is extra school for people too dumb to learn the

first time around," Dad said. Tyler stared at the floor, his face tense. Then his shoulders dropped, his face relaxed and he looked up; it seemed to me that he'd stepped out of himself. His eyes were soft, pleasant. I couldn't see him in there at all.

He listened to Dad, who settled into a lecture. "There's two kinds of them college professors," Dad said. "Those who know they're lying, and those who think they're telling the truth." Dad grinned. "Don't know which is worse, come to think of it, a bona fide agent of the Illuminati, who at least knows he's on the devil's payroll, or a high-minded professor who thinks his wisdom is greater than God's." He was still grinning. The situation wasn't serious; he just needed to talk some sense into his son.

Mother said Dad was wasting his time, that nobody could talk Tyler out of anything once his mind was made up. "You may as well take a broom and start sweeping dirt off the mountain," she said. Then she stood, took a few moments to steady herself, and trudged downstairs.

She had a migraine. She nearly always had a migraine. She was still spending her days in the basement, coming upstairs only after the sun had gone down, and even then she rarely stayed more than an hour before the combination of noise and exertion made her head throb. I watched her slow, careful progress down the steps, her back bent, both hands gripping the rail, as if she were blind and had to feel her way. She waited for both feet to plant solidly on one step before reaching for the next. The swelling in her face was nearly gone, and she almost looked like herself again, except for the rings, which had gradually faded from black to dark purple, and were now a mix of lilac and raisin.

An hour later Dad was no longer grinning. Tyler had not repeated his wish to go to college, but he had not promised to stay, either. He was just sitting there, behind that vacant expression, riding it out. "A man can't make a living out of books and scraps of paper," Dad said. "You're going to be the head of a family. How can you support a wife and children with *books*?"

Tyler tilted his head, showed he was listening, and said nothing.

"A son of mine, standing in line to get brainwashed by socialists and Illuminati spies—"

"The s-s-school's run by the ch-ch-church," Tyler interrupted. "How b-bad can it b-be?"

Dad's mouth flew open and a gust of air rushed out. "You don't think the Illuminati have infiltrated the church?" His voice was booming; every word reverberated with a powerful energy. "You don't think the first place they'd go is that school, where they can raise up a whole generation of socialist Mormons? I raised you better than that!"

I will always remember my father in this moment, the potency of him, and the desperation. He leans forward, jaw set, eyes narrow, searching his son's face for some sign of agreement, some crease of shared conviction. He doesn't find it.

The story of how Tyler decided to leave the mountain is a strange one, full of gaps and twists. It begins with Tyler himself, with the bizarre fact of him. It happens sometimes in families: one child who doesn't fit, whose rhythm is off, whose meter is set to the wrong tune. In our family, that was Tyler. He was waltzing while the rest of us hopped a jig; he was deaf to the raucous music of our lives, and we were deaf to the serene polyphony of his.

Tyler liked books, he liked quiet. He liked organizing and arranging and labeling. Once, Mother found a whole shelf of matchboxes in his closet, stacked by year. Tyler said they contained his pencil shavings from the past five years, which he had collected to make fire starters for our "head for the hills" bags. The rest of the house was pure confusion: piles of unwashed laundry, oily and black from the junkyard, littered the bedroom floors; in the kitchen, murky jars of tincture lined every table and cabinet, and these were only cleared away to make space for even messier projects, perhaps to skin a deer carcass or strip Cosmoline off a rifle. But in the heart of this chaos, Tyler had half a decade's pencil shavings, cataloged by year.

My brothers were like a pack of wolves. They tested each other constantly, with scuffles breaking out every time some young pup hit a growth spurt and dreamed of moving up. When I was young these tussles usually ended with Mother screaming over a broken lamp or vase, but as I got older there were fewer things left to break. Mother said we'd owned a TV once, when I was a baby, until Shawn had put Tyler's head through it.

While his brothers wrestled, Tyler listened to music. He owned the only boom box I had ever seen, and next to it he kept a tall stack of CDs with strange words on them, like "Mozart" and "Chopin." One Sunday afternoon, when he was perhaps sixteen, he caught me looking at them. I tried to run, because I thought he might wallop me for being in his room, but instead he took my hand and led me to the stack. "W-which one do y-you like best?" he said.

One was black, with a hundred men and women dressed in white on the cover. I pointed to it. Tyler eyed me skeptically. "Th-th-this is ch-ch-choir music," he said.

He slipped the disc into the black box, then sat at his desk to read. I squatted on the floor by his feet, scratching designs into the carpet. The music began: a breath of strings, then a whisper of voices, chanting, soft as silk, but somehow piercing. The hymn was familiar to me—we'd sung it at church, a chorus of mismatched voices raised in worship—but *this* was different. It was worshipful, but it was also something else, something to do with study, discipline and collaboration. Something I didn't yet understand.

53

The song ended and I sat, paralyzed, as the next played, and the next, until the CD finished. The room felt lifeless without the music. I asked Tyler if we could listen to it again, and an hour later, when the music stopped, I begged him to restart it. It was very late, and the house quiet, when Tyler stood from his desk and pushed play, saying this was the last time.

"W-w-we can l-l-listen again tomorrow," he said.

Music became our language. Tyler's speech impediment kept him quiet, made his tongue heavy. Because of that, he and I had never talked much; I had not known my brother. Now, every evening when he came in from the junkyard, I would be waiting for him. After he'd showered, scrubbing the day's grime from his skin, he'd settle in at his desk and say, "W-w-what shall we l-l-listen t-t-to tonight?" Then I would choose a CD, and he would read while I lay on the floor next to his feet, eyes fixed on his socks, and listened.

I was as rowdy as any of my brothers, but when I was with Tyler I transformed. Maybe it was the music, the grace of it, or maybe it was *his* grace. Somehow he made me see myself through his eyes. I tried to remember not to shout. I tried to avoid fights with Richard, especially the kind that ended with the two of us rolling on the floor, him pulling my hair, me dragging my fingernails through the softness of his face.

I should have known that one day Tyler would leave. Tony and Shawn had gone, and they'd belonged on the mountain in a way that Tyler never did. Tyler had always loved what Dad called "book learning," which was something the rest of us, with the exception of Richard, were perfectly indifferent to.

There had been a time, when Tyler was a boy, when Mother had been idealistic about education. She used to say that we were kept at home so we could get a *better* education than other kids. But it was only Mother who said that, as Dad thought we should learn more practical skills. When I was very young, that was the battle between them: Mother trying to hold school every morning, and Dad herding the boys into the junkyard the moment her back was turned.

But Mother would lose that battle, eventually. It began with Luke, the fourth of her five sons. Luke was smart when it came to the mountain—he worked with animals in a way that made it seem like he was talking to them—but he had a severe learning disability and struggled to learn to read. Mother spent five years sitting with him at the kitchen table every morning, explaining the same sounds again and again, but by the time he was twelve, it was all Luke could do to cough out a sentence from the Bible during family scripture study. Mother couldn't understand it. She'd had no trouble teaching Tony and Shawn to read, and everyone else had just sort of picked it up. Tony had taught me to read when I was four, to win a bet with Shawn, I think.

Once Luke could scratch out his name and read short, simple phrases, Mother turned to math. What math I was ever taught I learned doing the breakfast dishes and listening to Mother explain, over and over, what a fraction is or how to use negative numbers. Luke never made any progress, and after a year Mother gave up. She stopped talking about us getting a better education than other kids. She began to echo Dad. "All that really matters," she said to me one morning, "is that you kids learn to read. That other twaddle is just brainwashing." Dad started coming in earlier and earlier to round up the boys until, by the time I was eight, and Tyler sixteen, we'd settled into a routine that omitted school altogether.

Mother's conversion to Dad's philosophy was not total, however, and occasionally she was possessed of her old enthusiasm. On those days, when the family was gathered around the table, eating breakfast, Mother would announce that today we were *doing school*. She kept a bookshelf in the basement, stocked with books on herbalism, along with a few old paperbacks. There were a few textbooks on math, which we shared, and an American history book that I never saw anyone read except Richard. There was also a science book, which must have been for young children because it was filled with glossy illustrations.

It usually took half an hour to find all the books, then we would divide them up and go into separate rooms to "do school." I have no idea what my siblings did when they did school, but when I did it I opened my math book and spent ten minutes turning pages, running my fingers down the center fold. If my finger touched fifty pages, I'd report to Mother that I'd done fifty pages of math.

"Amazing!" she'd say. "You see? That pace would never be possible in the public school. You can only do that at home, where you can sit down and really focus, with no distractions."

Mother never delivered lectures or administered exams. She never assigned essays. There was a computer in the basement with a program called Mavis Beacon, which gave lessons on typing.

Sometimes, when she was delivering herbs, if we'd finished our chores, Mother would drop us at the Carnegie library in the center of town. The basement had a room full of children's books, which we read. Richard even took books from upstairs, books for adults, with heavy titles about history and science.

Learning in our family was entirely self-directed: you could learn anything you could teach yourself, after your work was done. Some of us were more disciplined than others. I was one of the least disciplined, so by the time I was ten, the only subject I had studied systematically was Morse code, because Dad insisted that I learn it. "If the lines are cut, we'll be the only people in the valley who can communicate," he said, though I was never quite sure, if we were the only people learning it, who we'd be communicating with.

The older boys—Tony, Shawn and Tyler—had been raised

in a different decade, and it was almost as if they'd had different parents. Their father had never heard of the Weavers; he never talked about the Illuminati. He'd enrolled his three oldest sons in school, and even though he'd pulled them out a few years later, vowing to teach them at home, when Tony had asked to go back, Dad had let him. Tony had stayed in school through high school, although he missed so many days working in the junkyard that he wasn't able to graduate.

Because Tyler was the third son, he barely remembered school and was happy to study at home. Until he turned thirteen. Then, perhaps because Mother was spending all her time teaching Luke to read, Tyler asked Dad if he could enroll in the eighth grade.

Tyler stayed in school that whole year, from the fall of 1991 through the spring of 1992. He learned algebra, which felt as natural to his mind as air to his lungs. Then the Weavers came under siege that August. I don't know if Tyler would have gone back to school, but I know that after Dad heard about the Weavers, he never again allowed one of his children to set foot in a public classroom. Still, Tyler's imagination had been captured. With what money he had he bought an old trigonometry textbook and continued to study on his own. He wanted to learn calculus next but couldn't afford another book, so he went to the school and asked the math teacher for one. The teacher laughed in his face. "You can't teach yourself calculus," he said. "It's impossible." Tyler pushed back. "Give me a book, I think I can." He left with the book tucked under his arm.

The real challenge was finding time to study. Every morning at seven, my father gathered his sons, divided them into teams and sent them out to tackle the tasks of the day. It usually took about an hour for Dad to notice that Tyler was not among his brothers. Then he'd burst through the back door and stride into the house to where Tyler sat studying in his room. "What the hell are you doing?" he'd shout, tracking clumps of dirt onto Tyler's spotless carpet. "I got Luke loading I-beams by himself—one man doing a two-man job—and I come in here and find you sitting on your ass?"

If Dad had caught me with a book when I was supposed to be working, I'd have skittered, but Tyler was steady. "Dad," he'd say. "I'll w-w-work after l-l-lunch. But I n-n-need the morning to s-st-study." Most mornings they'd argue for a few minutes, then Tyler would surrender his pencil, his shoulders slumping as he pulled on his boots and welding gloves. But there were other mornings—mornings that always astonished me—when Dad huffed out the back door, alone.

I didn't believe Tyler would really go to college, that he would ever abandon the mountain to join the Illuminati. I figured Dad had all summer to bring Tyler to his senses, which he tried to do most days when the crew came in for lunch. The boys would putter around the kitchen, dishing up seconds and thirds, and Dad would stretch himself out on the hard linoleum—because he was tired and needed to lie down, but was too dirty for Mother's sofa—and begin his lecture about the Illuminati.

One lunch in particular has lodged in my memory. Tyler is assembling tacos from the fixings Mother has laid out: he lines up the shells on his plate, three in a perfect row, then adds the hamburger, lettuce and tomatoes carefully, measuring the amounts, perfectly distributing the sour cream. Dad drones steadily. Then, just as Dad reaches the end of his lecture and takes a breath to begin again, Tyler slides all three of the flawless tacos into Mother's juicer, the one she uses to make tinctures, and turns it on. A loud roar howls through the kitchen, imposing a kind of silence. The roar ceases; Dad resumes. Tyler pours the orange liquid into a glass and begins to drink, carefully, delicately, because his front teeth are still loose, still trying to jump out of his mouth. Many memories might be summoned to symbolize this period of our lives, but this is the one that has stayed with me: of Dad's voice rising up from the floor while Tyler drinks his tacos.

As spring turned to summer, Dad's resolve turned to denial—he acted as if the argument were over and he had won. He stopped talking about Tyler's leaving and refused to hire a hand to replace him.

One warm afternoon, Tyler took me to visit Grandma- and Grandpa-over-in-town, who lived in the same house where they'd raised Mother, a house that could not have been more different from ours. The decor was not expensive but it was well cared for—creamy white carpet on the floors, soft floral paper on the walls, thick, pleated curtains in the windows. They seldom replaced anything. The carpet, the wallpaper, the kitchen table and countertops—everything was the same as it was in the slides I'd seen of my mother's childhood.

Dad didn't like us spending time there. Before he retired Grandpa had been a mailman, and Dad said no one worth our respect would have worked for the Government. Grandma was even worse, Dad said. She was frivolous. I didn't know what that word meant, but he said it so often that I'd come to associate it with her—with her creamy carpet and soft petal wallpaper.

Tyler loved it there. He loved the calm, the order, the soft way my grandparents spoke to each other. There was an aura in that house that made me feel instinctively, without ever being told, that I was not to shout, not to hit anyone or tear through the kitchen at full speed. I *did* have to be told, and told repeatedly, to leave my muddy shoes by the door.

"Off to college!" Grandma said once we were settled onto the floral-print sofa. She turned to me. "You must be so proud of your brother!" Her eyes squinted to accommodate her smile. I could see every one of her teeth. *Leave it to Grandma to think getting yourself brainwashed is something to celebrate,* I thought.

"I need the bathroom," I said.

Alone in the hall I walked slowly, pausing with each step to let my toes sink into the carpet. I smiled, remembering that Dad had said Grandma could keep her carpet so white only because Grandpa had never done any real work. "My hands might be dirty," Dad had said, winking at me and displaying his blackened fingernails. "But it's honest dirt."

Weeks passed and it was full summer. One Sunday Dad called the family together. "We've got a good supply of food," he said. "We've got fuel and water stored away. What we don't got is money." Dad took a twenty from his wallet and crumpled it. "Not this fake money. In the Days of Abomination, this won't be worth a thing. People will trade hundred-dollar bills for a roll of toilet paper."

I imagined a world where green bills littered the highway like empty soda cans. I looked around. Everyone else seemed to be imagining that too, especially Tyler. His eyes were focused, determined. "I've got a little money saved," Dad said. "And your mother's got some tucked away. We're going to change it into silver. That's what people will be wishing they had soon, silver and gold."

A few days later Dad came home with the silver, and even some gold. The metal was in the form of coins, packed in small, heavy boxes, which he carried through the house and piled in the basement. He wouldn't let me open them. "They aren't for playing," he said.

Sometime after Tyler took several thousand dollars— nearly all the savings he had left after he'd paid the farmer for the tractor and Dad for the station wagon—and bought his own pile of silver, which he stacked in the basement next to the gun cabinet. He stood there for a long time, considering the boxes, as if suspended between two worlds.

Tyler was a softer target: I begged and he gave me a silver

60

coin as big as my palm. The coin soothed me. It seemed to me that Tyler's buying it was a declaration of loyalty, a pledge to our family that despite the madness that had hold of him, that made him want to go to school, ultimately he would choose us. Fight on our side when the End came. By the time the leaves began to change, from the juniper greens of summer to the garnet reds and bronzed golds of autumn, that coin shimmered even in the lowest light, polished by a thousand finger strokes. I'd taken comfort in the raw physicality of it, certain that if the coin was real, Tyler's leaving could not be.

I awoke one morning in August to find Tyler packing his clothes, books and CDs into boxes. He'd nearly finished by the time we sat down to breakfast. I ate quickly, then went into his room and looked at his shelves, now empty except for a single CD, the black one with the image of the people dressed in white, which I now recognized as the Mormon Tabernacle Choir. Tyler appeared in the doorway. "I'm l-l-leaving that f-f-for you," he said. Then he walked outside and hosed down his car, blasting away the Idaho dust until it looked as though it had never seen a dirt road.

Dad finished his breakfast and left without a word. I understood why. The sight of Tyler loading boxes into his car made me crazed. I wanted to scream but instead I ran, out the back door and up through the hills toward the peak. I ran until the sound of blood pulsing in my ears was louder than the thoughts in my head; then I turned around and ran back, swinging around the pasture to the red railroad car. I scrambled onto its roof just in time to see Tyler close his trunk and turn in a circle, as if he wanted to say goodbye but there was no one to say goodbye to. I imagined him calling my name and pictured his face falling when I didn't answer.

He was in the driver's seat by the time I'd climbed down, and the car was rumbling down the dirt road when I leapt out from behind an iron tank. Tyler stopped, then got out and hugged me—not the crouching hug that adults often give children but the other kind, both of us standing, him pulling me into him and bringing his face close to mine. He said he would miss me, then he let me go, stepping into his car and speeding down the hill and onto the highway. I watched the dust settle.

Tyler rarely came home after that. He was building a new life for himself across enemy lines. He made few excursions back to our side. I have almost no memory of him until five years later, when I am fifteen, and he bursts into my life at a critical moment. By then we are strangers.

It would be many years before I would understand what leaving that day had cost him, and how little he had understood about where he was going. Tony and Shawn had left the mountain, but they'd left to do what my father had taught them to do: drive semis, weld, scrap. Tyler stepped into a void. I don't know why he did it and neither does he. He can't explain where the conviction came from, or how it burned brightly enough to shine through the black uncertainty. But I've always supposed it was the music in his head, some hopeful tune the rest of us couldn't hear, the same secret melody he'd been humming when he bought that trigonometry book, or saved all those pencil shavings.

Summer waned, seeming to evaporate in its own heat. The days were still hot but the evenings had begun to cool, the frigid hours after sunset claiming more of each day. Tyler had been gone a month.

I was spending the afternoon with Grandma-over-in-town. I'd had a bath that morning, even though it wasn't Sunday, and I'd put on special clothes with no holes or stains so that, scrubbed and polished, I could sit in Grandma's kitchen and watch her make pumpkin cookies. The autumn sun poured in through gossamer curtains and onto marigold tiles, giving the whole room an amber glow.

After Grandma slid the first batch into the oven, I went to the bathroom. I passed through the hallway, with its soft white carpet, and felt a stab of anger when I remembered that the last time I'd seen it, I'd been with Tyler. The bathroom felt foreign. I took in the pearly sink, the rosy tint of the carpet, the peach-colored rug. Even the toilet peeked out from under a primrose covering. I took in my own reflection, framed by creamy tiles. I looked nothing like myself, and I wondered for a moment if *this* was what Tyler wanted, a pretty house with a pretty bathroom and a pretty sister to visit him. Maybe this was what he'd left for. I hated him for that.

Near the tap there were a dozen pink and white soaps, shaped like swans and roses, resting in an ivory-tinted shell. I picked up a swan, feeling its soft shape give under pressure from my fingers. It was beautiful and I wanted to take it. I pictured it in our basement bathroom, its delicate wings set against the coarse cement. I imagined it lying in a muddy puddle on the sink, surrounded by strips of curling yellowed wallpaper. I returned it to its shell.

Coming out, I walked into Grandma, who'd been waiting for me in the hall.

"Did you wash your hands?" she asked, her tone sweet and buttery.

"No," I said.

My reply soured the cream in her voice. "Why not?"

"They weren't dirty."

"You should always wash your hands after you use the toilet."

"It can't be that important," I said. "We don't even have soap in the bathroom at home."

"That's not true," she said. "I raised your mother better than that."

63

I squared my stance, ready to argue, to tell Grandma again that we didn't use soap, but when I looked up, the woman I saw was not the woman I expected to see. She didn't seem frivolous, didn't seem like the type who'd waste an entire day fretting over her white carpet. In that moment she was transformed. Maybe it was something in the shape of her eyes, the way they squinted at me in disbelief, or maybe it was the hard line of her mouth, which was clamped shut, determined. Or maybe it was nothing at all, just the same old woman looking like herself and saying the things she always said. Maybe her transformation was merely a temporary shift in my perspective—for that moment, perhaps the perspective was *his,* that of the brother I hated, and loved.

Grandma led me into the bathroom and watched as I washed my hands, then directed me to dry them on the rose-colored towel. My ears burned, my throat felt hot.

Dad picked me up soon after on his way home from a job. He pulled up in his truck and honked for me to come out, which I did, my head bent low. Grandma followed. I rushed into the passenger seat, displacing a toolbox and welding gloves, while Grandma told Dad about my not washing. Dad listened, sucking on his cheeks while his right hand fiddled with the gearshift. A laugh was bubbling up inside him.

Having returned to my father, I felt the power of his person. A familiar lens slid over my eyes and Grandma lost whatever strange power she'd had over me an hour before.

"Don't you teach your children to wash after they use the toilet?" Grandma said.

Dad shifted the truck into gear. As it rolled forward he waved and said, "I teach them not to piss on their hands."

6

Shield and Buckler

The winter after Tyler left, Audrey turned fifteen. She picked up her driver's license from the county courthouse and, on her way home, got a job flipping burgers. Then she took a second job milking cows at four A.M. every morning. For a year she'd been fighting with Dad, bucking under the restraints he put on her. Now she had money; she had her own car; we hardly saw her. The family was shrinking, the old hierarchy compressing.

Dad didn't have enough of a crew to build hay sheds, so he went back to scrapping. With Tyler gone, the rest of us were promoted: Luke, at sixteen, became the eldest son, my father's right hand, and Richard and I took his place as grunts.

I remember the first morning I entered the junkyard as one of my father's crew. The earth was ice, even the air felt stiff. We were in the yard above the lower pasture, which was overrun by hundreds of cars and trucks. Some were old and broken down but most had been wrecked and they looked it—bent, arched, twisted, the impression they gave was of crumpled paper, not steel. In the center of the yard there was a lake of debris, vast and deep: leaking car batteries, tangles of insulated copper wire, abandoned transmissions, rusted sheets of corrugated tin, antique faucets, smashed radiators, serrated lengths of luminous brass pipe, and on and on. It was endless, a formless mass.

Dad led me to its edge.

"You know the difference between aluminum and stainless steel?" he said.

"I think so."

"Come here." His tone was impatient. He was used to dictating to grown men. Having to explain his trade to a ten-year-old girl somehow made us both feel small.

He yanked out a chunk of shimmering metal. "This here's aluminum," he said. "See how it shines? Feel how light it is?" Dad put the piece into my hand. He was right; it was not as heavy as it looked. Next Dad handed me a dented pipe. "This here's steel," he said.

We began to sort the debris into piles—aluminum, iron, steel, copper—so it could be sold. I picked up a piece of iron. It was dense with bronze rust, and its jagged angles nibbled at my palms. I had a pair of leather gloves, but when Dad saw them he said they'd slow me down. "You'll get calluses real quick," he promised as I handed them over. I'd found a hard hat in the shop, but Dad took that, too. "You'll move slower trying to balance this silly thing on your head," he said.

Dad lived in fear of time. He felt it stalking him. I could see it in the worried glances he gave the sun as it moved across the sky, in the anxious way he appraised every length of pipe or cut of steel. Dad saw every piece of scrap as the money it could be sold for, minus the time needed to sort, cut and deliver it. Every slab of iron, every ring of copper tubing was a nickel, a dime, a dollar—less if it took more than two seconds to extract and classify—and he constantly weighed these meager profits against the hourly expense of running the house. He figured that to keep the lights on, the house warm, he needed to work at breakneck speed. I never saw

Dad carry anything to a sorting bin; he just chucked it, with all the strength he had, from wherever he was standing.

The first time I saw him do it, I thought it was an accident, a mishap that would be corrected. I hadn't yet grasped the rules of this new world. I had bent down, and was reaching for a copper coil, when something massive cut through the air next to me. When I turned to see where it had come from, I caught a steel cylinder full in the stomach.

The impact knocked me to the ground. "Oops!" Dad hollered. I rolled over on the ice, winded. By the time I'd scrambled to my feet, Dad had launched something else. I ducked but lost my footing and fell. This time I stayed down. I was shaking but not from cold. My skin was alive and tingling with the certainty of danger, yet when I looked for the source of that danger, all I could see was a tired old man, tugging on a broken light fixture.

I remembered all the times I'd seen one of my brothers burst through the back door, howling, pinching some part of his body that was gashed or squashed or broken or burned. I remembered two years before, when a man named Robert, who worked for Dad, had lost a finger. I remembered the otherworldly pitch of his scream as he ran to the house. I remembered staring at the bloody stump, and then at the severed finger, which Luke brought in and placed on the counter. It looked like a prop from a magic trick. Mother put it on ice and rushed Robert to town so the doctors could sew it back on. Robert's was not the only finger the junkyard had claimed. A year before Robert, Shawn's girlfriend, Emma, had come through the back door shrieking. She'd been helping Shawn and lost half her index. Mother had rushed Emma to town, too, but the flesh had been crushed, and there was nothing they could do.

I looked at my own pink fingers, and in that moment the junkyard shifted. As children, Richard and I had passed countless hours in the debris, jumping from one mangled car to the next, looting some, leaving others. It had been the backdrop for a thousand imagined battles—between demons and wizards, fairies and goons, trolls and giants. Now it was changed. It had ceased to be my childhood playground and had become its own reality, one whose physical laws were mysterious, hostile.

I was remembering the strange pattern the blood had made as it streaked down Emma's wrist, smearing across her forearm, when I stood and, still shaking, tried to pry loose the small length of copper tubing. I almost had it when Dad flung a catalytic converter. I leapt aside, cutting my hand on the serrated edge of a punctured tank. I wiped the blood on my jeans and shouted, "Don't throw them here! *I'm* here!"

Dad looked up, surprised. He'd forgotten I was there. When he saw the blood, he walked over to me and put a hand on my shoulder. "Don't worry, honey," he said. "God and his angels are here, working right alongside us. They won't let you get hurt."

I wasn't the only one whose feet were searching for solid ground. For six months after the car accident, Mother had improved steadily and we'd thought she would fully recover. The headaches had become less frequent, so that she was shutting herself in the basement only two or three days a week. Then the healing had slowed. Now it had been nine months. The headaches persisted, and Mother's memory was erratic. At least twice a week she'd ask me to cook breakfast long after everyone had eaten and the dishes had been cleared. She'd tell me to weigh a pound of yarrow for a client, and I'd remind her that we'd delivered the yarrow the day before. She'd begin mixing a tincture, then a minute later couldn't remember which ingredients she'd added, so that the whole batch had to be tossed. Sometimes she would ask me to stand next to her and watch, so I could say, "You already added the lobelia. Next is the blue vervain."

Mother began to doubt whether she would ever midwife again, and while she was saddened by this, Dad was devastated. His face sagged every time Mother turned a woman away. "What if I have a migraine when she goes into labor?" she told him. "What if I can't remember what herbs I've given her, or the baby's heart rate?"

In the end it wasn't Dad who convinced Mother to midwife again. She convinced herself, perhaps because it was a part of herself she couldn't surrender without some kind of struggle. That winter, she midwifed two babies that I remember. After the first she came home sickly and pale, as if bringing that life into the world had taken a measure of her own. She was shut in the basement when the second call came. She drove to the birth in dark glasses, trying to peer through the waves distorting her vision. By the time she arrived the headache was blinding, pulsing, driving out all thought. She locked herself in a back room and her assistant delivered the baby. After that, Mother was no longer the Midwife. On the next birth, she used the bulk of her fee to hire a second midwife, to supervise her. Everyone was supervising her now, it seemed. She had been an expert, an uncontested power; now she had to ask her ten-year-old daughter whether she'd eaten lunch. That winter was long and dark, and I wondered if sometimes Mother was staying in bed even when she didn't have a migraine.

At Christmas, someone gave her an expensive bottle of blended essential oils. It helped her headaches, but at fifty dollars for a third of an ounce, we couldn't afford it. Mother decided to make her own. She began buying single, unmixed oils—eucalyptus and helichrysum, sandalwood and ravensara—and the house, which for years had smelled of earthy bark and bitter leaves, suddenly smelled of lavender and chamomile. She spent whole days blending oils, making adjustments to achieve specific fragrances and attributes. She worked with a pad and pen so she could record every step as she took it. The oils were much more expensive than the tinctures; it was devastating when she had to throw out a batch because she couldn't remember whether she'd added the spruce. She made an oil for migraines and an oil for menstrual cramps, one for sore muscles and one for heart palpitations. In the coming years she would invent dozens more.

To create her formulas, Mother took up something called "muscle testing," which she explained to me as "asking the body what it needs and letting it answer." Mother would say to herself, aloud, "I have a migraine. What will make it better?" Then she would pick up a bottle of oil, press it to her chest and, with her eyes closed, say, "Do I need *this*?" If her body swayed forward it meant yes, the oil would help her headache. If her body swayed backward it meant no, and she would test something else.

As she became more skilled, Mother went from using her whole body to only her fingers. She would cross her middle and index fingers, then flex slightly to try to uncross them, asking herself a question. If the fingers remained entwined that meant yes; if they parted it was no. The sound produced by this method was faint but unmistakable: each time the pad of her middle finger slipped across the nail of her index, there was a fleshy *click*.

Mother used muscle testing to experiment with other methods of healing. Diagrams of chakras and pressure points appeared around the house, and she began charging clients for something called "energy work." I didn't know what that meant until one afternoon when Mother called me and Richard into the back room. A woman named Susan was there. Mother's eyes were closed and her left hand was resting on Susan's. The fingers on her other hand were crossed, and she

70

was whispering questions to herself. After a few she turned to the woman and said, "Your relationship with your father is damaging your kidneys. Think of him while we adjust the chakra." Mother explained that energy work is most effective when several people are present. "So we can draw from everyone's energy," she said. Mother pointed to my forehead and told me to tap the center, between my eyebrows, while with my other hand I was to grab Susan's arm. Richard was to tap a pressure point on his chest while reaching out to me with his other hand, and Mother was to hold a point in her palm while touching Richard with her foot. "That's it," she said as I took my brother's arm. We stood in silence for ten minutes, a human chain.

When I think of that afternoon, what I remember first is the awkwardness of it: Mother said she could feel the hot energy moving through our bodies, but I felt nothing. Mother and Richard stood still, eyes shut, breath shallow. They could feel the energy and were transported by it. I fidgeted. I tried to focus, then worried that I was ruining things for Susan, that I was a break in the chain, that Mother and Richard's healing power would never reach her because I was failing to conduct it. When the ten minutes were up, Susan gave Mother twenty dollars and the next customer came in.

If I was skeptical, my skepticism was not entirely my fault. It was the result of my not being able to decide which of my mothers to trust. A year before the accident, when Mother had first heard of muscle testing and energy work, she'd dismissed both as wishful thinking. "People want a miracle," she'd told me. "They'll swallow anything if it brings them hope, if it lets them believe they're getting better. But there's no such thing as magic. Nutrition, exercise and a careful study of herbal properties, that's all there is. But when they're suffering, people can't accept that."

Now Mother said that healing was spiritual and limitless.

Muscle testing, she explained to me, was a kind of prayer, a divine supplication. An act of faith in which God spoke through her fingers. In some moments I believed her, this wise woman with an answer to every question; but I could never quite forget the words of that other woman, that other mother, who was also wise. *There's no such thing as magic.*

One day Mother announced that she had reached a new skill level. "I no longer need to say the question aloud," she said. "I can just think it."

That's when I began to notice Mother moving around the house, her hand resting lightly on various objects as she muttered to herself, her fingers flexing in a steady rhythm. If she was making bread and wasn't sure how much flour she'd added. *Click click click.* If she was mixing oils and couldn't remember whether she'd added frankincense. *Click click click.* She'd sit down to read her scriptures for thirty minutes, forget what time she'd started, then muscle-test how long it had been. *Click click click.*

Mother began to muscle-test compulsively, unaware she was doing it, whenever she grew tired of a conversation, whenever the ambiguities of her memory, or even just those of normal life, left her unsatisfied. Her features would slacken, her face become vacant, and her fingers would click like crickets at dusk.

Dad was rapturous. "Them doctors can't tell what's wrong just by touching you," he said, glowing. "But Mother can!"

The memory of Tyler haunted me that winter. I remembered the day he left, how strange it was to see his car bumping down the hill loaded with boxes. I couldn't imagine where he was now, but sometimes I wondered if perhaps school was less evil than Dad thought, because Tyler was the least evil person I knew, and he loved school—loved it more, it seemed, than he loved us.

The seed of curiosity had been planted; it needed nothing more than time and boredom to grow. Sometimes, when I was stripping copper from a radiator or throwing the five hundredth chunk of steel into the bin, I'd find myself imagining the classrooms where Tyler was spending his days. My interest grew more acute with every deadening hour in the junkyard, until one day I had a bizarre thought: that I should enroll in the public school.

Mother had always said we could go to school if we wanted. We just had to ask Dad, she said. Then we could go.

But I didn't ask. There was something in the hard line of my father's face, in the quiet sigh of supplication he made every morning before he began family prayer, that made me think my curiosity was an obscenity, an affront to all he'd sacrificed to raise me.

I made some effort to keep up my schooling in the free time I had between scrapping and helping Mother make tinctures and blend oils. Mother had given up homeschooling by then, but still had a computer, and there were books in the basement. I found the science book, with its colorful illustrations, and the math book I remembered from years before. I even located a faded green book of history. But when I sat down to study I nearly always fell asleep. The pages were glossy and soft, made softer by the hours I'd spent hauling scrap.

When Dad saw me with one of those books, he'd try to get me away from them. Perhaps he was remembering Tyler. Perhaps he thought if he could just distract me for a few years, the danger would pass. So he made up jobs for me to do, whether they needed doing or not. One afternoon, after he'd caught me looking at the math book, he and I spent an hour hauling buckets of water across the field to his fruit trees, which wouldn't have been at all unusual except it was during a rainstorm.

But if Dad was trying to keep his children from being overly interested in school and books—from being seduced by the Illuminati, like Tyler had been—he would have done better to turn his attention to Richard. Richard was also supposed to spend his afternoons making tinctures for Mother, but he almost never did. Instead, he'd disappear. I don't know if Mother knew where he went, but I did. In the afternoons, Richard could nearly always be found in the dark basement, wedged in the crawl space between the couch and the wall, an encyclopedia propped open in front of him. If Dad happened by he'd turn the light off, muttering about wasted electricity. Then I'd find some excuse to go downstairs so I could turn it back on. If Dad came through again, a snarl would sound through the house, and Mother would have to sit through a lecture on leaving lights on in empty rooms. She never scolded me, which makes me wonder if she did know where Richard was. If I couldn't get back down to turn on the light, Richard would pull the book to his nose and read in the dark; he wanted to read that badly. He wanted to read the *encyclopedia* that badly.

Tyler was gone. There was hardly a trace he'd ever lived in the house, except one: every night, after dinner, I would close the door to my room and pull Tyler's old boom box from under my bed. I'd drag his desk into my room, and while the choir sang I would settle into his chair and study, just as I'd seen him do on a thousand nights. I didn't study history or math. I studied religion.

I read the Book of Mormon twice. I read the New Testament, once quickly, then a second time more slowly, pausing to make notes, to cross-reference, and even to write short essays on doctrines like faith and sacrifice. No one read the essays; I wrote them for myself, the way I imagined Tyler had studied for himself and himself only. I worked through the Old Testament next, then I read Dad's books, which were mostly compilations of the speeches, letters and journals of the early

Mormon prophets. Their language was of the nineteenth century—stiff, winding, but exact—and at first I understood nothing. But over time my eyes and ears adjusted, so that I began to feel at home with those fragments of my people's history: stories of pioneers, my ancestors, striking out across the American wilderness. While the stories were vivid, the lectures were abstract, treatises on obscure philosophical subjects, and it was to these abstractions that I devoted most of my study.

In retrospect, I see that *this* was my education, the one that would matter: the hours I spent sitting at a borrowed desk, struggling to parse narrow strands of Mormon doctrine in mimicry of a brother who'd deserted me. The skill I was learning was a crucial one, the patience to read things I could not yet understand.

By the time the snow on the mountain began to melt, my hands were thickly callused. A season in the junkyard had honed my reflexes: I'd learned to listen for the low grunt that escaped Dad's lips whenever he tossed something heavy, and when I heard it I hit the dirt. I spent so much time flat in the mud, I didn't salvage much. Dad joked I was as slow as molasses running uphill.

The memory of Tyler had faded, and with it had faded his music, drowned out by the crack of metal crashing into metal. Those were the sounds that played in my head at night now—the jingle of corrugated tin, the short tap of copper wire, the thunder of iron.

I had entered into the new reality. I saw the world through my father's eyes. I saw the angels, or at least I imagined I saw them, watching us scrap, stepping forward and catching the car batteries or jagged lengths of steel tubing that Dad launched across the yard. I'd stopped shouting at Dad for throwing them. Instead, I prayed.

I worked faster when I salvaged alone, so one morning

when Dad was in the northern tip of the yard, near the mountain, I headed for the southern tip, near the pasture. I filled a bin with two thousand pounds of iron; then, my arms aching, I ran to find Dad. The bin had to be emptied, and I couldn't operate the loader—a massive forklift with a telescopic arm and wide, black wheels that were taller than I was. The loader would raise the bin some twenty-five feet into the air and then, with the boom extended, tilt the forks so the scrap could slide out, raining down into the trailer with a tremendous clamor. The trailer was a fifty-foot flatbed rigged for scrapping, essentially a giant bucket. Its walls were made of thick iron sheets that reached eight feet from the bed. The trailer could hold between fifteen and twenty bins, or about forty thousand pounds of iron.

I found Dad in the field, lighting a fire to burn the insulation from a tangle of copper wires. I told him the bin was ready, and he walked back with me and climbed into the loader. He waved at the trailer. "We'll get more in if you settle the iron after it's been dumped. Hop in."

I didn't understand. He wanted to dump the bin with me in it? "I'll climb up after you've dumped the load," I said.

"No, this'll be faster," Dad said. "I'll pause when the bin's level with the trailer wall so you can climb out. Then you can run along the wall and perch on top of the cab until the dump is finished."

I settled myself on a length of iron. Dad jammed the forks under the bin, then lifted me and the scrap and began driving, full throttle, toward the trailer's head. I could barely hold on. On the last turn, the bucket swung with such force that a spike of iron was flung toward me. It pierced the inside of my leg, an inch below my knee, sliding into the tissue like a knife into warm butter. I tried to pull it out but the load had shifted, and it was partially buried. I heard the soft groaning of hydraulic pumps as the boom extended. The groaning stopped when the bin was level with the trailer. Dad was giving me time to climb onto the trailer wall but I was pinned. "I'm stuck!" I shouted, only the growl of the loader's engine was too loud. I wondered if Dad would wait to dump the bin until he saw me sitting safely on the semi's cab, but even as I wondered I knew he wouldn't. Time was still stalking.

The hydraulics groaned and the bin raised another eight feet. Dumping position. I shouted again, higher this time, then lower, trying to find a pitch that would pierce through the drone of the engine. The bin began its tilt, slowly at first, then quickly. I was pinned near the back. I wrapped my hands around the bin's top wall, knowing this would give me a ledge to grasp when the bin was vertical. As the bin continued to pitch, the scrap at the front began to slide forward, bit by bit, a great iron glacier breaking apart. The spike was still embedded in my leg, dragging me downward. My grip had slipped and I'd begun to slide when the spike finally ripped from me and fell away, smashing into the trailer with a tremendous crash. I was now free, but falling. I flailed my arms, willing them to seize something that wasn't plunging downward. My palm caught hold of the bin's side wall, which was now nearly vertical. I pulled myself toward it and hoisted my body over its edge, then continued my fall. Because I was now falling from the side of the bin and not the front, I hoped—I prayed—that I was falling toward the ground and not toward the trailer, which was at that moment a fury of grinding metal. I sank, seeing only blue sky, waiting to feel either the stab of sharp iron or the jolt of solid earth.

My back struck iron: the trailer's wall. My feet snapped over my head and I continued my graceless plunge to the ground. The first fall was seven or eight feet, the second perhaps ten. I was relieved to taste dirt.

I lay on my back for perhaps fifteen seconds before the engine growled to silence and I heard Dad's heavy step.

"What happened?" he said, kneeling next to me.

"I fell out," I wheezed. The wind had been knocked out of me, and there was a powerful throbbing in my back, as if I'd been cut in two.

"How'd you manage that?" Dad said. His tone was sympathetic but disappointed. I felt stupid. *I should have been able to do it,* I thought. *It's a simple thing.*

Dad examined the gash in my leg, which had been ripped wide as the spike had fallen away. It looked like a pothole; the tissue had simply sunk out of sight. Dad slipped out of his flannel shirt and pressed it to my leg. "Go on home," he said. "Mother will stop the bleeding."

I limped through the pasture until Dad was out of sight, then collapsed in the wheatgrass. I was shaking, gulping mouthfuls of air that never made it to my lungs. I didn't understand why I was crying. I was alive. I would be fine. The angels had done their part. So why couldn't I stop trembling?

I was light-headed when I crossed the last field and approached the house, but I burst through the back door, as I'd seen my brothers do, as Robert and Emma had done, shouting for Mother. When she saw the crimson footprints streaked across the linoleum, she fetched the homeopathic she used to treat hemorrhages and shock, called Rescue Remedy, and put twelve drops of the clear, tasteless liquid under my tongue. She rested her left hand lightly on the gash and crossed the fingers of her right. Her eyes closed. *Click click click.* "There's no tetanus," she said. "The wound will close. Eventually. But it'll leave a nasty scar."

She turned me onto my stomach and examined the bruise—a patch of deep purple the size of a human head—that had formed a few inches above my hip. Again her fingers crossed and her eyes closed. *Click click click.*

"You've damaged your kidney," she said. "We'd better make a fresh batch of juniper and mullein flower."

The gash below my knee had formed a scab—dark and shiny, a black river flowing through pink flesh—when I came to a decision.

I chose a Sunday evening, when Dad was resting on the couch, his Bible propped open in his lap. I stood in front of him for what felt like hours, but he didn't look up, so I blurted out what I'd come to say: "I want to go to school."

He seemed not to have heard me.

"I've prayed, and I want to go," I said.

Finally, Dad looked up and straight ahead, his gaze fixed on something behind me. The silence settled, its presence heavy. "In this family," he said, "we obey the commandments of the Lord."

He picked up his Bible and his eyes twitched as they jumped from line to line. I turned to leave, but before I reached the doorway Dad spoke again. "You remember Jacob and Esau?"

"I remember," I said.

He returned to his reading, and I left quietly. I did not need any explanation; I knew what the story meant. It meant that I was not the daughter he had raised, the daughter of faith. I had tried to sell my birthright for a mess of pottage.

7

The Lord Will Provide

It was a rainless summer. The sun blazed across the sky each afternoon, scorching the mountain with its arid, desiccating heat, so that each morning when I crossed the field to the barn, I felt stalks of wild wheat crackle and break beneath my feet.

I spent an amber morning making the Rescue Remedy homeopathic for Mother. I would take fifteen drops from the base formula—which was kept in Mother's sewing cupboard, where it would not be used or polluted—and add them to a small bottle of distilled water. Then I would make a circle with my index finger and my thumb, and push the bottle through the circle. The strength of the homeopathic, Mother said, depended on how many passes the bottle made through my fingers, how many times it drew on my energy. Usually I stopped at fifty.

Dad and Luke were on the mountain, in the junkyard above the upper pasture, a quarter mile from the house. They were preparing cars for the crusher, which Dad had hired for later that week. Luke was seventeen. He had a lean, muscular build and, when outdoors, an easy smile. Luke and Dad were draining gasoline from the tanks. The crusher won't take a car with the fuel tank attached, because there's a risk of explosion, so every tank had to be drained and removed. It was slow work, puncturing the tank with a hammer and stake, then waiting for the fuel to drip out so the tank could be safely removed with a cutting torch. Dad had devised a shortcut: an enormous skewer, eight feet tall, of thick iron. Dad would lift a car with the forklift, and Luke would guide him until the car's tank was suspended directly over the spike. Then Dad would drop the forks. If all went well, the car would be impaled on the spike and gasoline would gush from the tank, streaming down the spike and into the flat-bottom container Dad had welded in place to collect it.

By noon, they had drained somewhere between thirty and forty cars. Luke had collected the fuel in five-gallon buckets, which he began to haul across the yard to Dad's flatbed. On one pass he stumbled, drenching his jeans in a gallon of gas. The summer sun dried the denim in a matter of minutes. He finished hauling the buckets, then went home for lunch.

I remember that lunch with unsettling clarity. I remember the clammy smell of beef-and-potato casserole, and the jingle of ice cubes tumbling into tall glasses, which sweated in the summer heat. I remember Mother telling me I was on dish duty, because she was leaving for Utah after lunch to consult for another midwife on a complicated pregnancy. She said she might not make it home for dinner but there was hamburger in the freezer.

I remember laughing the whole hour. Dad lay on the kitchen floor cracking jokes about an ordinance that had recently passed in our little farming village. A stray dog had bitten a boy and everyone was up in arms. The mayor had decided to limit dog ownership to two dogs per family, even though the attacking dog hadn't belonged to anybody at all.

"These genius socialists," Dad said. "They'd drown staring up at the rain if you didn't build a roof over them." I laughed so hard at that my stomach ached.

Luke had forgotten all about the gasoline by the time he and Dad walked back up the mountain and readied the cutting torch, but when he jammed the torch into his hip and struck flint to steel, flames burst from the tiny spark and engulfed his leg.

The part we would remember, would tell and retell so many times it became family folklore, was that Luke was unable to get out of his gasoline-soaked jeans. That morning, like every morning, he had hitched up his trousers with a yard of baling twine, which is smooth and slippery, and needs a horseman's knot to stay in place. His footwear didn't help, either: bulbous steel-toed boots so tattered that for weeks he'd been duct-taping them on each morning, then cutting them off each night with his pocketknife. Luke might have severed the twine and hacked through the boots in a matter of seconds, but he went mad with panic and took off, dashing like a marked buck, spreading fire through the sagebrush and wheat grass, which were baked and brittle from the parched summer.

I'd stacked the dirty dishes and was filling the kitchen sink when I heard it—a shrill, strangled cry that began in one key and ended in another. There was no question it was human. I'd never heard an animal bellow like that, with such fluctuations in tone and pitch.

I ran outside and saw Luke hobbling across the grass. He screamed for Mother, then collapsed. That's when I saw that the jeans on his left leg were gone, melted away. Parts of the leg were livid, red and bloody; others were bleached and dead. Papery ropes of skin wrapped delicately around his thigh and down his calf, like wax dripping from a cheap candle.

His eyes rolled back in his head.

I bolted back into the house. I'd packed the new bottles of Rescue Remedy, but the base formula still sat on the counter.

I snatched it and ran outside, then dumped half the bottle between Luke's twitching lips. There was no change. His eyes were marble white.

One brown iris slipped into view, then the other. He began to mumble, then to scream. "It's on fire! It's on fire!" he roared. A chill passed through him and his teeth clattered; he was shivering.

I was only ten, and in that moment I felt very much a child. Luke was my big brother; I thought he would know what to do, so I grabbed his shoulders and shook him, hard. "Should I make you cold or make you hot?" I shouted. He answered with a gasp.

The burn was the injury, I reasoned. It made sense to treat it first. I fetched a pack of ice from the chest freezer on the patio, but when the pack touched his leg he screamed—a back-arching, eye-popping scream that made my brain claw at my skull. I needed another way to cool the leg. I considered unloading the chest freezer and putting Luke inside it, but the freezer would work only if the lid was shut, and then he'd suffocate.

I mentally searched the house. We had a large garbage can, a blue whale of a bin. It was splattered with bits of rotted food, so rank we kept it shut away in a closet. I sprinted into the house and emptied it onto the linoleum, noting the dead mouse Richard had tossed in the day before, then I carried the bin outside and sprayed it out with the garden hose. I knew I should clean it more thoroughly, maybe with dish soap, but looking at Luke, the way he was writhing on the grass, I didn't feel I had time. With the last bit of slop blasted away, I righted the bin and filled it with water.

Luke was scrambling toward me to put his leg in when I heard an echo of my mother's voice. She was telling someone that the real worry with a burn isn't the damaged tissue, but infection.

"Luke!" I shouted. "Don't! Don't put your leg in!"

He ignored me and continued crawling toward the bin. He had a cold look in his eye that said nothing mattered except the fire burning from his leg into his brain. I moved quickly. I shoved the bin, and a great wave of water heaved over the grass. Luke made a gargled noise, as if he were choking.

I ran back into the kitchen and found the bags that fit the can, then held one open for Luke and told him to put his leg in. He didn't move, but he allowed me to pull the bag over the raw flesh. I righted the can and stuffed the garden hose inside. While the bin filled, I helped Luke balance on one foot and lower his burned leg, now wrapped in black plastic, into the garbage can. The afternoon air was sweltering; the water would warm quickly; I tossed in the pack of ice.

It didn't take long—twenty minutes, maybe thirty—before Luke seemed in his right mind, calm and able to prop himself up. Then Richard wandered up from the basement. The garbage can was smack in the middle of the lawn, ten feet from any shade, and the afternoon sun was strong. Full of water, the can was too heavy for us to move, and Luke refused to take out his leg, even for a minute. I fetched a straw sombrero Grandma had given us in Arizona. Luke's teeth were still chattering so I also brought a wool blanket. And there he stood, a sombrero on his head, a wool blanket around his shoulders, and his leg in a garbage can. He looked something between homeless and on vacation.

The sun warmed the water; Luke began to shift uncomfortably. I returned to the chest freezer but there was no more ice, just a dozen bags of frozen vegetables, so I dumped them in. The result was a muddy soup with bits of peas and carrots.

Dad wandered home sometime after this, I couldn't say how long, a gaunt, defeated look on his face. Quiet now, Luke was resting, or as near to resting as he could be standing up. Dad wheeled the bin into the shade because, despite the hat, Luke's hands and arms had turned red with sunburn.

Dad said the best thing to do was leave the leg where it was until Mother came home.

Mother's car appeared on the highway around six. I met her halfway up the hill and told her what had happened. She rushed to Luke and said she needed to see the leg, so he lifted it out, dripping. The plastic bag clung to the wound. Mother didn't want to tear the fragile tissue, so she cut the bag away slowly, carefully, until the leg was visible. There was very little blood and even fewer blisters, as both require skin and Luke didn't have much. Mother's face turned a grayish yellow, but she was calm. She closed her eyes and crossed her fingers, then asked aloud whether the wound was infected. *Click click click*.

"You were lucky this time, Tara," she said. "But what were you thinking, putting a burn into a *garbage* can?"

Dad carried Luke inside and Mother fetched her scalpel. It took her and Dad most of the evening to cut away the dead flesh. Luke tried not to scream, but when they pried up and stretched bits of his skin, trying to see where the dead flesh ended and the living began, he exhaled in great gusts and tears slid from his eyes.

Mother dressed the leg in mullein and comfrey salve, her own recipe. She was good with burns—they were a specialty of hers—but I could tell she was worried. She said she'd never seen one as bad as Luke's. She didn't know what would happen.

Mother and I stayed by Luke's bed that first night. He barely slept, he was so delirious with fever and pain. For the fever we put ice on his face and chest; for the pain we gave him lobelia, blue vervain and skullcap. This was another of Mother's recipes. I'd taken it after I'd fallen from the scrap bin, to dull the throbbing in my leg while I waited for the gash to close, but as near as I could tell it had no effect.

I believed hospital drugs were an abomination to God, but

if I'd had morphine that night, I'd have given it to Luke. The pain robbed him of breath. He lay propped up in his bed, beads of sweat falling from his forehead onto his chest, holding his breath until he turned red, then purple, as if depriving his brain of oxygen was the only way he could make it through the next minute. When the pain in his lungs overtook the pain of the burn, he would release the air in a great, gasping cry—a cry of relief for his lungs, of agony for his leg.

I tended him alone the second night so Mother could rest. I slept lightly, waking at the first sounds of fussing, at the slightest shifting of weight, so I could fetch the ice and tinctures before Luke became fully conscious and the pain gripped him. On the third night, Mother tended him and I stood in the doorway, listening to his gasps, watching Mother watch him, her face hollow, her eyes swollen with worry and exhaustion.

When I slept, I dreamed. I dreamed about the fire I hadn't seen. I dreamed it was me lying in that bed, my body wrapped in loose bandages, mummified. Mother knelt on the floor beside me, pressing my plastered hand the way she pressed Luke's, dabbing my forehead, praying.

Luke didn't go to church that Sunday, or the Sunday after that, or the one after that. Dad told us to tell people Luke was sick. He said there'd be trouble if the Government found out about Luke's leg, that the Feds would take us kids away. That they would put Luke in a hospital, where his leg would get infected and he would die.

About three weeks after the fire, Mother announced that the skin around the edges of the burn had begun to grow back, and that she had hope for even the worst patches. By then Luke was sitting up, and a week later, when the first cold spell hit, he could stand for a minute or two on crutches. Before long, he was thumping around the house, thin as a string bean, swallowing buckets of food to regain the weight he'd lost. By then, the twine was a family fable.

"A man ought to have a real belt," Dad said at breakfast on the day Luke was well enough to return to the junkyard, handing him a leather strap with a steel buckle.

"Not Luke," Richard said. "He prefers twine, you know how fashionable he is."

Luke grinned. "Beauty's everything," he said.

For eighteen years I never thought of that day, not in any probing way. The few times my reminiscing carried me back to that torrid afternoon, what I remembered first was the belt. *Luke,* I would think. *You wild dog. I wonder, do you still wear twine?*

Now, at age twenty-nine, I sit down to write, to reconstruct the incident from the echoes and shouts of a tired memory. I scratch it out. When I get to the end, I pause. There's an inconsistency, a ghost in this story.

I read it. I read it again. And there it is.

Who put out the fire?

A long-dormant voice says, *Dad did.*

But Luke was alone when I found him. If Dad had been with Luke on the mountain, he would have brought him to the house, would have treated the burn. Dad was away on a job somewhere, that's why Luke had had to get himself down the mountain. Why his leg had been treated by a ten-year-old. Why it had ended up in a garbage can.

I decide to ask Richard. He's older than I, and has a sharper memory. Besides, last I heard, Luke no longer has a telephone.

I call. The first thing Richard remembers is the twine, which, true to his nature, he refers to as a "baling implement." Next he remembers the spilled gasoline. I ask how Luke managed to put out the fire and get himself down the mountain, given that he was in shock when I found him. Dad was with him, Richard says flatly.

87

Right.

Then why wasn't Dad at the house?

Richard says, Because Luke had run through the weeds and set the mountain afire. You remember that summer. Dry, scorching. You can't go starting forest fires in farm country during a dry summer. So Dad put Luke in the truck and told him to drive to the house, to Mother. Only Mother was gone.

Right.

I think it over for a few days, then sit back down to write. Dad is there in the beginning—Dad with his funny jokes about socialists and dogs and the roof that keeps liberals from drowning. Then Dad and Luke go back up the mountain, Mother drives away and I turn the tap to fill the kitchen sink. Again. For the third time it feels like.

On the mountain something is happening. I can only imagine it but I see it clearly, more clearly than if it were a memory. The cars are stacked and waiting, their fuel tanks ruptured and drained. Dad waves at a tower of cars and says, "Luke, cut off those tanks, yeah?" And Luke says, "Sure thing, Dad." He lays the torch against his hip and strikes flint. Flames erupt from nowhere and take him. He screams, fumbles with the twine, screams again, and takes off through the weeds.

Dad chases him, orders him to stand still. It's probably the first time in his whole life that Luke doesn't do something when Dad is telling him to. Luke is fast but Dad is smart. He takes a shortcut through a pyramid of cars and tackles Luke, slamming him to the ground.

I can't picture what happens next, because nobody ever told me how Dad put out the fire on Luke's leg. Then a memory surfaces—of Dad, that night in the kitchen, wincing as Mother slathers salve on his hands, which are red and blistering—and I know what he must have done.

Luke is no longer on fire.

I try to imagine the moment of decision. Dad looks at the weeds, which are burning fast, thirsty for flame in that quivering heat. He looks at his son. He thinks if he can choke the flames while they're young, he can prevent a wildfire, maybe save the house.

Luke seems lucid. His brain hasn't processed what's happened; the pain hasn't set in. *The Lord will provide,* I imagine Dad thinking. *God left him conscious.*

I imagine Dad praying aloud, his eyes drawn heavenward, as he carries his son to the truck and sets him in the driver's seat. Dad shifts the engine into first, the truck starts its roll. It's going at a good speed now, Luke is gripping the wheel. Dad jumps from the moving truck, hits the ground hard and rolls, then runs back toward the brushfire, which has spread wider and grown taller. *The Lord will provide,* he chants, then he takes off his shirt and begins to beat back the flames.[3]

8

Tiny Harlots

I wanted to get away from the junkyard and there was only one way to do that, which was the way Audrey had done it: by getting a job so I wouldn't be at the house when Dad rounded up his crew. The trouble was, I was eleven.

I biked a mile into the dusty center of our little village. There wasn't much there, just a church, a post office and a gas station called Papa Jay's. I went into the post office. Behind the counter was an older lady whose name I knew was Myrna Moyle, because Myrna and her husband Jay (Papa Jay) owned the gas station. Dad said they'd been behind the city ordinance limiting dog ownership to two dogs per family. They'd proposed other ordinances, too, and now every Sunday Dad came home from church shouting about Myrna and Jay Moyle, and how they were from Monterey or Seattle or wherever and thought they could impose West Coast socialism on the good people of Idaho.

I asked Myrna if I could put a card up on the board. She asked what the card was for. I said I hoped I could find jobs babysitting.

"What times are you available?" she said.

"Anytime, all the time."

"You mean after school?"

"I mean all the time."

Myrna looked at me and tilted her head. "My daughter Mary needs someone to tend her youngest. I'll ask her."

Mary taught nursing at the school, which Dad said was just about as brainwashed as a person could get, to be working for the Medical Establishment *and* the Government both. I thought maybe he wouldn't let me work for her, but he did, and pretty soon I was babysitting Mary's daughter every Monday, Wednesday and Friday morning. Then Mary had a friend, Eve, who needed a babysitter for her three children on Tuesdays and Thursdays.

A mile down the road, a man named Randy ran a business out of his home, selling cashews, almonds and macadamias. He stopped by the post office one afternoon and chatted with Myrna about how tired he was of packing the boxes himself, how he wished he could hire some kids but they were all tied up with football and band.

"There's at least one kid in this town who isn't," Myrna said. "And I think she'd be real eager." She pointed to my card, and soon I was babysitting from eight until noon Monday to Friday, then going to Randy's to pack cashews until supper. I wasn't paid much, but as I'd never been paid anything before, it felt like a lot.

People at church said Mary could play the piano beautifully. They used the word "professional." I didn't know what that meant until one Sunday when Mary played a piano solo for the congregation. The music stopped my breath. I'd heard the piano played countless times before, to accompany hymns, but when Mary played it, the sound was nothing like that formless clunking. It was liquid, it was air. It was rock one moment and wind the next.

The next day, when Mary returned from the school, I asked her if instead of money she would give me lessons. We perched on the piano bench and she showed me a few finger exercises.

Then she asked what else I was learning besides the piano. Dad had told me what to say when people asked about my schooling. "I do school every day," I said.

"Do you meet other kids?" she asked. "Do you have friends?"

"Sure," I said. Mary returned to the lesson. When we'd finished and I was ready to go, she said, "My sister Caroline teaches dance every Wednesday in the back of Papa Jay's. There are lots of girls your age. You could join."

That Wednesday, I left Randy's early and pedaled to the gas station. I wore jeans, a large gray T-shirt, and steel-toed boots; the other girls wore black leotards and sheer, shimmering skirts, white tights and tiny ballet shoes the color of taffy. Caroline was younger than Mary. Her makeup was flawless and gold hoops flashed through chestnut curls.

She arranged us in rows, then showed us a short routine. A song played from a boom box in the corner. I'd never heard it before but the other girls knew it. I looked in the mirror at our reflection, at the twelve girls, sleek and shiny, pirouetting blurs of black, white and pink. Then at myself, large and gray.

When the lesson finished, Caroline told me to buy a leotard and dance shoes.

"I can't," I said.

"Oh." She looked uncomfortable. "Maybe one of the girls can lend you one."

She'd misunderstood. She thought I didn't have money. "It isn't modest," I said. Her lips parted in surprise. *These Californian Moyles,* I thought.

"Well, you can't dance in boots," she said. "I'll talk to your mother."

A few days later, Mother drove me forty miles to a small shop whose shelves were lined with exotic shoes and strange acrylic costumes. Not one was modest. Mother went straight to the counter and told the attendant we needed a black leotard, white tights and jazz shoes.

"Keep those in your room," Mother said as we left the store. She didn't need to say anything else. I already understood that I should not show the leotard to Dad.

That Wednesday, I wore the leotard and tights with my gray T-shirt over the top. The T-shirt reached almost to my knees, but even so I was ashamed to see so much of my legs. Dad said a righteous woman never shows anything above her ankle.

The other girls rarely spoke to me, but I loved being there with them. I loved the sensation of conformity. Learning to dance felt like learning to belong. I could memorize the movements and, in doing so, step into their minds, lunging when they lunged, reaching my arms upward in time with theirs. Sometimes, when I glanced at the mirror and saw the tangle of our twirling forms, I couldn't immediately discern myself in the crowd. It didn't matter that I was wearing a gray T-shirt—a goose among swans. We moved together, a single flock.

We began rehearsals for the Christmas recital, and Caroline called Mother to discuss the costume. "The skirt will be how long?" Mother said. "And sheer? No, that's not going to work." I heard Caroline say something about what the other girls in the class would want to wear. "Tara can't wear that," Mother said. "If that's what the other girls are wearing, she will stay home."

On the Wednesday after Caroline called Mother, I arrived at Papa Jay's a few minutes early. The younger class had just finished, and the store was flooded with six-year-olds, prancing for their mothers in red velvet hats and skirts sparkling with sequins of deep scarlet. I watched them wiggle and leap through the aisles, their thin legs covered only by sheer tights. I thought they looked like tiny harlots.

The rest of my class arrived. When they saw the outfits, they rushed into the studio to see what Caroline had for *them*. Caroline was standing next to a cardboard box full of large gray sweatshirts. She began handing them out. "Here are your costumes!" she said. The girls held up their sweat-shirts, eyebrows raised in disbelief. They had expected chiffon or ribbon, not Fruit of the Loom. Caroline had tried to make the sweatshirts more appealing by sewing large Santas, bordered with glitter, on the fronts, but this only made the dingy cotton seem dingier.

Mother hadn't told Dad about the recital, and neither had I. I didn't ask him to come. There was an instinct at work in me, a learned intuition. The day of the recital, Mother told Dad I had a "thing" that night. Dad asked a lot of questions, which surprised Mother, and after a few minutes she admitted it was a dance recital. Dad grimaced when Mother told him I'd been taking lessons from Caroline Moyle, and I thought he was going to start talking about California socialism again, but he didn't. Instead he got his coat and the three of us walked to the car.

The recital was held at the church. Everyone was there, with flashing cameras and bulky camcorders. I changed into my costume in the same room where I attended Sunday school. The other girls chatted cheerfully; I pulled on my sweatshirt, trying to stretch the material a few more inches. I was still tugging it downward when we lined up on the stage.

Music played from a stereo on the piano and we began to dance, our feet tapping in sequence. Next we were supposed to leap, reach upward and spin. My feet remained planted. Instead of flinging my arms above my head, I lifted them only to my shoulders. When the other girls crouched to slap the stage, I tilted; when we were to cartwheel, I swayed, refusing to allow gravity to do its work, to draw the sweatshirt any higher up my legs.

The music ended. The girls glared at me as we left the stage—I had ruined the performance—but I could barely see them. Only one person in that room felt real to me, and that was Dad. I searched the audience and recognized him easily.

He was standing in the back, the lights from the stage flickering off his square glasses. His expression was stiff, impassive, but I could see anger in it.

The drive home was only a mile; it felt like a hundred. I sat in the backseat and listened to my father shout. How could Mother have let me sin so openly? Was this why she'd kept the recital from him? Mother listened for a moment, chewing her lip, then threw her hands in the air and said that she'd had no idea the costume would be so immodest. "I'm furious with Caroline Moyle!" she said.

I leaned forward to see Mother's face, wanting her to look at me, to see the question I was mentally asking her, because I didn't understand, not at all. I knew Mother wasn't furious with Caroline, because I knew Mother had seen the sweatshirt days before. She had even called Caroline and thanked her for choosing a costume I could wear. Mother turned her head toward the window.

I stared at the gray hairs on the back of Dad's head. He was sitting quietly, listening to Mother, who continued to insult Caroline, to say how shocking the costumes were, how obscene. Dad nodded as we bumped up the icy driveway, becoming less angry with every word from Mother.

The rest of the night was taken up by my father's lecture. He said Caroline's class was one of Satan's deceptions, like the public school, because it claimed to be one thing when really it was another. It *claimed* to teach dance, but instead it taught immodesty, promiscuity. Satan was shrewd, Dad said. By calling it "dance," he had convinced good Mormons to accept the sight of their daughters jumping about like whores in the Lord's house. That fact offended Dad more than anything else: that such a lewd display had taken place in a church.

After he had worn himself out and gone to bed, I crawled under my covers and stared into the black. There was a knock at my door. It was Mother. "I should have known better," she said. "I should have seen that class for what it was."

Mother must have felt guilty after the recital, because in the weeks that followed she searched for something else I could do, something Dad wouldn't forbid. She'd noticed the hours I spent in my room with Tyler's old boom box, listening to the Mormon Tabernacle Choir, so she began looking for a voice teacher. It took a few weeks to find one, and another few weeks to persuade the teacher to take me. The lessons were much more expensive than the dance class had been, but Mother paid for them with the money she made selling oils.

The teacher was tall and thin, with long fingernails that clicked as they flew across the piano keys. She straightened my posture by pulling the hair at the base of my neck until I'd tucked in my chin, then she stretched me out on the floor and stepped on my stomach to strengthen my diaphragm. She was obsessed with balance and often slapped my knees to remind me to stand powerfully, to take up my own space.

After a few lessons, she announced that I was ready to sing in church. It was arranged, she said. I would sing a hymn in front of the congregation that Sunday.

The days slipped away quickly, as days do when you're dreading something. On Sunday morning, I stood at the pulpit and stared into the faces of the people below. There was Myrna and Papa Jay, and behind them Mary and Caroline. They looked sorry for me, like they thought I might . humiliate myself.

Mother played the introduction. The music paused; it was time to sing. I might have had any number of thoughts at that moment. I might have thought of my teacher and her techniques—square stance, straight back, dropped jaw. Instead I thought of Tyler, and of lying on the carpet next to his desk, staring at his woolen-socked feet while the Mormon

Tabernacle Choir chanted and trilled. He'd filled my head with their voices, which to me were more beautiful than anything except Buck's Peak.

Mother's fingers hovered over the keys. The pause had become awkward; the congregation shifted uncomfortably. I thought of the voices, of their strange contradictions—of the way they made sound float on air, of how that sound was soft like a warm wind, but so sharp it pierced. I reached for those voices, reached into my mind—and there they were. Nothing had ever felt so natural; it was as if I *thought* the sound, and by thinking it brought it into being. But reality had never yielded to my thoughts before.

The song finished and I returned to our pew. A prayer was offered to close the service, then the crowd rushed me. Women in floral prints smiled and clasped my hand, men in square black suits clapped my shoulder. The choir director invited me to join the choir, Brother Davis asked me to sing for the Rotary Club, and the bishop—the Mormon equivalent of a pastor—said he'd like me to sing my song at a funeral. I said yes to all of them.

Dad smiled at everyone. There was scarcely a person in the church that Dad hadn't called a gentile—for visiting a doctor or for sending their kids to the public school—but that day he seemed to forget about California socialism and the Illuminati. He stood next to me, a hand on my shoulder, graciously collecting compliments. "We're very blessed," he kept saying. "Very blessed." Papa Jay crossed the chapel and paused in front of our pew. He said I sang like one of God's own angels. Dad looked at him for a moment, then his eyes began to shine and he shook Papa Jay's hand like they were old friends.

I'd never seen this side of my father, but I would see it many times after—every time I sang. However long he'd worked in the junkyard, he was never too tired to drive across the valley to hear me. However bitter his feelings toward socialists like Papa Jay, they were never so bitter that, should those people praise my voice, Dad wouldn't put aside the great battle he was fighting against the Illuminati long enough to say, "Yes, God has blessed us, we're very blessed." It was as if, when I sang, Dad forgot for a moment that the world was a frightening place, that it would corrupt me, that I should be kept safe, sheltered, at home. He wanted my voice to be heard.

The theater in town was putting on a play, *Annie,* and my teacher said that if the director heard me sing, he would give me the lead. Mother warned me not to get my hopes up. She said we couldn't afford to drive the twelve miles to town four nights a week for rehearsals, and that even if we could, Dad would never allow me to spend time in town, alone, with who knows what kind of people.

I practiced the songs anyway because I liked them. One evening, I was in my room singing, "The sun'll come out tomorrow," when Dad came in for supper. He chewed his meatloaf quietly, and listened.

"I'll find the money," he told Mother when they went to bed that night. "You get her to that audition."

9

Perfect in His Generations

The summer I sang the lead for *Annie* it was 1999. My father was in serious preparedness mode. Not since I was five, and the Weavers were under siege, had he been so certain that the Days of Abomination were upon us.

Dad called it Y2K. On January 1, he said, computer systems all over the world would fail. There would be no electricity, no telephones. All would sink into chaos, and this would usher in the Second Coming of Christ.

"How do you know the day?" I asked.

Dad said that the Government had programmed the computers with a six-digit calendar, which meant the year had only two digits. "When nine-nine becomes oh-oh," he said, "the computers won't know what year it is. They'll shut down."

"Can't they fix it?"

"Nope, can't be done," Dad said. "Man trusted his own strength, and his strength was weak."

At church, Dad warned everyone about Y2K. He advised Papa Jay to get strong locks for his gas station, and maybe some defensive weaponry. "That store will be the first thing looted in the famine," Dad said. He told Brother Mumford that every righteous man should have, at minimum, a ten-year supply of food, fuel, guns and gold. Brother Mumford just whistled. "We can't all be as righteous as you, Gene," he said. "Some of us are sinners!" No one listened. They went about their lives in the summer sun.

Meanwhile, my family boiled and skinned peaches, pitted apricots and churned apples into sauce. Everything was pressure-cooked, sealed, labeled, and stored away in a root cellar Dad had dug out in the field. The entrance was concealed by a hillock; Dad said I should never tell anybody where it was.

One afternoon, Dad climbed into the excavator and dug a pit next to the old barn. Then, using the loader, he lowered a thousand-gallon tank into the pit and buried it with a shovel, carefully planting nettles and sow thistle in the freshly tossed dirt so they would grow and conceal the tank. He whistled "I Feel Pretty" from *West Side Story* while he shoveled. His hat was tipped back on his head, and he wore a brilliant smile. "We'll be the only ones with fuel when The End comes," he said. "We'll be driving when everyone else is hotfooting it. We'll even make a run down to Utah, to fetch Tyler."

I had rehearsals most nights at the Worm Creek Opera House, a dilapidated theater near the only stoplight in town. The play was another world. Nobody talked about Y2K.

The interactions between people at Worm Creek were not at all what I was used to in my family. Of course I'd spent time with people outside my family, but they were like us: women who'd hired Mother to midwife their babies, or who came to her for herbs because they didn't believe in the Medical Establishment. I had a single friend, named Jessica. A few years before, Dad had convinced her parents, Rob and Diane, that public schools were little more than Government propaganda programs, and since then they had kept her at home. Before her parents had pulled Jessica from school, she was one of *them,* and I never tried to talk to her; but after, she was one of *us.* The normal kids stopped including her, and she was left with me.

I'd never learned how to talk to people who weren't like us—people who went to school and visited the doctor. Who weren't preparing, every day, for the End of the World. Worm Creek was full of these people, people whose words seemed ripped from another reality. That was how it felt the first time the director spoke to me, like he was speaking from another dimension. All he said was, "Go find FDR." I didn't move.

He tried again. "President Roosevelt. FDR."

"Is that like a JCB?" I said. "You need a forklift?"

Everyone laughed.

I'd memorized all my lines, but at rehearsals I sat alone, pretending to study my black binder. When it was my turn onstage, I would recite my lines loudly and without hesitation. That made me feel a kind of confidence. If *I* didn't have anything to say, at least Annie did.

A week before opening night, Mother dyed my brown hair cherry red. The director said it was perfect, that all I needed now was to finish my costumes before the dress rehearsal on Saturday.

In our basement I found an oversized knit sweater, stained and hole-ridden, and an ugly blue dress, which Mother bleached to a faded brown. The dress was perfect for an orphan, and I was relieved at how easy finding the costumes had been, until I remembered that in act two Annie wears beautiful dresses, which Daddy Warbucks buys for her. I didn't have anything like that.

I told Mother and her face sank. We drove a hundred miles round-trip, searching every secondhand shop along the way, but found nothing. Sitting in the parking lot of the last shop, Mother pursed her lips, then said, "There's one more place we can try."

We drove to my aunt Angie's and parked in front of the white picket fence she shared with Grandma. Mother knocked, then stood back from the door and smoothed her hair. Angie looked surprised to see us—Mother rarely visited her sister—but she smiled warmly and invited us in. Her front room reminded me of fancy hotel lobbies from the movies, there was so much silk and lace. Mother and I sat on a pleated sofa of pale pink while Mother explained why we'd come. Angie said her daughter had a few dresses that might do.

Mother waited on the pink sofa while Angie led me up-stairs to her daughter's room and laid out an armful of dresses, each so fine, with such intricate lace patterns and delicately tied bows, that at first I was afraid to touch them. Angie helped me into each one, knotting the sashes, fastening the buttons, plumping the bows. "You should take this one," she said, passing me a navy dress with white braided cords arranged across the bodice. "Grandma sewed this detailing." I took the dress, along with another made of red velvet collared with white lace, and Mother and I drove home.

The play opened a week later. Dad was in the front row. When the performance ended, he marched right to the box office and bought tickets for the next night. It was all he talked about that Sunday in church. Not doctors, or the Illuminati, or Y2K. Just the play over in town, where his youngest daughter was singing the lead.

Dad didn't stop me from auditioning for the next play, or the one after that, even though he worried about me spending so much time away from home. "There's no telling what kind of cavorting takes place in that theater," he said. "It's probably a den of adulterers and fornicators."

When the director of the next play got divorced, it confirmed Dad's suspicions. He said he hadn't kept me out of the public school for all these years just to see me corrupted on a stage. Then he drove me to the rehearsal. Nearly every night he said he was going to put a stop to my going, that one evening he'd just show up at Worm Creek and haul me home. But each time a play opened he was there, in the front row.

Sometimes he played the part of an agent or manager, correcting my technique or suggesting songs for my repertoire, even advising me about my health. That winter I caught a procession of sore throats and couldn't sing, and one night Dad called me to him and pried my mouth open to look at my tonsils.

"They're swollen, all right," he said. "Big as apricots." When Mother couldn't get the swelling down with echinacea and calendula, Dad suggested his own remedy. "People don't know it, but the sun is the most powerful medicine we have. That's why people don't get sore throats in summer." He nodded, as if approving of his own logic, then said, "If I had tonsils like yours, I'd go outside every morning and stand in the sun with my mouth open—let those rays seep in for a half hour or so. They'll shrink in no time." He called it a treatment.

I did it for a month.

It was uncomfortable, standing with my jaw dropped and my head tilted back so the sun could shine into my throat. I never lasted a whole half hour. My jaw would ache after ten minutes, and I'd half-freeze standing motionless in the Idaho winter. I kept catching more sore throats, and anytime Dad noticed I was a bit croaky, he'd say, "Well, what do you expect? I ain't seen you getting treatment all week!"

It was at the Worm Creek Opera House that I first saw him: a boy I didn't know, laughing with a group of public school kids, wearing big white shoes, khaki shorts and a wide grin. He wasn't in the play, but there wasn't much to do in town, and I saw him several more times that week when he turned up to visit his friends. Then one night, when I was wandering alone in the dark wings backstage, I turned a corner and found him sitting on the wooden crate that was a favorite haunt of mine. The crate was isolated—that was why I liked it.

He shifted to the right, making room for me. I sat slowly, tensely, as if the seat were made of needles.

"I'm Charles," he said. There was a pause while he waited for me to give my name, but I didn't. "I saw you in the last play," he said after a moment. "I wanted to tell you something." I braced myself, for what I wasn't sure, then he said, "I wanted to tell you that your singing is about the best I ever heard."

I came home one afternoon from packing macadamias to find Dad and Richard gathered around a large metal box, which they'd hefted onto the kitchen table. While Mother and I cooked meatloaf, they assembled the contents. It took more than an hour, and when they'd finished they stood back, revealing what looked like an enormous military-green telescope, with its long barrel set firmly atop a short, broad tripod. Richard was so excited he was hopping from one foot to the other, reciting what it could do. "Got a range more than a mile! Can bring down a helicopter!"

Dad stood quietly, his eyes shining.

"What is it?" I asked.

"It's a fifty-caliber rifle," he said. "Wanna try it?"

I peered through the scope, searching the mountainside, fixing distant stalks of wheat between its crosshairs.

The meatloaf was forgotten. We charged outside. It was past sunset; the horizon was dark. I watched as Dad lowered himself to the frozen ground, positioned his eye at the scope and, after what felt like an hour, pulled the trigger. The blast was thunderous. I had both palms pressed to my ears, but after the initial boom I dropped them, listening as the shot echoed through the ravines. He fired again and again, so that by the time we went inside my ears were ringing. I could barely hear Dad's reply when I asked what the gun was for.

"Defense," he said.

The next night I had a rehearsal at Worm Creek. I was perched on my crate, listening to the monologue being performed onstage, when Charles appeared and sat next to me.

"You don't go to school," he said.

It wasn't a question.

"You should come to choir. You'd like choir."

"Maybe," I said, and he smiled. A few of his friends stepped into the wing and called to him. He stood and said goodbye, and I watched him join them, taking in the easy way they joked together and imagining an alternate reality in which I was one of them. I imagined Charles inviting me to his house, to play a game or watch a movie, and felt a rush of pleasure. But when I pictured Charles visiting Buck's Peak, I felt something else, something like panic. What if he found the root cellar? What if he discovered the fuel tank? Then I understood, finally, what the rifle was for. That mighty barrel, with its special range that could reach from the mountain to the valley, was a defensive perimeter for the house, for our supplies, because Dad said we would be driving when everyone else was hotfooting it. We would have food, too, when everyone else was starving, looting. Again I imagined Charles climbing the hill to our house. But in my imagination I was on the ridge, and I was watching his approach through crosshairs.

Christmas was sparse that year. We weren't poor—Mother's business was doing well and Dad was still scrapping—but we'd spent everything on supplies.

Before Christmas, we continued our preparations as if every action, every minor addition to our stores might make the difference between surviving, and not; after Christmas, we waited. "When the hour of need arises," Dad said, "the time of preparation has passed."

The days dragged on, and then it was December 31. Dad was calm at breakfast but under his tranquillity I sensed excitement, and something like longing. He'd been waiting for so many years, burying guns and stockpiling food and warning others to do the same. Everyone at church had read the prophecies; they knew the Days of Abomination were coming. But still they'd teased Dad, they'd laughed at him. Tonight he would be vindicated.

After dinner, Dad studied Isaiah for hours. At around ten he closed his Bible and turned on the TV. The television was new. Aunt Angie's husband worked for a satellite-TV company, and he'd offered Dad a deal on a subscription. No one had believed it when Dad said yes, but in retrospect it was entirely characteristic for my father to move, in the space of a day, from no TV or radio to full-blown cable. I sometimes wondered if Dad allowed the television *that* year, specifically, because he knew it would all disappear on January 1. Perhaps he did it to give us a little taste of the world, before it was swept away.

Dad's favorite program was *The Honeymooners*, and that night there was a special, with episodes playing back to back. We watched, waiting for The End. I checked the clock every few minutes from ten until eleven, then every few seconds until midnight. Even Dad, who was rarely stirred by anything outside himself, glanced often at the clock.

11:59.

I held my breath. One more minute, I thought, before everything is gone.

Then it was 12:00. The TV was still buzzing, its lights dancing across the carpet. I wondered if our clock was fast. I went to the kitchen and turned on the tap. We had water. Dad stayed still, his eyes on the screen. I returned to the couch.

12:05.

How long would it take for the electricity to fail? Was there a reserve somewhere that was keeping it going these few extra minutes?

The black-and-white specters of Ralph and Alice Kramden argued over a meatloaf.

12:10.

I waited for the screen to flicker and die. I was trying to take it all in, this last, luxurious moment—of sharp yellow light, of warm air flowing from the heater. I was experiencing nostalgia for the life I'd had before, which I would lose at any second, when the world turned and began to devour itself.

The longer I sat motionless, breathing deeply, trying to inhale the last scent of the fallen world, the more I resented its continuing solidity. Nostalgia turned to fatigue.

Sometime after 1:30 I went to bed. I glimpsed Dad as I left, his face frozen in the dark, the light from the TV leaping across his square glasses. He sat as if posed, with no agitation, no embarrassment, as if there were a perfectly mundane explanation for why he was sitting up, alone, at near two in the morning, watching Ralph and Alice Kramden prepare for a Christmas party.

He seemed smaller to me than he had that morning. The disappointment in his features was so childlike, for a moment I wondered how God could deny him this. He, a faithful servant, who suffered willingly just as Noah had willingly suffered to build the ark.

But God withheld the flood.

10

Shield of Feathers

When January 1 dawned like any other morning, it broke Dad's spirit. He never again mentioned Y2K. He slipped into despondency, dragging himself in from the junkyard each night, silent and heavy. He'd sit in front of the TV for hours, a black cloud hovering.

Mother said it was time for another trip to Arizona. Luke was serving a mission for the church, so it was just me, Richard and Audrey who piled into the old Chevy Astro van Dad had fixed up. Dad removed the seats, except the two in front, and in their place he put a queen mattress; then he heaved himself onto it and didn't move for the rest of the drive.

As it had years before, the Arizona sun revived Dad. He lay out on the porch on the hard cement, soaking it up, while the rest of us read or watched TV. After a few days he began to improve, and we braced ourselves for the nightly arguments between him and Grandma. Grandma was seeing a lot of doctors these days, because she had cancer in her bone marrow.

"Those doctors will just kill you quicker," Dad said one evening when Grandma returned from a consultation. Grandma refused to quit chemotherapy, but she did ask Mother about herbal treatments. Mother had brought some with her, hoping Grandma would ask, and Grandma tried them—foot soaks in red clay, cups of bitter parsley tea, tinctures of horsetail and hydrangea.

"Those herbs won't do a damned thing," Dad said. "Herbals operate by faith. You can't put your trust in a doctor, then ask the Lord to heal you."

Grandma didn't say a word. She just drank her parsley tea.

I remember watching Grandma, searching for signs that her body was giving way. I didn't see any. She was the same taut, undefeated woman.

The rest of the trip blurs in my memory, leaving me with only snapshots—of Mother muscle-testing remedies for Grandma, of Grandma listening silently to Dad, of Dad sprawled out in the dry heat.

Then I'm in a hammock on the back porch, rocking lazily in the orange light of the desert sunset, and Audrey appears and says Dad wants us to get our stuff, we're leaving. Grandma is incredulous. "After what happened last time?" she shouts. "You're going to drive through the night *again*? What about the storm?" Dad says we'll beat the storm. While we load the van Grandma paces, cussing. She says Dad hasn't learned a damned thing.

Richard drives the first six hours. I lie in the back on the mattress with Dad and Audrey.

It's three in the morning, and we are making our way from southern to northern Utah, when the weather changes from the dry chill of the desert to the freezing gales of an alpine winter. Ice claims the road. Snowflakes flick against the windshield like tiny insects, a few at first, then so many the road disappears. We push forward into the heart of the storm. The van skids and jerks. The wind is furious, the view out the window pure white. Richard pulls over. He says we can't go any further.

Dad takes the wheel, Richard moves to the passenger seat,

and Mother lies next to me and Audrey on the mattress. Dad pulls onto the highway and accelerates, rapidly, as if to make a point, until he has doubled Richard's speed.

"Shouldn't we drive slower?" Mother asks.

Dad grins. "I'm not driving faster than our angels can fly." The van is still accelerating. To fifty, then to sixty.

Richard sits tensely, his hand clutching the armrest, his knuckles bleaching each time the tires slip. Mother lies on her side, her face next to mine, taking small sips of air each time the van fishtails, then holding her breath as Dad corrects and it snakes back into the lane. She is so rigid, I think she might shatter. My body tenses with hers; together we brace a hundred times for impact.

It is a relief when the van finally leaves the road.

I awoke to blackness. Something ice-cold was running down my back. *We're in a lake!* I thought. Something heavy was on top of me. The mattress. I tried to kick it off but couldn't, so I crawled beneath it, my hands and knees pressing into the ceiling of the van, which was upside down. I came to a broken window. It was full of snow. Then I understood: we were in a field, not a lake. I crawled through the broken glass and stood, unsteadily. I couldn't seem to gain my balance. I looked around but saw no one. The van was empty. My family was gone.

I circled the wreck twice before I spied Dad's hunched silhouette on a hillock in the distance. I called to him, and he called to the others, who were spread out through the field. Dad waded toward me through the snowdrifts, and as he stepped into a beam from the broken headlights I saw a six-inch gash in his forearm and blood slashing into the snow.

I was told later that I'd been unconscious, hidden under the mattress, for several minutes. They'd shouted my name. When I didn't answer, they thought I must have been thrown from the van, through the broken window, so they'd left to search for me.

Everyone returned to the wreck and stood around it awkwardly, shaking, either from the cold or from shock. We didn't look at Dad, didn't want to accuse.

The police arrived, then an ambulance. I don't know who called them. I didn't tell them I'd blacked out—I was afraid they'd take me to a hospital. I just sat in the police car next to Richard, wrapped in a reflective blanket like the one I had in my "head for the hills" bag. We listened to the radio while the cops asked Dad why the van wasn't insured, and why he'd removed the seats and seatbelts.

We were far from Buck's Peak, so the cops took us to the nearest police station. Dad called Tony, but Tony was trucking long-haul. He tried Shawn next. No answer. We would later learn that Shawn was in jail that night, having been in some kind of brawl.

Unable to reach his sons, Dad called Rob and Diane Hardy, because Mother had midwifed five of their eight children. Rob arrived a few hours later, cackling. "Didn't you folks damned near kill yerselves last time?"

A few days after the crash, my neck froze.

I awoke one morning and it wouldn't move. It didn't hurt, not at first, but no matter how hard I concentrated on turning my head, it wouldn't give more than an inch. The paralysis spread lower, until it felt like I had a metal rod running the length of my back and into my skull. When I couldn't bend forward or turn my head, the soreness set in. I had a constant, crippling headache, and I couldn't stand without holding on to something.

Mother called an energy specialist named Rosie. I was lying on my bed, where I'd been for two weeks, when she appeared in the doorway, wavy and distorted, as if I were looking at her through a pool of water. Her voice was high in pitch, cheerful. It told me to imagine myself, whole and healthy, protected by a white bubble. Inside the bubble I was to place all the objects I loved, all the colors that made me feel at peace. I envisioned the bubble; I imagined myself at its center, able to stand, to run. Behind me was a Mormon temple, and Kamikaze, Luke's old goat, long dead. A green glow lighted everything.

"Imagine the bubble for a few hours every day," she said, "and you will heal." She patted my arm and I heard the door close behind her.

I imagined the bubble every morning, afternoon and night, but my neck remained immobile. Slowly, over the course of a month, I got used to the headaches. I learned how to stand, then how to walk. I used my eyes to stay upright; if I closed them even for a moment, the world would shift and I would fall. I went back to work—to Randy's and occasionally to the junkyard. And every night I fell asleep imagining that green bubble.

During the month I was in bed I heard another voice. I remembered it but it was no longer familiar to me. It had been six years since that impish laugh had echoed down the hall.

It belonged to my brother Shawn, who'd quarreled with my father at seventeen and run off to work odd jobs, mostly trucking and welding. He'd come home because Dad had asked for his help. From my bed, I'd heard Shawn say that he would only stay until Dad could put together a real crew. This was just a favor, he said, until Dad could get back on his feet.

It was odd finding him in the house, this brother who was nearly a stranger to me. People in town seemed to know him better than I did. I'd heard rumors about him at Worm Creek.

People said he was trouble, a bully, a bad egg, that he was always hunting or being hunted by hooligans from Utah or even further afield. People said he carried a gun, either concealed on his body or strapped to his big black motorcycle. Once someone said that Shawn wasn't really bad, that he only got into brawls because he had a reputation for being unbeatable—for knowing all there was to know about martial arts, for fighting like a man who feels no pain—so every strung-out wannabe in the valley thought he could make a name for himself by besting him. It wasn't Shawn's fault, really. As I listened to these rumors, he came alive in my mind as more legend than flesh.

My own memory of Shawn begins in the kitchen, perhaps two months after the second accident.

I am making corn chowder. The door squeaks and I twist at the waist to see who's come in, then twist back to chop an onion.

"You gonna be a walking Popsicle stick forever?" Shawn says.

"Nope."

"You need a chiropractor," he says.

"Mom'll fix it."

"You need a chiropractor," he says again.

The family eats, then disperses. I start the dishes. My hands are in the hot, soapy water when I hear a step behind me and feel thick, calloused hands wrap around my skull. Before I can react, he jerks my head with a swift, savage motion. *CRACK!* It's so loud, I'm sure my head has come off and he's holding it. My body folds, I collapse. Everything is black but somehow spinning. When I open my eyes moments later, his hands are under my arms and he's holding me upright.

"Might be a while before you can stand," he says. "But when you can, I need to do the other side."

I was too dizzy, too nauseous, for the effect to be

immediate. But throughout the evening I observed small changes. I could look at the ceiling. I could cock my head to tease Richard. Seated on the couch, I could turn to smile at the person next to me.

That person was Shawn, and I was looking at him but I wasn't seeing him. I don't know what I saw—what creature I conjured from that violent, compassionate act—but I think it was my father, or perhaps my father as I wished he were, some longed-for defender, some fanciful champion, one who wouldn't fling me into a storm, and who, if I was hurt, would make me whole.

11

Instinct

When Grandpa-down-the-hill was a young man, there'd been herds of livestock spread across the mountain, and they were tended on horseback. Grandpa's ranching horses were the stuff of legend. Seasoned as old leather, they moved their burly bodies delicately, as if guided by the rider's thoughts.

At least, that's what I was told. I never saw them. As Grandpa got older he ranched less and farmed more, until one day he stopped farming. He had no need for horses, so he sold the ones that had value and set the rest loose. They multiplied, and by the time I was born there was a whole herd of wild horses on the mountain.

Richard called them dog-food horses. Once a year, Luke, Richard and I would help Grandpa round up a dozen or so to take to the auction in town, where they'd be sold for slaughter. Some years Grandpa would look out over the small, frightened herd bound for the meat grinder, at the young stallions pacing, coming to terms with their first captivity, and a hunger would appear in his eyes. Then he'd point to one and say, "Don't load that 'un. That 'un we'll break."

But feral horses don't yield easily, not even to a man like Grandpa. My brothers and I would spend days, even weeks, earning the horse's trust, just so we could touch it. Then we would stroke its long face and gradually, over more weeks, work our hands around its wide neck and down its muscular body. After a month of this we'd bring out the saddle, and the horse would toss its head suddenly and with such violence that the halter would snap or the rope break. Once a large copper stallion busted the corral fence, smashed through it as if it weren't there, and came out the other side bloody and bruised.

We tried not to name them, these beasts we hoped to tame, but we had to refer to them somehow. The names we chose were descriptive, not sentimental: Big Red, Black Mare, White Giant. I was thrown from dozens of these horses as they bucked, reared, rolled or leapt. I hit the dirt in a hundred sprawling postures, each time righting myself in an instant and skittering to the safety of a tree, tractor or fence, in case the horse was feeling vengeful.

We never triumphed; our strength of will faltered long before theirs. We got some so they wouldn't buck when they saw the saddle, and a few who'd tolerate a human on their back for jaunts around the corral, but not even Grandpa dared ride them on the mountain. Their natures hadn't changed. They were pitiless, powerful avatars from another world. To mount them was to surrender your footing, to move into their domain. To risk being borne away.

The first domesticated horse I ever saw was a bay gelding, and it was standing next to the corral, nibbling sugar cubes from Shawn's hand. It was spring, and I was fourteen. It had been many years since I'd touched a horse.

The gelding was mine, a gift from a great-uncle on my mother's side. I approached warily, certain that as I moved closer the horse would buck, or rear, or charge. Instead it sniffed my shirt, leaving a long, wet stain. Shawn tossed me a cube. The horse smelled the sugar, and the prickles from his chin tickled my fingers until I opened my palm.

"Wanna break him?" Shawn said.

I did *not*. I was terrified of horses, or I was terrified of what I thought horses were—that is, thousand-pound devils whose ambition was to dash brains against rock. I told Shawn he could break the horse. I would watch from the fence.

I refused to name the horse, so we called him the Yearling. The Yearling was already broke to a halter and lead, so Shawn brought out the saddle that first day. The Yearling pawed the dirt nervously when he saw it; Shawn moved slowly, letting him smell the stirrups and nibble curiously at the horn. Then Shawn rubbed the smooth leather across his broad chest, moving steadily but without hurry.

"Horses don't like things where they can't see 'em," Shawn said. "Best to get him used to the saddle in front. Then when he's real comfortable with it, with the way it smells and feels, we can move it around back."

An hour later the saddle was cinched. Shawn said it was time to mount, and I climbed onto the barn roof, sure the corral would descend into violence. But when Shawn hoisted himself into the saddle, the Yearling merely skittered. His front hooves raised a few inches off the dirt, as if he'd pondered rearing but thought better of it, then he dropped his head and his paws stilled. In the space of a moment, he had accepted our claim to ride him, to his being ridden. He had accepted the world as it was, in which he was an owned thing. He had never been feral, so he could not hear the maddening call of that *other* world, on the mountain, in which he could not be owned, could not be ridden.

I named him Bud. Every night for a week I watched Shawn and Bud gallop through the corral in the gray haze of dusk. Then, on a soft summer evening, I stood next to Bud, grasping the reins while Shawn held the halter steady, and stepped into the saddle.

*

Shawn said he wanted out of his old life, and that the first step was to stay away from his friends. Suddenly he was home every evening, looking for something to do. He began to drive me to my rehearsals at Worm Creek. When it was just the two of us floating down the highway, he was mellow, lighthearted. He joked and teased, and he sometimes gave me advice, which was mostly "Don't do what I did." But when we arrived at the theater, he would change.

At first he watched the younger boys with wary concentration, then he began to bait them. It wasn't obvious aggression, just small provocations. He might flick off a boy's hat or knock a soda can from his hand and laugh as the stain spread over the boy's jeans. If he was challenged—and he usually wasn't—he would play the part of the ruffian, a hardened "Whatcha gonna do about it?" expression disguising his face. But after, when it was just the two of us, the mask lowered, the bravado peeled off like a breastplate, and he was my brother.

It was his smile I loved best. His upper canines had never grown in, and the string of holistic dentists my parents had taken him to as a child had failed to notice until it was too late. By the time he was twenty-three, and he got himself to an oral surgeon, they had rotated sideways inside his gums and were ejecting themselves through the tissue under his nose. The surgeon who removed them told Shawn to preserve his baby teeth for as long as possible, then when they rotted out, he'd be given posts. But they never rotted out. They stayed, stubborn relics of a misplaced childhood, reminding anyone who witnessed his pointless, endless, feckless belligerence, that this man was once a boy.

It was a hazy summer evening, a month before I turned fifteen. The sun had dipped below Buck's Peak but the sky still held a few hours of light. Shawn and I were in the corral.

After breaking Bud that spring, Shawn had taken up horses in a serious way. All summer he'd been buying horses, Thoroughbreds and Paso Finos, most of them unbroken because he could pick them up cheap. We were still working with Bud. We'd taken him on a dozen rides through the open pasture, but he was inexperienced, skittish, unpredictable.

That evening, Shawn saddled a new horse, a copper-coated mare, for the first time. She was ready for a short ride, Shawn said, so we mounted, him on the mare, me on Bud. We made it about half a mile up the mountain, moving deliberately so as not to frighten the horses, winding our way through the wheat fields. Then I did something foolish. I got too close to the mare. She didn't like having the gelding behind her, and with no warning she leapt forward, thrusting her weight onto her front legs, and with her hind legs kicked Bud full in the chest.

Bud went berserk.

I'd been tying a knot in my reins to make them more secure and didn't have a firm hold. Bud gave a tremendous jolt, then began to buck, throwing his body in tight circles. The reins flew over his head. I gripped the saddle horn and squeezed my thighs together, curving my legs around his bulging belly. Before I could get my bearings, Bud took off at a dead run straight up a ravine, bucking now and then but running, always running. My foot slipped through a stirrup up to my calf.

All those summers breaking horses with Grandpa, and the only advice I remembered him giving was, "Whate'er you do, don't git your foot caught in the stirrup." I didn't need him to explain. I knew that as long as I came off clean, I'd likely be fine. At least I'd be on the ground. But if my foot got caught, I'd be dragged until my head split on a rock.

Shawn couldn't help me, not on that unbroken mare. Hysteria in one horse causes hysteria in others, especially in the young and spirited. Of all Shawn's horses, there was only one—a seven-year-old buckskin named Apollo—who might have been old enough, and calm enough, to do it: to explode in furious speed, a nostril-flapping gallop, then coolly navigate while the rider detached his body, lifting one leg out of the stirrup and reaching to the ground to catch the reins of another horse wild with fright. But Apollo was in the corral, half a mile down the mountain.

My instincts told me to let go of the saddle horn—the only thing keeping me on the horse. If I let go I'd fall, but I'd have a precious moment to reach for the flapping reins or try to yank my calf from the stirrup. *Make a play for it*, my instincts screamed.

Those instincts were my guardians. They had saved me before, guiding my movements on a dozen bucking horses, telling me when to cling to the saddle and when to pitch myself clear of pounding hooves. They were the same instincts that, years before, had prompted me to hoist myself from the scrap bin when Dad was dumping it, because they had understood, even if I had not, that it was better to fall from that great height rather than hope Dad would intervene. All my life those instincts had been instructing me in this single doctrine—that the odds are better if you rely only on yourself.

Bud reared, thrusting his head so high I thought he might tumble backward. He landed hard and bucked. I tightened my grip on the horn, making a decision, based on another kind of instinct, not to surrender my hold.

Shawn would catch up, even on that unbroken mare. He'd pull off a miracle. The mare wouldn't even understand the command when he shouted, "Giddy-yap!"; at the jab of his boot in her gut, which she'd never felt before, she would rear, twisting wildly. But he would yank her head down, and as soon as her hooves touched the dirt, kick her a second time, harder, knowing she would rear again. He would do this until she leapt into a run, then he would drive her forward, welcoming her wild acceleration, somehow guiding her even though she'd not yet learned the strange dance of movements that, over time, becomes a kind of language between horse and rider. All this would happen in seconds, a year of training reduced to a single, desperate moment.

I knew it was impossible. I knew it even as I imagined it. But I kept hold of the saddle horn.

Bud had worked himself into a frenzy. He leapt wildly, arching his back as he shot upward, then tossing his head as he smashed his hooves to the ground. My eyes could barely unscramble what they saw. Golden wheat flew in every direction, while the blue sky and the mountain lurched absurdly.

I was so disoriented that I felt, rather than saw, the powerful penny-toned mare moving into place beside me. Shawn lifted his body from the saddle and tilted himself toward the ground, holding his reins tightly in one hand while, with the other, he snatched Bud's reins from the weeds. The leather straps pulled taut; the bit forced Bud's head up and forward. With his head raised, Bud could no longer buck and he entered a smooth, rhythmic gallop. Shawn yanked hard on his own reins, pulling the mare's head toward his knee, forcing her to run in a circle. He pulled her head tighter on every pass, wrapping the strap around his forearm, shrinking the circle until it was so small, the pounding hooves stood still. I slid from the saddle and lay in the wheat, the itchy stalks poking through my shirt. Above my head the horses panted, their bellies swelling and collapsing, their hooves pawing at the dirt.

12

Fish Eyes

My brother Tony had taken out a loan to buy his own rig—a semi and trailer—but in order to make the payments, he had to keep the truck on the road, so that's where he was living, on the road. Until his wife got sick and the doctor she consulted (she had consulted a doctor) put her on bed rest. Tony called Shawn and asked if he could run the rig for a week or two.

Shawn hated trucking long-haul, but he said he'd do it if I came along. Dad didn't need me in the junkyard, and Randy could spare me for a few days, so we set off, heading down to Las Vegas, then east to Albuquerque, west to Los Angeles, then up to Washington State. I'd thought I would see the cities, but mostly I saw truck stops and interstate. The windshield was enormous and elevated like a cockpit, which made the cars below seem like toys. The sleeper cab, where the bunks were, was musty and dark as a cave, littered with bags of Doritos and trail mix.

Shawn drove for days with little sleep, navigating our fifty-foot trailer as if it were his own arm. He doctored the books whenever we crossed a checkpoint, to make it seem he was getting more sleep than he was. Every other day we stopped to shower and eat a meal that wasn't dried fruit and granola.

Near Albuquerque, the Walmart warehouse was backed up and couldn't unload us for two days. We were outside the city—there was nothing but a truck stop and red sand stretching out in all directions—so we ate Cheetos and played Mario Kart in the sleeper. By sunset on the second day, our bodies ached from sitting, and Shawn said he should teach me martial arts. We had our first lesson at dusk in the parking lot.

"If you know what you're doing," he said, "you can incapacitate a man with minimal effort. You can control someone's whole body with two fingers. It's about knowing where the weak points are, and how to exploit them." He grabbed my wrist and folded it, bending my fingers downward so they reached uncomfortably toward the inside of my forearm. He continued to add pressure until I twisted slightly, wrapping my arm behind my back to relieve the strain.

"See? This is a weak point," he said. "If I fold it any more, you'll be immobilized." He grinned his angel grin. "I won't, though, because it'd hurt like hell."

He let go and said, "Now you try."

I folded his wrist onto itself and squeezed hard, trying to get his upper body to collapse the way mine had. He didn't move.

"Maybe another strategy for you," he said.

He gripped my wrist a different way—the way an attacker might, he said. He taught me how to break the hold, where the fingers were weakest and the bones in my arm strongest, so that after a few minutes I could cut through even his thick fingers. He taught me how to throw my weight behind a punch, and where to aim to crush the windpipe.

The next morning, the trailer was unloaded. We climbed into the truck, picked up a new load and drove for another two days, watching the white lines disappear hypnotically beneath the hood, which was the color of bone. We had few forms of entertainment, so we made a game of talking. The game had only two rules. The first was that every statement had to have at least two words in which the first letters were switched.

"You're not my little sister," Shawn said. "You're my sittle lister." He pronounced the words lazily, blunting the *t*'s to *d*'s so that it sounded like "siddle lister."

The second rule was that every word that sounded like a number, or like it had a number in it, had to be changed so that the number was one higher. The word "to" for example, because it sounds like the number "two," would become "three."

"Siddle Lister," Shawn might say, "we should pay a-eleven-tion. There's a checkpoint ahead and I can't a-five-d a ticket. Time three put on your seatbelt."

When we tired of this, we'd turn on the CB and listen to the lonely banter of truckers stretched out across the interstate.

"Look out for a green four-wheeler," a gruff voice said, when we were somewhere between Sacramento and Portland. "Been picnicking in my blind spot for a half hour."

A four-wheeler, Shawn explained, is what big rigs call cars and pickups.

Another voice came over the CB to complain about a red Ferrari that was weaving through traffic at 120 miles per hour. "Bastard damned near hit a little blue Chevy," the deep voice bellowed through the static. "Shit, there's kids in that Chevy. Anybody up ahead wanna cool this hothead down?" The voice gave its location.

Shawn checked the mile marker. We were ahead. "I'm a white Pete pulling a fridge," he said. There was silence while everybody checked their mirrors for a Peterbilt with a reefer. Then a third voice, gruffer than the first, answered: "I'm the blue KW hauling a dry box."

"I see you," Shawn said, and for my benefit pointed to a navy-colored Kenworth a few cars ahead.

When the Ferrari appeared, multiplied in our many mirrors, Shawn shifted into high gear, revving the engine and pulling beside the Kenworth so that the two fifty-foot trailers were running side by side, blocking both lanes. The Ferrari honked, weaved back and forth, braked, honked again.

"How long should we keep him back there?" the husky voice said, with a deep laugh.

"Until he calms down," Shawn answered.

Five miles later, they let him pass.

The trip lasted about a week, then we told Tony to find us a load to Idaho.

"Well, Siddle Lister," Shawn said when we pulled into the junkyard, "back three work."

The Worm Creek Opera House announced a new play: *Carousel*. Shawn drove me to the audition, then surprised me by auditioning himself. Charles was also there, talking to a girl named Sadie, who was seventeen. She nodded at what Charles was saying, but her eyes were fixed on Shawn.

At the first rehearsal she came and sat next to him, laying her hand on his arm, laughing and tossing her hair. She was very pretty, with soft, full lips and large dark eyes, but when I asked Shawn if he liked her, he said he didn't.

"She's got fish eyes," he said.

"Fish eyes?"

"Yup, fish eyes. They're dead stupid, fish. They're beautiful, but their heads're as empty as a tire."

Sadie started dropping by the junkyard around quitting time, usually with a milkshake for Shawn, or cookies or cake. Shawn hardly even spoke to her, just grabbed whatever she'd brought him and kept walking toward the corral. She would follow and try to talk to him while he fussed over his horses, until one evening she asked if he would teach her to ride. I tried to explain that our horses weren't broke all the way, but she was determined, so Shawn put her on Apollo and the three of us headed up the mountain. Shawn ignored her and Apollo. He offered none of the help he'd given me, teaching me how to stand in the stirrups while going down steep ravines or how to squeeze my thighs when the horse leapt over a branch. Sadie trembled for the entire ride, but she pretended to be enjoying herself, restoring her lipsticked smile every time he glanced in her direction.

At the next rehearsal, Charles asked Sadie about a scene, and Shawn saw them talking. Sadie came over a few minutes later but Shawn wouldn't speak to her. He turned his back and she left crying.

"What's that about?" I said.

"Nothing," he said.

By the next rehearsal, a few days later, Shawn seemed to have forgotten it. Sadie approached him warily, but he smiled at her, and a few minutes later they were talking and laughing. Shawn asked her to cross the street and buy him a Snickers at the dime store. She seemed pleased that he would ask and hurried out the door, but when she returned a few minutes later and gave him the bar, he said, "What is this shit? I asked for a Milky Way."

"You didn't," she said. "You said Snickers."

"I want a Milky Way."

Sadie left again and fetched the Milky Way. She handed it to him with a nervous laugh, and Shawn said, "Where's my Snickers? What, you forgot again?"

"You didn't want it!" she said, her eyes shining like glass. "I gave it to Charles!"

"Go get it."

"I'll buy you another."

"No," Shawn said, his eyes cold. His baby teeth, which

usually gave him an impish, playful appearance, now made him seem unpredictable, volatile. "I want *that* one. Get it, or don't come back."

A tear slid down Sadie's cheek, smearing her mascara. She paused for a moment to wipe it away and pull up her smile. Then she walked over to Charles and, laughing as if it were nothing, asked if she could have the Snickers. He reached into his pocket and pulled it out, then watched her walk back to Shawn. Sadie placed the Snickers in his palm like a peace offering and waited, staring at the carpet. Shawn pulled her onto his lap and ate the bar in three bites.

"You have lovely eyes," he said. "Just like a fish."

Sadie's parents were divorcing and the town was awash in rumors about her father. When Mother heard the rumors, she said now it made sense why Shawn had taken an interest in Sadie. "He's always protected angels with broken wings," she said.

Shawn found out Sadie's class schedule and memorized it. He made a point of driving to the high school several times a day, particularly at those times when he knew she'd be moving between buildings. He'd pull over on the highway and watch her from a distance, too far for her to come over, but not so far that she wouldn't see him. It was something we did together, he and I, nearly every time we went to town, and sometimes when we didn't need to go to town at all. Until one day, when Sadie appeared on the steps of the high school with Charles. They were laughing together; Sadie hadn't noticed Shawn's truck.

I watched his face harden, then relax. He smiled at me. "I have the perfect punishment," he said. "I simply won't see her. All I have to do is not see her, and she will suffer."

He was right. When he didn't return her calls, Sadie became desperate. She told the boys at school not to walk with her, for fear Shawn would see, and when Shawn said he disliked one of her friends, she stopped seeing them.

Sadie came to our house every day after school, and I watched the Snickers incident play out over and over, in different forms, with different objects. Shawn would ask for a glass of water. When Sadie brought it, he'd want ice. When she brought that he'd ask for milk, then water again, ice, no ice, then juice. This could go on for thirty minutes before, in a final test, he would ask for something we didn't have. Then Sadie would drive to town to buy it—vanilla ice cream, fries, a burrito—only to have him demand something else the moment she got back. The nights they went out, I was grateful.

One night, he came home late and in a strange mood. Everyone was asleep except me, and I was on the sofa, reading a chapter of scripture before bed. Shawn plopped down next to me. "Get me a glass of water."

"You break your leg?" I said.

"Get it, or I won't drive you to town tomorrow."

I fetched the water. As I handed it over, I saw the smile on his face and without thinking dumped the whole thing on his head. I made it down the hall and was nearly to my room when he caught me.

"Apologize," he said. Water dripped from his nose onto his T-shirt.

"No."

He grabbed a fistful of my hair, a large clump, his grip fixed near the root to give him greater leverage, and dragged me into the bathroom. I groped at the door, catching hold of the frame, but he lifted me off the ground, flattened my arms against my body, then dropped my head into the toilet. "Apologize," he said again. I said nothing. He stuck my head in further, so my nose scraped the stained porcelain. I closed my eyes, but the smell wouldn't let me forget where I was.

I tried to imagine something else, something that would take me out of myself, but the image that came to mind was of Sadie, crouching, compliant. It pumped me full of bile. He held me there, my nose touching the bowl, for perhaps a minute, then he let me up. The tips of my hair were wet; my scalp was raw.

I thought it was over. I'd begun to back away when he seized my wrist and folded it, curling my fingers and palm into a spiral. He continued folding until my body began to coil, then he added more pressure, so that without thinking, without realizing, I twisted myself into a dramatic bow, my back bent, my head nearly touching the floor, my arm behind my back.

In the parking lot, when Shawn had shown me this hold, I'd moved only a little, responding more to his description than to any physical necessity. It hadn't seemed particularly effective at the time, but now I understood the maneuver for what it was: control. I could scarcely move, scarcely breathe, without breaking my own wrist. Shawn held me in position with one hand; the other he dangled loosely at his side, to show me how easy it was.

Still harder than if I were Sadie, I thought.

As if he could read my mind, he twisted my wrist further; my body was coiled tightly, my face scraping the floor. I'd done all I could do to relieve the pressure in my wrist. If he kept twisting, it would break.

"Apologize," he said.

There was a long moment in which fire burned up my arm and into my brain. "I'm sorry," I said.

He dropped my wrist and I fell to the floor. I could hear his steps moving down the hall. I stood and quietly locked the bathroom door, then I stared into the mirror at the girl clutching her wrist. Her eyes were glassy and drops slid down her cheeks. I hated her for her weakness, for having a heart to break. That he could hurt her, that anyone could hurt her like *that,* was inexcusable.

I'm only crying from the pain, I told myself. *From the pain in my wrist. Not from anything else.*

This moment would define my memory of that night, and of the many nights like it, for a decade. In it I saw myself as unbreakable, as tender as stone. At first I merely believed this, until one day it became the truth. Then I was able to tell myself, without lying, that it didn't affect me, that *he* didn't affect me, because nothing affected me. I didn't understand how morbidly right I was. How I had hollowed myself out. For all my obsessing over the consequences of that night, I had misunderstood the vital truth: that its not affecting me, that *was* its effect.

13

Silence in the Churches

In September the twin towers fell. I'd never heard of them until they were gone. Then I watched as planes sank into them, and I stared, bewildered, at the TV as the unimaginably tall structures swayed, then buckled. Dad stood next to me. He'd come in from the junkyard to watch. He said nothing. That evening he read aloud from the Bible, familiar passages from Isaiah, Luke, and the Book of Revelation, about wars and rumors of wars.

Three days later, when she was nineteen, Audrey was married—to Benjamin, a blond-haired farm boy she'd met waitressing in town. The wedding was solemn. Dad had prayed and received a revelation: "There will be a conflict, a final struggle for the Holy Land," he'd said. "My sons will be sent to war. Some of them will not come home."

I'd been avoiding Shawn since the night in the bathroom. He'd apologized. He'd come into my room an hour later, his eyes glassy, his voice croaking, and asked me to forgive him. I'd said that I would, that I already had. But I hadn't.

At Audrey's wedding, seeing my brothers in their suits, those black uniforms, my rage turned to fear, of some predetermined loss, and I forgave Shawn. It was easy to forgive: after all, it was the End of the World.

For a month I lived as if holding my breath. Then there was no draft, no further attacks. The skies didn't darken, the moon didn't turn to blood. There were distant rumblings of war but life on the mountain remained unchanged. Dad said we should stay vigilant, but by winter my attention had shifted back to the trifling dramas of my own life.

I was fifteen and I felt it, felt the race I was running with time. My body was changing, bloating, swelling, stretching, bulging. I wished it would stop, but it seemed my body was no longer mine. It belonged to itself now, and cared not at all how I felt about these strange alterations, about whether I *wanted* to stop being a child, and become something else.

That something else thrilled and frightened me. I'd always known that I would grow differently than my brothers, but I'd never thought about what that might mean. Now it was all I thought about. I began to look for cues to understand this difference, and once I started looking, I found them everywhere.

One Sunday afternoon, I helped Mother prepare a roast for dinner. Dad was kicking off his shoes and loosening his tie. He'd been talking since we left the church.

"That hemline was three inches above Lori's knee," Dad said. "What's a woman thinking when she puts on a dress like that?" Mother nodded absently while chopping a carrot. She was used to this particular lecture.

"And Jeanette Barney," Dad said. "If a woman wears a blouse that low-cut, she ought not bend over." Mother agreed. I pictured the turquoise blouse Jeanette had worn that day. The neckline was only an inch below her collarbone, but it was loose-fitting, and I imagined that if she bent it would give a full view. As I thought this I felt anxious, because although a tighter blouse would have made Jeanette's bending more modest, the tightness itself would have been less modest. Righteous women do not wear tight clothing. *Other* women do that.

I was trying to figure out exactly how much tightness

would be the right amount when Dad said, "Jeanette waited to bend for that hymnal until I was looking. She *wanted* me to see." Mother made a disapproving *tsk* sound with her teeth, then quartered a potato.

This speech would stay with me in a way that a hundred of its precursors had not. I would remember the words very often in the years that followed, and the more I considered them, the more I worried that I might be growing into the wrong sort of woman. Sometimes I could scarcely move through a room, I was so preoccupied with not walking or bending or crouching like *them*. But no one had ever taught me the modest way to bend over, so I knew I was probably doing it the bad way.

Shawn and I auditioned for a melodrama at Worm Creek. I saw Charles at the first rehearsal and spent half the evening working up the courage to talk to him. When I did, finally, he confided in me that he was in love with Sadie. This wasn't ideal, but it did give us something to talk about.

Shawn and I drove home together. He sat behind the wheel, glaring at the road as if it had wronged him.

"I saw you talking to Charles," he said. "You don't want people thinking you're that kind of girl."

"The kind that talks?"

"You know what I mean," he said.

The next night, Shawn came into my room unexpectedly and found me smudging my eyelashes with Audrey's old mascara.

"You wear *makeup* now?" he said.

"I guess."

He spun around to leave but paused in the doorframe. "I thought you were better," he said. "But you're just like the rest."

He stopped calling me Siddle Lister. "Let's go, Fish Eyes!" he shouted from across the theater one night. Charles looked around curiously. Shawn began to explain the name, so I started laughing—loud enough, I hoped, to drown him out. I laughed as if I loved the name.

The first time I wore lip gloss, Shawn said I was a whore. I was in my bedroom, standing in front of my mirror, trying it out, when Shawn appeared in the doorway. He said it like a joke but I wiped the color from my lips anyway. Later that night, at the theater, when I noticed Charles staring at Sadie, I reapplied it and saw Shawn's expression twist. The drive home that night was tense. The temperature outside had fallen well below zero. I said I was cold and Shawn moved to turn up the heat. Then he paused, laughed to himself, and rolled all the windows down. The January wind hit me like a bucket of ice. I tried to roll up my window, but he'd put on the child lock. I asked him to roll it up. "I'm cold," I kept saying, "I'm really, really cold." He just laughed. He drove all twelve miles like that, cackling as if it were a game, as if we were both in on it, as if my teeth weren't clattering.

I thought things would get better when Shawn dumped Sadie—I suppose I'd convinced myself that it was *her* fault, the things he did, and that without her he would be different. After Sadie, he took up with an old girlfriend, Erin. She was older, less willing to play his games, and at first it seemed I was right, that he was doing better.

Then Charles asked Sadie to dinner, Sadie said yes, and Shawn heard about it. I was working late at Randy's that night when Shawn turned up, frothing at the mouth. I left with him, thinking I could calm him, but I couldn't. He drove around town for two hours, searching for Charles's Jeep, cursing and swearing that when he found that bastard he was "gonna give him a new face." I sat in the passenger seat of his truck, listening to the engine rev as it guzzled diesel, watching the yellow lines disappear beneath the hood. I thought of my brother as he had been, as I remembered him, as I wanted to remember him. I thought of Albuquerque and Los Angeles, and of the miles of lost interstate in between.

A pistol lay on the seat between us, and when he wasn't shifting gears, Shawn picked it up and caressed it, sometimes spinning it over his index like a gunslinger before laying it back on the seat, where light from passing cars glinted off the steel barrel.

I awoke with needles in my brain. Thousands of them, biting, blocking out everything. Then they disappeared for one dizzying moment and I got my bearings.

It was morning, early; amber sunlight poured in through my bedroom window. I was standing but not on my own strength. Two hands were gripping my throat, and they'd been shaking me. The needles, that was my brain crashing into my skull. I had only a few seconds to wonder why before the needles returned, shredding my thoughts. My eyes were open but I saw only white flashes. A few sounds made it through to me.

"SLUT!

"WHORE!"

Then another sound. Mother. She was crying. "Stop! You're killing her! Stop!"

She must have grabbed him because I felt his body twist. I fell to the floor. When I opened my eyes, Mother and Shawn were facing each other, Mother wearing only a tattered bathrobe.

I was yanked to my feet. Shawn grasped a fistful of my hair—using the same method as before, catching the clump near my scalp so he could maneuver me—and dragged me into the hallway. My head was pressed into his chest. All I could see were bits of carpet flying past my tripping feet. My head pounded, I had trouble breathing, but I was starting to understand what was happening. Then there were tears in my eyes.

From the pain, I thought.

"Now the bitch cries," Shawn said. "Why? Because someone sees you for the slut you are?"

I tried to look at him, to search his face for my brother, but he shoved my head toward the ground and I fell. I scrambled away, then pulled myself upright. The kitchen was spinning; strange flecks of pink and yellow drifted before my eyes.

Mother was sobbing, clawing at her hair.

"I see you for what you are," Shawn said. His eyes were wild. "You pretend to be saintly and churchish. But I see you. I see how you prance around with Charles like a prostitute." He turned to Mother to observe the effect of his words on her. She had collapsed at the kitchen table.

"She does *not*," Mother whispered.

Shawn was still turned toward her. He said she had no idea of the lies I told, how I'd fooled her, how I played the good girl at home but in town I was a lying whore. I inched toward the back door.

Mother told me to take her car and go. Shawn turned to me. "You'll be needing these," he said, holding up Mother's keys.

"She's not going anywhere until she admits she's a whore," Shawn said.

He grabbed my wrist and my body slipped into the familiar posture, head thrust forward, arm coiled around my lower back, wrist folded absurdly onto itself. Like a dance step, my muscles remembered and raced to get ahead of the music. The air poured from my lungs as I tried to bend deeper, to give my wrist bone every possible inch of relief.

"Say it," he said.

But I was somewhere else. I was in the future. In a few hours, Shawn would be kneeling by my bed, and he'd be so very sorry. I knew it even as I hunched there.

"What's going on?" A man's voice floated up from the stairwell in the hall.

I turned my head and saw a face hovering between two wooden railings. It was Tyler.

I was hallucinating. Tyler never came home. As I thought that, I laughed out loud, a high-pitched cackle. What kind of lunatic would come back here once they'd escaped? There were now so many pink and yellow specks in my vision, it was as if I were inside a snow globe. That was good. It meant I was close to passing out. I was looking forward to it.

Shawn dropped my wrist and again I fell. I looked up and saw that his gaze was fixed on the stairwell. Only then did it occur to me that Tyler was real.

Shawn took a step back. He had waited until Dad and Luke were out of the house, away on a job, so his physicality could go unchallenged. Confronting his younger brother— less vicious but powerful in his own way—was more than he'd bargained for.

"What's going on?" Tyler repeated. He eyed Shawn, inching forward as if approaching a rattlesnake.

Mother stopped crying. She was embarrassed. Tyler was an outsider now. He'd been gone for so long, he'd been shifted to that category of people who we kept secrets from. Who we kept *this* from.

Tyler moved up the stairs, advancing on his brother. His face was taut, his breath shallow, but his expression held no hint of surprise. It seemed to me that Tyler knew exactly what he was doing, that he had done this before, when they were younger and less evenly matched. Tyler halted his forward march but he didn't blink. He glared at Shawn as if to say, *Whatever is happening here, it's done.*

Shawn began to murmur about my clothes and what I did in town. Tyler cut him off with a wave of his hand. "I don't want to know," he said. Then, turning to me: "Go, get out of here."

"She's not going anywhere," Shawn repeated, flashing the key rings.

Tyler tossed me his own keys. "Just go," he said.

I ran to Tyler's car, which was wedged between Shawn's truck and the chicken coop. I tried to back out, but I stomped too hard on the gas and the tires spun out, sending gravel flying. On my second attempt I succeeded. The car shot backward and circled around. I shifted into drive and was ready to shoot down the hill when Tyler appeared on the porch. I lowered the window. "Don't go to work," he said. "He'll find you there."

That night, when I came home, Shawn was gone. Mother was in the kitchen blending oils. She said nothing about that morning, and I knew I shouldn't mention it. I went to bed, but I was still awake hours later when I heard a pickup roar up the hill. A few minutes later, my bedroom door creaked open. I heard the click of the lamp, saw the light leaping over the walls, and felt his weight drop onto my bed. I turned over and faced him. He'd put a black velvet box next to me. When I didn't touch it, he opened the box and withdrew a string of milky pearls.

He said he could see the path I was going down and it was not good. I was losing myself, becoming like other girls, frivolous, manipulative, using how I looked to get things.

I thought about my body, all the ways it had changed. I hardly knew what I felt toward it: sometimes I *did* want it to be noticed, to be admired, but then afterward I'd think of Jeanette Barney, and I'd feel disgusted.

"You're special, Tara," Shawn said.

Was I? I wanted to believe I was. Tyler had said I was special once, years before. He'd read me a passage of scripture from the Book of Mormon, about *a sober child, quick to observe.* "This reminds me of you," Tyler had said.

The passage described the great prophet Mormon, a fact I'd found confusing. A woman could never be a prophet, yet here was Tyler, telling me I reminded him of one of the greatest prophets of all. I still don't know what he meant by it, but what I understood at the time was that I could trust myself: that there was something in me, something like what was in the prophets, and that it was not male or female, not old or young; a kind of worth that was inherent and unshakable.

But now, as I gazed at the shadow Shawn cast on my wall, aware of my maturing body, of its evils and of my desire to do evil with it, the meaning of that memory shifted. Suddenly that worth felt conditional, like it could be taken or squandered. It was not inherent; it was bestowed. What was of worth was not *me,* but the veneer of constraints and observances that obscured me.

I looked at my brother. He seemed old in that moment, wise. He knew about the world. He knew about worldly women, so I asked him to keep me from becoming one.

"Okay, Fish Eyes," he said. "I will."

When I awoke the next morning, my neck was bruised and my wrist swollen. I had a headache—not an ache *in* my brain but an actual aching *of* my brain, as if the organ itself was tender. I went to work but came home early and lay in a dark corner of the basement, waiting it out. I was lying on the carpet, feeling the pounding in my brain, when Tyler found me and folded himself onto the sofa near my head. I was not pleased to see him. The only thing worse than being dragged through the house by my hair was Tyler's having seen it. Given the choice between letting it play out, and having Tyler there to stop it, I'd have chosen to let it play out. Obviously I would have chosen that. I'd been close to passing out anyway, and then I could have forgotten about it. In a day or two it wouldn't even have been real. It would become a bad dream, and in a month, a mere echo of a bad dream. But Tyler had seen it, had made it real.

"Have you thought about leaving?" Tyler asked.

"And go where?"

"School," he said.

I brightened. "I'm going to enroll in high school in September," I said. "Dad won't like it, but I'm gonna go." I thought Tyler would be pleased; instead, he grimaced.

"You've said that before."

"I'm going to."

"Maybe," Tyler said. "But as long as you live under Dad's roof, it's hard to go when he asks you not to, easy to delay just one more year, until there aren't any years left. If you start as a sophomore, can you even graduate?"

We both knew I couldn't.

"It's time to go, Tara," Tyler said. "The longer you stay, the less likely you will ever leave."

"You think I need to leave?"

Tyler didn't blink, didn't hesitate. "I think this is the worst possible place for you." He'd spoken softly, but it felt as though he'd shouted the words.

"Where could I go?"

"Go where I went," Tyler said. "Go to college."

I snorted.

"BYU takes homeschoolers," he said.

"Is that what we are?" I said. "Homeschoolers?" I tried to remember the last time I'd read a textbook.

"The admissions board won't know anything except what we tell them," Tyler said. "If we say you were homeschooled, they'll believe it."

"I won't get in."

"You will," he said. "Just pass the ACT. One lousy test."

Tyler stood to go. "There's a world out there, Tara," he said. "And it will look a lot different once Dad is no longer whispering his view of it in your ear."

The next day I drove to the hardware store in town and bought a slide-bolt lock for my bedroom door. I dropped it on my bed, then fetched a drill from the shop and started fitting screws. I thought Shawn was out—his truck wasn't in the driveway—but when I turned around with the drill, he was standing in my doorframe.

"What are you doing?" he said.

"Doorknob's broke," I lied. "Door blows open. This lock was cheap but it'll do the trick."

Shawn fingered the thick steel, which I was sure he could tell was not cheap at all. I stood silently, paralyzed by dread but also by pity. In that moment I hated him, and I wanted to scream it in his face. I imagined the way he would crumple, crushed under the weight of my words and his own self-loathing. Even then I understood the truth of it: that Shawn hated himself far more than I ever could.

"You're using the wrong screws," he said. "You need long ones for the wall and grabbers for the door. Otherwise, it'll bust right off."

We walked to the shop. Shawn shuffled around for a few minutes, then emerged with a handful of steel screws. We walked back to the house and he installed the lock, humming to himself and smiling, flashing his baby teeth.

14

My Feet No Longer Touch Earth

In October Dad won a contract to build industrial granaries in Malad City, the dusty farmtown on the other side of Buck's Peak. It was a big job for a small outfit—the crew was just Dad, Shawn, Luke, and Audrey's husband, Benjamin—but Shawn was a good foreman, and with him in charge Dad had acquired a reputation for fast, reliable work.

Shawn wouldn't let Dad take shortcuts. Half the time I passed the shop, I'd hear the two of them shouting at each other, Dad saying Shawn was wasting time, Shawn screaming that Dad had damned near taken someone's head off.

Shawn worked long days cleaning, cutting and welding the raw materials for the granaries, and once construction began he was usually on-site in Malad. When he and Dad came home, hours after sunset, they were nearly always cussing. Shawn wanted to professionalize the operation, to invest the profits from the Malad job in new equipment; Dad wanted things to stay the same. Shawn said Dad didn't understand that construction was more competitive than scrapping, and that if they wanted to land real contracts, they needed to spend real money on real equipment—specifically, a new welder and a man lift with a basket.

"We can't keep using a forklift and an old cheese pallet," Shawn said. "It looks like shit, and it's dangerous besides."

Dad laughed out loud at the idea of a man basket. He'd been using a forklift and pallet for twenty years.

I worked late most nights. Randy planned to take a big road trip to find new accounts, and he'd asked me to manage the business while he was gone. He taught me how to use his computer to keep the books, process orders, maintain inventory. It was from Randy that I first heard of the Internet. He showed me how to get online, how to visit a webpage, how to write an email. The day he left, he gave me a cellphone so he could reach me at all hours.

Tyler called one night just as I was getting home from work. He asked if I was studying for the ACT. "I can't take the test," I said. "I don't know any math."

"You've got money," Tyler said. "Buy books and learn it."

I said nothing. College was irrelevant to me. I knew how my life would play out: when I was eighteen or nineteen, I would get married. Dad would give me a corner of the farm, and my husband would put a house on it. Mother would teach me about herbs, and also about midwifery, which she'd gone back to now the migraines were less frequent. When I had children, Mother would deliver them, and one day, I supposed, *I* would be the Midwife. I didn't see where college fit in.

Tyler seemed to read my thoughts. "You know Sister Sears?" he said. Sister Sears was the church choir director. "How do you think she knows how to lead a choir?"

I'd always admired Sister Sears, and been jealous of her knowledge of music. I'd never thought about how she'd learned it.

"She studied," Tyler said. "Did you know you can get a degree in music? If you had one, you could give lessons, you could direct the church choir. Even Dad won't argue with that, not much anyway."

Mother had recently purchased a trial version of AOL. I'd only ever used the Internet at Randy's, for work, but after Tyler hung up I turned on our computer and waited for the modem to dial. Tyler had said something about BYU's webpage. It only took a few minutes to find it. Then the screen was full of pictures—of neat brick buildings the color of sunstone surrounded by emerald trees, of beautiful people walking and laughing, with books tucked under their arms and backpacks slung over their shoulders. It looked like something from a movie. A happy movie.

The next day, I drove forty miles to the nearest bookstore and bought a glossy ACT study guide. I sat on my bed and turned to the mathematics practice test. I scanned the first page. It wasn't that I didn't know how to solve the equations; I didn't recognize the symbols. It was the same on the second page, and the third.

I took the test to Mother. "What's this?" I asked.

"Math," she said.

"Then where are the numbers?"

"It's algebra. The letters stand in for numbers."

"How do I do it?"

Mother fiddled with a pen and paper for several minutes, but she wasn't able to solve any of the first five equations.

The next day I drove the same forty miles, eighty roundtrip, and returned home with a large algebra textbook.

Every evening, as the crew was leaving Malad, Dad would phone the house so Mother could have dinner waiting when the truck bumped up the hill. I listened for that call, and when it came I would get in Mother's car and drive away. I didn't know why. I would go to Worm Creek, where I'd sit in the balcony and watch rehearsals, my feet on the ledge, a math book open in front of me. I hadn't studied math since long division, and the concepts were unfamiliar. I understood the theory of fractions but struggled to manipulate them, and seeing a decimal on the page made my heart race. Every night for a month I sat in the opera house, in a chair of red velvet, and practiced the most basic operations—how to multiply fractions, how to use a reciprocal, how to add and multiply and divide with decimals—while on the stage, characters recited their lines.

I began to study trigonometry. There was solace in its strange formulas and equations. I was drawn to the Pythagorean theorem and its promise of a universal—the ability to predict the nature of any three points containing a right angle, anywhere, always. What I knew of physics I had learned in the junkyard, where the physical world often seemed unstable, capricious. But here was a principle through which the dimensions of life could be defined, captured. Perhaps reality was not wholly volatile. Perhaps it could be explained, predicted. Perhaps it could be made to make sense.

The misery began when I moved beyond the Pythagorean theorem to sine, cosine and tangent. I couldn't grasp such abstractions. I could feel the logic in them, could sense their power to bestow order and symmetry, but I couldn't unlock it. They kept their secrets, becoming a kind of gateway beyond which I believed there was a world of law and reason. But I could not pass through the gate.

Mother said that if I wanted to learn trigonometry, it was her responsibility to teach me. She set aside an evening, and the two of us sat at the kitchen table, scratching at bits of paper and tugging our hair. We spent three hours on a single problem, and every answer we produced was wrong.

"I wasn't any good at trig in high school," Mother moaned, slamming the book shut. "And I've forgotten what little I knew."

Dad was in the living room, shuffling through blueprints for the granaries and mumbling to himself. I'd watched him sketch those blueprints, watched him perform the calculations, altering this angle or lengthening that beam. Dad had little formal education in mathematics but it was impossible to doubt his aptitude: somehow I knew that if I put the equation before my father, he would be able to solve it.

When I'd told Dad that I planned to go to college, he'd said a woman's place was in the home, that I should be learning about herbs—"God's pharmacy" he'd called it, smiling to himself—so I could take over for Mother. He'd said a lot more, of course, about how I was whoring after man's knowledge instead of God's, but still I decided to ask him about trigonometry. Here was a sliver of man's knowledge I was certain he possessed.

I scribbled the problem on a fresh sheet of paper. Dad didn't look up as I approached, so gently, slowly, I slid the paper over the blueprints. "Dad, can you solve this?"

He looked at me harshly, then his eyes softened. He rotated the paper, gazed at it for a moment, and began to scrawl, numbers and circles and great, arcing lines that doubled back on themselves. His solution didn't look like anything in my textbook. It didn't look like anything I had ever seen. His mustache twitched; he mumbled. Then he stopped scribbling, looked up and gave the correct answer.

I asked how he'd solved it. "I don't know how to *solve* it," he said, handing me the paper. "All I know is, that's the answer."

I walked back to the kitchen, comparing the clean, balanced equation to the mayhem of unfinished computations and dizzying sketches. I was struck by the strangeness of that page: Dad could command this science, could decipher its language, decrypt its logic, could bend and twist and squeeze from it the truth. But as it passed through him, it turned to chaos.

I studied trigonometry for a month. I sometimes dreamed about sine, cosine and tangent, about mysterious angles and concussed computations, but for all this I made no real progress. I could not self-teach trigonometry. But I knew someone who had.

Tyler told me to meet him at our aunt Debbie's house, because she lived near Brigham Young University. The drive was three hours. I felt uncomfortable knocking on my aunt's door. She was Mother's sister, and Tyler had lived with her during his first year at BYU, but that was all I knew of her.

Tyler answered the door. We settled in the living room while Debbie prepared a casserole. Tyler solved the equations easily, writing out orderly explanations for every step. He was studying mechanical engineering, set to graduate near the top of his class, and soon after would start a PhD at Purdue. My trig equations were far beneath his abilities, but if he was bored he didn't show it; he just explained the principles patiently, over and over. The gate opened a little, and I peeked through it.

Tyler had gone, and Debbie was pushing a plate of casserole into my hands, when the phone rang. It was Mother.

"There's been an accident in Malad," she said.

Mother had little information. Shawn had fallen. He'd landed on his head. Someone had called 9-11, and he'd been airlifted to a hospital in Pocatello. The doctors weren't sure if he would live. That was all she knew.

I wanted more, some statement of the odds, even if it was just so I could reason against them. I wanted her to say,

"They think he'll be fine" or even "They expect we'll lose him." Anything but what she was saying, which was, "They don't know."

Mother said I should come to the hospital. I imagined Shawn on a white gurney, the life leaking out of him. I felt such a wave of loss that my knees nearly buckled, but in the next moment I felt something else. Relief.

There was a storm coming, set to lay three feet of snow over Sardine Canyon, which guarded the entrance to our valley. Mother's car, which I had driven to Debbie's, had bald tires. I told Mother I couldn't get through.

The story of how Shawn fell would come to me in bits and pieces, thin lines of narrative from Luke and Benjamin, who were there. It was a frigid afternoon and the wind was fierce, whipping the fine dust up in soft clouds. Shawn was standing on a wooden pallet, twenty feet in the air. Twelve feet below him was a half-finished concrete wall, with rebar jutting outward like blunt skewers. I don't know for certain what Shawn was doing on the pallet, but he was probably fitting posts or welding, because that was the kind of work he did. Dad was driving the forklift.

I've heard conflicting accounts of why Shawn fell.[4] Someone said Dad moved the boom unexpectedly and Shawn pitched over the edge. But the general consensus is that Shawn was standing near the brink, and for no reason at all stepped backward and lost his footing. He plunged twelve feet, his body revolving slowly in the air, so that when he struck the concrete wall with its outcropping of rebar, he hit headfirst, then tumbled the last eight feet to the dirt.

This is how the fall was described to me, but my mind sketches it differently—on a white page with evenly spaced lines. He ascends, falls at a slope, strikes the rebar and returns to the ground. I perceive a triangle. The event makes sense when I think of it in these terms. Then the logic of the page yields to my father.

Dad looked Shawn over. Shawn was disoriented. One of his pupils was dilated and the other wasn't, but no one knew what that meant. No one knew it meant there was a bleed inside his brain.

Dad told Shawn to take a break. Luke and Benjamin helped him prop himself against the pickup, then went back to work.

The facts after this point are even more hazy.

The story I heard was that fifteen minutes later Shawn wandered onto the site. Dad thought he was ready to work and told him to climb onto the pallet, and Shawn, who never liked being told what to do, started screaming at Dad about everything—the equipment, the granary designs, his pay. He screamed himself hoarse, then just when Dad thought he had calmed down, he gripped Dad around the waist and flung him like a sack of grain. Before Dad could scramble to his feet Shawn took off, leaping and howling and laughing, and Luke and Benjamin, now sure something was very wrong, chased after him. Luke reached him first but couldn't hold him; then Benjamin added his weight and Shawn slowed a little. But it wasn't until all three men tackled him—throwing his body to the ground, where, because he was resisting, his head hit hard—that he finally lay still.

No one has ever described to me what happened when Shawn's head struck that second time. Whether he had a seizure, or vomited, or lost consciousness, I'm not sure. But it was so chilling that someone—maybe Dad, probably Benjamin—dialed 9-11, which no member of my family had ever done before.

They were told a helicopter would arrive in minutes. Later the doctors would speculate that when Dad, Luke and Benjamin had wrestled Shawn to the ground—and he'd sustained a concussion—he was already in critical condition. They said it was a miracle he hadn't died the moment his head hit the ground.

I struggle to imagine the scene while they waited for the chopper. Dad said that when the paramedics arrived, Shawn was sobbing, begging for Mother. By the time he reached the hospital, his state of mind had shifted. He stood naked on the gurney, eyes bulging, bloodshot, screaming that he would rip out the eyes of the next bastard who came near him. Then he collapsed into sobs and finally lost consciousness.

Shawn lived through the night.

In the morning I drove to Buck's Peak. I couldn't explain why I wasn't rushing to my brother's bedside. I told Mother I had to work.

"He's asking for you," she said.

"You said he doesn't recognize anyone."

"He doesn't," she said. "But the nurse just asked me if he knows someone named Tara. He said your name over and over this morning, when he was asleep and when he was awake. I told them Tara is his sister, and now they're saying it would be good if you came. He might recognize you, and that would be something. Yours is the only name he's said since he got to the hospital."

I was silent.

"I'll pay for the gas," Mother said. She thought I wouldn't come because of the thirty dollars it would cost in fuel. I was embarrassed that she thought that, but then, if it wasn't the money, I had no reason at all.

"I'm leaving now," I said.

I remember strangely little of the hospital, or of how my brother looked. I vaguely recall that his head was wrapped in gauze, and that when I asked why, Mother said the doctors had performed a surgery, cutting into his skull to relieve some pressure, or stop a bleed, or repair something—actually, I can't remember what she said. Shawn was tossing and turning like a child with a fever. I sat with him for an hour. A few times his eyes opened, but if he was conscious, he didn't recognize me.

When I came the next day, he was awake. I walked into the room and he blinked and looked at Mother, as if to check that she was seeing me, too.

"You came," he said. "I didn't think you would." He took my hand and fell asleep.

I stared at his face, at the bandages wrapped around his forehead and over his ears, and was bled of my bitterness. Then I understood why I hadn't come sooner. I'd been afraid of how I would feel, afraid that if he died, I might be glad.

I'm sure the doctors wanted to keep him in the hospital, but we didn't have insurance, and the bill was already so large that Shawn would be making payments a decade later. The moment he was stable enough to travel, we took him home.

He lived on the sofa in the front room for two months. He was physically weak—it was all he had in him to make it to the bathroom and back. He'd lost his hearing completely in one ear and had trouble hearing with the other, so he often turned his head when people spoke to him, orienting his better ear toward them, rather than his eyes. Except for this strange movement and the bandages from the surgery, he looked normal, no swelling, no bruises. According to the doctors, this was because the damage was very serious: a lack of external injuries meant the damage was all internal.

It took some time for me to realize that although Shawn looked the same, he wasn't. He seemed lucid, but if you listened carefully his stories didn't make sense. They weren't really stories at all, just one tangent after another.

I felt guilty that I hadn't visited him immediately in the

hospital, so to make it up to him I quit my job and tended him day and night. When he wanted water, I fetched it; if he was hungry, I cooked.

Sadie started coming around, and Shawn welcomed her. I looked forward to her visits because they gave me time to study. Mother thought it was important that I stay with Shawn, so no one interrupted me. For the first time in my life I had long stretches in which to learn—without having to scrap, or strain tinctures, or check inventory for Randy. I examined Tyler's notes, read and reread his careful explanations. After a few weeks of this, by magic or miracle, the concepts took hold. I retook the practice test. The advanced algebra was still indecipherable—it came from a world beyond my ability to perceive—but the trigonometry had become intelligible, messages written in a language I could understand, from a world of logic and order that only existed in black ink and on white paper.

The real world, meanwhile, plunged into chaos. The doctors told Mother that Shawn's injury might have altered his personality—that in the hospital, he had shown tendencies toward volatility, even violence, and that such changes might be permanent.

He did succumb to rages, moments of blind anger when all he wanted was to hurt someone. He had an intuition for nastiness, for saying the single most devastating thing, that left Mother in tears more nights than not. These rages changed, and worsened, as his physical strength improved, and I found myself cleaning the toilet every morning, knowing my head might be inside it before lunch. Mother said I was the only one who could calm him, and I persuaded myself that that was true. *Who better?* I thought. *He doesn't affect me.*

Reflecting on it now, I'm not sure the injury changed him that much, but I convinced myself that it had, and that any cruelty on his part was entirely new. I can read my journals from this period and trace the evolution—of a young girl rewriting her history. In the reality she constructed for herself nothing had been wrong before her brother fell off that pallet. *I wish I had my best friend back*, she wrote. *Before his injury, I never got hurt at all.*

15

No More a Child

There was a moment that winter. I was kneeling on the carpet, listening to Dad testify of Mother's calling as a healer, when my breath caught in my chest and I felt taken out of myself. I no longer saw my parents or our living room. What I saw was a woman grown, with her own mind, her own prayers, who no longer sat, childlike, at her father's feet.

I saw the woman's swollen belly and it was my belly. Next to her sat her mother, the midwife. She took her mother's hand and said she wanted the baby delivered in a hospital, by a doctor. I'll drive you, her mother said. The women moved toward the door, but the door was blocked—by loyalty, by obedience. By her father. He stood, immovable. But the woman was *his* daughter, and she had drawn to herself all his conviction, all his weightiness. She set him aside and moved through the door.

I tried to imagine what future such a woman might claim for herself. I tried to conjure other scenes in which she and her father were of two minds. When she ignored his counsel and kept her own. But my father had taught me that there are not two reasonable opinions to be had on any subject: there is Truth and there are Lies. So as I knelt on the carpet, listening to my father but studying this stranger, and felt suspended between them, drawn to each, repelled by both, I understood that no future could hold them; no destiny could tolerate him *and* her. I would remain a child, in perpetuity, always, or I would lose him.

I was lying on my bed, watching the shadows my feeble lamp cast on the ceiling, when I heard my father's voice at the door. Instinctively I jerked to my feet in a kind of salute, but once I was standing I wasn't sure what to do. There was no precedent for this: my father had never visited my room before.

He strode past me and sat on my bed, then patted the mattress next to him. I took my seat, nervously, my feet barely touching the floor. I waited for him to speak, but the moments passed silently. His eyes were closed, his jaw slackened, as if he were listening to seraphic voices. "I've been praying," he said. His voice was soft, a loving voice. "I've been praying about your decision to go to college."

His eyes opened. His pupils had dilated in the lamplight, absorbing the hazel of the iris. I'd never seen eyes so given over to blackness; they seemed unearthly, tokens of spiritual power.

"The Lord has called me to testify," he said. "He is displeased. You have cast aside His blessings to whore after man's knowledge. His wrath is stirred against you. It will not be long in coming."

I don't remember my father standing to leave but he must have, while I sat, gripped by fear. God's wrath had laid waste to cities, it had flooded the whole earth. I felt weak, then wholly powerless. I remembered that my life was not mine. I could be taken out of my body at any moment, dragged heavenward to reckon with a furious Father.

The next morning I found Mother mixing oils in the kitchen. "I've decided not to go to BYU," I said.

She looked up, fixing her eyes on the wall behind me, and whispered, "Don't say that. I don't want to hear that."

I didn't understand. I'd thought she would be glad to see me yield to God.

Her gaze shifted to me. I hadn't felt its strength in years and I was stunned by it. "Of all my children," she said, "you were the one I thought would burst out of here in a blaze. I didn't expect it from Tyler—that was a surprise—but *you*. Don't you stay. Go. Don't let anything stop you from going."

I heard Dad's step on the stairwell. Mother sighed and her eyes fluttered, as if she were coming out of a trance.

Dad took his seat at the kitchen table and Mother stood to fix his breakfast. He began a lecture about liberal professors, and Mother mixed batter for pancakes, periodically murmuring in agreement.

Without Shawn as foreman, Dad's construction business dwindled. I'd quit my job at Randy's to look after Shawn. Now I needed money, so when Dad went back to scrapping that winter, so did I.

It was an icy morning, much like the first, when I returned to the junkyard. It had changed. There were still pillars of mangled cars but they no longer dominated the landscape. A few years before, Dad had been hired by Utah Power to dismantle hundreds of utility towers. He had been allowed to keep the angle iron, and it was now stacked—four hundred thousand pounds of it—in tangled mountains all over the yard.

I woke up every morning at six to study—because it was easier to focus in the mornings, before I was worn out from scrapping. Although I was still fearful of God's wrath, I reasoned with myself that my passing the ACT was so unlikely, it would take an act of God. And if God acted, then surely my going to school was His will.

The ACT was composed of four sections: math, English, science and reading. My math skills were improving but they were not strong. While I could answer most of the questions on the practice exam, I was slow, needing double or triple the allotted time. I lacked even a basic knowledge of grammar, though I was learning, beginning with nouns and moving on to prepositions and gerunds. Science was a mystery, perhaps because the only science book I'd ever read had had detachable pages for coloring. Of the four sections, reading was the only one about which I felt confident.

BYU was a competitive school. I'd need a high score—a twenty-seven at least, which meant the top fifteen percent of my cohort. I was sixteen, had never taken an exam, and had only recently undertaken anything like a systematic education; still I registered for the test. It felt like throwing dice, like the roll was out of my hands. God would score the toss.

I didn't sleep the night before. My brain conjured so many scenes of disaster, it burned as if with a fever. At five I got out of bed, ate breakfast, and drove the forty miles to Utah State University. I was led into a white classroom with thirty other students, who took their seats and placed their pencils on their desks. A middle-aged woman handed out strange pink sheets I'd never seen before.

"Excuse me," I said when she gave me mine. "What is this?"

"It's a bubble sheet. To mark your answers."

"How does it work?" I said.

"It's the same as any other bubble sheet." She began to move away from me, visibly irritated, as if I were playing a prank.

"I've never used one before."

She appraised me for a moment. "Fill in the bubble of the correct answer," she said. "Blacken it completely. Understand?"

The test began. I'd never sat at a desk for four hours in a room full of people. The noise was unbelievable, yet I seemed to be the only person who heard it, who couldn't divert her attention from the rustle of turning pages and the scratch of pencils on paper.

When it was over I suspected that I'd failed the math, and I was positive that I'd failed the science. My answers for the science portion couldn't even be called guesses. They were random, just patterns of dots on that strange pink sheet.

I drove home. I felt stupid, but more than stupid I felt ridiculous. Now that I'd seen the other students—watched them march into the classroom in neat rows, claim their seats and calmly fill in their answers, as if they were performing a practiced routine—it seemed absurd that I had thought I could score in the top fifteen percent.

That was their world. I stepped into overalls and returned to mine.

There was an unusually hot day that spring, and Luke and I spent it hauling purlins—the iron beams that run horizontally along the length of a roof. The purlins were heavy and the sun relentless. Sweat dripped from our noses and onto the painted iron. Luke slipped out of his shirt, grabbed hold of the sleeves and tore them, leaving huge gashes a breeze could pass through. I wouldn't have dreamed of doing anything so radical, but after the twentieth purlin my back was sticky with sweat, and I flapped my T-shirt to make a fan, then rolled up my sleeves until an inch of my shoulders was visible. When Dad saw me a few minutes later, he strode over and yanked the sleeves down. "This ain't a whorehouse," he said.

I watched him walk away and, mechanically, as if I weren't making the decision, rerolled them. He returned an hour later, and when he caught sight of me he paused mid-step, confused. He'd told me what to do, and I hadn't done it. He stood uncertainly for a moment, then crossed over to me, took hold of both sleeves and jerked them down. He didn't make it ten steps before I'd rolled them up again.

I wanted to obey. I meant to. But the afternoon was so hot, the breeze on my arms so welcome. It was just a few inches. I was covered from my temples to my toes in grime. It would take me half an hour that night to dig the black dirt out of my nostrils and ears. I didn't feel much like an object of desire or temptation. I felt like a human forklift. How could an inch of skin matter?

I was hoarding my paychecks, in case I needed the money for tuition. Dad noticed and started charging me for small things. Mother had gone back to buying insurance after the second car accident, and Dad said I should pay my share. So I did. Then he wanted more, for registration. "These Government fees will break you," he said as I handed him the cash.

That satisfied Dad until my test results arrived. I returned from the junkyard to find a white envelope. I tore it open, staining the page with grease, and looked past the individual scores to the composite. Twenty-two. My heart was beating loud, happy beats. It wasn't a twenty-seven, but it opened up possibilities. Maybe Idaho State.

I showed Mother the score and she told Dad. He became agitated, then he shouted that it was time I moved out.

"If she's old enough to pull a paycheck, she's old enough to pay rent," Dad yelled. "And she can pay it somewhere else." At first Mother argued with him, but within minutes he'd convinced her.

I'd been standing in the kitchen, weighing my options, thinking about how I'd just given Dad four hundred dollars, a third of my savings, when Mother turned to me and said, "Do you think you could move out by Friday?"

Something broke in me, a dam or a levee. I felt tossed about, unable to hold myself in place. I screamed but the screams were strangled; I was drowning. I had nowhere to go. I couldn't afford to rent an apartment, and even if I could the only apartments for rent were in town. Then I'd need a car. I only had eight hundred dollars. I sputtered all this at Mother, then ran to my room and slammed the door.

She knocked moments later. "I know you think we're being unfair," she said, "but when I was your age I was living on my own, getting ready to marry your father."

"You were married at sixteen?" I said.

"Don't be silly," she said. "You are not sixteen."

I stared at her. She stared at me. "Yes, I am. I'm sixteen."

She looked me over. "You're at least twenty." She cocked her head. "Aren't you?"

We were silent. My heart pounded in my chest. "I turned sixteen in September," I said.

"Oh." Mother bit her lip, then she stood and smiled. "Well, don't worry about it then. You can stay. Don't know what your dad was thinking, really. I guess we forgot. Hard to keep track of how old you kids are."

Shawn returned to work, hobbling unsteadily. He wore an Aussie outback hat, which was large, wide-brimmed, and made of chocolate-brown oiled leather. Before the accident, he had worn the hat only when riding horses, but now he kept it on all the time, even in the house, which Dad said was disrespectful. Disrespecting Dad might have been the reason Shawn wore it, but I suspect another reason was that it was large and comfortable and covered the scars from his surgery.

He worked short days at first. Dad had a contract to build a milking barn in Oneida County, about twenty miles from Buck's Peak, so Shawn puttered around the yard, adjusting schematics and measuring I-beams.

Luke, Benjamin and I were scrapping. Dad had decided it was time to salvage the angle iron stacked all around the farm. To be sold, each piece had to measure less than four feet. Shawn suggested we use torches to cut the iron, but Dad said it would be too slow and cost too much in fuel.

A few days later Dad came home with the most frightening machine I've ever seen. He called it the Shear. At first glance it appeared to be a three-ton pair of scissors, and this turned out to be exactly what it was. The blades were made of dense iron, twelve inches thick and five feet across. They cut not by sharpness but by force and mass. They bit down, their great jaws propelled by a heavy piston attached to a large iron wheel. The wheel was animated by a belt and motor, which meant that if something got caught in the machine, it would take anywhere from thirty seconds to a minute to stop the wheel and halt the blades. Up and down they roared, louder than a passing train as they chewed through iron as thick as a man's arm. The iron wasn't being cut so much as snapped. Sometimes it would buck, propelling whoever was holding it toward the dull, chomping blades.

Dad had dreamed up many dangerous schemes over the years, but this was the first that really shocked me. Perhaps it was the obvious lethality of it, the certainty that a wrong move would cost a limb. Or maybe that it was utterly un-necessary. It was indulgent. Like a toy, if a toy could take your head off.

Shawn called it a death machine and said Dad had lost what little sense he'd ever had. "Are you *trying* to kill someone?" he said. "Because I got a gun in my truck that will make a lot less mess." Dad couldn't suppress his grin. I'd never seen him so enraptured.

Shawn lurched back to the shop, shaking his head. Dad began feeding iron through the Shear. Each length bucked him forward and twice he nearly pitched headfirst into the blades. I jammed my eyes shut, knowing that if Dad's head got caught, the blades wouldn't even slow, just hack through his neck and keep chomping.

Now that he was sure the machine worked, Dad motioned for Luke to take over, and Luke, ever eager to please, stepped forward. Five minutes later Luke's arm was gashed to the bone and he was running toward the house, blood spurting.

Dad scanned his crew. He motioned to Benjamin, but Benjamin shook his head, saying he liked his fingers attached, thanks anyway. Dad looked longingly at the house, and I imagined him wondering how long it would take Mother to stop the bleeding. Then his eyes settled on me.

"Come here, Tara."

I didn't move.

"Get over here," he said.

I stepped forward slowly, not blinking, watching the Shear as if it might attack. Luke's blood was still on the blade. Dad picked up a six-foot length of angle iron and handed me the end. "Keep a good hold on it," he said. "But if it bucks, let go."

The blades chomped, growling as they snapped up and down—a warning, I thought, like a dog's snarl, to get the hell away. But Dad's mania for the machine had carried him beyond the reach of reason.

"It's easy," he said.

I prayed when I fed the first piece to the blades. Not to avoid injury—there was no possibility of that—but that the injury would be like Luke's, a wedge of flesh, so I could go to the house, too. I chose smaller pieces, hoping my weight could control the lurch. Then I ran out of small pieces. I picked up the smallest of what was left, but the metal was still thick. I shoved it through and waited for the jaws to crash shut. The sound of solid iron fracturing was thunderous. The iron bucked, tossing me forward so both my feet left the ground. I let go and collapsed in the dirt, and the iron, now free, and being chewed violently by the blades, launched into the air then crashed down next to me.

"WHAT THE HELL IS GOING ON?" Shawn appeared

in the corner of my vision. He strode over and pulled me to my feet, then spun around to face Dad.

"Five minutes ago, this monster nearly ripped Luke's arm off! So you've put Tara on it?"

"She's made of strong stuff," Dad said, winking at me.

Shawn's eyes bulged. He was supposed to be taking it easy, but he looked apoplectic.

"It's going to take her head off!" he screamed. He turned to me and waved toward the ironworker in the shop. "Go make clips to fit those purlins. I don't want you coming near this thing again."

Dad moved forward. "This is *my* crew. You work for me and so does Tara. I told her to run the Shear, and she will run it."

They shouted at each other for fifteen minutes. It was different from the fights they'd had before—this was unrestrained somehow, hateful. I'd never seen anyone yell at my father like that, and I was astonished by, then afraid of, the change it wrought in his features. His face transformed, becoming rigid, desperate. Shawn had awoken something in Dad, some primal need. Dad could not lose this argument and save face. If I didn't run the Shear, Dad would no longer be Dad.

Shawn leapt forward and shoved Dad hard in the chest. Dad stumbled backward, tripped and fell. He lay in the mud, shocked, for a moment, then he climbed to his feet and lunged toward his son. Shawn raised his arms to block the punch, but when Dad saw this he lowered his fists, perhaps remembering that Shawn had only recently regained the ability to walk.

"I told her to do it, and she *will* do it," Dad said, low and angry. "Or she won't live under my roof."

Shawn looked at me. For a moment, he seemed to consider helping me pack—after all, he had run away from Dad at my age—but I shook my head. I wasn't leaving, not like that. I would work the Shear first, and Shawn knew it. He looked at the Shear, then at the pile next to it, about fifty thousand pounds of iron. "She'll do it," he said.

Dad seemed to grow five inches. Shawn bent unsteadily and lifted a piece of heavy iron, then heaved it toward the Shear.

"Don't be stupid," Dad said.

"If she's doing it, I'm doing it," Shawn said. The fight had left his voice. I'd never seen Shawn give way to Dad, not once, but he'd decided to lose this argument. He understood that if *he* didn't submit, I surely would.

"You're my foreman!" Dad shouted. "I need you in Oneida, not mucking with scrap!"

"Then shut down the Shear."

Dad walked away cursing, exasperated, but probably thinking that Shawn would get tired and go back to being foreman before supper. Shawn watched Dad leave, then he turned to me and said, "Okay, Siddle Liss. You bring the pieces and I'll feed them through. If the iron is thick, say a half inch, I'll need your weight on the back to keep me from getting tossed into the blades. Okay?"

Shawn and I ran the Shear for a month. Dad was too stubborn to shut it down, even though it cost him more to have his foreman salvaging than it would have cost him to cut the iron with torches. When we finished, I had some bruises but I wasn't hurt. Shawn seemed bled of life. It had only been a few months since his fall from the pallet, and his body couldn't take the wear. He was cracked in the head many times when a length of iron bucked at an unexpected angle. When that happened he'd sit for a minute in the dirt, his hands over his eyes, then he'd stand and reach for the next length. In the evenings he lay on the kitchen floor in his stained shirt and dusty jeans, too weary even to shower.

I fetched all the food and water he asked for. Sadie came

most evenings, and the two of us would run side by side when he sent us for ice, then to remove the ice, then to put the ice back in. We were both Fish Eyes.

The next morning Shawn and I would return to the Shear, and he would feed iron through its jaws, which chewed with such force that it pulled him off his feet, easily, playfully, as if it were a game, as if he were a child.

16

Disloyal Man, Disobedient Heaven

Construction began on the milking barn in Oneida. Shawn designed and welded the main frame—the massive beams that formed the skeleton of the building. They were too heavy for the loader; only a crane could lift them. It was a delicate procedure, requiring the welders to balance on opposite ends of a beam while it was lowered onto columns, then welded in place. Shawn surprised everyone when he announced that he wanted me to operate the crane.

"Tara can't drive the crane," Dad said. "It'll take half the morning to teach her the controls, and she still won't know what the hell she's doing."

"But she'll be careful," Shawn said, "and I'm done falling off shit."

An hour later I was in the man box, and Shawn and Luke were standing on either end of a beam, twenty feet in the air. I brushed the lever lightly, listening as the hydraulic cylinders hissed softly to protract. "Hold!" Shawn shouted when the beam was in place, then they nodded their helmets down and began to weld.

My operating the crane was one of a hundred disputes between Dad and Shawn that Shawn won that summer. Most were not resolved so peacefully. They argued nearly every day—about a flaw in the schematics or a tool that had been left at home. Dad seemed eager to fight, to prove who was in charge.

One afternoon Dad walked over and stood right next to Shawn, watching him weld. A minute later, for no reason, he started shouting: that Shawn had taken too long at lunch, that he wasn't getting the crew up early enough or working us hard enough. Dad yelled for several minutes, then Shawn took off his welding helmet, looked at him calmly and said, "You gonna shut up so I can work?"

Dad kept yelling. He said Shawn was lazy, that he didn't know how to run a crew, didn't understand the value of hard work. Shawn stepped down from his welding and ambled over to the flatbed pickup. Dad followed, still hollering. Shawn pulled off his gloves, slowly, delicately, one finger at a time, as if there weren't a man screaming six inches from his face. For several moments he stood still, letting the abuse wash over him, then he stepped into the pickup and drove off, leaving Dad to shout at the dust.

I remember the awe I felt as I watched that pickup roll down the dirt road. Shawn was the only person I had ever seen stand up to Dad, the only one whose force of mind, whose sheer tonnage of conviction, could make Dad give way. I had seen Dad lose his temper and shout at every one of my brothers. Shawn was the only one I ever saw walk away.

It was a Saturday night. I was at Grandma-over-in-town's, my math book propped open on the kitchen table, a plate of cookies next to me. I was studying to retake the ACT. I often studied at Grandma's so Dad wouldn't lecture me.

The phone rang. It was Shawn. Did I want to watch a movie? I said I did, and a few minutes later I heard a loud rumble and looked out the window. With his booming black motorcycle and his wide-brimmed Aussie hat, he seemed entirely out of place parking parallel to Grandma's white picket fence. Grandma started making brownies, and Shawn and I went upstairs to choose a movie.

We paused the movie when Grandma delivered the brownies. We ate them in silence, our spoons clicking loudly against Grandma's porcelain plates. "You'll get your twenty-seven," Shawn said suddenly when we'd finished.

"It doesn't matter," I said. "I don't think I'll go either way. What if Dad's right? What if I get brainwashed?"

Shawn shrugged. "You're as smart as Dad. If Dad's right, you'll know when you get there."

The movie ended. We told Grandma good night. It was a balmy summer evening, perfect for the motorcycle, and Shawn said I should ride home with him, we'd get the car tomorrow. He revved the engine, waiting for me to climb on. I took a step toward him, then remembered the math book on Grandma's table.

"You go," I said. "I'll be right behind you."

Shawn yanked his hat down on his head, spun the bike around and charged down the empty street.

I drove in a happy stupor. The night was black—that thick darkness that belongs only in backcountry, where the houses are few and the streetlights fewer, where starlight goes unchallenged. I navigated the winding highway as I'd done numberless times before, racing down the Bear River Hill, coasting through the flat stretch parallel to Fivemile Creek. Up ahead the road climbed and bent to the right. I knew the curve was there without looking for it, and wondered at the still headlights I saw shining in the blackness.

I began the ascent. There was a pasture to my left, a ditch to my right. As the incline began in earnest I saw three cars pulled off near the ditch. The doors were open, the cab lights on. Seven or eight people huddled around something on the gravel. I changed lanes to drive around them, but stopped when I saw a small object lying in the middle of the highway.

It was a wide-brimmed Aussie hat.

I pulled over and ran toward the people clustered by the ditch. "Shawn!" I shouted.

The crowd parted to let me through. Shawn was facedown on the gravel, lying in a pool of blood that looked pink in the glare from the headlights. He wasn't moving. "He hit a cow coming around the corner," a man said. "It's so dark tonight, he didn't even see it. We've called an ambulance. We don't dare move him."

Shawn's body was contorted, his back twisted. I had no idea how long an ambulance might take, and there was so much blood. I decided to stop the bleeding. I dug my hands under his shoulder and heaved but I couldn't lift him. I looked up at the crowd and recognized a face. Dwain.[5] He was one of *us*. Mother had midwifed four of his eight children.

"Dwain! Help me turn him."

Dwain hefted Shawn onto his back. For a second that contained an hour, I stared at my brother, watching the blood trickle out of his temple and down his right cheek, pouring over his ear and onto his white T-shirt. His eyes were closed, his mouth open. The blood was oozing from a hole the size of a golf ball in his forehead. It looked as though his temple had been dragged on the asphalt, scraping away skin, then bone. I leaned close and peered inside the wound. Something soft and spongy glistened back at me. I slipped out of my jacket and pressed it to Shawn's head.

When I touched the abrasion, Shawn released a long sigh and his eyes opened.

"Sidlister," he mumbled. Then he seemed to lose consciousness.

My cellphone was in my pocket. I dialed. Dad answered.

I must have been frantic, sputtering. I said Shawn had crashed his bike, that he had a hole in his head.

"Slow down. What happened?"

I said it all a second time. "What should I do?"

"Bring him home," Dad said. "Your mother will deal with it."

I opened my mouth but no words came out. Finally, I said, "I'm not joking. His brain, I can see it!"

"Bring him home," Dad said. "Your mother can handle it." Then: the dull drone of a dial tone. He'd hung up.

Dwain had overheard. "I live just through this field," he said. "Your mother can treat him there."

"No," I said. "Dad wants him home. Help me get him in the car."

Shawn groaned when we lifted him but he didn't speak again. Someone said we should wait for the ambulance. Someone else said we should drive him to the hospital ourselves. I don't think anyone believed we would take him home, not with his brain dribbling out of his forehead.

We folded Shawn into the backseat. I got behind the wheel, and Dwain climbed in on the passenger side. I checked my rearview mirror to pull onto the highway, then reached up and shoved the mirror downward so it reflected Shawn's face, blank and bloodied. My foot hovered over the gas.

Three seconds passed, maybe four. That's all it was.

Dwain was shouting, "Let's go!" but I barely heard him. I was lost to panic. My thoughts wandered wildly, feverishly, through a fog of resentment. The state was dreamlike, as if the hysteria had freed me from a fiction that, five minutes before, I had needed to believe.

I had never thought about the day Shawn had fallen from the pallet. There was nothing to think about. He had fallen because God wanted him to fall; there was no deeper meaning in it than that. I had never imagined what it would have been like to be there. To see Shawn plunge, grasping at air. To watch him collide, then fold, then lie still. I had never allowed myself to imagine what happened *after*—Dad's decision to leave him by the pickup, or the worried looks that must have passed between Luke and Ben.

Now, staring at the creases in my brother's face, each a little river of blood, I remembered. I remembered that Shawn had sat by the pickup for a quarter of an hour, his brain bleeding. Then he'd had that fit and the boys had wrestled him to the ground, so that he'd fallen, sustained a second injury, the injury the doctors said should have killed him. It was the reason Shawn would never quite be Shawn again.

If the first fall was God's will, whose was the second?

I'd never been to the hospital in town, but it was easy to find.

Dwain had asked me what the hell I was doing when I flipped a U-turn and accelerated down the hillside. I'd listened to Shawn's shallow breathing as I raced through the valley, along Fivemile Creek, then shot up the Bear River Hill. At the hospital, I parked in the emergency lane, and Dwain and I carried Shawn through the glass doors. I shouted for help. A nurse appeared, running, then another. Shawn was conscious by then. They took him away and someone shoved me into the waiting room.

There was no avoiding what had to be done next. I called Dad.

"You nearly home?" he said.

"I'm at the hospital."

There was silence, then he said, "We're coming."

Fifteen minutes later they were there, and the three of us waited awkwardly together, me chewing my fingernails on a pastel-blue sofa, Mother pacing and clicking her fingers, and Dad sitting motionless beneath a loud wall clock.

The doctor gave Shawn a CAT scan. He said the wound was nasty but the damage was minimal, and then I remembered what the last doctors had told me—that with head injuries, often the ones that look the worst are actually less severe—and I felt stupid for panicking and bringing him here. The hole in the bone was small, the doctor said. It might grow over on its own, or a surgeon could put in a metal plate. Shawn said he'd like to see how it healed, so the doctor folded the skin over the hole and stitched it.

We took Shawn home around three in the morning. Dad drove, with Mother next to him, and I rode in the backseat with Shawn. No one spoke. Dad didn't yell or lecture; in fact, he never mentioned that night again. But there was something in the way he fixed his gaze, never looking directly at me, that made me think a fork had come along in the road, and I'd gone one way and he the other. After that night, there was never any question of whether I would go or stay. It was as if we were living in the future, and I was already gone.

When I think of that night now, I don't think of the dark highway, or of my brother lying in a pool of his own blood. I think of the waiting room, with its ice-blue sofa and pale walls. I smell its sterilized air. I hear the ticking of a plastic clock.

Sitting across from me is my father, and as I look into his worn face it hits me, a truth so powerful I don't know why I've never understood it before. The truth is this: that I am not a good daughter. I am a traitor, a wolf among sheep; there is something different about me and that difference is not good. I want to bellow, to weep into my father's knees and promise never to do it again. But wolf that I am, I am still above lying, and anyway he would sniff the lie. We both know that if I ever again find Shawn on the highway, soaked in crimson, I will do exactly what I have just done.

I am not sorry, merely ashamed.

The envelope arrived three weeks later, just as Shawn was getting back on his feet. I tore it open, feeling numb, as if I were reading my sentence after the guilty verdict had already been handed down. I scanned down to the composite score. Twenty-eight. I checked it again. I checked my name. There was no mistake. Somehow—and a miracle was the only way I could account for it—I'd done it.

My first thought was a resolution: I resolved to never again work for my father. I drove to the only grocery store in town, called Stokes, and applied for a job bagging groceries. I was only sixteen, but I didn't tell the manager that and he hired me for forty hours a week. My first shift started at four o'clock the next morning.

When I got home, Dad was driving the loader through the junkyard. I stepped onto the ladder and grabbed hold of the rail. Over the roar of the engine, I told him I'd found a job but that I would drive the crane in the afternoons, until he could hire someone. He dropped the boom and stared ahead.

"You've already decided," he said without glancing at me. "No point dragging it out."

I applied to BYU a week later. I had no idea how to write the application, so Tyler wrote it for me. He said I'd been educated according to a rigorous program designed by my mother, who'd made sure I met all the requirements to graduate.

My feelings about the application changed from day to day, almost from minute to minute. Sometimes I was sure God wanted me to go to college, because He'd given me that twenty-eight. Other times I was sure I'd be rejected, and that God would punish me for applying, for trying to abandon my own family. But whatever the outcome, I knew I would leave. I would go somewhere, even if it wasn't to school. Home had changed the moment I'd taken Shawn to that hospital instead of to Mother. I had rejected some part of it; now it was rejecting me.

The admissions committee was efficient; I didn't wait long. The letter arrived in a normal envelope. My heart sank when I saw it. Rejection letters are small, I thought. I opened it and read "Congratulations." I'd been admitted for the semester beginning January 5.

Mother hugged me. Dad tried to be cheerful. "It proves one thing at least," he said. "Our home school is as good as any public education."

Three days before I turned seventeen, Mother drove me to Utah to find an apartment. The search took all day, and we arrived home late to find Dad eating a frozen supper. He hadn't cooked it well and it was mush. The mood around him was charged, combustible. It felt like he might detonate at any moment. Mother didn't even kick off her shoes, just rushed to the kitchen and began shuffling pans to fix a real dinner. Dad moved to the living room and started cursing at the VCR. I could see from the hallway that the cables weren't connected. When I pointed this out, he exploded. He cussed and waved his arms, shouting that in a man's house the cables should *always* be hooked up, that a man should never have to come into a room and find the cables to his VCR unhooked. Why the hell had I unhooked them anyway?

Mother rushed in from the kitchen. "*I* disconnected the cables," she said.

Dad rounded on her, sputtering. "Why do you always take her side! A man should be able to expect support from his wife!"

I fumbled with the cables while Dad stood over me, shouting. I kept dropping them. My mind pulsed with panic, which overpowered every thought, so that I could not even remember how to connect red to red, white to white.

Then it was gone. I looked up at my father, at his purple face, at the vein pulsing in his neck. I still hadn't managed to attach the cables. I stood, and once on my feet, didn't care whether the cables were attached. I walked out of the room. Dad was still shouting when I reached the kitchen. As I moved down the hall I looked back. Mother had taken my place, crouching over the VCR, groping for the wires, as Dad towered over her.

Waiting for Christmas that year felt like waiting to walk off the edge of a cliff. Not since Y2K had I felt so certain that something terrible was coming, something that would obliterate everything I'd known before. And what would replace it? I tried to imagine the future, to populate it with professors, homework, classrooms, but my mind couldn't conjure them. There *was* no future in my imagination. There was New Year's Eve, then there was nothing.

I knew I should prepare, try to acquire the high school education Tyler had told the university I had. But I didn't know how, and I didn't want to ask Tyler for help. He was starting a new life at Purdue—he was even getting married—and I doubted he wanted responsibility for mine.

I noticed, though, when he came home for Christmas, that he was reading a book called *Les Misérables,* and I decided that it must be the kind of a book a college student reads. I bought my own copy, hoping it would teach me about history or literature, but it didn't. It couldn't, because I was unable to distinguish between the fictional story and the factual backdrop. Napoleon felt no more real to me than Jean Valjean. I had never heard of either.

PART TWO

17

To Keep It Holy

On New Year's Day, Mother drove me to my new life. I didn't take much with me: a dozen jars of home-canned peaches, bedding, and a garbage bag full of clothes. As we sped down the interstate I watched the landscape splinter and barb, the rolling black summits of the Bear River Mountains giving way to the razor-edged Rockies. The university was nestled in the heart of the Wasatch Mountains, whose white massifs jutted mightily out of the earth. They were beautiful, but to me their beauty seemed aggressive, menacing.

My apartment was a mile south of campus. It had a kitchen, living room and three small bedrooms. The other women who lived there—I knew they would be women because at BYU all housing was segregated by gender—had not yet returned from the Christmas holiday. It took only a few minutes to bring in my stuff from the car. Mother and I stood awkwardly in the kitchen for a moment, then she hugged me and drove away.

I lived alone in the quiet apartment for three days. Except it wasn't quiet. *Nowhere* was quiet. I'd never spent more than a few hours in a city and found it impossible to defend myself from the strange noises that constantly invaded. The chirrup of crosswalk signals, the shrieking of sirens, the hissing of air brakes, even the hushed chatter of people strolling on the sidewalk—I heard every sound individually. My ears, accustomed to the silence of the peak, felt battered by them.

I was starved for sleep by the time my first roommate arrived. Her name was Shannon, and she studied at the cosmetology school across the street. She was wearing plush pink pajama bottoms and a tight white tank with spaghetti straps. I stared at her bare shoulders. I'd seen women dressed this way before—Dad called them gentiles—and I'd always avoided getting too near them, as if their immorality might be catching. Now there was one in my house.

Shannon surveyed me with frank disappointment, taking in my baggy flannel coat and oversized men's jeans. "How old are you?" she said.

"I'm a freshman," I said. I didn't want to admit I was only seventeen, and that I should be in high school, finishing my junior year.

Shannon moved to the sink and I saw the word "Juicy" written across her rear. That was more than I could take. I backed away toward my room, mumbling that I was going to bed.

"Good call," she said. "Church is early. I'm usually late."

"*You* go to church?"

"Sure," she said. "Don't you?"

"Of course I do. But you, you really go?"

She stared at me, chewing her lip, then said, "Church is at eight. Good night!"

My mind was spinning as I shut my bedroom door. How could *she* be a Mormon?

Dad said there were gentiles everywhere—that most Mormons were gentiles, they just didn't know it. I thought about Shannon's tank and pajamas, and suddenly realized that probably everyone at BYU was a gentile.

My other roommate arrived the next day. Her name was

Mary and she was a junior studying early childhood education. She dressed like I expected a Mormon to dress on Sunday, in a floral skirt that reached to the floor. Her clothes were a kind of shibboleth to me; they signaled that she was not a gentile, and for a few hours I felt less alone.

Until that evening. Mary stood suddenly from the sofa and said, "Classes start tomorrow. Time to stock up on groceries." She left and returned an hour later with two paper bags. Shopping was forbidden on the Sabbath—I'd never purchased so much as a stick of gum on a Sunday—but Mary casually unpacked eggs, milk and pasta without acknowledging that every item she was placing in our communal fridge was a violation of the Lord's Commandments. When she withdrew a can of Diet Coke, which my father said was a violation of the Lord's counsel for health, I again fled to my room.

The next morning, I got on the bus going the wrong direction. By the time I'd corrected my mistake, the lecture was nearly finished. I stood awkwardly in the back until the professor, a thin woman with delicate features, motioned for me to take the only available seat, which was near the front. I sat down, feeling the weight of everyone's eyes. The course was on Shakespeare, and I'd chosen it because I'd heard of Shakespeare and thought that was a good sign. But now I was here I realized I knew nothing about him. It was a word I'd heard, that was all.

When the bell rang, the professor approached my desk. "You don't belong here," she said.

I stared at her, confused. Of course I didn't belong, but how did she know? I was on the verge of confessing the whole thing—that I'd never gone to school, that I hadn't really met the requirements to graduate—when she added, "This class is for seniors."

"There are classes for seniors?" I said.

She rolled her eyes as if I were trying to be funny. "This is 382. You should be in 110."

It took most of the walk across campus before I understood what she'd said, then I checked my course schedule and, for the first time, noticed the numbers next to the course names.

I went to the registrar's office, where I was told that every freshman-level course was full. What I should do, they said, was check online every few hours and join if someone dropped. By the end of the week I'd managed to squeeze into introductory courses in English, American history, music and religion, but I was stuck in a junior-level course on art in Western civilization.

Freshman English was taught by a cheerful woman in her late twenties who kept talking about something called the "essay form," which, she assured us, we had learned in high school.

My next class, American history, was held in an auditorium named for the prophet Joseph Smith. I'd thought American history would be easy because Dad had taught us about the Founding Fathers—I knew all about Washington, Jefferson, Madison. But the professor barely mentioned them at all, and instead talked about "philosophical underpinnings" and the writings of Cicero and Hume, names I'd never heard.

In the first lecture, we were told that the next class would begin with a quiz on the readings. For two days I tried to wrestle meaning from the textbook's dense passages, but terms like "civic humanism" and "the Scottish Enlightenment" dotted the page like black holes, sucking all the other words into them. I took the quiz and missed every question.

That failure sat uneasily in my mind. It was the first indication of whether I would be okay, whether whatever I had in my head by way of *education* was enough. After the quiz, the answer seemed clear: it was not enough. On realizing this, I might have resented my upbringing but I didn't. My loyalty to my father had increased in proportion to the miles between us. On the mountain, I could rebel. But here, in this loud, bright place, surrounded by gentiles disguised as saints, I clung to every truth, every doctrine he had given me. Doctors were Sons of Perdition. Homeschooling was a commandment from the Lord.

Failing a quiz did nothing to undermine my new devotion to an old creed, but a lecture on Western art did.

The classroom was bright when I arrived, the morning sun pouring in warmly through a high wall of windows. I chose a seat next to a girl in a high-necked blouse. Her name was Vanessa. "We should stick together," she said. "I think we're the only freshmen in the whole class."

The lecture began when an old man with small eyes and a sharp nose shuttered the windows. He flipped a switch and a slide projector filled the room with white light. The image was of a painting. The professor discussed the composition, the brushstrokes, the history. Then he moved to the next painting, and the next and the next.

Then the projector showed a peculiar image, of a man in a faded hat and overcoat. Behind him loomed a concrete wall. He held a small paper near his face but he wasn't looking at it. He was looking at us.

I opened the picture book I'd purchased for the class so I could take a closer look. Something was written under the image in italics but I couldn't understand it. It had one of those black-hole words, right in the middle, devouring the rest. I'd seen other students ask questions, so I raised my hand.

The professor called on me, and I read the sentence aloud. When I came to the word, I paused. "I don't know this word," I said. "What does it mean?"

There was silence. Not a hush, not a muting of the noise,

but utter, almost violent silence. No papers shuffled, no pencils scratched.

The professor's lips tightened. "Thanks for *that*," he said, then returned to his notes.

I scarcely moved for the rest of the lecture. I stared at my shoes, wondering what had happened, and why, whenever I looked up, there was always someone staring at me as if I was a freak. Of course I *was* a freak, and I knew it, but I didn't understand how *they* knew it.

When the bell rang, Vanessa shoved her notebook into her pack. Then she paused and said, "You shouldn't make fun of that. It's not a joke." She walked away before I could reply.

I stayed in my seat until everyone had gone, pretending the zipper on my coat was stuck so I could avoid looking anyone in the eye. Then I went straight to the computer lab to look up the word "Holocaust."

I don't know how long I sat there reading about it, but at some point I'd read enough. I leaned back and stared at the ceiling. I suppose I was in shock, but whether it was the shock of learning about something horrific, or the shock of learning about my own ignorance, I'm not sure. I do remember imagining for a moment, not the camps, not the pits or chambers of gas, but my mother's face. A wave of emotion took me, a feeling so intense, so unfamiliar, I wasn't sure what it was. It made me want to shout at her, at my own mother, and that frightened me.

I searched my memories. In some ways the word "Holocaust" wasn't wholly unfamiliar. Perhaps Mother *had* taught me about it, when we were picking rosehips or tincturing hawthorn. I did seem to have a vague knowledge that Jews had been killed somewhere, long ago. But I'd thought it was a small conflict, like the Boston Massacre, which Dad talked about a lot, in which half a dozen people had been martyred by a tyrannical government. To have misunderstood it on this scale—five versus six million—seemed impossible.

I found Vanessa before the next lecture and apologized for the joke. I didn't explain, because I couldn't explain. I just said I was sorry and that I wouldn't do it again. To keep that promise, I didn't raise my hand for the rest of the semester.

That Saturday, I sat at my desk with a stack of homework. Everything had to be finished that day because I could not violate the Sabbath.

I spent the morning and afternoon trying to decipher the history textbook, without much success. In the evening, I tried to write a personal essay for English, but I'd never written an essay before—except for the ones on sin and repentance, which no one had ever read—and I didn't know how. I had no idea what the teacher meant by the "essay form." I scribbled a few sentences, crossed them out, then began again. I repeated this until it was past midnight.

I knew I should stop—this was the Lord's time—but I hadn't even started the assignment for music theory, which was due at seven A.M. on Monday. The Sabbath begins when I wake up, I reasoned, and kept working.

I awoke with my face pressed to the desk. The room was bright. I could hear Shannon and Mary in the kitchen. I put on my Sunday dress and the three of us walked to church. Because it was a congregation of students, everyone was sitting with their roommates, so I settled into a pew with mine. Shannon immediately began chatting with the girl behind us. I looked around the chapel and was again struck by how many women were wearing skirts cut above the knee.

The girl talking to Shannon said we should come over that afternoon to see a movie. Mary and Shannon agreed but I shook my head. I didn't watch movies on Sunday.

Shannon rolled her eyes. "She's *very* devout," she whispered.

I'd always known that my father believed in a different

God. As a child, I'd been aware that although my family attended the same church as everyone in our town, our religion was not the same. They *believed* in modesty; we practiced it. They believed in God's power to heal; we left our injuries in God's hands. They believed in preparing for the Second Coming; we were actually prepared. For as long as I could remember, I'd known that the members of my own family were the only true Mormons I had ever known, and yet for some reason, here at this university, in this chapel, for the first time I felt the immensity of the gap. I understood now: I could stand with my family, or with the gentiles, on the one side or the other, but there was no foothold in between.

The service ended and we filed into Sunday school. Shannon and Mary chose seats near the front. They saved me one but I hesitated, thinking of how I'd broken the Sabbath. I'd been here less than a week, and already I had robbed the Lord of an hour. Perhaps *that* was why Dad hadn't wanted me to come: because he knew that by living with them, with people whose faith was *less*, I risked becoming like them.

Shannon waved to me and her V-neck plunged. I walked past her and folded myself into a corner, as far from Shannon and Mary as I could get. I was pleased by the familiarity of the arrangement: me, pressed into the corner, away from the other children, a precise reproduction of every Sunday school lesson from my childhood. It was the only sensation of familiarity I'd felt since coming to this place, and I relished it.

18

Blood and Feathers

After that, I rarely spoke to Shannon or Mary and they rarely spoke to me, except to remind me to do my share of the chores, which I never did. The apartment looked fine to me. So what if there were rotting peaches in the fridge and dirty dishes in the sink? So what if the smell slapped you in the face when you came through the door? To my mind if the stench was bearable, the house was clean, and I extended this philosophy to my person. I never used soap except when I showered, usually once or twice a week, and sometimes I didn't use it even then. When I left the bathroom in the morning, I marched right past the hallway sink where Shannon and Mary always—*always*—washed their hands. I saw their raised eyebrows and thought of Grandma-over-in-town. *Frivolous*, I told myself. *I don't pee on my hands.*

The atmosphere in the apartment was tense. Shannon looked at me like I was a rabid dog, and I did nothing to reassure her.

My bank account decreased steadily. I had been worried that I might not pass my classes, but a month into the semester, after I'd paid tuition and rent and bought food and books, I began to think that even if I did pass I wouldn't be coming back to school for one obvious reason: I couldn't afford it. I looked up the requirements for a scholarship online. A full-tuition waiver would require a near-perfect GPA.

I was only a month into the semester, but even so I knew a scholarship was comically out of reach. American history was getting easier, but only in that I was no longer failing the quizzes outright. I was doing well in music theory, but I struggled in English. My teacher said I had a knack for writing but that my language was oddly formal and stilted. I didn't tell her that I'd learned to read and write by reading only the Bible, the Book of Mormon, and speeches by Joseph Smith and Brigham Young.

The real trouble, however, was Western Civ. To me, the lectures were gibberish, probably because for most of January, I thought Europe was a country, not a continent, so very little of what the professor said made sense. And after the Holocaust incident, I wasn't about to ask for clarification.

Even so, it was my favorite class, because of Vanessa. We sat together for every lecture. I liked her because she seemed like the same kind of Mormon I was: she wore high-necked, loose-fitting clothing, and she'd told me that she never drank Coke or did homework on Sunday. She was the only person I'd met at the university who didn't seem like a gentile.

In February, the professor announced that instead of a single midterm he would be giving monthly exams, the first of which would be the following week. I didn't know how to prepare. There wasn't a textbook for the class, just the picture book of paintings and a few CDs of classical compositions. I listened to the music while flipping through the paintings. I made a vague effort to remember who had painted or composed what, but I didn't memorize spelling. The ACT was the only exam I'd ever taken, and it had been multiple choice, so I assumed all exams were multiple choice.

The morning of the exam, the professor instructed everyone

to take out their blue books. I barely had time to wonder what a blue book was before everyone produced one from their bags. The motion was fluid, synchronized, as if they had practiced it. I was the only dancer on the stage who seemed to have missed rehearsal. I asked Vanessa if she had a spare, and she did. I opened it, expecting a multiple-choice exam, but it was blank.

The windows were shuttered; the projector flickered on, displaying a painting. We had sixty seconds to write the work's title and the artist's full name. My mind produced only a dull buzz. This continued through several questions: I sat completely still, giving no answers at all.

A Caravaggio flickered onto the screen—*Judith Beheading Holofernes*. I stared at the image, that of a young girl calmly drawing a sword toward her body, pulling the blade through a man's neck as she might have pulled a string through cheese. I'd beheaded chickens with Dad, clutching their scabby legs while he raised the ax and brought it down with a loud *thwack,* then tightening my grip, holding on with all I had, when the chicken convulsed with death, scattering feathers and spattering my jeans with blood. Remembering the chickens, I wondered at the plausibility of Caravaggio's scene: no one had *that* look on their face—that tranquil, disinterested expression—when taking off something's head.

I knew the painting was by Caravaggio but I remembered only the surname and even that I couldn't spell. I was certain the title was *Judith Beheading Someone* but could not have produced *Holofernes* even if it had been my neck behind the blade.

Thirty seconds left. Perhaps I could score a few points if I could just get something—anything—on the page, so I sounded out the name phonetically: "Carevajio." That didn't look right. One of the letters was doubled up, I remembered, so I scratched that out and wrote "Carrevagio." Wrong again.

I auditioned different spellings, each worse than the last. Twenty seconds.

Next to me, Vanessa was scribbling steadily. Of course she was. She belonged here. Her handwriting was neat, and I could read what she'd written: Michelangelo Merisi da Caravaggio. And next to it, in equally pristine print, *Judith Beheading Holofernes*. Ten seconds. I copied the text, not including Caravaggio's full name because, in a selective display of integrity, I decided that would be cheating. The projector flashed to the next slide.

I glanced at Vanessa's paper a few more times during the exam but it was hopeless. I couldn't copy her essays, and I lacked the factual and stylistic know-how to compose my own. In the absence of skill or knowledge, I must have scribbled down whatever occurred to me. I don't recall whether we were asked to evaluate *Judith Beheading Holofernes*, but if we were I'm sure I would have given my impressions: that the calm on the girl's face didn't sit well with my experience slaughtering chickens. Dressed in the right language this might have made a fantastic answer—something about the woman's serenity standing in powerful counterpoint to the general realism of the piece. But I doubt the professor was much impressed by my observation that, "When you chop a chicken's head off, you shouldn't smile because you might get blood and feathers in your mouth."

The exam ended. The shutters were opened. I walked outside and stood in the winter chill, gazing up at the pinnacles of the Wasatch Mountains. I wanted to stay. The mountains were as unfamiliar and menacing as ever, but I wanted to stay.

I waited a week for the exam results, and twice during that time I dreamed of Shawn, of finding him lifeless on the asphalt, of turning his body and seeing his face alight in crimson. Suspended between fear of the past and fear of the future, I recorded the dream in my journal. Then, without any explanation, as if the connection between the two were obvious, I wrote, *I don't understand why I wasn't allowed to get a decent education as a child.*

The results were handed back a few days later. I had failed.

One winter, when I was very young, Luke found a great horned owl in the pasture, unconscious and half frozen. It was the color of soot, and seemed as big as me to my child eyes. Luke carried it into the house, where we marveled at its soft plumage and pitiless talons. I remember stroking its striped feathers, so smooth they were waterlike, as my father held its limp body. I knew that if it were conscious, I would never get this close. I was in defiance of nature just by touching it.

Its feathers were soaked in blood. A thorn had lanced its wing. "I'm not a vet," Mother said. "I treat *people*." But she removed the thorn and cleaned the wound. Dad said the wing would take weeks to mend, and that the owl would wake up long before then. Finding itself trapped, surrounded by predators, it would beat itself to death trying to get free. It was wild, he said, and in the wild that wound was fatal.

We laid the owl on the linoleum by the back door and, when it awoke, told Mother to stay out of the kitchen. Mother said hell would freeze over before she surrendered her kitchen to an owl, then marched in and began slamming pots to make breakfast. The owl flopped about pathetically, its talons scratching the door, bashing its head in a panic. We cried, and Mother retreated. Two hours later Dad had blocked off half the kitchen with plywood sheets. The owl convalesced there for several weeks. We trapped mice to feed it, but sometimes it didn't eat them, and we couldn't clear away the carcasses. The smell of death was strong and foul, a punch to the gut.

The owl grew restless. When it began to refuse food, we opened the back door and let it escape. It wasn't fully healed, but Dad said its chances were better with the mountain than with us. It didn't belong. It couldn't be taught to belong.

I wanted to tell someone I'd failed the exam, but something stopped me from calling Tyler. It might have been shame. Or it might have been that Tyler was preparing to be a father. He'd met his wife, Stefanie, at Purdue, and they'd married quickly. She didn't know anything about our family. To me, it felt as though he preferred his new life—his new family—to his old one.

I called home. Dad answered. Mother was delivering a baby, which she was doing more and more now the migraines had stopped.

"When will Mother be home?" I said.

"Don't know," said Dad. "Might as well ask the Lord as me, as He's the one deciding." He chuckled, then asked, "How's school?"

Dad and I hadn't spoken since he'd screamed at me about the VCR. I could tell he was trying to be supportive, but I didn't think I could admit to him that I was failing. I wanted to tell him it was going well. *So easy,* I imagined myself saying.

"Not great," I said instead. "I had no idea it would be this hard."

The line was silent, and I imagined Dad's stern face hardening. I waited for the jab I imagined he was preparing, but instead a quiet voice said, "It'll be okay, honey."

"It won't," I said. "There will be no scholarship. I'm not even going to pass." My voice was shaky now.

"If there's no scholarship, there's no scholarship," he said. "Maybe I can help with the money. We'll figure it out. Just be happy, okay?"

"Okay," I said.

"Come on home if you need."

I hung up, not sure what I'd just heard. I knew it wouldn't

last, that the next time we spoke everything would be different, the tenderness of this moment forgotten, the endless struggle between us again in the foreground. But tonight he wanted to help. And that was something.

In March, there was another exam in Western Civ. This time I made flash cards. I spent hours memorizing odd spellings, many of them French (France, I now understood, was a part of Europe). Jacques-Louis David and François Boucher: I couldn't say them but I could spell them.

My lecture notes were nonsensical, so I asked Vanessa if I could look at hers. She looked at me skeptically, and for a moment I wondered if she'd noticed me cheating off her exam. She said she wouldn't give me her notes but that we could study together, so after class I followed her to her dorm room. We sat on the floor with our legs crossed and our notebooks open in front of us.

I tried to read from my notes but the sentences were incomplete, scrambled. "Don't worry about your notes," Vanessa said. "They aren't as important as the textbook."

"What textbook?" I said.

"*The* textbook," Vanessa said. She laughed as if I were being funny. I tensed because I wasn't.

"I don't have a textbook," I said.

"Sure you do!" She held up the thick picture book I'd used to memorize titles and artists.

"Oh that," I said. "I looked at that."

"You *looked* at it? You didn't read it?"

I stared at her. I didn't understand. This was a class on music and art. We'd been given CDs with music to listen to, and a book with pictures of art to look at. It hadn't occurred to me to read the art book any more than it had to read the CDs.

"I thought we were just supposed to look at the pictures." This sounded stupid when said aloud.

"So when the syllabus assigned pages fifty through eighty-five, you didn't think you had to *read* anything?"

"I looked at the pictures," I said again. It sounded worse the second time.

Vanessa began thumbing through the book, which suddenly looked very much like a textbook.

"That's your problem then," she said. "You have to read the textbook." As she said this, her voice lilted with sarcasm, as if this blunder, after everything else—after joking about the Holocaust and glancing at her test—was too much and she was done with me. She said it was time for me to go; she had to study for another class. I picked up my notebook and left.

"Read the textbook" turned out to be excellent advice. On the next exam I scored a B, and by the end of the semester I was pulling A's. It was a miracle and I interpreted it as such. I continued to study until two or three A.M. each night, believing it was the price I had to pay to earn God's support. I did well in my history class, better in English, and best of all in music theory. A full-tuition scholarship was unlikely, but I could maybe get half.

During the final lecture in Western Civ, the professor announced that so many students had failed the first exam, he'd decided to drop it altogether. And *poof*. My failing grade was gone. I wanted to punch the air, give Vanessa a high five. Then I remembered that she didn't sit with me anymore.

19

In the Beginning

When the semester ended I returned to Buck's Peak. In a few weeks BYU would post grades; then I'd know if I could return in the fall.

I filled my journals with promises that I would stay out of the junkyard. I needed money—Dad would have said I was broker than the Ten Commandments—so I went to get my old job back at Stokes. I turned up at the busiest hour in the afternoon, when I knew they'd be understaffed, and sure enough, the manager was bagging groceries when I found him. I asked if he'd like me to do that, and he looked at me for all of three seconds, then lifted his apron over his head and handed it to me. The assistant manager gave me a wink: she was the one who'd suggested I ask during the rush. There was something about Stokes—about its straight, clean aisles and the warm people who worked there—that made me feel calm and happy. It's a strange thing to say about a grocery store, but it felt like home.

Dad was waiting for me when I came through the back door. He saw the apron and said, "You're working for me this summer."

"I'm working at Stokes," I said.

"Think you're too good to scrap?" His voice was raised. "*This* is your family. You belong here."

Dad's face was haggard, his eyes bloodshot. He'd had a spectacularly bad winter. In the fall, he'd invested a large sum of money in new construction equipment—an excavator, a man lift and a welding trailer. By spring it was all gone. Luke had accidentally lit the welding trailer on fire, burning it to the ground; the man lift had come off a trailer because someone—I never asked who—hadn't secured it properly; and the excavator had joined the scrap heap when Shawn, pulling it on an enormous trailer, had taken a corner too fast and rolled the truck and trailer both. With the luck of the damned, Shawn had crawled from the wreckage, although he'd hit his head and couldn't remember the days before the accident. Truck, trailer and excavator were totaled.

Dad's determination was etched into his face. It was in his voice, in the harshness of it. He *had* to win this standoff. He'd convinced himself that if I was on the crew, there'd be fewer accidents, fewer setbacks. "You're slower than tar running uphill," he'd told me a dozen times. "But you get the job done without smashing anything."

But I couldn't do the job, because to do it would be to slide backward. I had moved home, to my old room, to my old life. If I went back to working for Dad, to waking up every morning and pulling on steel-toed boots and trudging out to the junkyard, it would be as if the last four months had never happened, as if I had never left.

I pushed past Dad and shut myself in my room. Mother knocked a moment later. She stepped into the room quietly and sat so lightly on the bed, I barely felt her weight next to me. I thought she would say what she'd said last time. Then I'd remind her I was only seventeen, and she'd tell me I could stay.

"You have an opportunity to help your father," she said. "He needs you. He'll never say it but he does. It's your choice what to do." There was silence, then she added, "But if you don't help, you can't stay here. You'll have to live somewhere else."

The next morning, at four A.M., I drove to Stokes and worked a ten-hour shift. It was early afternoon, and raining heavily, when I came home and found my clothes on the front lawn. I carried them into the house. Mother was mixing oils in the kitchen, and she said nothing as I passed by with my dripping shirts and jeans.

I sat on my bed while the water from my clothes soaked into the carpet. I'd taken a phone with me, and I stared at it, unsure what it could do. There was no one to call. There was nowhere to go and no one to call.

I dialed Tyler in Indiana. "I don't want to work in the junkyard," I said when he answered. My voice was hoarse.

"What happened?" he said. He sounded worried; he thought there'd been another accident. "Is everyone okay?"

"Everyone's fine," I said. "But Dad says I can't stay here unless I work in the junkyard, and I can't do that anymore." My voice was pitched unnaturally high, and it quivered.

Tyler said, "What do you want me to do?"

In retrospect I'm sure he meant this literally, that he was asking how he could help, but my ears, solitary and suspicious, heard something else: *What do you expect me to do?* I began to shake; I felt light-headed. Tyler had been my lifeline. For years he'd lived in my mind as a last resort, a lever I could pull when my back was against the wall. But now that I had pulled it, I understood its futility. It did nothing after all.

"What happened?" Tyler said again.

"Nothing. Everything's fine."

I hung up and dialed Stokes. The assistant manager answered. "You done working today?" she said brightly. I told her I quit, said I was sorry, then put down the phone. I opened my closet and there they were, where I'd left them four months before: my scrapping boots. I put them on. It felt as though I'd never taken them off.

Dad was in the forklift, scooping up a stack of corrugated

tin. He would need someone to place wooden blocks on the trailer so he could offload the stack. When he saw me, he lowered the tin so I could step onto it, and I rode the stack up and onto the trailer.

My memories of the university faded quickly. The scratch of pencils on paper, the *clack* of a projector moving to the next slide, the peal of the bells signaling the end of class—all were drowned out by the clatter of iron and the roar of diesel engines. After a month in the junkyard, BYU seemed like a dream, something I'd conjured. Now I was awake.

My daily routine was exactly what it had been: after breakfast I sorted scrap or pulled copper from radiators. If the boys were working on-site, sometimes I'd go along to drive the loader or forklift or crane. At lunch I'd help Mother cook and do the dishes, then I'd return, either to the junkyard or to the forklift.

The only difference was Shawn. He was not what I remembered. He never said a harsh word, seemed at peace with himself. He was studying for his GED, and one night when we were driving back from a job, he told me he was going to try a semester at a community college. He wanted to study law.

There was a play that summer at the Worm Creek Opera House, and Shawn and I bought tickets. Charles was also there, a few rows ahead of us, and at intermission when Shawn moved away to chat up a girl, he shuffled over. For the first time I was not utterly tongue-tied. I thought of Shannon and how she'd talked to people at church, the friendly merriment of her, the way she laughed and smiled. *Just be Shannon,* I thought to myself. And for five minutes, I was.

Charles was looking at me strangely, the way I'd seen men look at Shannon. He asked if I'd like to see a movie on Saturday. The movie he suggested was vulgar, worldly, one I would never want to see, but I was being Shannon, so I said I'd love to.

I tried to be Shannon on Saturday night. The movie was terrible, worse than I'd expected, the kind of movie only a gentile would see. But it was hard for me to see Charles as a gentile. He was just Charles. I thought about telling him the movie was immoral, that he shouldn't be seeing such things, but—still being Shannon—I said nothing, just smiled when he asked if I'd like to get ice cream.

Shawn was the only one still awake when I got home. I was smiling when I came through the door. Shawn joked that I had a boyfriend, and it was a real joke—he wanted me to laugh. He said Charles had good taste, that I was the most decent person he knew, then he went to bed.

In my room, I stared at myself in the mirror for a long time. The first thing I noticed was my men's jeans and how they were nothing like the jeans other girls wore. The second thing I noticed was that my shirt was too large and made me seem more square than I was.

Charles called a few days later. I was standing in my room after a day of roofing. I smelled of paint thinner and was covered in dust the color of ash, but he didn't know that. We talked for two hours. He called the next night, and the one after. He said we should get a burger on Friday.

On Thursday, after I'd finished scrapping, I drove forty miles to the nearest Walmart and bought a pair of women's jeans and two shirts, both blue. When I put them on, I barely recognized my own body, the way it narrowed and curved. I took them off immediately, feeling that somehow they were immodest. They weren't, not technically, but I knew why I wanted them—for my body, so it would be noticed—and that seemed immodest even if the clothes were not.

The next afternoon, when the crew had finished for the day, I ran to the house. I showered, blasting away the dirt, then I laid the new clothes on my bed and stared at them.

After several minutes, I put them on and was again shocked by the sight of myself. There wasn't time to change so I wore a jacket even though it was a warm evening, and at some point, though I can't say when or why, I decided that I didn't need the jacket after all. For the rest of the night, I didn't have to remember to be Shannon; I talked and laughed without pretending at all.

Charles and I spent every evening together that week. We haunted public parks and ice cream shops, burger joints and gas stations. I took him to Stokes, because I loved it there, and because the assistant manager would always give me the unsold doughnuts from the bakery. We talked about music—about bands I'd never heard of and about how he wanted to be a musician and travel the world. We never talked about us—about whether we were friends or something else. I wished he would bring it up but he didn't. I wished he would let me know some other way—by gently taking my hand or putting an arm around me—but he didn't do that, either.

On Friday we stayed out late, and when I came home the house was dark. Mother's computer was on, the screen saver casting a green light over the living room. I sat down and mechanically checked BYU's website. Grades had been posted. I'd passed. More than passed. I'd earned A's in every subject except Western Civ. I would get a scholarship for half of my tuition. I could go back.

Charles and I spent the next afternoon in the park, rocking lazily in tire swings. I told him about the scholarship. I'd meant it as a brag, but for some reason my fears came out with it. I said I shouldn't even be in college, that I should be made to finish high school first. Or to at least start it.

Charles sat quietly while I talked and didn't say anything for a long time after. Then he said, "Are you angry your parents didn't put you in school?"

"It was an advantage!" I said, half-shouting. My response

was instinctive. It was like hearing a phrase from a catchy song: I couldn't stop myself from reciting the next line. Charles looked at me skeptically, as if asking me to reconcile that with what I'd said only moments before.

"Well, I'm angry," he said. "Even if you aren't."

I said nothing. I'd never heard anyone criticize my father except Shawn, and I wasn't able to respond to it. I wanted to tell Charles about the Illuminati, but the words belonged to my father, and even in my mind they sounded awkward, rehearsed. I was ashamed at my inability to take possession of them. I believed then—and part of me will always believe— that my father's words ought to be my own.

Every night for a month, when I came in from the junkyard, I'd spend an hour scrubbing grime from my fingernails and dirt from my ears. I'd brush the tangles from my hair and clumsily apply makeup. I'd rub handfuls of lotion into the pads of my fingers to soften the calluses, just in case that was the night Charles touched them.

When he finally did, it was early evening and we were in his jeep, driving to his house to watch a movie. We were just coming parallel to Fivemile Creek when he reached across the gearshift and rested his hand on mine. His hand was warm and I wanted to take it, but instead I jerked away as if I'd been burned. The response was involuntary, and I wished immediately that I could take it back. It happened again when he tried a second time. My body convulsed, yielding to a strange, potent instinct.

The instinct passed through me in the form of a word, a bold lyric, strong, declarative. The word was not new. It had been with me for a while now, hushed, motionless, as if asleep, in some remote corner of memory. By touching me Charles had awakened it, and it throbbed with life.

I shoved my hands under my knees and leaned into the

window. I couldn't let him near me—not that night, and not any night for months—without shuddering as that word, my word, ripped its way into remembrance. *Whore.*

We arrived at his house. Charles turned on the TV and settled onto the sofa; I perched lightly on one side. The lights dimmed, the opening credits rolled. Charles inched toward me, slowly at first, then more confidently, until his leg brushed mine. In my mind I bolted, I ran a thousand miles in a single heartbeat. In reality I merely flinched. Charles flinched, too—I'd startled him. I repositioned myself, driving my body into the sofa arm, gathering my limbs and pressing them away from him. I held that unnatural pose for perhaps twenty seconds, until he understood, hearing the words I couldn't say, and moved to the floor.

20

Recitals of the Fathers

Charles was my first friend from that other world, the one my
father had tried to protect me from. He was conventional in
all the ways and for all the reasons my father despised con-
ventionality: he talked about football and popular bands
more than the End of Days; he loved everything about high
school; he went to church, but like most Mormons, if he was
ill, he was as likely to call a doctor as a Mormon priest.

I couldn't reconcile his world with mine so I separated
them. Every evening I watched for his red jeep from my
window, and when it appeared on the highway I ran for the
door. By the time he'd bumped up the hill I'd be waiting on
the lawn, and before he could get out I'd be in the jeep, arguing with him about my seatbelt. (He refused to drive unless I
wore one.)

Once, he arrived early and made it to the front door. I
stammered nervously as I introduced him to Mother, who
was blending bergamot and ylang-ylang, clicking her fingers
to test the proportions. She said hello but her fingers kept
pulsing. When Charles looked at me as if to ask why, Mother
explained that God was speaking through her fingers. "Yesterday I tested that I'd get a migraine today if I didn't have a

bath in lavender," she said. "I took the bath and guess what? No headache!"

"Doctors can't cure a migraine before it happens," Dad chimed in, "but the Lord can!"

As we walked to his jeep, Charles said, "Does your house always smell like that?"

"Like what?"

"Like rotted plants."

I shrugged.

"You must have smelled it," he said. "It was *strong*. I've smelled it before. On you. You always smell of it. Hell, I probably do, too, now." He sniffed his shirt. I was quiet. I hadn't smelled anything.

Dad said I was becoming "uppity." He didn't like that I rushed home from the junkyard the moment the work was finished, or that I removed every trace of grease before going out with Charles. He knew I'd rather be bagging groceries at Stokes than driving the loader in Blackfoot, the dusty town an hour north where Dad was building a milking barn. It bothered him, knowing I wanted to be in another place, dressed like someone else.

On the site in Blackfoot, he dreamed up strange tasks for me to do, as if he thought my doing them would remind me who I was. Once, when we were thirty feet in the air, scrambling on the purlins of the unfinished roof, not wearing harnesses because we never wore them, Dad realized that he'd left his chalk line on the other side of the building. "Fetch me that chalk line, Tara," he said. I mapped the trip. I'd need to jump from purlin to purlin, about fifteen of them, spaced four feet apart, to get the chalk, then the same number back. It was exactly the sort of order from Dad that was usually met with Shawn saying, "She's not doing that."

"Shawn, will you run me over in the forklift?"

"You can fetch it," Shawn said. "Unless your fancy school and fancy boyfriend have made you too good for it." His features hardened in a way that was both new and familiar.

I shimmied the length of a purlin, which took me to the framing beam at the barn's edge. This was more dangerous in one sense—if I fell to the right, there would be no purlins to catch me—but the framing beam was thicker, and I could walk it like a tightrope.

That was how Dad and Shawn became comrades, even if they only agreed on one thing: that my brush with education had made me uppity, and that what I needed was to be dragged through time. Fixed, anchored to a former version of myself.

Shawn had a gift for language, for using it to define others. He began searching through his repertoire of nicknames. "Wench" was his favorite for a few weeks. "Wench, fetch me a grinding wheel," he'd shout, or "Raise the boom, Wench!" Then he'd search my face for a reaction. He never found one. Next he tried "Wilbur." Because I ate so much, he said. "That's *some* pig," he'd shout with a whistle when I bent over to fit a screw or check a measurement.

Shawn took to lingering outside after the crew had finished for the day. I suspect he wanted to be near the driveway when Charles drove up it. He seemed to be forever changing the oil in his truck. The first night he was out there, I ran out and jumped into the jeep before he could say a word. The next night he was quicker on the draw. "Isn't Tara beautiful?" he shouted to Charles. "Eyes like a fish and she's nearly as smart as one." It was an old taunt, blunted by overuse. He must have known I wouldn't react on the site so he'd saved it, hoping that in front of Charles it might still have sting.

The next night: "You going to dinner? Don't get between Wilbur and her food. Won't be nothin' left of you but a splat on the pavement."

Charles never responded. We entered into an unspoken agreement to begin our evenings the moment the mountain disappeared in the rearview mirror. In the universe we explored together there were gas stations and movie theaters; there were cars dotting the highway like trinkets, full of people laughing or honking, always waving, because this was a small town and everybody knew Charles; there were dirt roads dusted white with chalk, canals the color of beef stew, and endless wheat fields glowing bronze. But there was no Buck's Peak.

During the day, Buck's Peak was all there was—that and the site in Blackfoot. Shawn and I spent the better part of a week making purlins to finish the barn roof. We used a machine the size of a mobile home to press them into a Z shape, then we attached wire brushes to grinders and blasted away the rust so they could be painted. When the paint was dry we stacked them next to the shop, but within a day or two the wind from the peak had covered them in black dust, which turned to grime when it mixed with the oils on the iron. Shawn said they had to be washed before they could be loaded, so I fetched a rag and a bucket of water.

It was a hot day, and I wiped beads of sweat from my forehead. My hairband broke. I didn't have a spare. The wind swept down the mountain, blowing strands in my eyes, and I reached across my face and brushed them away. My hands were black with grease, and each stroke left a dark smudge.

I shouted to Shawn when the purlins were clean. He appeared from behind an I-beam and raised his welding shield. When he saw me, his face broke into a wide smile. "Our Nigger's back!" he said.

The summer Shawn and I had worked the Shear, there'd been an afternoon when I'd wiped the sweat from my face so many times that, by the time we quit for supper, my nose and cheeks had been black. That was the first time Shawn called me "Nigger." The word was surprising but not unfamiliar. I'd heard Dad use it, so in one sense I knew what it meant. But in another sense, I didn't understand it as meaning anything at all. I'd only ever seen one black person, a little girl, the adoptive daughter of a family at church. Dad obviously hadn't meant her.

Shawn had called me Nigger that entire summer: "Nigger, run and fetch those C-clamps!" or "It's time for lunch, Nigger!" It had never given me a moment's pause.

Then the world had turned upside down: I had entered a university, where I'd wandered into an auditorium and listened, eyes wide, mind buzzing, to lectures on American history. The professor was Dr. Richard Kimball, and he had a resonant, contemplative voice. I knew about slavery; I'd heard Dad talk about it, and I'd read about it in Dad's favorite book on the American founding. I had read that slaves in colonial times were happier and more free than their masters, because the masters were burdened with the cost of their care. That had made sense to me.

The day Dr. Kimball lectured on slavery, he filled the overhead screen with a charcoal sketch of a slave market. The screen was large; as in a movie theater it dominated the room. The sketch was chaotic. Women stood, naked or half naked, and chained, while men circled them. The projector clacked. The next image was a photograph, black and white and blurred with age. Faded and overexposed, the image is iconic. In it a man sits, stripped above the waist, exposing for the camera a map of raised, crisscrossing scars. The flesh hardly looks like flesh, from what has been done to it.

I saw many more images in the coming weeks. I'd heard of the Great Depression years before when I'd played Annie, but the slides of men in hats and long coats lined up in front of soup kitchens were new to me. When Dr. Kimball lectured on World War II, the screen showed rows of fighter planes interspersed with the skeletal remains of bombed cities. There were faces mixed in—FDR, Hitler, Stalin. Then World War II faded with the lights of the projector.

The next time I entered the auditorium there were new faces on the screen and they were black. There hadn't been a black face on that screen—at least none that I remembered—since the lectures on slavery. I'd forgotten about them, these other Americans who were foreign to me. I had not tried to imagine the end of slavery: surely the call of justice had been heard by all, and the issue had been resolved.

This was my state of mind when Dr. Kimball began to lecture on something called the civil rights movement. A date appeared on the screen: 1963. I figured there'd been a mistake. I recalled that the Emancipation Proclamation had been issued in 1863. I couldn't account for that hundred years, so I assumed it was a typo. I copied the date into my notes with a question mark, but as more photographs flashed across the screen, it became clear which century the professor meant. The photos were black and white but their subjects were modern—vibrant, well defined. They were not dry stills from another era; they captured movement. Marches. Police. Firefighters turning hoses on young men.

Dr. Kimball recited names I'd never heard. He began with Rosa Parks. An image appeared of a policeman pressing a woman's finger into an ink sponge. Dr. Kimball said she'd taken a seat on a bus. I understood him as saying she had stolen the seat, although it seemed an odd thing to steal.

Her image was replaced by another, of a black boy in a white shirt, tie and round-brimmed hat. I didn't hear his story. I was still wondering at Rosa Parks, and how someone could steal a bus seat. Then the image was of a corpse and I heard Dr. Kimball say, "They pulled his body from the river."

There was a date beneath the image: 1955. I realized that Mother had been four years old in 1955, and with that realization, the distance between me and Emmett Till collapsed. My proximity to this murdered boy could be measured in the lives of people I knew. The calculation was not made with reference to vast historical or geological shifts—the fall of civilizations, the erosion of mountains. It was measured in the wrinkling of human flesh. In the lines on my mother's face.

The next name was Martin Luther King Jr. I had never seen his face before, or heard his name, and it was several minutes before I understood that Dr. Kimball didn't mean Martin Luther, who I *had* heard of. It took several more minutes for me to connect the name with the image on the screen—of a dark-skinned man standing in front of a white marble temple and surrounded by a vast crowd. I had only just understood who he was and why he was speaking when I was told he had been murdered. I was still ignorant enough to be surprised.

"Our Nigger's back!"

I don't know what Shawn saw on my face—whether it was shock, anger or a vacant expression. Whatever it was, he was delighted by it. He'd found a vulnerability, a tender spot. It was too late to feign indifference.

"Don't call me that," I said. "You don't know what it means."

"Sure I do," he said. "You've got black all over your face, like a nigger!"

For the rest of the afternoon—for the rest of the summer—I was Nigger. I'd answered to it a thousand times before with indifference. If anything, I'd been amused and thought Shawn was clever. Now it made me want to gag him.

Or sit him down with a history book, as long as it wasn't the one Dad still kept in the living room, under the framed copy of the Constitution.

I couldn't articulate how the name made me feel. Shawn had meant it to humiliate me, to lock me in time, into an old idea of myself. But far from fixing me in place, that word transported me. Every time he said it—"Hey Nigger, raise the boom" or "Fetch me a level, Nigger"—I returned to the university, to that auditorium, where I had watched human history unfold and wondered at my place in it. The stories of Emmett Till, Rosa Parks and Martin Luther King were called to my mind every time Shawn shouted, "Nigger, move to the next row." I saw their faces superimposed on every purlin Shawn welded into place that summer, so that by the end of it, I had finally begun to grasp something that should have been immediately apparent: that someone had opposed the great march toward equality; someone had been the person from whom freedom had to be wrested.

I did not think of my brother as that person; I doubt I will ever think of him that way. But something had shifted none-theless. I had started on a path of awareness, had perceived something elemental about my brother, my father, myself. I had discerned the ways in which we had been sculpted by a tradition given to us by others, a tradition of which we were either willfully or accidentally ignorant. I had begun to under-stand that we had lent our voices to a discourse whose sole purpose was to dehumanize and brutalize others—because nurturing that discourse was easier, because retaining power always *feels* like the way forward.

I could not have articulated this, not as I sweated through those searing afternoons in the forklift. I did not have the language I have now. But I understood this one fact: that a thousand times I had been called Nigger, and laughed, and now I could not laugh. The word and the way Shawn said it hadn't changed; only my ears were different. They no longer heard the jingle of a joke in it. What they heard was a signal, a call through time, which was answered with a mounting conviction: that never again would I allow myself to be made a foot soldier in a conflict I did not understand.

21

Skullcap

Dad paid me the day before I returned to BYU. He didn't have the money to give what he'd promised, but it was enough to cover the half tuition I owed. I spent my last day in Idaho with Charles. It was a Sunday, but I didn't go to church. I'd had an earache for two days, and during the night it had changed from a dull twinge to a constant sharp stab. I had a fever. My vision was distorted, sensitive to light. That's when Charles called. Did I want to come to his house? I said I couldn't see well enough to drive. He picked me up fifteen minutes later.

I cupped my ear and slouched in the passenger seat, then took off my jacket and put it over my head to block the light. Charles asked what medicine I'd taken.

"Lobelia," I said. "And skullcap."

"I don't think they're working," he said.

"They will. They take a few days."

He raised his eyebrows but said nothing.

Charles's house was neat and spacious, with large, bright windows and shiny floors. It reminded me of Grandma-over-in-town's house. I sat on a stool, my head pressed against the cold counter. I heard the *creak* of a cabinet opening and the *pop* of a plastic lid. When I opened my eyes, two red pills were on the counter in front of me.

"This is what people take for pain," Charles said.

"Not us."

"Who is this *us*?" Charles said. "You're leaving tomorrow. You're not one of them anymore."

I closed my eyes, hoping he would drop it.

"What do you think will happen if you take the pills?" he said.

I didn't answer. I didn't know what would happen. Mother always said that medical drugs are a special kind of poison, one that never leaves your body but rots you slowly from the inside for the rest of your life. She told me if I took a drug now, even if I didn't have children for a decade, they would be deformed.

"People take drugs for pain," he said. "It's *normal*."

I must have winced at the word "normal," because he went quiet. He filled a glass of water and set it in front of me, then gently pushed the pills forward until they touched my arm. I picked one up. I'd never seen a pill up close before. It was smaller than I'd expected.

I swallowed it, then the other.

For as long as I could remember, whenever I was in pain, whether from a cut or a toothache, Mother would make a tincture of lobelia and skullcap. It had never lessened the pain, not one degree. Because of this, I had come to respect pain, even revere it, as necessary and untouchable.

Twenty minutes after I swallowed the red pills, the earache was gone. I couldn't comprehend its absence. I spent the afternoon swinging my head from left to right, trying to jog the pain loose again. I thought if I could shout loudly enough, or move quickly enough, perhaps the earache would return and I would know the medicine had been a sham after all.

Charles watched in silence but he must have found my behavior absurd, especially when I began to pull on my ear, which still ached dully, so I could test the limits of this strange witchcraft.

Mother was supposed to drive me to BYU the next morning, but during the night, she was called to deliver a baby. There was a car sitting in the driveway—a Kia Sephia Dad had bought from Tony a few weeks before. The keys were in the ignition. I loaded my stuff into it and drove it to Utah, figuring the car would just about make up for the money Dad owed me. I guess he figured that, too, because he never said a word about it.

I moved into an apartment half a mile from the university. I had new roommates. Robin was tall and athletic, and the first time I saw her she was wearing running shorts that were much too short, but I didn't gape at her. When I met Jenni she was drinking a Diet Coke. I didn't stare at that, either, because I'd seen Charles drink dozens of them.

Robin was the oldest, and for some reason she was sympathetic to me. Somehow she understood that my missteps came from ignorance, not intention, and she corrected me gently but frankly. She told me exactly what I would need to do, or not do, to get along with the other girls in the apartment. No keeping rotten food in the cupboards or leaving rancid dishes in the sink.

Robin explained this at an apartment meeting. When she'd finished another roommate, Megan, cleared her throat.

"I'd like to remind everyone to wash their hands after they use the bathroom," she said. "And not just with water, but with soap."

Robin rolled her eyes. "I'm sure *everyone* here washes their hands."

That night, after I left the bathroom, I stopped at the sink in the hall and washed my hands. With soap.

The next day was the first day of class. Charles had

designed my course schedule. He'd signed me up for two music classes and a course on religion, all of which he said would be easy for me. Then he'd enrolled me in two more challenging courses—college algebra, which terrified me, and biology, which didn't but only because I didn't know what it was.

Algebra threatened to put an end to my scholarship. The professor spent every lecture muttering inaudibly as he paced in front of the chalkboard. I wasn't the only one who was lost, but I was more lost than anyone else. Charles tried to help, but he was starting his senior year of high school and had his own schoolwork. In October I took the midterm and failed it.

I stopped sleeping. I stayed up late, twisting my hair into knots as I tried to wrest meaning from the textbook, then lying in bed and brooding over my notes. I developed stomach ulcers. Once, Jenni found me curled up on a stranger's lawn, halfway between campus and our apartment. My stomach was on fire; I was shaking with the pain, but I wouldn't let her take me to a hospital. She sat with me for half an hour, then walked me home.

The pain in my stomach intensified, burning through the night, making it impossible to sleep. I needed money for rent, so I got a job as a janitor for the engineering building. My shift began every morning at four. Between the ulcers and the janitorial work, I barely slept. Jenni and Robin kept saying I should see a doctor but I didn't. I told them I was going home for Thanksgiving and that my mother would cure me. They exchanged nervous glances but didn't say anything.

Charles said my behavior was self-destructive, that I had an almost pathological inability to ask for help. He told me this on the phone, and he said it so quietly it was almost a whisper.

I told him he was crazy.

"Then go talk to your algebra professor," he said. "You're failing. Ask for help."

It had never occurred to me to talk to a professor—I didn't realize we were allowed to talk to them—so I decided to try, if only to prove to Charles I could do it.

I knocked on his office door a few days before Thanksgiving. He looked smaller in his office than he did in the lecture hall, and more shiny: the light above his desk reflected off his head and glasses. He was shuffling through the papers on his desk, and he didn't look up when I sat down. "If I fail this class," I said, "I'll lose my scholarship." I didn't explain that without a scholarship, I couldn't come back.

"I'm sorry," he said, barely looking at me. "But this is a tough school. It might be better if you come back when you're older. Or transfer."

I didn't know what he meant by "transfer," so I said nothing. I stood to go, and for some reason this softened him. "Truthfully," he said, "a lot of people are failing." He sat back in his chair. "How about this: the final covers all the material from the semester. I'll announce in class that anyone who gets a perfect score on the final—not a ninety-eight but an actual one hundred—will get an A, no matter how they performed on the midterm. Sound good?"

I said it did. It was a long shot, but I was the queen of long shots. I called Charles. I told him I was coming to Idaho for Thanksgiving and I needed an algebra tutor. He said he would meet me at Buck's Peak.

22

What We Whispered and What We Screamed

When I arrived at the peak, Mother was making the Thanksgiving meal. The large oak table was covered with jars of tincture and vials of essential oil, which I cleared away. Charles was coming for dinner.

Shawn was in a mood. He sat on a bench at the table, watching me gather the bottles and hide them. I'd washed Mother's china, which had never been used, and I began laying it out, eyeing the distance between each plate and knife.

Shawn resented my making a fuss. "It's just Charles," he said. "His standards aren't that high. He's with you, after all."

I fetched glasses. When I put one in front of him, Shawn jabbed a finger into my ribs, digging hard. "Don't touch me!" I shrieked. Then the room turned upside down. My feet were knocked out from under me and I was swept into the living room, just out of Mother's sight.

Shawn turned me onto my back and sat on my stomach, pinning my arms at my sides with his knees. The shock of his weight forced the breath from my chest. He pressed his forearm into my windpipe. I sputtered, trying to gulp enough air to shout, but the airway was blocked.

"When you act like a child, you force me to treat you like one."

Shawn said this loudly, he almost shouted it. He was saying it *to* me, but he was not saying it *for* me. He was saying it for Mother, to define the moment: I was a misbehaving child; he was setting the child right. The pressure on my windpipe eased and I felt a delicious fullness in my lungs. He knew I would not call out.

"Knock it off," Mother hollered from the kitchen, though I wasn't sure whether she meant Shawn or me.

"Yelling is rude," Shawn said, again speaking to the kitchen. "You'll stay down until you apologize." I said I was sorry for yelling at him. A moment later I was standing.

I folded napkins from paper towels and put one at each setting. When I placed one at Shawn's plate, he again jabbed his finger into my ribs. I said nothing.

Charles arrived early—Dad hadn't even come in from the junkyard yet—and sat at the table across from Shawn, who glared at him, never blinking. I didn't want to leave them alone together, but Mother needed help with the cooking, so I returned to the stove but devised small errands to bring me back to the table. On one of those trips I heard Shawn telling Charles about his guns, and on another, about all the ways he could kill a man. I laughed loudly at both, hoping Charles would think they were jokes. The third time I returned to the table, Shawn pulled me onto his lap. I laughed at that, too.

The charade couldn't last, not even until supper. I passed Shawn carrying a large china plate of dinner rolls, and he stabbed my gut so hard it knocked the wind out of me. I dropped the plate. It shattered.

"Why did you do that?" I shouted.

It happened so quickly, I don't know how he got me to the floor, but again I was on my back and he was on top of me. He demanded that I apologize for breaking the plate. I whispered the apology, quietly, so Charles wouldn't hear, but this enraged Shawn. He grabbed a fistful of my hair, again near the scalp, for leverage, and yanked me upright, then dragged me toward the bathroom. The movement was so abrupt, Charles had no time to react. The last thing I saw as my head hurled down the hall was Charles leaping to his feet, eyes wide, face pale.

My wrist was folded, my arm twisted behind my back. My head was shoved into the toilet so that my nose hovered above the water. Shawn was yelling something but I didn't hear what. I was listening for the sound of footsteps in the hall, and when I heard them I became deranged. Charles could not see me like this. He could not know that for all my pretenses—my makeup, my new clothes, my china place settings—*this* is who I was.

I convulsed, arching my body and ripping my wrist away from Shawn. I'd caught him off guard; I was stronger than he'd expected, or maybe just more reckless, and he lost his hold. I sprang for the door. I'd made it through the frame and had taken a step into the hallway when my head shot backward. Shawn had caught me by the hair, and he yanked me toward him with such force that we both tumbled back and into the bathtub.

The next thing I remember, Charles was lifting me and I was laughing—a shrill, demented howl. I thought if I could just laugh loudly enough, the situation might still be saved, that Charles might yet be convinced it was all a joke. Tears streamed from my eyes—my big toe was broken—but I kept cackling. Shawn stood in the doorway looking awkward.

"Are you okay?" Charles kept saying.

"Of course I am! Shawn is so, so, so—*funny*." My voice strangled on the last word as I put weight on my foot and a wave of pain swept through me. Charles tried to carry me but I pushed him off and walked on the break, grinding my teeth to stop myself from crying out, while I slapped playfully at my brother.

Charles didn't stay for supper. He fled to his jeep and I

didn't hear from him for several hours, then he called and asked me to meet him at the church. He wouldn't come to Buck's Peak. We sat in his jeep in the dark, empty parking lot. He was crying.

"You didn't see what you thought you saw," I said.

If someone had asked me, I'd have said Charles was the most important thing in the world to me. But he wasn't. And I would prove it to him. What *was* important to me wasn't love or friendship, but my ability to lie convincingly to myself: to believe I was strong. I could never forgive Charles for knowing I wasn't.

I became erratic, demanding, hostile. I devised a bizarre and ever-evolving rubric by which I measured his love for me, and when he failed to meet it, I became paranoid. I surrendered to rages, venting all my savage anger, every fearful resentment I'd ever felt toward Dad or Shawn, at him, this bewildered bystander who'd only ever helped me. When we argued, I screamed that I never wanted to see him again, and I screamed it so many times that one night, when I called to change my mind, like I always did, he wouldn't let me.

We met one final time, in a field off the highway. Buck's Peak loomed over us. He said he loved me but this was over his head. He couldn't save me. Only I could.

I had no idea what he was talking about.

Winter covered campus in thick snow. I stayed indoors, memorizing algebraic equations, trying to live as I had before—to imagine my life at the university as disconnected from my life on Buck's Peak. The wall separating the two had been impregnable. Charles was a hole in it.

The stomach ulcers returned, burning and aching through the night. Once, I awoke to Robin shaking me. She said I'd been shouting in my sleep. I touched my face and it was wet. She wrapped me in her arms so tight I felt cocooned.

The next morning, Robin asked me to go with her to a doctor—for the ulcers but also for an X-ray of my foot, because my big toe had turned black. I said I didn't need a doctor. The ulcers would heal, and someone had already treated the toe.

Robin's eyebrow rose. "Who? Who treated it?"

I shrugged. She assumed my mother had, and I let her believe it. The truth was, the morning after Thanksgiving, I had asked Shawn to tell me if it was broken. He'd knelt on the kitchen floor and I'd dropped my foot into his lap. In that posture he seemed to shrink. He examined the toe for a moment, then he looked up at me and I saw something in his blue eyes. I thought he was about to say he was sorry, but just when I expected his lips to part he grasped the tip of my toe and yanked. It felt as if my foot had exploded, so intense was the shock that shot through my leg. I was still trying to swallow spasms of pain when Shawn stood, put a hand on my shoulder and said, "Sorry, Siddle Lister, but it hurts less if you don't see it coming."

A week after Robin asked to take me to the doctor, I again awoke to her shaking me. She gathered me up and pressed me to her, as if her body could hold me together, could keep me from flying apart.

"I think you need to see the bishop," she said the next morning.

"I'm fine," I said, making a cliché of myself the way not-fine people do. "I just need sleep."

Soon after, I found a pamphlet for the university counseling service on my desk. I barely looked at it, just knocked it into the trash. I could *not* see a counselor. To see one would be to ask for help, and I believed myself invincible. It was an elegant deception, a mental pirouette. The toe was not broken because it was not breakable. Only an X-ray could prove otherwise. Thus, the X-ray would break my toe.

My algebra final was swept up in this superstition. In my mind, it acquired a kind of mystical power. I studied with the intensity of the insane, believing that if I could best *this* exam, win that impossible perfect score, even with my broken toe and without Charles to help me, it would prove that I was above it all. Untouchable.

The morning of the exam I limped to the testing center and sat in the drafty hall. The test was in front of me. The problems were compliant, pliable; they yielded to my manipulations, forming into solutions, one after the other. I handed in my answer sheet, then stood in the frigid hallway, staring up at the screen that would display my score. When it appeared, I blinked, and blinked again. One hundred. A perfect score.

I was filled with an exquisite numbness. I felt drunk with it and wanted to shout at the world: *Here's the proof:* nothing *touches me.*

Buck's Peak looked the way it always did at Christmas—a snowy spire, adorned with evergreens—and my eyes, increasingly accustomed to brick and concrete, were nearly blinded by the scale and clarity of it.

Richard was in the forklift as I drove up the hill, moving a stack of purlins for the shop Dad was building in Franklin, near town. Richard was twenty-two, and one of the smartest people I knew, but he lacked a high school diploma. As I passed him in the drive, it occurred to me that he'd probably be driving that forklift for the rest of his life.

I'd been home for only a few minutes when Tyler called. "I'm just checking in," he said. "To see if Richard is studying for the ACT."

"He's gonna take it?"

"I don't know," Tyler said. "Maybe. Dad and I have been working on him."

"Dad?"

Tyler laughed. "Yeah, Dad. He wants Richard to go to college."

I thought Tyler was joking until an hour later when we sat down to dinner. We'd only just started eating when Dad, his mouth full of potatoes, said, "Richard, I'll give you next week off, paid, if you'll use it to study them books."

I waited for an explanation. It was not long in coming. "Richard is a genius," Dad told me a moment later, winking. "He's five times smarter than that Einstein was. He can disprove all them socialist theories and godless speculations. He's gonna get down there and blow up the whole damn system."

Dad continued with his raptures, oblivious to the effect he was having on his listeners. Shawn slumped on a bench, his back against the wall, his face tilted toward the floor. To look at him was to imagine a man cut from stone, so heavy did he seem, so void of motion. Richard was the miracle son, the gift from God, the Einstein to disprove Einstein. Richard would move the world. Shawn would not. He'd lost too much of his mind when he'd fallen off that pallet. One of my father's sons would be driving the forklift for the rest of his life, but it wouldn't be Richard.

Richard looked even more miserable than Shawn. His shoulders hunched and his neck sank into them, as if he were compressing under the weight of Dad's praise. After Dad went to bed, Richard told me that he'd taken a practice test for the ACT. He'd scored so low, he wouldn't tell me the number.

"Apparently I'm Einstein," Richard said, his head in his hands. "What do I do? Dad is saying I'm going to blow this thing out of the water, and I'm not even sure I can pass."

Every night was the same. Through dinner, Dad would list all the false theories of science that his genius son would disprove; then after dinner, I would tell Richard about college, about classes, books, professors, things I knew would appeal to his innate need to learn. I was worried: Dad's expectations were so high, and Richard's fear of disappointing him so intense, it seemed possible that Richard might not take the ACT at all.

The shop in Franklin was ready to roof, so two days after Christmas I forced my toe, still crooked and black, into a steel-toed boot, then spent the morning on a roof driving threading screws into galvanized tin. It was late afternoon when Shawn dropped his screw gun and shimmied down the loader's extended boom. "Time for a break, Siddle Liss," he shouted up from the ground. "Let's go into town."

I hopped onto the pallet and Shawn dropped the boom to the ground. "You drive," he said, then he leaned his seat back and closed his eyes. I headed for Stokes.

I remember strange details about the moment we pulled into the parking lot—the smell of oil floating up from our leather gloves, the sandpaper feel of dust on my fingertips. And Shawn, grinning at me from the passenger seat. Through the city of cars I spy one, a red jeep. Charles. I pass through the main lot and turn into the open asphalt on the north side of the store, where employees park. I pull down the visor to evaluate myself, noting the tangle the windy roof has made of my hair, and the grease from the tin that has lodged in my pores, making them fat and brown. My clothes are heavy with dirt.

Shawn sees the red jeep. He watches me lick my thumb and scrub dirt from my face, and he becomes excited. "Let's go!" he says.

"I'll wait in the car."

"You're coming in," Shawn says.

Shawn can smell shame. He knows that Charles has never

seen me like this—that every day all last summer, I rushed home and removed every stain, every smudge, hiding cuts and calluses beneath new clothes and makeup. A hundred times Shawn has seen me emerge from the bathroom unrecognizable, having washed the junkyard down the shower drain.

"You're coming in," Shawn says again. He walks around the car and opens my door. The movement is old-fashioned, vaguely chivalrous.

"I don't want to," I say.

"Don't want your boyfriend to see you looking so glamorous?" He smiles and jabs me with his finger. He is looking at me strangely, as if to say, *This is who you are. You've been pretending that you're someone else. Someone better. But you are just this.*

He begins to laugh, loudly, wildly, as if something funny has happened but nothing has. Still laughing, he grabs my arm and draws it upward, as if he's going to throw me over his back and carry me in fireman-style. I don't want Charles to see that so I end the game. I say, flatly, "Don't touch me."

What happens next is a blur in my memory. I see only snapshots—of the sky flipping absurdly, of fists coming at me, of a strange, savage look in the eyes of a man I don't recognize. I see my hands grasping the wheel, and I feel strong arms wrenching my legs. Something shifts in my ankle, a crack or a pop. I lose my grip. I'm pulled from the car.

I feel icy pavement on my back; pebbles are grinding into my skin. My jeans have slid down past my hips. I'd felt them peeling off me, inch by inch, as Shawn yanked my legs. My shirt has risen up and I look at myself, at my body spread flat on the asphalt, at my bra and faded underwear. I want to cover myself but Shawn has pinned my hands above my head. I lie still, feeling the cold seep into me. I hear my voice begging him to let me go, but I don't sound like myself. I'm listening to the sobs of another girl.

I am dragged upward and set on my feet. I claw at my clothing. Then I'm doubled over and my wrist is being folded back, bending, bent as far as it will go and bending still. My nose is near the pavement when the bone begins to bow. I try to regain my balance, to use the strength in my legs to push back, but when my ankle takes weight, it buckles. I scream. Heads turn in our direction. People crane to see what the commotion is. Immediately I begin to laugh—a wild, hysterical cackle that despite all my efforts still sounds a little like a scream.

"You're going in," Shawn says, and I feel the bone in my wrist crack.

I go with him into the bright lights. I laugh as we pass through aisle after aisle, gathering the things he wants to buy. I laugh at every word he says, trying to convince anyone who might have been in the parking lot that it was all a joke. I'm walking on a sprained ankle, but the pain barely registers.

We do not see Charles.

The drive back to the site is silent. It's only five miles but it feels like fifty. We arrive and I limp toward the shop. Dad and Richard are inside. I'd been limping before because of my toe, so my new hobble isn't so noticeable. Still, Richard takes one look at my face, streaked with grease and tears, and knows something is wrong; Dad sees nothing.

I pick up my screw gun and drive screws with my left hand, but the pressure is uneven, and with my weight gathered on one foot, my balance is poor. The screws bounce off the painted tin, leaving long, twisting marks like curled ribbons. Dad sends me home after I ruin two sheets.

That night, with a heavily wrapped wrist, I scratch out a journal entry. I ask myself questions. Why didn't he stop when I begged him? *It was like getting beaten by a zombie,* I write. *Like he couldn't hear me.*

Shawn knocks. I slide my journal under the pillow. His shoulders are rounded when he enters. He speaks quietly. It was a game, he says. He had no idea he'd hurt me until he saw me cradling my arm at the site. He checks the bones in my wrist, examines my ankle. He brings me ice wrapped in a dish towel and says that next time we're having fun, I should tell him if something is wrong. He leaves. I return to my journal. *Was it really fun and games?* I write. *Could he not tell he was hurting me? I don't know. I just don't know.*

I begin to reason with myself, to doubt whether I had spoken clearly: what had I whispered and what had I screamed? I decide that if I had asked differently, been more calm, he would have stopped. I write this until I believe it, which doesn't take long because I *want* to believe it. It's comforting to think the defect is mine, because that means it is under my power.

I put away my journal and lie in bed, reciting this narrative as if it is a poem I've decided to learn by heart. I've nearly committed it to memory when the recitation is interrupted. Images invade my mind—of me, pinned, arms pressed above my head. Then I'm back in the parking lot. I look down at my white stomach, then up at my brother. His expression is un-forgettable: not anger or rage. There is no fury in it. Only pleasure, unperturbed. Then a part of me understands, even as I begin to argue against it, that my humiliation was the cause of that pleasure. It was not an accident or side effect. It was the objective.

This half-knowledge works in me like a kind of posses-sion, and for a few minutes I'm taken over by it. I rise from my bed, retrieve my journal, and do something I have never done before: I write what happened. I do not use vague, shadowy language, as I have done in other entries; I do not hide behind hints and suggestion. I write what I remember: *There was one point when he was forcing me from the car, that he had both hands pinned above my head and my shirt rose up. I asked him to let me fix it but it was like he couldn't hear me. He just stared at it like a great big jerk. It's a good thing I'm as small as I am. If I was larger, at that moment, I would have torn him apart.*

"I don't know what you've done to your wrist," Dad told me the next morning, "but you're no good on the crew like that. You might as well head back to Utah."

The drive to BYU was hypnotic; by the time I arrived, my memories of the previous day had blurred and faded.

They were brought into focus when I checked my email. There was a message from Shawn. An apology. But he'd apologized already, in my room. I had never known Shawn to apologize twice.

I retrieved my journal and I wrote another entry, opposite the first, in which I revised the memory. It was a misunderstanding, I wrote. If I'd asked him to stop, he would have.

But however I chose to remember it, that event would change everything. Reflecting on it now I'm amazed by it, not by what happened, but that I wrote what happened. That from somewhere inside that brittle shell—in that girl made vacant by the fiction of invincibility—there was a spark left.

The words of the second entry would not obscure the words of the first. Both would remain, *my* memories set down alongside *his*. There was a boldness in not editing for consistency, in not ripping out either the one page or the other. To admit uncertainty is to admit to weakness, to powerlessness, and to believe in yourself despite both. It is a frailty, but in this frailty there is a strength: the conviction to live in your own mind, and not in someone else's. I have often wondered if the most powerful words I wrote that night came not from anger or rage, but from doubt: *I don't know. I just don't know.*

Not knowing for certain, but refusing to give way to those who claim certainty, was a privilege I had never allowed myself. My life was narrated for me by others. Their voices were forceful, emphatic, absolute. It had never occurred to me that my voice might be as strong as theirs.

23

I'm from Idaho

On Sunday, a week later, a man at church asked me to dinner. I said no. It happened a second time a few days later with a different man. Again I said no. I couldn't say yes. I didn't want either of them anywhere near me.

Word reached the bishop that there was a woman in his flock who was set against marriage. His assistant approached me after the Sunday service and said I was wanted in the bishop's office.

My wrist was still tender when I shook the bishop's hand. He was a middle-aged man with a round face and dark, neatly parted hair. His voice was soft like satin. He seemed to know me before I even opened my mouth. (In a way he did; Robin had told him plenty.) He said I should enroll in the university counseling service so that one day I might enjoy an eternal marriage to a righteous man.

He talked and I sat, wordless as a brick.

He asked about my family. I didn't answer. I had already betrayed them by failing to love them as I should; the least I could do was stay silent.

"Marriage is God's plan," the bishop said, then he stood. The meeting was over. He asked me to return the following Sunday. I said I would, but knew I wouldn't.

My body felt heavy as I walked to my apartment. All my life I had been taught that marriage was God's will, that to refuse it was a kind of sin. I was in defiance of God. And yet, I didn't want to be. I wanted children, my own family, but even as I longed for it I knew I would never have it. I was not capable. I could not be near any man without despising myself.

I had always scoffed at the word "whore." It sounded guttural and outmoded even to me. But even though I silently mocked Shawn for using it, I had come to identify with it. That it was old-fashioned only strengthened the association, because it meant I usually only heard the word in connection with myself.

Once, when I was fifteen, after I'd started wearing mascara and lip gloss, Shawn had told Dad that he'd heard rumors about me in town, that I had a reputation. Immediately Dad thought I was pregnant. He should never have allowed those plays in town, he screamed at Mother. Mother said I was trustworthy, modest. Shawn said no teenage girl was trustworthy, and that in his experience those who seemed pious were sometimes the worst of all.

I sat on my bed, knees pressed to my chest, and listened to them shout. Was I pregnant? I wasn't sure. I considered every interaction I'd had with a boy, every glance, every touch. I walked to the mirror and raised my shirt, then ran my fingers across my abdomen, examining it inch by inch and thought, *Maybe.*

I had never kissed a boy.

I had witnessed birth, but I'd been given none of the facts of conception. While my father and brother shouted, ignorance kept me silent: I couldn't defend myself, because I didn't understand the accusation.

Days later, when it was confirmed that I was not pregnant, I evolved a new understanding of the word "whore," one that was less about actions and more about essence. It was not that I had *done* something wrong so much as that I *existed* in the wrong way. There was something impure in the fact of my being.

It's strange how you give the people you love so much power over you, I had written in my journal. But Shawn had more power over me than I could possibly have imagined. He had defined me to myself, and there's no greater power than that.

I stood outside the bishop's office on a cold night in February. I didn't know what had taken me there.

The bishop sat calmly behind his desk. He asked what he could do for me, and I said I didn't know. No one could give me what I wanted, because what I wanted was to be remade.

"I can help," he said, "but you'll need to tell me what's bothering you." His voice was gentle, and that gentleness was cruel. I wished he would yell. If he yelled, it would make me angry, and when angry I felt powerful. I didn't know if I could do this without feeling powerful.

I cleared my throat, then talked for an hour.

The bishop and I met every Sunday until spring. To me he was a patriarch with authority over me, but he seemed to surrender that authority the moment I passed through his door. I talked and he listened, drawing the shame from me like a healer draws infection from a wound.

When the semester ended, I told him I was going home for the summer. I was out of money; I couldn't pay rent. He looked tired when I told him that. He said, "Don't go home, Tara. The church will pay your rent."

I didn't want the church's money. I'd made the decision. The bishop made me promise only one thing: that I wouldn't work for my father.

My first day in Idaho, I got my old job back at Stokes. Dad scoffed, said I'd never earn enough to return to school. He was right, but the bishop had said God would provide a way and I believed it. I spent the summer restocking shelves and walking elderly ladies to their cars.

I avoided Shawn. It was easy because he had a new girlfriend, Emily, and there was talk of a wedding. Shawn was twenty-eight; Emily was a senior in high school. Her temperament was compliant. Shawn played the same games with her he'd played with Sadie, testing his control. She never failed to follow his orders, quivering when he raised his voice, apologizing when he screamed at her. That their marriage would be manipulative and violent, I had no doubt—although those words were not mine. They had been given to me by the bishop, and I was still trying to wrest meaning from them.

When the summer ended, I returned to BYU with only two thousand dollars. On my first night back, I wrote in my journal: *I have so many bills I can't imagine how I'm going to pay them. But God will provide either trials for growth or the means to succeed.* The tone of that entry seems lofty, high-minded, but in it I detect a whiff of fatalism. Maybe I would have to leave school. That was fine. There were grocery stores in Utah. I would bag groceries, and one day I'd be manager.

I was shocked out of this resignation two weeks into the fall semester, when I awoke one night to a blinding pain in my jaw. I'd never felt anything so acute, so electrifying. I wanted to rip my jaw from my mouth, just to be rid of it. I stumbled to a mirror. The source was a tooth that had been chipped many years before, but now it had fractured again, and deeply. I visited a dentist, who said the tooth had been rotting for years. It would cost fourteen hundred dollars to repair. I couldn't afford to pay half that and stay in school.

I called home. Mother agreed to lend me the money, but

Dad attached terms: I would have to work for him next summer. I didn't even consider it. I said I was finished with the junkyard, finished for life, and hung up.

I tried to ignore the ache and focus on my classes, but it felt as though I were being asked to sit through a lecture while a wolf gnawed on my jaw.

I'd never taken another ibuprofen since that day with Charles, but I began to swallow them like breath mints. They helped only a little. The pain was in the nerves, and it was too severe. I hadn't slept since the ache began, and I started skipping meals because chewing was unthinkable. That's when Robin told the bishop.

He called me to his office on a bright afternoon. He looked at me calmly from across his desk and said, "What are we going to do about your tooth?" I tried to relax my face.

"You can't go through the school year like this," he said. "But there's an easy solution. Very easy, in fact. How much does your father make?"

"Not much," I said. "He's been in debt since the boys wrecked all the equipment last year."

"Excellent," he said. "I have the paperwork here for a grant. I'm sure you're eligible, and the best part is, you won't have to pay it back."

I'd heard about Government grants. Dad said that to accept one was to indebt yourself to the Illuminati. "That's how they get you," he'd said. "They give you free money, then the next thing you know, they *own* you."

These words echoed in my head. I'd heard other students talk about their grants, and I'd recoiled from them. I would leave school before I would allow myself to be purchased.

"I don't believe in Government grants," I said.

"Why not?"

I told him what my father said. He sighed and looked heavenward. "How much will it cost to fix the tooth?"

"Fourteen hundred," I said. "I'll find the money."

"The church will pay," he said quietly. "I have a discretionary fund."

"That money is sacred."

The bishop threw his hands in the air. We sat in silence, then he opened his desk drawer and withdrew a checkbook. I looked at the heading. It was for his personal account. He filled out a check, to me, for fifteen hundred dollars.

"I will *not* allow you to leave school over this," he said.

The check was in my hand. I was so tempted, the pain in my jaw so savage, that I must have held it for ten seconds before passing it back.

I had a job at the campus creamery, flipping burgers and scooping ice cream. I got by between paydays by neglecting overdue bills and borrowing money from Robin, so twice a month, when a few hundred dollars went into my account, it was gone within hours. I was broke when I turned nineteen at the end of September. I had given up on fixing the tooth; I knew I would never have fourteen hundred dollars. Besides, the pain had lessened: either the nerve had died or my brain had adjusted to its shocks.

Still, I had other bills, so I decided to sell the only thing I had of any value—my horse, Bud. I called Shawn and asked how much I could get. Shawn said a mixed breed wasn't worth much, but that I could send him to auction like Grandpa's dog-food horses. I imagined Bud in a meat grinder, then said, "Try to find a buyer first." A few weeks later Shawn sent me a check for a few hundred dollars. When I called Shawn and asked who he'd sold Bud to, he mumbled something vague about a guy passing through from Tooele.

I was an incurious student that semester. Curiosity is a luxury reserved for the financially secure: my mind was absorbed with more immediate concerns, such as the exact balance of my bank account, who I owed how much, and whether there was anything in my room I could sell for ten or twenty dollars. I submitted my homework and studied for my exams, but I did so out of a terror—of losing my scholarship should my GPA fall a single decimal—not from real interest in my classes.

In December, after my last paycheck of the month, I had sixty dollars in my account. Rent was $110, due January 7. I needed quick cash. I'd heard there was a clinic near the mall that paid people for plasma. A clinic sounded like a part of the Medical Establishment, but I reasoned that as long as they were taking things out, not putting anything in, I'd be okay. The nurse stabbed at my veins for twenty minutes, then said they were too small.

I bought a tank of gas with my last thirty dollars and drove home for Christmas. On Christmas morning, Dad gave me a rifle—I didn't take it out of the box, so I have no idea what kind. I asked Shawn if he wanted to buy it off me, but Dad gathered it up and said he'd keep it safe.

That was it, then. There was nothing left to sell, no more childhood friends or Christmas presents. It was time to quit school and get a job. I accepted that. My brother Tony was living in Las Vegas, working as a long-haul trucker, so on Christmas Day I called him. He said I could live with him for a few months and work at the In-N-Out Burger across the street.

I hung up and was walking down the hall, wishing I'd asked Tony if he could lend me the money to get to Vegas, when a gruff voice called to me. "Hey, Siddle Lister. Come here a minute."

Shawn's bedroom was filthy. Dirty clothes littered the floor, and I could see the butt of a handgun poking out from under a pile of stained T-shirts. The bookshelves strained under boxes of ammo and stacks of Louis L'Amour paperbacks. Shawn was sitting on the bed, his shoulders hunched, his legs bowed outward. He looked as if he'd been holding that posture for some time, contemplating the squalor. He let out a sigh, then stood and walked toward me, lifting his right arm. I took an involuntary step back, but he had only reached into his pocket. He pulled out his wallet, opened it and extracted a crisp hundred-dollar bill.

"Merry Christmas," he said. "You won't waste this like I will."

I believed that hundred dollars was a sign from God. I was supposed to stay in school. I drove back to BYU and paid my rent. Then, because I knew I wouldn't be able to pay it in February, I took a second job as a domestic cleaner, driving twenty minutes north three days a week to scrub expensive homes in Draper.

The bishop and I were still meeting every Sunday. Robin had told him that I hadn't bought my textbooks for the semester. "This is ridiculous," he said. "Apply for the grant! You're poor! That's why these grants exist!"

My opposition was beyond rational, it was visceral.

"I make a lot of money," the bishop said. "I pay a lot of taxes. Just think of it as my money." He had printed out the application forms, which he gave to me. "Think about it. You need to learn to accept help, even from the Government."

I took the forms. Robin filled them out. I refused to send them.

"Just get the paperwork together," she said. "See how it feels."

I needed my parents' tax returns. I wasn't even sure my parents filed taxes, but if they did, I knew Dad wouldn't give them to me if he knew why I wanted them. I thought up a dozen fake reasons for why I might need them, but none were believable. I pictured the returns sitting in the large gray filing cabinet in the kitchen. Then I decided to steal them.

I left for Idaho just before midnight, hoping I would arrive at around three in the morning and the house would be quiet. When I reached the peak, I crept up the driveway, wincing each time a bit of gravel snapped beneath my tires. I eased the car door open noiselessly, then padded across the grass and slipped through the back door, moving silently through the house, reaching my hand out to feel my way to the filing cabinet.

I had only made it a few steps when I heard a familiar *clink*.

"Don't shoot!" I shouted. "It's me!"

"Who?"

I flipped the light switch and saw Shawn sitting across the room, pointing a pistol at me. He lowered it. "I thought you were . . . someone else."

"Obviously," I said.

We stood awkwardly for a moment, then I went to bed.

The next morning, after Dad left for the junkyard, I told Mother one of my fake stories about BYU needing her tax returns. She knew I was lying—I could tell because when Dad came in unexpectedly and asked why she was copying the returns, she said the duplicates were for her records.

I took the copies and returned to BYU. Shawn and I exchanged no words before I left. He never asked why I'd been sneaking into my own house at three in the morning, and I never asked who he'd been waiting for, sitting up in the middle of the night, with a loaded pistol.

The forms sat on my desk for a week before Robin walked with me to the post office and watched me hand them to the postal worker. It didn't take long, a week, maybe two. I was cleaning houses in Draper when the mail came, so Robin left the letter on my bed with a note that I was a Commie now.

I tore open the envelope and a check fell onto my bed. For four thousand dollars. I felt greedy, then afraid of my greed. There was a contact number. I dialed it.

"There's a problem," I told the woman who answered. "The check is for four thousand dollars, but I only need fourteen hundred."

The line was silent.

"Hello? Hello?"

"Let me get this straight," the woman said. "You're saying the check is for too *much* money? What do you want me to do?"

"If I send it back, could you send me another one? I only need fourteen hundred. For a root canal."

"Look, honey," she said. "You get that much because that's how much you get. Cash it or don't, it's up to you."

I had the root canal. I bought my textbooks, paid rent, and had money left over. The bishop said I should treat myself to something, but I said I couldn't, I had to save the money. He told me I could afford to spend some. "Remember," he said, "you can apply for the same amount next year." I bought a new Sunday dress.

I'd believed the money would be used to control me, but what it did was enable me to keep my word to myself: for the first time, when I said I would never again work for my father, I believed it.

I wonder now if the day I set out to steal that tax return wasn't the first time I left *home* to go to Buck's Peak. That night I had entered my father's house as an intruder. It was a shift in mental language, a surrendering of where I was from.

My own words confirmed it. When other students asked where I was from, I said, "I'm from Idaho," a phrase that, as many times as I've had to repeat it over the years, has never felt comfortable in my mouth. When you are part of a place, growing that moment in its soil, there's never a need to say you're from there. I never uttered the words "I'm from Idaho" until I'd left it.

24

A Knight, Errant

I had a thousand dollars in my bank account. It felt strange just to think that, let alone say it. A thousand dollars. Extra. That I did not immediately need. It took weeks for me to come to terms with this fact, but as I did, I began to experience the most powerful advantage of money: the ability to think of things besides money.

My professors came into focus, suddenly and sharply; it was as if before the grant I'd been looking at them through a blurred lens. My textbooks began to make sense, and I found myself doing more than the required reading.

It was in this state that I first heard the term bipolar disorder. I was sitting in Psychology 101 when the professor read the symptoms aloud from the overhead screen: depression, mania, paranoia, euphoria, delusions of grandeur and persecution. I listened with a desperate interest.

This is my father, I wrote in my notes. *He's describing Dad.*

A few minutes before the bell rang, a student asked what role mental disorders might have played in separatist movements. "I'm thinking of famous conflicts like Waco, Texas, or Ruby Ridge, Idaho," he said.

Idaho isn't famous for many things, so I figured I'd have heard of whatever "Ruby Ridge" was. He'd said it was a conflict. I searched my memory, trying to recall if I'd ever heard the words. There was something familiar in them. Then images appeared in my mind, weak and distorted, as if the transmission were being disrupted at the source. I closed my eyes and the scene became vivid. I was in our house, crouching behind the birch wood cabinets. Mother was kneeling next to me, her breath slow and tired. She licked her lips and said she was thirsty, then before I could stop her she stood and reached for the tap. I felt the tremor of gunfire and heard myself shout. There was a thud as something heavy fell to the floor. I moved her arm aside and gathered up the baby.

The bell rang. The auditorium emptied. I went to the computer lab. I hesitated for a moment over the keyboard—struck by a premonition that this was information I might regret knowing—then typed "Ruby Ridge" into the browser. According to Wikipedia, Ruby Ridge was the site of a deadly standoff between Randy Weaver and a number of Federal agencies, including the U.S. Marshals Service and the FBI.

The name Randy Weaver was familiar, and even as I read it I heard it falling from my father's lips. Then the story as it had lived in my imagination for thirteen years began replaying in my mind: the shooting of a boy, then of his father, then of his mother. The Government had murdered the entire family, parents and children, to cover up what they had done.

I scrolled past the backstory to the first shooting. Federal agents had surrounded the Weaver cabin. The mission was surveillance only, and the Weavers were unaware of the agents until a dog began to bark. Believing the dog had sensed a wild animal, Randy's fourteen-year-old son, Sammy, charged into the woods. The agents shot the dog, and Sammy, who was carrying a gun, opened fire. The resulting conflict left two dead: a federal agent and Sammy, who was retreating, running up the hill toward the cabin, when he was shot in the back.

I read on. The next day, Randy Weaver was shot, also in the back, while trying to visit his son's body. The corpse was in the shed, and Randy was lifting the latch on the door, when a sniper took aim at his spine and missed. His wife, Vicki, moved toward the door to help her husband and again the sniper opened fire. The bullet struck her in the head, killing her instantly as she held their ten-month-old daughter. For nine days the family huddled in the cabin with their mother's body, until finally negotiators ended the standoff and Randy Weaver was arrested.

I read this last line several times before I understood it. Randy Weaver was alive? Did Dad know?

I kept reading. The nation had been outraged. Articles had appeared in nearly every major newspaper blasting the government's callous disregard for life. The Department of Justice had opened an investigation, and the Senate had held hearings. Both had recommended reforms to the rules of engagement, particularly concerning the use of deadly force.

The Weavers had filed a wrongful death suit for $200 million but settled out of court when the government offered Vicki's three daughters $1 million each. Randy Weaver was awarded $100,000 and all charges, except two related to court appearances, were dropped. Randy Weaver had been interviewed by major news organizations and had even co-written a book with his daughter. He now made his living speaking at gun shows.

If it was a cover-up, it was a very bad one. There had been media coverage, official inquiries, oversight. Wasn't that the measure of a democracy?

There was one thing I still didn't understand: Why had federal agents surrounded Randy Weaver's cabin in the first place? Why had Randy been targeted? I remembered Dad saying it could just as easy be us. Dad was always saying that one day the Government would come after folks who resisted its brainwashing, who didn't put their kids in school. For thirteen years, I'd assumed that this was why the Government had come for Randy: to force his children into school.

I returned to the top of the page and read the whole entry again, but this time I didn't skip the backstory. According to all the sources, including Randy Weaver himself, the conflict had begun when Randy sold two sawed-off shotguns to an undercover agent he'd met at an Aryan Nations gathering. I read this sentence more than once, many times in fact. Then I understood: white supremacy was at the heart of this story, not homeschool. The government, it seemed, had never been in the habit of murdering people for not submitting their children to a public education. This seemed so obvious to me now, it was difficult to understand why I had ever believed anything else.

For one bitter moment, I thought Dad had lied. Then I remembered the fear on his face, the heavy rattling of his breath, and I felt certain that he'd really believed we were in danger. I reached for some explanation and strange words came to mind, words I'd learned only minutes before: *paranoia, mania, delusions of grandeur and persecution.* And finally the story made sense—the one on the page, and the one that had lived in me through childhood. Dad must have read about Ruby Ridge or seen it on the news, and somehow as it passed through his feverish brain, it had ceased to be a story about someone else and had become a story about *him.* If the Government was after Randy Weaver, surely it must also be after Gene Westover, who'd been holding the front line in the war with the Illuminati for years. No longer content to read about the brave deeds of others, he had forged himself a helmet and mounted a nag.

I became obsessed with bipolar disorder. We were required to write a research paper for Psychology and I chose it as my subject, then used the paper as an excuse to interrogate every neuroscientist and cognitive specialist at the university. I described Dad's symptoms, attributing them not to my father but to a fictive uncle. Some of the symptoms fit perfectly; others did not. The professors told me that every case is different.

"What you're describing sounds more like schizophrenia," one said. "Did your uncle ever get treatment?"

"No," I said. "He thinks doctors are part of a Government conspiracy."

"That does complicate things," he said.

With all the subtlety of a bulldozer I wrote my paper on the effect bipolar parents have on their children. It was accusative, brutal. I wrote that children of bipolar parents are hit with double risk factors: first, because they are genetically predisposed to mood disorders and second, because of the *stressful environment and poor parenting of parents with such disorders.*

In class I had been taught about neurotransmitters and their effect on brain chemistry; I understood that disease is not a choice. This knowledge might have made me sympathetic to my father, but it didn't. I felt only anger. *We* were the ones who'd paid for it, I thought. Mother. Luke. Shawn. We had been bruised and gashed and concussed, had our legs set on fire and our heads cut open. We had lived in a state of alert, a kind of constant terror, our brains flooding with cortisol because we knew that any of those things might happen at any moment. Because Dad always put faith before safety. Because he believed himself right, and he kept on believing himself right—after the first car crash, after the second, after the bin, the fire, the pallet. And it was us who paid.

I visited Buck's Peak the weekend after I submitted my paper. I had been home for less than an hour when Dad and I got into an argument. He said I owed him for the car. He really only mentioned it but I became crazed, hysterical. For the first time in my life I shouted at my father—not about the car, but about the Weavers. I was so suffocated by rage, my words didn't come out as words but as choking, sputtering sobs. Why are you like this? Why did you terrify us like that? Why did you fight so hard against made-up monsters, but do nothing about the monsters in your own house?

Dad gaped at me, astonished. His mouth sagged and his hands hung limply at his sides, twitching, as if he wanted to raise them, to do something. I hadn't seen him look so help-less since he'd crouched next to our wrecked station wagon, watching Mother's face bulge and distend, unable even to touch her because electrified cables were sending a deadly pulse through the metal.

Out of shame or anger, I fled. I drove without stopping back to BYU. My father called a few hours later. I didn't answer. Screaming at him hadn't helped; maybe ignoring him would.

When the semester ended, I stayed in Utah. It was the first summer that I didn't return to Buck's Peak. I did not speak to my father, not even on the phone. This estrangement was not formalized: I just didn't feel like seeing him, or hearing his voice, so I didn't.

I decided to experiment with normality. For nineteen years I'd lived the way my father wanted. Now I would try some-thing else.

I moved to a new apartment on the other side of town where no one knew me. I wanted a new start. At church my first week, my new bishop greeted me with a warm hand-shake, then moved on to the next newcomer. I reveled in his disinterest. If I could just pretend to be normal for a little while, maybe it would feel like the truth.

It was at church that I met Nick. Nick had square glasses and dark hair, which he gelled and teased into neat spikes.

Dad would have scoffed at a man wearing hair gel, which is perhaps why I loved it. I also loved that Nick wouldn't have known an alternator from a crankshaft. What he *did* know were books and video games and clothing brands. And words. He had an astonishing vocabulary.

Nick and I were a couple from the beginning. He grabbed my hand the second time we met. When his skin touched mine, I prepared to fight that primal need to push him away, but it never came. It was strange and exciting, and no part of me wanted it to end. I wished I were still in my old congregation, so I could rush to my old bishop and tell him I wasn't broken anymore.

I overestimated my progress. I was so focused on what *was* working, I didn't notice what wasn't. We'd been together a few months, and I'd spent many evenings with his family, before I ever said a word about mine. I did it without thinking, casually mentioned one of Mother's oils when Nick said he had an ache in his shoulder. He was intrigued—he'd been waiting for me to bring them up—but I was angry at myself for the slip, and didn't let it happen again.

I began to feel poorly toward the end of May. A week passed in which I could hardly drag myself to my job, an internship at a law firm. I slept from early evening until late morning, then yawned through the day. My throat began to ache and my voice dropped, roughening into a deep crackle, as if my vocal cords had turned to sandpaper.

At first Nick was amused that I wouldn't see a doctor, but as the illness progressed his amusement turned to worry, then confusion. I blew him off. "It's not that serious," I said. "I'd go if it were serious."

Another week passed. I quit my internship and began sleeping through the days as well as the nights. One morning, Nick showed up unexpectedly.

"We're going to the doctor," he said.

I started to say I wouldn't go, but then I saw his face. He looked as though he had a question but knew there was no point in asking it. The tense line of his mouth, the narrowing of his eyes. *This is what distrust looks like,* I thought.

Given the choice between seeing an evil socialist doctor, and admitting to my boyfriend that I believed doctors were evil socialists, I chose to see the doctor.

"I'll go today," I said. "I promise. But I'd rather go alone."

"Fine," he said.

He left, but now I had another problem. I didn't know *how* to go to a doctor. I called a friend from class and asked if she'd drive me. She picked me up an hour later and I watched, perplexed, as she drove right past the hospital a few blocks from my apartment. She took me to a small building north of campus, which she called a "clinic." I tried to feign nonchalance, act as though I'd done this before, but as we crossed the parking lot I felt as though Mother were watching me.

I didn't know what to say to the receptionist. My friend attributed my silence to my throat and explained my symptoms. We were told to wait. Eventually a nurse led me to a small white room where she weighed me, took my blood pressure, and swabbed my tongue. Sore throats this severe were usually caused by strep bacteria or the mono virus, she said. They would know in a few days.

When the results came back, I drove to the clinic alone. A balding middle-aged doctor gave me the results. "Congratulations," he said. "You're positive for strep *and* mono. Only person I've seen in a month to get both."

"Both?" I whispered. "How can I have both?"

"Very, very bad luck," he said. "I can give you penicillin for the strep, but there's not much I can do for the mono. You'll have to wait it out. Still, once we've cleared out the strep, you should feel better."

247

The doctor asked a nurse to bring some penicillin. "We should start you on the antibiotics right away," he said. I held the pills in my palm and was reminded of that afternoon when Charles had given me ibuprofen. I thought of Mother, and of the many times she'd told me that antibiotics poison the body, that they cause infertility and birth defects. That the spirit of the Lord cannot dwell in an unclean vessel, and that no vessel is clean when it forsakes God and relies on man. Or maybe Dad had said that last part.

I swallowed the pills. Perhaps it was desperation because I felt so poorly, but I think the reason was more mundane: curiosity. There I was, in the heart of the Medical Establishment, and I wanted to see, at long last, what it was I had always been afraid of. Would my eyes bleed? My tongue fall out? Surely something awful would happen. I needed to know what.

I returned to my apartment and called Mother. I thought confessing would alleviate my guilt. I told her I'd seen a doctor, and that I had strep and mono. "I'm taking penicillin," I said. "I just wanted you to know."

She began talking rapidly but I didn't hear much of it, I was so tired. When she seemed to be winding down, I said "I love you" and hung up.

Two days later a package arrived, express from Idaho. Inside were six bottles of tincture, two vials of essential oil, and a bag of white clay. I recognized the formulas—the oils and tinctures were to fortify the liver and kidneys, and the clay was a foot soak to draw toxins. There was a note from Mother: *These herbs will flush the antibiotics from your system. Please use them for as long as you insist on taking the drugs. Love you.*

I leaned back into my pillow and fell asleep almost instantly, but before I did I laughed out loud. She hadn't sent any remedies for the strep or the mono. Only for the penicillin.

*

I awoke the next morning to my phone ringing. It was Audrey.

"There's been an accident," she said.

Her words transported me to another moment, to the last time I'd answered a phone and heard those words instead of a greeting. I thought of that day, and of what Mother had said next. I hoped Audrey was reading from a different script.

"It's Dad," she said. "If you hurry—leave right now—you can say goodbye."

25

The Work of Sulphur

There's a story I was told when I was young, told so many times and from such an early age, I can't remember who told it to me first. It was about Grandpa-down-the-hill and how he got the dent above his right temple.

When Grandpa was a younger man, he had spent a hot summer on the mountain, riding the white mare he used for cowboy work. She was a tall horse, calmed with age. To hear Mother tell it that mare was steady as a rock, and Grandpa didn't pay much attention when he rode her. He'd drop the knotted reins if he felt like it, maybe to pick a burr out of his boot or sweep off his red cap and wipe his face with his shirt-sleeve. The mare stood still. But tranquil as she was, she was terrified of snakes.

"She must have glimpsed something slithering in the weeds," Mother would say when she told the story, "because she chucked Grandpa clean off." There was an old set of harrows behind him. Grandpa flew into them and a disc caved in his forehead.

What exactly it was that shattered Grandpa's skull changed every time I heard the story. In some tellings it was harrows, but in others it was a rock. I suspect nobody knows for sure. There weren't any witnesses. The blow rendered Grandpa unconscious, and he doesn't remember much until Grandma found him on the porch, soaked to his boots in blood.

Nobody knows how he came to be on that porch.

From the upper pasture to the house is a distance of a mile—rocky terrain with steep, unforgiving hills, which Grandpa could not have managed in his condition. But there he was. Grandma heard a faint scratching at the door, and when she opened it there was Grandpa, lying in a heap, his brains dripping out of his head. She rushed him to town and they fitted him with a metal plate.

After Grandpa was home and recovering, Grandma went looking for the white mare. She walked all over the mountain but found her tied to the fence behind the corral, tethered with an intricate knot that nobody used except her father, Lott.

Sometimes, when I was at Grandma's eating the forbidden cornflakes and milk, I'd ask Grandpa to tell me how he got off the mountain. He always said he didn't know. Then he'd take a deep breath—long and slow, like he was settling into a mood rather than a story—and he'd tell the whole tale from start to finish. Grandpa was a quiet man, near silent. You could pass a whole afternoon clearing fields with him and never hear ten words strung together. Just "Yep" and "Not that one" and "I reckon so."

But ask how he got down the mountain that day and he'd talk for ten minutes, even though all he remembered was lying in the field, unable to open his eyes, while the hot sun dried the blood on his face.

"But I tell you this," Grandpa would say, taking off his hat and running his fingers over the dent in his skull. "I heard things while I was lyin' in them weeds. Voices, and they was talking. I recognized one, because it was Grandpa Lott. He was a tellin' somebody that Albert's son was in trouble. It was Lott sayin' that, I know it sure as I know I'm standing here."

Grandpa's eyes would shine a bit, then he'd say, "Only thing is, Lott had been dead near ten years."

This part of the story called for reverence. Mother and Grandma both loved to tell it but I liked Mother's telling best. Her voice hushed in the right places. It was angels, she would say, a small tear falling to the corner of her smile. Your great-grandpa Lott sent them, and they carried Grandpa down the mountain.

The dent was unsightly, a two-inch crater in his forehead. As a child, when I looked at it, sometimes I imagined a tall doctor in a white coat banging on a sheet of metal with a hammer. In my imagination the doctor used the same corrugated sheets of tin that Dad used to roof hay sheds.

But that was only sometimes. Usually I saw something else. Proof that my ancestors walked that peak, watching and waiting, angels at their command.

I don't know why Dad was alone on the mountain that day.

The car crusher was coming. I suppose he wanted to remove that last fuel tank, but I can't imagine what possessed him to light his torch without first draining the fuel. I don't know how far he got, how many of the iron belts he managed to sever, before a spark from the torch made it into the tank. But I know Dad was standing next to the car, his body pressed against the frame, when the tank exploded.

He was wearing a long-sleeved shirt, leather gloves and a welding shield. His face and fingers took the brunt of the blast. The heat from the explosion melted through the shield as if it were a plastic spoon. The lower half of his face liquefied: the fire consumed plastic, then skin, then muscle. The same process was repeated with his fingers—the leather gloves were no match for the inferno that passed over and through them— then tongues of flame licked across his shoulders and chest.

When he crawled away from the flaming vehicle, I imagine he looked more like a corpse than a living man.

It is unfathomable to me that he was able to move, let alone drag himself a quarter mile through fields and over ditches. If ever a man needed angels, it was that man. But against all reason he did it, and—as his father had years before—huddled outside his wife's door, unable to knock.

My cousin Kylie was working for my mother that day, filling vials of essential oil. A few other women worked nearby, weighing dried leaves or straining tinctures. Kylie heard a soft tap on the back door, as if someone was bumping it with their elbow. She opened it but has no memory of what was on the other side. "I've blocked it out," she would later tell me. "I can't remember what I saw. I only remember what I thought, which was, *He has no skin*."

My father was carried to the couch. Rescue Remedy—the homeopathic for shock—was poured into the lipless cavity that had been his mouth. They gave him lobelia and skullcap for the pain, the same mixture Mother had given Luke years before. Dad choked on the medicine. He couldn't swallow. He'd inhaled the fiery blast, and his insides were charred.

Mother tried to take him to the hospital, but between rasping breaths he whispered that he'd rather die than see a doctor. The authority of the man was such that she gave way.

The dead skin was gently cut away and he was slathered in salve—the same salve Mother had used on Luke's leg years before—from his waist to the tip of his head, then bandaged. Mother gave him ice cubes to suck on, hoping to hydrate him, but the inside of his mouth and throat were so badly burned, they absorbed no liquid, and without lips or muscles he couldn't hold the ice in his mouth. It would slide down his throat and choke him.

They nearly lost him many times that first night. His

breathing would slow, then stop, and my mother—and the heavenly host of women who worked for her—would fly about, adjusting chakras and tapping pressure points, anything to coax his brittle lungs to resume their rattle.

That morning was when Audrey called me.[6] His heart had stopped twice during the night, she told me. It would probably be his heart that killed him, assuming his lungs didn't give out first. Either way, Audrey was sure he'd be dead by midday.

I called Nick. I told him I had to go to Idaho for a few days, for a family thing, nothing serious. He knew I wasn't telling him something—I could hear the hurt in his voice that I wouldn't confide in him—but I put him out of my mind the moment I hung up the phone.

I stood, keys in hand, hand on the doorknob, and hesitated. The strep. What if I gave it to Dad? I had been taking the penicillin for nearly three days. The doctor had said that after twenty-four hours I would no longer be contagious, but then he was a doctor, and I didn't trust him.

I waited a day. I took several times the prescribed dose of penicillin, then called Mother and asked what I should do.

"You should come home," she said, and her voice broke. "I don't think the strep will matter tomorrow."

I don't recall the scenery from the drive. My eyes barely registered the patchwork of corn and potato fields, or the dark hills covered in pine. Instead I saw my father, the way he'd looked the last time I'd seen him, that twisted expression. I remembered the searing pitch of my voice as I'd screamed at him.

Like Kylie, I don't remember what I saw when I first looked at my father. I know that when Mother had removed the gauze that morning, she'd found that his ears were so burned, the skin so glutinous, they had fused to the syrupy tissue behind them. When I walked through the back door, the first thing I saw was Mother grasping a butter knife, which she was using

254

to pry my father's ears from his skull. I can still picture her gripping the knife, her eyes fixed, focused, but where my father should be, there's an aperture in my memory.

The smell in the room was powerful—of charred flesh, and of comfrey, mullein and plantain. I watched Mother and Audrey change his remaining bandages. They began with his hands. His fingers were slimy, coated in a pale ooze that was either melted skin or pus. His arms were not burned and neither were his shoulders or back, but a thick swath of gauze ran over his stomach and chest. When they removed it, I was pleased to see large patches of raw, angry skin. There were a few craters from where the flames must have concentrated in jets. They gave off a pungent smell, like meat gone to rot, and were filled with white pools.

But it was his face that visited my dreams that night. He still had a forehead and nose. The skin around his eyes and partway down his cheeks was pink and healthy. But below his nose, nothing was where it should be. Red, mangled, sagging, it looked like a plastic drama mask that had been held too close to a candle.

Dad hadn't swallowed anything—no food, no water—for nearly three days. Mother called a hospital in Utah and begged them to give her an IV. "I need to hydrate him," she said. "He'll die if he doesn't get water."

The doctor said he would send a chopper that very minute but Mother said no. "Then I can't help you," the doctor said. "You're going to kill him, and I want no part of it."

Mother was beside herself. In a final, desperate act, she gave Dad an enema, pushing the tube in as far as she dared trying to flush enough liquid through his rectum to keep him alive. She had no idea if it would work—if there was even an organ in that part of the body to absorb the water—but it was the only orifice that hadn't been scorched.

I slept on the living room floor that night so I could be

there, in the room, when we lost him. I awoke several times to gasps and flights of movements and murmurs that it had happened again, he'd stopped breathing.

Once, an hour before dawn, his breath left him and I was sure it was the end: he was dead and would not be raised. I rested my hand on a small patch of bandages while Audrey and Mother rushed around me, chanting and tapping. The room was not at peace, or maybe it's just that I wasn't. For years my father and I had been locked in conflict, an endless battle of wills. I thought I had accepted it, accepted our relationship for what it was. But in that moment, I realized how much I'd been counting on that conflict coming to an end, how deeply I believed in a future in which we would be a father and daughter at peace.

I watched his chest, prayed for him to breathe, but he didn't. Then too much time had passed. I was preparing to move away, to let my mother and sister say goodbye, when he coughed—a brittle, rasping hack that sounded like crepe paper being crinkled. Then, like Lazarus reanimated, his chest began to rise and fall.

I told Mother I was leaving. Dad might survive, I said. And if he does, strep can't be what kills him.

Mother's business came to a halt. The women who worked for her stopped concocting tinctures and bottling oils and instead made vats of salve—a new recipe, of comfrey, lobelia and plantain, that Mother had concocted specifically for my father. Mother smeared the salve over Dad's upper body twice a day. I don't remember what other treatments they used, and I don't know enough about the energy work to give an account. I know they went through seventeen gallons of salve in the first two weeks, and that Mother was ordering gauze in bulk.

Tyler flew in from Purdue. He took over for Mother, changing the bandages on Dad's fingers every morning, scraping away the layers of skin and muscle that had necrotized during the night. It didn't hurt. The nerves were dead. "I scraped off so many layers," Tyler told me, "I was sure that one morning I'd hit bone."

Dad's fingers began to bow, bending unnaturally backward at the joint. This was because the tendons had begun to shrivel and contract. Tyler tried to curl Dad's fingers, to elongate the tendons and prevent the deformity from becoming permanent, but Dad couldn't bear the pain.

I came back to Buck's Peak when I was sure the strep was gone. I sat by Dad's bed, dripping teaspoons of water into his mouth with a medical dropper and feeding him pureed vegetables as if he were a toddler. He rarely spoke. The pain made it difficult for him to focus; he could hardly get through a sentence before his mind surrendered to it. Mother offered to buy him pharmaceuticals, the strongest analgesics she could get her hands on, but he declined them. This was the Lord's pain, he said, and he would feel every part of it.

While I was away, I had scoured every video store within a hundred miles until I'd found the complete box set of *The Honeymooners*. I held it up for Dad. He blinked to show me he'd seen it. I asked if he wanted to watch an episode. He blinked again. I pushed the first tape into the VCR and sat beside him, searching his warped face, listening to his soft whimpers, while on the screen Alice Kramden outfoxed her husband again and again.

26

Waiting for Moving Water

Dad didn't leave his bed for two months unless one of my brothers was carrying him. He peed in a bottle, and the enemas continued. Even after it became clear that he would live, we had no idea what kind of life it would be. All we could do was wait, and soon it felt as though everything we did was just another form of waiting—waiting to feed him, waiting to change his bandages. Waiting to see how much of our father would grow back.

It was difficult to imagine a man like Dad—proud, strong, physical—permanently impaired. I wondered how he would adjust if Mother were forever cutting his food for him; if he could live a happy life if he wasn't able to grasp a hammer. So much had been lost.

But mixed in with the sadness, I also felt hope. Dad had always been a hard man—a man who knew the truth on every subject and wasn't interested in what anybody else had to say. *We* listened to *him*, never the other way around: when he was not speaking, he required silence.

The explosion transformed him from lecturer to observer. Speaking was difficult for him, because of the constant pain but also because his throat was burned. So he watched, he listened. He lay, hour after hour, day after day, his eyes alert, his mouth shut.

Within a few weeks, my father—who years earlier had not been able to guess my age within half a decade—knew about my classes, my boyfriend, my summer job. I hadn't told him any of it, but he'd listened to the chatter between me and Audrey as we changed his bandages, and he'd remembered.

"I'd like to hear more about them classes," he rasped one morning near the end of the summer. "It sounds real interesting."

It felt like a new beginning.

Dad was still bedridden when Shawn and Emily announced their engagement. It was suppertime, and the family was gathered around the kitchen table, when Shawn said he guessed he'd marry Emily after all. There was silence while forks scraped plates. Mother asked if he was serious. He said he wasn't, that he figured he'd find somebody better before he actually had to go through with it. Emily sat next to him, wearing a warped smile.

I didn't sleep that night. I kept checking the bolt on the door. The present seemed vulnerable to the past, as if it might be overwhelmed by it, as if I might blink, and when my eyes opened I would be fifteen.

The next morning Shawn said he and Emily were planning a twenty-mile horse ride to Bloomington Lake. I surprised both of us by saying I wanted to go. I felt anxious when I imagined all those hours in the wilderness with Shawn, but I pushed the anxiety aside. There was something I had to do.

Fifty miles feels like five hundred on a horse, particularly if your body is more accustomed to a chair than a saddle. When we arrived at the lake, Shawn and Emily slipped nimbly off their horses and began to make camp; it was all I could do to unhitch Apollo's saddle and ease myself onto a fallen tree. I watched Emily set up the tent we were to share. She was tall and unthinkably slight, with long, straight hair so blond it was nearly silver.

We built a fire and sang campfire songs. We played cards. Then we went to our tents. I lay awake in the dark next to Emily, listening to the crickets. I was trying to imagine how to begin the conversation—how to tell her she shouldn't marry my brother—when she spoke. "I want to talk to you about Shawn," she said. "I know he's got some problems."

"He does," I said.

"He's a spiritual man," Emily said. "God has given him a special calling. To help people. He told me how he helped Sadie. And how he helped you."

"He didn't help me." I wanted to say more, to explain to Emily what the bishop had explained to me. But they were his words, not mine. I had no words. I had come fifty miles to speak, and was mute.

"The devil tempts him more than other men," Emily said. "Because of his gifts, because he's a threat to Satan. That's why he has problems. Because of his righteousness."

She sat up. I could see the outline of her long ponytail in the dark. "He said he'll hurt me," she said. "I know it's because of Satan. But sometimes I'm scared of him, I'm scared of what he'll do."

I told her she shouldn't marry someone who scares her, that no one should, but the words left my lips stillborn. I believed them, but I didn't understand them well enough to make them live.

I stared into the darkness, searching it for her face, trying to understand what power my brother had over her. He'd had that power over me, I knew. He had some of it still. I was neither under his spell, nor free of it.

"He's a spiritual man," she said again. Then she slipped into her sleeping bag, and I knew the conversation was over.

I returned to BYU a few days before the fall semester. I drove directly to Nick's apartment. We'd hardly spoken. Whenever he called, I always seemed to be needed somewhere to change a bandage or make salve. Nick knew my father had been burned, but he didn't know the severity of it. I'd withheld more information than I'd given, never saying that there had been an explosion, or that when I "visited" my father it wasn't in a hospital but in our living room. I hadn't told Nick about his heart stopping. I hadn't described the gnarled hands, or the enemas, or the pounds of liquefied tissue we'd scraped off his body.

I knocked and Nick opened the door. He seemed surprised to see me. "How's your dad?" he asked after I'd joined him on the sofa.

In retrospect, this was probably the most important moment of our friendship, the moment I could have done one thing, the better thing, and I did something else. It was the first time I'd seen Nick since the explosion. I might have told him everything right then: that my family didn't believe in modern medicine; that we were treating the burn at home with salves and homeopathy; that it had been terrifying, worse than terrifying; that for as long as I lived I would never forget the smell of charred flesh. I could have told him all that, could have surrendered the weight, let the relationship carry it and grow stronger. Instead I kept the burden for myself, and my friendship with Nick, already anemic, underfed and underused, dwindled in obsolescence.

I believed I could repair the damage—that now I was back, *this* would be my life, and it wouldn't matter that Nick understood nothing of Buck's Peak. But the peak refused to give me up. It clung to me. The black craters in my father's chest often materialized on chalkboards, and I saw the sagging cavity of his mouth on the pages of my textbooks. This remembered world was somehow more vivid than the physical world I inhabited, and I phased between them. Nick would take my hand, and for a moment I would be there with him, feeling the surprise of his skin on mine. But when I looked at our joined fingers, something would shift so that the hand was not Nick's. It was bloody and clawed, not a hand at all.

When I slept, I gave myself wholly to the peak. I dreamed of Luke, of his eyes rolling back in his head. I dreamed of Dad, of the slow rattle in his lungs. I dreamed of Shawn, of the moment my wrist had cracked in the parking lot. I dreamed of myself, limping beside him, laughing that high, horrible cackle. But in my dreams I had long, silvery hair.

The wedding was in September.

I arrived at the church full of anxious energy, as though I'd been sent through time from some disastrous future to this moment, when my actions still had weight and my thoughts, consequences. I didn't know what I'd been sent to do, so I wrung my hands and chewed my cheeks, waiting for the crucial moment. Five minutes before the ceremony, I vomited in the women's bathroom.

When Emily said "I do," the vitality left me. I again became a spirit, and drifted back to BYU. I stared at the Rockies from my bedroom window and was struck by how implausible they seemed. Like paintings.

A week after the wedding I broke up with Nick—callously, I'm ashamed to say. I never told him of my life before, never sketched for him the world that had invaded and obliterated the one he and I had shared. I could have explained. I could have said, "That place has a hold on me, which I may never break." That would have got to the heart of it. Instead I sank through time. It was too late to confide in Nick, to take him with me wherever I was going. So I said goodbye.

27

If I Were a Woman

I'd come to BYU to study music, so that one day I could direct a church choir. But that semester—the fall of my junior year—I didn't enroll in a single music course. I couldn't have explained why I dropped advanced music theory in favor of geography and comparative politics, or gave up sight-singing to take History of the Jews. But when I'd seen those courses in the catalog, and read their titles aloud, I had felt something infinite, and I wanted a taste of that infinity.

For four months I attended lectures on geography and history and politics. I learned about Margaret Thatcher and the Thirty-Eighth Parallel and the Cultural Revolution; I learned about parliamentary politics and electoral systems around the world. I learned about the Jewish diaspora and the strange history of *The Protocols of the Elders of Zion*. By the end of the semester the world felt big, and it was hard to imagine returning to the mountain, to a kitchen, or even to a piano in the room next to the kitchen.

This caused a kind of crisis in me. My love of music, and my desire to study it, had been compatible with my idea of what a woman is. My love of history and politics and world affairs was not. And yet they called to me.

A few days before finals, I sat for an hour with my friend

Josh in an empty classroom. He was reviewing his applications for law school. I was choosing my courses for the next semester.

"If you were a woman," I asked, "would you still study law?"

Josh didn't look up. "If I were a woman," he said, "I wouldn't *want* to study it."

"But you've talked about nothing except law school for as long as I've known you," I said. "It's your dream, isn't it?"

"It is," he admitted. "But it wouldn't be if I were a woman. Women are made differently. They don't have this ambition. Their ambition is for children." He smiled at me as if I knew what he was talking about. And I did. I smiled, and for a few seconds we were in agreement.

Then: "But what if you were a woman, and somehow you felt exactly as you do now?"

Josh's eyes fixed on the wall for a moment. He was really thinking about it. Then he said, "I'd know something was wrong with me."

I'd been wondering whether something was wrong with me since the beginning of the semester, when I'd attended my first lecture on world affairs. I'd been wondering how I could be a woman and yet be drawn to unwomanly things.

I knew someone must have the answer so I decided to ask one of my professors. I chose the professor of my Jewish history class, because he was quiet and soft-spoken. Dr. Kerry was a short man with dark eyes and a serious expression. He lectured in a thick wool jacket even in hot weather. I knocked on his office door quietly, as if I hoped he wouldn't answer, and soon was sitting silently across from him. I didn't know what my question was, and Dr. Kerry didn't ask. Instead he posed general questions—about my grades, what courses I was taking. He asked why I'd chosen Jewish history, and without thinking I blurted that I'd learned of the Holocaust only a few semesters before and wanted to learn the rest of the story.

"You learned of the Holocaust when?" he said.

"At BYU."

"They didn't teach about it in your school?"

"They probably did," I said. "Only I wasn't there."

"Where were you?"

I explained as best I could, that my parents didn't believe in public education, that they'd kept us home. When I'd finished, he laced his fingers as if he were contemplating a difficult problem. "I think you should stretch yourself. See what happens."

"Stretch myself how?"

He leaned forward suddenly, as if he'd just had an idea. "Have you heard of Cambridge?" I hadn't. "It's a university in England," he said. "One of the best in the world. I organize a study abroad program there for students. It's highly competitive and extremely demanding. You might not be accepted, but if you are, it may give you some idea of your abilities."

I walked to my apartment wondering what to make of the conversation. I'd wanted moral advice, someone to reconcile my calling as a wife and mother with the call I heard of something else. But he'd put that aside. He'd seemed to say, "First find out what you are capable of, then decide who you are."

I applied to the program.

Emily was pregnant. The pregnancy was not going well. She'd nearly miscarried in the first trimester, and now that she was approaching twenty weeks, she was beginning to have contractions. Mother, who was the midwife, had given her Saint-John's-wort and other remedies. The contractions lessened but continued.

When I arrived at Buck's Peak for Christmas, I expected to find Emily on bed rest. She wasn't. She was standing at the kitchen counter straining herbs, along with half a dozen other women. She rarely spoke and smiled even more rarely, just moved about the house carrying vats of cramp bark and motherwort. She was quiet to the point of invisibility, and after a few minutes, I forgot she was there.

It had been six months since the explosion, and while Dad was back on his feet, it was clear he would never be the man he was. He could scarcely walk across a room without gasping for air, so damaged were his lungs. The skin on his lower face had regrown, but it was thin and waxy, as if someone had taken sandpaper and rubbed it to the point of transparency. His ears were thick with scars. He had thin lips and his mouth drooped, giving him the haggard appearance of a much older man. But it was his right hand, more than his face, that drew stares: each finger was frozen in its own pose, some curled, some bowed, twisting together into a gnarled claw. He could hold a spoon by wedging it between his index finger, which bowed upward, and his ring finger, which curved downward, but he ate with difficulty. Still, I wondered whether skin grafts could have achieved what Mother had with her comfrey and lobelia salve. It was a miracle, everyone said, so that was the new name they gave Mother's recipe: after Dad's burn it was known as Miracle Salve.

At dinner my first night on the peak, Dad described the explosion as a tender mercy from the Lord. "It was a blessing," he said. "A miracle. God spared my life and extended to me a great calling. To testify of His power. To show people there's another way besides the Medical Establishment."

I watched as he tried and failed to wedge his knife tightly enough to cut his roast. "I was never in any danger," he said. "I'll prove it to you. As soon as I can walk across the yard without near passing out, I'll get a torch and cut off another tank."

The next morning when I came out for breakfast, there was a crowd of women gathered around my father. They listened with hushed voices and glistening eyes as Dad told of the heavenly visitations he'd received while hovering between life and death. He had been ministered to by angels, he said, like the prophets of old. There was something in the way the women looked at him. Something like adoration.

I watched the women throughout the morning and became aware of the change my father's miracle had wrought in them. Before, the women who worked for my mother had always approached her casually, with matter-of-fact questions about their work. Now their speech was soft, admiring. Dramas broke out between them as they vied for my mother's esteem, and for my father's. The change could be summed up simply: before, they had been employees; now they were followers.

The story of Dad's burn had become something of a founding myth: it was told over and over, to newcomers but also to the old. In fact, it was rare to spend an afternoon in the house without hearing some kind of recitation of the miracle, and occasionally these recitations were less than accurate. I heard Mother tell a room of devoted faces that sixty-five percent of Dad's upper body had been burned to the third degree. That was not what I remembered. In my memory the bulk of the damage had been skin-deep—his arms, back and shoulders had hardly been burned at all. It was only his lower face and hands that had been third-degree. But I kept this to myself.

For the first time, my parents seemed to be of one mind. Mother no longer moderated Dad's statements after he left the room, no longer quietly gave her own opinion. She had been transformed by the miracle—transformed into him. I remembered her as a young midwife, so cautious, so meek about the lives over which she had such power. There was little of that meekness in her now. The Lord Himself guided her hands, and no misfortune would occur except by the will of God.

A few weeks after Christmas, the University of Cambridge wrote to Dr. Kerry, rejecting my application. "The competition was very steep," Dr. Kerry told me when I visited his office.

I thanked him and stood to go.

"One moment," he said. "Cambridge instructed me to write if I felt there were any gross injustices."

I didn't understand, so he repeated himself. "I could only help one student," he said. "They have offered you a place, if you want it."

It seemed impossible that I would really be allowed to go. Then I realized that I would need a passport, and that without a real birth certificate, I was unlikely to get one. Someone like me did not belong at Cambridge. It was as if the universe understood this and was trying to prevent the blasphemy of my going.

I applied in person. The clerk laughed out loud at my Delayed Certificate of Birth. "Nine years!" she said. "Nine years is *not* a delay. Do you have any other documentation?"

"Yes," I said. "But they have different birth dates. Also, one has a different name."

She was still smiling. "Different date and different name? No, that's not gonna work. There's no way you're gonna get a passport."

I visited the clerk several more times, becoming more and more desperate, until, finally, a solution was found. My aunt Debbie visited the courthouse and swore an affidavit that I was who I said I was. I was issued a passport.

*

In February, Emily gave birth. The baby weighed one pound, four ounces.

When Emily had started having contractions at Christmas, Mother had said the pregnancy would unfold according to God's will. His will, it turned out, was that Emily give birth at home at twenty-six weeks' gestation.

There was a blizzard that night, one of those mighty mountain storms that clears the roads and closes the towns. Emily was in the advanced stages of labor when Mother realized she needed a hospital. The baby, which they named Peter, appeared a few minutes later, slipping from Emily so easily that Mother said she "caught" him more than delivered him. He was still, and the color of ash. Shawn thought he was dead. Then Mother felt a tiny heartbeat—actually she *saw* his heart beating through a thin film of skin. My father rushed to the van and began scraping at the snow and ice. Shawn carried Emily and laid her on the back seat, then Mother placed the baby against Emily's chest and covered him, creating a makeshift incubator. Kangaroo care, she called it later.

My father drove; the storm raged. In Idaho we call it a whiteout: when the wind whips the snowfall so violently it bleaches the road, covers it as if with a veil, and you can't see the asphalt, or the fields or rivers; you can't see anything except billows of white. Somehow, skidding through snow and sleet, they made it to town but the hospital there was rural, unequipped to care for such a faint whimper of life. The doctors said they had to get him to McKay-Dee in Ogden as soon as possible, there was no time. He could not go by chopper because of the blizzard, so the doctors sent him in an ambulance. In fact they sent *two* ambulances, a second in case the first succumbed to the storm.

Many months would pass, and countless surgeries would be performed, before Shawn and Emily would bring home the little twig of flesh that I was told was my nephew. By then he was out of danger, but the doctors said his lungs might never develop fully. He might always be frail.

Dad said God had orchestrated the birth just as He had orchestrated the explosion. Mother echoed him, adding that God had placed a veil over her eyes so she wouldn't stop the contractions. "Peter was supposed to come into the world this way," she said. "He is a gift from God, and God gives His gifts in whatever way He chooses."

28

Pygmalion

The first time I saw King's College, Cambridge, I didn't think I was dreaming, but only because my imagination had never produced anything so grand. My eyes settled on a clock tower with stone carvings. I was led to the tower, then we passed through it and into the college. There was a lake of perfectly clipped grass and, across the lake, an ivory-tinted building I vaguely recognized as Greco-Roman. But it was the Gothic chapel, three hundred feet long and a hundred feet high, a stone mountain, that dominated the scene.

I was taken past the chapel and into another courtyard, then up a spiral staircase. A door was opened, and I was told that this was my room. I was left to make myself comfortable. The kindly man who'd given me this instruction did not realize how impossible it was.

Breakfast the next morning was served in a great hall. It was like eating in a church, the ceiling was cavernous, and I felt under scrutiny, as if the hall knew I was there and I shouldn't be. I'd chosen a long table full of other students from BYU. The women were talking about the clothes they had brought. Marianne had gone shopping when she learned she'd been accepted to the program. "You need different *pieces* for Europe," she said.

Heather agreed. Her grandmother had paid for her plane ticket, so she'd spent that money updating her wardrobe. "The way people dress here," she said, "it's more refined. You can't get away with jeans."

I thought about rushing to my room to change out of the sweatshirt and Keds I was wearing, but I had nothing to change into. I didn't own anything like what Marianne and Heather wore—bright cardigans accented with delicate scarves. I hadn't bought new clothes for Cambridge, because I'd had to take out a student loan just to pay the fees. Besides, I understood that even if I had Marianne's and Heather's clothes, I wouldn't know how to wear them.

Dr. Kerry appeared and announced that we'd been invited to take a tour of the chapel. We would even be allowed on the roof. There was a general scramble as we returned our trays and followed Dr. Kerry from the hall. I stayed near the back of the group as we made our way across the courtyard.

When I stepped inside the chapel, my breath caught in my chest. The room—if such a space can be called a room—was voluminous, as if it could hold the whole of the ocean. We were led through a small wooden door, then up a narrow spiraling staircase whose stone steps seemed numberless. Finally the staircase opened onto the roof, which was heavily slanted, an inverted V enclosed by stone parapets. The wind was gusting, rolling clouds across the sky; the view was spectacular, the city miniaturized, utterly dwarfed by the chapel. I forgot myself and climbed the slope, then walked along the ridge, letting the wind take me as I stared out at the expanse of crooked streets and stone courtyards.

"You're not afraid of falling," a voice said. I turned. It was Dr. Kerry. He had followed me, but he seemed unsteady on his feet, nearly pitching with every rush of wind.

"We can go down," I said. I ran down the ridge to the flat walkway near the buttress. Again Dr. Kerry followed but his steps were strange. Rather than walk facing forward, he rotated his body and moved sideways, like a crab. The wind continued its attack. I offered him an arm for the last few steps, so unsteady did he seem, and he took it.

"I meant it as an observation," he said when we'd made it down. "Here you stand, upright, hands in your pockets." He gestured toward the other students. "See how they hunch? How they cling to the wall?" He was right. A few were venturing onto the ridge but they did so cautiously, taking the same ungainly side steps Dr. Kerry had, tipping and swaying in the wind; everyone else was holding tightly to the stone parapet, knees bent, backs arched, as if unsure whether to walk or crawl.

I raised my hand and gripped the wall.

"You don't need to do that," he said. "It's not a criticism."

He paused, as if unsure he should say more. "Everyone has undergone a change," he said. "The other students were relaxed until we came to this height. Now they are uncomfortable, on edge. You seem to have made the opposite journey. This is the first time I've seen you at home in yourself. It's in the way you move: it's as if you've been on this roof all your life."

A gust of wind swept over the parapet and Dr. Kerry teetered, clutching the wall. I stepped up onto the ridge so he could flatten himself against the buttress. He stared at me, waiting for an explanation.

"I've roofed my share of hay sheds," I said finally.

"So your legs are stronger? Is that why you can stand in this wind?"

I had to think before I could answer. "I can stand in this wind, because I'm not trying to stand in it," I said. "The wind is just wind. You could withstand these gusts on the ground, so you can withstand them in the air. There is no difference. Except the difference you make in your head."

He stared at me blankly. He hadn't understood.

"I'm just standing," I said. "You are all trying to compensate, to get your bodies lower because the height scares you. But the crouching and the sidestepping are not natural. You've made yourselves vulnerable. If you could just control your panic, this wind would be nothing."

"The way it is nothing to you," he said.

I wanted the mind of a scholar, but it seemed that Dr. Kerry saw in me the mind of a roofer. The other students belonged in a library; I belonged in a crane.

The first week passed in a blur of lectures. In the second week, every student was assigned a supervisor to guide their research. My supervisor, I learned, was the eminent Professor Jonathan Steinberg, a former vice-master of a Cambridge college, who was much celebrated for his writings on the Holocaust.

My first meeting with Professor Steinberg took place a few days later. I waited at the porter's lodge until a thin man appeared and, producing a set of heavy keys, unlocked a wooden door set into the stone. I followed him up a spiral staircase and into the clock tower itself, where there was a well-lit room with simple furnishings: two chairs and a wooden table.

I could hear the blood pounding behind my ears as I sat down. Professor Steinberg was in his seventies but I would not have described him as an old man. He was lithe, and his eyes moved about the room with probing energy. His speech was measured and fluid.

"I am Professor Steinberg," he said. "What would you like to read?"

I mumbled something about historiography. I had decided to study not history, but historians. I suppose my interest came from the sense of groundlessness I'd felt since learning about the Holocaust and the civil rights movement—since realizing that what a person knows about the past is limited, and will always be limited, to what they are told by others. I knew what it was to have a misconception corrected—a misconception of such magnitude that shifting it shifted the world. Now I needed to understand how the great gatekeepers of history had come to terms with their own ignorance and partiality. I thought if I could accept that what they had written was not absolute but was the result of a biased process of conversation and revision, maybe I could reconcile myself with the fact that the history most people agreed upon was not the history I had been taught. Dad could be wrong, and the great historians Carlyle and Macaulay and Trevelyan could be wrong, but from the ashes of their dispute I could construct a world to live in. In knowing the ground was not ground at all, I hoped I could stand on it.

I doubt I managed to communicate any of this. When I finished talking, Professor Steinberg eyed me for a moment, then said, "Tell me about your education. Where did you attend school?"

The air was immediately sucked from the room.

"I grew up in Idaho," I said.

"And you attended school there?"

It occurs to me in retrospect that someone might have told Professor Steinberg about me, perhaps Dr. Kerry. Or perhaps he perceived that I was avoiding his question, and that made him curious. Whatever the reason, he wasn't satisfied until I had admitted that I'd never been to school.

"How marvelous," he said, smiling. "It's as if I've stepped into Shaw's Pygmalion."

For two months I had weekly meetings with Professor Steinberg. I was never assigned readings. We read only what I asked to read, whether it was a book or a page.

None of my professors at BYU had examined my writing the way Professor Steinberg did. No comma, no period, no adjective or adverb was beneath his interest. He made no distinction between grammar and content, between form and substance. A poorly written sentence was a poorly conceived idea, and in his view the grammatical logic was as much in need of correction. "Tell me," he would say, "why have you placed this comma here? What relationship between these phrases are you hoping to establish?" When I gave my explanation sometimes he would say, "Quite right," and other times he would correct me with lengthy explanations of syntax.

After I'd been meeting with Professor Steinberg for a month, I wrote an essay comparing Edmund Burke with Publius, the persona under which James Madison, Alexander Hamilton and John Jay had written *The Federalist Papers*. I barely slept for two weeks: every moment my eyes were open, I was either reading or thinking about those texts.

From my father I had learned that books were to be either adored or exiled. Books that were of God—books written by the Mormon prophets or the Founding Fathers—were not to be studied so much as cherished, like a thing perfect in itself. I had been taught to read the words of men like Madison as a cast into which I ought to pour the plaster of my own mind, to be reshaped according to the contours of their faultless model. I read them to learn what to think, not how to think for myself. Books that were not of God were banished; they were a danger, powerful and irresistible in their cunning.

To write my essay I had to read books differently, without giving myself over to either fear or adoration. Because Burke had defended the British monarchy, Dad would have said he was an agent of tyranny. He wouldn't have wanted the book in the house. There was a thrill in trusting myself to read the words. I felt a similar thrill in reading Madison, Hamilton and Jay, especially on those occasions when I discarded their conclusions in favor of Burke's, or when it seemed to me that their ideas were not really different in substance, only in form. There were wonderful suppositions embedded in this method of reading: that books are not tricks, and that I was not feeble.

I finished the essay and sent it to Professor Steinberg. Two days later, when I arrived for our next meeting, he was subdued. He peered at me from across the table. I waited for him to say the essay was a disaster, the product of an ignorant mind, that it had overreached, drawn too many conclusions from too little material.

"I have been teaching in Cambridge for thirty years," he said. "And this is one of the best essays I've read."

I was prepared for insults but not for this.

Professor Steinberg must have said more about the essay but I heard nothing. My mind was consumed with a wrenching need to get out of that room. In that moment I was no longer in a clock tower in Cambridge. I was seventeen, in a red jeep, and a boy I loved had just touched my hand. I bolted.

I could tolerate any form of cruelty better than kindness. Praise was a poison to me; I choked on it. I wanted the professor to shout at me, wanted it so deeply I felt dizzy from the deprivation. The ugliness of me had to be given expression. If it was not expressed in his voice, I would need to express it in mine.

I don't remember leaving the clock tower, or how I passed the afternoon. That evening there was a black-tie dinner. The hall was lit by candlelight, which was beautiful, but it cheered me for another reason: I wasn't wearing formal clothing, just a black shirt and black pants, and I thought people might not notice in the dim lighting. My friend Laura arrived late. She explained that her parents had visited and taken her to

France. She had only just returned. She was wearing a dress of rich purple with crisp pleats in the skirt. The hemline bounced several inches above her knee, and for a moment I thought the dress was whorish, until she said her father had bought it for her in Paris. A gift from one's father could not be whorish. A gift from one's father seemed to me the definitive signal that a woman was not a whore. I struggled with this dissonance—a whorish dress, gifted to a loved daughter—until the meal had been finished and the plates cleared away.

At my next supervision, Professor Steinberg said that when I applied for graduate school, he would make sure I was accepted to whatever institution I chose. "Have you visited Harvard?" he said. "Or perhaps you prefer Cambridge?"

I imagined myself in Cambridge, a graduate student wearing a long black robe that swished as I strode through ancient corridors. Then I was hunching in a bathroom, my arm behind my back, my head in the toilet. I tried to focus on the student but I couldn't. I couldn't picture the girl in the whirling black gown without seeing that *other* girl. Scholar or whore, both couldn't be true. One was a lie.

"I can't go," I said. "I can't pay the fees."

"Let me worry about the fees," Professor Steinberg said.

In late August, on our last night in Cambridge, there was a final dinner in the great hall. The tables were set with more knives, forks and goblets than I'd ever seen; the paintings on the wall seemed ghostly in the candlelight. I felt exposed by the elegance and yet somehow made invisible by it. I stared at the other students as they passed, taking in every silk dress, every heavily lined eye. I obsessed over the beauty of them.

At dinner I listened to the cheerful chatter of my friends while longing for the isolation of my room. Professor

Steinberg was seated at the high table. Each time I glanced at him, I felt that old instinct at work in me, tensing my muscles, preparing me to take flight.

I left the hall the moment dessert was served. It was a relief to escape all that refinement and beauty—to be allowed to be unlovely and not a point of contrast. Dr. Kerry saw me leave and followed.

It was dark. The lawn was black, the sky blacker. Pillars of chalky light reached up from the ground and illuminated the chapel, which glowed, moonlike, against the night sky.

"You've made an impression on Professor Steinberg," Dr. Kerry said, falling into step beside me. "I only hope he has made some impression on you."

I didn't understand.

"Come this way," he said, turning toward the chapel. "I have something to say to you."

I walked behind him, noticing the silence of my own footfalls, aware that my Keds didn't click elegantly on stone the way the heels worn by other girls did.

Dr. Kerry said he'd been watching me. "You act like someone who is impersonating someone else. And it's as if you think your life depends on it."

I didn't know what to say, so I said nothing.

"It has never occurred to you," he said, "that you might have as much right to be here as anyone." He waited for an explanation.

"I would enjoy serving the dinner," I said, "more than eating it."

Dr. Kerry smiled. "You should trust Professor Steinberg. If he says you're a scholar—'pure gold,' I heard him say—then you are."

"This is a magical place," I said. "Everything shines here."

"You must stop yourself from thinking like that," Dr. Kerry said, his voice raised. "You are not fool's gold, shining only under a particular light. Whomever you become, whatever you make yourself into, that is who you always were. It was always in you. Not in Cambridge. In *you*. You are gold. And returning to BYU, or even to that mountain you came from, will not change who you are. It may change how others see you, it may even change how you see yourself—even gold appears dull in some lighting—but *that* is the illusion. And it always was."

I wanted to believe him, to take his words and remake myself, but I'd never had that kind of faith. No matter how deeply I interred the memories, how tightly I shut my eyes against them, when I thought of my *self*, the images that came to mind were of *that* girl, in the bathroom, in the parking lot.

I couldn't tell Dr. Kerry about that girl. I couldn't tell him that the reason I couldn't return to Cambridge was that being here threw into great relief every violent and degrading moment of my life. At BYU I could almost forget, allow what had been to blend into what was. But the contrast here was too great, the world before my eyes too fantastical. The memories were more real—more believable—than the stone spires.

To myself I pretended there were other reasons I couldn't belong at Cambridge, reasons having to do with class and status: that it was because I was poor, had grown up poor. Because I could stand in the wind on the chapel roof and not tilt. *That* was the person who didn't belong in Cambridge: the roofer, not the whore. *I can go to school,* I had written in my journal that very afternoon. *And I can buy new clothes. But I am still Tara Westover. I have done jobs no Cambridge student would do. Dress us any way you like, we are not the same.* Clothes could not fix what was wrong with me. Something had rotted on the inside, and the stench was too powerful, the core too rancid, to be covered up by mere dressings.

Whether Dr. Kerry suspected any part of this, I'm not sure. But he understood that I had fixated on clothes as the symbol of why I didn't, and couldn't, belong. It was the last thing he said to me before he walked away, leaving me rooted, astonished, beside that grand chapel.

"The most powerful determinant of who you are is inside you," he said. "Professor Steinberg says this is Pygmalion. Think of the story, Tara." He paused, his eyes fierce, his voice piercing. "She was just a cockney in a nice dress. Until she believed in herself. Then it didn't matter what dress she wore."

29

Graduation

The program ended and I returned to BYU. Campus looked the way it always had, and it would have been easy to forget Cambridge and settle back into the life I'd had there. But Professor Steinberg was determined that I not forget. He sent me an application for something called the Gates Cambridge Scholarship, which, he explained, was a little like the Rhodes Scholarship, but for Cambridge instead of Oxford. It would provide full funding for me to study at Cambridge, including tuition, room and board. As far as I was concerned it was comically out of reach for someone like me, but he insisted that it was not, so I applied.

Not long after, I noticed another difference, another small shift. I was spending an evening with my friend Mark, who studied ancient languages. Like me, and almost everyone at BYU, Mark was Mormon.

"Do you think people should study church history?" he asked.

"I do," I said.

"What if it makes them unhappy?"

I thought I knew what he meant, but I waited for him to explain.

"Many women struggle with their faith after they learn

about polygamy," he said. "My mother did. I don't think she's ever understood it."

"I've never understood it, either," I said.

There was a tense silence. He was waiting for me to say my line: that I was praying for faith. And I *had* prayed for it, many, many times.

Perhaps both of us were thinking of our history, or perhaps only I was. I thought of Joseph Smith, who'd had as many as forty wives. Brigham Young had had fifty-five wives and fifty-six children. The church had ended the *temporal* practice of polygamy in 1890, but it had never recanted the doctrine. As a child I'd been taught—by my father but also in Sunday school—that in the fullness of time God would restore polygamy, and in the afterlife, I would be a plural wife. The number of my sister wives would depend on my husband's righteousness: the more nobly he lived, the more wives he would be given.

I had never made my peace with it. As a girl I had often imagined myself in heaven, dressed in a white gown, standing in a pearly mist across from my husband. But when the camera zoomed out there were ten women standing behind us, wearing the same white dress. In my fantasy I was the first wife but I knew there was no guarantee of that; I might be hidden anywhere in the long chain of wives. For as long as I could remember, this image had been at the core of my idea of paradise: my husband, and his wives. There was a sting in this arithmetic: in knowing that in the divine calculus of heaven, one man could balance the equation for countless women.

I remembered my great-great-grandmother. I had first heard her name when I was twelve, which is the year that, in Mormonism, you cease to be a child and become a woman. Twelve was the age when lessons in Sunday school began to include words like *purity* and *chastity*. It was also the age that

I was asked, as part of a church assignment, to learn about one of my ancestors. I asked Mother which ancestor I should choose, and without thinking she said, "Anna Mathea." I said the name aloud. It floated off my tongue like the beginning of a fairy tale. Mother said I should honor Anna Mathea because she had given me a gift: her voice.

"It was her voice that brought our family to the church," Mother said. "She heard Mormon missionaries preaching in the streets of Norway. She prayed, and God blessed her with faith, with the knowledge that Joseph Smith was His prophet. She told her father, but he'd heard stories about the Mormons and wouldn't allow her to be baptized. So she sang for him. She sang him a Mormon hymn called 'O My Father.' When she finished singing, her father had tears in his eyes. He said that any religion with music so beautiful must be the work of God. They were baptized together."

After Anna Mathea converted her parents, the family felt called by God to come to America and meet the prophet Joseph. They saved for the journey, but after two years they could bring only half the family. Anna Mathea was left behind.

The journey was long and harsh, and by the time they made it to Idaho, to a Mormon settlement called Worm Creek, Anna's mother was sick, dying. It was her last wish to see her daughter again, so her father wrote to Anna, begging her to take what money she had and come to America. Anna had fallen in love and was to be married, but she left her fiancé in Norway and crossed the ocean. Her mother died before she reached the American shore.

The family was now destitute; there was no money to send Anna to her fiancé, to the marriage she had given up. Anna was a financial burden on her father, so a bishop persuaded her to marry a rich farmer as his second wife. His first wife was barren, and she flew into a jealous rage when Anna became pregnant. Anna worried the first wife might hurt her baby, so she returned to her father, where she gave birth to twins, though only one would survive the harsh winter on the frontier.

Mark was still waiting. Then he gave up and mumbled the words I was supposed to say, that he didn't understand fully, but that he knew polygamy was a principle from God.

I agreed. I said the words, then braced myself for a wave of humiliation—for that image to invade my thoughts, of me, one of many wives standing behind a solitary, faceless man— but it didn't come. I searched my mind and discovered a new conviction there: I would never be a plural wife. A voice declared this with unyielding finality; the declaration made me tremble. What if God commanded it? I asked. *You wouldn't do it,* the voice answered. And I knew it was true.

I thought again of Anna Mathea, wondering what kind of world it was in which she, following a prophet, could leave her lover, cross an ocean, enter a loveless marriage as a second mistress, then bury her first child, only to have her granddaughter, in two generations, cross the same ocean an unbeliever. I was Anna Mathea's heir: she had given me her voice. Had she not given me her faith, also?

I was put on a short list for the Gates scholarship. There would be an interview in February in Annapolis. I had no idea how to prepare. Robin drove me to Park City, where there was an Ann Taylor discount outlet, and helped me buy a navy pantsuit and matching loafers. I didn't own a handbag so Robin lent me hers.

Two weeks before the interview my parents came to BYU. They had never visited me before, but they were passing through on their way to Arizona and stopped for dinner. I took them to the Indian restaurant across the street from my apartment.

The waitress stared a moment too long at my father's face, then her eyes bulged when they dropped to his hands. Dad ordered half the menu. I told him three mains would be enough, but he winked and said money was not a problem. It seemed the news of my father's miraculous healing was spreading, earning them more and more customers. Mother's products were being sold by nearly every midwife and natural healer in the Mountain West.

We waited for the food, and Dad asked about my classes. I said I was studying French. "That's a socialist language," he said, then he lectured for twenty minutes on twentieth-century history. He said Jewish bankers in Europe had signed secret agreements to start World War II, and that they had colluded with Jews in America to pay for it. They had engineered the Holocaust, he said, because they would benefit financially from worldwide disorder. They had sent their own people to the gas chambers for money.

These ideas were familiar to me, but it took me a moment to remember where I'd heard them: in a lecture Dr. Kerry had given on *The Protocols of the Elders of Zion*. The *Protocols*, published in 1903, purported to be a record of a secret meeting of powerful Jews planning world domination. The document was discredited as a fabrication but still it spread, fueling anti-Semitism in the decades before World War II. Adolf Hitler had written about the *Protocols* in *Mein Kampf*, claiming they were authentic, that they revealed the true nature of the Jewish people.

Dad was talking loudly, at a volume that would have suited a mountainside but was thunderous in the small restaurant. People at nearby tables had halted their own conversations and were sitting in silence, listening to ours. I regretted having chosen a restaurant so near my apartment.

Dad moved on from World War II to the United Nations, the European Union, and the imminent destruction of the world. He spoke as if the three were synonyms. The curry arrived and I focused my attention on it. Mother had grown tired of the lecture, and asked Dad to talk about something else.

"But the world is about to end!" he said. He was shouting now.

"Of course it is," Mother said. "But let's not discuss it over dinner."

I put down my fork and stared at them. Of all the strange statements from the past half hour, for some reason this was the one that shocked me. The mere fact of them had never shocked me before. Everything they did had always made sense to me, adhering to a logic I understood. Perhaps it was the backdrop: Buck's Peak was theirs and it camouflaged them, so that when I saw them there, surrounded by the loud, sharp relics of my childhood, the setting seemed to absorb them. At least it absorbed the noise. But here, so near the university, they seemed so unreal as to be almost mythic.

Dad looked at me, waiting for me to give an opinion, but I felt alienated from myself. I didn't know who to be. On the mountain I slipped thoughtlessly into the voice of their daughter and acolyte. But here, I couldn't seem to find the voice that, in the shadow of Buck's Peak, came easily.

We walked to my apartment and I showed them my room. Mother shut the door, revealing a poster of Martin Luther King Jr. that I'd put up four years before, when I'd learned of the civil rights movement.

"Is that Martin Luther King?" Dad said. "Don't you know he had ties to communism?" He chewed the waxy tissue where his lips had been.

They departed soon after to drive through the night. I watched them go, then took out my journal. *It's astonishing that I used to believe all this without the slightest suspicion,* I wrote. *The whole world was wrong; only Dad was right.*

I thought of something Tyler's wife, Stefanie, had told me over the phone a few days before. She said it had taken her years to convince Tyler to let her immunize their children, because some part of him still believed vaccines are a conspiracy by the Medical Establishment. Remembering that now, with Dad's voice still ringing in my ears, I sneered at my brother. *He's a scientist!* I wrote. *How can he not see beyond their paranoia!* I reread what I had written, and as I did so my scorn gave way to a sense of irony. *Then again,* I wrote. *Perhaps I could mock Tyler with more credibility if I had not remembered, as I did just now, that to this day I have never been immunized.*

My interview for the Gates scholarship took place at St. John's College in Annapolis. The campus was intimidating, with its immaculate lawns and crisp colonial architecture. I sat nervously in the corridor, waiting to be called in for my interview; I felt stiff in the pantsuit and clung awkwardly to Robin's handbag. But in the end, Professor Steinberg had written such a powerful letter of recommendation that there was little left for me to do.

I received confirmation the next day: I'd won the scholarship.

The phone calls began—from BYU's student paper and the local news. I did half a dozen interviews. I was on TV. I awoke one morning to find my picture plastered on BYU's homepage. I was the third BYU student ever to win a Gates scholarship, and the university was taking full advantage of the press. I was asked about my high school experience, and which of my grade school teachers had prepared me for my success. I dodged, I parried, I lied when I had to. I didn't tell a single reporter that I'd never gone to school.

I didn't know why I couldn't tell them. I just couldn't stand the thought of people patting me on the back, telling me how impressive I was. I didn't want to be Horatio Alger in someone's tear-filled homage to the American dream. I wanted my life to make sense, and nothing in that narrative made sense to me.

A month before my graduation, I visited Buck's Peak. Dad had read the articles about my scholarship, and what he said was, "You didn't mention home school. I'd think you'd be more grateful that your mother and I took you out of them schools, seeing how it's worked out. You should be telling people that's what done it: home school."

I said nothing. Dad took it as an apology.

He disapproved of my going to Cambridge. "Our ancestors risked their lives to cross the ocean, to escape those socialist countries. And what do you do? You turn around and go back?"

Again, I said nothing.

"I'm looking forward to your graduation," he said. "The Lord has a few choice rebukes for me to give them professors."

"You will not," I said quietly.

"If the Lord moves me, I will stand and speak."

"You will not," I repeated.

"I won't go anywhere that the Lord's spirit isn't welcome."

That was the conversation. I hoped it would blow over, but Dad was so hurt that I hadn't mentioned homeschooling in my interviews that this new wound festered.

There was a dinner the night before my graduation where I was to receive the "most outstanding undergraduate" award from the history department. I waited for my parents at the entrance, but they never appeared. I called Mother, thinking they were running late. She said they weren't coming. I went to the dinner and was presented with a plaque. My table had the only empty seats in the hall. The next day there was a luncheon for honors graduates, and I was seated with the college dean and the director of the honors program. Again, there were two empty seats. I said my parents had had car trouble.

I phoned my mother after the luncheon.

"Your father won't come unless you apologize," she said. "And I won't, either."

I apologized. "He can say whatever he wants. But please come."

They missed most of the ceremony; I don't know if they saw me accept my diploma. What I remember is waiting with my friends before the music began, watching their fathers snap pictures and their mothers fix their hair. I remember that my friends were wearing colorful leis and recently gifted jewelry.

After the ceremony I stood alone on the lawn, watching the other students with their families. Eventually I saw my parents. Mother hugged me. My friend Laura snapped two photos. One is of me and Mother, smiling our forced smiles; the other is of me wedged between my parents, looking squeezed, under pressure.

I was leaving the Mountain West that night. I had packed before graduation. My apartment was empty, my bags by the door. Laura had volunteered to drive me to the airport, but my parents asked if they could take me.

I expected them to drop me at the curb, but Dad insisted that they walk with me through the airport. They waited while I checked my bags, then followed me to the security gate. It was as if Dad wanted to give me until the last second to change my mind. We walked in silence. When we arrived at security I hugged them both and said goodbye. I removed my shoes, laptop, camera, then I passed through the checkpoint, reassembled my pack, and headed for the terminal.

It was only then that I glanced back and saw Dad, still standing at the checkpoint, watching me walk away, his hands in his pockets, his shoulders slumping, his mouth slackened. I waved and he stepped forward, as if to follow, and I was reminded of the moment, years before, when power lines had covered the station wagon, with Mother inside it, and Dad had stood next to her, exposed.

He was still holding that posture when I turned the corner. That image of my father will always stay with me: that look on his face, of love and fear and loss. I knew why he was afraid. He'd let it slip my last night on Buck's Peak, the same night he'd said he wouldn't come to see me graduate.

"If you're in America," he'd whispered, "we can come for you. Wherever you are. I've got a thousand gallons of fuel buried in the field. I can fetch you when The End comes, bring you home, make you safe. But if you cross the ocean . . ."

PART THREE

30

Hand of the Almighty

A stone gate barred the entrance to Trinity College. Cut into the gate was a small wooden door. I stepped through it. A porter in a black overcoat and bowler hat showed me around the college, leading me through Great Court, the largest of the courtyards. We walked through a stone passageway and into a covered corridor whose stone was the color of ripe wheat.

"This is the north cloister," the porter said. "It is here that Newton stomped his foot to measure the echo, calculating the speed of sound for the first time."

We returned to the Great Gate. My room was directly opposite it, up three flights of stairs. After the porter left I stood, bookended by my suitcases, and stared out my little window at the mythic stone gate and its otherworldly battlements. Cambridge was just as I remembered: ancient, beautiful. I was different. I was not a visitor, not a guest. I was a member of the university. My name was painted on the door. According to the paperwork, I belonged here.

I dressed in dark colors for my first lecture, hoping I wouldn't stand out, but even so I didn't think I looked like the other students. I certainly didn't *sound* like them, and not just because they were British. Their speech had a lilting cadence that made me think of singing more than speaking. To my ears they sounded refined, educated; I had a tendency to mumble, and when nervous, to stutter.

I chose a seat around the large square table and listened as the two students nearest me discussed the lecture topic, which was Isaiah Berlin's two concepts of liberty. The student next to me said he'd studied Isaiah Berlin at Oxford; the other said he'd already heard this lecturer's remarks on Berlin when he was an undergraduate at Cambridge. I had never heard of Isaiah Berlin.

The lecturer began his presentation. He spoke calmly but moved through the material quickly, as if he assumed we were already familiar with it. This was confirmed by the other students, most of whom were not taking notes. I scribbled down every word.

"So what are Isaiah Berlin's two concepts?" the lecturer asked. Nearly everyone raised a hand. The lecturer called on the student who had studied at Oxford. "Negative liberty," he said, "is the freedom from external obstacles or constraints. An individual is free in this sense if they are not physically prevented from taking action." I was reminded for a moment of Richard, who had always seemed able to recite with exactness anything he'd ever read.

"Very good," the lecturer said. "And the second?"

"Positive liberty," another student said, "is freedom from internal constraints."

I wrote this definition in my notes, but I didn't understand it.

The lecturer tried to clarify. He said positive liberty is self-mastery—the rule of the self, by the self. To have positive liberty, he explained, is to take control of one's own mind; to be liberated from irrational fears and beliefs, from addictions, superstitions and all other forms of self-coercion.

I had no idea what it meant to self-coerce. I looked around the room. No one else seemed confused. I was one of the few students taking notes. I wanted to ask for further explanation, but something stopped me—the certainty that to do so would be to shout to the room that I didn't belong there.

After the lecture, I returned to my room, where I stared out my window at the stone gate with its medieval battlements. I thought of positive liberty, and of what it might mean to self-coerce, until my head thrummed with a dull ache.

I called home. Mother answered. Her voice rose with excitement when she recognized my weepy "Hello, Mom." I told her I shouldn't have come to Cambridge, that I didn't understand anything. She said she'd been muscle-testing and had discovered that one of my chakras was out of balance. She could adjust it, she said. I reminded her that I was five thousand miles away.

"That doesn't matter," she said. "I'll adjust the chakra on Audrey and wing it to you."

"You'll what it to me?"

"*Wing* it," she said. "Distance is nothing to living energy. I can send the corrected energy to you from here."

"How fast does energy travel?" I asked. "At the speed of sound, or is it more like a jetliner? Does it fly direct, or will it have to lay over in Minneapolis?"

Mother laughed and hung up.

I studied most mornings in the college library, near a small window. I was there on a particular morning when Drew, a friend from BYU, sent me a song via email. He said it was a classic but I had never heard of it, nor of the singer. I played the song through my headphones. It gripped me immediately. I listened to it over and over while staring out at the north cloister.

> Emancipate yourselves from mental slavery
> None but ourselves can free our mind

I scratched those lines into notebooks, into the margins of the essays I was writing. I wondered about them when I should have been reading. From the Internet I learned about the cancer that had been discovered on Bob Marley's foot. I also learned that Marley had been a Rastafarian, and that Rastafari believe in a "whole body," which is why he had refused surgery to amputate the toe. Four years later, at age thirty-six, he died.

Emancipate yourselves from mental slavery. Marley had written that line a year before his death, while an operable melanoma was, at that moment, metastasizing to his lungs, liver, stomach and brain. I imagined a greedy surgeon with sharp teeth and long, skeletal fingers urging Marley to have the amputation. I shrank from this frightening image of the doctor and his corrupt medicine, and only then did I understand, as I had not before, that although I had renounced my father's world, I had never quite found the courage to live in this one.

I flipped through my notebook to the lecture on negative and positive liberty. In a blank corner I scratched the line, *None but ourselves can free our mind.* Then I picked up my phone and dialed.

"I need to get my vaccinations," I told the nurse.

I attended a seminar on Wednesday afternoons, where I noticed two women, Katrina and Sophie, who nearly always sat together. I never spoke to them until one afternoon a few weeks before Christmas, when they asked if I'd like to get a coffee. I'd never "gotten a coffee" before—I'd never even tasted coffee, because it is forbidden by the church—but I followed them across the street and into a café. The cashier was impatient so I chose at random. She passed me a doll-sized cup with a tablespoon of mud-colored liquid in it, and I looked longingly at the foamy mugs Katrina and Sophie carried to our table. They debated concepts from the lecture; I debated whether to drink my coffee.

They used complex phrases with ease. Some of them, like "the second wave," I'd heard before even if I didn't know what they meant; others, like "the hegemonic masculinity," I couldn't get my tongue around let alone my mind. I'd taken several sips of the grainy, acrid fluid before I understood that they were talking about feminism. I stared at them as if they were behind glass. I'd never heard anyone use the word "feminism" as anything but a reprimand. At BYU, "You sound like a feminist" signaled the end of the argument. It also signaled that I had lost.

I left the café and went to the library. After five minutes online and a few trips to the stacks, I was sitting in my usual place with a large pile of books written by what I now understood to be second-wave writers—Betty Friedan, Germaine Greer, Simone de Beauvoir. I read only a few pages of each book before slamming it shut. I'd never seen the word "vagina" printed out, never said it aloud.

I returned to the Internet and then to the shelves, where I exchanged the books of the second wave for those that preceded the first—Mary Wollstonecraft and John Stuart Mill. I read through the afternoon and into the evening, developing for the first time a vocabulary for the uneasiness I'd felt since childhood.

From the moment I had first understood that my brother Richard was a boy and I was a girl, I had wanted to exchange his future for mine. My future was motherhood; his, fatherhood. They sounded similar but they were not. To be one was to be a decider. To preside. To call the family to order. To be the other was to be among those called.

I knew my yearning was unnatural. This knowledge, like so much of my self-knowledge, had come to me in the voice of people I knew, people I loved. All through the years that voice had been with me, whispering, wondering, worrying. That I was *not right*. That my dreams were perversions. That voice had many timbres, many tones. Sometimes it was my father's voice; more often it was my own.

I carried the books to my room and read through the night. I loved the fiery pages of Mary Wollstonecraft, but there was a single line written by John Stuart Mill that, when I read it, moved the world: "It is a subject on which nothing final can be known." The subject Mill had in mind was the nature of women. Mill claimed that women have been coaxed, cajoled, shoved and squashed into a series of feminine contortions for so many centuries, that it is now quite impossible to define their natural abilities or aspirations.

Blood rushed to my brain; I felt an animating surge of adrenaline, of possibility, of a frontier being pushed outward. *Of the nature of women, nothing final can be known.* Never had I found such comfort in a void, in the black absence of knowledge. It seemed to say: whatever you are, you are woman.

In December, after I had submitted my last essay, I took a train to London and boarded a plane. Mother, Audrey and Emily picked me up at the airport in Salt Lake City, and together we skidded onto the interstate. It was nearly midnight when the mountain came into view. I could only just make out her grand form against the inky sky.

When I entered the kitchen I noticed a gaping hole in the wall, which led to a new extension Dad was building. Mother walked with me through the hole and switched on the light.

"Amazing, isn't it?" she said. "Amazing" was the word.

It was a single massive room the size of the chapel at church, with a vaulted ceiling that rose some sixteen feet into the air. The size of the room was so ridiculous, it took me a moment to notice the decor. The walls were exposed Sheetrock, which contrasted spectacularly with the wood paneling on the vaulted ceiling. Crimson suede sofas sat cordially next to the stained upholstery love seat my father had dragged in from the dump many years before. Thick rugs with intricate patterns covered half the floor, while the other half was raw cement. There were several pianos, only one of which looked playable, and a television the size of a dining table. The room suited my father perfectly: it was larger than life and wonderfully incongruous.

Dad had always said he wanted to build a room the size of a cruise ship but I'd never thought he'd have the money. I looked to Mother for an explanation but it was Dad who answered. The business was a roaring success, he explained. Essential oils were popular, and Mother had the best on the market. "Our oils are so good," he said, "we've started eating into the profits of the large corporate producers. They know all about them Westovers in Idaho." Dad told me that one company had been so alarmed by the success of Mother's oils, they had offered to buy her out for an astonishing three million dollars. My parents hadn't even considered it. Healing was their calling. No amount of money could tempt them. Dad explained that they were taking the bulk of their profits and reconsecrating them to God in the form of supplies— food, fuel, may be even a real bomb shelter. I suppressed a grin. From what I could tell, Dad was on track to become the best-funded lunatic in the Mountain West.

Richard appeared on the stairwell. He was finishing his undergraduate degree in chemistry at Idaho State. He'd come home for Christmas, and he'd brought his wife, Kami, and their one-month-old son, Donavan. When I'd met Kami a year before, just before the wedding, I'd been struck by how *normal* she was. Like Tyler's wife, Stefanie, Kami was an outsider: she was a Mormon, but she was what Dad would have called "mainstream." She thanked Mother for her herbal advice but seemed oblivious to the expectation that she renounce doctors. Donavan had been born in a hospital.

I wondered how Richard was navigating the turbulent waters between his normal wife and his abnormal parents. I watched him closely that night, and to me it seemed he was trying to live in both worlds, to be a loyal adherent to all creeds. When my father condemned doctors as minions of Satan, Richard turned to Kami and gave a small laugh, as if Dad were joking. But when my father's eyebrows rose, Richard's expression changed to one of serious contemplation and accord. He seemed in a state of constant transition, phasing in and out of dimensions, unsure whether to be my father's son or his wife's husband.

Mother was overwhelmed with holiday orders, so I passed my days on Buck's Peak just as I had as a child: in the kitchen, making homeopathics. I poured the distilled water and added the drops from the base formula, then passed the tiny glass bottle through the ring made by my thumb and index fingers, counting to fifty or a hundred, then moving on to the next. Dad came in for a drink of water. He smiled when he saw me.

"Who knew we'd have to send you to Cambridge to get you in the kitchen where you belong?" he said.

In the afternoons, Shawn and I saddled the horses and fought our way up the mountain, the horses half-jumping to clamber through snowdrifts that reached their bellies. The mountain was beautiful and crisp; the air smelled of leather and pine. Shawn talked about the horses, about their training, and about the colts he expected in the spring, and I remembered that he was always at his best when he was with his horses.

I had been home about a week when the mountain was gripped by an intense cold spell. The temperature plunged, dropping to zero, then dropping further still. We put the horses away, knowing that if they worked up a sweat, it would turn to ice on their backs. The trough froze solid. We broke the ice but it refroze quickly, so we carried buckets of water to each horse.

That night everyone stayed indoors. Mother was blending oils in the kitchen. Dad was in the extension, which I had begun to jokingly call the Chapel. He was lying on the crimson sofa, a Bible resting on his stomach, while Kami and Richard played hymns on the piano. I sat with my laptop on the love seat, near Dad, and listened to the music. I had just begun a message to Drew when something struck the back door. The door burst open, and Emily flew into the room.

Her thin arms were wrapped around her body and she was shaking, gasping for breath. She wore no coat, no shoes, nothing but jeans, an old pair I'd left behind, and one of my worn T-shirts. Mother helped her to the sofa, wrapping her in the nearest blanket. Emily bawled, and for several minutes not even Mother could get her to say what had happened. Was everyone all right? Where was Peter? He was fragile, half the size he should have been, and he wore oxygen tubes because his lungs had never fully developed. Had his tiny lungs collapsed, his breathing stopped?

The story came out haltingly, between erratic sobs and the clattering of teeth. From what I could tell, when Emily had gone to Stokes that afternoon to buy groceries, she had returned home with the wrong crackers for Peter. Shawn had exploded. "How can he grow if you can't buy the right food!" he had screamed, then he'd gathered her up and flung her from their trailer, into a snowbank. She'd pounded on the door, begging to be let in, then she'd run up the hillside to the house. I stared at her bare feet as she said this. They were so red, they looked as if they'd been burned.

My parents sat with Emily on the sofa, one on each side of her, patting her shoulders and squeezing her hands. Richard paced a few feet behind them. He seemed frustrated, anxious, as if he wanted to explode into action and was only just being held in check.

Kami was still seated at the piano. She was staring at the group huddled on the couch, confused. She had not understood Emily. She did not understand why Richard was pacing, or why he paused every few seconds to glance at Dad, waiting for a word or gesture—any signal of what should be done.

I looked at Kami and felt a tightening in my chest. I resented her for witnessing this. I imagined myself in Emily's place, which was easy to do—I couldn't stop myself from doing it—and in a moment I was in a parking lot, laughing my high-pitched cackle, trying to convince the world that my wrist wasn't breaking. Before I knew what I was doing I had crossed the room. I grasped my brother's arm and pulled him with me to the piano. Emily was still sobbing, and I used her sobs to muffle my whispers. I told Kami that what we were witnessing was private, and that Emily would be embarrassed by it tomorrow. For Emily's sake, I said, we should all go to our rooms and leave it in Dad's hands.

Kami stood. She had decided to trust me. Richard hesitated, giving Dad a long look, then he followed her from the room.

I walked with them down the hallway then I doubled back. I sat at the kitchen table and watched the clock. Five minutes passed, then ten. *Come on, Shawn,* I chanted under my breath. *Come now.*

I'd convinced myself that if Shawn appeared in the next few minutes, it would be to make sure Emily had made it to the house—that she hadn't slipped on the ice and broken a leg, wasn't freezing to death in a field. But he didn't come.

Twenty minutes later, when Emily finally stopped shaking, Dad picked up the phone. "Come get your wife!" he shouted into it. Mother was cradling Emily's head against her shoulder.

Dad returned to the sofa and patted Emily's arm. As I stared at the three of them huddling together, I had the impression that all of this had happened before, and that everyone's part was well rehearsed. Even mine.

It would be many years before I would understand what had happened that night, and what my role in it had been. How I had opened my mouth when I should have stayed silent, and shut it when I should have spoken out. What was needed was a revolution, a reversal of the ancient, brittle roles we'd been playing out since my childhood. What was needed—what Emily needed—was a woman emancipated from pretense, a woman who could show herself to be a man. Voice an opinion. Take action in scorn of deference. A father.

The French doors my father had installed squawked as they opened. Shawn shuffled in wearing heavy boots and a thick winter coat. Peter emerged from the folds of thick wool, where Shawn had been shielding him from the cold, and reached out for Emily. She clung to him. Dad stood. He motioned for Shawn to take the seat next to Emily. I stood and went to my room, pausing to take a last look at my father, who was inhaling deeply, readying himself to deliver a lengthy lecture.

"It was very stern," Mother assured me twenty minutes later, when she appeared at my door asking if I could lend Emily a pair of shoes and a coat. I fetched them and watched from the kitchen as she disappeared, tucked under my brother's arm.

31
Tragedy Then Farce

The day before I returned to England, I drove seven miles along the mountain range, then turned onto a narrow dirt road and stopped in front of a powder-blue house. I parked behind an RV that was nearly as large as the house itself. I knocked; my sister answered.

She stood in the doorway in flannel pajamas, a toddler on her hip and two small girls clinging to her leg. Her son, about six, stood behind her. Audrey stepped aside to let me pass, but her movements were stiff, and she avoided looking directly at me. We'd spent little time together since she'd married.

I moved into the house, stopping abruptly in the entryway when I saw a three-foot hole in the linoleum that plunged to the basement. I walked past the hole and into the kitchen, which was filled with the scent of our mother's oils—birch, eucalyptus, ravensara.

The conversation was slow, halting. Audrey asked me no questions about England or Cambridge. She had no frame of reference for my life, so we talked about hers—how the public school system was corrupt so she was teaching her children herself, at home. Like me, Audrey had never attended a public school. When she was seventeen, she had made a fleeting effort to get her GED. She had even enlisted the help

306

of our cousin Missy, who had come up from Salt Lake City to tutor her. Missy had worked with Audrey for an entire summer, at the end of which she'd declared that Audrey's education hovered somewhere between the fourth- and fifth-grade levels, and that a GED was out of the question. I chewed my lip and stared at her daughter, who had brought me a drawing, wondering what education she could hope to receive from a mother who had none herself.

We made breakfast for the children, then played with them in the snow. We baked, we watched crime dramas and designed beaded bracelets. It was as if I had stepped through a mirror and was living a day in the life I might have had, if I'd stayed on the mountain. But I hadn't stayed. My life had diverged from my sister's, and it felt as though there was no common ground between us. The hours passed; it was late afternoon; and still she felt distant from me, still she refused to meet my gaze.

I had brought a small porcelain tea set for her children, and when they began to quarrel over the teapot, I gathered up the pieces. The oldest girl reminded me that she was five now, which she said was too old to have a toy taken away. "If you act like a child," I said, "I'll treat you like one."

I don't know why I said it; I suppose Shawn was on my mind. I regretted the words even as they left my lips, hated myself for saying them. I turned to pass the tea set to my sister, so she could administer justice however she saw fit, but when I saw her expression I nearly dropped it. Her mouth hung open in a perfect circle.

"Shawn used to say that," she said, fixing her eyes on mine.

That moment would stay with me. I would remember it the next day, when I boarded a plane in Salt Lake City, and it would still be on my mind when I landed in London. It was the shock of it that I couldn't shake. Somehow, it had never occurred to me that my sister might have lived my life before I did.

*

That term, I presented myself to the university like resin to a sculptor. I believed I could be remade, my mind recast. I forced myself to befriend other students, clumsily introducing myself again and again until I had a small circle of friends. Then I set out to obliterate the barriers that separated me from them. I tasted red wine for the first time, and my new friends laughed at my pinched face. I discarded my high-necked blouses and began to wear more fashionable cuts—fitted, often sleeveless, with less restrictive necklines. In photos from this period I'm struck by the symmetry: I look like everyone else.

In April I began to do well. I wrote an essay on John Stuart Mill's concept of self-sovereignty, and my supervisor, Dr. David Runciman, said that if my dissertation was of the same quality, I might be accepted to Cambridge for a PhD. I was stunned: I, who had sneaked into this grand place as an impostor, might now enter through the front door. I set to work on my dissertation, again choosing Mill as the topic.

One afternoon near the end of term, when I was eating lunch in the library cafeteria, I recognized a group of students from my program. They were seated together at a small table. I asked if I could join them, and a tall Italian named Nic nodded. From the conversation I gathered that Nic had invited the others to visit him in Rome during the spring holiday. "You can come, too," he said.

We handed in our final essays for the term, then boarded a plane. On our first evening in Rome, we climbed one of the seven hills and looked out over the metropolis. Byzantine domes hovered over the city like rising balloons. It was nearly dusk; the streets were bathed in amber. It wasn't the color of a modern city, of steel, glass and concrete. It was the color of sunset. It didn't look real. Nic asked me what I thought of his home, and that was all I could say: it didn't look real.

At breakfast the next morning, the others talked about

their families. Someone's father was a diplomat; another's was an Oxford don. I was asked about my parents. I said my father owned a junkyard.

Nic took us to the conservatory where he'd studied violin. It was in the heart of Rome and was richly furnished, with a grand staircase and resonant halls. I tried to imagine what it would have been like to study in such a place, to walk across marble floors each morning and, day after day, come to associate learning with beauty. But my imagination failed me. I could only imagine the school as I was experiencing it now, as a kind of museum, a relic from someone else's life.

For two days we explored Rome, a city that is both a living organism and a fossil. Bleached structures from antiquity lay like dried bones, embedded in pulsating cables and thrumming traffic, the arteries of modern life. We visited the Pantheon, the Roman Forum, the Sistine Chapel. My instinct was to worship, to venerate. That was how I felt toward the whole city: that it should be behind glass, adored from a distance, never touched, never altered. My companions moved through the city differently, aware of its significance but not subdued by it. They were not hushed by the Trevi Fountain; they were not silenced by the Colosseum. Instead, as we moved from one relic to the next, they debated philosophy— Hobbes and Descartes, Aquinas and Machiavelli. There was a kind of symbiosis in their relationship to these grand places: they gave life to the ancient architecture by making it the backdrop of their discourse, by refusing to worship at its altar as if it were a dead thing.

On the third night there was a rainstorm. I stood on Nic's balcony and watched streaks of lightning race across the sky, claps of thunder chasing them. It was like being on Buck's Peak, to feel such power in the earth and sky.

The next morning was cloudless. We took a picnic of wine and pastries to the grounds of the Villa Borghese. The sun was hot, the pastries ambrosial. I could not remember ever feeling more present. Someone said something about Hobbes, and without thinking I recited a line from Mill. It seemed the natural thing, to bring this voice from the past into a moment so saturated with the past already, even if the voice was mixed with my own. There was a pause while everyone checked to see who had spoken, then someone asked which text the line was from, and the conversation moved forward.

For the rest of the week, I experienced Rome as they did: as a place of history, but also as a place of life, of food and traffic and conflict and thunder. The city was no longer a museum; it was as vivid to me as Buck's Peak. The Piazza del Popolo. The Baths of Caracalla. Castel Sant'Angelo. These became as real to my mind as the Princess, the red railway car, the Shear. The world they represented, of philosophy, science, literature—an entire civilization—took on a life that was distinct from the life I had known. At the Galleria Nazionale d'Arte Antica, I stood before Caravaggio's *Judith Beheading Holofernes* and did not once think about chickens.

I don't know what caused the transformation, why suddenly I could engage with the great thinkers of the past, rather than revere them to the point of muteness. But there was something about that city, with its white marble and black asphalt, crusted with history, ablaze in traffic lights, that showed me I could admire the past without being silenced by it.

I was still breathing in the fustiness of ancient stone when I arrived in Cambridge. I rushed up the staircase, anxious to check my email, knowing there would be a message from Drew. When I opened my laptop, I saw that Drew had written, but so had someone else: my sister.

I opened Audrey's message. It was written in one long paragraph, with little punctuation and many spelling errors, and at first I fixated on these grammatical irregularities as a way to mute the text. But the words would not be hushed; they shouted at me from the screen.

Audrey said she should have stopped Shawn many years ago, before he could do to me what he'd done to her. She said that when she was young, she'd wanted to tell Mother, to ask for help, but she'd thought Mother wouldn't believe her. She'd been right. Before her wedding, she'd experienced nightmares and flashbacks, and she'd told Mother about them. Mother had said the memories were false, impossible. *I should have helped you,* Audrey wrote. *But when my own mother didn't believe me, I stopped believing myself.**

It was a mistake she was going to correct. *I believe God will hold me accountable if I don't stop Shawn from hurting anyone else,* she wrote. She was going to confront him, and our parents, and she was asking me to stand with her. *I am doing this with or without you. But without you, I will probably lose.*

I sat in the dark for a long time. I resented her for writing me. I felt she had torn me from one world, one life, where I was happy, and dragged me back into another.

I typed a response. I told her she was right, that of course we should stop Shawn, but I asked her to do nothing until I could return to Idaho. I don't know why I asked her to wait, what benefit I thought time would yield. I don't know what I thought would happen when we talked to our parents, but I understood instinctively what was at stake. As long as we had never asked, it was possible to believe that they would help. To tell them was to risk the unthinkable: it was to risk learning that they already knew.

Audrey did not wait, not even a day. The next morning she

* The italics used on this page indicate that the language from the referenced email is paraphrased, not directly quoted.

showed my email to Mother. I cannot imagine the details of that conversation, but I know that for Audrey it must have been a tremendous relief, laying my words before our mother, finally able to say, I'm not crazy. It happened to Tara, too.

For all of that day, Mother pondered it. Then she decided she had to hear the words from me. It was late afternoon in Idaho, nearly midnight in England, when my mother, unsure how to place an international call, found me online. The words on the screen were small, confined to a tiny text box in the corner of the browser, but somehow they seemed to swallow the room. She told me she had read my letter. I braced myself for her rage.

It is painful to face reality, she wrote. *To realize there was something ugly, and I refused to see it.**

I had to read those lines a number of times before I understood them. Before I realized that she was not angry, not blaming me, or trying to convince me I had only imagined. She believed me.

Don't blame yourself, I told her. Your mind was never the same after the accident.

Maybe, she said. *But sometimes I think we choose our illnesses, because they benefit us in some way.*

I asked Mother why she'd never stopped Shawn from hurting me.

Shawn always said you picked the fights, and I guess I wanted to believe that, because it was easier. Because you were strong and rational, and anyone could see that Shawn was not.

That didn't make sense. If I had seemed rational, why had Mother believed Shawn when he'd told her I was picking fights? That I needed to be subdued, disciplined.

* The italicized language in the description of the referenced text exchange is paraphrased, not directly quoted.

I'm a mother, she said. *Mothers protect. And Shawn was so damaged.*

I wanted to say that she was also *my* mother but I didn't. I don't think Dad will believe any of this, I typed.

He will, she wrote. *But it's hard for him. It reminds him of the damage his bipolar has caused to our family.*

I had never heard Mother admit that Dad might be mentally ill. Years before, I had told her what I'd learned in my psychology class about bipolar disorder and schizophrenia, but she had shrugged it off. Hearing her say it now felt liberating. The illness gave me something to attack besides my father, so when Mother asked why I hadn't come to her sooner, why I hadn't asked for help, I answered honestly.

Because you were so bullied by Dad, I said. You were not powerful in the house. Dad ran things, and he was not going to help us.

I am stronger now, she said. *I no longer run scared.*

When I read this, I imagined my mother as a young woman, brilliant and energetic, but also anxious and complying. Then the image changed, her body thinning, elongating, her hair flowing, long and silver.

Emily is being bullied, I wrote.

She is, Mother said. *Like I was.*

She is you, I said.

She is me. But we know better now. We can rewrite the story.

I asked about a memory. It was from the weeks before I'd left for BYU, after Shawn had had a particularly bad night. He'd brought Mother to tears, then plopped onto the sofa and turned on the TV. I'd found her sobbing at the kitchen table, and she'd asked me not to go to BYU. "You're the only one strong enough to handle him," she'd said. "I can't, and your father can't. It has to be you."

I typed slowly, reluctantly: Do you remember telling me

not to go to school, that I was the only one who could handle Shawn?

Yes, I remember that.

There was a pause, then more words appeared—words I hadn't known I needed to hear, but once I saw them, I realized I'd been searching my whole life for them.

You were my child. I should have protected you.

I lived a lifetime in the moment I read those lines, a life that was not the one I had actually lived. I became a different person, who remembered a different childhood. I didn't understand the magic of those words then, and I don't understand it now. I know only this: that when my mother told me she had not been the mother to me that she wished she'd been, she became that mother for the first time.

I love you, I wrote, and closed my laptop.

Mother and I spoke only once about that conversation, on the phone, a week later. "It's being dealt with," she said. "I told your father what you and your sister said. Shawn will get help."

I put the issue from my mind. My mother had taken up the cause. She was strong. She had built that business, with all those people working for her, and it dwarfed my father's business, and all the other businesses in the whole town; she, that docile woman, had a power in her the rest of us couldn't contemplate. And Dad. He had changed. He was softer, more prone to laugh. The future could be different from the past. Even the past could be different from the past, because my memories could change: I no longer remembered Mother listening in the kitchen while Shawn pinned me to the floor, pressing my windpipe. I no longer remembered her looking away.

My life in Cambridge was transformed—or rather, I was transformed into someone who believed she belonged in Cambridge. The shame I'd long felt about my family leaked out of me almost overnight. For the first time in my life I talked openly about where I'd come from. I admitted to my friends that I'd never been to school. I described Buck's Peak, with its many junkyards, barns, corrals. I even told them about the root cellar full of supplies in the wheat field, and the gasoline buried near the old barn.

I told them I'd been poor, I told them I'd been ignorant, and in telling them this I felt not the slightest prick of shame. Only then did I understand where the shame had come from: it wasn't that I hadn't studied in a marble conservatory, or that my father wasn't a diplomat. It wasn't that Dad was half out of his mind, or that Mother followed him. It had come from having a father who shoved me toward the chomping blades of the shear, instead of pulling me away from them. It had come from those moments on the floor, from knowing that Mother was in the next room, closing her eyes and ears to me, and choosing, for that moment, not to be my mother at all.

I fashioned a new history for myself. I became a popular dinner guest, with my stories of hunting and horses, of scrapping and fighting mountain fires. Of my brilliant mother, midwife and entrepreneur; of my eccentric father, junkman and zealot. I thought I was finally being honest about the life I'd had before. It wasn't the truth exactly, but it was true in a larger sense: true to what *would* be, in the future, now that everything had changed for the better. Now that Mother had found her strength.

The past was a ghost, insubstantial, unaffecting. Only the future had weight.

32

A Brawling Woman in a Wide House

When I next returned to Buck's Peak, it was autumn and Grandma-down-the-hill was dying. For nine years she had battled the cancer in her bone marrow; now the contest was ending. I had just learned that I'd won a place at Cambridge to study for a PhD when Mother wrote to me. "Grandma is in the hospital again," she said. "Come quick. I think this will be the last time."

When I landed in Salt Lake, Grandma was drifting in and out of consciousness. Drew met me at the airport. We were more than friends by then, and Drew said he would drive me to Idaho, to the hospital in town.

I hadn't been back there since I'd taken Shawn years before, and as I walked down its white, antiseptic hallway, it was difficult not to think of him. We found Grandma's room. Grandpa was seated at her bedside, holding her speckled hand. Her eyes were open and she looked at me. "It's my little Tara, come all the way from England," she said, then her eyes closed. Grandpa squeezed her hand but she was asleep. A nurse told us she would likely sleep for hours.

Drew said he would drive me to Buck's Peak. I agreed, and it wasn't until the mountain came into view that I wondered whether I'd made a mistake. Drew had heard my stories, but still there was a risk in bringing him here: this was not a story, and I doubted whether anyone would play the part I had written for them.

The house was in chaos. There were women everywhere, some taking orders over the phone, others mixing oils or straining tinctures. There was a new annex on the south side of the house, where younger women were filling bottles and packaging orders for shipment. I left Drew in the living room and went to the bathroom, which was the only room in the house that still looked the way I remembered it. When I came out I walked straight into a thin old woman with wiry hair and large, square glasses.

"This bathroom is for senior management only," she said. "Bottle fillers must use the bathroom in the annex."

"I don't work here," I said.

She stared at me. Of course I worked here. Everyone worked here.

"This bathroom is for senior management," she repeated, straightening to her full height. "*You* are not allowed to leave the annex."

She walked away before I could reply.

I still hadn't seen either of my parents. I weaved my way back through the house and found Drew on the sofa, listening to a woman explain that aspirin can cause infertility. I grasped his hand and pulled him behind me, cutting a path through the strangers.

"Is this place for real?" he said.

I found Mother in a windowless room in the basement. I had the impression that she was hiding there. I introduced her to Drew and she smiled warmly. "Where's Dad?" I said. I suspected that he was sick in bed, as he had been prone to pulmonary illnesses since the explosion had charred his lungs.

"I'm sure he's in the fray," she said, rolling her eyes at the ceiling, which thrummed with the thudding of feet.

Mother came with us upstairs. The moment she appeared on the landing, she was hailed by several of her employees with questions from clients. Everyone seemed to want her opinion—about their burns, their heart tremors, their underweight infants. She waved them off and pressed forward. The impression she gave as she moved through her own house was of a celebrity in a crowded restaurant, trying not to be recognized.

My father's desk was the size of a car. It was parked in the center of the chaos. He was on the phone, which he'd wedged between his cheek and shoulder so it wouldn't slip through his waxy hands. "Doctors can't help with them diabetes," he said, much too loudly. "But the Lord can!"

I looked sideways at Drew, who was smiling. Dad hung up and turned toward us. He greeted Drew with a large grin. He radiated energy, feeding off the general bedlam of the house. Drew said he was impressed with the business, and Dad seemed to grow six inches. "We've been blessed for doing the Lord's work," he said.

The phone rang again. There were at least three employees tasked with answering it, but Dad leapt for the receiver as if he'd been waiting for an important call. I'd never seen him so full of life.

"The power of God on earth," he shouted into the mouthpiece. "That's what these oils are: God's pharmacy!"

The noise in the house was disorienting, so I took Drew up the mountain. We strolled through fields of wild wheat and from there into the skirt of pines at the mountain base. The fall colors were soothing and we stayed for hours, gazing down at the quiet valley. It was late afternoon when we finally made our way back to the house and Drew left for Salt Lake City.

I entered the Chapel through the French doors and was surprised by the silence. The house was empty, every phone disconnected, every workstation abandoned. Mother sat alone in the center of the room.

"The hospital called," she said. "Grandma's gone."

My father lost his appetite for the business. He started getting out of bed later and later, and when he did, it seemed it was only to insult or accuse. He shouted at Shawn about the junk-yard and lectured Mother about her management of the employees. He snapped at Audrey when she tried to make him lunch, and barked at me for typing too loudly. It was as if he wanted to fight, to punish himself for the old woman's death. Or maybe the punishment was for her life, for the conflict that had been between them, which had only ended now she was dead.

The house slowly filled again. The phones were reconnected, and women materialized to answer them. Dad's desk remained empty. He spent his days in bed, gazing up at the stucco ceiling. I brought him supper, as I had as a child, and wondered now, as I'd wondered then, whether he knew I was there.

Mother moved about the house with the vitality of ten people, mixing tinctures and essential oils, directing her employees between making funeral arrangements and cooking for every cousin and aunt who dropped in unannounced to reminisce about Grandma. As often as not I'd find her in an apron, hovering over a roast with a phone in each hand, one a client, the other an uncle or friend calling to offer condolences. Through all this my father remained in bed.

Dad spoke at the funeral. His speech was a twenty-minute sermon on God's promises to Abraham. He mentioned my grandmother twice. To strangers it must have seemed he was hardly affected by the loss of his mother, but we knew better, we who could see the devastation.

When we arrived home from the service, Dad was incensed

that lunch wasn't ready. Mother scrambled to serve the stew she'd left to slow-cook, but after the meal Dad seemed equally frustrated by the dishes, which Mother hurriedly cleaned, and then by his grandchildren, who played noisily while Mother dashed about trying to hush them.

That evening, when the house was empty and quiet, I listened from the living room as my parents argued in the kitchen.

"The least you could do," Mother said, "is fill out these thank-you cards. It was *your* mother, after all."

"That's wifely work," Dad said. "I've never heard of a man writing cards."

He had said the exact wrong thing. For ten years, Mother had been the primary breadwinner, while continuing to cook meals, clean the house, do the laundry, and I had never once heard her express anything like resentment. Until now.

"Then you should do the *husband's work*," she said, her voice raised.

Soon they were both shouting. Dad tried to corral her, to subdue her with a show of anger, the way he always had, but this only made her more stubborn. Eventually she tossed the cards on the table and said, "Fill them out or don't. But if you don't, no one will." Then she marched downstairs. Dad followed, and for an hour their shouts rose up through the floor. I'd never heard my parents shout like that—at least, not my mother. I'd never seen her refuse to give way.

The next morning I found Dad in the kitchen, dumping flour into a glue-like substance I assumed was supposed to be pancake batter. When he saw me, he dropped the flour and sat at the table. "You're a woman, ain'tcha?" he said. "Well, this here's a kitchen." We stared at each other and I contemplated the distance that had sprung up between us—how natural those words sounded to his ears, how grating to mine.

It wasn't like Mother to leave Dad to make his own

breakfast. I thought she might be ill and went downstairs to check on her. I'd barely made it to the landing when I heard it: deep sobs coming from the bathroom, muffled by the steady drone of a blow-dryer. I stood outside the door and listened for more than a minute, paralyzed. Would she want me to leave, to pretend I hadn't heard? I waited for her to catch her breath, but her sobs only grew more desperate.

I knocked. "It's me," I said.

The door opened, a sliver at first, then wider, and there was my mother, her skin glistening from the shower, wrapped in a towel that was too small to cover her. I had never seen my mother so exposed, and instinctively I closed my eyes. The world went black. I heard a thud, the cracking of plastic, and opened my eyes. Mother had dropped the blow-dryer and it had struck the floor, its roar now doubled as it rebounded off the exposed concrete. I looked at her, and as I did she pulled me to her and held me. The wet from her body seeped into my clothes, and I felt droplets slide from her hair and onto my shoulder.

33

Sorcery of Physics

I didn't stay long on Buck's Peak, maybe a week. On the day I left the mountain, Audrey asked me not to go. I have no memory of the conversation, but I remember writing the journal entry about it. I wrote it my first night back in Cambridge, while sitting on a stone bridge and staring up at King's College Chapel. I remember the river, which was calm; I remember the slow drift of autumn leaves resting on the glassy surface. I remember the scratch of my pen moving across the page, recounting in detail, for a full eight pages, precisely what my sister had said. But the memory of her saying it is gone: it is as if I wrote in order to forget.

Audrey asked me to stay. Shawn was too strong, she said, too persuasive, for her to confront him alone. I told her she wasn't alone, she had Mother. Audrey said I didn't understand. No one had believed us after all. If we asked Dad for help, she was sure he'd call us both liars. I told her our parents had changed and we should trust them. Then I boarded a plane and took myself five thousand miles away.

If I felt guilty to be documenting my sister's fears from such a safe distance, surrounded by grand libraries and ancient chapels, I gave only one indication of it, in the last line of the entry: *Cambridge is less beautiful tonight.*

Drew had come with me to Cambridge, having been admitted to a master's program in Middle Eastern studies. I told him about my conversation with Audrey. He was the first boyfriend in whom I confided about my family—really confided, the truth and not just amusing anecdotes. Of course all that is in the past, I said. My family is different now. But you should know. So you can watch me. In case I do something crazy.

The first term passed in a flurry of dinners and late-night parties, punctuated by even later nights in the library. To qualify for a PhD, I had to produce a piece of original academic research. In other words, having spent five years reading history, I was now being asked to write it.

But to write what? While reading for my master's thesis, I'd been surprised to discover echoes of Mormon theology in the great philosophers of the nineteenth century. I mentioned this to David Runciman, my supervisor. "*That's* your project," he said. "You can do something no one has done: you can examine Mormonism not just as a religious movement, but as an intellectual one."

I began to reread the letters of Joseph Smith and Brigham Young. As a child I'd read those letters as an act of worship; now I read them with different eyes, not the eyes of a critic, but also not the eyes of a disciple. I examined polygamy, not as a doctrine but as a social policy. I measured it against its own aims, as well as against other movements and theories from the same period. It felt like a radical act.

My friends in Cambridge had become a kind of family, and I felt a sense of belonging with them that, for many years, had been absent on Buck's Peak. Sometimes I felt damned for those feelings. No natural sister should love a stranger more than a brother, I thought, and what sort of daughter prefers a teacher to her own father?

But although I wished it were otherwise, I did not want to go home. I preferred the family I had chosen to the one I had been given, so the happier I became in Cambridge, the more my happiness was made fetid by my feeling that I had betrayed Buck's Peak. That feeling became a physical part of me, something I could taste on my tongue or smell on my own breath.

I bought a ticket to Idaho for Christmas. The night before my flight, there was a feast in my college. One of my friends had formed a chamber choir that was to sing carols during dinner. The choir had been rehearsing for weeks, but on the day of the feast the soprano fell ill with bronchitis. My phone rang late that afternoon. It was my friend. "Please tell me you know someone who can sing," he said.

I had not sung for years, and never without my father to hear me, but a few hours later I joined the chamber choir on a platform near the rafters, above the massive Christmas tree that dominated the hall. I treasured the moment, taking pleasure in the lightness I felt to have music once again floating up from my chest, and wondering whether Dad, if he were here, would have braved the university and all its socialism to hear me sing. I believed he would.

Buck's Peak was unchanged. The Princess was buried in snow but I could see the deep contours of her legs. Mother was in the kitchen when I arrived, stirring a stew with one hand and with the other holding the phone and explaining the properties of motherwort. Dad's desk was still empty. He was in the basement, Mother said, in bed. Something had hold of his lungs.

A burly stranger shuffled through the back door. Several seconds passed before I recognized my brother. Luke's beard was so thick, he looked like one of his goats. His left eye was white and dead: he'd been shot in the face with a paintball gun a few months before. He crossed the room and clapped me on the back, and I stared into his remaining eye, looking for something familiar. But it wasn't until I saw the raised scar on his forearm, a curved check mark two inches wide from where the Shear had bitten his flesh, that I was sure this man was my brother.[7] He told me he was living with his wife and a pack of kids in a mobile home behind the barn, making his money working oil rigs in North Dakota.

Two days passed. Dad came upstairs every evening and settled himself into a sofa in the Chapel, where he would cough and watch TV or read the Old Testament. I spent my days studying or helping Mother.

On the third evening I was at the kitchen table, reading, when Shawn and Benjamin shuffled through the back door. Benjamin was telling Shawn about a punch he'd thrown after a fender bender in town. He said that before climbing out of his truck to confront the other driver, he'd slipped his handgun into the waistband of his jeans. "The guy didn't know what he was getting into," Benjamin said, grinning.

"Only an idiot brings a gun into a mess like that," Shawn said.

"I wasn't gonna use it," Benjamin muttered.

"Then don't bring it," Shawn said. "Then you *know* you won't use it. If you bring it you *might* use it, that's how things are. A fistfight can turn into a gunfight real quick."

Shawn spoke calmly, thoughtfully. His blond hair was filthy and uncut, growing wild, and his face was covered in stubble the color of shale. His eyes shone from under the oil and dirt, blazes of blue in clouds of ash. His expression, as well as his words, seemed to belong to a much older man, a man whose hot blood had cooled, who was at peace.

Shawn turned to me. I had been avoiding him, but

suddenly that seemed unfair. He had changed; it was cruel to pretend he hadn't. He asked if I'd like to go for a drive, and I said I would. Shawn wanted ice cream so we got milkshakes. The conversation was calm, comfortable, like it had been years before on those dusky evenings in the corral. He told me about running the crew without Dad, about Peter's frail lungs—about the surgeries and the oxygen tubes he still wore at night.

We were nearly home, only a mile from Buck's Peak, when Shawn cranked the wheel and the car skidded on the ice. He accelerated through the spin, the tires caught, and the car leapt onto a side road.

"Where we going?" I asked, but the road only went one place.

The church was dark, the parking lot deserted.

Shawn circled the lot, then parked near the main entrance. He switched off the ignition and the headlights faded. I could barely make out the curve of his face in the dark.

"You talk much to Audrey?" he said.

"Not really," I said.

He seemed to relax, then he said, "Audrey is a lying piece of shit."

I looked away, fixing my eyes on the church spire, visible against the light from the stars.

"I'd put a bullet in her head," Shawn said, and I felt his body shift toward me. "But I don't want to waste a good bullet on a worthless bitch."

It was crucial that I not look at him. As long as I kept my eyes on the spire, I almost believed he couldn't touch me. Almost. Because even while I clung to this belief, I waited to feel his hands on my neck. I knew I would feel them, and soon, but I didn't dare do anything that might break the spell of waiting. In that moment part of me believed, as I had always believed, that it would be me who broke the spell, who caused it to break. When the stillness shattered and his fury rushed at me, I would know that something I had done was the catalyst, the cause. There is hope in such a superstition; there is the illusion of control.

I stayed still, without thought or motion.

The ignition clicked, the engine growled to life. Warm air flooded through the vents.

"You feel like a movie?" Shawn said. His voice was casual. I watched the world revolve as the car spun around and lurched back to the highway. "A movie sounds just right," he said.

I said nothing, unwilling to move or speak lest I offend the strange sorcery of physics that I still believed had saved me. Shawn seemed unaware of my silence. He drove the last mile to Buck's Peak chatting cheerfully, almost playfully, about whether to watch *The Man Who Knew Too Little,* or not.

34

The Substance of Things

I didn't feel particularly brave as I approached my father in the Chapel that night. I saw my role as reconnaissance: I was there to relay information, to tell Dad that Shawn had threatened Audrey, because Dad would know what to do.

Or perhaps I was calm because I was not there, not really. Maybe I was across an ocean, on another continent, reading Hume under a stone archway. Maybe I was racing through King's College, the *Discourse on Inequality* tucked under my arm.

"Dad, I need to tell you something."

I said that Shawn had made a joke about shooting Audrey, and that I thought it was because Audrey had confronted him about his behavior. Dad stared at me, and the skin where his lips had been tightened. He shouted for Mother and she appeared. Her mood was somber; I couldn't understand why she wouldn't look me in the eye.

"What exactly are you saying?" Dad said.

From that moment it was an interrogation. Every time I suggested that Shawn was violent or manipulative in any way, Dad shouted at me: "Where's your proof? Do you have proof?"

"I have journals," I said.

"Get them, I'm going to read them."

"I don't have them with me." This was a lie; they were under my bed.

"What the hell am I supposed to think if you ain't got proof?" Dad was still shouting. Mother sat on the sofa's edge, her mouth open in a slant. She looked in agony.

"You don't need proof," I said quietly. "You've seen it. You've both seen it."

Dad said I wouldn't be happy until Shawn was rotting in prison, that I'd come back from Cambridge just to raise hell. I said I didn't want Shawn in prison but that some type of intervention was needed. I turned to Mother, waiting for her to add her voice to mine, but she was silent. Her eyes were fixed on the floor as if Dad and I were not there.

There was a moment when I realized she would not speak, that she would sit there and say nothing, that I was alone. I tried to calm Dad but my voice trembled, cracked. Then I was wailing—sobs erupted from somewhere, some part of me I had not felt in years, that I had forgotten existed. I thought I might vomit.

I ran to the bathroom. I was shaking from my feet to my fingers.

I had to strangle the sobs quickly—Dad would never take me seriously if I couldn't—so I stopped the bawling using the old methods: staring my face down in the mirror and scolding it for every tear. It was such a familiar process, that in doing it I shattered the illusion I'd been building so carefully for the past year. The fake past, the fake future, both gone.

I stared at the reflection. The mirror was mesmeric, with its triple panels trimmed with false oak. It was the same mirror I'd gazed into as a child, then as a girl, then as a youth, half woman, half girl. Behind me was the same toilet Shawn had put my head in, holding me there until I confessed I was a whore.

I had often locked myself in this bathroom after Shawn let me go. I would move the panels until they showed my face three times, then I would glare at each one, contemplating what Shawn had said and what he had made me say, until it all began to feel true instead of just something I had said to make the pain stop. And here I was still, and here was the mirror. The same face, repeated in the same three panels.

Except it wasn't. This face was older, and floating above a soft cashmere sweater. But Dr. Kerry was right: it wasn't the clothes that made this face, this woman, different. It was something behind her eyes, something in the set of her jaw—a hope or belief or conviction—that a life is not a thing unalterable. I don't have a word for what it was I saw, but I suppose it was something like *faith*.

I had regained a fragile sense of calm, and I left the bathroom carrying that calmness delicately, as if it were a china plate balancing on my head. I walked slowly down the hall, taking small, even steps.

"I'm going to bed," I said when I'd made it to the Chapel. "We'll talk about this tomorrow."

Dad was at his desk, holding a phone in his left hand. "We'll talk about it now," he said. "I told Shawn what you said. He is coming."

I considered making a run for it. Could I get to my car before Shawn made it to the house? Where were the keys? I need my laptop, I thought, with my research. *Leave it,* the girl from the mirror said.

Dad told me to sit and I did. I don't know how long I waited, paralyzed with indecision, but I was still wondering if there was time to escape when the French doors opened and Shawn walked in. Suddenly the vast room felt tiny. I looked at my hands. I couldn't raise my eyes.

I heard footsteps. Shawn had crossed the room and was

now sitting next to me on the sofa. He waited for me to look at him, and when I didn't he reached out and took my hand. Gently, as if he were unfolding the petals of a rose, he peeled open my fingers and dropped something into them. I felt the cold of the blade before I saw it, and sensed the blood even before I glimpsed the red streak staining my palm.

The knife was small, only five or six inches long and very thin. The blade glowed crimson. I rubbed my thumb and index finger together, then brought them to my nose and inhaled. Metallic. It was definitely blood. Not mine—he'd merely handed me the knife—but whose?

"If you're smart, Siddle Lister," Shawn said, "you'll use this on yourself. Because it will be better than what I'll do to you if you don't."

"That's uncalled for," Mother said.

I gaped at Mother, then at Shawn. I must have seemed like an idiot to them, but I couldn't grasp what was happening well enough to respond to it. I half-wondered if I should return to the bathroom and climb through the mirror, then send out the other girl, the one who was sixteen. *She* could handle this, I thought. She would not be afraid, like I was. She would not be hurt, like I was. She was a thing of stone, with no fleshy tenderness. I did not yet understand that it was this fact of being tender—of having lived some years of a life that allowed tenderness—that would, finally, save me.

I stared at the blade. Dad began a lecture, pausing often so Mother could ratify his remarks. I heard voices, among them my own, chanting harmonies in an ancient hall. I heard laughter, the slosh of wine being poured from a bottle, the tinkle of butter knives tapping porcelain. I heard little of my father's speech, but I remember exactly, as if it were happening now, being transported over an ocean and back through three sunsets, to the night I had sung with my friends in the chamber choir. *I must have fallen asleep,* I thought. *Too much wine. Too much Christmas turkey.*

Having decided I was dreaming, I did what one does in dreams: I tried to understand and use the rules of this queer reality. I reasoned with the strange shadows impersonating my family, and when reasoning failed, I lied. The impostors had bent reality. Now it was my turn. I told Shawn I hadn't said anything to Dad. I said things like "I don't know how Dad got that idea" and "Dad must have misheard me," hoping that if I rejected their percipience, they would simply dissipate. An hour later, when the four of us were still seated on the sofas, I finally came to terms with their physical persistence. They were here, and so was I.

The blood on my hands had dried. The knife lay on the carpet, forgotten by everyone except me. I tried not to stare at it. Whose was the blood? I studied my brother. He had not cut himself.

Dad had begun a new lecture, and this time I was present enough to hear it. He explained that little girls need to be instructed in how to behave appropriately around men, so as not to be too inviting. He'd noticed indecent habits in my sister's daughters, the oldest of whom was six. Shawn was calm. He had been worn down by the sheer duration of Dad's droning. More than that, he felt protected, justified, so that when the lecture finally ended he said to me, "I don't know what you said to Dad tonight, but I can tell just by looking at you that I've hurt you. And I'm sorry."

We hugged. We laughed like we always did after a fight. I smiled at him like I'd always done, like *she* would have. But *she* wasn't there, and the smile was a fake.

I went to my room and shut the door, quietly sliding the bolt, and called Drew. I was nearly incoherent with panic but eventually he understood. He said I should leave, right now, and he'd meet me halfway. I can't, I said. At this moment things are calm. If I try to run off in the middle of the night, I don't know what will happen.

I went to bed but not to sleep. I waited until six in the morning, then I found Mother in the kitchen. I'd borrowed the car I was driving from Drew, so I told Mother something had come up unexpectedly, that Drew needed his car in Salt Lake. I said I'd be back in a day or two.

A few minutes later I was driving down the hill. The highway was in sight when I saw something and stopped. It was the trailer where Shawn lived with Emily and Peter. A few feet from the trailer, near the door, the snow was stained with blood. Something had died there.

From Mother I would later learn it was Diego, a German shepherd Shawn had purchased a few years before. The dog had been a pet, much beloved by Peter. After Dad had called, Shawn had stepped outside and slashed the dog to death, while his young son, only feet away, listened to the dog scream. Mother said the execution had nothing to do with me, that it had to be done because Diego was killing Luke's chickens. It was a coincidence, she said.

I wanted to believe her but didn't. Diego had been killing Luke's chickens for more than a year. Besides, Diego was a purebred. Shawn had paid five hundred dollars for him. He could have been sold.

But the real reason I didn't believe her was the knife. I'd seen my father and brothers put down dozens of dogs over the years—strays mostly, that wouldn't stay out of the chicken coop. I'd never seen anyone use a knife on a dog. We shot them, in the head or the heart, so it was quick. But Shawn chose a knife, and a knife whose blade was barely bigger than his thumb. It was the knife you'd choose to experience a slaughter, to feel the blood running down your hand the moment the heart stopped beating. It wasn't the knife of a farmer, or even of a butcher. It was a knife of rage.

I don't know what happened in the days that followed. Even now, as I scrutinize the components of the confrontation—the threat, the denial, the lecture, the apology—it is difficult to relate them. When I considered it weeks later, it seemed I had made a thousand mistakes, driven a thousand knives into the heart of my own family. Only later did it occur to me that whatever damage was done that night might not have been done solely by me. And it was more than a year before I understood what should have been immediately apparent: that my mother had not confronted my father and my father had not confronted Shawn. Dad had never promised to help me and Audrey. Mother had lied.

Now, when I reflect on my mother's words, remembering the way they appeared as if by magic on the screen, one detail stands above the rest: that Mother described my father as bipolar. It was the exact disorder that I myself suspected. It was *my* word, not hers. Then I wonder if perhaps my mother, who had always reflected so perfectly the will of my father, had that night merely been reflecting mine.

No, I tell myself. They were her words. But hers or not, those words, which had so comforted and healed me, were hollow. I don't believe they were faithless, but sincerity failed to give them substance, and they were swept away by other, stronger currents.

35
West of the Sun

I fled the mountain with my bags half packed and did not retrieve anything that was left behind. I went to Salt Lake and spent the rest of the holidays with Drew.

I tried to forget that night. For the first time in fifteen years, I closed my journal and put it away. Journaling is contemplative, and I didn't want to contemplate anything.

After the New Year I returned to Cambridge, but I withdrew from my friends. I had seen the earth tremble, felt the preliminary shock; now I waited for the seismic event that would transform the landsape. I knew how it would begin. Shawn would think about what Dad had told him on the phone, and sooner or later he would realize that my denial—my claim that Dad had misunderstood me—was a lie. When he realized the truth, he would despise himself for perhaps an hour. Then he would transfer his loathing to me.

It was early March when it happened. Shawn sent me an email. It contained no greeting, no message whatsoever. Just a chapter from the Bible, from Matthew, with a single verse set apart in bold: *O generation of vipers, how can ye, being evil, speak good things?* It froze my blood.

Shawn called an hour later. His tone was casual, and we talked for twenty minutes about Peter, about how his lungs were developing. Then he said, "I have a decision to make, and I'd like your advice."

"Sure."

"I can't decide," he said. He paused, and I thought perhaps the connection had failed. "Whether I should kill you myself, or hire an assassin." There was a static-filled silence. "It might be cheaper to hire someone, when you figure in the cost of the flight."

I pretended I hadn't understood, but this only made him aggressive. Now he was hurling insults, snarling. I tried to calm him but it was pointless. We were seeing each other at long last. I hung up on him but he called again, and again and again, each time repeating the same lines, that I should watch my back, that his assassin was coming for me. I called my parents.

"He didn't mean it," Mother said. "Anyway, he doesn't have that kind of money."

"Not the point," I said.

Dad wanted evidence. "You didn't record the call?" he said. "How am I supposed to know if he was serious?"

"He sounded like he did when he threatened me with the bloody knife," I said.

"Well, he wasn't serious about that."

"Not the point," I said again.

The phone calls stopped, eventually, but not because of anything my parents did. They stopped when Shawn cut me out of his life. He wrote, telling me to stay away from his wife and child, and to stay the hell away from him. The email was long, a thousand words of accusation and bile, but by the end his tone was mournful. He said he loved his brothers, that they were the best men he knew. I loved you the best of all of them, he wrote, but you had a knife in my back the whole time.

It had been years since I'd had a relationship with my brother, but the loss of it, even with months of foreknowledge, stunned me.

My parents said he was justified in cutting me off. Dad said I was hysterical, that I'd thrown thoughtless accusations when it was obvious my memory couldn't be trusted. Mother said my rage was a real threat and that Shawn had a right to protect his family. "Your anger that night," she told me on the phone, meaning the night Shawn had killed Diego, "was twice as dangerous as Shawn has ever been."

Reality became fluid. The ground gave way beneath my feet, dragging me downward, spinning fast, like sand rushing through a hole in the bottom of the universe. The next time we spoke, Mother told me that the knife had never been meant as a threat. "Shawn was trying to make you more comfortable," she said. "He knew you'd be scared if *he* were holding a knife, so he gave it to you." A week later she said there had never been any knife at all.

"Talking to you," she said, "your reality is so *warped*. It's like talking to someone who wasn't even there."

I agreed. It was exactly like that.

I had a grant to study that summer in Paris. Drew came with me. Our flat was in the sixth arrondissement, near the Luxembourg Gardens. My life there was entirely new, and as near to a cliché as I could make it. I was drawn to those parts of the city where one could find the most tourists so I could throw myself into their center. It was a hectic form of forgetting, and I spent the summer in pursuit of it: of losing myself in swarms of travelers, allowing myself to be wiped clean of all personality and character, of all history. The more crass the attraction, the more I was drawn to it.

I had been in Paris for several weeks when, one afternoon, returning from a French lesson, I stopped at a café to check my email. There was a message from my sister.

My father had visited her—this I understood immediately—but I had to read the message several times before I understood what exactly had taken place. Our father had testified to her that Shawn had been cleansed by the Atonement of Christ, that he was a new man. Dad had warned Audrey that if she ever again brought up the past, it would destroy our entire family. It was God's will that Audrey and I forgive Shawn, Dad said. If we did not, ours would be the greater sin.

I could easily imagine this meeting, the gravity of my father as he sat across from my sister, the reverence and power in his words.

Audrey told Dad that she had accepted the power of the Atonement long ago, and had forgiven her brother. She said that I had provoked her, had stirred up anger in her. That I had betrayed her because I'd given myself over to fear, the realm of Satan, rather than walking in faith with God. I was dangerous, she said, because I was controlled by that fear, and by the Father of Fear, Lucifer.

That is how my sister ended her letter, by telling me I was not welcome in her home, or even to call her unless someone else was on the line to supervise, to keep her from succumbing to my influence. When I read this, I laughed out loud. The situation was perverse but not without irony: a few months before, Audrey had said that Shawn should be supervised around children. Now, after our efforts, the one who would be supervised was me.

When I lost my sister, I lost my family.

I knew my father would pay my brothers the same visit he'd paid her. Would they believe him? I thought they would. After all, Audrey would confirm it. My denials would be meaningless, the rantings of a stranger. I'd wandered too far, changed too much, bore too little resemblance to the scabby-kneed girl they remembered as their sister.

There was little hope of overpowering the history my father and sister were creating for me. Their account would claim my brothers first, then it would spread to my aunts, uncles, cousins, the whole valley. I had lost an entire kinship, and for what?

It was in this state of mind that I received another letter: I had won a visiting fellowship to Harvard. I don't think I have ever received a piece of news with more indifference. I knew I should be drunk with gratitude that I, an ignorant girl who'd crawled out of a scrap heap, should be allowed to study there, but I couldn't summon the fervor. I had begun to conceive of what my education might cost me, and I had begun to resent it.

After I read Audrey's letter, the past shifted. It started with my memories of her. They transformed. When I recalled any part of our childhood together, moments of tenderness or humor, of the little girl who had been me with the little girl who had been her, the memory was immediately changed, blemished, turned to rot. The past became as ghastly as the present.

The change was repeated with every member of my family. My memories of them became ominous, indicting. The female child in them, who had been me, stopped being a child and became something else, something threatening and ruthless, something that would consume them.

This monster child stalked me for a month before I found a logic to banish her: that I was likely insane. If I was insane, everything could be made to make sense. If I was sane, nothing could. This logic seemed damning. It was also a relief. I was not evil; I was clinical.

I began to defer, always, to the judgment of others. If Drew remembered something differently than I did, I would immediately concede the point. I began to rely on Drew to tell me the facts of our lives. I took pleasure in doubting myself about whether we'd seen a particular friend last week or the week before, or whether our favorite *crêperie* was next to the library or the museum. Questioning these trivial facts, and my ability to grasp them, allowed me to doubt whether anything I remembered had happened at all.

My journals were a problem. I knew that my memories were not memories only, that I had recorded them, that they existed in black and white. This meant that more than my memory was in error. The delusion was deeper, in the core of my mind, which invented in the very moment of occurrence, then recorded the fiction.

In the month that followed, I lived the life of a lunatic. Seeing sunshine, I suspected rain. I felt a relentless desire to ask people to verify whether they were seeing what I was seeing. Is this book blue? I wanted to ask. Is that man tall?

Sometimes this skepticism took the form of uncompromising certainty: there were days when the more I doubted my own sanity, the more violently I defended my own memories, my own "truth," as the only truth possible. Shawn was violent, dangerous, and my father was his protector. I couldn't bear to hear any other opinion on the subject.

In those moments I searched feverishly for a reason to think myself sane. Evidence. I craved it like air. I wrote to Erin—the woman Shawn had dated before and after Sadie, who I hadn't seen since I was sixteen. I told her what I remembered and asked her, bluntly, if I was deranged. She replied immediately that I was not. To help me trust myself, she shared her memories—of Shawn screaming at her that she was a whore. My mind snagged on that word. I had not told her that that was *my* word.

Erin told me another story. Once, when she had talked back to Shawn—just a little, she said, as if her manners were on trial—he'd ripped her from her house and slammed her head against a brick wall so hard she'd thought he was going to kill her. His hands locked around her throat. *I was lucky,* she wrote. *I had screamed before he began choking me, and my grandpa heard it and stopped him in time. But I know what I saw in his eyes.*

Her letter was like a handrail fixed to reality, one I could reach out and grasp when my mind began to spin. That is, until it occurred to me that she might be as crazy as I was. She was damaged, obviously, I told myself. How could I trust her account after what she'd been through? I could not give this woman credence because I, of all people, knew how crippling her psychological injuries were. So I continued searching for testimony from some other source.

Four years later, by pure chance, I would get it.

While traveling in Utah for research, I would meet a young man who would bristle at my last name.

"Westover," he would say, his face darkening. "Any relation to Shawn?"

"My brother."

"Well, the last time I saw your *brother*," he would say, emphasizing this last word as if he were spitting on it, "he had both hands wrapped around my cousin's neck, and he was smashing her head into a brick wall. He would have killed her, if it weren't for my grandfather."

And there it was. A witness. An impartial account. But by the time I heard it, I no longer needed to hear it. The fever of self-doubt had broken long ago. That's not to say I trusted my memory absolutely, but I trusted it as much as I trusted anybody else's, and more than some people's.

But that was years away.

36

Four Long Arms, Whirling

It was a sunny September afternoon when I heaved my suitcase through Harvard Yard. The colonial architecture felt foreign but also crisp and unimposing compared to the Gothic pinnacles of Cambridge. The central library, called the Widener, was the largest I had ever seen, and for a few minutes I forgot the past year and stared up at it, wonderstruck.

My room was in the graduate dorms near the law school. It was small and cavelike—dark, moist, frigid, with ashen walls and cold tiles the color of lead. I spent as little time in it as possible. The university seemed to offer a new beginning, and I intended to take it. I enrolled in every course I could squeeze into my schedule, from German idealism to the history of secularism to ethics and law. I joined a weekly study group to practice French, and another to learn knitting. The graduate school offered a free course on charcoal sketching. I had never drawn in my life but I signed up for that, too.

I began to read—Hume, Rousseau, Smith, Godwin, Wollstonecraft and Mill. I lost myself in the world they had lived in, the problems they had tried to solve. I became obsessed with their ideas about the family—with how a person ought to weigh their special obligations to kin against their obligations to society as a whole. Then I began to write, weaving the strands I'd found in Hume's *Principles of Morals* with filaments from Mill's *The Subjection of Women*. It was good work, I knew it even as I wrote it, and when I'd finished I set it aside. It was the first chapter of my PhD.

I returned from my sketching class one Saturday morning to find an email from my mother. We're coming to Harvard, she said. I read that line at least three times, certain she was joking. My father did not travel—I'd never known him to go anywhere except Arizona to visit his mother—so the idea that he would fly across the country to see a daughter he believed taken by the devil seemed ludicrous. Then I understood: he was coming to save me. Mother said they had already booked their flights and would be staying in my dorm room.

"Do you want a hotel?" I asked. They didn't.

A few days later, I signed in to an old chat program I hadn't used in years. There was a cheerful jingle and a name turned from gray to green. *Charles is online,* it said. I'm not sure who started the chat, or who suggested moving the conversation to the phone. We talked for an hour, and it was as if no time had passed.

He asked where I was studying; when I answered, he said, "Harvard! Holy hell!"

"Who woulda thought?" I said.

"I did," he said, and it was true. He had always seen me like that, long before there was any reason to.

I asked what he'd done after graduating from college and there was a strained silence. "Things didn't go the way I planned," he said. He'd never graduated. He'd dropped out his sophomore year after his son was born, because his wife was sick and there was a mound of medical bills. He'd signed on to work the oil rigs in Wyoming. "It was only supposed to be for a few months," he said. "That was a year ago."

I told him about Shawn, how I'd lost him, how I was losing the rest of my family. He listened quietly, then let out a long sigh and said, "Have you ever thought maybe you should just let them go?"

I hadn't, not once. "It's not permanent," I said. "I can fix it."

"Funny how you can change so much," Charles said, "but still sound the same as when we were seventeen."

My parents arrived as the leaves began to turn, when campus was at its most beautiful, the reds and yellows of autumn mingling with the burgundy of colonial brick. With his hay-seed grammar, denim shirt and lifetime-member NRA cap, Dad would have always been out of place at Harvard, but his scarring intensified the effect. I had seen him many times in the years since the explosion, but it wasn't until he came to Harvard, and I saw him set against my life there, that I realized how severely he'd disfigured himself. That awareness reached me through the eyes of others—strangers whose faces changed when he passed them in the street, who turned to get a second look. Then I would look at him, too, and notice how the skin on his chin was taut and plastic; how his lips lacked natural roundness; how his cheeks sucked inward at an angle that was almost skeletal. His right hand, which he often raised to point at some feature or other, was knotted and twisted, and when I gazed at it, set against Harvard's antediluvian steeples and columns, it seemed to me the claw of some mythical creature.

Dad had little interest in the university, so I took him into the city. I taught him how to take the T—how to feed his card through the slot and push through the rotating gate. He laughed out loud, as if it were a fabulous technology. A home-less man passed through our subway car and asked for a dollar. Dad gave him a crisp fifty.

"You keep that up in Boston, you won't have any money left," I said.

"Doubt it," Dad said with a wink. "The business is rolling. We got more than we can spend!"

Because his health was fragile, my father took the bed. I had purchased an air mattress, which I gave to Mother. I slept on the tile floor. Both my parents snored loudly, and I lay awake all night. When the sun finally rose I stayed on the floor, eyes closed, breathing slow, deep breaths, while my parents ransacked my mini fridge and discussed me in hushed tones.

"The Lord has commanded me to testify," Dad said. "She may yet be brought to the Lord."

While they plotted how to reconvert me, I plotted how to let them. I was ready to yield, even if it meant an exorcism. A miracle would be useful: if I could stage a convincing rebirth, I could dissociate from everything I'd said and done in the last year. I could take it all back—blame Lucifer and be given a clean slate. I imagined how esteemed I would be, as a newly cleansed vessel. How loved. All I had to do was swap my memories for theirs, and I could have my family.

My father wanted to visit the Sacred Grove in Palmyra, New York—the forest where, according to Joseph Smith, God had appeared and commanded him to found the true church. We rented a car and six hours later entered Palmyra. Near the grove, off the highway, there was a shimmering temple topped by a golden statue of the angel Moroni. Dad pulled over and asked me to cross the temple grounds. "Touch the temple," he said. "Its power will cleanse you."

I studied his face. His expression was stretched—earnest, desperate. With all that was in him, he was willing me to touch the temple and be saved.

My father and I looked at the temple. He saw God; I saw granite. We looked at each other. He saw a woman damned;

I saw an unhinged old man, literally disfigured by his beliefs. And yet, triumphant. I remembered the words of Sancho Panza: *An adventuring knight is someone who's beaten and then finds himself emperor.*

When I reflect on that moment now, the image blurs, reconstituting itself into that of a zealous knight astride a steed, charging into an imaginary battle, striking at shadows, hacking into thin air. His jaw is set, his back straight. His eyes blaze with conviction, throwing sparks that burn where they lie. My mother gives me a pale, disbelieving look, but when he turns his gaze on her they become of one mind, then they are both tilting at windmills.

I crossed the grounds and held my palm to the temple stone. I closed my eyes and tried to believe that this simple act could bring the miracle my parents prayed for. That all I had to do was touch this relic and, by the power of the Almighty, all would be put right. But I felt nothing. Just cold rock.

I returned to the car. "Let's go," I said.

When life itself seems lunatic, who knows where madness lies?

In the days that followed, I wrote that passage everywhere—unconsciously, compulsively. I find it now in books I was reading, in my lecture notes, in the margins of my journal. Its recitation was a mantra. I willed myself to believe it—to believe there was no real difference between what I knew to be true and what I knew to be false. To convince myself that there was some dignity in what I planned to do, in surrendering my own perceptions of right and wrong, of reality, of sanity itself, to earn the love of my parents. For them I believed I could don armor and charge at giants, even if I saw only windmills.

We entered the Sacred Grove. I walked ahead and found a bench beneath a canopy of trees. It was a lovely wood, heavy with history. It was the reason my ancestors had come to

America. A twig snapped, my parents appeared. They sat, one on either side of me.

My father spoke for two hours. He testified that he had beheld angels and demons. He had seen physical manifestations of evil and had been visited by the Lord Jesus Christ, like the prophets of old, like Joseph Smith had been in this very grove. His faith was no longer a faith, he said, but a perfect knowledge.

"You have been taken by Lucifer," he whispered, his hand on my shoulder. "I could feel it the moment I entered your room."

I thought of my dorm room—of the murky walls and frigid tiles, but also of the sunflowers Drew had sent, and of the textile wall hanging a friend from Zimbabwe had brought from his village.

Mother said nothing. She stared at the dirt, her eyes glossy, her lips pursed. Dad prodded me for a response. I searched myself, reaching deep, groping for the words he needed to hear. But they were not in me, not yet.

Before we returned to Harvard, I convinced my parents to take a detour to Niagara Falls. The mood in the car was heavy, and at first I regretted having suggested the diversion, but the moment Dad saw the falls he was transformed, elated. I had a camera. Dad had always hated cameras but when he saw mine his eyes shone with excitement. "Tara! Tara!" he shouted, running ahead of me and Mother. "Get yourself a picture of this angle. Ain't that pretty!" It was as if he realized we were making a memory, something beautiful we might need later. Or perhaps I'm projecting, because that was how I felt. *There are some photos from today that might help me forget the grove,* I wrote in my journal. *There's a picture of me and Dad happy, together. Proof that's possible.*

When we returned to Harvard, I offered to pay for a hotel. They refused to go. For a week we stumbled over one another in my dorm room. Every morning my father trudged up a flight of stairs to the communal shower in nothing but a small white towel. This would have humiliated me at BYU, but at Harvard I shrugged. I had transcended embarrassment. What did it matter who saw him, or what he said to them, or how shocked they were? It was *his* opinion I cared about; he was the one I was losing.

Then it was their last night, and still I had not been reborn.

Mother and I shuffled around the shared kitchen making a beef and potato casserole, which we brought into the room on trays. My father studied his plate quietly, as if he were alone. Mother made a few observations about the food, then she laughed nervously and was silent.

When we'd finished, Dad said he had a gift for me. "It's why I came," he said. "To offer you a priesthood blessing."

In Mormonism, the priesthood is God's power to act on earth—to advise, to counsel, to heal the sick, and to cast out demons. It is given to men. This was the moment: if I accepted the blessing, he would cleanse me. He would lay his hands on my head and cast out the evil thing that had made me say what I had said, that had made me unwelcome in my own family. All I had to do was yield, and in five minutes it would be over.

I heard myself say no.

Dad gaped at me in disbelief, then he began to testify—not about God, but about Mother. The herbs, he said, were a divine calling from the Lord. Everything that happened to our family, every injury, every near death, was because we had been chosen, we were special. God had orchestrated all of it so we could denounce the Medical Establishment and testify of His power.

"Remember when Luke burned his leg?" Dad said, as if I could forget. "That was the Lord's plan. It was a curriculum.

348

For your mother. So she would be ready for what would happen to me."

The explosion, the burn. It was the highest of spiritual honors, he said, to be made a living testament of God's power. Dad held my hands in his mangled fingers and told me that his disfiguration had been foreordained. That it was a tender mercy, that it had brought souls to God.

Mother added her testimony in low, reverent whispers. She said she could stop a stroke by adjusting a chakra; that she could halt heart attacks using only energy; that she could cure cancer if people had faith. She herself had had breast cancer, she said, and she had cured it.

My head snapped up. "You have cancer?" I said. "You're sure? You had it tested?"

"I didn't need to have it tested," she said. "I muscle-tested it. It was cancer. I cured it."

"We could have cured Grandma, too," Dad said. "But she turned away from Christ. She lacked faith and that's why she's dead. God won't heal the faithless."

Mother nodded but never looked up.

"Grandma's sin was serious," Dad said. "But your sins are more serious still, because you were given the truth and have turned from it."

The room was quiet except for the dull hum of traffic on Oxford Street.

Dad's eyes were fixed on me. It was the gaze of a seer, of a holy oracle whose power and authority were drawn from the very universe. I wanted to meet it head-on, to prove I could withstand its weight, but after a few seconds something in me buckled, some inner force gave way, and my eyes dropped to the floor.

"I am called of God to testify that disaster lies ahead of you," Dad said. "It is coming soon, very soon, and it will break you, break you utterly. It will knock you down into the depths of humility. And when you are there, when you are lying broken, you will call on the Divine Father for mercy." Dad's voice, which had risen to fever pitch, now fell to a murmur. "And He will not hear you."

I met his gaze. He was burning with conviction; I could almost feel the heat rolling off him. He leaned forward so that his face was nearly touching mine and said, "But I will."

The silence settled, undisturbed, oppressive.

"I will offer, one final time, to give you a blessing," he said.

The blessing was a mercy. He was offering me the same terms of surrender he had offered my sister. I imagined what a relief it must have been for her, to realize she could trade her reality—the one she shared with me—for his. How grateful she must have felt to pay such a modest price. I could not judge her for her choice, but in that moment I knew I could not choose it for myself. Everything I had worked for, all my years of study, had been to purchase for myself this one privilege: to see and experience more truths than those given to me by my father, and to use those truths to construct my own mind. I had come to believe that the ability to evaluate many ideas, many histories, many points of view, was at the heart of what it means to self-create. If I yielded now, I would lose more than an argument. I would lose custody of my own mind. This was the price I was being asked to pay, I understood that now. What my father wanted to cast from me wasn't a demon: it was me.

Dad reached into his pocket and withdrew a vial of consecrated oil, which he placed in my palm. I studied it. This oil was the only thing needed to perform the ritual, that and the holy authority resting in my father's misshapen hands. I imagined my surrender, imagined closing my eyes and recanting my blasphemies. I imagined how I would describe my change, my divine transformation, what words of gratitude I would shout. The words were ready, fully formed and waiting to leave my lips.

But when my mouth opened they vanished.

"I love you," I said. "But I can't. I'm sorry, Dad."

My father stood abruptly.

He said again there was an evil presence in my room, that he couldn't stay another night. Their flight was not until morning, but Dad said it was better to sleep on a bench than with the devil.

My mother bustled about the room, shoveling shirts and socks into their suitcase. Five minutes later, they were gone.

37

Gambling for Redemption

Someone was screaming, a long, steady holler, so loud it woke me up. It was dark. There were streetlights, pavement, the rumble of distant cars. I was standing in the middle of Oxford Street, half a block from my dorm room. My feet were bare, and I was wearing a tank top and flannel pajama bottoms. It felt like people were gawking at me, but it was two in the morning and the street was empty.

Somehow I got back into my building, then I sat on my bed and tried to reconstruct what had happened. I remembered going to sleep. I remembered the dream. What I did *not* remember was flying from my bed and sprinting down the hall and into the street, shouting, but that is what I had done.

The dream had been of home. Dad had built a maze on Buck's Peak and trapped me inside it. The walls were ten feet high and made of supplies from his root cellar—sacks of grain, cases of ammunition, drums of honey. I was searching for something, something precious I could never replace. I had to escape the maze to recover it, but I couldn't find the way out, and Dad was pursuing me, sealing the exits with sacks of grain stacked into barricades.

*

I stopped going to my French group, then to my sketching class. Instead of reading in the library or attending lectures, I watched TV in my room, working my way through every popular series from the past two decades. When one episode ended, I would begin the next without thinking, the way one breath follows another. I watched TV eighteen or twenty hours a day. When I slept I dreamed of home, and at least once a week I awoke standing in the street in the middle of the night, wondering if it was my own cry that I'd heard just before waking.

I did not study. I tried to read but the sentences meant nothing. I needed them to mean nothing. I couldn't bear to string sentences into strands of thought, or to weave those strands into ideas. Ideas were too similar to reflection, and my reflections were always of the expression on my father's stretched face the moment before he'd fled from me.

The thing about having a mental breakdown is that no matter how obvious it is that you're having one, it is somehow not obvious to you. *I'm fine,* you think. *So what if I watched TV for twenty-four straight hours yesterday. I'm not falling apart. I'm just lazy.* Why it's better to think yourself lazy than think yourself in distress, I'm not sure. But it *was* better. More than better: it was vital.

By December I was so far behind in my work that, pausing one night to begin a new episode of *Breaking Bad,* I realized that I might fail my PhD. I laughed maniacally for ten minutes at this irony: that having sacrificed my family to my education, I might lose that, also.

After a few more weeks of this, I stumbled from my bed one night and decided that I'd made a mistake, that when my father had offered me the blessing, I should have accepted it. But it wasn't too late. I could repair the damage, put it right.

I purchased a ticket to Idaho for Christmas. Two days before the flight, I awoke in a cold sweat. I'd dreamed I was in a hospital, lying on crisp white sheets. Dad was at the foot of the gurney, telling a policeman I had stabbed myself. Mother echoed him, her eyes panicked. I was surprised to hear Drew's voice, shouting that I needed to be moved to another hospital. "He'll find her here," he kept saying.

I wrote to Drew, who was living in the Middle East. I told him I was going to Buck's Peak. When he replied his tone was urgent and sharp, as if he was trying to cut through whatever fog I was living in. *My dear Tara,* he wrote. *If Shawn stabs you, you won't be taken to a hospital. You'll be put in the basement and given some lavender for the wound.* He begged me not to go, saying a hundred things I already knew and didn't care about, and when that didn't work, he said: *You told me your story so I could stop you if you ever did something crazy. Well, Tara, this is it. This is crazy.*

I can still fix this, I chanted as the plane lifted off the tarmac.

It was a bright winter morning when I arrived on Buck's Peak. I remember the crisp smell of frozen earth as I approached the house and the feel of ice and gravel crunching beneath my boots. The sky was a shocking blue. I breathed in the welcome scent of pine.

My gaze dropped below the mountain and my breath caught. When Grandma had been alive, she had, by nagging, shouting and threats, kept my father's junkyard contained. Now refuse covered the farm and was creeping toward the mountain base. The rolling hills, once perfect lakes of snow, were dotted with mangled trucks and rusted septic tanks.

Mother was ecstatic when I stepped through the door. I hadn't told her I was coming, hoping that, if no one knew, I might avoid Shawn. She talked rapidly, nervously. "I'm going to make you biscuits and gravy!" she said, then flew to the kitchen.

"I'll help in a minute," I said. "I just need to send an email."

The family computer was in the old part of the house, what had been the front room before the renovation. I sat down to write Drew, because I'd promised, as a kind of compromise between us, that while on the mountain I would write to him every two hours. I nudged the mouse and the screen flickered on. The browser was already open; someone had forgotten to sign out. I moved to open a different browser but stopped when I saw my name. It was in the message that was open on the screen, which Mother had sent only moments before. To Shawn's ex-girlfriend Erin.

The premise of the message was that Shawn had been re-born, spiritually cleansed. That the Atonement had healed our family, and that all had been restored. All except me. *The spirit has whispered to me the truth about my daughter,* Mother wrote. *My poor child has given herself over to fear, and that fear has made her desperate to validate her misperceptions. I do not know if she is a danger to our family, but I have reasons to think she might be.**

I had known, even before reading the message, that my mother shared my father's dark vision, that she believed the devil had a hold of me, that I was dangerous. But there was something in seeing the words on the page, in reading them and hearing *her* voice in them, the voice of my mother, that turned my body cold.

There was more to the email. In the final paragraph, Mother described the birth of Emily's second child, a daughter, who had been born a month before. Mother had midwifed the child. The birth had taken place at home and, according to Mother, Emily had nearly bled to death before

---

* The italicized language in the description of the referenced email exchange is paraphrased, not directly quoted.

they could get to a hospital. Mother finished the story by testifying: God had worked through her hands that night, she said. The birth was a testament of His power.

I remembered the drama of Peter's birth: how he'd slipped out of Emily weighing little more than a pound; how he'd been such a shocking shade of gray, they'd thought he was dead; how they'd fought through a snowstorm to the hospital in town, only to be told it wasn't enough, and there were no choppers flying; how two ambulances had been dispatched to McKay-Dee in Ogden. That a woman with this medical history, a woman so obviously high-risk, should be advised to attempt a second birth at home seemed reckless to the point of delusion.

If the first fall was God's will, whose was the second?

I was still wondering at the birth of my niece when Erin's response appeared. *You are right about Tara,* she said. *She is lost without faith.* Erin told Mother that my doubting myself—my writing to her, Erin, to ask if I might be mistaken, if my memories might be false—was evidence that my soul was in jeopardy, that I couldn't be trusted: *She is building her life on fear. I will pray for her.* Erin ended the message by praising my mother's skill as a midwife. *You are a true hero,* she wrote.

I closed the browser and stared at the wallpaper behind the screen. It was the same floral print from my childhood. For how long had I been dreaming of seeing it? I had come to reclaim that life, to save it. But there was nothing here to save, nothing to grasp. There was only shifting sand, shifting loyalties, shifting histories.

I remembered the dream, the maze. I remembered the walls made of grain sacks and ammunition boxes, of my father's fears and paranoias, his scriptures and prophecies. I had wanted to escape the maze with its disorienting switchbacks, its ever-modulating pathways, to find the precious thing. But now I understood: the precious thing, that was the maze. That's all that was left of the life I'd had here: a puzzle whose rules I would never understand, because they were not rules at all but a kind of cage meant to enclose me. I could stay, and search for what had been home, or I could go, now, before the walls shifted and the way out was shut.

Mother was sliding biscuits into the oven when I entered the kitchen. I looked around, mentally searching the house. *What do I need from this place?* There was only one thing: my memories. I found them under my bed, in a box, where I had left them. I carried them to the car and put them in the backseat.

"I'm going for a drive," I told Mother. I tried to keep my voice smooth. I hugged her, then took a long look at Buck's Peak, memorizing every line and shadow. Mother had seen me take my journals to the car. She must have known what that meant, must have sensed the farewell in it, because she fetched my father. He gave me a stiff hug and said, "I love you, you know that?"

"I do," I said. "That has never been the issue."

Those words are the last I said to my father.

I drove south; I didn't know where I was going. It was nearly Christmas. I had decided to go to the airport and board the next flight to Boston when Tyler called.

I hadn't spoken to my brother in months—after what happened with Audrey, it had seemed pointless to confide in my siblings. I was sure Mother would have told every brother, cousin, aunt and uncle the story she had told Erin: that I was possessed, dangerous, taken by the devil. I wasn't wrong: Mother *had* warned them. But then she made a mistake.

After I left Buck's Peak, she panicked. She was afraid I might contact Tyler, and that if I did, he might sympathize with me. She decided to get to Tyler first, to deny anything I might tell him, but she miscalculated. She didn't stop to think how the denials would sound, coming from nowhere like that.

"Of course Shawn didn't stab Diego and threaten Tara with the knife," Mother reassured Tyler, but to Tyler, who had never heard any part of this story, not from me or anyone else, this was somewhat less than reassuring. A moment after he said goodbye to Mother, Tyler called me, demanding to know what had happened and why I hadn't come to him.

I thought he'd say I was lying but he didn't. He accepted almost immediately the reality I'd spent a year denying. I didn't understand why he was trusting me, but then he told me his own stories and I remembered: Shawn had been *his* older brother, too.

In the weeks that followed, Tyler began to test my parents in the subtle, nonconfrontational way that was uniquely his. He suggested that perhaps the situation had been mishandled, that perhaps I was not possessed. Perhaps I was not evil at all.

I might have taken comfort in Tyler's trying to help me, but the memory of my sister was too raw, and I didn't trust him. I knew that if Tyler confronted my parents—really confronted them—they would force him to choose between me and them, between me and the rest of the family. And from Audrey I had learned: he would not choose me.

My fellowship at Harvard finished in the spring. I flew to the Middle East, where Drew was completing a Fulbright. It took some effort, but I managed to hide from Drew how poorly I was doing, or at least I thought I did. I probably didn't. He was, after all, the one chasing me through his flat when I awoke in the middle of the night, screaming and sprinting, with no idea where I was but a desperate need to escape it.

We left Amman and drove south. We were in a Bedouin

camp in the Jordanian desert on the day the navy SEALs killed bin Laden. Drew spoke Arabic, and when the news broke he spent hours in conversation with our guides. "He's no Muslim," they told Drew as we sat on cold sand watching the dying flames of a campfire. "He does not understand Islam, or he would not do the terrible things he's done."

I watched Drew talk with the Bedouins, heard the strange, smooth sounds falling from his lips, and was struck by the implausibility of my presence there. When the twin towers had fallen ten years before, I had never heard of Islam. Now I was drinking sugary tea with Zalabia Bedouins and squatting on a sand drift in Wadi Rum, the Valley of the Moon, less than twenty miles from the Saudi Arabian border.

The distance—physical and mental—that had been traversed in the last decade nearly stopped my breath, and I wondered if perhaps I had changed *too* much. All my studying, reading, thinking, traveling, had it transformed me into someone who no longer belonged anywhere? I thought of the girl who, knowing nothing beyond her junkyard and her mountain, had stared at a screen, watching as two planes sailed into strange white pillars. Her classroom was a heap of junk. Her textbooks, slates of scrap. And yet she had something precious that I—despite all my opportunities, or maybe because of them—did not.

I returned to England, where I continued to unravel. My first week back in Cambridge, I awoke nearly every night in the street, having run there, shouting, asleep. I developed headaches that lasted for days. My dentist said I was grinding my teeth. My skin broke out so severely that twice perfect strangers stopped me in the street and asked if I was having an allergic reaction. No, I said. I always look like this.

One evening, I got into an argument with a friend about something trivial, and before I knew what was happening I had pressed myself into the wall and was hugging my knees to my chest, trying to keep my heart from leaping out of my body. My friend rushed toward me to help and I screamed. It was an hour before I could let her touch me, before I could will myself away from the wall. *So that's a panic attack,* I thought the next morning.

Soon after, I sent a letter to my father. I'm not proud of that letter. It's full of rage, a fractious child screaming, "I hate you" at a parent. It's filled with words like "thug" and "tyrant," and it goes on for pages, a torrent of frustration and abuse.

That is how I told my parents I was cutting off contact with them. Between insults and fits of temper, I said I needed a year to heal myself; then perhaps I could return to their mad world to try to make sense of it.

My mother begged me to find another way. My father said nothing.

38
Family

I was failing my PhD.

If I had explained to my supervisor, Dr. Runciman, why I was unable to work, he would have helped me, would have secured additional funding, petitioned the department for more time. But I didn't explain, I couldn't. He had no idea why it had been nearly a year since I'd sent him work, so when we met in his office one overcast July afternoon, he suggested that I quit.

"The PhD is exceptionally demanding," he said. "It's okay if you can't do it."

I left his office full of fury at myself. I went to the library and gathered half a dozen books, which I lugged to my room and arranged on my desk. But my mind was made nauseous by rational thought, and by the next morning the books had moved to my bed, where they propped up my laptop while I worked steadily through *Buffy the Vampire Slayer.*

That autumn, Tyler confronted my father. He talked to Mother first, on the phone. He called me after and related their conversation. He said Mother was "on our side," that she thought the situation with Shawn was unacceptable and had convinced Dad to do something. "Dad is taking care of it," Tyler said. "Everything is going to be fine. You can come home."

My phone rang again two days later, and I paused *Buffy* to answer it. It was Tyler. The whole thing had exploded in his face. He had felt uneasy after his conversation with Mother, so he had called Dad to see exactly what was being done about Shawn. Dad had become angry, aggressive. He'd shouted at Tyler that if he brought this up again, he would be disowned, then he'd hung up the phone.

I dislike imagining this conversation. Tyler's stutter was always worse when he talked to our father. I picture my brother hunched over the receiver, trying to concentrate, to push out the words that have jammed in his throat, while his father hurls an arsenal of ugly words.

Tyler was still reeling from Dad's threat when his phone rang. He thought it was Dad calling to apologize, but it was Shawn. Dad had told him everything. "I can have you out of this family in two minutes," Shawn said. "You know I can do it. Just ask Tara."

I listened to Tyler relate this story while staring at the frozen image of Sarah Michelle Gellar. Tyler talked for a long time, moving through the events quickly but lingering in a wasteland of rationalization and self-recrimination. Dad must have misunderstood, Tyler said. There had been a mistake, a miscommunication. Maybe it was *his* fault, maybe he hadn't said the right thing in the right way. That was it. *He* had done this, and *he* could repair it.

As I listened, I felt a strange sensation of distance that bordered on disinterestedness, as if my future with Tyler, this brother I had known and loved all my life, was a film I had already seen and knew the ending of. I knew the shape of this drama because I had lived it already, with my sister. This was the moment I had lost Audrey: this was the moment the costs had become real, when the tax was levied, the rent due.

This was the moment she had realized how much easier it was to walk away: what a poor trade it was to swap an entire family for a single sister.

So I knew even before it happened that Tyler would go the same way. I could hear his hand-wringing through the long echo of the telephone. He was deciding what to do, but I knew something he did not: that the decision had already been made, and what he was doing now was just the long work of justifying it.

It was October when I got the letter.

It came in the form of a PDF attached to an email from Tyler and Stefanie. The message explained that the letter had been drafted carefully, thoughtfully, and that a copy would be sent to my parents. When I saw that, I knew what it meant. It meant Tyler was ready to denounce me, to say my father's words, that I was possessed, dangerous. The letter was a kind of voucher, a pass that would admit him back into the family.

I couldn't get myself to open the attachment; some instinct had seized my fingers. I remembered Tyler as he'd been when I was young, the quiet older brother reading his books while I lay under his desk, staring at his socks and breathing in his music. I wasn't sure I could bear it, to hear *those* words in *his* voice.

I clicked the mouse, the attachment opened. I was so far removed from myself that I read the entire letter without understanding it: *Our parents are held down by chains of abuse, manipulation, and control. . . . They see change as dangerous and will exile anyone who asks for it. This is a perverted idea of family loyalty. . . . They claim faith, but this is not what the gospel teaches. Keep safe. We love you.*

From Tyler's wife, Stefanie, I would learn the story of this letter, how in the days after my father had threatened disownment, Tyler had gone to bed every night saying aloud to himself, over and over, "What am I supposed to do? She's my sister."

When I heard this story, I made the only good decision I

had made for months: I enrolled in the university counseling service. I was assigned to a sprightly middle-aged woman with tight curls and sharp eyes, who rarely spoke in our sessions, preferring to let me talk it out, which I did, week after week, month after month. The counseling did nothing at first—I can't think of a single session I would describe as "helpful"—but their collective power over time was undeniable. I didn't understand it then, and I don't understand it now, but there was something nourishing in setting aside that time each week, in the act of admitting that I needed something I could not provide for myself.

Tyler did send the letter to my parents, and once committed he never wavered. That winter I spent many hours on the phone with him and Stefanie, who became a sister to me. They were available whenever I needed to talk, and back then I needed to talk quite a lot.

Tyler paid a price for that letter, though the price is hard to define. He was not disowned, or at least his disownment was not permanent. Eventually he worked out a truce with my father, but their relationship may never be the same.

I've apologized to Tyler more times than I can count for what I've cost him, but the words are awkwardly placed and I stumble over them. What is the proper arrangement of words? How do you craft an apology for weakening someone's ties to his father, to his family? Perhaps there aren't words for that. How do you thank a brother who refused to let you go, who seized your hand and wrenched you upward just as you had decided to stop kicking, and sink? There aren't words for that, either.

Winter was long that year, the dreariness punctuated only by my weekly counseling sessions and the odd sense of loss, almost bereavement, I felt whenever I finished one TV series and had to find another.

Then it was spring, then summer, and finally as summer turned to fall, I found I could read with focus. I could hold thoughts in my head besides anger and self-accusation. I returned to the chapter I had written nearly two years before at Harvard. Again I read Hume, Rousseau, Smith, Godwin, Wollstonecraft and Mill. Again I thought about the family. There was a puzzle in it, something unresolved. What is a person to do, I asked, when their obligations to their family conflict with *other* obligations—to friends, to society, to themselves?

I began the research. I narrowed the question, made it academic, specific. In the end, I chose four intellectual movements from the nineteenth century and examined how they had struggled with the question of family obligation. One of the movements I chose was nineteenth-century Mormonism. I worked for a solid year, and at the end of it I had a draft of my thesis: "The Family, Morality, and Social Science in Anglo-American Cooperative Thought, 1813–1890."

The chapter on Mormonism was my favorite. As a child in Sunday school, I'd been taught that all history was a preparation for Mormonism: that every event since the death of Christ had been fashioned by God to make possible the moment when Joseph Smith would kneel in the Sacred Grove and God would restore the one true church. Wars, migrations, natural disasters—these were mere preludes to the Mormon story. On the other hand, secular histories tended to overlook spiritual movements like Mormonism altogether.

My dissertation gave a different shape to history, one that was neither Mormon nor anti-Mormon, neither spiritual nor profane. It didn't treat Mormonism as the objective of human history, but neither did it discount the contribution Mormonism had made in grappling with the questions of the age. Instead, it treated the Mormon ideology as a chapter in the larger human story. In my account, history did not set

Mormons apart from the rest of the human family; it bound them to it.

I sent Dr. Runciman the draft, and a few days later we met in his office. He sat across from me and, with a look of astonishment, said it was good. "Some parts of it are very good," he said. He was smiling now. "I'll be surprised if it doesn't earn a doctorate."

As I walked home carrying the heavy manuscript, I remembered attending one of Dr. Kerry's lectures, which he had begun by writing, "Who writes history?" on the blackboard. I remembered how strange the question had seemed to me then. My idea of a historian was not human; it was of someone like my father, more prophet than man, whose visions of the past, like those of the future, could not be questioned, or even augmented. Now, as I passed through King's College, in the shadow of the enormous chapel, my old diffidence seemed almost funny. *Who writes history?* I thought. *I do.*

On my twenty-seventh birthday, the birthday I had chosen, I submitted my PhD dissertation. The defense took place in December, in a small, simply furnished room. I passed and returned to London, where Drew had a job and we'd rented a flat. In January, nearly ten years to the day since I'd set foot in my first classroom at BYU, I received confirmation from the University of Cambridge: I was Dr. Westover.

I had built a new life, and it was a happy one, but I felt a sense of loss that went beyond family. I had lost Buck's Peak, not by leaving but by leaving silently. I had retreated, fled across an ocean and allowed my father to tell my story for me, to define me to everyone I had ever known. I had conceded too much ground—not just the mountain, but the entire province of our shared history.

It was time to go home.

39

Watching the Buffalo

It was spring when I arrived in the valley. I drove along the highway to the edge of town, then pulled over at the drop-off overlooking the Bear River. From there I could look out over the basin, a patchwork of expectant fields stretching to Buck's Peak. The mountain was crisp with evergreens, which were luminous set against the browns and grays of shale and limestone. The Princess was as bright as I'd ever seen her. She stood facing me, the valley between us, radiating permanence.

The Princess had been haunting me. From across the ocean I'd heard her beckoning, as if I were a troublesome calf who'd wandered from her herd. Her voice had been gentle at first, coaxing, but when I didn't answer, when I stayed away, it had turned to fury. I had betrayed her. I imagined her face contorted with rage, her stance heavy and threatening. She had been living in my mind like this for years, a deity of contempt.

But seeing her now, standing watch over her fields and pastures, I realized that I had misunderstood her. She was not angry with me for leaving, because *leaving* was a part of her cycle. Her role was not to corral the buffalo, not to gather and confine them by force. It was to celebrate their return.

*

I backtracked a quarter mile into town and parked beside Grandma-over-in-town's white picket fence. In my mind it was still *her* fence, even though she didn't live here anymore: she had been moved to a hospice facility near Main Street.

I had not seen my grandparents in three years, not since my parents had begun telling the extended family that I was possessed. My grandparents loved their daughter. I was sure they had believed her account of me. So I had surrendered them. It was too late to reclaim Grandma—she was suffering from Alzheimer's and would not have known me—so I had come to see my grandfather, to find out whether there would be a place for me in his life.

We sat in the living room; the carpet was the same crisp white from my childhood. The visit was short and polite. He talked about Grandma, whom he had cared for long after she ceased to recognize him. I talked about England. Grandpa mentioned my mother, and when he spoke of her it was with the same look of awe that I had seen in the faces of her followers. I didn't blame him. From what I'd heard, my parents were powerful people in the valley. Mother was marketing her products as a spiritual alternative to Obamacare, and she was selling product as fast as she could make it, even with dozens of employees.

God had to be behind such a wondrous success, Grandpa said. My parents must have been called by the Lord to do what they have done, to be great healers, to bring souls to God. I smiled and stood to go. He was the same gentle old man I remembered, but I was overwhelmed by the distance between us. I hugged him at the door, and gave him a long look. He was eighty-seven. I doubted whether, in the years he had left, I would be able to prove to him that I was not what my father said I was, that I was not a wicked thing.

*

Tyler and Stefanie lived a hundred miles north of Buck's Peak, in Idaho Falls. It was there I planned to go next, but before leaving the valley, I wrote my mother. It was a short message. I said I was nearby and wanted her to meet me in town. I wasn't ready to see Dad, I said, but it had been years since I'd seen her face. Would she come?

I waited for her reply in the parking lot at Stokes. I didn't wait long.

It pains me that you think it is acceptable to ask this. A wife does not go where her husband is not welcome. I will not be party to such blatant disrespect.*

The message was long and reading it made me tired, as if I'd run a great distance. The bulk of it was a lecture on loyalty: that families forgive, and that if I could not forgive mine, I would regret it for the rest of my life. *The past,* she wrote, *whatever it was, ought to be shoveled fifty feet under and left to rot in the earth.*

Mother said I was welcome to come to the house, that she prayed for the day when I would run through the back door, shouting, "I'm home!"

I wanted to answer her prayer—I was barely more than ten miles from the mountain—but I knew what unspoken pact I would be making as I walked through that door. I could have my mother's love, but there were terms, the same terms they had offered me three years before: that I trade my reality for theirs, that I take my own understanding and bury it, leave it to rot in the earth.

Mother's message amounted to an ultimatum: I could see her *and* my father, or I would never see her again. She has never recanted.

*

* The italicized language in the description of the referenced exchange is paraphrased, not directly quoted.

The parking lot had filled while I was reading. I let her words settle, then started the engine and pulled onto Main Street. At the intersection I turned west, toward the mountain. Before I left the valley, I would set eyes on my home.

Over the years I'd heard many rumors about my parents: that they were millionaires, that they were building a fortress on the mountain, that they had hidden away enough food to last decades. The most interesting, by far, were the stories about Dad hiring and firing employees. The valley had never recovered from the recession; people needed work. My parents were one of the largest employers in the county, but from what I could tell Dad's mental state made it difficult for him to maintain employees long-term: when he had a fit of paranoia, he tended to fire people with little cause. Months before, he had fired Diane Hardy, Rob's ex-wife, the same Rob who'd come to fetch us after the second accident. Diane and Rob had been friends with my parents for twenty years. Until Dad fired Diane.

It was perhaps in another such fit of paranoia that Dad fired my mother's sister Angie. Angie had spoken to Mother, believing her sister would never treat family that way. When I was a child it had been Mother's business; now it was hers and Dad's together. But at this test of whose it was really, my father won: Angie was dismissed.

It is difficult to piece together what happened next, but from what I later learned, Angie filed for unemployment benefits, and when the Department of Labor called my parents to confirm that she had been terminated, Dad lost what little reason remained to him. It was not the Department of Labor on the phone, he said, but the Department of Homeland Security, pretending to be the Department of Labor. Angie had put his name on the terrorist watch list, he said. The Government was after him now—after his money and his guns and his fuel. It was Ruby Ridge all over again.

I pulled off the highway and onto the gravel, then stepped out of the car and gazed up at Buck's Peak. It was clear immediately that at least some of the rumors were true—for one, that my parents were making huge sums of money. The house was massive. The home I'd grown up in had had five bedrooms; now it had been expanded in all directions and looked as though it had at least forty.

It would only be a matter of time, I thought, before Dad started using the money to prepare for the End of Days. I imagined the roof lined with solar panels, laid out like a deck of cards. "We need to be self-sufficient," I imagined Dad would say as he dragged the panels across his titanic house. In the coming year, Dad would spend hundreds of thousands of dollars buying equipment and scouring the mountain for water. He didn't want to be dependent on the Government, and he knew Buck's Peak must have water, if he could only find it. Gashes the size of football fields would appear at the mountain base, leaving a desolation of broken roots and upturned trees where once there had been a forest. He was probably chanting, "Got to be self-reliant" the day he climbed into a crawler and tore into the fields of satin wheat.

Grandma-over-in-town died on Mother's Day.

I was doing research in Colorado when I heard the news. I left immediately for Idaho, but while traveling realized I had nowhere to stay. It was then that I remembered my aunt Angie, and that my father was telling anyone who would listen that she had put his name on a terrorist watch list. Mother had cast her aside; I hoped I could reclaim her.

Angie lived next door to my grandfather, so again I parked along the white picket fence. I knocked. Angie greeted me

371

politely, the way Grandpa had done. It was clear that she had heard much about me from my mother and father in the past five years.

"I'll make you a deal," I said. "I'll forget everything my dad has said about you, if you'll forget everything he's said about me." She laughed, closing her eyes and throwing back her head in a way that nearly broke my heart, she looked so much like my mother.

I stayed with Angie until the funeral.

In the days before the service, my mother's siblings began to gather at their childhood home. They were my aunts and uncles, but some of them I hadn't seen since I was a child. My uncle Daryl, who I barely knew, suggested that his brothers and sisters should spend an afternoon together at a favorite restaurant in Lava Hot Springs. My mother refused to come. She would not go without my father, and he would have nothing to do with Angie.

It was a bright May afternoon when we all piled into a large van and set off on the hour-long drive. I was uncomfortably aware that I had taken my mother's place, going with her siblings and her remaining parent on an outing to remember her mother, a grandmother I had not known well. I soon realized that my not knowing her was wonderful for her children, who were bursting with remembrances and loved answering questions about her. With every story my grandmother came into sharper focus, but the woman taking shape from their collective memories was nothing like the woman I remembered. It was then I realized how cruelly I had judged her, how my perception of her had been distorted, because I'd been looking at her through my father's harsh lens.

During the drive back, my aunt Debbie invited me to visit her in Utah. My uncle Daryl echoed her. "We'd love to have you in Arizona," he said. In the space of a day, I had reclaimed a family—not mine, hers.

The funeral was the next day. I stood in a corner and watched my siblings trickle in.

There were Tyler and Stefanie. They had decided to home school their seven children, and from what I'd seen, the children were being educated to a very high standard. Luke came in next, with a brood so numerous I lost count. He saw me and crossed the room, and we made small talk for several minutes, neither of us acknowledging that we hadn't seen each other in half a decade, neither of us alluding to why. *Do you believe what Dad says about me?* I wanted to ask. *Do you believe I'm dangerous?* But I didn't. Luke worked for my parents, and without an education, he needed that job to support his family. Forcing him to take a side would only end in heartache.

Richard, who was finishing a PhD in chemistry, had come down from Oregon with Kami and their children. He smiled at me from the back of the chapel. A few months before, Richard had written to me. He'd said he was sorry for believing Dad, that he wished he'd done more to help me when I needed it, and that from then on, I could count on his support. We were family, he said.

Audrey and Benjamin chose a bench near the back. Audrey had arrived early, when the chapel was empty. She had grabbed my arm and whispered that my refusing to see our father was a grave sin. "He is a great man," she said. "For the rest of your life you will regret not humbling yourself and following his counsel." These were the first words my sister had said to me in years, and I had no response to them.

Shawn arrived a few minutes before the service, with Emily and Peter and a little girl I had never met. It was the first time I had been in a room with him since the night he'd killed Diego. I was tense, but there was no need. He did not look at me once during the service.

My oldest brother, Tony, sat with my parents, his five

373

children fanning out in the pew. Tony had a GED and had built a successful trucking company in Las Vegas, but it hadn't survived the recession. Now he worked for my parents, as did Shawn and Luke and their wives, as well as Audrey and her husband, Benjamin. Now I thought about it, I realized that all my siblings, except Richard and Tyler, were economically dependent on my parents. My family was splitting down the middle—the three who had left the mountain, and the four who had stayed. The three with doctorates, and the four without high school diplomas. A chasm had appeared, and was growing.

A year would pass before I would return to Idaho.

A few hours before my flight from London, I wrote to my mother—as I always did, as I always will do—to ask if she would see me. Again, her response was swift. She would not, she would never, unless I would see my father. To see me without him, she said, would be to disrespect her husband.

For a moment it seemed pointless, this annual pilgrimage to a home that continued to reject me, and I wondered if I should go. Then I received another message, this one from Aunt Angie. She said Grandpa had canceled his plans for the next day, and was refusing even to go to the temple, as he usually did on Wednesdays, because he wanted to be at home in case I came by. To this Angie added: *I get to see you in about twelve hours! But who's counting?*

40

Educated

When I was a child, I waited for my mind to grow, for my experiences to accumulate and my choices to solidify, taking shape into the likeness of a person. That person, or that likeness of one, had belonged. I was *of* that mountain, the mountain that had made me. It was only as I grew older that I wondered if how I had started is how I would end—if the first shape a person takes is their only true shape.

As I write the final words of this story, I've not seen my parents in years, since my grandmother's funeral. I'm close to Tyler, Richard and Tony, and from them, as well as from other family, I hear of the ongoing drama on the mountain— the injuries, violence and shifting loyalties. But it comes to me now as distant hearsay, which is a gift. I don't know if the separation is permanent, if one day I will find a way back, but it has brought me peace.

That peace did not come easily. I spent two years enumerating my father's flaws, constantly updating the tally, as if reciting every resentment, every real and imagined act of cruelty, of neglect, would justify my decision to cut him from my life. Once justified, I thought the strangling guilt would release me and I could catch my breath.

But vindication has no power over guilt. No amount of

375

anger or rage directed at others can subdue it, because guilt is never about *them*. Guilt is the fear of one's own wretchedness. It has nothing to do with other people.

I shed my guilt when I accepted my decision on its own terms, without endlessly prosecuting old grievances, without weighing his sins against mine. Without thinking of my father at all. I learned to accept my decision for my own sake, because of me, not because of him. Because I needed it, not because he deserved it.

It was the only way I could love him.

When my father was in my life, wrestling me for control of that life, I perceived him with the eyes of a soldier, through a fog of conflict. I could not make out his tender qualities. When he was before me, towering, indignant, I could not remember how, when I was young, his laugh used to shake his gut and make his glasses shine. In his stern presence, I could never recall the pleasant way his lips used to twitch, before they were burned away, when a memory tugged tears from his eyes. I can only remember those things now, with a span of miles and years between us.

But what has come between me and my father is more than time or distance. It is a change in the self. I am not the child my father raised, but he is the father who raised her.

If there was a single moment when the breach between us, which had been cracking and splintering for two decades, was at last too vast to be bridged, I believe it was that winter night, when I stared at my reflection in the bathroom mirror, while, without my knowing it, my father grasped the phone in his knotted hands and dialed my brother. Diego, the knife. What followed was very dramatic. But the real drama had already played out in the bathroom.

It had played out when, for reasons I don't understand, I was unable to climb through the mirror and send out my sixteen-year-old self in my place.

Until that moment she had always been there. No matter how much I appeared to have changed—how illustrious my education, how altered my appearance—I was still *her*. At best I was two people, a fractured mind. *She* was inside, and emerged whenever I crossed the threshold of my father's house.

That night I called on her and she didn't answer. She left me. She stayed in the mirror. The decisions I made after that moment were not the ones she would have made. They were the choices of a changed person, a new self.

You could call this selfhood many things. Transformation. Metamorphosis. Falsity. Betrayal.

I call it an education.

Acknowledgments

To my brothers Tyler, Richard and Tony I owe the greatest debt for making this book possible, first in the living of it, then in the writing of it. From them and their wives, Stefanie, Kami and Michele, I learned much of what I know about family.

Tyler and Richard in particular were generous with their time and their memories, reading multiple drafts, adding their own details, and in general helping me make the book as accurate as possible. Though our perspectives may have differed in some particulars, their willingness to verify the facts of this story enabled me to write it.

Professor David Runciman encouraged me to write this memoir and was among the first to read the manuscript. Without his confidence in it, I might never have had confidence in it myself.

I am grateful to those who make books their life's work and who gave a portion of that life to this book: my agents, Anna Stein and Karolina Sutton; and my wonderful editors, Hilary Redmon and Andy Ward at Random House, and Jocasta Hamilton at Hutchinson; as well as the many other people who worked to edit, typeset and launch this story. Most notably, Boaty Boatright at ICM was a tireless champion. Special thanks are owed to Ben Phelan, who was given the difficult task of fact checking this book, and who did so rigorously but with great sensitivity and professionalism.

I am especially grateful to those who believed in this book before it was a book, when it was just a jumble of home-printed papers. Among those early readers are Dr. Marion Kant, Dr. Paul Kerry, Annie Wilding, Livia Gainham, Sonya Teich, Dunni Alao and Suraya Sidhi Singh.

My aunts Debbie and Angie came back into my life at a crucial moment, and their support means everything. For believing in me, always, thanks to Professor Jonathan Steinberg. For granting me haven, emotional as well as practical, in which to write this book, I am indebted to my dear friend, Drew Mecham.

Notes

1   p. 2 Except for my sister Audrey, who broke an arm and
a leg when she was young. She was taken to get a cast.

2   p. 24 While everyone agrees that there were many years
in which my parents did not have a phone, there is
considerable disagreement in the family about which
years they were. I've asked my brothers, aunts, uncles
and cousins, but I have not been able to definitively
establish a timeline, and have therefore relied on my own
memories.

3   p. 89 Since the writing of this story, I have spoken to
Luke about the incident. His account differs from both
mine and Richard's. In Luke's memory, Dad took Luke
to the house, administered a homeopathic for shock,
then put him in a tub of cold water, where he left him to
go fight the fire. This goes against my memory, and
against Richard's. Still, perhaps our memories are in
error. Perhaps I found Luke in a tub, alone, rather than
on the grass. What everyone agrees upon, strangely, is
that somehow Luke ended up on the front lawn, his leg
in a garbage can.

4   p. 148 My account of Shawn's fall is based on the story as
it was told to me at the time. Tyler was told the same story;
in fact, many of the details in this account come from his
memory. Asked fifteen years later, others remember it

differently. Mother says Shawn was not standing on a pallet, only on forklift tines. Luke remembers the pallet, but substitutes a metal drain, with the grating removed, in place of the rebar. He says the fall was twelve feet, and that Shawn began acting strangely as soon as he regained consciousness. Luke has no memory of who dialed 9-11, but says there were men working in a nearby mill, and he suspects that one of them called immediately after Shawn fell.

5 p. 169 Asked fifteen years later, Dwain did not recall being there. But he is there, vividly, in my memory.

6 p. 254 It is possible that my timeline is off here by one or two days. According to some who were there, although my father was horribly burned, he did not seem in any real danger until the third day, when the scabbing began, making it difficult to breathe. Dehydration compounded the situation. In this account, it was then that they feared for his life, and that is when my sister called me, only I misunderstood and assumed that the explosion had happened the day before.

7 p. 325 I remember this as the scar Luke got from working the Shear; however, it might have come from a roofing accident.

A Note on the Text

Certain footnotes have been included to give a voice to memories that differ from mine. The notes concerning two stories—Luke's burn and Shawn's fall from the pallet—are significant and require additional commentary.

In both events, the discrepancies between accounts are many and varied. Take Luke's burn. Everyone who was there that day either saw someone who wasn't there, or failed to see someone who was. Dad saw Luke, and Luke saw Dad. Luke saw me, but I did not see Dad and Dad did not see me. I saw Richard and Richard saw me, but Richard did not see Dad, and neither Dad nor Luke saw Richard. What is one to make of such a carousel of contradiction? After all the turning around and round, when the music finally stops, the only person everyone can agree was actually present that day, is Luke.

Shawn's fall from the pallet is even more bewildering. I was not there. I heard my account from others, but was confident it was true because I'd heard it told that way for years, by many people, and because Tyler had heard the same story. He remembered it the way I did, fifteen years later. So I put it in writing. Then this other story appeared. *There was no waiting*, it insists. *The chopper was called right away.*

I'd be lying if I said these details are unimportant; that the "big picture" is the same no matter which version you believe.

These details matter. Either my father sent Luke down the mountain alone, or he did not; either he left Shawn in the sun with a serious head injury, or he did not. A different father, a different man, is born from those details.

I don't know which account of Shawn's fall to believe. More remarkably, I don't know which account of Luke's burn to believe, and *I was there*. I can return to that moment. Luke is on the grass. I look around me. There is no one else, no shadow of my father, not even the idea of him pushing in on the periphery of my memory. He is not there. But in Luke's memory he *is* there, laying him gently in the bathtub, administering a homeopathic for shock.

What I take from this is a correction, not to my memory but to my understanding. We are all of us more complicated than the roles we are assigned in the stories other people tell. This is especially true in families. When one of my brothers first read my account of Shawn's fall, he wrote to me: "I can't imagine Dad calling 9-11. Shawn would have died first." But maybe not. Maybe, after hearing his son's skull crack, the desolate thud of bone and brain on concrete, our father was not the man we thought he would be, and assumed he had been for years after. I have always known that my father loves his children and powerfully; I have always believed that his hatred of doctors was more powerful. But maybe not. Maybe, in that moment, a moment of real crisis, his love subdued his fear and hatred both.

Maybe the real tragedy is that he could live in our minds this way, in my brother's and mine, because his response in other moments—thousands of smaller dramas and lesser crises—had led us to see him in that role. To believe that should *we* fall, he would not intervene. We would die first.

We are all more complicated than the roles we are assigned in stories. Nothing has revealed that truth to me more than writing this memoir—trying to pin down the people I love on paper, to capture the whole meaning of them in a few words, which is of course impossible. This is the best I can do: to tell that *other* story next to the one I remember. Of a summer day, a fire, the smell of charred flesh, and a father helping his son down the mountain.

THE
CANALS OF SOUTH
AND
SOUTH EAST ENGLAND

by

Charles Hadfield

DAVID & CHARLES : NEWTON ABBOT

7153   4693   8

This book is a considerably extended version of part of *The Canals of Southern England* 1955. A companion volume, *The Canals of South West England*, was published in 1967

© *Charles Hadfield* 1969

REPL.

2 4 NOV

WESTON-S-MARE
PUBLIC LIBRARIES

45975

386.46.   A⅁

HJ

69-27741

Printed in Great Britain by
Latimer Trend & Company Limited Plymouth
for David & Charles (Publishers) Limited
South Devon House Newton Abbot Devon

This book
is respectfully dedicated
to the memory of
THE EARL OF EGREMONT,
CHARLES DUNDAS, LORD AMESBURY
and
JAMES PERRY
promoters of Inland Navigation
and of
JOSIAH CLOWES, JOHN RENNIE,
WILLIAM TIERNEY CLARK
and
WILLIAM WHITWORTH
civil engineers

CONTENTS

		Page
	List of Illustrations	9
	Preface	13
Chapter		
I.	Introduction to a Pattern	15
II.	Waterways of the South East	30
	River Adur and Baybridge Canal—River Ouse (Sussex)—River Cuckmere—Eastern Rother and Brede—Royal Military Canal—Weald of Kent Canal project—River Stour (Kent)—Dartford & Crayford Navigation	
III.	The River Medway	60
IV.	The Thames & Medway Canal	81
V.	Round London	102
	Grand Surrey Canal—Surrey Iron Railway—Croydon Canal—Wimbledon & Wandsworth Canal project—Royal Clarence Ship Canal project	
VI.	The London–Portsmouth Line	118
	River Wey—River Arun—River Rother (Western)—The London–Portsmouth schemes of 1803 and 1810—Wey & Arun Junction Canal—Portsmouth & Arundel Canal—The Ship Canal projects of 1823–8—Langstone Docks & Ship Canal project	
VII.	The Basingstoke Canal	151
VIII.	Hampshire Waterways	160
	River Itchen—River Avon (Hampshire)—Andover Canal—Proposed links between the Basingstoke Canal and the Itchen or the Andover Canal—Salisbury & Southampton Canal—Schemes for canals from Bristol to Salisbury or the Andover Canal	
IX.	The River Thames and the Canals	188
X.	The Kennet & Avon Canal	221

7

8 CONTENTS

Chapter   *page*

XI. The Somersetshire Coal Canal   262

XII. The Wilts & Berks Canal   276

XIII. The Stroudwater Navigation   295

XIV. The Thames & Severn Canal   315

XV. The Gloucester & Berkeley Canal   341

    Author's Notes & Acknowledgments   354

    Notes   356

APPENDICES

I. Summary of Facts about the Canals and Navigations
    of the South and South East   370

II. Principal Engineering Works   380

    Index   381

ILLUSTRATIONS

PLATES

page

The Royal Military Canal   17

Canterbury Navigation Company share certificate   17

Old Maidstone lock on the Upper Medway Navigation   18

Thames & Medway Canal; trains and barges both use the tunnels   18

Gravesend basin, Thames & Medway Canal   35

Croydon Canal, looking towards Deptford   35

Wey Navigation, barges unload at Coxe's lock mill, 1963   36

Thames lock, Weybridge, 1950   36

A barge on the Arun   69

Portsea Canal sea-lock, about 1900   69

Repairing lock gates on the Basingstoke Canal at Woking, about 1912   70

Basingstoke Canal at Byfleet, about 1930   70

Itchen Navigation, view from the Blackbridge wharf, Winchester   87

Rooksbury bridge, Andover Canal, 1833   87

Upper Thames Navigation in 1875   88

Upper Thames Navigation in 1875   88

Thames pleasure boating at Henley regatta, 1880   121

Thames pleasure boating at Boulter's lock, about 1905–10   121

Newbury lock on the Kennet & Avon Canal, about 1900   122

Kennet & Avon Canal at Devizes flight, about 1880–90   122

Upper Midford bridge on the Somersetshire Coal Canal   139

9

page

Plan of Combe Hay in 1884, Somersetshire Coal Canal   139

Calne from the Wilts & Berks Canal, about 1820   140

Fleet Street bridge, Swindon, on the Wilts & Berks Canal   140

Stroudwater Navigation, committee-boat passing Stonehouse church, 1781   205

Stroudwater Navigation, a barge in Framilode basin, about
1900   205

Stroudwater Navigation, *Gertrude* at Ebley, about 1900   206

Thames & Severn Canal, South Cerney locks, about 1875   206

Gloucester & Berkeley Canal, *Sally* in Sharpness dry-dock,
1875   223

Gloucester & Berkeley Canal, Sharpness new docks under
construction, 1872   223

Gloucester docks, narrow boats being towed   224

Barges and a trow on the Gloucester & Berkeley Canal   224

TEXT ILLUSTRATIONS AND MAPS

1. Sutherland's reports on the Kent & Sussex Junction
   Canal   43

2. Inland navigation in the south east   44–5

3. The St Nicholas Bay and Canterbury scheme is promoted   50

4. Telford reports in 1824 on the Canterbury Navigation
   scheme   53

5. The Canterbury Navigation Company explain their
   position   55

6. A Dartford ship canal is projected   58

7. The Upper Medway Act of 1740   63

8. James Christie's card   71

9. The Upper Medway Company is attacked   73

10. Three routes for the Thames & Medway Canal   83

11. A Thames & Medway toll-sheet of 1825   91

12. Design for the staging that carried the Gravesend &
    Rochester Railway through Strood and Higham
    tunnels   98

13. Seal of the Croydon Canal   104

14. A Croydon Canal barge is sold   114

15. Rennie's report on the Grand Southern Canal   131

16. Inland navigation in the Hampshire basin   162

17. Andover Canal waybill of 1859   172

18. Notice is given to close the Andover Canal   175

19. Seal of the Thames Navigation Commissioners   189

20. Brindley reports in 1770 on the Thames   191

21. Routes of the Reading–Monkey Island–Isleworth canal
    schemes of 1770 and 1771   193

22. The Thames and its links with Severn and Avon   196–7

23. Zachary Allnutt describes the upper Thames in 1810   209

24. Praise for the Thames Commissioners   214

25. Shooting a Thames weir in a pleasure boat—if you were
    unlucky   218

26. The same—if you were lucky   219

27. John Hore's complaint against the Kennet proprietors   229

28. An early scheme for a Thames and Avon canal   233

29. A meeting of what became the Kennet & Avon com-
    pany   234

30. The ride to Devizes   236

31. Two title-pages from the time of the canal mania   237–8

32. A letter to the Kennet & Avon's committee chairman   247–8

33. Weldon's lift on the Somersetshire Coal Canal   266

34. Wilts & Berks Canal share certificate   278

page

35. Swindon at the time the Wilts & Berks was built   279

36. Pleasure cruising on the North Wilts Canal, 1893   293

37. The Saul crossing soon after 1820   303

38. Landowners meet in 1825 to encourage competition
    with the Stroudwater Navigation   308

39. The eastern portal of Sapperton tunnel on the Thames
    & Severn Canal   318

40. Route of the proposed Bristol–Cirencester Canal of 1793   321

41. Thames & Severn barge-owners' notice of about 1812   327

42. Notice by a fly-boat owner on the London to Gloucester
    route   331

43. Pleasure cruising tolls on the Thames & Severn, 1908   339

PREFACE

WHEN *The Canals of Southern England* was published in 1955, only a few specialized studies existed in local and learned journals. But now, as the old book comes to be re-cast, four full-length books are in print on aspects of the subject: Mr P. A. L. Vine's *London's Lost Route to the Sea* and *London's Lost Route to Basingstoke*, Mr Kenneth R. Clew's *Kennet and Avon Canal*, and Mr Humphrey Household's *Thames and Severn Canal*; I have also had access to the manuscript of a fifth, Mr Clew's *The Somersetshire Coal Canal*. In addition, F. S. Thacker's scarce two-volume history of the Thames navigation has been reprinted, and a number of excellent articles or booklets have appeared.

This book has been completely rewritten, but in it I have naturally done most new work on the waterways which have not yet been the subject of special studies. There are much fuller accounts of the Medway, the Thames & Medway Canal, and the various schemes for improving or by-passing the Kentish Stour and building a Weald of Kent Canal; the Croydon Canal; some of the Hampshire waterways; and the Stroudwater Navigation; but readers will, I hope, find additional information throughout the volume.

Because of coming decimalization, I have rounded up figures to the nearest pound when the shillings and pence element is unimportant. In other cases, except within a quotation, the decimal equivalent of 6d, and of sums of 1s and over, is given in brackets.

One advantage of rewriting an old book is that former contacts are renewed. I have had much pleasure from meeting or corresponding with old friends, while gaining new ones; pleasure also from revisiting waterways I had not seen for many years. My many obligations are acknowledged later in the book, but the companionship of my wife, the efficiency of my secretary, Mrs Whittaker, the help of so many members of the Railway & Canal Historical Society and the encouragement of my publisher are with me always. No one could be more fortunate.

CHARLES HADFIELD

13

CHAPTER I

Introduction to a Pattern

✦

In this book I have followed the Thames from its mouth to Lechlade, and the canal line thence to Gloucester; the Severn to the Bristol Avon, and from Bath drawn a zigzag line to the English Channel running west of Radstock but east of Frome and then straight to the sea at Christchurch. The atlas or the mind's eye shows that the area is nearly enclosed by the sea, the Severn or the Thames, and that no place in it is very far from one of the three. It was natural, then, that a water-transport system should grow inland from the sea or to join Severn to Thames.

In the middle of the eighteenth century the small ports were more important than they are now, for poor inland transport meant that each had to import and export the goods which concerned its immediate hinterland. Many on the south coast had an actually or potentially navigable river behind them: London on the Thames, Chatham and Rochester on the Medway, Sandwich on the Stour, Rye on the Eastern Rother, Newhaven or Lewes on the Ouse, Arundel on the Arun, Shoreham on the Adur, Southampton on the Itchen, and Bristol on the Avon were the most important.

For foreign trade the more important ports were London, Bristol and Southampton. The craft of the coasting trade, however, moved ceaselessly between the ports, great and small, and continued to do so throughout our period, carrying coal, timber, building materials and agricultural products. Insofar as inland navigations led inland from such ports as these, coasting craft and barges were complementary; but when a through line of inland navigation was completed, as from London to Bristol or Portsmouth, it had to compete against vessels making the same voyage by sea.

Again, the existence of London, Bristol and Bath within the area, and its prosperity in the middle and late eighteenth century, were incentives to the improvement of roads at a rate faster than in the country as a whole. This meant that by the end of the Napoleonic Wars, the south country was relatively well supplied with turnpikes. Therefore land carriage was always a competitor with canals, and after 1815 very seriously so.

These turnpike roads were maintained not by the statute labour of the parishes* but by groups of trustees originally appointed by Parliament. These raised money by loan to build proper roads and paid the interest from the tolls they levied upon the traffic passing through their toll-gates. In the eighteenth century the system had been developing, but many important roads had not yet been turnpiked, and the turnpike trusts in being were mostly local affairs, each as self-sufficient as were the smaller canals. But as the century drew to its end and the new one began, various pressures welded them into the beginnings of a national system, and at the same time were making the individual roads more efficient and better able to bear heavy traffic. The running of coaches at steadily increasing speeds; the necessity for goods to go by road when no alternative was available; the influence of the Board of Agriculture in introducing Macadam and his ideas to the turnpike trusts; and the pressure of the Post Office, anxious for improved deliveries of the mails, all had their effect. The increases in the length of turn-pike roads for three southern counties between 1814 and 1839 were as follows:[1]

	Surrey miles	Sussex miles	Hants miles
1814			
Length of turnpike roads and paved streets	248	558	497
1839			
Length of turnpike roads and paved streets	386¾	728¼	837

By 1840 22,000 miles of roads throughout the country had been turnpiked, and the trusts had a total debt of £7 million.

The growth of the system and the improvement of road surfaces made it easier and cheaper to run road waggons, which therefore began to compete more effectively with the waterways, and especially with the canals, which had higher interest charges and costs of upkeep than the river navigations. One hardly ever finds a southern canal company complaining seriously of the competition of land carriage before 1815, but the falling prices of peace combined with the improved road system to produce a state of affairs in which the waterways, though still increasing each

---

* Sometimes all the inhabitants turned out, more often many of them commuted their service for a money payment with which men were hired. The liability to statute labour was abolished in 1835.

Page 17 (above) The Royal Military Canal and military road near Ruckinge. The curves enabled guns to be so placed that they could prevent a crossing by firing down each stretch of canal; (*below*) a share certificate of the Canterbury Navigation & Sandwich Harbour Company

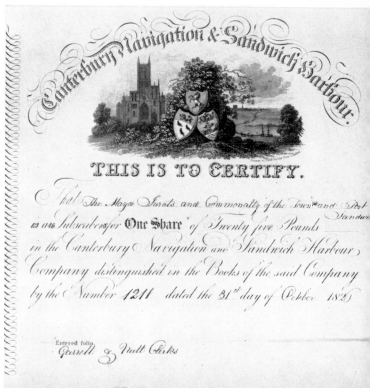

Canterbury Navigation & Sandwich Harbour

THIS IS TO CERTIFY.

That The Mayor Jurats and Commonalty of the Town and Port ... Sandwich ... are Subscribers for **One Share** of Twenty five Pounds in the Canterbury Navigation and Sandwich Harbour Company distinguished in the Books of the said Company by the Number 1211 dated the 31st day of October 1825

Entered folio
Garrett & Nutt Clerks

All Transfers of Shares must be registered at the Office

Page 18 (above) Old Maidstone lock on the Upper Medway Navigation, removed in 1881; *(below)* for most of 1845 trains and barges shared Higham and Strood tunnels on the Thames & Medway Canal

year the total tonnage they carried, were losing to the roads a bigger percentage of the total traffic available.

We have, therefore, to look at canal history within the south and south east of England against the background of a widespread coasting trade and a better than average road system. These are two of the reasons why it is one of few successes and many comparative failures, whereas the opposite was the case in the midlands and the north.

In addition, the south of England was a declining industrial area during the canal age. The iron industry of Sussex and Kent had diminished to extinction before the end of the eighteenth century, while the floating of timber down such rivers as the Adur and the Arun lessened as the forests were exhausted. The woollen industry of Gloucestershire, Hampshire, and Wiltshire was giving way to the developing north.

The coal mines of Somerset, the only ones of any importance in the south, had a greater output relative to the total for the country then than now. In 1800 they produced about 140,000 tons a year against a total of 10m tons. As the century grew, however, the Somerset field declined relatively as it felt increasingly the competition of collieries in south Wales, the Forest of Dean and the Midlands. The real unfolding of the Industrial Revolution was taking place where there were coal and iron together, and swift streams for water power. The powerful industrial motive for canal-building, that drove to completion such early ventures as the Duke of Bridgewater's Canal and the Trent & Mersey, was therefore absent in the south. Its place was partially taken by the less powerful Agricultural Revolution.

The south of England was predominantly an agricultural area. It is easy to forget that while the countryside was well populated for those days, the towns, with the exception of London and Bristol, were all very small. In 1801 London had a population of 865,000 and Bristol 64,000, but in that year a town of such importance to waterways as Reading, standing at the junction of the Kennet with the Thames, had only 10,827 people. Even in 1851, when the canal age was over, its population was only 21,456.

The countryside produced wheat, barley, oats, hops, butter, cheese, and other commodities not only for its own use and that of the towns in its midst, but also for London and Bristol. Many inland navigations were therefore conceived of as a means of exporting agricultural produce either to the great towns or to local markets, and of bringing domestic coal and other needed goods in exchange. At the time of enthusiasm for canals, agricultural pro-

B

duction was growing, and with it the need of all classes for commodities brought from outside the rural districts. Once the Napoleonic Wars were over, however, agricultural production in the south seems no longer to have increased at the same rate, and the needs of London, Bristol, and the other growing towns were met partly by imports from abroad, and partly by supplies from other parts of the United Kingdom. This unforeseen failure of output falsified the hopes of many canal promoters in the south, and its effects were added to by the growing poverty of the lower classes as the agricultural revolution and its consequences took effect.

Even during the period of high agricultural productivity of the Wars themselves, W. Stevenson, writing of the Croydon Canal in his *General View of the Agriculture of Surrey*, published in 1809, was perspicacious enough to say:

It is evident that all the canals which are or may be made in this country, if they terminate within it, must depend almost entirely upon the goods conveyed *from* the metropolis for their support. . . . Of the advantage to the county itself, from canals, there can be no doubt: the easy and cheap conveyance, even of coals and manure, would be a great means both of improving the land, and increasing the comforts of the inhabitants; but it may be doubted, whether a county purely agricultural, except under very peculiar and favourable circumstances, can maintain a sufficient *export trade* to keep up a canal.

Within this general framework, we may consider some incentives to the building and working of inland navigations in the south. The first, and by far the most important, was to distribute coal. The demand for fuel was not primarily from industry but from the householder. As villages grew into towns, and towns into larger towns; as the population increased and standards of life rose; and as the supply of wood for fuel fell away, so the demand for coal for heating increased. To carry such a cheap and bulky commodity by waggon was far too expensive; water transport was the answer. The need to bring coal to a neighbourhood, with special reference to the resulting benefit to the poor, was always a reason for building canals, and a reduction in the price of coal was always a principal result of their construction and a cause of local rejoicing.

Two demands for coal besides the domestic accounted for large quantities. From about 1810 gasworks began to be built, and streets and houses to be lit by gas. If one looks at the sites of present-day gasworks, one often finds them alongside a canal or navigable river. Towns without water carriage usually had to wait for their gas till the railway came. Again, lime, the universal fertilizer of the agricultural revolution that accompanied the industrial, was produced by burning either limestone or chalk with imported coal (usually the small coal and slack called culm) at the many limekilns that are to be found on the banks of estuaries where limestone was imported or along canals and rivers where they penetrated the chalk ridges or where limestone was quarried. The pressure to improve agricultural output, and so the demand for lime, was especially heavy during the Napoleonic Wars, and it remained a major factor throughout the canal age. With the introduction of railways came centralization, and at the same time the introduction of artificial fertilizers.

A second great incentive to canal building was the desire to distribute the produce of the land. The growth of towns, especially London and Bristol, led to the replacement of the more or less self-sufficient economy of the countryside by a trading economy, by which food was exported to the towns, and their products, visible or invisible, were imported in exchange. We remember Cobbett's complaints of the draining away of the wealth of the countryside by the towns, and especially the Great Wen. The barges that brought coal, therefore, returned with corn, flour, wool, cheese, cider, and much else, till this business was lessened by the increasing consumption of their own products in the country districts, and of imported foods in the big towns.

Another agricultural influence was the need to improve land drainage. It was often found, as in Kent and Sussex, that rivers could be improved both for drainage purposes and for navigation at the same time, or that drainage schemes had made it easier to build navigations.

Three other common cargoes each had some influence on canal building. The development of the turnpike road and the road engineering techniques of Macadam, Telford, and others, created a heavy demand for roadstone to be carried from quarries to the nearest point to the road where it was to be used. The carriage of this stone gave a steadily increasing tonnage to many canals. Sometimes the roads thus improved were ancillary to the waterways; more often they were competitive.

The growth of population and the increasing wealth of the upper and middle classes led to extensive house-building. Often, as in the Cotswolds, the material used was so local that it did not need water transport, but the carriage of bricks, slates, roofing tiles, and timber was common. The timber was sometimes grown not far from the place where it was to be used, but as the forests disappeared, so imported wood was substituted, and the lines of trade changed.

Again, the food for man and beast which everyone in the south had to import was salt, usually from Worcestershire by way of the Severn, and salthouses stand beside many old wharves.

Finally, two other kinds of cargo were carried mainly on the trunk waterways, the Thames, the Kennet & Avon and the Gloucester & Berkeley: what were usually classified as groceries, that is, sugar, imported fruit, wines and spirits, and so on; and manufactured goods, most of them either from the Bristol area or, deriving from the Midlands and the north, coming on to our system from the Oxford Canal or by way of the Severn.

Within the framework of these conditions and motives, the pattern of waterways described in this book becomes easier to follow. It could hardly be more variegated: old river navigations like the Itchen, Medway, Kentish Stour or Hampshire Avon; trunk lines like the great Kennet & Avon or the little Wey & Arun Junction; short canals that were successes, like the Stroud-water, comparative failures, like the Croydon, or disasters like the Salisbury & Southampton; the Gloucester & Berkeley, the biggest ship canal that had so far been built in England; two of her three longest canal tunnels; and, dominating and conditioning the development of three-quarters of the whole system, the indispensable Thames.

After the Oxford–Burcot Commission had, in the 1620s, built three of the earliest pound-locks in the country between Oxford and Abingdon, the Thames was considered reasonably navigable over its whole length for the boats of the time. Earlier still, about 1200, the bishop of Winchester had enabled commercial craft to use the Itchen, though the river passage had decayed since then; the Arun had about 1570 been made navigable to Pallingham quay, and about 1594 the Kentish Stour to Canterbury, though only temporarily. In 1627 a partially successful attempt was made to improve the Medway upwards from Maidstone, and in 1653 the Wey was opened to Guildford. After the Restoration there was a flood of navigation schemes, some of which included a canal-building element: to link London and Bristol, connect the Adur, Arun, Mole and Wey, open the Medway and Hampshire Avon, and reopen the Itchen. Not much came of them, though the Avon was navigable to Salisbury for a time after 1684, but failed to survive.

The first seventy years of the eighteenth century saw solid work done. The Kennet was made navigable to Newbury in 1723, the

Bristol Avon to Bath in 1727, the Medway to Tonbridge about 1750, the Wey extended to Godalming in 1763. And then, a few years later, the canal age began, not yet with construction, but with little groups of enterprising local promoters employing the few experienced engineers of the time to make surveys: Smeaton's combined land drainage and navigation study of the lower Sussex Ouse and Brindley's of a Salisbury to the sea canal in 1768, Whitworth's for an Andover Canal in 1770, Brindley's, on behalf of the City corporation, for a London Canal from below Maidenhead to Isleworth to by-pass the lower Thames, Whitworth's for a connecting Maidenhead to Reading canal, and Davis's for one from Maidenhead to Basingstoke. Bills for the last two, the first practicable canal Bills within the area covered by this book, in 1771 met in Parliament another to reorganize the Thames Commissioners upon the basis they were to keep until they gave way to the Conservancy in 1866. The canal Bills failed, but that for the river succeeded, and out of that year's legislation came the eight Thames locks built from Boulter's at Maidenhead upwards to below Reading in 1772 and 1773.

Then followed the difficult political period that led up to and through the war of American Independence. To the east little happened except that two more Thames locks were built, this time above Reading, and, in 1778, an Act passed to authorize a Basingstoke Canal, now to the Wey, though times were too discouraging for construction to begin. But in the west they were thinking less of present troubles and more of what might be. Between 1776 and 1779 the Stroudwater Navigation, a river scheme that became a true canal, was opened from the Severn to Stroud, and in 1781 that company ordered a survey to be made of the ground over the Cotswolds from Stroud to the Thames. The result was the Thames & Severn Canal Act of 1783 and the linked but unsuccessful bill of 1785 to bypass the upper Thames from Kempsford on the canal to Abingdon. The developing prospect of a water connection between Severn and Thames, Bristol or Coalbrookdale and London, was made actual on 19 November 1789 when the Thames & Severn opened.

By that year also the Oxford Canal had been completed from Banbury to a junction with the Thames by way of the Duke's Cut above Oxford, and along it at once began to flow a trade to and from Birmingham and the Black Country, the Potteries and Lancashire. Anticipating this, the Thames Commissioners had built further new locks between Reading and Oxford, and were soon to rebuild the old ones of the Oxford–Burcot Commission. The end of 1789 therefore saw the opening of two trunk routes through the south country, from the Severn and from the Oxford Canal, meeting in the Thames. The first was to prove of small importance; the second for a few years of much more, until it was bypassed from 1800 onwards by the opening of an all-canal route from the Midlands to London by way of the Grand Junction Canal. Even then, however, a good deal of trade passed on to the river at Oxford for Abingdon, Reading and other Thames-side wharves.

All over our area local activity was now beginning. In 1788 work started on the Basingstoke Canal; in 1789 on the Andover; in 1790 the Arun Navigation was opened through to Newbridge by way of Hardham tunnel, and an Act passed to make navigable the Sussex Ouse above Lewes, followed a year later by another for the western Rother.

From 1788 also, interest in canals was everywhere increasing, the Thames and other rivers were being improved, schemes were proliferating, possible trunk lines were being surveyed, solid investment possibilities were being overlaid by speculation, until the whole exploded into the get-rich-quick frenzy of the canal mania in the last quarter of 1792. Out of it all emerged, at the cost of a million pounds, the Kennet & Avon, a great trunk canal from Bath on the Bristol Avon to Newbury on the Kennet, which, after its opening in 1810, offered a good barge communication between Bristol and London far straighter and easier than the roundabout Thames & Severn route. Emerged also the Wilts & Berks, again fully opened in 1810, a narrow waterway from the Kennet & Avon near Trowbridge through the Vale of White Horse to the Thames at Abingdon, a company with trunk-line aspirations without the facilities, who for the time being had to limit themselves to carrying agricultural produce and also coal from the third of the mania canals based on the Bristol–Bath area, the Somersetshire Coal Canal opened in 1806. There had been many plans also for another east–west trunk route, using the Basingstoke Canal, completed in 1794, and then a waterway to Salisbury with a link to Southampton, or to the Itchen at Winchester and so via Southampton to Salisbury again, and on to Bristol direct or by a junction with the Kennet & Avon at Pewsey. But nothing came of these except the unfinished Salisbury & Southampton.

Out of the mania, this time at Gloucester, also came the remarkable achievement of the Gloucester & Berkeley ship canal that avoided the difficult navigation of the lower Severn, and provided improved access from the river to the Stroudwater Navigation and the Thames & Severn Canal.

In 1799 and 1800 Ralph Dodd, an engineer with more vision than practical ability, put forward three schemes for canals near London, all of which were built in some form: from the Thames at Rotherhithe to Croydon; again from Rotherhithe to Vauxhall and Mitcham, partly made as the Grand Surrey; and from the Thames at Gravesend to the Medway near Rochester, opened after many tribulations in 1824. Dodd's ideas were supplemented by others of Sutherland's and Rennie's, for a trunk canal to link the Medway, through the Weald of Kent, to the eastern Rother towards Rye, but these got nowhere.

Fear of invasion by Napoleon built the Royal Military Canal in Kent between 1804 and 1806. Otherwise it was not until a minor repetition of the canal mania in 1810, encouraged by the opening in that year of the Kennet & Avon and the Wilts & Berks, that progress was made. That year saw numerous schemes that failed, most of them deservedly: for a ship canal from Canterbury to the sea; a canal link between the Kennet & Avon and the Grand Junction, or the Basingstoke, or even the Grand Surrey; several possible connections with the Wilts & Berks, from the Bristol coalfield, the Thames & Severn Canal, the Stratford-upon-Avon Canal or the Grand Junction; for Rennie's Medway–Portsmouth Grand Southern Canal; and for a Bath to Bristol canal. Out of it all came two results. One, the 9-mile long North Wilts, opened in 1819, connected the Thames & Severn to the Wilts & Berks, so giving the former an all-canal route that avoided the Thames above Abingdon, and enabling improved services between London and Gloucester. The other was the Wey & Arun Junction.

Rennie's Grand Southern scheme of 1810 for a Medway–Portsmouth canal had failed, as had an earlier one of his in 1803 for a line from Portsmouth to the Croydon Canal, but the war with France and its accompanying danger of privateers in the Channel, sharply increased interest in an internal water transport means of carrying goods between London and the great naval base. A step towards this was taken when the Wey & Arun was authorized in 1813, a canal from the Wey Navigation above Guildford to the Arun and so to the Channel at Littlehampton below Arundel. Opened in 1816, it was followed in the next year by an Act for a Portsmouth & Arundel Canal, to continue the line from the Arun below Arundel to the sea near Chichester, and then by what Americans would call an intracoastal waterway to Portsmouth. This London–Portsmouth route was opened throughout in 1823, and proved an immediate failure.

The mixed value of what existed was, however, for a time

obscured by the impressiveness of what might be. The boom year
of 1824 was a time of big ship canal projects, helped perhaps by
the encouraging progress then being made with the Gloucester &
Berkeley Canal, thanks to Government loans, and the completion
of the Thames & Medway. From 1823 to 1828 the public read
with interest several proposals for a ship canal from London to
Portsmouth, and for others from Canterbury to the sea and to
bypass part of the lower Thames between Woolwich and Erith.
Elsewhere in England, too, men were talking widely about similar
canals to Manchester, and across the peninsula of Devon and
Somerset. They read the plans, discussed them, listened to the
promoters—but kept their money in their pockets.

The opening of the Gloucester & Berkeley in 1827 ended canal
building in the south. A few years later active railway construction
began. The construction of main lines from London to the towns
of Kent, Surrey and Sussex, to Southampton, Salisbury, Reading,
Oxford, Bath, Bristol and Gloucester, drove the trunk waterways
back upon local trade. Then followed an intricate system of inter-
connecting branches which attacked the smaller navigations' business. They had the same effect upon the coasting trade, as for
instance when much of the coal that had formerly come by sea
from Newcastle or south Wales to be distributed by river or canal
began to come by rail. It was the same with the turnpikes:

In 1833, Turnpike Roads were the chief means of communication throughout the kingdom for the transit of goods and
passengers; much expense and skill has been bestowed in adapt-
ing the roads to the increased traffic of goods, and the more
speedy passage of the mails and stage coaches. From this period
railways have gradually superseded the use of Turnpike Roads
for the conveyance of goods and passengers, except for short
distances and local convenience.[2]

The fall in turnpike trust income between 1837 and 1854 was as
follows:[3]

	per cent		per cent
Sussex	41·35	Kent	37·87
Hants	41·09	Glos	34·33
Surrey	38·22	Wilts	33·81

In 1836 occurred the first major closure, of the Croydon Canal
to enable the London & Croydon Railway to use its bed. Unlike
what happened in the Midlands and north, few southern waterways were bought by railway companies: apart from the Croydon,
the Kennet & Avon in 1852, the Thames & Severn in extreme old

age and the Somersetshire Coal Canal after the company had gone into liquidation; while the Thames & Medway and Andover concerns turned themselves into railway companies and built their own competing lines. The rest were too independent, like the Thames or the Medway, or too unimportant. Instead, the competing railways crept along the canal routes: the Vale of White Horse, the Golden Valley, the valley of the Bristol Avon, beside the rivers of the south, taking the slow-moving barges' trade, until too little remained to pay maintenance expenses.

The second half of the nineteenth century saw closure after closure as traffic died, but also effort at reorganization and revival. The Thames & Severn was intended for conversion to a railway, re-started as a canal, re-planned once more as a railway, sold to the Great Western, who wanted it to stay an ineffective canal, bought back again by a group of navigation concerns and local authorities, and finished up in the hands of the Gloucestershire County Council. Several groups tried to make the Wilts & Berks pay, and failed; others did the same on the upper Medway until a number of local authorities, led by the Kent County Council, completely rebuilt the navigation. Even then it did not attract commercial traffic. As for the Basingstoke Canal, its somewhat humble self appeared and reappeared under different names and increasingly speculative dresses, detrimentally to many investors and without commercial success, until all its traffic had gone.

Finally, the 1900s saw two schemes for big new barge canals using electric haulage, one from London to Southampton, the other, which got as far as an Act, from the Medway to the Thames.

From that time, commercial traffic continued to fall away where it still existed, and closures to take place: the Wilts & Berks, for instance, in 1914, the Thames & Severn in 1927 and 1933, the Stroudwater in 1954. On some waterways pleasure traffic began to replace it, notably of course on the Thames, but also on the Wey and the upper Medway, and a little elsewhere. As I write, the same possibility opens before the Kennet & Avon and is suggested for the Basingstoke. Of all the waterways this book describes, commercial traffic only passes now on the Gloucester & Berkeley, the lowest part of the Thames above Teddington, the Grand Surrey, and the Medway to Tovil just beyond Maidstone. The table on page 28 summarizes the story. It is arranged on the same basis as that used in the other volumes of this series.

Excluding the Thames, there were at their fullest extent about 472 miles of navigable waterway in south and south eastern England: in Great Britain about 3,875. Our group therefore accounted

*Canals and Waterways Open in the South and South East by type of Waterway**

Date	*Ship Canal miles*	*Broad Canal miles*	*Narrow Canal miles*	*Tub-boat Canal miles*	*River Nav. miles*	*Total miles*
1760					211⅞	211⅞
1770					216⅜	216⅜
1780		8			216⅜	224⅜
1790		38¼			229⅜	267⅝
1800		90¾	28		245⅛	363⅞
1810		155⅞	106½		243⅞	506¼
1820		174⅜	108¼		267⅛	549¾
1830	27¾	184¾	108¼		276¼	597
1840	27¾	184¾	99		276¼	587¾
1850	20¾	175	99		279¼	574
1900	16¾	156½	66½		212½	452¼

* The canals and navigations listed are those of Appendix I. For classification purposes a ship canal is a canal that admits seagoing ships; a broad canal one with locks at least 12 ft wide; a narrow canal one with locks less than 12 ft wide; and a tub-boat canal one taking small boats carrying a few tons each. See *British Canals*, 4th ed., 1969, for a fuller description.

for about one-eighth of the total. The tonnage (if one makes no attempt to eliminate the same goods carried on more than one waterway) probably amounted to about 1,650,000 tons a year in 1845.* Of this, about 700,000 tons passed along some portion of the trunk routes: the Kennet & Avon, Wilts & Berks, Thames & Severn, Somersetshire Coal Canal, or the Stroudwater, though probably not more than 50,000 tons a year at most moved between the extremities of London and Bristol or Gloucester. About 500,000 tons passed on the Gloucester & Berkeley Canal, and perhaps we may estimate some 450,000 tons on all the other waterways. No figure of the tonnage carried in the whole of Great Britain at the same time is available, but that of 30,000,000 tons is probably a reasonable estimate.† If so, one-eighth of the waterways of Great Britain carried under one-fifteenth of the traffic. This lack of traffic was the basic reason why the canals of the south failed during their lives to pay their proprietors an adequate return, and so quickly collapsed before the competition of railways, whereas those elsewhere put up a stiffer and more often a

* I have excluded the tonnage on the Grand Surrey Canal, which is more in the nature of an extended dock.

† See article 'Canals: Their Cost, Their Dividends, and their Traffic', *Railway News*, 30 April 1864, which gives this figure. The Canal Returns of 1888 estimate it as 34,800,000.

successful fight. If we still exclude the Thames, and leave a broad margin for error, we can say that the river navigations of the south and south-east cost £211,000 to build, and the canals about £4m, the figure for the rivers being so small partly because it was much cheaper to make a river navigable than to build a canal, some of the work having been done by nature, and partly because they were mostly built at low eighteenth-century wage rates. Against this initial cost of some £4¼m, and ignoring subsequent capital expenditure on the canals themselves or on other operations such as carrying or trading, it is not likely that at their most flourishing time, about 1842, the total sums being paid in dividends and interest on loans by the southern waterway concerns exceeded £110,000, of which about £45,000 or over one-third would be attributable to two canals, the Kennet & Avon and the Somersetshire Coal Canal. The average remuneration of capital, prior charge and risk alike, therefore, was not more than 2½ per cent, and may have been less. Indeed, the figure would not have been so high if some of the river navigations with low initial costs, like the Kennet, the Avon, the Medway and the Wey, had not been good earners. Of the canals, only the Stroudwater and the Somersetshire Coal Canal were consistent payers of dividends of over 5 per cent.

The pattern we have to study is more intricate, perhaps, than in any other region of Britain. Yet what the waterways of the south and south east lose in economic importance, they gain in their interest for the canal enthusiast, the local historian and the industrial archaeologist. Let us, then, start our exploration with the smaller ones of the Sussex and Kent coast.

CHAPTER II

Waterways of the South East

+++++++++++++++++++++++++++++++++++++++◆++

River Adur and Baybridge Canal

THE natural river Adur was carrying timber in Defoe's day, but it was probably the fair success with which other nearby rivers had been made navigable that led to an Act[1] of 1807 to do the same for the Adur for 14 miles from Shoreham to Bines bridge for barges drawing 3 ft of water, and to improve the drainage of the surrounding lands. Seventy-nine trustees, together with the Commissioners of Sewers for the Rape of Bramber, were appointed to carry it out, and as with other drainage schemes, they were empowered to raise money by levying rates on the lands to be benefited. The Adur was tidal to Bines bridge, and the improvements consisted of dredging, embanking, and making a towpath. There were to be no locks or cuts. In spite of the low rate of authorized toll—a maximum of 1d for the whole length—the work was done, and an actual depth of 4 ft achieved.

Toll receipts started well, but fell away, as the following table[2] shows:

Year	Tolls £	Year	Tolls £
1812	523	1827	154
1815	475	1830	174
1818	315	1833	229
1821	330	1836	186
1824	206	1839	258

In 1825 seven promoters led by Lord Selsey and Sir Charles and Walter Burrell, both MPs, had subscribed £5,250 and obtained an Act to form the Baybridge Canal Company. In spite of its name and the wording of the Act,[3] the preamble of which said that it would be useful if 'a navigable Cut or Canal was made . . . from and out of the said River Adur . . . to or near Baybridge' on the Worthing–Horsham road by West Grinstead, and 5 miles from Horsham, the deposited plan shows only a widening of the Adur in places upwards from Bines bridge, and a number of small cuts and straightenings over a length of 3⅜ miles. May Upton's estimate was £5,958 for a navigation 28 ft wide, 4 ft deep, and with two locks 75 ft × 12 ft 6 in, each having a 7 ft rise, and for the rebuilding of Bines bridge. A capital of £6,000 was authorized, and £3,000 more if necessary.

The Brighton Railway opened in 1861 from Shoreham to join the Horsham–Pulborough railway near Horsham. This line competed directly with the Adur, which in 1865 ceased to pay interest on its loan debt. The Baybridge Canal was little used after 1861, and was closed from and after 1 September 1875. Of the three petitioners for a closure Act,[4] two bore names of original shareholders, Sir Percy Burrell and C. G. Eversfield. In 1905, 12,989 tons were carried on the Adur in barges drawn by a tug and working to a cement works at Beeding and to Shoreham. This specialized use of the river, together with a very little general traffic, continued until 1929.

River Ouse (Sussex)

In the eighteenth century and afterwards, the Ouse below Lewes was a tidal navigation. Smeaton, reporting in 1768 on suggested land drainage improvements, suggested a lock should be built at Piddinghoe, but this was not done, and the river remained open.

On the Ouse above Lewes, a map of 1724[5] shows boats (probably very small ones) navigating to Maresfield Forge above Shortbridge, and a lock (presumably a flash-lock) is marked. The preamble to the Ouse Act of 1790, however, implies that the river was then only used to Barcombe mills.

In 1788 William Jessop, then engineer of the Trent Navigation, was called in to suggest how best to make the Ouse above Lewes navigable. He surveyed a possible navigation from Lewes past Barcombe mill to Pilstye bridge just beyond the Cuckfield–Balcombe road, 4 ft deep and a minimum of 24 ft wide, to take 30-ton craft, 45 ft × 12 ft, the navigation to be made by cutting off sharp curves, some widening, a number of short cuts, and 25 locks. The cost, he thought, would be £14,400 exclusive of parliamentary expenses. However, he seems himself to have been doubtful whether it was wise to extend the navigation higher than Lindfield, with 18 locks at a cost of £9,271. He saw the traffic as mainly chalk for use on the land, supplemented by timber, coal and the usual commerce of a country navigation, and thought that by carrying these a good dividend could be paid.

Barges could not pass below Lewes to Newhaven for about half of every month, during the time of neap tides. He proposed therefore also to widen, deepen and straighten this tidal section for an additional £1,980, mainly by making a 1,000 yd cut and by dredging, though he also provided for a towing path as far down as Piddinghoe.

Jessop's report was followed by an Act[6] of 1790 to make the upper river navigable from Lewes past Barcombe mill to the further boundary of Cuckfield parish beyond Hammer bridge, at a cost of £25,000, and a year later another for improving the navigation of the lower river from Lewes to Newhaven,[7] mainly by about 1,100 yd of new cutting. This second measure was as much concerned with drainage as navigation, and the work of embanking and straightening the river was financed by tolls and drainage rates in roughly equal shares. No locks were built on the lower river.

In May 1790 a contract was advertised for building 20 locks and other works, making new cuts, and widening and deepening the Ouse between Lewes and Slaugham. The Pinkertons, who were so often associated with Jessop, took the contract, and soon began work above Lewes. In July 1791 tolls were first taken at Hamsey, the lock nearest Lewes. But not long afterwards the committee

Resolved That Messrs Pinkertons have neglected their Undertaking on the River Ouse, that a Considerable part of the Work has failed and other parts have been injudiciously done.[8]

By April 1793 the river seems to have been navigable from Lewes to Sheffield bridge, and some work had been done 'between that place and Hammer Bridge in deepening and widening the River, Building locks and other works'.[9] Over £20,000 had been spent, but the tolls for 1793–6 averaged only £236 pa, and the shareholders were exhausted. It took from 1793 to 1805 to raise the few hundred pounds necessary to extend a further 1½ miles to Freshfield bridge, and meanwhile the navigation had from 1797 been in the hands of a receiver. The extension improved receipts, and in 1806 it was decided to go forward for a Bill authorizing the raising of another £30,000 to complete the navigation to Hammer bridge, but to abandon the powers to extend beyond. The Bill was approved in the same year.

In 1808 the lethargy caused by floods, failures, and finance was thrown off. William Smith the geologist, formerly of the Somersetshire Coal Canal, was appointed engineer, and Dymoke Wells, a local man already connected with the navigation, contracted to carry it upwards to Lindfield mill, taking only one-third of the cost in cash, and the rest equally in bonds and shares. Money was raised, the old creditors were given bonds and withdrew their receiver, and by the end of the year 1809 the navigation was open to that point. The tolls for 1809 had been £751 without the receipts from the extension.

Now a quarrel with the first Lord Sheffield broke out, He had been the leader in the early days, but he seems to have quarrelled with his associates, and to have then set himself to harry them. In 1810 the committee had to say:

That the Company know no cause for Lord Sheffield's restless endeavours to harass them unless it be that he has no longer the management of the Navigation. . . . That it is the Opinion of this Meeting that the Navigation did not prosper under his Lordship's management, that it did never advance beyond his own Wharf at Sheffield Bridge. . . . That to rescue the Navigation . . . several of the Proprietors advanced among themselves a Sum . . . for the purpose of forming the Navigation to Freshfield Bridge, to which Lord Sheffield refused to contribute. . . . That they effected this object not only without the assistance but in spite of every obstruction from his Lordship.[10]

The quarrel went on for some years, but by 1823 the second Lord Sheffield was back on the committee.

The navigation was further extended about 1812 to Upper Ryelands bridge near the Haywards Heath–Balcombe road by Dymoke Wells on the same terms. It was now 22½ miles long, with a ¾-mile branch to Shortbridge (for Uckfield) and some other shorter branches. Eighteen locks were built, 52 ft 6 in by 13 ft 6 in, taking barges carrying about 18 tons. The figures suggest that the navigation was not deepened to the extent Jessop had recommended, for he had proposed barges 45 ft × 12 ft to draw 3 ft 6 in, and carry 30 tons. There are almost no revenue figures available, but in 1811 the tolls were let for one year at £1,625, and in 1812 for two years at £1,250. It seems to have been enough to pay interest on the money borrowed to extend upwards from Sheffield bridge, some £10,000, but not to pay dividends, and the shareholders received nothing. The upward traffic was mainly coal, chalk and road material, the downward agricultural produce.

In 1825 there was a curious proposal for a canal from Lewes, rising by 29 locks from the Ouse and then passing through a 2½-mile tunnel to reach Brighton on the level.

The Ouse maintained a small and local business till the London & Brighton Railway was built, and indeed carried building material for the great viaduct at Hayward's Heath. When this line was opened there was said to have been some trade which passed up the river to the end of the navigation to be transferred to the rails, and back again. In 1846, however, this traffic was ended by the railway line built along the coast from Brighton to Lewes and Hastings (the bridge over the Ouse, like that over the Arun, had a telescopic opening section), and some competition ensued between the river and the railway to Brighton and thence to the Ouse valley. In 1844 the tolls on coal and timber had been reduced from 1½d to 1d a ton per mile, and in 1846 the revenue was about £800, about a third less than thirty years before. In 1849 the coal toll was again reduced to ¾d. Direct competition began when in 1858 a branch line was opened which joined Lewes to Uckfield, and in the following year, after a last reduction of the coal toll to ½d, the company's books cease. In 1861 the upper part of the navigation above Lindfield became disused, and the rest of the river above Lewes about 1868, when the last barge went up to Lindfield. A line was built in 1882 branching from the Lewes–Uckfield railway and running past the upper river to East Grinstead, but by this time there was no water-borne traffic.

River Cuckmere

In 1791–2 there was a proposal for a canal from the river Ouse below Lewes to Horsebridge and Hellingly on the Cuckmere, with a branch to Selmeston, and in 1813 it was suggested that the Cuckmere should be made navigable from the tideway to Horsebridge, perhaps in connection with the Act for the enclosure of Dicker Common passed in the same year.

The Eastern Rother and Brede

The Eastern Rother[11] was navigable from very early times from Rye past Appledore and round the north of the Isle of Oxhey to Newenden, Bodiam, Udiam and beyond. The Romans certainly used it to Bodiam and probably further, and in Saxon, Norman and later times it was navigable at least to Etchingham for small boats. Records exist of the carriage by water of stone for the building of Bodiam Castle in the late fourteenth century, and of the shipment of mid-sixteenth century cargoes of iron from Udiam and Bodiam. Iron also came down, before and after 1635, from Etchingham, Robertsbridge, Hawkhurst and Biddenden to be shipped at Udiam, where an iron-store was built in the seventeenth

Page 35 (*above*) Gravesend basin and sea lock on the Thames & Medway Canal, about 1956. The canal leads off to the right; (*below*) looking towards Deptford on the Croydon Canal, from a print published in 1815

Page 36 Wey Navigation: (*above*) barges unload grain from London docks at Coxe's lock mill, 1963; (*below*) one of William Stevens' barges in Thames lock, Weybridge, in 1950

century, or Newenden. There was also trade to Rolvenden from Maytham wharf and to Tenterden from Small Hythe. About 1695 the course of the Rother was shortened by about five miles by bringing it round the south of the Isle of Oxhey, the old north channel becoming the Reading Sewer.

The Brede was also navigable from very early times. From the Tudor period to 1766 there was an iron furnace at Brede itself, and 'from 1747 to 1766 barges came up the river from Strand Wharf, Rye, loaded with iron ore for the furnaces, also groceries for the village shop-keepers . . . and loading back guns brought from the Brede furnace.'[12]

Later, the navigation of the river and its tributaries was mainly by Rye sailing barges about 45 ft × 12 ft, drawing 2 ft 9 in, and carrying some 20 tons. About 1800[13] there seems to have been navigation to Appledore and Reading Street; to Maytham wharf, Newenden and Bodiam; to Small Hythe; and up the Newmill Channel towards Tenterden. A pamphlet of 1802 says:

. . . previous to the last ten years three barges only were employed on the Rother navigations. Owing to the increased and still increasing demand for manures, fuel, and mendment for the roads, there are actually at this time no less than sixteen barges employed, chiefly in conveying those commodities.[14]

Towing was by men; there was no horse path. When the Royal Military Canal was built, barges worked up the Rother through Scots Float sluice (lock) and then through Iden lock* on to the canal, on which they traded probably as far as Bonnington. In October 1804 Rennie described Scots Float sluice as being 'very inconvenient and illadapted to the present Vessels which navigate the Rother.'

The Rother Levels Acts of 1826 and 1830 laid certain obligations upon the Commissioners of the Rother Levels to maintain navigation between Scots Float and Bodiam bridge, and a minimum bridge headroom of 5 ft, although they charged no tolls. In two reports of 1830, the Rennies said that the admission of tidal water through Scots Float sluice to the upper Rother was prejudicial. There were shoals below the sluice, and above it the channel was 'circuitous and irregular and for the most part too small; it is moreover full of shoals; the Bridges are built obliquely' so causing flooding and navigation difficulties.[15] In 1844, Scots Float sluice was rebuilt as the present lock by William Cubitt and James Elliott, the latter of whom had in that year been appointed

---

* *The Encyclopaedia Britannica* of 1842 said that these two locks, 72 ft × 16 ft, 'are only required for the tide, and the fluctuations of the Rother.'

C

Expenditor of the Rother Levels. There was navigation up the Rother to Maytham at least to the 1920s. In 1933, land drainage needs were given priority over navigation above Scots Float.

The Rother was involved in three canal schemes, none of which came to anything. From 1800 onwards versions of the Weald of Kent Canal scheme (see p. 42) proposed junctions between the Medway and the Rother; in 1813 Netlam Giles, working for Rennie, surveyed for a canalization of the river from Newenden bridge through Robertsbridge to near Mayfield; and in late 1834 a shorter canalization was suggested from Bodiam to Robertsbridge. This was advertised as the Rye & Robertsbridge Canal with a capital of £10,000, plans and prospectuses being offered— unsuccessfully.[16]

The Rye Harbour Act of 1833 required the Commissioners of Sewers for the Levels of Brede and Pett to make Brede sluice navigable, and the Brede able to take barges to Brede bridge. These obligations were effectively abrogated in 1933, when land drainage needs were given priority over the maintenance of a navigable depth. During the nineteenth century there had been some navigation up the Brede to Brede village, and the Tillingham to Marshall's Farm.[17]

Navigation responsibility on the rivers is now with the Kent River Authority. Neither Brede nor Tillingham sluice is now navigable.

Royal Military Canal

The war, first with the French Republic and then with Napoleon, had another influence upon canal building besides stimulating schemes for joining London to Portsmouth, or for crossing the peninsula of the south-west or the Great Glen of Scotland. There was a time after the resumption of the war in 1803 when invasion was seriously feared. A glance at the map will show the advantages presented to an enemy by the great flat expanse of Romney Marsh, as a coastline upon which to land and an area upon which to consolidate a beach-head. Martello towers were therefore built along the coast and the Royal Military Canal was dug from the sea at Shorncliffe along the line of the high ground behind the marsh to the line of the Rother, and again from the Brede to Cliff End beyond Winchelsea. The historian J. Holland Rose says that the formation of the canal was probably due to the extreme importance attached to the defence of that part of Kent by Dumouriez, the French revolutionary general who was antiinvasion adviser to the British Government.[18]

The idea for the canal apparently came from Lt-Col. Brown, Assistant Quartermaster-General, and a member of the newly-formed Royal Staff Corps of field engineers.[19] He surveyed the south Kent coast and proposed a canal in a report dated 19 September 1804, for which he got the support of General Sir David Dundas commanding the Southern District. Brown's proposal was mainly for a canal from Shorncliffe in front of Hythe and under Lympne Heights to West Hythe, 60 ft wide at top and 9 ft deep. He said, however, that it would be advantageous if it could be extended to join the river Rother, whence there would be a communication with the sea. He also proposed to build a great military road on the inside with a parapet between.* Sir David Dundas, in supporting the recommendation, said:

> Such a Ditch or Canal would not be totally unproductive and be of use for Commercial or Husbandry purposes. Floating Defences would be moveable and manageable, and contribute much to its strength and the quick movement of troops.

He went on to say that the total cost including a road would be about £80,000, and

> at any Rate the execution of the part recommended in the Neighbourhood of Hithe is essential and within a very moderate expence.

These two reports were sent on 27 September by the Commander-in-Chief, Frederick, Duke of York, to Lord Camden, Minister at War. The Commander-in-Chief wrote in his covering letter:

> In regard to the Proposal of cutting a Canal betwixt Hithe and the River Rother, for the purpose of Military Defence, by separating an Enemy landed upon the Coast of Romney Marsh from the Interior of the Country, I am to press this Measure most earnestly upon the consideration of His Majesty's Government. . . . The first advantage to be proposed from this Measure, is the necessity being done away of Innundating previous to the moment that the Enemy's Attempt is deemed certain. Secondly, Should his Force not prove very considerable this measure of Ruinous Consequence may possibly be altogether avoided.
>
> But however desirable, I beg your Lordship will not dwell upon the Expectation of our being enabled to depart from a Precaution of such Importance, should the Enemy conduct his Operation with vigour and in Formidable numbers. As this Canal will at most give a defensible line of great strength, But

---

* The canal and its parapet were built so that gun positions were provided at the end of each length to flank the crossings.

not one from which the same Body of Troops could be spared in support of other Points, were the same extent of country protected by Innundation.

He then goes on to say that should an armed flotilla be stationed in the port of Rye for the defence of Pevensey Bay, gun vessels might be able to move up and down the canal to defend the whole of Romney Marsh.

On the same day the Commander-in-Chief himself obtained Pitt's authority to start work, and wrote a second and less pleasant letter to Lord Camden:

By his desire, the different Measures proposed were immediately authorised for the purpose of avoiding Delay which must other-wise have attended the receiving of Your Lordship's Official Sanction. But which you will be pleased to remark it is necessary should be sent.

John Rennie was now retained as consultant. By the end of October there was talk of extending the canal from the Rother to Cliff End and by this date work had already begun. The Com-mander-in-Chief writes on 31 October:

Its progress may (be) expected to be rapid and when completed, (it) may be fairly considered as an almost insurmountable Barrier against an Enemy's penetrating into the Country. From the difficulty of approach across the Marsh, the Time that will be afforded for assembly from every Quarter and the numbers that may thus oppose him; it ought to operate as a great dis-couragement from making any Effort by this the shortest Line of Passage.

In a letter of 15 November the Commander-in-Chief estimates the total cost to Cliff End at £200,000 and says that three con-tractors are at work who had been employed in building the London and West India docks. He proposed to build the canal from Shorncliffe to three miles west of Lympne Hill by 1 March 1805, and the whole by 1 June.

The work fell behind. In March 1805 Rennie wrote:

In respect to the Contractors, I am sorry to say they have greatly disappointed my expectations, founded upon the dili-gence and accuracy with which I have seen other great Works done by them.

and about the middle of the year Lord Camden and Pitt agreed that more contractors should be employed. On 15 July, however, the Commander-in-Chief wrote to Castlereagh that Lt-Col. Brown, in charge of the work, considered he could complete the canal without using new contractors. Later those already engaged were withdrawn, and the work was finished under the direction of the Quartermaster-General of the Forces. The canal seems to have been completed about October 1806, for the major disbursements end after December, and these may be guessed to fall three months after the work was done.

It was in two canal sections, the first from Shorncliffe to the Rother, including Iden lock into the Rother that was part of the canal for defensive purposes, the second from the river Brede at Winchelsea to Cliff End. This section had no entrance lock, and therefore no navigable connection with the Brede. It was probably never navigated. The net cost of the canal to 30 June 1807, when an account was made up,[20] was £140,871, to which an estimated £50,000 as an outside price was added for land. The canal was therefore completed within its estimate, and reflects credit on Lt-Col. Brown, who was in charge of the section from Shorncliffe to Rye, and Lt-Col. Nicolay, in charge from Rye to Cliff End, and their superiors.

After 1805 the main invasion danger passed away as Napoleon turned eastwards, though on 30 May 1808 the Commander-in-Chief proposed to Lord Chatham 'two respectable works' at the ends of the canal. Before this, however, the Government had taken steps to earn what revenue was to be obtained from the waterway while keeping it available for its original purpose. An Act of 1807[21] established

the Speaker of the House of Commons, the Lord High Treasurer of Great Britain, the First Commissioner of the Treasury, the Chancellor of the Exchequer, His Majesty's Principal Secretaries of State, the Commander in Chief of His Majesty's Forces, the Lord Warden of the Cinque Ports, the Secretary at War, the Master General of the Ordnance, and the Quartermaster General of His Majesty's Forces, for the Time being respectively

as an impressive body of commissioners to maintain the canal and road, to set up toll-gates and to charge tolls, except on manure and produce for the owners or occupiers of lands along its route. Three main sources of revenue were tolls from the canal, those from one and later two turnpike gates near Rye on the military road, and sales of grass from the parapet and land. Some revenue figures are given in the table on page 42.

Expenditure on the canal was high in early years, but for 1815–19 it averaged £1,644.[22]

The commissioners owned a few barges, sometimes towed by horses of the Royal Waggon Train which also used the military

	Canal tolls £	Road tolls £	Grass £	Other revenue £	Total £
1811	421	163	172	14	770
1812	576	194	213	58	1041
1813	426	294	189	78	987
1814	377	305	165	60	907
1815	305	316	197	21	839
1816	292	316	253	20	881
1817	359	299	263	59	980
1818	316	367	306	56	1045
1819	458	378	356	31	1223
1820	536	352			

road, in which sand was carried inland from a beach they owned at Rye. Other traffics on the canal were bricks, stone and timber.

In 1837 a further Act transferred responsibility for the canal and its works from the commissioners of 1807 to the principal officers of the Ordnance, and in the following year we know that there were 21 barges licensed to trade on the canal, with tonnages from 21 to 38. The last toll at Iden lock, connecting the eastern section with the Rother, was taken on 15 December 1909 for 27 tons of shingle on the barge *Vulture*. Later, the lock was replaced by a sluice which does not allow craft to pass. The eastern part of this section is owned by Hythe corporation and used by local pleasure craft, the western end from Appledore to Iden lock partly by the Kent River Authority and partly by private owners, the part west of Rye by private owners.

The Weald of Kent Canal project

From the beginning of the nineteenth century there were proposals, encouraged by the proposed Thames & Medway Canal, to link the rivers Thames and Medway with the eastern Rother to make a through waterway from London to Rye harbour. In September 1800 the plan of such a canal, surveyed by Alexander Sutherland, was deposited, and in July 1801 a meeting of promoters, with Sir William Geary in the chair and Lords Romney and Camden supporting, decided that it was practicable. The proposed 28-mile long Kent & Sussex Junction Canal was to run from the Medway between Brandbridges and Yalding to the New-mill channel of the Rother near Tenterden, with branches 11 miles long to Lamberhurst by making the river Teise navigable, and one mile to Headcorn. To take 40-ton Medway barges, the main

REPORTS,

WITH

ESTIMATES, PLANS, AND SECTIONS, &c.

FIRST, OF THE PROPOSED

CANAL THROUGH THE WEALD OF KENT,

INTENDED TO FORM A

JUNCTION OF THE RIVERS MEDWAY AND ROTHER,

FROM NEAR

YALDING IN KENT,

TO THE TIDEWAY NEAR THE PORT OF

RYE IN SUSSEX;

SECONDLY, OF A

BRANCH FROM THE CANAL BY THE RIVER TEISE

TO THE

TOWN OF LAMBERHURST IN KENT AND SUSSEX;

THIRDLY, OF A

BRANCH FROM THE CANAL

TO THE TOWN OF HEDCORN;

AND FOURTHLY, OF A

Branch from the Canal to the Town of CRANBROOK:

DEMONSTRATING THEIR PRACTICABILITY.

TOGETHER WITH SOME

General Observations

ON THEIR GREAT LOCAL AND NATIONAL IMPORTANCE.

LONDON:

PRINTED BY R. B. SCOTT, NO. 27, ST. CLEMENT'S LANE, STRAND.

1802.

1. Title page of Alexander Sutherland's reports upon the proposed Kent & Sussex Junction Canal

2. Inland navigation in the south east: (1) Portsmouth & Arundel Canal; (2) Arun River; River; (8) Adur River; (9) Baybridge Canal; (10) Croydon and Grand Surrey Canals; (11) C Military Canal; (16) Stour Rive

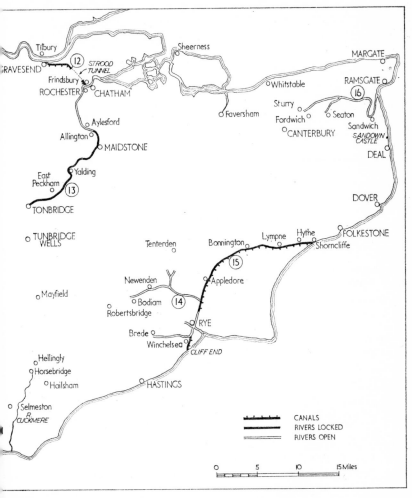

n Rother River; (4) Wey & Arun Canal; (5) Wey River; (6) Basingstoke Canal; (7) Thames ; (12) Thames & Medway Canal; (13) Medway River; (14) Eastern Rother River; (15) Royal artford & Crayford Navigation line and branches were to cost £103,412. The main purposes were to connect London and Rye by avoiding the sea passage, carry chalk, lime and coal into the Weald, and bring timber and agricultural produce out of it. Sutherland estimated the revenue at £8,050.[23]

In 1802 Geary commissioned Rennie to check Sutherland's work, which was surveyed for him by Francis and Netlam Giles. Rennie confirmed Sutherland's main line and Lamberhurst branch, but added another to Ashford and Wye, so increasing the cost to £175,653. Tolls, however, he estimated at only £6,241 to give about 3 per cent on capital. However, he hoped that Geary might be able to interest public-spirited landowners and traders in the canal as a development project. He also saw a possibility of junction by way of the Wye branch with Canterbury and the proposed canal thence to the sea, or with Faversham, and of the canal ending in the Royal Military Canal instead of the Rother.[24]

The figures were so discouraging, however, that the scheme lay dormant until 1809. It was then taken up again, and a Bill introduced in 1811 for a line from Brandbridges to Iden on the Rother, with branches to Wye and Hope Mill (Goudhurst). The Commissioners of the Royal Military Canal then suggested that the proposed canal should rather end in their own waterway near Appledore and, the promoters having agreed, the Bill was withdrawn for that session. A few days earlier, that for Rennie's Grand Southern Canal from the Medway to Portsmouth had been decisively defeated (see p. 130).

The scheme was reintroduced in 1812 as the Weald of Kent Canal, 30½ miles long with 24 locks from Brandbridges to Appledore on the Military Canal, with a 14¼-mile long branch to the chalk hills near Wye (where there were to be feeder railroads) and another, 2⅞ miles long to near Hope Mill (Goudhurst). The estimate was now £305,108, which included £37,114 for four reservoirs. But only £83,500 had so far been subscribed, some of it by those, like Geary and Lord Romney, connected with the Thames & Medway Canal, who probably saw the new project as benefiting the older one. No connection was now proposed to the St Nicholas Bay Harbour & Canterbury Canal, though this navigation from Canterbury to the sea had been authorized in the previous year. Rennie, perpetually hopeful about the most unlikely projects, told the Lords Committee that 'it is without exception the finest piece of Country to cut a Canal through I ever saw,' and the Act[25] was passed, authorizing a capital of £305,800, which had to be raised within three years before work could start, and

£160,000 more if necessary. Authority was granted the company to lengthen Iden lock where the Royal Military Canal joined the Rother.

In 1815 the promoters were back in Parliament for an extension of time Bill, though they had only raised another £20,400, most of it from the same subscribers, and were faced with withdrawals of an almost equal amount. The attempt was then dropped, but the idea lingered on. In 1823, for example, a letter in the *Maidstone Journal*[26] urged its building, now that the Thames & Medway Canal was nearly finished, so that hops could be more easily transported from Kent to the Midlands; others in 1824 saw a connection with the future Canterbury Navigation.

River Stour (Kent)

The Stour appears always to have been navigable after a fashion for twelve miles from the sea at Sandwich to Fordwich, some 2½ miles from Canterbury, which from very early times had had a quay and public crane, and was the city's port. In 1515 an Act[27] was obtained by Canterbury corporation

> to make that part of the river between Fordwich and Canterbury answerable to that below the former; that is, to cleanse, deepen and enlarge it, and to remove all mills and other annoyances on it, insomuch that lighters and boats might be brought to both alike.[28]

In 1576 the Court of Sewers ordered every lighter working between Fordwich and Sandwich once each summer to pull an iron harrow behind it, to clear weeds and even the river's bottom.[29] In 1588, the enthusiasm of Alderman Rose, sometime mayor of Canterbury, caused a rate to be levied on the inhabitants and the proceeds to be laid out in scouring the river. Mr Rose died in 1591, and left £300 towards the work, while the corporation spent about £700 in 1592 and more in the following year. In 1594 we learn from Hasted that there were locks (these would be flash-locks at Sturry and Barton) and that lighters went between Canterbury and Fordwich.

The improvement must have been temporary, for in 1625 John Gason

> covenanted with the mayor and commonalty, within two years to make the river navigable for boats and other vessels of the burthen of twelve tons, from Sandwich to Canterbury.[30]

In 1638 Arnold Spencer made a similar agreement, and in 1695 the mayor and commonalty leased their powers for forty-one years to Thomas Rogers, who engaged to make the river navigable from Sandwich to Browning's mill. But he had trouble with Fordwich corporation, who tried to stop his lighters going beyond their town, and seems to have ruined himself in the enterprise, having found in the end that road transport from Fordwich to Canterbury was just as cheap.[31]

All the same, the tolls collected at Fordwich quay grew during the seventeenth century: imports included coal from the northeast coast, Norwegian timber, merchandise from Holland and wines from France and Spain.[32] Defoe tells us that in the 1720s coal and timber went up the Stour and then by road to Canterbury, though groceries and other London goods were carried by road from Whitstable, because there was less danger than by sea.[33] In 1776 a petition from inhabitants of Sandwich and others interested in the Stour navigation was presented against the Sandwich Drainage Bill, which was to authorize the Stonar drainage cut near Richborough to avoid the river's great meander near Sandwich, on the grounds that the proposed works would take so much water from the river that the 'Haven would become choaked with Mud, Sand and Dirt'.[34] According to Telford in 1824, the cut did just that, and it seems that the whole river navigation became more difficult after it was made.

During the eighteenth and early nineteenth centuries, Canterbury functioned as an economic focal point for east Kent; therefore its trading links, mainly by sea, with London were close. Hence plans to better water access to the city, by improving the Stour or by building a canal, and so make the London trade safer, were discussed throughout the canal age, and were only ended when the Canterbury & Whitstable Railway was built for the same purpose. In 1787 there were discussions, and in 1792 Joseph Hodskinson signed a deposited plan for a 4-mile cut upwards from below Fordwich to Barton mill below Canterbury. He said in his report that though it would be cheaper to make the river navigable with two locks above Fordwich, there were too many shallows for efficiency, and he therefore recommended a canal at a cost of £4,638. He added:

the present method of haling by men being attended by considerable delay, I am informed, that a boat is seldom less than four days, often considerably more, in making a voyage from Fordwich to Sandwich and back

and said that the 6,000 or so chaldrons of coal consumed at Canterbury mostly came by road from Whitstable or Herne.[35]

It seems a pity that Hodskinson's modest canal was not quickly built. Instead, men turned to something more elaborate, designed to be more accessible to London than was Sandwich. In 1797 a newspaper announced that 'a Canal is about to be made from Canterbury to the sea at Reculver, from which much benefit is expected.'³⁶ Early in the new century Alderman Simmons employed Robert Whitworth jun to survey a small ship-canal upon which 100-ton vessels could reach Canterbury. He proposed a line to St Nicholas Bay west of Margate. Interest in the scheme grew, not only because Canterbury needed better transport, but because of a possible connection with a Medway–Rother canal. Rennie's opinion was therefore asked. He approved Whitworth's general line, but proposed to increase the canal's size to take 150-ton craft, have a side-lock to the Stour, and a dock at the sea entrance. His estimate was therefore £86,000, double Whitworth's. He mentioned the possibility of joining his planned Weald of Kent Canal, and thought a 1½ mile cut from Sandwich to the sea north of Sandown Castle would also be useful.

In the minor canal mania of 1810 Samuel Jones was called in to do a detailed survey of the same line.* Having agreed to his still more elaborate plans, a meeting held on 6 June 1810 decided to raise £120,000: London interests included the Heygates, bankers, of the firm of Pares & Heygate. These were then interested in other canal schemes, including the Grand Surrey, the Bristol & Taunton, and the Grand Western. Pares interests centred on Leicester, and the firm were bankers to local canals there. J. Z. Plummer, a local solicitor, wrote of the raising of Canterbury's £50,000 share of this sum,

the Books for Subscription were opened here this Morning about 9 o'clock and were filled before 10 o'clock . . . I understand a Premium has been offered and refused of £1 per cent . . . I think my neighbours are mad.'³⁷

Rennie, called back, upgraded these plans also, till they were to cost £155,207 to carry out, of which £94,178 was for the harbour and wet dock, £54,042 for the barge canal and branch, and £6,987 for an approach road to the basin at Canterbury. The company, having worked out that the city paid £20,850 pa for its present land carriage, and would save £5,906 pa were it all transferred to their waterway, went ahead and introduced a Bill in 1811.

This authorized a new canal from the barracks at Canterbury along the north side of the river by Sturry to Upstreet, and then straight to St Nicholas Bay, about half way between Reculver and

---

* He also suggested a second harbour at Deal, and a ship canal 18 ft deep thence to St Nicholas Bay to cut off the Goodwin Sands and the North Foreland.

ST. NICHOLAS BAY, HARBOUR,

AND

CANAL, TO CANTERBURY,

IN THE COUNTY OF KENT.

At the City of London Tavern, the 6th Day of June, 1810,

PRESENT:

EDMOND THOMAS WATERS, ESQ. IN THE CHAIR.

&c. &c. &c.

THE Minutes of former Meetings, a printed Report, and divers Communications, with Charts and Plans prepared by Mr. Samuel Jones, Engineer, of a proposed Harbour at Saint Nicholas Bay, in the Isle of Thanet, and a Navigable Canal from thence to Canterbury, in the County of Kent, having been read and considered, and the Co-operation and Concurrence of divers principal Persons of that City and Vicinity having been communicated by Mr. James Lawrence, of that City,

IT WAS RESOLVED UNANIMOUSLY,

That the Plan proposed by Mr. Samuel Jones appeared to be practicable, and highly advantageous to the Public, to the City of Canterbury, and to the Individuals concerned.

That the Sum of £.120,000 be raised in Shares of 100*l.* each.

That a Reservation of 10,000*l.* of that Sum be made for the Land Owners on the Line of Canal.

That the Sum of 50,000*l.* of the above Sum, be reserved for the Inhabitants of Canterbury and its Vicinity.

That no Person be permitted to hold more than Twenty Shares.

That Books for Subscription be opened at Messrs. Pares and Heygate, Bankers, Aldermanbury; and that they be appointed TREASURERS to this Concern.

That Books be also opened at the Banks at Canterbury, to receive the reserved Subscriptions for that Place and Vicinity of 50,000*l.*

That a Deposit of 2*l.* per Cent. be made at the Time of Subscription, towards defraying Preliminary Expences.

That the following Gentlemen be appointed a Temporary Committee, viz.

Messrs. Edmond Thomas Waters	Messrs. James Heygate, Jun.
James Innes	George Palmer
Henry Hinckley	James Gibson
William Heygate	James Lawrence.
John Gray	

with Power to add to their Number; and that any Five of them be a Quorum, present at the Hour of Summons.

That Mr. ANTHONY HIGHMORE, Solicitor, No. 33, Ely Place, London; be appointed Solicitor and Secretary to this Concern.

That Mr. SAMUEL JONES be appointed Engineer to this Concern.

Adjourned to the 8th Instant.

At the

3. The St Nicholas Bay and Canterbury scheme is promoted

Westgate on Sea. A branch was to be provided to the Stour near Upstreet. £150,000 had been subscribed, £80,000 in London and £70,000 in Kent, mainly in Canterbury itself.

Fordwich and Sandwich, seeing the river trade likely to be lost, opposed the Bill, as did Margate Pier & Harbour Commissioners, but London and Canterbury interests supported it. The commissioners managed to extract £620 pa from the new company as compensation for loss of prospective trade while the Bill was going through, to which the latter felt bound to agree because of House of Commons suspicions: 'the failure of wild and impracticable Schemes, eagerly patronized in former years, had generated a spirit of mistrust.'[38]

The Act[39] passed in June, and the St Nicholas Bay Harbour & Canterbury Canal Company was created, with a capital of £160,000 and £80,000 more if needed. Exceptionally, their Act required them to report regularly to Parliament on their expenditure of capital, building progress, and toll changes. However, they did not need to. Whitworth had said the harbour at St Nicholas Bay would require piling over the whole area; Rennie in 1804 that the bottom was chalk; Jones in 1810, tenacious clay. Now, after the Act, Rennie found it to be a quicksand. One of the directors, S. R. Lushington, then proposed a smaller harbour. Rennie supported this, for which, he said, 'he took not the merit of the abridgement to himself, it was a justice due to Mr Whitworth, from whose plans he had imbibed the idea.' It seems a pity he had not read Whitworth's report more thoroughly before.

Given this setback the project looked too hugely formidable, and the shareholders, faced with many defaulters on calls, decided to delay. In December 1813 they were, however, 'determined to proceed with all practicable dispatch'; in 1814 they were waiting for peace before making up their minds; in 1817 they were trying to borrow money from the Exchequer Bill Loan Commissioners, and again in 1818, when they were also wondering whether a canal to Nagden Creek near Faversham would give a better communication with the Thames & Medway. But Telford, having surveyed four hilly and difficult lines to Nagden for them, had said bluntly that 'an improved land carriage to Whitstable, or even to Nagden, would supersede, or so far divide the business, as to render it unadvisable to incur the expense.' He was in favour of the original line, given a better site for the entrance.[40]

No action followed, until in 1823 a committee was got together at Canterbury, who made contact with others at Sandwich, and called a joint meeting. Their ideas were more modest than those of 1811. At the time the Stour was being used by barges able to carry about 30 tons to Fordwich. They foresaw a waterway able to take coasting vessels 'constructed like the Dutch Traders', but in the meantime considered that a steam tug to tow such barges, a cut past Sturry mill just above Fordwich, and some dredging (or, alternatively, a cut from below Fordwich as Hodskinson had suggested) would provide a useful navigation to Canterbury.[41]

A meeting at Canterbury in January 1824 included not only the Canterbury and Sandwich committees, but also directors of the 1811 company. These approved a modest prospectus.[42] The united committee then employed James Morgan, engineer of the Regent's Canal, to survey the line. Unfortunately, he went much further than the prospectus by suggesting that the winding and shallow river course between Sandwich and the sea should be avoided by a new cut from Sandwich to just north of Sandown Castle above Deal, where piers and an entrance basin would be built to take ships of 400–500 tons. This idea of a harbour near Sandown Castle was not new. John Smeaton says in 1791 that

in the time of King Edward 6th it is said there was an attempt to make a Harbour from Sandwich into the Downs, and that the evident traces of a canal, which still subsist in the level grounds, between Sandwich and Sandown Castle, are the remains of that attempt.[43]

There was a proposal in 1736–8 which included a canal and basin, and others later in the century for a harbour only. From the harbour Morgan proposed, the cut to Sandwich would carry 300–400 ton craft moving in and out on the tide. Upwards from the town the river was to be made suitable for 100-ton coasting vessels by dredging the section nearest Fordwich, and making new river cuts with two locks 80 ft × 20 ft thence to Canterbury.

A meeting on 9 March accepted Morgan's scheme and estimate of £45,777 for the cost and £4,441 pa for revenue, and appointed him chief engineer, while a paper signed by the new company's vice-chairman promised the inhabitants of Canterbury that their coal would be 10s (50p) a chaldron cheaper were the canal to be built. The old 1811 company now dissolved itself so as not to obstruct the new enterprise, and a Bill was introduced in May, but then withdrawn because of opposition from the Commission of Sewers, whose engineer, Benjamin Bevan, had not yet reported upon the drainage aspects of the navigation scheme.

Thomas Telford was then called in to check Morgan's work and help him to satisfy the commissioners. He agreed with it, but elaborated it further by increasing the dimensions of the entrance

STOUR NAVIGATION,

And Sandwich Harbour.

---❦---

REPORT

OF

MR. T. TELFORD, ENGINEER,

ON THE PRACTICABILITY, AND ADVANTAGES OF OPENING, AND IMPROVING THE NAVIGATION OF THE RIVER STOUR;

TOGETHER WITH

THE QUERIES SUBMITTED TO HIM,

BY THE COMMITTEE,

FOR HIS OPINION AS TO THE EFFECTS ON THE LEVELS

AND DRAINAGE.

Also a Statement of the Revenue.

---❦---

SANDWICH:

PRINTED BY W. COCKING, EXCHANGE-OFFICE, MARKET PLACE.

1824.

4. Telford reports in 1824

D

piers, basin and channel to Sandwich, and produced an estimate of
£67,650 for the 18 mile long navigation, with one of £5,371 pa of
revenue.[44] He strongly commended the project, and a provisional
shareholders' meeting on 28 September approved his plan, agreed
to raise another £30,000, and to go back to Parliament. To allow
for compensation, Telford's estimate was later raised to £76,858,
and after William Chapman had been called in to adjudge between
the Commission of Sewers and the company, an Act[45] was passed
in 1825, authorizing a capital of £100,000, with £40,000 more if
necessary. At this time £66,925 had actually been subscribed.

At the news of the royal assent, guns were fired and flags put
up, and in the following month

> a procession was formed and proceeded through Canterbury
> with flags and a band of music to Fordwich, where the party
> embarked on board a barge for Grove Ferry. Several gentlemen
> also proceeded on horseback and in carriages to the latter place
> where there was a dinner in celebration of the passing of the
> Navigation Act.[46]

At the Mayor's dinner at Canterbury on Michaelmas Day, a
speaker said he hoped that barges would be coming to the city
within a year.[47]

While the Bill had been going through, it had been agreed that
the new Canterbury Navigation & Sandwich Harbour Company
should not interfere with the Stour itself until the cut had been
completed from Sandwich to the sea, together with the basin
there. This daunting proviso, presumably the result of the nervousness of the Commission of Sewers that the work might be
left unfinished, the ending of the boom of 1824, and the fact that
tenders showed the work would cost more than the estimate,
prevented it from starting. The committee were indeed prepared
to go ahead, but a large number of shareholders lived in London,
and four of these had been elected directors. The extract below
from a report of the following year shows some of the troubles of
a company floated in a speculative period:

> The Board regretted that only one of those gentlemen had
> hitherto attended its meetings. On the 25th. of May, however,
> one more of the London Directors attended, and was furnished
> with every information he required, as to the proceedings of the
> Board; and in availing himself of the opportunity of expressing
> his opinion thereon, it was soon discovered that he had views
> far different from those of the majority of the Directors: his
> object was to dissolve the Company! theirs to fulfil the purposes
> for which it was incorporated. He acknowledged that a certain

A SHORT

EXPOSITION

OF THE

PRESENT STATE

OF THE

CANTERBURY NAVIGATION

AND

𝕾𝖆𝖓𝖉𝖜𝖎𝖈𝖍 𝕳𝖆𝖗𝖇𝖔𝖚𝖗

COMPANY;

AND OF

The Proceedings of the Directors

Of the said Company,

DRAWN UP BY PERMISSION OF THE BOARD;

—»)●●●(«—

ADDRESSED TO

The Shareholders & Public in General;

BUT MORE ESPECIALLY TO

Those who are resident in Canterbury, Sandwich,
and the Towns and Districts contiguous to the
intended improvements.

—»)●●●(«—

Sandwich:

PRINTED BY E. A. GIRAUD, MARKET-STREET.

1826.

5. The Canterbury Navigation Company explain their position

portion of Subscribers, by whom he had been requested to attend the Board, had taken shares, not with a view of an investment of the amount for the benefit of the undertaking, but with an intention of disposing of them at a premium, when they could be offered in the Market;—that the late disastrous change had defeated this intention;—that it would now be inconvenient to pay up the instalments of their shares;—and they in consequence resolved to put a stop to the proceedings, by every legal impediment they could interpose.[48]

The directors in 1826 explain that the delay in beginning work has been due to this group of speculative shareholders, and to the slump that made money more difficult to get. But the beginnings of the Canterbury & Whitstable Railway may also have been a major factor. This line was proposed in 1823 by William James, and got its Act in 1825, including provision for a harbour at Whitstable.[49] Since the capital first applied for, £31,000, was considerably less than the estimated cost of the Canterbury Navigation & Sandwich Harbour, the railway must have looked the more economical proposition, though the canal company were quite prepared to face the competition:

but when they both enter the lists of competition in fair and open rivalry, it will be found that each has its peculiar advantages. Where expedition is the object, for light and expensive commodities from the London Market, the Rail Road will find its supporters; but where bulky and heavy goods are to be transported, the Navigation will evidently have a preference.

A general meeting of 5 June 1827 agreed to postpone the canal scheme, and no more was heard of it.

At the beginning of 1825 a group of Deal men had met others from Sandwich to ask whether a branch ship canal from the proposed Sandown Castle harbour to Deal would be acceptable to the promoters of the bill. The latter agreed, and a public meeting at Deal on 19 January opened a subscription for a survey. This was done by James Morgan, who reported early in February that such a Deal Junction Canal, which would also be used as a wet-dock, 1¾ miles long, to take 500-ton craft, would cost £30,535. The Canterbury company then took the view that this scheme would prejudice their own, while the Deal promoters refused to lessen their own ideas, or to agree to the company's expensive conditions. The proposal was therefore dropped.[50]

In 1864 the Downs Dock Act[51] authorized a dock, piers, branch railway and other works near Sandown Castle, and a canal thence to the Stour at Sandwich, the company to have an initial capital of

£240,000. But no canal resulted from this last flicker of an old idea.

In the 1840s, coal and timber were going up the Stour—probably quite considerable amounts of the former, for in 1845, 12,000 tons were imported at Sandwich, together with 1,600 tons of merchandize from London and 750 tons of timber, far more than a town of about 3,000 people could use.[52] The Rev. C. E. Woodruff, writing in 1895, said:

Within living memory as many as seven barges were regularly engaged in plying between Sandwich and Fordwich bridge. . . . The last Fordwich barge disappeared nearly twenty years ago.[53]

At some time before 1825 the Little Stour, Seaton or Ickham Navigation was made without Parliamentary authority from Seaton to the Stour below Stourmouth, six miles long. Seaton was an alternative riverhead to Fordwich, where goods were transferred to waggons to be carried to Canterbury (in that year Edward Kingsford had a 'Water Corn Mill, Wharfs, and Warehouses' there),[54] and so, seemingly, in favourable conditions[55] were Wingham and Littlebourne on the Sandwich–Canterbury road.

Dartford & Crayford Navigation

Before 1835 the river Darenth (known as Dartford Creek) was about 3½ miles long, a winding tidal channel which could be used up to Dartford wharves at spring tides by barges carrying 50 tons. At other times craft with 20 to 40 tons had to anchor at Hibbert's wharf about a quarter mile below the head of navigation at Phoenix mills to tranship their cargoes into smaller punts of 10 to 12 tons.

In November 1835, when the trade was about 50,000–60,000 tons a year, a local engineer, Edward Hall, proposed a ship canal from the creek's entrance to Dartford, and later defined his scheme as a waterway 100 ft wide and 12 ft deep to take vessels of 300–400 tons. A company, the Dartford & Crayford Ship Canal & Kent & Essex Ferry Company, was formed with a capital of £65,000; £37,675 was subscribed and a Bill introduced. There was, however, criticism of the scheme, and in 1839 a more modest plan, put to a public meeting on 5 September 1839, suggested that cuts should reduce the length of Dartford Creek by ¾ mile and Crayford Creek, branching from it below the town and the channel of the river Cray, by ½ mile, and that dredging would enable 150 ton barges to reach the wharves. The cost was estimated at £12,000.

The plan was approved, and an Act[56] of 1840 set up commissioners with power to improve both creeks, build a diversion,

A LETTER

TO THE

INHABITANTS OF DARTFORD,

&c. &c.

DARTFORD, KENT,
November, 30, 1835.

MY FELLOW TOWNSMEN,

NOW that the excitement attendant on Two Public Meetings has subsided, and we are put in possession of all the leading points connected with our intended grand improvement, "the Ship Canal," I will sit down and calmly give you my ideas upon the subject, that now engrosses so much of our attention, and in order to be more correctly understood, I shall divide my letter into three parts:—

First, I shall endeavour to show the necessity of engaging in the undertaking in order to keep pace with the spirit of improvement going on around us.

Secondly, The advantages resulting therefrom.

Thirdly, A word of Friendly Advice to the land-owners and agriculturists of our own locality and to the county of Kent generally.

First. If the gentleman to whom we are indebted for launching this project before the public, had attempted it ten years since, it would have been considered as the effect of a disordered brain, and instead of receiving the thanks of one of the largest and most respectable meetings that has been held in Dartford for some years, he would at the least have been consigned to the ridicule of his fellow-townsmen; but such is the spirit of improvement going forward, that no sooner was the project fairly laid open, than the inhabitants of Dartford (to their honour be it spoken,) hailed the proposal, sanctioned the proceedings, and at once showed themselves worthy of being ranked amongst the number of the improvables of the day.

6. The opening pages of Richard Penny's pamphlet of 1835 upon the projected Dartford ship canal

and levy tolls. Using these, the commissioners made a new 95 ft cut to shorten the upper part of Dartford Creek, dredged the channel, and made other improvements. The work was done by 25 March 1844, when a toll of 3d a ton began to be collected.

Later, in 1895, a lock was completed just below Dartford, 169 ft × 24½ ft, to create a floating basin above it, at a cost of £8,162. Since then some 200,000 tons a year of goods have been carried on the navigation.[57]

CHAPTER III

The River Medway

THE river is tidal nearly to Maidstone, and has been navigable up to the town from time immemorial for craft up to 50 tons. Between 1565 and 1619 the town's waterborne trade greatly increased, while higher up, in the Weald, was a considerable iron industry, and timber that needed to be carried to the dockyards for ship-building, and to London for fuel and building construction. Because land carriage of heavy goods was so difficult, and Acts of 1584 and 1597 required cash payments and contributions of materials for the repair of roads according to use, the ironmasters and timber growers turned towards water transport. Their first aim was to make the Medway passable, by removing fish weirs, fallen trees, and other obstructions, up to Yalding, six miles from Maidstone, which small boats had intermittently been able to reach since about 1580. Beyond that, they hoped for navigation to Tonbridge or even Penshurst.[1]

Commissions of Sewers were primarily concerned with the free flow of the river, and not with its navigation. Those of 1580 and 1597 had done some clearance and made limited navigation possible, but the riparian landowners, claiming the river as private property, were unco-operative, and replaced many of the obstructions. In 1600 a group on the commission were in favour of navigation, but though they obtained government support, local interests were stronger, and they only succeeded in reducing flooding.

In 1627 a new commission was appointed. Preparations were going on for a French war, and the government were therefore interested in more efficient transport from the Weald. Letters were read at the commission's meeting on 23 May at Tonbridge from the King and the Duke of Buckingham:

> We are given to understand that the River Meadway in Kent from Maidstone and Tonbridge upward may be made passable and useful for Boates, to carry and recarry the Commodities of

that part of Kent, and the part of Sussex next adjoining, all the
Year because the highways are bad and the bridges dangerous.
There is a Quantity of Timber, Iron, Ordinance, and other
Commodities in those Parts, wch woud come cheaper and more
readily for the Service of our Navy at Chatham all the Year,
than now they are brought.

They recommended the commissioners to make the river navigable to Tonbridge, and were supported by those who were
interested in the Wealden products.

The commission ordered obstructions to be removed, while a
group of them agreed with a contractor, Michael Cole, to make
the river navigable for 4-ton craft up to Penshurst, and to build
towing paths, in exchange for a 33-year carrying monopoly at
agreed charges. He was to buy four obstructing mills and build
locks where necessary. Landowners were to be compensated.

The commission set to work to get obstacles removed, but came
up against opposition from local landowners. Meanwhile, Cole
and his supporters realized that an Act was necessary if navigation
works were to be successfully built, and introduced a Bill in 1628.
But it came at a time when Crown and Parliament were quarrelling
about monopolies, was ruled to be establishing a monopoly, and
dropped. All the same, Cole began work, and the government
supported him, so that by 1630 small barges seem to have been
reaching Yalding. But Cole got no further, and the riparian owners
continued to obstruct what had been done.

After the Restoration another attempt was made, when the
ironmasters and others concerned with the products of the Weald
got an Act[2] early in 1665 to make the river navigable

> for carriage of Iron, Ordinance, Balls, Timber, Wood, Corn and
> grain, Hay, Hops, Wool, Leather and all other Provisions there
> had growing and accruing from thence, as of Coals, Lime
> Stone, Wares and all other Necessaries and Commodities
> thither.

Ten local landowners were named as undertakers, who were to
make the river navigable in exchange for a monopoly of carrying.
It was stipulated that the charges should not exceed two-thirds of
the cost of land carriage in the summer and half in the winter.

Again no action followed, and a second Act[3] was passed in
1740, authorizing the river to be made navigable to Forest Row,
three miles south-east of East Grinstead and 15 miles above Tonbridge. The capital was to be £30,000 in 300 shares. The carriage
of timber for the navy was given as the principal object, and the
excessive cost of carrying it by land the reason. Undertakers were

appointed, and this time the work was done as far as Tonbridge, fourteen locks being built to take barges of about 40 tons. Scarcity of water, doubts about traffic, and the number of mills, probably deterred the company from doing any work higher up the river.* No horse towing path was built, towing being done by men. Of the capital, 213 £100 shares were issued but 55 of these were forfeited, leaving 158 held by 40 shareholders. Calls of £70 had been made on each, and a total of £11,725 spent.

The main trade of the river at the time was in coal, timber, and iron, and from the beginning this company of enterprising men went not only into the business of carrying in their own craft, but also into that of merchanting. They began in 1743, with coal, both north-east coast and Welsh, into which they put their profits for many years, and created a monopoly of supplying it upon the river, for only they, as merchants, carriers, and toll-owners, could quote a competitive price. As we shall see, this coal merchanting lasted till late in the nineteenth century. By 1767 they could declare a dividend of £4 per share, so beginning a record of continuous dividends that was to last till 1869.

Trading in coal was so successful that in 1768 the company went also into the business of importing iron and deals from Norway and Russia, so founding a second lucrative, though shorter-lived, business. Their appetite was whetted, and the buying and selling of chalk for lime-burning was added in the same year, and about this time trading in roadstone. By 1770 coal was being bought by the shipload, and the proprietors of the navigation felt themselves strong enough to begin a policy that later brought many protests, that of enforcing the full Parliamentary tolls authorized by their Act against outside carriers, thereby making sure that there would not be too much competition with their own trading businesses. By 1774 the company was carrying stocks valued at: coal, £632; deals, £212; iron, £573; stone, £3, and was the owner of a developing navigation and of the foundation of many good trading businesses.

The lower Medway below Maidstone remained a natural tidal navigation until an Act[4] of 1792 empowered trustees to improve it from below Aylesford bridge to Maidstone, and to borrow £8,000. They did raise this sum, but it was soon thought best to convert the trust into a company and the mortgagees to shareholders, and a further Act[5] of 1802 enabled this to be done and another £5,000 to be raised. It also authorized the rebuilding of Aylesford bridge, a hindrance to navigation, set out maximum

* Later, barges could reach Barden bridge, a mile or so above Tonbridge.

Anno decimo tertio

Georgii II. Regis.

An Act to revive, explain, and amend an Act made in the Sixteenth and Seventeenth Years of the Reign of his late Majesty King *Charles* the Second, intituled, *An Act for making the River of* Medway *navigable, in the Counties of* Kent *and* Suffex.

Hereas an Act of Parliament was made in the Sixteenth and Seventeenth Years of the Reign of his late Majesty King Charles the Second, intituled, An Act for making the River of *Medway* navigable, in the Counties of *Kent* and *Suffex*; whereby, after reciting, that making the River Medway, and all other Rivers, Streams, and Water-courses falling thereinto, in the Counties of Kent and Suffex, navigable, had been upon View found to be feasable, and would be of great Use for the better and more easy and speedy Portage of Iron Ordnance, Balls, Timber, and other Materials, in Places adjacent, made, forged, and provided for His Majesty's Service at all Times, and more especially at such Times and Seasons in the Year as the same could not otherwise be brought out of those Parts; and would be advantageous to the Inhabitants, and all others concerned, as well for Carriage of the Commodities aforesaid, as of Wood, Corn, and Grain, Hay, Hops, Wooll, Leather, and all other Provisions, growing and accruing from thence; as also of Coals, Lime, Stone Wares, and all other Necessaries and Commodities

Preamble reciting the Act 16 & 17 *Car.* II.

6 N 2 ties

7. The first page of the Upper Medway Navigation Act of 1740

tolls, and limited dividends to 10 per cent. Under these Acts, Allington tidal lock below Maidstone was built, which enabled craft to reach Maidstone* at all states of the tide and not just at springs, and to remain afloat there at all times. A start also seems to have been made with a towpath, but not much more.

In 1820 and later the Lower Medway company had made moves towards rebuilding Aylesford bridge and removing shoals near it, and then done nothing. With the Thames & Medway Canal nearing completion† and greater traffic to and from Maidstone therefore likely, a meeting of indignant Maidstone inhabitants in October 1823 demanded action to improve the navigation below the town, by at last rebuilding Maidstone bridge, removing shoals below Allington lock, making new cuts lower down the river near New Hythe, and building a horse towing path from thereabouts up to the town. Either the Lower Medway Company should do the work, they thought, or others should be allowed to. On behalf of the company, it was pointed out that they had already spent £18,000 on improvements,‡ of which £2,000 had been paid off, and that a reasonable return on the remainder swallowed most of their annual income of some £1,400 pa. In the end, the meeting appointed a committee to meet the company. The latter made difficulties still, but after much talk of forming a new concern, and the exercise of great tact by Lord Romney, who acted as honest broker, they agreed to go to Parliament for additional powers to raise money.[6]

An Act[7] of 1824 authorized increased tolls and the raising of another £12,000, reduced the maximum dividend to 7½ per cent until the money had been repaid and tolls lowered, and extended the company's jurisdiction downwards to Halling. Work then began briskly, on the shoals in the same year, Aylesford bridge in 1825 (two arches were removed, and a single bigger one substituted), and the towing path in 1826 from Maidstone as far down as Millhall below Aylesford. It was later extended. All this had cost £10,322. The company then settled down to pay off the mortgage they had raised, and to declare dividends of 5 per cent from 1824 to 1830, 6 per cent from 1831 to 1835, and 7½ per cent thereafter, to the owners of the 160 shares. It was not until 1842, when the mortgage debt had been reduced to £5,200, and after further protests from the town, and perhaps hurried on by pros-

---

* The original boundary with the Upper Medway was below Maidstone bridge, near Faith Street, but in 1907 this was changed to a line about 300 yd above the bridge.

† It was opened on 14 October 1824.

‡ I find it difficult to think how this money was spent.

pective railway competition, that they began to make the authorized cuts at Haystack Hole and New Hythe. Both were completed
by June 1845, and the company then seems within the next few
years to have rebuilt Allington lock, and made a third cut between
Millhall and New Hythe. Here is the Lower Medway's averaged
record of tolls received:

Mid-year	Tolls £	Mid-year	Tolls £
1809–11*	1,323	1830–32	2,839
1812–14	1,313	1833–35	3,066
1815–17	1,242	1836–38	3,398
1818–20	1,468	1839–41	3,253
1821–23	1,368	1842–44	3,455
1824–26	2,067	1845–47	3,501
1827–29†	2,669	1848–50	2,985

* Years 1810 and 1811 only.
† Tolls were increased in 1825 under the 1824 Act.

The rise in receipts from 1827 onwards reflects the benefit of the
improvements made in the lower Medway, and probably also the
stimulus given to trade by the Thames & Medway Canal. This
was not great, but it was perceptible.

Meanwhile the upper Medway company continued on its prosperous way. Among their steady worries were thefts of coal, which
they took especially seriously because they owned as well as
carried the commodity:

Ordered, that the Coals delivered out by the Bargemen at
each Wharfe, shall be Measured as they are delivered out of
their Barges, and that the utmost Care at each Wharfe shall be
taken to prevent the Coals being stolen.

and also the visits of the press-gang. The Company possessed only
ten protections for their bargemen working near the dockyard,
and on 18 December 1780 the Committee were told

that a Press Gang from Maidstone had lately been up the River
and taken . . . four . . . Persons out of the Company's Service
. . . and the Committee being convinced that unless a Stop be
put to the Press Gangs coming up the River to Impress the
Company's Watermen that a very great Obstruction will be
occasioned to the Company's trade which is carried on principally in freighting and transporting Timber and other Stores to
His Majesty's Yards at Chatham and Sheerness and it not having
been usual for Impresses to be made so high up the
River.

They therefore applied for twenty protections, but met with

masterly obstruction from the Navy authorities, for they were still urging their request ten years later.

In 1792, when the first Act was passed for the Lower Medway, the Upper Medway Company had clauses inserted in it giving themselves preferential tolls on their own craft. Thenceforward it is notable that there was little contact between the two companies responsible for the navigation of the river, and they only came together on formal occasions or at times of quarrel.

In 1798 Hasted, the historian of Kent, describes the river at Maidstone as follows:

> a considerable traffic is carried on by it from hence to Rochester, Chatham, and so on to London, and from the several large corn-mills here abundance of meal and flour is shipped off for the use of those towns, the dock and navy there, as well as great quantities sent weekly to London. The fulling and paper mills in and near this town . . . send all their manufacture hither to be transported from hence to London. The vast quantities of timber brought hither from the Weald of Kent and its neighbourhood, by land carriage, as well as water, are conveyed from hence by the navigation of the Medway to the dock at Chatham, and other more distant parts. Besides which there are several large hoys, of fifty tons burthen and upwards, which sail weekly to and from London for the convenience of this town and other adjacent country.[8]

The Upper Medway Company had ceased to deal in iron in 1797, but their other trading concerns were flourishing, and that in roadstone had greatly developed with the improvement of highways. Their stocks in 1800 stood at: coal, £1,813; deals, £419; stone, £351; chalk, £46, and their dividend had risen to £12. In 1802 the company decided to eliminate middlemen on its two principal businesses, and to order deals and fir timber by the shipload direct from Norway, and coal by the shipload from the pits. Indeed, in 1804 they went further and bought a ship to carry coal, in which the company had a seven-eighths interest and the captain the remainder, at the same time calling another £17 on each share (making £89 paid up) and temporarily cutting dividends in order to increase the capital they were using in these trading activities. These are the stock figures for 1807: coal, £2,337; deals, £3,759; stone, £328; chalk, £43. In this year also they advertised that

> they have fitted up a Barge to carry Shop Goods, ironmongery and Goods in General from Maidstone to Tonbridge and Places between which will load at Maidstone every Monday . . . Goods

sent to the Wharfs in London where the Maidstone Hoys are in
the Habit of taking in Lading will be regularly forwarded to
Maidstone and delivered by the Tonbridge Medway Navigation.[9]

This barge ran for many years, and in 1828 was supplemented by
weekly through company barges from Tonbridge to London. An
advertisement of September 1828[10] gives hops as the downwards
traffic (it was the hop season), and wheat, beans, peas, malt, oats,
barley, linseed, shop and other goods as upward traffics. By 1833
these were running twice a week. Independent carriers also operated barges once or twice a week between Maidstone and London;
during the hop season many offered a daily service. There were
also occasional coastal, or even foreign, sailings direct from
Maidstone.

A picturesque annual outing on the river was organized each
year by the Maidstone Commonalty Society. They were accustomed to spend a convivial day going up or down river on a
decorated barge, accompanied by a fleet of smaller pleasure boats,
and finishing up at night with fireworks and fun. Other bodies,
such as the Non-Freemen, occasionally did the same thing.

Profits were now high, those of a prosperous business being
supplemented by those of war. Dividends four times reached £20
per share between 1806–7 and 1814–15, and the main difficulty of
the company during this period was shortage of working capital
because of their rapidly expanding trade. Then there was a setback,
followed by another advance in the twenties, during which £38
per share was returned to the shareholders. Trading in chalk ended
in 1813, and in deals in 1824, the capital employed being presumably part of that returned. Another £5 went back in 1833,
after which the shares' paid-up value was £46. Dividends rose in
the twenties and thirties, absolutely and as a percentage, and,
together with their alleged conservatism, were to cause the company much trouble. The record from 1767, averaged over three-
year periods, is set out on page 68.

In 1828 a rather mysterious character, James Christie, decided
to buy Tonbridge mill—for which he paid a high figure—and led
a group of people calling themselves the Penshurst Canal Company, who proposed to make the river navigable for six miles to
that place from Tonbridge under the powers of the Upper Medway's Act, which allowed others to do so if the company itself did
not. He started to buy land for the new navigation, and in March
1829, navvies having heard of jobs likely to be going and having
arrived for work, cutting began. It stopped during the winter and

Years	Dividend £ s d		Paid-up capital per £100 share £	Dividend per cent £ s d	
1767–69	4 0 0		70	5 14 4	(£5.71½)
1770–72	4 13 4	(£4.66½)	70	6 13 4	(£6.66½)
1773–75	4 0 0		70	5 14 4	(£5.71½)
1776–78	5 0 0		70	7 2 11	(£7.14½)
1779–81	8 13 4	(£8.66½)	70	12 7 7	(£12.38)
1782–84	9 6 8	(£9.33½)	70	13 6 8	(£13.33½)
1785–87	6 10 0	(£6.50)	70	9 5 8	(£9.28½)
1788–90	8 6 8	(£8.33½)	70	12 1 1	(£12.05½)
1791–93	9 0 0		70	12 17 1	(£12.85½)
1794–96	8 6 8	(£8.33½)	70	12 1 1	(£12.05½)
1797–99	7 6 8	(£7.33½)	70	10 9 7	(£10.48)
1800–02	11 6 8	(£11.33½)	70	16 3 11	(£16.19½)
1803–05	5 0 0		80	6 5 0*	(£6.25)
1806–08	13 6 8	(£13.33½)	89	15 0 0	
1809–11	15 0 0		89	16 17 1	(£16.85½)
1812–14	15 0 0		89	16 17 1	(£16.85½)
1815–17	15 6 8	(£15.33½)	89	17 3 10	(£17.19)
1818–20	16 0 0		89	17 19 7	(£17.98)
1821–23	15 13 4	(£15.66½)	66⅓	23 12 6*	(£23.62½)
1824–26	18 0 0		44⅓	40 12 7*	(£40.63)
1827–29	23 0 0		43⅓	53 2 0*	(£53.10)
1830–32	22 0 0		43	51 0 4	(£51.01½)
1833–35	24 13 4	(£24.66½)	38	64 18 2*	(£64.91)

* During these years, when capital was being called or repaid, it is not clear whether capital movements preceded or followed the dividend payments. These figures are therefore approximate.

began again in 1830, the first stone of the lower of two locks being laid on 12 May amidst the free distribution of 400 gallons of whisky and several pipes of cider.[11] Work probably stopped during this year. It seems likely that he built three cuts: the first, with the lock unfinished, about a mile above Tonbridge; the second just beyond, and the third near Penshurst, but there is no evidence that barges ever reached the town. Including the £20,000 he spent on Tonbridge mill, he is said to have spent about £50,000, though the figure seems doubtful. His real motives were unknown even to his engineer, James Walker: 'I never knew, nor do I know at this moment, what Mr Christie's ultimate object was', and 'there was a kind of secret about the ultimate object of that large sum of money which Mr Christie expended on that navigation.'[12] A letter to the press in 1829, probably written by Christie, however, gives us the clue that he had in mind an extension to Portsmouth.[13] We must remember that Rennie's Grand Southern Canal of 1810 (see

Page 69 (*above*) A barge on the Arun passes Arundel castle, c 1864; (*below*) the sea-lock of the Portsea Canal, c 1900

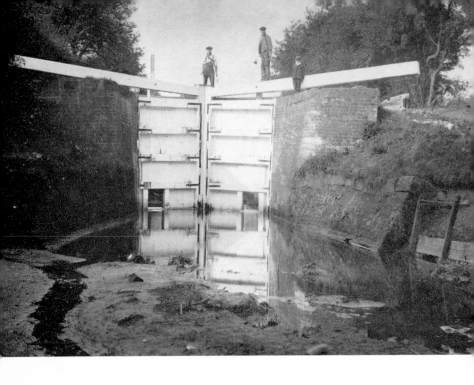

Page 70 Basingstoke Canal: (*above*) repairing lock gates at Woking, c 1912; (*below*) at Byfleet, c 1930

MR JAMES CHRISTIE.

Huckbridge,
Carshalton,

8. James Christie's card

p. 130) had envisaged a similar connection, and that the Portsmouth & Arundel Canal (see p. 135) had recently been opened, so that a line from Penshurst by Forest Row to the Arun would have served. If this was his scheme, he was as hare-brained as Walker clearly thought he was. By 1832 he had dropped the Penshurst extension as a practical possibility: an advertisement of April of that year offered land for sale at Haysden which includes 'parts of the Navigable Canal from Tonbridge to Penshurst, and prospective buyers are told they will have command over the canal.'[14]

Christie had also asked the Upper Medway Company for preferential rates for his barges, and went on to offer to lease that company's whole property. They indeed offered such a lease, but at unacceptable terms. Then a fight began between the two, arising out of Christie's occupation of Tonbridge mill. The company thought that his works near the mill would give him control over the supply of water to their upper pounds, refused to allow him to connect his navigation to theirs, and began legal proceedings which lasted with intervals from 1829 to 1831. Christie then broadened his front, and denounced the company as an inefficient and expensive monopoly, which moreover was trading in coal without legal sanction. In a broadsheet he published about this time he attacks the lack of a towing path, the delays due to short water, and goes on:

The Public being deprived of the advantageous use of the Navigation, the same is used by the Company themselves as a monopoly, and they are themselves Traders, though unauthorized by the Act, particularly in the Article of Coals, in which they are the sole Dealers at Tonbridge, charging what they

E

please and taxing the public if they bring up Coals the full
Toll. . . . All competition is consequently prevented and the
Public are at the mercy of the Company. The Company have, as
may be supposed, become from such monopoly very rich. . . .
In great truth the Medway Navigation is the worst Navigation
in England. 40 Ton Barges, towed by men, occupied two days
in going 16 miles. The Locks in the most disgraceful state. Few
places where two Barges can pass each other, and yet the Public
are charged higher rate of Tolls than on any other Canal where
expedition is great and the Navigation certain and in all respects
good.

Faced by these accusations and the threat of filing a Bill in
Chancery to stop the coal trade, the committee called in an engineer to suggest improvements to the navigation, some of which
were done, and made toll reductions. They decided, however, to
continue the carrying and coal trade businesses, 'which is in ac-
cordance with the usage of the Company from its commence-
ment', and they saw no need for horse towing paths 'because
little or nothing would be gained by them, the whole length of the
navigation from Maidstone to Tonbridge being accomplished in
considerably under a day' or for reservoirs, as water was not a
serious problem.[15]

By this time Christie seems to have gone bankrupt, and trouble
died down, till in 1834 the company learned with a shock that two
petitions had been presented to Parliament, one complaining that
the company had imposed excessive charges on the public, and
made enormous profits by employing their surplus funds (which
should have been used to improve the navigation and lower tolls)
as trading capital 'for carrying on a monopoly in limestone, timber
and particularly coals, so as to exclude competition, thereby rendering their . . . navigation a source of great injury to the public',
and one asking leave to introduce a Bill to amend the company's
Acts over their head. T. L. Hodges, MP, in his supporting speech,
alleged a gross act of oppression against an individual trading on
the river (presumably Christie) and extortion against the public,
and was supported by the *Brighton Guardian*[16] which was consistently on Christie's side, and wrote:

We understand that this Company charge the enormous toll of
6s od per ton on coals, having never expended more than
£11,000 on the navigation, and divide 56½% per annum . . . in
order to avoid the exaction of the Medway Company, the inhabitants in the immediate neighbourhood of their navigation
prefer carting their coals from Mill-Hill, below Maidstone.

The Company have, as may be supposed, become from such monopoly very rich. There are about 158 Shares in the hands of about 40 individuals. The Company's affairs are conducted by a Committee of ⟨?⟩, who hold the majority of Shares, and they control and do as they please.

The Shares were issued as £100 Shares, but £74 only ⅌ Share was subscribed by each Shareholder towards the original expenses, and the returns have been very large : for many years the Average Annual Division has been £20 ⅌ Share—last year it was £31 ⅌ Share—and besides the actual Division, a Capital of £16,000 is embarked in the Coal Trade, and more in other Properties.

In great truth is the Medway Navigation the worst Navigation in England. 40 Ton Barges, towed by men, occupied two days in going 16 miles. The Locks in the most disgraceful state. Few places where two Barges can pass each other, and yet the Public are charged higher rate of Tolls than on any other Canal where expedition is great and the Navigation certain and in all respects good.

9. The last paragraphs of the Christie-inspired attack on the Upper Medway Company

The committee of the company immediately resolved that the truth of the Allegations ought to be forthwith enquired into, and that the State of the Navigation and its management, the Tolls and Freights charged to the public, and generally the Affairs of the Company in all respects ought to be made subjects of the most attentive inquiry and consideration of the Committee as early as possible.

Counsel's opinion was taken, favourably, on the legality of the coal trade, a warehouse was built at Tonbridge for storing goods belonging to the public, and the 6d (2½p) per ton per mile toll from Brandbridges to Tonbridge was reduced to 4d. Christie in 1834 nevertheless gave notice of his Bill forcibly to reduce the tolls and freights on the river, to make reservoirs and a towing path, and to extend the navigation to Forest Row. The Bill was introduced and referred to a committee, which threw it out, but warned the Medway Company to put its affairs in order if they were not to take a more favourable view of another such application. The company took a deep breath, reduced their coal charge from 6s (30p) to 5s (25p) early in 1835, announced that there was no advantage in a towpath, and invited the two local Members of Parliament to look at the river. Neither came. Instead, the Bill was again introduced in 1836, and was lost by the small margin of 55 votes to 41. Soon afterwards some widenings were carried out, and later a horse towing path was at last built. By this time Christie had gone to America.

The company put in to the parliamentary committee of 1836 figures which showed that the river's business was rapidly increasing, but that within the total figures the share carried by the company either for its own trade or for others had dropped as a proportion of the whole: doubtless they had felt it wise to see that it did.

	1822 tons*	1830 tons*	1835 tons*
Coal carried independently	3,661	3,799	5,367
Goods carried independently	3,104	7,517	16,632
Goods carried by company for the public	1,177	10,027	17,162
Goods carried by company for its own trade	925	289	—
Coal carried by company for its own trade	7,527	10,506	10,975
Total	16,394	32,138	50,136

* Figures are given for coal in chaldrons, for goods in tons and loads, but all three seem to have been equal.

For the same three years, toll receipts were as follows: 1822, £3,119; 1830, £4,916; 1835, £5,571.

A new threat now arose, for in 1837 a railway was projected from the South Eastern line near Tonbridge to Maidstone, though it was not opened till 1844. Before that, the company had been asked by the railway if they would supply coke under contract for ten years. This was so clearly within their trading scope that their reply can only mean that they did not intend to help a rival:

the Committee do not consider they have the power as a Committee, nor would they deem it expedient, to enter into such a contract on behalf of the Proprietors.[17]

Meanwhile in 1839–40 and 1841–42 the company's dividends reached their highest level at £36 a share, or almost 95 per cent.

It was in 1840 that the company, aware perhaps of present prosperity and future dangers, agreed to pay £20 a year, later increased to £40, towards the stipend of the minister of the proposed new church at East Peckham,

being desirous of procuring for the . . . Laborers employed on the Navigation and their families at the earliest possible period the benefits of such new church so as to ensure two full Services there on Sundays.[18]

The prosperity of the Upper Medway Navigation caused the proprietors of the navigation to take a forward line with the South Eastern Railway. They proposed to make use of the railway to extend their coal business further afield in competition with new businesses set up to sell railway-hauled coal, and it was therefore necessary to make a physical link between Tonbridge wharf and the railway line there. This was built in 1844 as a tramroad. Land for coal wharves was bought at Edenbridge, Penshurst, Marden, Godstone, and later at Paddock Wood and Tunbridge Wells, and even before the tramroad was ready the Medway company had asked for coal trucks to be made available. They began a series of obstructions by the railway, who wished for a longer haul of coal on their rails than from riverhead at Tonbridge to the new coal wharves. For instance, the stationmaster at Tonbridge writes to the Medway in September 1843:

In consequence of our Stock of Waggons being so limited that it is impossible to supply them for the conveyance of Coal from Tonbridge I am desired by Captain Charlewood to decline carrying Coal from hence until I receive further instructions from him on the subject.[19]

The Medway Company then provided themselves with trucks that they appear to have hired, and applied to have them hauled by railway locomotives; meanwhile they supplied Edenbridge wharf, already open, by land carriage. The railway countered by quoting excessive prices for locomotive power, to which the navigation replied

> That as the South Eastern Railway's scale of Charges . . . for locomotive power must operate very injuriously against the Medway Company, Resolved that unless Mr. Bull* be able to effect a proper modification of such Charges he be authorized to provide an Engine for the Medway Company's use.[20]

It was possible under the railway's Act to run such an independent locomotive. Meanwhile the Medway company corresponded with the Board of Trade upon the inequity of the railway being able to vary its charges for locomotive power according to the customer, but thought prospects were good enough largely to increase its orders with the supplying collieries for coal, and to buy a steam tug for £1,345.

Negotiations with the railway were unsatisfactory, and in April 1845 an engine was bought, and a shed to house it and a cottage for the driver were built at Paddock Wood. Under the railway's Act it was necessary for them to give a certificate of fitness to the engine, and this was applied for in a letter from Mr Bull

> stating that the Medway Navigation Company's Locomotive Engine had arrive in London and would be ready to set to work in a few days . . .

> 'Resolved: That it is the opinion of this Board,† that under the peculiar circumstances of the case, and for the reasons embodied in their letter to the Board of Trade, every practicable resistance should be offered to the claim of the Medway Navigation Company. Resolved accordingly: That the letter of Mr. Bull be referred to Mr. Fearon with instructions to answer it in such terms, and to adopt such further course in this matter as he shall, with additional legal advice if he deems it necessary, consider best calculated to throw upon the Medway Navigation Company the onus of attempting to establish their claim before some competent tribunal.[21]

In May the navigation company therefore applied for a mandamus to compel the railway company to issue a certificate. Meanwhile the engine was borrowed by the contractor working on the new Tonbridge and Tunbridge Wells line, and the railway company were providing locomotives at a high charge to maintain the

* The navigation's agent.
† The South Eastern Railway.

coal trade at the new wharves. All these developments had caused the Medway to raise about £20,000 of new capital.

The mandamus was granted in November, but the railway did nothing directly. Indirectly, they offered Mr Bull a job at three times his salary (which he took, so leaving the river's employment under a cloud), and made an offer to lease the navigation. They offered £3,000 a year clear and half the profits above that sum. It would have been wise of the proprietors to agree, but they asked for £4,000 a year clear and half the profits above the sum, and the railway broke off negotiations. The Medway company then took proceedings to enforce the mandamus, and lost them. The minute book sadly records:

> The unfavourable result of the proceedings on the Mandamus was stated to the Meeting and Mr. Wildash was directed to dispose of the Engine on the best terms he can obtain.[22]

However, the Medway's opposition to the South Eastern Bills then before Parliament was strong enough to make the railway agree to abolish differential tolls for coal in favour of a maximum if the Medway would withdraw, which it did. The tug had been a failure, and was also sold in 1847.

Meanwhile, the railway had come to Maidstone. In 1842 a horse-bus service was established between a station then called Maidstone Road on the main South Eastern line and Maidstone. A branch line followed, which was opened on 25 September 1844, from Maidstone Road, now renamed Paddock Wood, to what is now Maidstone West station, and caused the Upper Medway to cut its tolls. The day before the line opened, Simmonds & Jackson, one of the river carriers, advertised in the Maidstone paper that they would be carrying hops, corn, fruit, vegetables and goods by rail, though they also advertised their barge services. In spite of their reverses, however, the company was still prosperous, and in the year ending June 1851 earned a profit of £2,545 and paid a dividend of £10 per share. Then a decline began. The next twenty years saw the virtual ending of the coal business at the railway wharves, and its withdrawal back to the river itself. Profits fell, and the weight of the mortgage debt created about 1845 to finance the extended coal business began to be felt; £15,000 remained in 1870, but by 1888 it had been cleared. In that year there was a net profit of £127 on a revenue of £2,414, all from tolls. Tonnage was 54,722, 21,561 of which was carried by the company. But in 1869, for the first time in over a hundred years, no dividend had been paid. About 1880 the rebuilding of Allington lock to much larger size by the Lower Medway Company enabled the Upper Medway to remove Maidstone lock in 1881. In 1892 the concern was reconstructed as a new company, and again in 1899, a year after the coal business had closed down, when the business was transferred to a new Medway Navigation Co Ltd. This, however, went into liquidation in 1903[23] and was replaced by another of the same name. The leading figure of the second was Harry Le Marchant, who had come late to its predecessor, and who joined E. J. V. Earle, another of the former directors, in an effort to turn the river's fortunes.

They commissioned plans and estimates for increasing the size and reducing the number of locks, and for modernizing the river. These were submitted in 1903, whereupon Le Marchant and Earle tried to raise £18,000 to get the work done. But less than £2,000 came in, and they could do little. In 1905 the company, still doing its own carrying with one steam barge and some horse-drawn ones, said that bye-traders seldom went further than Maidstone, because of the size of the locks, that traffics were agricultural manures and feeding stuffs, coal, timber and lamp oil, and that the existence of the navigation kept down the SER's rates. Traffic had sometimes to be refused because smaller barges were not immediately available to carry it. Toll receipts from 1904 to 1908 averaged £1,130 pa, and the company managed to pay 10 per cent dividends on its small capital for 1907, 1908 and 1909.

In the winter of 1909–10 East Farleigh lock collapsed. It was closed for three months, and the traffic diverted to the roads, to which the traction engines used did a good deal of damage. There was some public alarm lest the river should be closed and, thanks largely to the efforts of Mr O. E. d'Avigdor-Goldsmid* of the council, the Kent County Council agreed to promote a Bill to transfer the management of the Upper Medway from the company to a publicly-controlled Conservancy Board, composed of representatives of the County Council and other interested local authorities. It was argued by the county surveyor that the County Council would gain some £500 pa by the lower cost of transporting roadstone on the improved river, and save about £430 pa more in wear on the roads, arguments very similar to those that had been used ten years earlier when the Gloucestershire County Council were taking over the Thames & Severn Canal.

The new Conservancy was set up by the Upper Medway Navigation & Conservancy Act of 1911, which authorized the winding up of the old company and the payment of 2s (10p) per £10 share.

---

* Later Sir Osmond d'Avigdor-Goldsmid.

However, it was not until 1923 that its barges were sold and the proceeds distributed, or until 1927 that it was dissolved.[24]

The new Conservancy adopted plans drawn up by the county surveyor, which were based upon those prepared in 1903. These provided for the removal of the 13 old locks, and the building of ten* new ones 105 ft × 21 ft 6 in to take craft 80 ft × 18 ft 6 in, alterations to bridges, and a navigable depth of 7 ft, so that barges of 120 tons, then able to reach Maidstone, could continue to Tonbridge. At the same time, flood control would be improved. There were contingent plans to continue to Penshurst after the rest of the work had been done. The estimated cost was some £31,000, with a further £17,000 for the Penshurst extension.

The Conservancy took over the river on 12 June 1911 and closed it. Money was borrowed from local authorities and the government, and work began upwards from Maidstone. Unfortunately, apart from serious damage from floods during construction, the engineer in charge adopted a design of curved iron lock gate and sluice which proved unworkable, and had to be scrapped in 1913 after several locks had been rebuilt, ordinary wooden gates being substituted. The lower part of the river was reopened about the end of 1913, and the whole on 1 September 1915 by the tug *Keston* towing the 75-ft barge *Beaver* laden with 120 tons of ballast, though seemingly with a navigable depth of 6 ft only to take craft of 5 ft draught. The cost, some £93,000, had far exceeded the estimate. In January 1916 it was reported that 'the first two toll-paying barges since 1911 had been through from Maidstone to Tonbridge, and had returned.'[25]

But the war had made the revival of navigation even more difficult than would normally have been the case, for barges were scarce and men were fighting. Toll revenue proved small: £238 for 1917, £184 for 1918, £108 for 1919, and the considerable annual losses had to be borne by the contributing local authorities. Indeed, in 1921 the Conservancy almost gave up, but was rescued at the last minute by these bodies. Losses then lessened as sales of dredged gravel were built up, and some pleasure cruising revenue began to come in (the first hire cruiser appeared at Tonbridge in 1923). Commercial tolls averaged £188 between 1925 and 1932, though the last toll-paying barge passed to Tonbridge in 1927 and

---

* Brandbridges, New and Child's locks were eliminated. Stoneham lock, with a fall of 1 ft 9 in, was put out of use in 1934–35, the weir and sluices being demolished and the river being allowed to run through the lock, so that there are now nine locks above Maidstone.

to Yalding and Brandbridges in 1928. On 1 April 1934 the Conservancy ceased to exist, its property being transferred to the River Medway Catchment Board established in December 1930. Mr d'Avigdor-Goldsmid's chairmanship had lasted throughout the Conservancy's whole life, though his seat had often been empty while he was away at the war.

Under the Catchment Board the draught for vessels above Yalding was reduced to 4 ft 6 in.* In March 1950 a tug and empty 200-ton barge went up to Tonbridge in an experiment by the Gas Board to find out whether coal could be taken to the local gasworks by water. But neither the small tug nor the type of steel barge used was considered suitable, and the idea was not followed up. The navigation is now controlled by the Kent River Authority, who maintain it above Maidstone for pleasure craft, while barges still come up to Tovil just above the town.

The Lower Medway Company's receipts kept steady from the early 1850s to the late 1880s at an average of about £2,800, and their dividend at 7½ per cent. In 1881 the lower river was divided, the Lower Medway Company being confined to the stretch above Hawkwood, four miles below Allington lock, the rest of the lower river being put under the control of a new Medway Conservancy, which replaced the ancient jurisdiction of Rochester. By the end of the century the Lower Medway's debt had been paid off, 7½ per cent dividends continued, and over 300,000 tons of goods a year were passing over its waters. Today they are still used for commercial traffic.

* It is now 4 ft.

CHAPTER IV

The Thames & Medway Canal

✦

RALPH DODD, who in 1799 published a pamphlet[1] to advocate a Thames and Medway canal, was born in 1756 in London, and in 1795 published a rare *Account of the principal Canals in the known World, with reflections on the great utility of Canals.* He invented a canal cutting machine in 1794, surveyed a Tyne–Wear canal in 1795, and part of one from Newcastle to the Solway Firth, reported on Sunderland and Hartlepool harbours and the port of London between 1794 and 1799, and in 1800 got support for a Mersey bridge at Runcorn. Round London he pressed four proposals at once in 1799 and 1800: what became the Thames & Medway, Grand Surrey and Croydon canals, and a tunnel under the Thames at Gravesend. But he was a failure as a practical engineer, and after diversions towards a harbour at Brighton, piers and jetties there and at Grimsby, water supply matters and the causes of dry rot in timber, he died at Cheltenham in 1822, almost penniless.[2]

His present proposal was for a canal to save the passage of some 47 miles between Gravesend on the Thames and Strood on the Medway. He had not taken a survey, he said, but it was possible to build a canal six miles long on the level 'through as fine a stratum as can well be wished for: the lower levels will need no puddling, the upper Line of chalk will pay for its own excavation' —he meant, because it could be sold for use on the land. Such a canal would be useful to the government for shortening the distance between Deptford and Chatham, but commercial men must judge its general utility, though 'upon inquiry, I find the commerce that would employ this canal is immense; probably few canals in this kingdom would have greater traffic.' In a report later in the year to the subscribers who had by then been got together, he estimated the cost of a canal 48 ft wide at top and 7 ft deep, with river locks and basins, at £24,576, thought over 65,260 tons a year would be carried, and reckoned the waterway could be built within two years.

By the time the proposal got to Parliament in 1800, preceded by a petition arguing that trade between London and Rochester would be helped and cheapened by avoiding the 'long and circuitous, and sometimes dangerous' sea passage round the Isle of Grain, and that the neighbouring country would be improved 'by the Conveyance of Manure',*[3] the level line extended to $8\frac{5}{8}$ miles, running from Gravesend by a curve to Higham and Silver Street to enter the Medway at the bottom of Limehouse Reach opposite Rochester. A branch, then called the White Wall cut, was to join the river further north, in Chatham Reach. No tunnelling was envisaged, but cutting through the chalk reaching a maximum depth near Silver Street of 84 ft. Though Dodd intended to remove nearly 600,000 cu yd of soil from a 5,000 yd long deep cutting, his estimate was still only £33,819, or £45,972 should a wider angle of slope prove necessary in the cuttings, this sum to include locks and basins at each end.

Dodd's backers, led by Sir William Geary and Charles Marsham who became Lord Romney, had already subscribed £35,400 (Dodd put his name down for £500), and in spite of some opposition from landowners, the Act[4] passed, granting a capital of £40,000 in £100 shares and £20,000 more if necessary. There were 155 subscribers at the time of the Bill, very many of them for £100. Only three people were willing to put up £1,000 or more. Authorized tolls were on the high side: stone, manure, sand, slates, 2d per ton per mile; coal, timber, iron, 3d; flour and corn, 4d; and merchandize, 6d (2½p), with additional charges for mooring in the basins. Passenger carrying was authorized, and tolls for foot passengers along the towpath.

Rennie was then consulted. He confirmed Dodd's line, but recommended that unless the ground proved very stable, 2,000 yd of cutting should be replaced by a tunnel, which 'will be more certain in the Execution than open cutting, as well as in standing after it is finished.'[5] He also raised the estimate to £57,433. Dodd now began cutting, and by the end of 1801 four miles had been completed from Gravesend to Higham, together with the basin at Gravesend. Then Ralph Walker was called in, and reported that a great deal more money would be necessary. In face of this the shareholders became despondent, and many abandoned their shares. In this year of 1803, John Phillips the canal historian appraised the usefulness of the canal:

This canal may answer the purpose for government when at war, but never will for the purpose of trade, as barges would

* Chalk was meant.

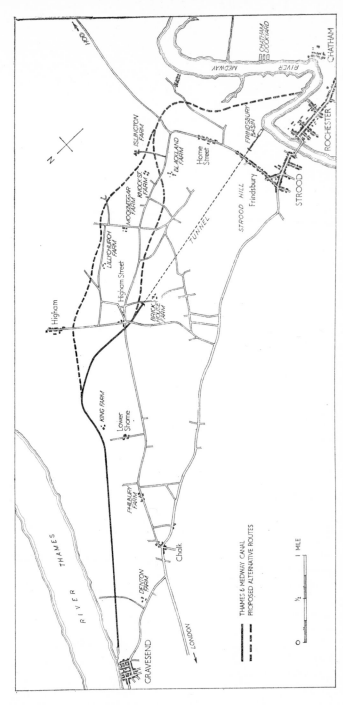

10. Three lines for the Thames & Medway Canal: Dodd's farthest to the east, Walker's first line in the middle, Walker's second line, as built, to the west

get to the mouth of the Medway by low water in the same tide that they must enter the canal at Gravesend, and be ready to go up to Chatham the beginning of the flood-tide, and be at Chatham by the time (or very near, and sometimes sooner) than a barge can go on the canal, without the additional expense of lock-dues, horses and attendance in being drawn along, and this in most instances, except when it blows a gale of wind at east or north-east for a short time in winter: this is not my own opinion only, but, from inquiry I made of several barge-men and barge-masters at Maidstone and Rochester, I found it general.[6]

Walker suggested a deviation to shorten Dodd's line by ⅜ mile, doing so by increasing the cutting, which would now involve moving some 1·4 million cu yd of material at depths up to 100 ft, but without a tunnel. Though the whole £60,000 of the original Act had not been raised, that of 1804[7] authorized an additional £60,000, and gave power to make the deviation. Dodd had probably left by this time, his departure accelerated by the failure of his Thames tunnel, the Gravesend shaft of which was abandoned in 1803 after £15,243 had been spent upon it.

The works then languished until early in 1808, when 'a spirited individual raised it again into action, and, with the assistance of some who had always seen its value, recommenced this promising work.'[8] This spirited individual may have been Edward Smith, already connected with the Croydon Canal. He was certainly spirited, writing to a friend on 18 July 1808:

I have just rec^d your favor on my return from Town, were I have meet an Able Engineer on The Subject of the Thames & Medway Canal which as an Old proprietor I did not chuse to give up, unheard, or without a Survey & due consideration. My *friends* are all purchasers. I have since I saw you bought 10 shares of Mr Tappenden of Faversham, and intend to purchase 3 or 4 Thousand pounds in the Concern. . . . I never was nor will I enter into new Speculations but in this Case as in the Croydon Canal . . . I am an *old* proprietor & will never give *them* up.[9]

The committee again consulted Ralph Walker, and then recommended

that much of the Line proposed by the last Act . . . should be abandoned, and that it should be formed in a line commencing from Higham Street . . . into Strood Marsh, on the South of Frindsbury Church, and open into the Medway about a quarter of a Mile to the West of Rochester Bridge—that this line, if

adopted, will be attended with much advantage in point of
saving a considerable Expence, and be upwards of one Mile and
one quarter less in length.[10]
There was now to be a tunnel. To finish it, they thought another
£40,000 should be raised by creating new £100 shares, £30 paid
up, to rank with the original issue of £100 shares, £80 paid up.
These were offered first to old shareholders, and 934 out of the
1,320 created were taken up almost at once, Lords Romney, Marsham, Barham and Radnor taking 110 between them to lead the
way. On 27 November 1809 the first stone of the entrance lock at
Gravesend was laid by the chairman, Joseph Stonard, and the
committee in Ralph Walker's presence.

The alteration in line was made by an Act of 1810,[11] which
followed Walker's recommendations, and envisaged larger dimensions. By that time, however, Walker had increased his estimate of
the money required, providing £37,715 for the tunnel, and
£16,989 for other work: all the same, it was his opinion before the
Parliamentary committee that the deviation and tunnel would be
made for half the cost of the previous line.[12] In all, however,
£113,400 was raised before the tunnel was begun or the Frindsbury basin made.

In 1817 William Tierney Clark was engaged as engineer, and
estimated a further £97,755 for completion. An Act of 1818[13]
therefore allowed £100,000 more, and granted higher rates for
goods landed at or transhipped in the basins, and upon craft using
them; this presumably because Gravesend basin was the company's main source of revenue, yielding £452 in 1817.

Money was then raised by £40 notes convertible within 5 years
to £100 ordinary shares, and work began early in 1819, when we
get a glimpse of how money went. In February a special jury was
called out to settle the price of 7 acres of land at Frindsbury, and
awarded £1,260 to the landowner. That settled, it was reported

we understand it to be the intention of the Canal Company to
commence the work at the Rochester end immediately, and to
prosecute it to completion with the greatest energy.[14]

The tunnel contractors were Pritchard & Hoof, and a man
called Williams, each with about half, but it seems that by the time
it was finished, only Pritchard & Hoof were at work. The contract
was interesting because the company intended to sell some of the
excavated chalk. Hence it provided for the contractor to sort this
into block, combles and rubbish, and also to pick out white and
brown flints, and deliver each to the company.

Work began on the tunnel itself in April, and by November

1820 the header, 7 ft square, had been completed,[15] after which 'many persons, impelled by curiosity . . . walked through it with lamps.'[16]

This canal tunnel was the second longest in Britain, 3,931 yd in length (see note on p. 94), exceeded only by Standedge on the Huddersfield Canal. In dimensions, however, it was far the largest. The interior measurements varied somewhat in different places, but the usual figures given are: bed of canal to top of arch, 35 ft, 8 ft of which was water; 26 ft 6 in from one wall to the other, which included a towpath 5 ft wide, or 30 ft at the widest part of the span.

Probably for the first time in Britain, an astronomer's transit telescope, mounted in an observatory that commanded the whole site, was used to lay out the tunnel line and select the points at which shafts should be sunk.[17] Tunnelling was done from each end and from nine working shafts, up and down which men and materials were moved by horse-operated drums or whims. The ground was mainly chalk, with some fuller's earth. The former was so compacted beneath the highest parts of the hills that gunpowder had to be used to break it, and these sections were later left unlined. But where the overlying land came lower, the chalk was loose, and brick lining of various thicknesses had to be built, springing either from the bottom of the tunnel in the worst places, or from above the towing path level. The brickwork was usually 14 in thick at the arch, and 18 in at the springing. The space above the brick arch was filled in with chalk and lime mortar as the vaulting advanced, and the chalk above was pinned up as securely as possible. An iron railing to the towpath was provided soon after opening.

It was found in all cases necessary to secure a portion of the roof, right and left of the working shafts, with brickwork; which no doubt prevented the occurrence of many accidents: a few, however, could not be avoided. Notwithstanding every possible precaution was taken to ascertain the soundness of the chalk during the progress of the work, and no expense was spared for timber for securing the workmen from injury, yet no human foresight could anticipate the probability of a fall before it took place. Some serious accidents occurred, both from the fool-hardiness of the miners, and from the wanton and wicked acts of others, in cutting the whim ropes nearly through, by which several were severely hurt, and one killed. In works of such magnitude it is scarcely possible to arrive at completion without occasional accidents.[18]

Page 87 (*above*) Itchen Navigation, view from Blackbridge wharf, Winchester; (*below*) a scene near Rooksbury bridge on the Andover Canal, 1833

Page 88 Upper Thames Navigation in 1875: (*above*) a narrow boat approaches a lock; (*below*) lifting the paddles of a flash-lock

In December 1822 Frindsbury basin was advertised as being open to receive vessels of 300 tons, and having 'accommodation for loading and ballasting Vessels of every description, with the greatest despatch', and half a mile of tunnel at that end of the canal were reported navigable.[19] Soon afterwards a canal road was made from the basin for about 500 yd towards Strood. In November of that year, and again in February 1823, the company were advertising to attract craft to enter the canal basin to load

The very best White Flints for the Porcelain Manufactories, Superior Block Chalk, Cobble ditto for Lime, Chalk Rubbish for Manure. Also Loam for Ballast.

Such advertisements were put in the Worcester newspaper, presumably because of the porcelain works there.[20]

In November 1822 the company applied to the Exchequer Bill Loan Commissioners for a loan to finish the works. Telford, the Commissioners' engineer, went down to see the canal. At that time the company had raised £177,757 out of an authorized capital of £220,000, incurred £17,553 of debt, and paid £3,000 of interest on optional loan notes. They had cut the open canal section, made both basins and locks, Frindsbury being bigger to take larger craft, and cut 1,121 yd of finished tunnel out of a then estimated total of 4,013 yd. The company's income for 1821 had been:

	£
Rent of land and warehouses	351
Sale of 38,535 tons of chalk and flint	3,261
Dock and canal dues (Gravesend end)	534
Income at Rochester end of canal	500
	£4,646

They estimated that when their canal was open, they would obtain three-quarters of the available traffic, the total being assessed at 2,570 tons a week as recorded at Rochester customs. At an average of 8d a ton, they counted on a toll income of £7,515 and a total income of £15,515 pa 'independent of all other advantages that may accrue from the Levant Trade, etc'.[21]

By the beginning of 1823, however, hope was short and money was low. A large shareholder at that time circularized the other shareholders, and said:

The Money raised by Loan has been comparatively from a very few Individuals (about 25 or 30 Subscribers) and those chiefly belonging to the Committee, the general body not having contributed any thing towards the improvement of their own

F

Property, ought now to come forward to its support, as it cannot be expected that those Gentlemen, who have already done so much, can continue to render their assistance.

Complaints have been made that the Canal will never be finished, and certainly these complaints are justly founded, while the mass of proprietors do nothing towards it, and the progress of the concern has at times been impeded for want of means. There has been more money expended than was expected, but when the impossibility of estimating correctly the cost of Tunnelling is considered, this complaint will vanish: however, the capability of now finishing it, and at the present estimate, is reduced to a moral certainty.

Perhaps in response to this circular, opinion seems to have rallied, for a newspaper letter of July 1823[22] refers to those disappointed of admission to the final subscription. It was not, however, final, for in January 1824 the company realized that they would not have enough money to finish, owing to the 'great expense which would be occasioned by an extra quantity of brick arching in the tunnel, and for other unforeseen circumstances,'[23] and promoted a late Bill to enable them to raise another £50,000.[24] On 6 May the tunnel was finished[25] and on 14 October 1824 the canal was opened with much rejoicing.*

It was some 7 miles long, 51 ft wide at top surface and 7 ft deep except in the tunnel, taking 60-ton sailing barges measuring 94 ft 8 in × 22 ft 8 in. The older Gravesend lock was 109 ft × 23 ft and admitted 200 ton craft to the basin there, whereas that at Frindsbury was 131 ft × 30 ft and allowed 300 ton vessels to enter. The sills of the entrance locks were 2 ft 10 in below low water level. The Frindsbury lock had cast-iron gates from the start; those of Gravesend were originally of oak, but these became so seriously affected by worm that they were replaced by cast-iron gates in 1819. At that time it was intended to supply the canal with water by filling it right up during spring tides and allowing it then to act as a reservoir during neaps, but in early years it was found that it could lose 4 in of water in 24 hours, and diminish to 3 ft in the canal and 4 ft in the tunnel before it could be refilled, whereas loaded Medway barges needed 3 ft 6 in to 5 ft, and the bigger corn barges 6 ft.[26] A steam-engine to pump water into the canal was therefore installed at Gravesend before 1835, probably about 1827, though the tides were still used to fill the canal when they could. It was expensive. For the year 1843 it worked 3,666 hours, used 444 tons of coal, and cost £520 to run exclusive of wages. Cost of

* For an account of the opening ceremony, see *British Canals*, 4th ed, pp. 49–51.

1825.

THAMES AND MEDWAY CANAL.

RATES OF TONNAGE.

SPECIES OF GOODS.	Per Ton. Per Mile.	Whole Length of Canal.	SPECIES OF GOODS.	Per Ton. Per Mile.	Whole Length of Canal.
Freestone.........	.. 1d. ..	5d. per Ton.	Flour.............	.. 2d. ..	1s 2d per Ton.
Limestone	.. 1d. ..	5d. ditto.	Wheat............	.. 2d. ..	1s 2d ditto
Chalk...	.. 1d. ..	5d. bitto.	Barley............	.. 2d. ..	1s 2d ditto
Bricks	.. 1d. ..	5d. ditto.	Oats.............	.. 2d. ..	1s 2d ditto
Tiles	.. 1d. ..	5d. ditto.	Beans............	.. 2d. ..	1s 2d ditto
Slates............	.. 1d. ..	5d. ditto.	Peas	.. 2d. ..	1s 2d ditto
Sand	.. 1d. ..	5d. ditto.	Malt.............	.. 2d. ..	1s 2d ditto
Stones............	.. 1d. ..	5d. ditto.	Corn in the Straw .	.. 2d. ..	1s 2d ditto
Clay....	.. 1d. ..	5d. ditto.	Hay	.. 2d. ..	1s 2d ditto
Dung..	.. 1d. ..	5d. ditto.	Straw............	.. 2d. ..	1s 2d ditto
Manure	.. 1d. ..	5d. ditto.	Faggots	.. 2d. ..	1s 2d ditto
Tin..	.. 1d. ..	5d. ditto.			
Iron Stone.	.. 1d. ..	5d. ditto.			
Pig Iron..	. 1d. ..	5d. ditto.	Fruit.............	.. 3d. ..	1s 9d per Ton.
Pig Lead ..	.. 1d. ..	5d. ditto.	Coke.............	.. 3d. ..	1s 9d ditto
Lime	.. 1d. ..	7d. ditto.	Timber, rough	.. 3d. ..	1s 9d ditto
			Hemp............	.. 3d. ..	1s 9d ditto
			Bark.............	.. 3d. ..	1s 9d ditto
Cattle	.. 2d. ..	1s. per Ton.	Coals	.. 3d. ..	1s 9d ditto
Potatoes..... ...	.. 2d. ..	1s. ditto.	Culm	.. 3d. ..	1s 9d ditto
Goods	.. 2d. ..	1s. ditto.			
Wares....	.. 2d. ..	1s. ditto.	Hops.............	.. 6d. ..	2s 6d per Ton.
Merchandize	.. 2d. ..	1s. ditto.	Wool.............	.. 6d. ..	2s 6d ditto

N. B. If Landed or Shipped from the Company's Premises, 2d. per Ton for Wharfage, extra.
Vessels not exceeding 18 feet in breadth and 100 feet in length, and drawing not more than 5 feet water, may pass along the whole line of the Canal.
An empty return Barge or Vessel, having passed the Canal loaded.......Nil.
An empty Barge or Vessel, going for and returning with Lading........Nil.
An empty Barge or Vessel passing, to be considered as 20 Tons, at 6d. per Ton, 10s.—and such empty Barge or Vessel returning without Lading within 24 hours, Nil.

11. A Thames & Medway Canal toll-sheet of 1825

the canal at opening was probably about £260,000. Contemporary figures up to £350,000 or more are found,[27] but these are exaggerated. We may note that the canal was just outside the City of London's coal limits: coal could therefore be landed without paying the City dues. The limit, to the north-west of the basin at Gravesend, was marked by an old tree until it was burnt in 1824, and after that by a stone obelisk.

The opening ceremony did not end the company's troubles. Four months later, the Frindsbury end had to be closed for about six weeks for improvements at Frindsbury basin, whatever these were. Then the cutting of the tunnel was found to have deprived of water wells on three estates at Frindsbury and Strood whose bottoms were above the canal level, and they had to be deepened at the company's expense. When the canal was filled with water on a spring-tide this water then began to find its way into the wells. Claims for compensation were brought against the company, who meanwhile were having to provide a service of water carriers. Eventually, in 1826, the complainants, who had claimed £1,527, were awarded £979.[28] It seems likely that the canal had been closed during this episode, for not until a few days after the case had been settled did an advertisement appear on 6 June that the canal was completely open.[29]

At that time the City of London claimed the conservancy of the Thames down to Yantlet Creek beyond Gravesend, then by a line down that winding tidal channel to Colemouth Creek on the Medway, and up that river to Upnor below Rochester, these channels marking the ancient boundary between the Isle of Grain and the Hundred of Hoo. In 1823, after having been petitioned by fishermen to reopen what was claimed to be an ancient navigation, but seemingly with the main motive of preserving their claim, they hired John Pinkerton and some canal cutters, and on 17 September cut through an embankment across the channel, where once a bridge had stood, amidst the objections of local landowners.

A few boats and barges then managed to get through the channel from one river to the other, but the landowners brought and won an action at Surrey Assizes in August 1824. The City obtained a retrial in the King's Bench in July 1825, but lost that also, for they could only prove one previous transit of the channels, in 1778, and assert the likelihood that these were in use in and before 1716.

The Court of Aldermen never seem to have been officially told in 1823 that the Thames & Medway Canal was nearly finished, or even of its existence, and evidence about it was excluded from the law cases. Again, it was not mentioned when in November 1826 the whole Court, having had Sir Edward Banks's advice, decided to seek a Bill to build a canal about a mile long to link the two creeks. But no Bill was in fact introduced, clearly because the Thames & Medway was by then free of its legal troubles and fully open.[30] A subscription for £15,000 also followed immediately the law case was over, in promissory or optional notes at favourable rates, the latter with the option to convert within 5 years to £100 shares at £25 each. Money must have come in, for in October the company decided to get trade started by building six barges to be used in the hop-carrying and general goods trades from Maidstone and Rochester to London. They then set up Henry Drury as a carrier at Maidstone, and in January 1827 he advertised that from the 27th he was starting a weekly sailing barge service between Maidstone and London:

> To obviate the present dilatory and irregular mode of conveying goods by Water between Maidstone and London, and to ensure despatch and certainty, his Vessels will positively sail on such days as they are advertised for, *whether full or not*, and pass through the Thames and Medway Canal, thereby saving about 50 miles of an uncertain, tedious and dangerous navigation.[31]

The inevitable exponent of the old way being best, another carrier from Maidstone, John Barlow, who was not going to use the canal, then advertised that one of his barges

> arrived at Maidstone BEFORE the *fast sailing* Vessells of the Thames and Medway Canal Wharf, although they both started at the same time.[32]

Drury riposted by explaining that his first voyage had been delayed by 'an accident arising from inexperience in the new navigation',[33] and then by advertising voyage times for his barges from Maidstone to London or return, 28 hours, 25 and 23 and a freak 11, but with an average of 29. He was successful, for in February he put on two barges a week, and in March he was followed by the first of his competitors, when Henry Simmonds of Maidstone announced that his vessels would in future sail twice weekly 'in 24 hours, by way of the new Canal'.[34] Later, he was to say that he had refused to follow Drury's example until the canal company had reduced their 'very exorbitant charge of tonnage' by about 1s (5p) a ton.[35] Before long, the old firms changed over and new firms started up, until half a dozen were working barges from Maidstone to London and back once or twice a week out of season, and daily during the hop harvest. There were also twice-weekly hoy services from Strood to London and from Gravesend to Maidstone.[36]

In 1828 there was a further subscription of £13,000 in shares or notes, new shares now being issued at £3 10s (£3.50) each ranking *pari passu*. Part of the money was used to pay debts, and part to build a passing place.[37] Given that vessels tended, because of the tide times, to arrive together at the canal entrances, at peak periods enough delay was threatened in passing boats through the tunnel to cancel the canal's advantage in time. As well as the waiting basin they had at Higham, the company had earlier intended to build a passing place for barges, 200 ft long and 50 ft wide, within the tunnel itself, but the idea had been dropped because of the cost. Such a passing place was now found essential, and between 9 February and 18 April 1830 the canal was closed for the centre of the tunnel to be opened up by cutting down from the lowest part of the valley above. The original tunnel was thus divided into two, of 1,515 and 2,347 yd,* at a probable cost of about £13,000. 'The sides of this opening, about 100 feet high, are perpendicular or nearly so, and have stood like solid rock since it was first executed.'[38]

The new trade used sailing barges of 40–60 tons, and therefore many of the old seagoing hoys became obsolete: a news item of August 1828 says that several hoys formerly used in the London trade are for sale at Rochester, having been replaced by barges on account of the canal.[39] Nevertheless the older term 'the hoying trade', persisted for the business that succeeded it. In 1829 Drury announced that he was building boats to carry fruit four times a week for the London market,[40] baskets to be returned free, but these soon drop out of the advertisements, and presumably failed to pay.

The company seem to have employed a towing contractor to provide towing services on the canal. He is said to have held a beer licence, and to have lived in the house that later became Higham station.[41] At some time also they put on a steam tug, probably to help craft through the tunnels. This was still working when the line closed.

It is said that when the canal opened, a small steamboat carried

* The present lengths of the tunnels are Higham, 1,530 yd, and Strood, 2,329 yd, with a gap, the old passing place, of 72 yd, or 3,931 in all. There have, however, been changes since canal days. Major-General Pasley, inspector general of railways, in his report of 9 August 1845, gives the respective lengths as 1,514 yd 2 ft 9 in and 2,346 yd 2 ft 8 in. The scaled length of the passing place on the deposited plan of 1846 is about 85 yd, giving an original total length of 3,946 yd. On the other hand, John Pinkerton, who had worked on the tunnel, writing about 1825 from the canal company's office and on their notepaper, gave the length as 4,004 yd. It is therefore possible that it was slightly shortened in canal days. It seems best to take the figure of 3,946 for the purpose of this book. The figure formerly given, of 3,909 yd, was made up of the present lengths of the two tunnels and an estimated 50 yd for the passing place.

passengers between Gravesend and Strood in connection with the Thames steamers, but that it was discontinued because of bank damage. However, the tunnels were popular with excursionists, who walked through them, rowed to them,* or visited them on a pleasure trip. In August 1831 a public excursion was run from Maidstone to Sheerness through the canal in the steamboat *Adelaide*, taking 3½ hours for the trip, and offering refreshments on board and a band. It was advertised as to examine

> that stupendous work of art, the *Thames and Medway Canal* and *Tunnel*,

but the appearance of the paddle-wheeler also created much excitement as she left Aylesford wharf to the firing of a cannon. She entered the canal at Frindsbury, the newspaper report tells us, through the magnificent lock and basin and entered the sombre gloom of the tunnel, where torches were used to throw their lurid glare. The vessel almost filled the channel, and the passengers, what with the reverberation of the noise of the paddles, the indistinct light, and the consciousness of traversing the bowels of the earth, experienced a

> very odd and certainly novel sensation,

but were elevated by observing that fragments of flint sparkling in the chalk roof resembled Magri's description of the celebrated grotto of Antiparos.[43] In 1836 a canal shareholder, in spite of his lack of dividends, spoke proudly of 'the finest tunnel in the world'.[44]

In the thirties the hop and general trades via the canal remained busy, with six firms operating from Maidstone through the canal, though the upper Medway company's own craft used it only for the hop trade and in exceptional conditions. Speed was presumably not so necessary for them, though the toll of 1s a ton seems reasonable enough. In 1837 the growing Medway paper trade appears in advertisements, as:

> Simmonds and Masters have appropriated a part of Kent Wharf, Southwark, exclusively to the Paper business, and having Carts at all times in readiness on the arrival of the Vessels . . . to deliver to the Trade,[45]

while in 1842 a Maidstone firm is advertising chemical manures and saltpetre brought from London by way of the canal.[46] Drury probably died at the beginning of 1840, for in February his wharf was advertised to let: it was then said to be doing 3,000 tons a year of business, and was soon taken.

I have been able to find few details of the company's finances.

* A guide book of 1835[42] told its readers that they could visit the canal by boat on application at the Canal Tavern, Gravesend, or at Strood.

Surviving loan notes of 1819 and 1826 are endorsed with interest payments, for the former to April 1826, for the latter to January 1827.[47] It is probable that little interest was paid thereafter,[48] and certainly no dividends, surpluses being used for improvements, though a surviving account for 1844[49] shows £194 paid as interest on bonds, a very small amount. In 1843 the canal carried 58,078 tons, 37,890 of which had entered from Gravesend and 20,188 from Frindsbury. In addition, 21,611 tons had been handled at Gravesend basin, and 4,002 at Frindsbury—83,691 tons in all, 6,380 less than the year before. Revenue was £3,410, £186 less than 1842, of which £2,032 was for canal tolls, and the balance for wharfages and rents. There was a small balance on working which went to debt reduction. The company had during the year bought land near the passing place as a preliminary, they reported, to opening a further section of tunnel. The final cost of canal and tunnel, including the things done after it was opened, was given in 1846 as £285,439.[50]

In January 1842, the canal shareholders met with J. U. Rastrick to discuss possible conversion to a railway at a cost of £120,000, and seemingly agreed at once to form the Gravesend & Rochester Railway Company with a capital of £150,000 for this purpose. Its prospectus appeared a few days later.[51] This essay seems to have had no consequences in action, but in the autumn of that year, Maidstone was busy discussing a rail link with Rochester and Gravesend to connect with the steamers for London, in the hope of replacing the current 'laborious day's work' with a three hours journey by train and river. A letter to the newspaper then suggested that such a line should pass through the canal tunnels, but Joseph Locke's survey of a Maidstone, Rochester & Gravesend Railway at the end of the year proposed a short tunnel crossing obliquely over those of the canal and then a long viaduct at Higham.[52] But this scheme dropped, and Maidstone got its first railway by a branch from Paddock Wood on 25 September 1844, though in the 1843 hop season the water carriers had already been offering reduced rates.

In January 1844 a meeting of Thames & Medway shareholders were considering a contractor's offer to convert their canal to a railway, be paid entirely in loan notes, and then lease it for 99 years. They decided not to convert, but immediately afterwards two other railway companies put up competing schemes, and a further meeting on 9 February reversed the earlier decision. It was now agreed that the company would itself make the railway, using the same contractor, Fox, Henderson & Co, and a new prospectus was issued asking for subscriptions to loan notes convertible to preference shares. A net revenue of £16,000 pa was estimated, which after servicing the money to be raised would yield £12,750 pa to the existing share and loan note holders.[53]

By April the contract was signed to the satisfaction of the company's engineer, J. U. Rastrick, whereby the contractors would make the line and provide working stock for £65,528, £30,000 of which was to be paid in 5 per cent loan notes. An offer from the South Eastern Railway for the canal was refused, and the single-track Gravesend & Rochester Railway was then built alongside the canal from Gravesend, where a temporary station was constructed alongside the basin, to Higham, and then through the tunnels themselves with one rail on the towpath and the other on supports placed in the canal bed so as not to interfere with traffic, though the navigable width was reduced to 16½ ft. A passing place was provided at Higham, and at the Medway end the lines swung away from the Frindsbury basin to a station at Strood. Passengers at Gravesend changed to and from the London steamboats, and at Strood to another, subsidized by the company, to Chatham or made their way by road over the bridge to Rochester. The company realized that more convenient stations would have to be built, and early in 1844 had made provisional arrangements with the Terrace Pier company for one at Gravesend near the pier. The tunnels now had no towpath, but on the open canal a new one was built on the north side, and in use by June 1844.

The conversion proposal started a lot of rumours that the tunnels would be dangerous for trains. For instance, the *Railway Times* told its readers that 'the tunnel, we are positively assured by competent judges who have no interest in the matter, is unsafe,' and called for a Board of Trade inspection.[54] It got several,[55] though no serious slips had occurred under the canal company. At the time of conversion a few short sections had been lined, making the total lined portions just under a mile in length, and leaving about 1¼ miles unlined. Major General Pasley, on behalf of the Board of Trade, thoroughly tested the tunnels by going through them at night on a barge carrying a special inspection bridge, and then by firing small blank mortars at the chalk to see if he could shift it. He could not, and pronounced it perfectly safe, though he required the staging that carried the railway rails over the canal to be strengthened. He noted that the original tunnel shafts had been covered over and partly filled up.

The line was to have been opened on 23 January 1845, but a pay dispute led to thirty or forty navvies taking possession of a station

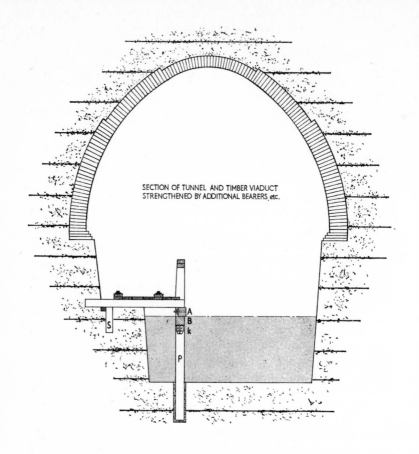

SECTION OF TUNNEL AND TIMBER VIADUCT
STRENGTHENED BY ADDITIONAL BEARERS, etc.

ELEVATION OF IMPROVED VIADUCT

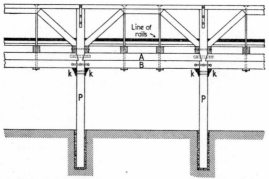

12. Final design of the staging that carried the outer rails of the Gravesend &
Rochester Railway through Strood and Higham tunnels

and threatening to destroy it, a foreman to steal part of a locomotive to prevent it running, and the contractor to refuse to give
up the line to the company until the dispute was ended. However,
the magistrates sensibly told two from each side to settle the
trouble.[56] They did so, and after some experimental runs carrying
passengers free, the public service began on 10 February with
three engines, whose chimneys were fitted with shields to deflect
the smoke sideways, and carriages with windows barred on the
towpath side of the tunnels. Only passengers were carried in the
early days. Here are figures:

Period	Trains run	No of Passengers	Receipts £
10 Feb–30 June 1845	2,791	114,817	2,971
1 July–31 Dec 1845	7,118	253,867	6,201
1 Jan–30 June 1846	8,047	217,214	5,319

In the same year of 1845 an Act[57] was obtained to raise £170,000
in shares and a further £56,666 on mortgage on certain conditions,
to liquidate the railway debt and provide more capital. In this,
power was given to abandon the canal from Strood to Higham
except for Frindsbury basin, and this section was closed on 15
November. It was then estimated that two-thirds of the former
revenue would still be got from the rest of the canal and the two
basins.[58]

Meanwhile, the South Eastern Railway was expanding. In May
1844 that company had:

Resolved: that an application be made to the Thames and Medway Canal Company . . . asking them on what terms they would
be willing to dispose of their interests to this Company,[59]

and later in the same year a deputation was received from what
was now the Gravesend & Rochester Railway and Canal Company
which was sent to

ascertain whether the Line running along the route of the
Thames and Medway Canal from Rochester to Gravesend could
not be adopted by this Company as part of the Lines contemplated by them from Maidstone to Gravesend and from London
to Chatham, Faversham and Chilham. The Deputation were
informed that this Company were prepared to take an independent course, unless satisfactory arrangements were made
with them for working the Traffic over their Line and a double
Line laid down. The latter the Deputation stated they intended
to do and proposed applying to Parliament for powers in the
next Session.[60]

A year later, on 4 December 1845, an agreement was made whereby the South Eastern bought the Gravesend & Rochester for £310,000,* ten per cent to be paid in cash and the remainder in railway bonds at 3½ per cent. Since the interest on the loan notes and the preference shares of the smaller railway was in arrears, the sum paid by the South Eastern reflects the strategic value of the line and tunnels, an SER statement of January 1846 saying that the canal railway 'now necessarily occupies an important position with reference to the North Kent lines'.[61] The authorizing Act[62] was passed on 3 August 1846.

The canal from Higham to Frindsbury was now filled in, and a double track laid down as part of what was then called the North Kent line. It was opened on 23 August 1847. This is, I think, the only important instance in Great Britain of a railway line being laid through a canal tunnel, though many such proposals were made, notably for the Sapperton tunnel on the Thames & Severn.† In 1861 the East Kent Railway completed a line from Strood to Dover, and by arrangement with the South Eastern, through London–Dover trains began running by way of the old canal tunnels. Soon, however, the company that was to become the London, Chatham & Dover sought access to London independently of the South Eastern, and left the Gravesend route. The Gravesend–Higham section of the canal remained open under the name of the Gravesend & Rochester Canal, and was used for a time by local farmers to carry manure and produce, while coal was unloaded in the basins from schooners and small sailing vessels. Some canalside industries grew up at Gravesend, and here boat repairing was done at the basin, and rowing boats could be hired out from the occupant of a curious little house made from an inverted boat.[63] Finally, the rest of the canal was authorized to be abandoned by a Southern Railway Act of 1934, and only Gravesend basin is still used by pleasure boats.

In 1902 a group of industrialists with works on the Medway, led by Col. T. J. Holland, of Townshend, Hook & Co, paper makers, and Harold Le Marchant, of Martineau & Co, cement manufacturers, (who was in 1903 also to be concerned in the new Upper Medway company) promoted a new Medway & Thames Canal, 5⅛ miles long with two tunnels, to run slightly to the east of the old canal, at an estimated cost of £245,310. Its purpose was to enable something over 2m tons a year of coal, cement, pulp and

---

* Afterwards increased by various payments to £325,000.
† There was one other, the 66-yd Combe Hay tunnel on the Somersetshire Coal Canal, through which a railway was laid, and opened in 1910.

paper which then passed round the Isle of Grain in sailing barges carrying 70 to 180 tons, or in lighters carrying 160 to 240 tons pulled by tugs, losing time and sometimes being damaged by salt water, to be carried quickly by electric traction. The project was authorized by an Act of 1902, but went no further.

CHAPTER V

Round London

IT is said that Canute sailed up the river Effra to Brixton, and that Queen Elizabeth I did the same when she visited Raleigh. In 1664 Lord Loughborough, who held the manor of Water Lambeth or Lambeth Wick, got a private Act[1] to make a navigable canal of the Effra from the Thames to near Brixton Causeway.[2]

In 1778 Smeaton had been called in to judge between two possible routes for a canal from Kingston on the Thames to Ewell. No action followed, but in the late 1790s Ralph Dodd, whom we have met on the Thames & Medway, proposed a canal from Deptford by Clapham to Kingston, with a branch to Epsom by way of Ewell, another by way of Mitcham to Croydon, and other shorter cuts, which would show a 10 per cent return to the shareholders. At the same time there was a proposal for a canal from Wandsworth to Croydon, which was surveyed by Jessop and Rennie, who both considered it impracticable because of water shortage unless the sources of the Wandle were tapped, which would interfere with the many mills on its banks. In 1799 also there was talk of a horse railway from London to Portsmouth by way of Croydon. Again, in 1796, William Jessop, giving evidence before the Select Committee on the Port of London, proposed a canal from Rotherhithe to Vauxhall.[3]

These ideas crystallized into three projects, for a canal from Rotherhithe to Mitcham, the Grand Surrey; a canal from Rotherhithe to Croydon, the Croydon Canal; and a horse railway from Wandsworth to Croydon along the Wandle valley, the Surrey Iron Railway. All three obtained their Acts in 1801.

Grand Surrey Canal

The authorized route of the Grand Surrey, at the time of its Act[4] called the Surrey & Kent Canal, and estimated at £60,000, was from the Thames at Rotherhithe by way of Camberwell,

Kennington, Clapham and Tooting to Mitcham, with branches to Deptford, Peckham, the Borough, and the river again at Vauxhall. An intended branch to Kingston, which would have provided a canal bypass through London to the Thames again above Teddington, had to be taken out while the Bill was going through, as did one from Mitcham to Croydon. Strict protective clauses for the Wandle's water were also inserted.

Ralph Dodd was the engineer, being paid the high salary of £600 pa, while Robert Dodd, presumably a relation, was his clerk of works. A third Dodd, George, presumably Ralph's brother, then only 18 years old, and later to be Rennie's assistant on Waterloo bridge, gave evidence in favour of the Bill. Ralph was not a success, and in April 1802 he was dismissed with a gratuity. There is evidence that he did work without authority, and it is said that he quarrelled with the chairman, but the official reasons given were that he was engaged in too many other activities, and was too expensive. Robert Dodd was also dismissed. Soon after this, Ralph Dodd attacked the new engineer, John Rowe, and the committee upon the state of the works, and Jessop had to be called in to restore the shareholders' confidence. In spite of this, Dodd was later employed in small jobs for the company.

The influence of a shipowner, John Hall, now became strong. He submitted in June 1802 a plan for a basin for ships on the canal near the entrance lock. The London docks were being built, and for about a year the committee hovered between wishing to develop their canal plans and wishing to create a dock business. In October 1803, however, they decided to build a 3-acre basin and a ship-lock, and these were opened in 1807. The dock business had won.

Meanwhile the necessity of providing a waterway to the Thames for the Croydon Canal, the proprietors of which had agreed to join the Grand Surrey near New Cross instead of building an independent entrance at Rotherhithe, caused the latter canal to be completed past the proposed junction to the Old Kent Road in 1807. There was now traffic to and from the Croydon, though that canal was not completed till 1809, and a steady bickering went on between the two companies because the Croydon barges were obstructed by floating timber and craft lying in the basin. It was not till 1810 that the Grand Surrey's line was completed to Camberwell. This lethargy was caused by the profitableness of the dock business. For instance, the committee report to the 1810 General Assembly said:

It is known to every one who has attended to the concerns of

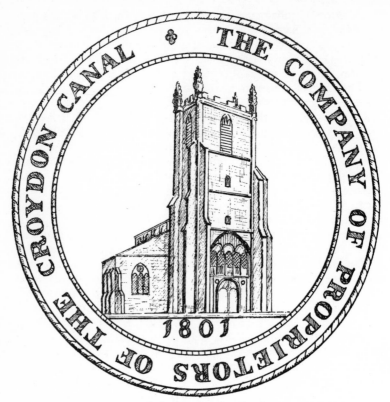

13. Seal of the Croydon Canal

the Company that their greatest and principal revenue arises from the Bason and Shipping. It is known also that the Canal has hitherto been not merely unproductive, but a heavy weight attached to the Bason. The Committee however have great pleasure in announcing that the Canal is now open to Camberwell, and that it has at present better prospects of being productive than it ever had.[5]

In spite of this unproductiveness, the company had up to this time taken a sporadic interest in the line to Mitcham, and more consistently in an extension to Kennington and then along the Washway (parallel with Brixton Road), up Brixton Hill by a deviation to the south of the road and an inclined plane at Rushey Green, to a point where the canal was to pass under the road near the present waterworks on its way to Tooting. They bought some land along this line, as also along one of the Deptford branches. In 1810 there was a revival of interest in canals, and even a discussion between the Grand Surrey and Kennet & Avon companies about a junction, presumably by way of the Basingstoke and the old idea of a canal from Kingston to Camberwell.

The original share capital had been £60,000 with power to raise a further £30,000. Soon after the foundation stone of the entrance lock had been laid on 7 November 1804 the company had spent all its resources, and after various devices for raising money had been discarded, the committee reported that if money could not be raised 'there is no alternative but that the property will be seized by the Creditors immediately.'[6] The shareholders put up some money on mortgage, and the Heygates, bankers, active in the City corporation and in canal finance, some more, till on 13 March 1807 the entrance lock and basin were opened:

Early in the morning, every thing about the works denoted the approaching festivity: two colours were seen flying at the entrance lock, and the royal standard was displayed on a staff in the middle of the island.* At two o'clock the ship intended to take the lead in entering, began to dress in the colours of various nations, and the remaining ships also followed the example, though in a plainer style. About the same time, the company assembled on the insular wharfage, where marquees and a cold collation were prepared for their accommodation. At length the tide rose to a level with the water in the bason, the gates were thrown open, and guns were fired as a signal for the vessels to enter. At half past three o'clock, the *Argo*, a fine brig of 242 tons burthen, the property of Mr John Hall, made her entry amidst the acclamations of the spectators. She was saluted by the discharge of cannon on shore, which was returned by the vessel, whilst a band of martial music on the deck played 'God Save the King' and 'Rule Britannia'. Four of the vessels, named the *Equity*, the *British Tar*, the *Nautilus* and the Cumberland yatch, all handsomely ornamented with colours, immediately followed. The whole made a very interesting appearance, riding in the capacious channels of the commercial bason, which is a great improvement to the port of London, and promises the most ample accommodation to the trade of the river Thames.[7]

In 1807 another £60,000 was authorized, and further sums as the docks were extended. By 25 March 1811 the dock and canal so far built had cost £121,167, of which just over £40,000 was for land. In 1808 the company got powers to supply water to areas

* In the dock.

G

near the canal. Later, new timber ponds were formed, and in November 1812 the company opened a second dock and connecting lock, after having had to close the canal for two months to make it. Angling tickets were now issued at a guinea each, a tribute to the canal water of the time. In 1817 and 1818 the company seriously considered an extension of the Camberwell arm for 1,245 yd further to Kennington Common, but high land prices and the deep cutting needed meant that not enough land would be available for wharves, and the idea was dropped, though in 1819 the company opposed the Surrey & Sussex road Bill for a new road crossing their Parliamentary line to Vauxhall until they got a clause protecting them should they decide to extend 'at a future period'.

Thereafter, while timber remained a useful source of revenue, corn to the docks and coal to the canal became increasingly important. Demand for canalside wharves increased, and the canal trade grew. In August 1825, therefore, the company started to build the Peckham branch, and by May 1826 had completed it, 5 furlongs in length, 40 ft wide, with a basin 450 ft by 80 ft at its end. In 1830 the South Metropolitan Gas Company took a site on the Camberwell line to build a gasworks, and were much encouraged by the company because of the prospect of an increasing coal trade.

When in March 1835 the London & Croydon Railway's Bill, which included power to buy and close the Croydon Canal, came to Parliament, the Grand Surrey sought protective clauses to cover the railway's crossing, and also to indemnify them against loss of trade. This last the railway flatly refused to do, but they agreed to build an interchange basin at the railway junction where coal and merchandize could be transferred.

In August 1835 the company were approached by the engineer Henry H. Price with a scheme which interested the directors—who by that time included Nathan Rothschild—enough for them to put it before a shareholders' meeting on 29 October. As a result, a prospectus appeared for the Grand Surrey Dock, Canal & Junction Railway Company, with a capital of £600,000, and Price as engineer. It proposed to extend the canal to the Thames at Vauxhall and also at Deptford, so providing both wharves for local trade and a waterway to bypass the Thames through London and save 2½ miles of distance on a tidal river; and also to build a railway, mostly on the canal's north bank, from the London & Southampton's line at Vauxhall to Deptford (this was later altered to a connection with the London & Greenwich), and a branch to the Elephant & Castle. In it, the Grand Surrey Company were said to have agreed to turn themselves into a new company for this purpose, accepting 1,521 £50 shares fully paid up, equal to £76,050, for their interest, the new company to take over their £140,000 of 4 per cent loan notes. Profits were estimated at 14 per cent, and the cost at £547,589, but the public were uninterested: 'from the very few Shares paid upon it would have been folly to attempt to bring in a Bill or proceed further in the present Session.'[8] The railway portion of the project, from the London & Southampton to the London & Greenwich, was then brought forward again in February 1836 by another group of projectors as the South London Union, but had no better future.

In 1850 a prospectus[9] appeared for a company to build a canal from the Thames near Deptford dockyard to the Kennet & Avon at Reading using part of the Grand Surrey line, reducing the distance to 22 miles from 42 by the river. There would be branches to the Thames at Vauxhall, Wandsworth, Mortlake, Richmond, Staines, Datchet and Maidenhead. Oddly, the Deptford end of the canal was to be open to the tides.

Arguments used by the promoter, John Martin, and engineer, William Sowerby, were that continuous wharves could be provided in the metropolitan area, whereas railways could only offer separated stations, that the canal would allow the Thames water to become cleaner and so make its use for water supply possible again, and that screw passenger steamers could be worked on it. Capital was to be £500,000—one would have thought a very considerable underestimate.

John Martin's final paragraph refers to the Grand Junction, Bridgewater, Basingstoke, Regent's and Kennet & Avon Canals, 'all of which are in a prosperous condition and pay a very handsome dividend': the shareholders of the Basingstoke, Regent's and Kennet & Avon must have been surprised to hear of their prosperity.

In June 1849 a hand-operated vertical lift bridge which had been installed on the Thames Junction branch of the LBSCR where it crossed over the canal near its junction with the Croydon Canal, was brought into use. When raised, it increased the waterway headroom from 4 ft 2½ in to 9 ft 6 in. Its installation had been bitterly opposed by the canal company, who wanted a swing bridge, but allowed by the Railway Commissioners. It worked well, and its electrically powered successor still exists.[10]

Apart from a half-year's payment to 25 March 1811, no dividend was paid until the 2 per cent of 1819; 3 per cent was distributed for 1820 to 1822, then amounts of £3 or less in most years. Strong competition between the various London docks kept their rates low and so their dividends. In 1864 the extension of the Greenland dock absorbed the canal, which thenceforward led out of that dock. In 1855 the company became the Grand Surrey Docks & Canal Company, and in 1864 it amalgamated with its chief rival, the Commercial Docks Company, to control and construct the great Surrey commercial docks system that later passed into the hands of the Port of London Authority.

Surrey Iron Railway

The Grand Surrey's tramroad contemporary was laid down from the river Thames at Wandsworth Creek, where a tide-lock and basin capable of holding thirty barges were built, by way of Mitcham to Croydon, with a branch to Hackbridge. The line was nearly 9 miles long, and the cost some £60,000. Its purpose was to carry coal to Croydon and to bring back lime, chalk, flint, fuller's earth, and agricultural products.

The line was built by William Jessop as a double-track horse-operated plateway. The main line was opened on 26 July 1803, the first public railway to be authorized independently of a canal, and the first railway company in the world, all previous lines having been privately owned, and built to carry the commodities of the owner, usually the products of a coal-mine or an ironworks. Phillips, the historian of inland navigation, records the opening of the river-lock and basin at Wandsworth, and then goes on:

> The iron rail-ways are of great advantage to the country in general, and are made at an expense of about £300* per mile. The advantages they give for the conveyance of goods by carts and waggons, seem even to surpass, in some instances, those of boat carriage by canals.[11]

In the year of its opening another Act was passed for a connecting railway, largely promoted by the principal shareholders of the Surrey Iron Railway. This was the Croydon, Merstham & Godstone, to run from Croydon to Reigate, with a branch from Merstham to Godstone. The company failed to raise the necessary money, however, and it was only built with a single track from Croydon to the Greystone limeworks at Merstham at a cost of £45,500. It was opened in July 1805. In 1837 the London & Brighton Railway was authorized to buy the Croydon–Merstham

---

* In fact, the Surrey Iron Railway cost a great deal more. The amount is not certainly known, and is put at figures from £4,500 to £7,000 a mile.

line; in 1846 traffic ended on the Surrey Iron, and the company was effectively dissolved in 1848.[12]

Croydon Canal

Five weeks after the Surrey Iron Railway had been authorized, the Act[13] for the Croydon Canal was passed, though the town that had to support these two lines of communication had a population of only 7,000. For the first time in Britain there was to be direct competition on very equal terms between the two forms of transport. A contemporary writer described it thus:

> This magnificent undertaking was set on foot in the year 1800 by the spirited enterprise of a few gentlemen residing in the neighbourhood of Croydon, who, flattered with the prospect of an abundant supply of water, and with the great increase of the traffic in the town and parts adjacent, were solicitous of availing themselves of these circumstances to open a new communication between that place and the metropolis. The scheme went forward with great enthusiasm.[14]

The original plan by Ralph Dodd in 1799 was for a small canal taking 10 to 20-ton boats, 24 ft wide and 3½ ft deep. It was to run west of Beckenham and Sydenham, east of Lewisham and west of Deptford to Rotherhithe, with two inclined planes, one near Deptford and one at New Cross. The estimate was £25,000 for 12 miles. John Rennie was then called in, and on 8 October 1800 reported both on a canal with planes, and one with locks on a different line through Penge Common, Sydenham, Brockley, New Cross and Deptford to Rotherhithe. For the former, he recommended planes able to work boats of only 5 to 7 tons, as was done at that time on the planes at work in Shropshire,[15] or locks 75 ft × 7 ft to take boats carrying 20 to 25 tons, the canal to be of about the same dimensions in either case. His estimates were then £46,516 for the canal with planes, or £64,100 with locks. He was, however, lukewarm about the canal's prospects, saying:

> If the Lock Canal is adopted, I do not apprehend there will ever be more than five Boats pass up and down daily on the average.

He went on:

> If . . . from the expence which I have stated, it appears eligible to have a Canal at all, I apprehend it will be determined in favour of one with Inclined Planes, or some other such substitute for Locks,[16]

his reason being the scarcity of water on the summit level. This was the result, for the deposited plan for the 1801 bill shows a

canal 11 miles long from the Thames at Rotherhithe, level for the
first 2½ miles, with one plane at New Cross and a second at
Deptford, followed by a level 7 miles to Croydon. While the Bill
was going through Parliament, however, that for the Grand
Surrey passed, and the Croydon's line was therefore shortened to
join it near New Cross. The Act also allowed the canal company
to supply water, to be pumped from the Thames, to Sydenham,
Streatham, Dulwich and Norwood.

Rennie's Parliamentary estimate was £50,847 for the canal, proposed to be 34 ft wide (44 ft on the Rotherhithe level) and 6 ft
deep, including £4,500 for the planes and £6,200 for 'Two Steam
Engines for Hauling the Boats up the Planes, and for Supplying
the Canal with Water when not working the Planes, with their
Shafts and Tunnels,' with another £9,235 for the water supply
side.[17] The capital authorized, however, in the Act of 1801, was
£50,000 with power to raise another £30,000, including the water
supply costs; presumably the estimate had been reduced to take
account of the shortened length. Shares were widely spread: there
were 200 holders, none having more than 5 £100 shares.

After the Act had been passed, the company decided that, were
reservoirs to be built, water for canal use could be found to fill
them without pumping from the Thames, so they dropped the
steam engines, and with them the inclined planes and their water
supply plans. They could now build locks and have bigger boats,
but they also concluded that 20–25 ton craft would offer little
economy over road transport, because they would be too small,
especially to carry large timber, which 'as this Canal passes near the
King's Yard at Deptford, was a consideration of great importance.'[18]

A lock canal 9¼ miles long to take 30–35 ton barges was therefore built by Dudley Clark as engineer. From the Grand Surrey it
rose 167 ft by 26 locks in a little over 2½ miles to Forest Hill,
whence there was a level stretch of 5½ miles to Selhurst, and then
another 2 locks on the last stretch into Croydon. Depth was now
5 ft, and the locks were made to take craft 60 ft × 9 ft, an unusual
size. Reservoirs were built at Sydenham and Norwood, and a
pumping station at Croydon.

In 1808, having borrowed £20,357 and raised £47,508 from the
shareholders, the company had run out of money, and obtained
an Act enabling them to raise another £30,000.

On 22 October 1809 the canal was opened. The proprietors
'met at Sydenham . . . and there embarked, in one of the company's barges, which was handsomely decorated with flags, etc.'
It was followed

by a great many barges, loaded some of them with coals, others
with stone, corn, etc. . . . After passing a wharf, erected at Penge
Common by John Scott, Esq., by means of which, the towns of
Beckenham, Bromley, and a considerable part of Kent are accommodated with coals, manure, and all articles of merchandise
. . . the gay fleet of barges entered Penge Forest. The Canal
passes through this forest in a part of it so elevated, that it
affords the most extensive prospects, comprehending Beckenham, and several beautiful scattered villages and seats, Shooter's-
hill, Addington-hills, Banstead Downs, and numerous other
picturesque objects . . . they were deprived of this grand scenery
only by . . . finding themselves gliding through the deepest
recesses of the forest, where nothing met the eye but the elegant
windings of the still and clear Canal . . . It is impossible to
describe, adequately, the scene which presented itself, and the
feelings which prevailed, when the Proprietors' barge was entering the basin, at which instant the band was playing 'God
Save the King', the guns were firing, the bells of the churches
were ringing; and this immense concourse of delighted persons
were hailing by universal and hearty, and long continued
shouts, the dawn of their commerce and prosperity.

About 160 shareholders had dinner at the Greyhound, with
Edward Smith in the chair. Healths were drunk, and songs sung,
including an impromptu of which the first verse ran:

> *All hail this grand day when with gay colours flying,*
> *The barges are seen on the current to glide,*
> *When with fond emulation all parties are vying,*
> *To make our Canal of Old England the pride.*
> *Long down its fair stream may the rich vessel glide,*
> *And the Croydon Canal be of England the pride.*

The Duke of Norfolk, Lord Gwydir, Sir Thomas Turton, John
Brickwood and the chairman were thanked for their help in
getting the canal authorized and built, and, it

having been stated to the meeting that circumstances are now
favourable for the extension of the Croydon Canal to Portsmouth; and the prodigious advantages of such a measure, both
as affecting public commerce and the commercial and agricultural improvements of the counties through which it will pass,
being universally acknowledged, the following toast was accompanied by the most lively acclamations: 'The union of the
River Thames and the English Channel through the Croydon
Canal'.[19]

The canal carried stone, lime, fuller's earth and timber from Croydon and brought coal and general merchandise back. The company were, however, in debt and needed more money to complete their works. In 1811 a third Act stated that £110,366 had been raised, they owed £25,700, and needed £27,343 to enlarge reservoirs, build a wharf at Rotherhithe, warehouses at Croydon, wharves at Sydenham and New Cross, and a road from Croydon wharf to Church Street. They were empowered to raise £80,000. If this sum was in fact raised and spent, total expenditure, about £127,000 at opening, must have reached some £160,000.

From its opening, the canal and the Iron Railway were serious competitors, both comparatively unsuccessful, for the canal's £100 shares and the railway's £94 shares each seem never to have received a dividend of more than 1 per cent.

Some time between 1809 and 1811 a branch was built from the Iron Railway at Pitlake to the basin of the canal at Croydon, especially for the service of the Croydon, Merstham & Godstone Railway:

> The trucks were generally drawn by large mules. Nearing the wharf, the trucks used to be hauled by a windlass up a short incline, on to the platform, where their contents of lime, timber, stone, or fuller's earth . . . were unloaded into barges, that afterwards came back from Deptford laden with coals.[20]

The branch was closed as from 22 August 1836. The site is now occupied by Tamworth Road.

In the autumn of 1812 the company took action against the Grand Surrey, who had closed their canal for two months between September and November to make their new dock. However, the matter was 'adjusted upon terms of mutual accommodation'.[21]

Four sets of annual accounts which have survived, for 1819–20, 1821–22, 1822–23, and 1823–4,*[22] throw light on the company's working. For 1819 the toll revenue was £3,319 (1818 had been about £100 more), for 1821 £2,402, for 1822 £2,080 and for 1823 £2,910; in addition, the company received about £350 pa in rents, about £80 from selling osiers, and a few pounds by licences for pleasure boats and fishing. The osiers were specially cultivated— 'setts for increased plantation, cleaning and trenching' are included in the accounts. The company were themselves carriers, and provided warehouse and wharf accommodation and labour; they seem to have owned the barges, but to have hired crews and horses. Their gross income and expenditure from carrying comes out as follows:

* The company's financial year ended on 31 March.

	Income	Expenditure*
	£	£
1819–20	1,818	1,741
1821–22	877	968
1822–23	730	558
1823–24	729	785

* These figures include Croydon and Grand Surrey tolls.

There seems to have been special activity in 1818 and 1819, judging by the toll and carrying receipts, and in April 1820 the Grand Surrey company referred to the 'falling off of the Trade of the Croydon Canal'.

The company was paying no dividend, and in these years was still settling debts. In 1819 a non-recurring item of £2,138 was paid for 'sundry rents, taxes, etc.' and in 1823 £300 to their engineer Dudley Clark, presumably as arrears of fees, as no payments are shown for 1819, 1821 or 1822. They only employed two lock-keepers.

Their pumping station was expensive to run. The engine-men, coal and repairs cost:

	£
1819–20	350
1821–22	313
1822–23	278
1823–24	275

Nevertheless, in spite of pumping and their reservoirs, leakage seems to have left the canal often short of water.[23]

The Croydon Canal and the Surrey Iron Railway competed against each other for some twenty years, and horses pulling boats kept even with horses pulling trucks, with little gain to either set of shareholders. In 1834, however, Joseph Gibbs surveyed a new railway line to Croydon which would make use of the bed of the Croydon Canal. His report was accepted by the board of the proposed London & Croydon Railway, and after resolving:

That this Committee feels it due to the high respectability & reputation of those Gentlemen, to waive all the usual methods of bargaining for the purchase of the Canal, & to offer them at once the sum of £30,000 for the whole of the Canal and its appendages of Land, Stations, etc.,[24]

they asked the Croydon Canal shareholders to meet them. The terms were rejected by the canal representatives, and an increased offer of £35,000 was also rejected, the canal company asking for £40,000. A deadlock followed, till the railway decided to go ahead

Croydon,

SURREY.

To Coal Merchants, Lightermen, & Others.
Trading on the Croydon Canal.

TO BE

Sold by Auction,

(PEREMPTORILY,)

BY

Messrs. Blake,

AT THE CROYDON CANAL WHARF,

NORTH-END, CROYDON.

On WEDNESDAY, the 27th. JANUARY. 1819,

At ELEVEN for TWELVE o'CLOCK.

One Capital Canal

BARGE,

35 TONS.

May be Viewed till the Sale by applying to the Wharfinger
at the Basin.

• *Conditions of Sale as usual.*

Annual. Printer, Croydon.

old to Mr Edward pritland for £94. 0 0

14. A Croydon Canal barge is sold

with their Bill and leave the terms to be settled during its passage.
Meanwhile the owners of the 37 barges working on the canal
asked for and received a promise of compensation for the value of
the barges.* In July 1835 the railway and the canal committees
agreed that the price should be settled by an independent jury, the
former reporting to its shareholders that

we are persuaded that it will be determined, not by the original

* It looks as if the company had by this time ceased to carry.

cost, or assumed value of the Canal, but by the actual worth of the Land and materials.[25]

In support of their view that the value of the canal was only the value of its land and materials, they had it valued by three different people, who all gave a figure between £16,000 and £18,000. The railway made offers of these amounts, which were rejected by the canal company, which in turn now asked £52,500 including compensation. Too late the railway realized that the jury would value the canal as a navigation; it did so, and fixed the figure at £40,250. The purchase was completed on 21 July 1836, and the canal was formally stopped on 22 August. In May of the following year the railway committee recorded that

> some of the men employed on the Canal may be discharged as far as the Canal business is concerned . . . to inform the Head Engineer that the company will have no occasion for his services at the end of a week or ten days.[26]

It was fortunate for the canal company that they were no longer responsible when on Thursday 26 January 1837 the canal overflowed after heavy rain, and

> the inhabitants of the Broadway, and Tanner's hill, Deptford, were thrown into the utmost alarm by a large torrent of water rushing completely through their premises . . . in upwards of 200 homes the water was 3 or in many instances 5 feet deep.[27]

The station at West Croydon was built upon the site of the canal basin and warehouses and the railway from Croydon to Anerley made use of the canal bed. The line was opened in 1839. Soon afterwards the railway speaks:

> *What! knows't thou not me, thy country's salvation,*
> *The genius of railroads and civilization,*
> *The spirit of energy, industry, wealth,*
> *Of swiftness, of happiness, cheapness, and health,*
> *That blessings produce and traffic creates,*
> *Though folly opposes, and ignorance hates,*
> *And bigots may fancy they like just as well,*
> *To travel by coach, or the Croydon Canal?'*

> *Then spake the Canal,—'Thou worst of my foes,*
> *Dost taunt my misfortunes and brag to my nose:*
> *Base, rascally railroad, my tears were thy laughter.*
> *Like surgeons, you bought me, to cut me up after.*
> *At present you manage it all your own way,*
> *But perhaps after all the concern might not pay . . .*

The railway again:

> *Thou doz y old god—the water, 'tis plain,*
> *(What little is left) has got on your brain.*
> *Suppose we did buy you! pooh! nonsense and stuff!*
> *Why, every one says we gave more than enough:*
> *Though we tapped and dissected you, who can be blind,*
> *Like surgeons we cut, for the good of mankind?*

And the author:

> *The magic steam whistle has sounded his knell,*
> *And the spirit is lost of the Croydon Canal.*[28]

From its early days the canal seems to have been much more used for recreation than was usual at the time: this is how an old man remembered it:

This Canal was a source of delight to the inhabitants, who derived much pleasure from it, whether they were angler,* bather, skater, boatman or pedestrian. . . . Boats could be hired, and parties were made up to enjoy pleasant rows to Forest Hill, through a beautiful country, with scarcely a house to be seen on the journey . . . taking their tea in pretty and extensive gardens then connected with the Dartmouth Arms Tavern. The walk on the Banks, or towing path, of the Canal from its terminus to Norwood or farther on could not be surpassed in the neighbourhood. Norwood and its grand woods were on one side, and wide, well-cultivated fields on the other. Nor was it a monotonous walk; the passing and repassing of loaded barges diversified it; parties in pleasure boats rowed on the canal surface; and patient anglers sat on the banks anxiously watching for a nibble.[29]

Indeed, the angling outlasted the canal, for in *Robinson's Railway Directory* for 1840 there is an advertisement for day tickets on the line which allowed passengers to alight at intermediate stations to see the scenery, which added:

MARQUEES &c ARE ERECTED IN THE WOOD, Close to the Anerley Station, and Parties using the Railway will be permitted to ANGLE IN THE ADJACENT CANAL, WHICH ABOUNDS IN FISH.

Wimbledon & Wandsworth Canal project

In 1865 plans were deposited[30] for a canal from Wandsworth Basin (built by the Surrey Iron Railway company, and now owned

* As early as 1814 the canal company had sold angling licences at a guinea each.

by Mr MacMurray, a paper manufacturer, and called MacMurray's Canal) parallel to the Wandle to near Plough Lane, Wimbledon, 2⅜ miles long with two locks above the basin. With a new road also for part of the way, the scheme was estimated at £53,000 by the engineer J. W. Wilson.

The promoters were connected with the Wandsworth gasworks company, and seem to have had in mind the improvement of Wandsworth Basin for their own traffic, freedom from Mr Mac-Murray's ownership, and the supply of the paper, copper and other works on the Wandle, and Wimbledon gasworks, with raw materials. A Bill was introduced, but lost in committee in March 1866 through MacMurray's hostility.

In 1867, with Hamilton H. Fulton, who had taken part in the earlier Parliamentary proceedings, as engineer, new plans were deposited which also included a road and tramway from Wandsworth High Street to Wimbledon, and a sewer, at an estimated cost of £117,800. The scheme seems to have stopped there.

Royal Clarence Ship Canal project

The Royal Clarence Ship Canal was planned in 1812 to shorten and make easier the navigation of the Thames by a cut from below Woolwich Arsenal to Erith. In 1813 a railway from the canal to limekilns at Plumstead Wood was added, and in 1815 the scheme included a second and shorter cut from below Greenwich to above the Arsenal. Presumably the ending of the war also ended the scheme.

CHAPTER VI

The London-Portsmouth Line

THE navigable river Wey, running south from the Thames to Guildford and Godalming, had at first little relation to the Arun between Littlehampton and Newbridge. But with their junction by the Wey & Arun Canal, and later extension through the Portsmouth & Arundel Canal to Portsmouth, they became part of a water route often talked about, for a brief period a practical reality, for even less time the subject of inflated plans for a great ship canal. The idea of a London–Portsmouth waterway, however, influenced so much development, especially during the twenty years of the French Wars, that it seems convenient to group the canals and navigations concerned, along with the related western Rother, in a single chapter.[1]

River Wey

The river from its junction with the Thames at Weybridge to Guildford was made navigable under an Act of 1651. The initiative came from a local landowner, Sir Richard Weston, and he and three partners began the work. The Act allowed a maximum toll of 4s (20p) for the fifteen miles—a lower rate per mile than for the Bristol Avon sixty years later—and also fixed a charge for passengers. The Wey undertakers might themselves run barges and take a fixed rate for freight.[2]

Sir Richard died in 1652, the lead was taken by another partner, James Pitson, and by November 1653 twelve pound locks had been built and the work done, at a cost of about £15,000, though financial repercussions and recriminations lasted for years. In 1671, to clear up the muddle, an Act[3] vested the river in six trustees, and a board was set up to adjudge claims. This Act also contained an exceptional provision which granted the town of Guildford a toll of one penny to pay for the damage done to the roads by carts coming to the river, and because the Corporation and Inhabitants would be burthened with poor more than before the Navigation, by the poverty of the barge-men, their families and others occasioned by the Navigation.

Timber was a principal traffic throughout the pre-canal period. Dr Willan states that 4,000 loads of timber passed down the river in 1664; Defoe says:

> by this navigation a very great quantity of timber is brought down to London, not from the neighbourhood of this town* only, but even from the woody parts of Sussex and Hampshire above thirty miles from it, the country carriages bringing it hither in the summer by land[4]

and in 1776 the Rev. W. Gilpin, in search of the picturesque, finds it:

> navigable as far as Guildford; and beyond it, for timber, which is brought down the river from the contiguous parts of the country. Floats of timber are among the pleasing appendages of a river, when the trunks are happily disposed. This disposition, however, I fear, must be the result of chance, rather than of art. It is hardly possible to pack a float picturesquely by design. These cumbrous machines are navigated each by a single man with a pole; and as they glide gently down the stream, the tremulous reflections they form on the still surface of the water, and their contrast with trees, bushes, and pasturage, as they float along, are pleasing.[5]

Among the other traffics, which included coal upwards, and hoops, bark, and paper downwards, was flour, of which Defoe says:

> This navigation is also a mighty support to the great corn-market at Farnham . . . as the meal-men and other dealers buy the corn at that market, much of it is brought to the mills on this river; which is not above seven miles distant, and being first ground and dress'd, is then sent down in the meal by barges to London; the expence of which is very small.[4]

In 1759 a Bill was presented to Parliament to extend the navigation for 4½ miles above Guildford to Godalming. It was lost, but another[6] passed in 1760. Richard Steadman and, at first, John Smeaton were engaged upon it; four locks were built, and the waterway opened in the autumn of 1763 at a cost of £6,450. Control was by commissioners, but a body separate from those managing the Wey below Guildford. The basic trades were still corn, coal and timber, but flour, iron, hoops and bark for tanning were growing downstream traffics. During the War of American

* Guildford.

Independence, from 1780 to peace in 1783, a large tonnage of war stores moved up the Thames and Wey to Godalming to be carried thence by land to Portsmouth.

From 1763, when the Godalming extension was opened, the Wey Navigation made a good living largely by carrying agricultural products and timber downwards, and bringing back the needs of Guildford, Godalming, and the villages along its banks.* The opening in 1794 of the Basingstoke Canal, which entered it three miles above its junction with the Thames, brought additional tolls, and as the war was causing goods to travel overland to the south and west that would normally have gone by sea, the average profits rose as follows:

Years	Average profits £
1794–98	2,046
1799–1803	2,598
1804–08	3,713
1809–13	4,079

The building and opening of the Wey & Arun Canal (see p. 130) brought further trade to the Wey, which became a most prosperous waterway. Here are representative figures of receipts and tonnages:

Year	Receipts £	Tonnages tons
1780	3,349	24,006
1790	4,236	32,981
1800	5,860	57,500
1812	6,009	65,279
1820	5,678	56,400
1830	5,571	55,035

If we look at the navigation as it was in 1831, we find that 827 loaded boats passed into the river, almost all from London, carrying 31,544½ tons of goods. Of this tonnage, 12,859¼ tons were coal, 6,155¼ tons corn, and 5,719¼ tons groceries. The destinations were as set out in the table on page 123.

Some interesting conclusions can be drawn. When the Wey & Arun was projected, the supply of Guildford and Godalming with cheaper coal was one of the objects, and when the canal was opened it was reported that the price of fuel fell at Guildford. Clearly coal from London was costing too much, and it was hoped

* In 1783 the Basingstoke Canal Committee said 'the River Wey . . . is well known to have very lately succeeded the most sanguine Expectations of the Owners.'

Page 121 Thames pleasure boating: (*above*) during Henley regatta, July 1880; (*below*) Boulter's lock, c 1905–10

Page 122 Kennet & Avon Canal: (*above*) a wide boat in Newbury lock, c 1900; (*below*) *Caroline* and butty working up Devizes flight, c 1880–90

	Coal tons	Corn tons	Groceries tons
Wharves below Guildford	2,392¾	2,584	50½
Guildford	2,505½	754½	279¾
Wharves above Guildford (Godalming or Wey & Arun)	1,507½	2,349¼	3,360½
Basingstoke Canal	6,453½	467½	2,028½

that that brought by way of the Arun, probably from south Wales, would compete. We can see that the effort failed, for coal is now passing from the Thames not only to Guildford but beyond it, and the records of the Wey & Arun confirm that this coal ascended the canal as far as Loxwood, where it met that carried up the Arun. Again, one notices the tonnage of groceries coming up from London and passing above Guildford to be distributed as far as Arundel. Thirdly, we can see the amount of imported corn that was coming upstream, most of it to be ground in the mills along the Wey.

Downwards, 26,644¾ tons were carried in 1831 in 867 loaded boats, a very balanced trade. Of this total, timber in various forms accounted for 9,632½ tons, to which should be added 4,761 tons of hoops and 2,797¾ tons of bark, presumably for tanning. Much of this timber trade, and nearly all that in barrel hoops and bark, came from the Wey & Arun Canal. The other big downward traffic was in flour; this amounted to 5,593¼ tons, which must have included a good deal from home-grown as well as imported corn. The origins of these traffics were:

	Timber tons	Hoops tons	Bark tons	Flour tons
Wharves below Guildford	1,240¾	279¾	36¼	1,316½
Guildford	8¾	106¾	56¾	104½
Wharves above Guildford (Godalming or Wey & Arun)	5,342	3,800¼	2,262¼	2,980½
Basingstoke Canal	3,041	574¼	442½	1,191¾

The principal manufactured products carried to the Thames were spokes and other parts of carts (589¼ tons), mainly from the Wey & Arun; ale (482 tons) mainly, and pottery (86¾ tons) entirely, from the Basingstoke Canal; and powder (79¼ tons) from the mills at Shalford.

The story of the middle years can be read in the toll and tonnage figures set out at the top of the next page.

In 1845 the Guildford Junction Railway was opened from the main line at Woking to Guildford in competition with the Wey, and in 1849 was extended to Godalming. Later, with the closing

H

Years	Average tolls £	Average tonnage tons
1830–32	5,790	57,749
1833–35	6,111	64,512
1836–38	7,401	79,233
1839–41	6,574	73,124
1842–44	5,256	62,497
1845–47	4,854	64,442
1848–50	3,579	52,337
1851–53	2,640	42,863

of the Wey & Arun Canal in 1871, and the decay of the Basingstoke Canal, the navigation was driven back upon local traffic.
For the later years, ten-yearly figures tell the story:

Years	Average tolls £	Average tonnage tons
1854–63	2,861	56,800
1864–73	2,032	41,803
1874–83	1,541	31,305
1884–93	1,165	26,231
1894–1903	1,113	30,568
1904–13	1,188	36,406
1914–23	1,646	45,504
1924–33	1,721	50,335
1934–43	1,218	37,634
1944–53	1,235	23,603

The toll figures for 1890 onwards include substantial amounts for pleasure craft, £371 in 1893. That the waterway did so well in its later years was due to the management of the Stevens family, who controlled the river for a century and have been associated with it since 1812.

The Wey was transferred to the National Trust in 1963, and the Godalming Navigation in 1969. The last barge passed beyond Guildford in 1950, and to the town in 1958. By 1965 barges went no further than Weybridge. The old navigation is, however, increasingly used by pleasure traffic.

River Arun

The lower part of the river Arun, probably to Ford, was navigable at the time of the Norman Conquest. In the thirty years from 1544 Henry Fitzalan, Earl of Arundel, made that town something of a port by improving the river channel and building town wharves. He then made the river passable, and toll-free, upwards to Pallingham Quay for craft of about 15 tons carrying timber, though the many flash-locks caused difficulties. In the early 1600s there was an unsuccessful attempt to make the river navigable higher still, to Newbridge.

In 1785 an Act[7] was obtained by a group of local men which, while leaving the river between Arundel and Houghton bridge uncontrolled, enabled the proprietors to make the river navigable for craft of up to 30 tons to Newbridge, though the Arun itself was to remain toll-free to Pallingham. Their object was to make easier the carriage of coal, chalk and lime upwards, and of agricultural produce downwards. The company made a separate canal beside the river upwards from Pallingham to Newbridge, with three locks and an aqueduct at Orfold, and a cut lower down between Coldwaltham and Hardham which saved three miles, and included a 375-yd tunnel and three more locks. The upper canal was opened on 1 August 1787, the Hardham cut during the summer of 1790. The cost had been some £16,000.

There were proposals in 1791 to extend the navigation by a canal to North Chapel, north of Petworth, and in 1792 to Horsham: John Rennie surveyed the line and estimated it at £18,133. Satisfactory terms could not be negotiated with the Arun company, however, and the project was dropped in 1794.

A first dividend of 2 per cent had been paid for the year 1 August 1787–8, apparently out of capital, before the navigation was finished, and regular payments were made from 1792. For the five years 1792–6 the average tolls were £893, and the average dividend 3·1 per cent. Then the Earl of Egremont, having bought about a third of the shares, took over the chairmanship, and dividends ceased while the mortgage debt was paid off. They did not restart until 1830, except for a simple payment of 3 per cent for 1821. The opening of the Wey & Arun Junction Canal in 1816, and efforts to start a Portsmouth trade, increased the traffic carried; takings rose, and good dividends were paid, as the figures in table (a) on page 126 show.

The upper part of the Arun Navigation was first affected by railway competition when in 1857 the Mid-Sussex Railway was authorized to build a line from Horsham to Pulborough and Petworth; it was opened in 1859. A link from Pulborough to Ford and on to Littlehampton, parallel to the rest of the Arun, was opened in 1863. The effect is shown by the figures set out in table (b) overleaf.

table (a)

Year Nov–Oct	Average tolls received £	Average dividend paid per cent
1830–35	1,572	10·7
1835–40	2,044	11·8
1840–45	1,643	8·4
1845–50	1,686	9·2
1850–55	1,134	5·9

table (b)

Year Nov–Oct	Average tolls received £	Average dividend paid per cent
1850–55	1,134	5·9
1855–60	1,224	6·5
1860–65	1,023	5·6
1865–70	563	1·8
1870–75	389	1·0

The waterways competed with the railways for some years, but the Arun closed, in the sense of the company ceasing to maintain, on 1 January 1888. In March 1888 the last barge passed out of the Rother, and on 20 June of the same year the last from Pallingham to Newbridge, and through Hardham tunnel on 29 January 1889. A Board of Trade closing order was made in 1896. Thenceforth the upper river had no controlling authority, but some navigation was carried on to Harwoods Green brickworks until 1905, Bury and Houghton until the late 1920s, and on the lower river to Arundel until 1936.

River Rother (Western)

In 1615, soon after the Arun had been made navigable to Pallingham, craft could also reach Fittleworth on the Rother. In 1783 William Jessop was called in to report on the lower part of the river to Petworth mills, and again in 1790, this time to Midhurst. This year saw the Arun navigation completed, and in 1791 the Earl of Egremont, whose seat was at Petworth House, obtained an Act[8] to make the Rother navigable, and build a branch canal to Petworth. He was the sole proprietor, and because his interest was to develop the country and not to make money, the authorized tolls and wharfage rates were low. Since he owned 'a very large proportion of the Lands situate on or near the Banks', the Earl was given a free hand to choose the lines of his cuts and branch, so long as he did not take gardens or enclosed grounds. The main line from Stopham, the junction with the Arun, to Midhurst, was 11¼ miles long, with 8 locks and a total rise of 54 ft. It mainly followed the natural course of the river, with less than two miles of cuts. The navigation was opened in 1794 at a cost of £13,300, and carried coal upwards, and downwards timber, corn, and that 'beautiful variegated fossil limestone, well known in London by the name of Petworth Marble'.[9]

The Earl also built a branch canal, 1¼ miles long, from above Stopham lock, the third coming upwards, to Haslingbourne bridge to serve the town of Petworth. With two locks, it was opened in 1793, having cost nearly £5,000 more, but ceased to be used in a few years because a diverted turnpike road gave easier access to the town. The Earl also had it in mind to connect Petworth by canal with the Wey near Guildford, with a branch to Horsham and a link to the head of the Arun at Newbridge. This forerunner of the Wey & Arun Canal was surveyed by Jessop about 1795, but made no progress.

The Earl used his own men to make the navigation, and the Rev. A. Young, author of *A General View of the Agriculture of Sussex*, published in 1808, comments as follows:

Let us for a moment reflect upon the advantages which result from the employment of between one and two hundred workmen, all natives of Sussex. In the usual method of cutting canals, these men are a constant nuisance to the neighbourhood, and the terror of all other descriptions of people. But in Lord Egremont's canal, the men are all drawn from amongst his own workmen, and have none of that turbulence and riot with which foreign workmen are inspired; . . . the expenses of the job are much less to the employer, whilst the weekly wages of the men in this business, instead of 8s. or 9s. rise up to 14s. or 15s.

The Earl was a remarkable man. Born in 1751, he succeeded to the title at the age of 11. He gave much time and money to improving agricultural methods and stockbreeding, and turned Petworth House into a meeting place for those interested in agricultural progress. This interest led him to promote navigations, first his own Rother and the Petworth Canal, then the London–Portsmouth route. He was a chief mover in the Arun Navigation, and the Wey & Arun and Portsmouth & Arundel Canals, and altogether invested over £100,000 in waterways. The adulation of Mr Young was solidly based when he wrote:

It is impossible not to feel great respect, in contemplating the energy of an individual of the highest rank and fortune, animated with such ideas, and expending his income in so meritorious a manner, forming navigations, rewarding industry in the lower classes, improving the breeds of live-stock by bounties, encouraging all useful and mechanical artisans; setting on foot multiplied experiments to ascertain the comparative merit of different agricultural implements; introducing improvements, by extending the knowledge of new plants, animals, or implements, all of them in so many and various shapes contributing their assistance to national prosperity. The thought of one man having been instrumental in the improvement of his country, and still exerting himself in the same career, must be a constant fund of gratification to every benevolent mind; and that long may he live to enjoy the fruits of his labour in the service of his country, is the wish of every man in the county. He died in 1837.

The gross earnings of the Rother for the years 1802–31 averaged about £550 pa. Railways came to Petworth in 1859, when the Mid-Sussex line was opened from Horsham by way of Pulborough. The river became disused in the late 1880s, though it was not abandoned until 15 April 1936.

The London–Portsmouth Schemes of 1803 and 1810

Plans for connecting London and Portsmouth go back to the eighteenth century. For instance, a news item appeared in 1785:

> We are well informed, that the Minister is in possession of a Plan for making a navigable Canal from Reading . . . to Portsmouth; by which, in Time of War, Provisions and Stores . . . may be conveyed to the Fleet at no Hazard, and at less Expence. . . . The Cargoes also of the Norway and West India Ships may be transported to London by the same Communication.[10]

A little later, a scheme to connect the Basingstoke with the Andover Canal (see p. 174) opened the possibility of a waterway to Southampton and Portsmouth.

The simultaneous promotion of the Surrey Iron Railway and the Croydon Canal, however, gave such ideas a new direction, for John Rennie, planning the latter in October 1800, then thought it likely to be extended beyond Croydon. In 1802–3 rival schemes were put forward for a communication between London and Portsmouth, Rennie[11] planning a canal, and Jessop[12] a railway. Rennie's plan was for a canal, the London & Portsmouth, 100 miles long with 41 locks and a 4,400-yd tunnel between Coulsdon and Merstham, running from the Croydon Canal, then being built, via Merstham, Crawley, Ifield, Horsham Common, Pulborough, Arundel Bridge (using the Arun for 1¼ miles), Yapton, Barnham, Mundham, Chichester, Emsworth, Havant to Portsmouth 'just above His Majesty's dockyard'. From this line he suggested branches could be run to the Medway, Ouse, Adur, and Arun, but these were not estimated for. No details of expected traffic were given, but there was mention of naval stores, goods for the East India Co's ships at Spithead, marine timber, chalk and coal, and revenue was estimated at £100,000 a year. Two estimates were given: £720,649 for a broad and £571,621 for a narrow canal. Though the *Lewes Journal* not unreasonably found itself 'at a loss to know from whence the tolls are to arise to pay the interest of the immense sums which will be required,'[13] a Bill was introduced, with support from some Croydon Canal shareholders, but subscriptions were insufficient, and it was thrown out on 15 March 1804. Later, in 1810, Rennie was to write:

> A powerful opposition arose, which stopped the Bill in its early progress, and since then, the project, though not abandoned by its original promoters, has not been actively prosecuted.[14]

Jessop's line for a railway arose out of proposals made in 1802 by supporters of the Surrey Iron Railway. At a meeting on 3 June 1802, it was stated:

> That it had been thought adviseable to enquire whether the iron railway now establishing from Wandsworth to Croydon might not be extended through Surrey, Sussex and Hants, so as to open a communication with seaports in the Channel and particularly with Portsmouth.[15]

Later in the year the proposal forked, on the one hand to pursue the limited extension that became the Croydon, Merstham & Godstone Iron Railway, on the other hand to consider further the big scheme. That the main line of the CM & GIR was to run to Reigate shows the influence of the Portsmouth scheme upon it.

The original Portsmouth plan proposed that at the London end* the railway should leave the SIR at Mitcham and cross the Thames upon the already contemplated bridge that was later to be named after Waterloo; thence it was to run to Tottenham Court Road to join the proposed London Railway, which was to link London Docks with the basin of the Grand Junction Canal at Paddington and which later became the Regent's Canal.[16] Jessop's

---

* This proposed extension to the metropolis was strongly opposed by the Grand Surrey and Croydon Canal companies.

final proposal was for a terminus in Stamford Street, approximately where Waterloo now is. The estimated cost was £430,000. Its supporters criticized the canal project, pointing out the difficulties of the long tunnel through Merstham Hill, the danger of diverting water from the Wandle, the slowness with which the Croydon Canal was being built and Rennie's probable underestimate of the cost. Its opponents said that sixty tons of corn could not be carried from London to Portsmouth for less than £125·50 on a railway, but for £49·25 by canal.

In 1810, at a time when he was working also on a Medway–Eastern Rother project that was to become the Weald of Kent Canal scheme of 1812 (see p. 42), Rennie revived his scheme of 1803 in altered form. A branch to the Medway had been part of it, and he now published a proposal for a Grand Southern Canal from the Medway to Portsmouth.[17] He suggested a line 95¾ miles long from Tonbridge through Edenbridge to Horsham, thence to Pulborough and a cut to Newbridge on the Arun, Arundel, Chichester, Emsworth, Havant, and Portsmouth. Branches were proposed to the Adur, Ouse, the Croydon Canal and the Weald of Kent Canal, 'by which an inland navigation will at all times be had from the Royal dockyard at that place to Chatham, without the hazardous navigation of the narrow parts of the British Channel to the Metropolis.'[18] 'I propose', wrote Rennie, 'the Canal to be of a size capable of admitting the Thames Barges to Navigate.' The estimate was £585,500, and it is said that £650,000 was actually subscribed, but the Bill was defeated on second reading by 100 votes to 17. The parallel Medway–Rother Bill, in Parliament at the same time, was withdrawn soon afterwards. The failure of both this and the 1803 scheme was attributed in a Portsmouth & Arundel Canal document of 1817 to the powerful opposition of certain landowners.

In the same year E. (later Sir Edward) Banks,* instructed by the two iron railway companies, first suggested a canal extension of the railways to Horsham, and later a 12-mile link between Rennie's line at Copthorne Common and Merstham on the Croydon, Merstham & Godstone Iron Railway, where an inclined plane and tunnel would join the canal branch to the railway. The estimated cost was £72,500.[19]

Wey & Arun Junction Canal

The idea of linking Wey and Arun dates back to 1641, when a

* Joliffe & Banks had the limeworks at Merstham.

Report and Estimate

OF THE

GRAND SOUTHERN CANAL,

PROPOSED TO BE MADE BETWEEN

TUNBRIDGE AND PORTSMOUTH:

BY MEANS OF WHICH AND THE

River Medway,

AN

INLAND NAVIGATION WILL BE OPENED

BETWEEN

The River Thames and Portsmouth.

BY

JOHN RENNIE, Civil Engineer,

And F. R. S. &c. &c. &c.

LONDON:

PRINTED BY E. BLACKADER, TOOK'S COURT, CHANCERY LANE.
1810.

15. John Rennie's report on the Grand Southern Canal

Bill to authorize a 2-mile canal to join tributaries of the two rivers was introduced and reached Committee stage before being dropped. There was another, to join the rivers Adur, Arun, Mole and Wey, in 1663.

Though in 1810 Rennie had said that 'the Arun is a very bad navigation, and barges navigating it, experience great detention, from the floods in winter and droughts in summer,' after the failure of the London and Portsmouth schemes of 1803 and 1810 men's minds began to turn to ways of connecting it with London.

The first scheme, surveyed by Netlam and Francis Giles in 1811 and promoted at a meeting at Horsham on 3 January 1812, was for a reduced Grand Southern scheme, a 37-mile long canal from the bottom of an inclined plane from the Croydon, Merstham & Godstone Railway at Merstham by way of Three Bridges, Crawley and Horsham to the upper Arun at Parthings, and then down the valley to the navigation at Newbridge. It got no further than a Parliamentary petition.

The second was to join together the two existing and working navigations of the Wey and the Arun, as Lord Egremont had already foreshadowed, to give a through waterway from London to Arundel or Littlehampton, whence goods could be transhipped for Portsmouth. That done, the Arun would be linked to Portsmouth to bring a through navigation into existence at last.

The line of the Wey & Arun Junction Canal was from Shalford Powder Mills between Guildford and Godalming to Newbridge on the Arun. It was originally projected in the autumn of 1810, was temporarily checked by the Grand Southern scheme, but got under way after a meeting at Guildford on 1 June 1811, with Lord Egremont in the chair, at which he announced that the Arun proprietors would charge only 6d (2½p) a ton on goods to the Wey. Even before the Wey & Arun Bill had been introduced, hopeful promoters of a branch from it at Drungewick, 4½ miles above Newbridge, to Horsham, had petitioned in December 1812, but then waited. A similar scheme was discussed in 1817 and 1839, but in the end Horsham never got water transport, its nearest navigation being five miles away at the head of the Baybridge Canal at West Grinstead.

In the Wey & Arun's prospectus it was hoped that one-twelfth of the London–Portsmouth trade, estimated at 1,200,000 tons a year, would pass by the canal, as well as 30,000 tons of local traffic. Josias Jessop, one of William's sons, was appointed consulting engineer in 1811, and made an estimate of £71,217* for

* Later revised to £86,132 after part of the route had been changed.

cost, and 7 per cent for yield. A prospectus was issued in October, and a month later the £90,500 subscription was full, Lord Egremont having contributed £20,000. The Act[20] of 1813 authorized a further £9,500 if required. Work began in July 1813 with May Upton as resident engineer and a local man, Zachariah Keppel, as contractor. Later, Keppel went bankrupt, but Upton carried on, and the canal was opened on 29 September 1816, when the Earl of Egremont

with a numerous company of friends and shareholders, attended by the Mayor and Aldermen of Guildford, assembled at Alfold, where, after having provided a plentiful entertainment for the navigators, consisting of a roasted ox and 200 gallons of ale, they embarked on the canal in four barges, enlivened by two bands of music. The weather in the early part of the morning was rather inauspicious, but towards noon it cleared up, and the procession, a little after three, was discerned from St. Catherine's hill near Guildford. The sunshine which now broke out, combined with the unrivalled scenery of the favourite spot, the music, and numerous assemblage of spectators, and the merry peal of the bells of Guildford, Shalford, and Godalming, all heard at this time, gave an effect to the scene which could not be contemplated but with the most lively and pleasing emotions. About four o'clock, the interesting spectacle reached Guildford Bridge, when the Mayor and Aldermen landed, and having assumed the regalia of the corporation, and being joined by the other branches of it, accompanied by one of the town Members, neighbouring gentry, and magistrates, and attended by a band of music and colours, they welcomed the arrival of Lord Egremont and his friends. The whole then went in procession to the White Hart inn, where one hundred and thirty persons partook of a sumptuous dinner . . . One of its leading advantages will be a great reduction in the price of fuel, as coals, which within a month sold at Guildford at £3 3s, per chaldron, are now offered at 50s. It will also afford a facility to the agriculturalist for the disposal of his produce by the easy communication thus opened with the market of Guildford.[21]

The Wey & Arun Canal, 18½ miles long with 23 locks, was built during a time of falling prices, which kept down the usual excess of cost over estimate. Total expenditure was about £103,000, found by calling £110 on each share and raising the balance by mortgages that were not fully paid off until 1842. Lord Egremont, after having taken up some forfeited shares, held 28 per cent of the capital.

The hopes of through London–Portsmouth traffic on the canal did not justify themselves. Barge capacity, at about 30 tons, was too low; there were too many hindrances to navigation, artificial like the small size of Hardham tunnel and Stopham bridge on the Arun, or natural, like floods or drought; too many authorities to whom tolls had to be paid; while on the canal itself, the lockage was heavy and the water supply uncertain. On the other hand, the coasting trade was easier, now that the war was over, while improvements to the Thames and reductions in coal prices along the Wey meant that coal came that way to Guildford and not from Arundel via the Wey & Arun.

Receipts from tolls were as follows:

Y.e. 30 *April*	*Average tolls* £
1817–21	1,251
1822–26	1,838
1827–31	1,991
1832–36	2,060
1837–41	2,301

Dividends, only one of which, largely out of capital, was paid before 1828, never exceeded 1 per cent, and the tonnage carried averaged 15,000 tons a year from 1816 to 1871, only exceeding 20,000 tons between 1837–40 and 1855–57. Far the greater part of it passed to and from the Wey.

In the early forties, as a result of the railway competition with the Wey, and probably also of road transport pressure, the Wey & Arun made heavy toll reductions, which were clearly meant to preserve the through traffic, for some were made conditional upon reductions by other companies, and others fixed a low maximum toll for passage over the whole length of the canal. The goods actually carried for the year May 1849–April 1850 were as follows:

	£
Coal	547
Timber	284
Groceries	106
Hoops	120
Corn	15
Sundries	189
	1,261

The receipts of the canal reached their highest point in 1839–40 with £2,524. By 1841–2, before the toll reductions, they had fallen to £1,713, and the tonnage carried from about 23,250 to 15,750.

Thenceforward there was a slow decline in receipts, but not in tonnage, to 1850–1, when the figures were £1,036 and 15,121 tons. At that level the canal maintained its local traffic sufficiently to keep open and to pay in most years a few shillings of dividend. At last, in 1860, the Horsham & Guildford Direct Railway was formed to build a line between those places along the route of the canal, and in October 1865 the railway, now bought by the London, Brighton & South Coast Company, was opened. The effect was nearly to halve the remaining receipts of the canal, from £807 in 1864–5 to £463 in 1866–7, reduce the tonnage carried from about 16,000 to about 8,750, and make the dividend of 6s (30p) per £110 share for 1864–5 the last that could be paid. It was now impossible for the canal to operate at a profit, and in 1868 an Act was passed authorizing its closure. The year before, Mr Dashwood had passed through it in his pleasure boat.[22] The canal finally closed on 22 July 1871, though coal came up to Bramley wharf till June 1872. The company was not formally dissolved until 1910.

Portsmouth & Arundel Canal

With the authorization of the Wey & Arun, an inland water line from London to Portsmouth was coming nearer. What was now needed was a canal from the Arun to Portsmouth. In 1815 promoters of such a line sought Admiralty approval; the latter in turn consulted Rennie, who recommended in favour. The promoters then seem to have asked him direct for his advice, for he employed Francis and Netlam Giles on a survey, and then reported early in 1816.

He would have preferred the old Grand Southern line of 1810 from Arundel by Chichester, Emsworth and Havant to Portsmouth Harbour, a distance of 30¾ miles, but because of landowners' objections that had defeated previous schemes he proposed a barge canal from the tidal Arun at Ford below Arundel to Salterns in Chichester Harbour, with a branch from Hunston to Chichester itself. From Salterns, barges were to be sailed or towed along dredged bargeways above Thorney and Hayling islands, already used by a considerable coasting trade, and then across Langstone Harbour to Eastney lake, where they would enter a Portsea island canal and pass to Halfway Houses in Portsmouth. There would also be another cut, 1½ miles long, with two locks, from Langstone Harbour by Cosham to give access to Portsmouth Harbour.

His estimate was £118,990 (of which £15,188 was for the Cosham cut); this was subsequently increased to £125,452. His recommendation was wildly out:

> I have no doubt that when the Wey and Arun Canal is compleated the Proprietors of the River Navigations with which it communicates will improve their respective Navigations. I trust therefore the Trade through the intended Navigation will give an ample return to those who may be inclined to venture their Money in the project, while to the Merchants of London and Portsmouth as well as to the Traders in all the Towns near which the Canal will pass and to the Country in general the advantages will greatly exceed any reasonable calculation that may be made . . . I think it cannot fail to give a fair return for the Money it is likely to cost.[23]

Like the Wey & Arun, the canal was conceived as part of a through communication, and little local trade was envisaged other than that to Chichester. Between this town and the sea a canal had been talked of in the reign of Elizabeth I, and again in 1801, 1805 and 1811. Currently, about 18,000 tons a year of coal and 1,650 tons of merchandise were discharged into lighters at Itchenor, about seven miles from the city. These took them to Dell Quay, where they were moved by road waggons for the last two miles, incidentally through a turnpike gate.

Lord Egremont and the Cutfields, the latter large shareholders in the Arun, were big subscribers. The project seems also to have been especially interesting to those connected with the Navy. Many shareholders were thus Portsmouth or Devonport people, and some were naval officers—Captain John Bligh was one of them.

The Act[24] was passed in 1817, by which time £101,250 had been subscribed. It authorized a capital of £126,000 in £50 shares, and £40,000 more on mortgage if required. On 5 August the committee issued a statement which reveals that they had some doubts about the possible revenue now that the war had ended, for they worked hard to justify the speculation. Their estimate of revenue was some £21,000 gross or £10,575 net from carrying 80,000 tons, a substantial part of which was to come from goods formerly carried by sea, not only between London and Portsmouth, but between London and western ports such as Poole, Plymouth and Falmouth, which the promoters hopefully thought would now come by inland waterway to Portsmouth for transhipment there. This estimate was derived from the customs and excise returns on coastwise trade of 75,259 tons, which, taken at 5·7s (28½p) per ton, would have yielded £21,150 pa. The committee refer to the

Chichester trade; they say that for the trade to the western ports the intended canal will afford the means of forwarding such goods with a dispatch equal to that of the present Land Carriage, and at less than one-sixth part of the expence,

they point out that the London merchants will desire to use the canal, particularly during contrary winds, and to send goods to Portsmouth in four days; they mention the transport of warlike stores, and end that

they are strongly of opinion that there is every reasonable expectation of a very abundant and satisfactory interest on the capital to be expended, even in times of peace; but to those persons whose chief object in becoming Subscribers might be future advantage to their children, the Committee submit the consideration of the inevitable and greatly increased value that must attend Shares in this undertaking, whenever the country might be again in a state of warfare.

Others were less enthusiastic:

If the design is entered upon, it will have at least *one* beneficial effect, viz: that of employing a number of the poor and labouring classes of society.[25]

It then occurred to the promoters that they might meet a bigger demand if the Salterns–Chichester and Langston Harbour–Portsmouth sections were enlarged to small ship canal standard, the former for 100, the latter for 150-ton craft. These changes were authorized in a second Act[26] of June 1819, which also included a toll agreement with the Wey & Arun Company. The extra cost was balanced by the dropping of the Cosham cut. Although these changes were made to get additional traffic, the creation of a through London to Portsmouth trade was a major preoccupation. In 1818 the Arun proprietors had agreed to make a number of basic improvements, including better depth and width of channel and the evening up of lock and bridge dimensions. The toll agreement with the Wey & Arun, as stated in the Act, read:

The agreement between this company and the Wey and Arun is confirmed, whereby the Wey and Arun Company consent to receive for all descriptions of goods conveyed from the Port of Portsmouth through their canal into the river Thames 4s. 6d. a ton . . . in time of peace; but in war the rates secured to them by Act of Parliament, shall be demanded; the Portsmouth and Arundel Company also covenant for themselves that they will only charge 3d. per ton per mile, for all goods conveyed from the Port of Portsmouth into and through the said Wey and Arun Canal, and vice versa.[27]

The Arun company, however, took no action until it was sure that the Ford section of the Portsmouth & Arundel would actually be opened; then they made a second agreement early in 1821, which was confirmed by an Act[28] in May, which empowered them to do the work, and, when it was finished, to receive 1s 6d (7½p) a ton (instead of 1s [5p]) on all goods passing on and throughout the Arun and the Wey & Arun to the Wey. The Arun company borrowed £3,000, but probably spent nearer £5,000, and with James Hollinsworth as engineer completed the improvements in the summer of 1823; the loans were repaid between 1825 and 1831. Barge capacity had now been raised from about 30 to 40 tons on their river, and business increased.

On August 20th, 1818, the work was commenced at Ford, the eastern extremity of the Canal, the first spade being put into the ground by Mr. J. Williams, the projector of the enterprise,[29] and on 1 September on the Chichester line. On 27 December 1821, water was let into the basin at Chichester, and on 9 April 1822 the Salterns–Chichester ship canal section was opened, rather unfortunately, for half the procession, coming from Milton, Portsmouth, behind the tug *Egremont* through the Channels, ran aground and never arrived, though the other half went up the canal to the celebrations at Southgate basin, Chichester. On 19 September 1822 the Portsea Canal, expensive in land costs as in cutting, was opened, and the Hunston–Ford section on 26 May 1823. The whole line was now complete. It had cost some £170,000, £40,000 of which had been borrowed from the Exchequer Bill Loan Commissioners on Lord Egremont's guarantee.

The Chichester ship canal, which took craft of 8 ft draught, was 4 miles long from the basin, 399 ft by 199 ft, to Salterns lock, the lower of the two that gave access to the sea, the branch itself being 1⅜ miles long from Hunston to the city. From Hunston the barge canal, 33 ft wide and 5 ft deep, ran for 9¾ miles to Ford, where two locks took it down to the Arun. There was a 40 hp steam pumping engine here, but the Arun being tidal, it could only work at certain hours if fresh but not salt water were to be lifted to the canal. Even so, salt percolated to the surrounding farmlands, and some compensation had to be paid. In 1827 the Rennies said that some of the Ford–Hunston section had been only partially puddled, and part not at all, though it ran through loose porous soil 'incapable of holding water'. Percolation of salt water was therefore made easier by the canal's leaky state.

The bargeway from Salterns through the Thorney and Hayling Channels, 13 miles long, was navigable with safety and

Page 139 Somersetshire Coal Canal: (*above*) upper Midford bridge; (*below*) plan of Combe Hay in 1884. The three bottom locks, on the right, were built at the time when the rest of the rise was to have been obtained by Weldon-pattern lifts. The bottom of the inclined plane was near the figure 126, the top just below Caisson House

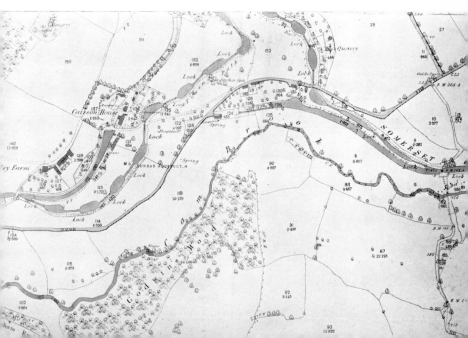

Page 140 Wilts & Berks Canal: (*above*) Calne from the canal, c 1820; (*below*) Fleet Street bridge, Swindon

regularity at low water springs, though the Rennies reported in 1827 that about 2,200 yd needed dredging by some 18 in. The second intended passage, from Langstone to Portsmouth harbours, was not then made.

The bargeway ended at the Portsea Canal. Craft then entered the Portsea ship canal through two locks, and passed for 2⅜ miles to a basin where the Commercial Road end of Arundel Street, Portsmouth, now is. Its dimensions were 517 ft × 77 ft, and the company built two warehouses beside it. Just above the second lock there was another 40 hp steam engine, pumping from a large well supplied by a freshwater spring, but nevertheless salt water percolated into the canal here also, and so into some of the town's drinking water, at much the same time that the Thames & Medway Canal was suffering from the same trouble. Again, compensation had to be paid.

By 1827 £176,314 had been spent, and more realistic estimates produced likely expenses of £1,500 pa, and revenues of £5,500, which might yield about 1¾ per cent after improvements had been carried out. These the Rennies estimated at £28,333, including £6,159 for the Portsbridge cut to Portsmouth harbour that was to replace the Portsea Canal as well as the proposed Cosham cut, and £18,148 for work on the Ford–Salterns main line. In 1828 a fourth Act[30] authorized an additional £50,000 in £25 preference shares.* It seems that £112,650 was raised in £50 shares, the balance of 267 shares having been forfeited or assigned to the company, and £20,325 in £25 shares, together with the £40,000 loan. The shareholders' register in 1855, when dealings ceased, shows very widespread ownership. There were then 589 shareholders, holding an average of less than 5 shares each. Only six had holdings of £2,000 or more.

The full opening in May 1823 naturally led to great hopes of a developing London and Portsmouth trade. It began, maintained itself for two years, and then fell away, to be somewhat revived in 1832 and 1833 before finally collapsing, as the figures overleaf show. Those in table (a) are the toll receipts at Newbridge, where the Wey & Arun entered the Arun. The second group, set out in table (b), are taken from the Wey Navigation ledgers, and show the tonnages passing between the Thames and the Portsmouth & Arundel Canal, see table (b) on page 142.

There were three main difficulties: the competition of the coasting trade, now free from war risks and offering cheap rates; the sheer difficulty of the inland water route, with its tidal waters,

* 6 per cent for 10 years, then 5 per cent.

table (a)

	£			£
1822	1,193		1829	1,180
1823	1,158		1830	not known
1824	1,609*		1831	1,243
1825	1,630		1832	1,437
1826	not known		1833	1,325
1827	not known		1834	1,217
1828	not known			

* Figures for February and August defective, and averaged.

table (b)

Year	To London tons	From London tons	Total tons	Year	To London tons	From London tons	Total tons
1823	425	1,475	1,900	1832	670	1,335	2,005
1824	1,158	2,492	3,650	1833	1,102	1,458	2,560
1825	1,001	1,581	2,582	1834	820	1,130	1,950
1826	421	958	1,379	1835	409	721	1,130
1827	193	78	271	1836	547	636	1,183
1828	285	95	380	1837	303	602	905
1829	125	77	202	1838	259	494	753
1830	101	92	193	1839	285	502	787
1831	115	296	411	1840	192	282	474

locks and tunnel, operated by six authorities and taking an average of four days for the 116 miles; and the unbalanced nature of the trade. Corn, groceries and other goods moved to Portsmouth, but there was little to take back except bullion. One enterprising effort tried by Lord Egremont and some of the canal's committeemen was to extend the communication beyond Portsmouth by creating a steam packet service thence to Plymouth and Falmouth. Some £5,000 was subscribed, and the sail-steamer *Sir Francis Drake*, equipped to carry 80 tons of goods and 27 passengers, began running in 1824. But the canal-packet route remained more expensive for cargo than by through coaster, and the passenger trade was knocked out by competition in 1826.

Meanwhile the canal company was in trouble. As a result of continuing complaints about sea-water in some of Portsmouth's wells, they had had to drain the Portsea Canal, and when the Rennies saw it at the end of July 1827

there was no water in it, nor has it, we understand, been used to any considerable extent on account of the very defective manner in which it has been executed, as it is incapable of holding water.

In 1825 a Bill to raise more capital failed amidst the outcry. In this year also a principal carrier sold his craft, and in 1826 Lord Egremont, having had enough of the Portsmouth & Arundel, surrendered his 315 shares, which had cost him £15,750, and agreed to pay the £40,000 the company owed the Exchequer Bill Loan Commissioners without making any future claim on them. 'The sole condition required on the part of his Lordship is that they shall cause the canal to be rendered complete and efficient, as originally contemplated.'[31] Another threat now appeared, for there was talk of a London–Portsmouth ship canal (see p. 146) which might end the waterway altogether. However, this died as a practical proposition almost before it had lived, and in 1828, when the fourth Act passed, enough people still thought the canal had a future, now that the prior charge had been lifted, to subscribe some £20,000 of new money. They were optimists, for the company's early results could hardly have been worse:

Year	Revenue
	£
1822 (May–Dec)	142
1823	669
1824	827
1825	944
1826	1,010
1827 (Jan–July)	534

The 1826 revenue from 13,351 tons of goods, was derived as follows:

	£
Salterns to Chichester (the ship canal)	428
Salterns to Ford	18
Ford or Chichester to Salterns	564

There was no revenue from the Portsea Canal, which was probably empty, and of course no toll income from the Channels run.

A renewed effort was begun in 1829 to obtain a through trade, by meetings between the navigations concerned to negotiate lower tolls. Some were arranged, but they had little effect. By 1831 it was clear that the hoped-for traffic was not going to be won from the coasting vessels or created new by the unaided efforts of the canal carriers. In October of that year, therefore, the Portsmouth & Arundel Company took the initiative in persuading the Arun, Wey & Arun, Wey (Godalming) and Wey concerns, but not the Thames Commissioners, to follow its own example and carry through goods for six months free of toll, in order to get a traffic started. The only advantage the route, by way of six navigations, had over the coasters was one of speed, and in fact this could not be maintained against the manifold difficulties of the line. The Portsmouth & Arundel Company itself was now doing the carrying, as no carrier could be persuaded to venture, and a letter from them of 5 April 1832 to the Wey & Arun explains some of the difficulties:

> my calculations, though well founded, have been baffled by awkward circumstances . . . I therefore would for the present, merely advert to the temporary stoppage of your Canal, to the various floods which have occasioned detention of goods—to the interruptions at the Tunnel—to the impositions of the Commanders of Barges and generally to many vexatious circumstances which have taken place and which could not be guarded against in the infancy of a trade, commenced by parties not practically acquainted with its details.

Another letter of the same time says:

> The Steamer's* boiler is worn out—there must be a new one . . . we are obliged to hire till arrangements are made.

At this time the failure of the trade led to recriminations and divisions between members of the committee. George Palmer, the largest shareholder, who wrote the letter from which I have quoted, and who was making frantic efforts to get a trade started, wrote to James Mangles, deputy-chairman of the Wey & Arun, also a shareholder in the P & A, on 11 April 1833:

> I have exerted myself by day and by night. I have sacrificed my own business frequently to attend to the affairs of the Company and I can now retreat with honor. I only wish that every proprietor will take the trouble of making themselves masters of the actual state of things and either prosecute or abandon the concern altogether. I will neither drive a starved horse nor whip a skeleton.

On the 29th of the same month Admiral Sir Peter Halkett, a shareholder and mortgagee, wrote to Mangles:

> It is to be regretted that Mr. Palmer did not sooner acquaint you as a Member of the Committee that he was not supported . . . I cordially wish that Mr. Palmer, yourself, and others in Town engaged in the concern would endeavourt o recommend an efficient Committee. Many men of business unoccupied in Portsmouth would materially assist. The General Meeting is on 3rd. Tuesday of May to arrange these matters, it is most desirable to have you and Mr. Palmer present and any other

* Presumably the *Egremont*.

Gentlemen with knowledge in such affairs, or we will be at our last gasp.

They were. The through trade actually created was negligible in quantity and ephemeral in time.

While these efforts were being made, the Portsea canal was closed in 1830, it having hardly been used in its eight years of life, and replaced by a channel dredged through Portsea Creek at a cost of over £1,000, so that craft could pass from Langstone to Portsmouth harbours as the Rennies had recommended in 1827. The company thus got rid of water complaints and saved its maintenance. But the Portsmouth trade had no future, and the *Egremont* was broken up in 1840.

It was now the age of the railway. Portsmouth first got rail communication by the London & Southampton to Gosport and the ferry, a route initiated in November 1841. In 1841, also, the London & Brighton Railway was opened, and three years later an extension was projected to Chichester; it was opened on 8 June 1846. A curious single-track telescopic timber bridge was built over the Arun, which could be withdrawn to leave a clear passage for shipping.[32] It was replaced in 1862 by a double-track iron drawbridge, which was last opened on 5 April 1936 to allow a vessel to pass, and which was rebuilt as a fixed bridge in 1938. This line was directly competitive with the Ford–Chichester portion of the canal, which ceased to be used commercially after 1847, though it probably remained navigable until 1856, leaving only the 4 miles of larger canal from Chichester to Salterns lock. The railway was extended to Portsmouth over the Portsea Creek channel at Portsbridge, and opened in 1847. The direct route by way of Godalming had to wait until 1859.

Thomas Edgcumbe, who had been clerk since the company's formation, had in later years great difficulty in getting valid shareholders' meetings together, for lack of a quorum, and therefore in getting committees elected. After 1845 there was no general meeting until 1851, when the prospect of selling some land to the LBSCR caused a meeting to succeed and a committee to be elected. Others followed until 1855, and after that none, though Thomas Smith Edgcumbe, who succeeded his father in 1851, advertised them for some years. Land sales about this time did enable the company to discharge its remaining bonds, most of which had been waived by Lord Egremont in 1826.

At Chichester the company's wharfinger, Richard Purchase, took tolls of about £10 a month and paid himself and other expenses from the proceeds. In 1868, 7,070 tons came up the line. This had fallen to about 4,000 tons in 1888, but Chichester Corporation had an interest in the line, not only for the lime, shingle, bricks and coal for the gasworks that it carried, but because they were paid basin dues and city tolls direct by the users, these yielding about £50 pa in the early 1880s.

In 1888 three shareholders applied for a winding-up order, which was granted. By an Act of 1892 the Chichester line was transferred without charge to the Corporation. The company's remaining property was disposed of, which with money in hand from accumulated rents and land sales, including one in Portsmouth to the LSWR, enabled a dividend of £2 11s 4½d (£2.57) to be paid on the £50 shares, and £1 5s 8¼d (£1.28½) on those of £25, the only payment they ever received. The company was finally dissolved on 3 November 1896.[33]

In 1898 the tonnage on the Chichester line had fallen to 704 of sand and grit, and about 1906 the canal became disused. It was abandoned by the corporation on 6 June 1928, and sold in 1957 to the West Sussex County Council. The lower reach from Cutfield bridge to Salterns lock was reopened in 1932 and is used for berthing yachts.

The Ship Canal Projects of 1823–8

Between the date of opening of the Portsmouth & Arundel Canal and the early thirties, when it proved a failure, a fantastic group of schemes was projected, beginning in 1823 with William James's *Report, or Essay, to illustrate the advantages of direct inland communication through Kent, Surrey, Sussex, and Hants, to connect the Metropolis with ports of Shoreham, (Brighton), Rochester, (Chatham) and Portsmouth, by a line of Engine Rail-road, and to render the Grand Surrey Canal, Wandsworth and Merstham Rail-road, Shoreham Harbour, and Waterloo Bridge shares productive property.*

This was a proposal for two intersecting lines of railway, one from Waterloo to Shoreham and Brighton, the other from Chatham to Portsmouth. On the one hand it was the forerunner, by way of the proposal of 1825 for a Surrey, Sussex & Hants Railroad Company, of the London & Brighton Railway; on the other it was followed by various schemes for a ship canal from London to Portsmouth, which became more grandiose as their improbability increased, and which caused much ill-feeling among rival engineers. Only the boom of 1823–4 made their appearance possible, and the subsequent slump expedited their exits. They owed something to the slightly earlier schemes for a westcountry ship canal, the English & Bristol Channels,*[34] but the main arguments in their favour were their value in supplying military and naval stores to Portsmouth in time of war, the losses of sailing ships making the passage by sea, and the improvement of the supply of produce to the capital.

The first was James Elmes's plan of the autumn of 1824, for a tidal ship canal estimated to cost £4m or £5, which his rival, the engineer N. W. Cundy, described as:

> purporting to be made by Imbanking up all the Rivers on his proposed line into one stream, without a Lock, Dock, or Basin; distance, 100 miles; and the elevation of the country, from Croydon to near Horsham, is from 200 to 400 feet above the Tides, for the distance of 25 to 30 miles.

Very soon after this was published, Cundy announced his own Grand Ship Canal from London to Arundel Bay. Elmes, undeterred, went ahead, subscriptions for shares came in, and a provisional committee was appointed to take the scheme further. Cundy also issued a preliminary report in 1824. He claimed the original idea, probably inaccurately, as his, and went on:

> This Canal, and the several works connected therewith, are intended to accommodate vessels of the largest dimensions, when fully loaded, so as to enable them to pass each other; for this purpose 28 feet depth of water will be required,† and about 150 feet in width, with about four locks, 300 feet in length and 64 in breadth, up to the summit level.

This was to be 21 miles long at 360 ft, part of it through a cutting over 100 ft deep.

The 78-mile long line was to run from two entrances at Cherry Garden stairs, Rotherhithe, and Deptford, by Ewell, Epsom, Leatherhead, Dorking, Newbridge, Pulborough, Arundel (with a branch to the bay), Chichester, Emsworth, Langstone Harbour and Spithead, but alternative lines by Bromley and Reigate on the one hand, and the Wey and Guildford on the other, were suggested. Cundy estimated that the expense to shipowners of taking their vessels round the Foreland was £940,000 pa, while that through the canal would be £350,000. The construction cost he gave as just under £4m, the annual revenue as £518,025, and expenditure as £40,000.

A third plan was proposed in March 1825 by George and the

---

* In the first quarter of 1825, *The Times* was carrying news not only of this and the London to Portsmouth, but of three other projected ship canals, to Manchester, across Ireland, and across the isthmus of Panama.

† The depth of the Manchester Ship Canal is 30 ft from Eastham to Ince and 28 ft from Ince to Manchester. Its locks are 600 ft × 65 ft.

younger John (later Sir John) Rennie, *A Proposal for a Ship Canal from London to Portsmouth, capable of conveying Line of Battleships and the largest Merchantmen*, with a line 86 miles long, 300 ft wide and 24 ft deep, by Guildford, Loxwood and the valley of the Arun, longer than Cundy's but with a lower summit. They put the cost of their bigger waterway higher, at £7m, the estimated revenue lower, at £350,000, and thought the voyage could be made in two days by horse haulage, or in one by using a steam tug.

The three groups decided to meet together in the same month, and agreed:

That upon the examination of several Engineers and Surveyors, and other circumstantial evidence laid before this Meeting, that the plan of a Ship Canal between London and Portsmouth is practicable, and can be executed within the estimated expense of £5,000,000, given by Mr. John Rennie, Mr. Elms, and Mr. Cundy; and that such an undertaking would be of great advantage to the Commerce of London.

The Rennies were asked to survey the alternative lines and schemes and to recommend the best. They in turn asked Francis Giles to take the levels. Meanwhile, £1 subscriptions carrying an option to buy shares were sought towards survey costs, but only £120 came in, apart from £100 from one of the committee. After some months had passed, and five routes had been examined, the Rennies recommended their original line at a cost of £6m to £6½m because, though longer than Cundy's, its summit level was only 174 ft above the tideway, against his 382 ft, and because they thought it would be cheaper. Cundy then issued another report in September, in which he accused the Rennies of surveying by going over the line in a carriage, paying no attention to geology, and misrepresenting his proposals. He argued against their Guildford route, and against delay, saying:

land has already advanced in price, and property advertised for sale has been postponed in consequence, until the proprietors can ascertain the probability of the work being commenced.

The idea then dropped, though both Cundy's and the Rennies' scheme had a brief revival in 1827, when hopeful paragraphs began to appear, such as the following in *Aris's Birmingham Gazette*:

The making of a ship canal from London to Portsmouth, it is understood, is to take place, supported by several Government Offices, the East India Company, the Bank of England, several other public establishments, and the Commercial and Shipping Interests . . . The expence estimated at 4,000,000£, and it will employ 20,000 workmen 4 years.[35]

Cundy now issued a third report, in which he left reason even further behind. He had now seen the Duke of Clarence, who, as Lord High Admiral, was interested, ordered it to be called the Grand Imperial Ship Canal, and commanded Cundy to consult Sir Edwin Owen and the engineers of the Ordnance Department. This must have got to the ears of the Portsmouth & Arundel company, who then, with support from Lord Egremont and others, approached the Admiralty to suggest that they might take over the canal, whether or not the bigger project were to be built. The Duke then asked the Admiralty to consult the Rennies. They surveyed the canal company's property and prospects, and returned the discouraging answer that the company was

> not of a nature sufficiently encouraging to induce the Government to embark in the concern with a view of deriving profit; if, however, they are content to make common cause with the rest of the proprietors or to grant assistance by way of Loan at a Low rate of Interest we think that the money would be well bestowed in a national point of view towards the completion of this Great Undertaking.[36]

The Admiralty took no further action, and the ship canal project itself died early in 1828, after Cundy had presented it to the Commons in a petition of 15 February.[37]

So did the Rennies' scheme for their Portsmouth Ship Canal. Of the latter, Sir John Rennie later wrote in his *Autobiography*:

> The world had not then been accustomed to the enormous sums since spent on railways, and then they would never have believed that £16,000,000 would be spent upon the London, Chatham and Dover Railway, only the same length as the proposed canal.

The Rennies wrote to the *Morning Herald* on 3 November 1827:

> all relish for speculation of any sort was gone by . . . As for the original supporters of the measure, it only remains to say, that perceiving the time gone by for such matters, and feeling that it was impossible to raise the immense sum of money required, even on the cheapest plan, without extensive aid from Government, which it was not disposed to afford, they abandoned all notion of it for the present, took every farthing of the expense incurred upon themselves, and left the £220, which remained untouched, to the inadequate remuneration of the survey.

Langstone Docks & Ship Canal project

In 1846 a scheme was prepared to provide Portsmouth with new docks which would be accessible to large ships which were then hindered by the harbour bar at Portsmouth and the difficult entrance to Langstone Harbour. The promoters proposed a ship canal having its entrance at Spithead about ½ mile below Southsea Castle, and then running eastwards by the sea to Eastney Lake, and so to two docks, which in turn would communicate with Langstone Harbour, thus giving access from either direction.

Sir John Rennie was concerned with the scheme, which died in 1849 when the Admiralty refused to agree to the entrance into Portsmouth Harbour.[38]

CHAPTER VII

The Basingstoke Canal

THE first effort to build a Basingstoke Canal[1] was made in 1770 in connection with the schemes then being discussed for canals to by-pass the Thames navigation between Reading and Monkey Island below Bray, and between Monkey Island and Isleworth. Benjamin Davis, who surveyed it, chose Monkey Island rather than the nearer Sonning because most of the expected traffic would be downwards, and would thereby have a shorter voyage. His proposed barge canal ran for 29 miles from Basingstoke down the Loddon valley to Ruscombe and then past White Waltham to the Thames.[2] He estimated that it would cost £51,000, and reduce the costs of carriage by three-quarters.

On 11 October 1770 a meeting at the town hall, Basingstoke, approved the scheme, and in November a petition for a Bill was presented to Parliament. This sought a canal

which will enable the petitioners, and others, to furnish Timber for the Service of the Navy, and also to supply the London Markets with Flour and Grain, at a cheaper Rate.[3]

But the improvement of the Thames itself between Sonning and Monkey Island carried the day against both the Basingstoke and the Reading–Monkey Island Bills, which were lost.

From about the time that war began in 1776, a group of promoters encouraged a new line of canal, now to run from Basingstoke to the river Wey. It was surveyed by Joseph Parker. At the beginning of 1778 a meeting of the inhabitants of Reading protested against it, presumably on the grounds that it would divert trade, but an Act was passed. This[4] authorized a canal nearly 44 miles long from Basingstoke by way of Odiham, Frimley and Woking to near Weybridge on the Wey, with a branch to Turgis Green, the capital to be £86,000, with power to raise £40,000 more if necessary. It also bound the Wey proprietors in the size of their locks and the charges they could make on their river for Basingstoke Canal traffic.

The petition to Parliament of 2 February 1778, repeating the 1770 wording, had said that the canal

will enable the petitioners, and others, to furnish timber for the service of the Navy; and also to supply the London markets with flour and grain at a cheaper rate than they can do at present,

and a witness before the Parliamentary committee, asked why he thought the canal would be useful, claimed that the cost of carrying timber, corn, and all other heavy goods between Hampshire and London would be reduced by two-thirds.[5] There was, however, some scepticism outside.

The war discouraged activity, and for several years nothing was done. In 1783 the canal committee published *An Address to the Public, on the Basingstoke Canal Navigation*, which said:

The Company, seeing the Impropriety of pushing the Scheme, at a Time when the Nation had occasion for every Resource of Men and Money for the expensive and complicated War in which it was then engaged, postponed all thoughts of executing it until the Return of Peace, which desirable Event having now taken place, they propose to set about the Work.

They did not do so, however, until after an estimate had been published in June 1787 forecasting a traffic of 30,700 tons (of which 6,500 were coal, 6,300 flour and 5,500 timber) and a revenue of £7,783 pa to yield 7½ per cent. At this time also it was decided to drop the authorized loop of canal from Odiham in the direction of the Turgis Green branch and then back through Newnham, and to substitute a 1,230 yd tunnel through the base of the loop at Greywell, thereby reducing the total length from about 44 miles to a little over 37.

Capital was then raised, partly locally, partly in London. William Jessop was appointed engineer and did the final survey, advertisements for contractors appeared in August 1788, in October John Pinkerton, who often worked with Jessop, was appointed contractor, and work began. It must have been soon afterwards that the Rev. S. Shaw on his travels to the west observed the canal under construction, and remarked improvingly:

The contractor, agreeable to the request of the company of proprietors, gives the preference to all the natives who are desirous of this work, but such is the power of use over nature, that while these industrious poor are by all their efforts incapable of earning a sustenance, those who are brought from similar works, cheerfully obtain a comfortable support.[6]

At this time and during the early 1790s, the company had hopes that its line, by an extension to the Itchen or the Andover Canal, might be connected to Southampton and Salisbury and even form part of a through route to Bristol (see p. 186), but these were fading fast by the time they had managed to finish their existing canal, and never had enough impetus to get beyond paper and meetings.

In 1791 the first tolls were taken at the Wey navigation end, and by 27 August 1792 about 32 miles of the canal and 24 locks had been completed, and part of Greywell tunnel cut. The canal was opened on 4 September 1794, though two severe slips, the first only six weeks after opening, partially closed it until the summer of 1795. The waterway, 37½ miles long, fell 195 ft from Basingstoke by 29 locks to the river Wey above Weybridge, and took barges of 50 tons, 82 ft 6 in × 14 ft 6 in, and drawing 3 ft.

Before the opening, prospective carriers were asked to attend to have their craft recorded, and to receive rules and regulations. They were told that wharves for receiving goods were at Basingstoke, Basing, Odiham, Winchfield, Crookham, Farnham road, Ash, Frimley and Horsell, where warehousing sheds were being built. The company itself also engaged in carrying with some dozen barges, and in 1796 were busy encouraging land carriers to take goods on regularly from Basingstoke wharf to Winchester, Southampton, Salisbury, Romsey and Andover. But by April 1797 they had disposed of their craft. In 1799, however, they were offering to build barges for sale or hire to carriers.

The original capital of £86,000 had been spent by 1792. Additional money was then raised mainly by bonds, and a number of these were also issued in settlement of unpaid interest on calls, while a debt of £7,500 was incurred. A second Act[7] of 1793 authorized a further £60,000 in addition to the £126,000 of that of 1778. Without interest on calls, the cost had been £153,462; with it, about £190,000. For the rest of its life the company struggled first to pay off the debts, then to pay interest on the bonds—even partial interest was not possible until 1808, and full interest was never paid—and then to buy bonds in at low rates and cancel them. It only partially succeeded in this, while the shareholders never received a dividend.

From the beginning the canal failed to carry the tonnage or earn the tolls that had been estimated in 1787. The actual results after the canal had been open for some years were as shown on page 154. For only a few years in the 1830s did the tonnage exceed 30,000, and the net revenue was seldom more than £2,000. When it is remembered that the canal carried goods not only to and from Basingstoke and other places along its line, but also, using Basing-

	Tonnage tons	Net Revenue before Bond Interest £
Lady Day 1799–1800	17,877	1,345
Lady Day 1800–1801	18,638	2,038
Lady Day 1801–02	18,737	1,925

stoke as the distributive centre, for many other places in Hampshire and Wiltshire, it can be seen how small was the potential traffic on a mainly agricultural canal at the time.

Peace was a threat to this company, for much of its carrying was in competition with the coasting trade. The Peace of Amiens in 1802 was commented upon as follows in a report:

the Return of Peace, by giving Security to the Coasting Trade, may induce many of the Customers to the Canal, to prefer that Mode of sending their Goods, as being much cheaper than by the Canal,

and

a considerable Quantity of the Goods consigned to the Isle of Wight, Jersey, Guernsey, etc., which used to go up the Canal to Basingstoke, and thence by Waggons to Southampton, are now sent directly from the Thames in Vessels trading to those Islands.

Much the same was said after Waterloo, and thenceforward life was an even greater struggle. In 1818 the chairman referred to 'our miserable State', and now the competition of land carriage was added to that of the coasting ships:

the number of Waggons and Vans has been greatly increased upon the principal roads in the neighbourhood of the Canal, and the prices of conveyance of Goods have been reduced by the Waggon-Proprietors far below the amount absolutely necessary to maintain their Establishments, notwithstanding the cheapness of Horse-keep . . . the Committee beg leave to state, that one hundred weight of Goods is conveyed from London to Farnham by land, for one shilling and sixpence, which by the Canal, the same quantity must cost one shilling and threepence . . . In ordinary times, the expense of conveyance on land was about three times as much as by water.[8]

In terms of speed there could not have been much difference, for in 1810 Zachary Allnutt had recorded that barges took three to four days from London to Basingstoke.

The best hope of the company was to make their canal a part of a through waterway. There were a number of such plans, the most likely being the proposed Hants & Berks Junction Canal (see p. 213) from Old Basing to Newbury, to which the company subscribed £10,000. When this failed to pass through Parliament in 1825 the last opportunity of strengthening a precarious position had gone.

On 22 September 1831 an extraordinary general meeting of the Basingstoke Canal proprietors was held,

> to adopt such measures as may be necessary for the Interests of this Company, in regard to the proposed Railway, from London to Southampton.

The clerk, in summoning the meeting, wrote:

> As, in all probability, the proposed Railway from London to Southampton, will either afford an opportunity for securing the best interests of this Navigation, or greatly injure them, your attendance at this meeting is highly desirable.

This scheme, begun in 1830, did not reach Parliament till 1834, when it was authorized as the London & Southampton Railway, to run from Nine Elms beside the Thames through Woking, Basingstoke and Winchester. At Frimley the Basingstoke Canal would have to be carried over the line on an aqueduct.* The Act empowered the railway company to buy the canal by agreement. The engineer was Francis Giles, who had in 1825 been the engineer of the projected canal to join the Kennet & Avon at Newbury to the Basingstoke Canal at Old Basing. It is odd that the London & Southampton Railway in 1835 tried to get through Parliament a Bill for a branch railway from their line at Basingstoke to Newbury and so by Hungerford and Devizes to Bath and Bristol, the line of the proposed canal and of the Kennet & Avon which had supported it. Giles had, however, been so wrong in the evidence he had given in Parliament against the Liverpool & Manchester Railway Bill that he failed to command the confidence of the Manchester shareholders of the L & S, and was replaced by Joseph Locke in 1837. The railway's amendment Act of that year compelled them to build banks and walls where the line ran alongside the canal, so that the horses would not be frightened.

The London & Southampton threatened not only the canal but the road carrier: a pamphlet of 1834, criticizing the railway scheme, says that the whole traffic between London and Southampton is at present carried on by eight stage coaches, four waggons per week, and one barge weekly on the Basingstoke Canal.[9] Another writer,

---

* The aqueduct was doubled in width, probably in 1900, by the LSWR to keep traffic moving while its own line was widened, as a cheaper alternative than incurring the penalties of closing it.

after saying that there were in Hampshire in 1835 810 miles of turnpiked roads under 36 trusts, with an annual income of £30,321, goes on:

> Should the opening of the railway render the conveyance of goods less costly, the number of stage-waggons which will in course of time be discontinued will be much greater than in most other parts of the country where a complete line of artificial navigation is in existence. It is calculated that the number of stage-waggons

that will be thrown out of employment by the railway on the London and Southampton line of road will be about 82.[10]

While the line was being built, the canal did well by carrying construction material. It was completed from London to Basingstoke on 10 June 1839, and to Southampton on 11 May 1840, thereby doing mortal damage to the Basingstoke Canal in the traffic from London to that town as well as in that consigned to Southampton, and also to the Itchen Navigation from Winchester to Southampton. In the year ending 30 September 1836, the Basingstoke Canal had carried 33,809 tons, 11,144 more than in 1835. The annual report says:

> A great portion of this increase is from the Materials for the Southampton Railway having been conveyed on the Canal . . . had not the competition of the road waggons much reduced the price of carriage, the revenues of the Canal would have been still larger.

At this period fly-boats were running on the canal. In September 1835 'Wallis and White, Basingstoke Canal Fly Boats' were advertising in the Maidstone paper that they would carry hops from London to Weyhill Fair at 2s 3d per cwt delivered.[11] Ten days before the railway was opened to Basingstoke, the canal company cut its tolls, and again the following year. The Wey did the same, but the Thames Commissioners, controlling the third part of the route to London, made no move. In the first year of competition, to 31 March 1840, the canal receipts fell from their inflated figure of £5,416 to £3,763. In comparison, the receipts of the railway for the second half of 1840 were £16,131 as well as £115,016 from passengers. Further damage was done when the LSWR opened its line from near Guildford by way of Ash Junction to Farnham (with a branch to Farnborough) in 1849, and later extended it to Alton. While the tonnage carried on the canal only fell between 1839–40 and 1865–6 from 26,965 to 20,598, railway competition caused the tolls to fall to £1,212, a point below survival. An average toll of 3·2s (16p) per ton in 1835 had become 2·79s (14p) per ton in 1839 and 1·03s (5p) per ton in 1865.* The company went into liquidation in 1866. After a period in the hands of the liquidator, it was bought in 1874 by William St Aubyn, who formed the Surrey & Hants Canal Company. He too failed, and it was back with a receiver in 1878, the year that also saw the winding up of the original company. In early 1880 it was bought by Messrs Dixon and Ward, who sold it to J. B. Smith for £14,800. Smith was the nominee for three men, B. A. Grant, G. D. Cardew and William Leeming, who seem to have come from Lancashire to use the canal as a means of removing money from the public. At that time London was becoming short of water. Using the water rights of the canal as their talking point to those who were ignorant of how short of water it had always been, they floated the Surrey & Hampshire Canal Corporation Ltd in 1880,[12] with a capital of £100,000 in preference and ordinary shares. Its object was mainly to supply water to London from its alleged springs, seemingly in pipes laid along the canal bed so as not to interfere with traffic.

The promoters then bought the canal from their own nominee for £150,000, half in short-term bonds, half in fully-paid shares. He then re-sold the shares to the public, while they raised £100,000 in debentures, mostly to repay the bonds. When the winding-up came in 1882, one of the petitioners said that the shares and debentures were sold

> in distant parts of the country, particularly in and near Lancashire, but I believe that none of the shareholders or bond-holders for any material amount resided near the . . . Canal.

Until a burst at Aldershot stopped traffic, business was carried on, but the directors added to their takings by selling surplus lands, trees, and some of the carrying plant. In the end the shareholders lost all their money, while the debenture holders and other creditors collected a small dividend from the liquidator, who had meanwhile had the breach mended and re-started trade.

Some of the creditors tried to save something from the wreck by forming, in 1883, the London & Hampshire Canal & Water Co Ltd.[13] When the canal was auctioned, they bought it for £15,000 with money raised from those share and debenture holders of the old corporation who were willing to subscribe 10 per cent of their former holdings in cash, in exchange for new debentures. It was an honest effort to retrieve the situation, but sufficient revenue did not exist, and in 1887 this company went into voluntary liquidation. In 1888 only 4,187 tons were carried.

---

* These figures are not exactly comparable because of differences in length of haul and class of goods, but they show the trend clearly enough.

K

The receiver had it until it was bought in 1895 by Sir Frederick Hunt, who re-floated it—if one can so put it—as the Woking, Aldershot & Basingstoke Canal & Navigation Company. Barges were built or hired, and traffic increased, especially in timber and bricks from the brickfields at Up Nately and Nately Scures which were now worked by another company formed by Hunt. Just before the turn of the century over 20,000 tons were being carried, mostly by the canal company, who in 1898 made a loss of £3,077. In 1900 they went into liquidation, and were followed by the brickmaking concern in 1901. It was now that commercial traffic to Basingstoke virtually ended.

In 1905 the company was bought from the liquidator by one William Carter, who resold it to Horatio Bottomley's Joint Stock Trust & Finance Corporation for a million 5s shares. After various vicissitudes in the hands of that regrettable financier, it emerged as the London & South Western Canal Company with a capital of £100,000, and caused a number of gullible people to lose their money before being wound up in 1909, William Carter having a mortgage and therefore retaining an interest in the canal.

In 1914 the last boat passed to Basingstoke, having taken three months to get there. In that year the canal was taken over by the Basingstoke Canal Syndicate Ltd,[14] with a nominal capital of £15,000 in ordinary shares and £20,000 in debentures. This concern seems to have paid upwards of £15,000 for the canal, and to have been interested in it more as property than as a navigation. Only four of the shares were ever subscribed, but all the debentures. The leading figure was Shurmer Sibthorp, a City man who was also a director of the Transcaucasian Syndicate, and whose interests were therefore not parochial. Some repairs were done, and fair business on the canal during the war. By October 1919 a receiver had been appointed, though he did not take possession until February 1921. Some tolls were received for the period up to 28 October of that year, but none thereafter until the receiver was discharged in October 1923, by which time £3,500 of the debentures had been repaid by the proceeds of land sales. The company was dissolved in 1926.

In 1923 the canal, back with William Carter, was sold to A. J. Harmsworth, whose family had had a long working connection with it. Thenceforward there was no commercial traffic above Woking, but tonnage carried reached 25,200 tons in 1935. Greywell tunnel fell in during 1932, after which parts of the canal above it were sold, including the wharf at Basingstoke. In 1937 Harmsworth formed the Weybridge, Woking & Aldershot Canal Company, but about that time the canal's trade fell away badly as coal ceased to be carried to Woking's gasworks. The last loaded barge passed to Woking in 1949, and the company went into voluntary liquidation in 1950.

The canal was sold in 1949 to the New Basingstoke Canal Co Ltd, and since then has been used for supplying water. It is only navigable over short stretches.

CHAPTER VIII

Hampshire Waterways

++++++++++++++++++++++++++++++++++++++◆+++++++++++++++++++++++++++++++++++++

HAMPSHIRE waterways ran north and south, from Winchester, Andover and Salisbury to the sea. Efforts to provide lateral connections, or to join them at Basingstoke to a London route or at Pewsey to the Kennet & Avon Canal, came to nothing.

River Itchen

The Itchen[1] seems to have been made navigable by Godfrey de Lucy, Bishop of Winchester from 1189 to 1204. He built a reservoir of some 200 acres at Alresford with an embankment 78 yd long and 20 ft high, part of which can still be seen, and made the river navigable from Southampton to that town. In consideration of his enterprise he was given by King John the right to levy tolls on goods

> that shall or may hereafter be conveyed up or down the river Itchen which the said Bishop hath now caused to be first trenched and made navigable at his own expense.

For a time the Winchester trade in leather and wool grew, but after 1353, when the staple was moved to Calais and Melcombe Regis, it declined. So did the navigation, which by 1452 was in a bad state. It seems likely that mills on the banks increasingly obstructed it. Certainly in 1617, in a report to the Commissioners of Sewers, impediments to a free passage were mentioned.[2]

In 1664-5 an Act was passed to make a number of rivers navigable, among them the Itchen. This named undertakers, and also appointed commissioners from the justices, who were to confirm the charges levied. The undertakers seem not to have been successful, but about 1710 the navigation was at last made to Winchester by building artificial cuts and locks, and providing a horse towing path. By 1767 the undertakers' rights had been concentrated in the hands of one owner, who had created a carrying and trading monopoly, which was considered to be worth £12,000, and which, local opinion felt, had to be curbed. Mr Pyott carries on a considerable Trade and Commerce in Goods, Wares and Merchandize, carried and conveyed by Water, in and upon the said River, and who, acting and appearing, as the sole Owner and Proprietor of the said Navigation, and for the Carriage and Freight of Goods . . . doth not only demand and impose exorbitant Rates and Duties . . . but frequently refuses to carry and convey by Water, Coals and other such Goods . . . as interfere with his own Trade, Dealing and Commerce, whereby he has in a great Measure obtained and acquired the Monopoly of several of the Necessaries of Life to his own Use and Benefit, to the great Damage and Oppression of several poor and indigent Persons, and to the great Loss and Prejudice of the Inhabitants of the City of Winchester, and several other Places . . . which are within the Limits and Influence of the said Navigation.[3]

The Act of 1767,[4] from the preamble to which this quotation has been taken, is exceptional in that it was clearly obtained over the head of the proprietor; there was later to be a similar but unsuccessful case on the Medway. A group of local justices and Winchester dignitaries was formed into a new commission to fix tolls and freight rates. The owner was to accept all goods for carriage without preference, and if there were not enough boats, the Commission could require the owner to provide more; if he did not, they could license others. Boats should not be of a size to carry more than thirty tons or less than twenty. Lastly, the commission could order the erection of locks, wharves, warehouses or other facilities. Mr Pyott had clearly gone too far.

The commissioners laid down rates which were 'found by Experience not only to be very moderate, but highly satisfactory to the public,'[5] though it is doubtful how much controlling they really did. It seems that the merchants who had promoted the Act of 1767 themselves leased the river from Pyott for a time, after which he took it again, recouping himself on the freight for the lowness of the tolls. At Edward Pyott's death James d'Arcy, who had married the widow of one of Pyott's sons, bought the family interest and became sole proprietor, though he had to pay an annuity of £200 a year to Pyott's widow and interest on £4,666 worth of mortgages held by other members of the family.

It is probable that between 1767 and 1795 more locks were added to those already in place, bringing the total to fifteen. In its final state, the navigation had three masonry and twelve turf-sided locks, and two single-gated or half locks. The navigation was now 10⅜ miles long from Winchester, of which 2¾ miles were artificial

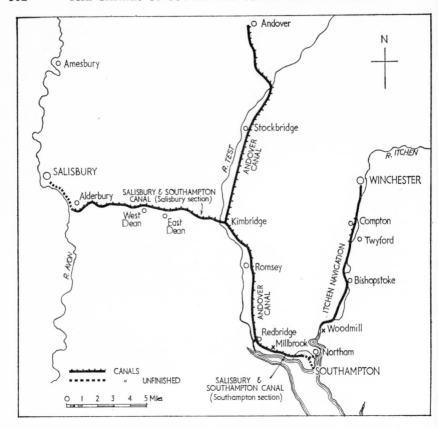

16. Inland navigation in the Hampshire basin

cut and a great deal more made use of secondary streams. It ended at Woodmill, where a tide-lock with an extra pair of gates facing the sea communicated with the estuary. Thence barges worked down on the stream for two miles to Northam, or were punted against it. At Northam were the wharves and warehouses of the navigation.

In September 1790 a newspaper notice says that the navigation 'is now in the hands of the proprietors', who want tolls paid in cash 'as it could be highly inconvenient to keep any accounts open for the carriage of goods upon the said River.'[6] This sounds as if d'Arcy had for a time leased the tolls. He did so again, to Edward Knapp, before again taking over himself late in 1794.

In 1795 an Act[7] granted powers to canalize the river from

Woodmill down to Northam, probably because it was then thought that a traffic would develop from Southampton quay by way of the Northam branch of the Salisbury & Southampton Canal. D'Arcy was also empowered to raise more capital by loans or shares. If the latter, then a shareholders' managing committee was to be appointed. The commissioners could also set one up if he failed to provide enough barges. Some shares were now sold, though a complaint to the commissioners in 1799 showed that d'Arcy had not yet formed a committee.

About 1796, when the first schemes were being talked about for joining the Itchen and the Basingstoke Canal, so making a through navigation from London, the prospects for the river seemed good, and its value was put at £24,000. D'Arcy wanted to live in Ireland, so he sold first a half-share, and then all his interest, to George Hollis, his agent, who had Harry Baker as sleeping partner. Hollis became sole proprietor in 1804. About this time* the river was carrying an average of 18,310 tons of goods annually in four barges, the trade being made up as follows:

	tons
Coal and culm	10,300
Salt	350
Chalk	1,710
Other goods	5,950
	18,310

The average annual revenue was stated to be £3,735, but I assume that the proprietors' freight takings, as well as tolls, are included in this figure.

Hollis now proposed to give up his near-monopoly position and make the navigation an open one. He therefore obtained the Act[8] of 1802. This listed the tolls to be taken and ended the fixing of rates by the commissioners. The Act provided that the river must be put in order within three years, and seems to have been followed by a lease for a time to a group of merchants. About 1808 a number of manœuvres by Hollis's enemies culminated in their employing engineers to report the river as a poor navigation in order that they might attack the revived plan to link the navigation with the Basingstoke Canal in which Hollis was interested. In this way they hoped to bring financial pressure on Hollis to concede water rights to mills and land owned by his attackers.[9] From now on the river seems to have declined. In 1811 Hollis got an Act[10]

* I think the figures refer to 1802.

allowing him to raise tolls, though the deepening and improving of the river were not yet finished.

In March 1819 he was again in difficulties, and explained why he wanted once more to increase charges to a meeting in the Guildhall at Winchester. He told the audience that he was not then receiving 5 per cent on the £12,000 at which the river was valued. Since 1811 trade had greatly decreased: 'a large proportion of this decrease might be attributed to the establishment of the Basingstoke Canal'; trade was also unbalanced, being almost all upwards to Winchester with the barges returning empty, while maintenance was expensive. The merchants agreed that he ought to get his 5 per cent, but claimed that bad management was the trouble. After an argument, a group of them agreed to pay Hollis £1,200 for one year inclusive of tolls, wharfage and rent, he to spend some £600 in repairs (the balance being 5 per cent on £12,000). In return, he would postpone his Bill for one year.[11] It seems that Hollis proved to be right, for in July 1820 a new Act[12] authorized increased tolls, though simultaneously the commissioners reduced freight rates: they therefore intended that Hollis should get more income, and the barge-owners less.

A number of mortgages were raised, presumably to pay for these improvements, but by 1833, when no carrying was being done by the owner, the receipts were only £1,870, and in 1839, the last full year before the opening of the London & Southampton Railway, £1,821. Of these last years of the river before railway competition began a contemporary said:

By starting from the Wharf,* and proceeding along the navigable branch of the Itchen, the stranger will be able to form some idea, probably not a very high one, of the commerce of Winchester, restricted as it is to coals and corn, and a few other bulky articles, for the use of the immediate vicinity.[13]

The opening of the railway to Southampton coincided with an internal squabble among the owners of the Itchen Navigation. In 1839 George Hollis had handed over all his property in the navigation to members of his family. From 1832 to 1841 his son, F. J. Hollis, was manager, but in 1841 he was succeeded by W. W. Bulpett, a member of the banking firm of Knapp, Bulpett & Markham of Winchester, who was himself a mortgagee and who agreed to manage the river free of charge, whereas F. W. Hollis had been charging £150 a year. He seems to have made a good job of it. In 1847, however, the Hollis family gave him notice to quit, which as a mortgagee he refused to do. After many years, F. W.

* At Winchester.

Hollis, who already held a quarter of the shares, bought up others at a nominal price from members of the family, and about 1860 brought an action against Bulpett, alleging that he had not informed the shareholders, kept proper accounts, or adequately maintained the river.

Receipts began to fall sharply after the railway was opened. Soon the shareholders, and later the mortgagees, ceased to receive anything, while lessening sums were spent on repairs and management as funds got low. These are the figures, averaged over three-year periods. The expenses shown are the actual payments of the year, and are more or less than the receipts as the balance in hand changes.

Date	Receipts £	Repairs and Expenses £	To Mortgagees £	To Shareholders £
1842–4	1,012	418	450	554
1845–7	824	374	392	58
1848–50	739	332	389	115
1851–3	532	231	244	—
1854–6	422	210	178	—
1857–9	371	184	191	—
1860–2	430	585*	—	—

* The heavy spending on repairs in this period was apparently due to the manager trying to avoid the accusation that not enough money had been spent on maintenance.

In 1863, while the case was still on, Mr Clarke, the last manager of the Andover Canal, was made manager in place of Bulpett. By this time the navigation had only two full-time employees, a carpenter at £1 3s (£1.15) a week and a lock-keeper and earthworker at 11s (55p), and only two barges were in use. Bulpett won the case, and was then reinstated as manager, but the days of the navigation were nearly done, and the last tolls seem to have been taken for January 1869. At this time there were still mortgages of £19,708 on the navigation, of which £2,607 dated from the Pyott ownership, apart from the shares. In 1871 J. R. Stebbing of Southampton negotiated to buy the waterway, but his plans fell through.

An optimistic Southsea estate agent, Patrick O'Carroll, had in June 1909 obtained an option to buy the Itchen Navigation from C. W. L. Bulpett, 'who is believed to be the only person entitled to an indisputable interest therein', for £4,890. With some Portsmouth and Southampton associates he then registered a company, the Itchen Navigation Ltd, with a nominal capital of £20,000, to which he gave an option to re-purchase the navigation from himself for £6,000 cash and 6,000 fully-paid £1 shares. But the plan never got off the ground, for the options expired because the promoters 'had great trouble and difficulty in Clearing the Titles of the Navigation', and were indeed unable to do so. The company therefore never traded, and was finally wound up in 1925.[14]

River Avon (Hampshire)

Salisbury has been unfortunate in her search after water communication. In early times the efforts to make the Hampshire Avon[15] navigable were only temporarily successful, in the early canal age the Salisbury & Southampton Canal hardly affected the city, and the projects for a branch from the Kennet & Avon Canal came to nothing.

In 1535 a Commission was appointed for the river, to order the removal of all weirs and obstructions, presumably with navigation in mind. But it is unlikely that anything happened.

Early in the next century both Francis Mathew and John Taylor the water-poet proposed that the river be made navigable. Taylor was persuaded by a fellow-waterman, Gregory Bastable, to visit Salisbury to see whether it would be feasible. The two, accompanied by others, rowed from London to Christchurch and up the river in a wherry in 1623. In his subsequent pamphlet, *A New Discovery by Sea*,[16] Taylor says that the river could be made navigable without much difficulty, forecasts cargoes of timber, coal, bricks, beer and corn, and strongly urges the townsmen to make it so.

It was not until 1664–5 that an Act[17] was obtained which authorized the Earl of Clarendon as undertaker for making the Avon navigable from Christchurch to Salisbury, and the Earl of Pembroke and Montgomery to do the same for the Wylye between Salisbury and Wilton. Clarendon did some work on Christchurch quay under this Act, but none on the Avon. In 1675 Andrew Yarranton, who had built navigation works on the Worcestershire Stour and elsewhere, and was thoroughly interested in water transport, surveyed the river at the request of Lord Salisbury. He thought it was practicable to make it navigable, and envisaged timber and ironstone as among the likely cargoes. It was probably now that Salisbury Corporation took it up, trying to get subscriptions to pay for the work, and undertakers to carry it out. They then decided to make a start themselves, at a cost of £2,000, and appointed Samuel Fortrey engineer.

On 20 September 1675, the first spit was cut by the bishop, 'the Mayor and other persons of quality doing the like'; and the corporation then wrote to various important people who might be interested to tell them 'of the great worke of the navigation undertaken by this Corporation and of the vast charge they are likely to be at about it, in hopes that they will be pleased to lend their assistance to so good and publiq a worke.'

A start was apparently made, but enough assistance was not forthcoming, and in 1677 the council decided not to continue without help. In the same year, certain private individuals agreed to take over the work and make the river navigable for boats of ten tons. They were some years at the task, spent £3,500 on it, and seem to have done the work after a fashion, for two 25-ton barges are said to have come up river to Salisbury in 1684, while in 1687 a Code of Regulation and Tolls was issued. However, in 1693 another group of undertakers had it in hand. Clear proof that the navigation carried barges at this time comes from depositions made in a lawsuit in 1737; they refer to the river at Standlynch, between Alderbury and Downton.

Robert Tanner . . . Saith . . . they used to go through the weir gap with their boats when the hatches were up, and when they were down they used to halle their boats over the mead. Saith he has formerly for upwards of 40 years since seen barges go through the weir gap.

Andrew Bourne . . . Saith he remembers two barges going through the weir gap when it was a lock.

Tho. Hatcher . . . Saith he was at the building of the Navigation Bridges about 35 years ago. Saith he remembers Barges about 45 years ago coming from Salisbury to Christchurch and from Christchurch to Salisbury for several years together, that the Navigators failing, the Navigation ceased, and some time after it was revived and barges navigated as before.

Farmer Arnold . . . Saith the navigation was begun about 45 years ago and he remembers Barges navigating the river and coming through Standlynch where they were hauled through by a windlass.[18]

From these depositions, it seems likely that the main navigation cuts on the river were made by the 1693 group of undertakers, who made the river navigable with flash-locks at the mills, as at Standlynch, and also some pound-locks,* and fined landowners for not keeping up the ancient weirs, or cutting weeds in the river. They also built 'a small Key and Alehouse' at a haven or creek below Christchurch, and

---

* At Britford, and perhaps at Fordingbridge and Winkton, are remains of what appear to be pound-locks.

made a new Cut from the Sea to the said Haven, with Design . . . to make a better Haven; but the Undertakers, finding the Work impossible, left the same off, and more dangerous passage by the new Cut, whereby the sand is brought in, and the Haven like to be utterly spoiled for want of the Current through the Old Passage.

In 1699 the undertakers introduced a Bill into Parliament to increase their powers. Salisbury corporation supported them, saying that because of the deficiencies of the former Act 'the said Navigation hath been retarded, though brought to some Perfection; on the finishing whereof the Trade of the . . . City doth greatly depend,'[19] but the undertakers had annoyed too many landowners, and also the shipowners who had been charged tolls for using the haven (perhaps Mudeford), though they alleged it was worse than before owing to silting, and that the former Act's powers had not extended below Christchurch. The Bill got no further than committee. It is likely that the undertakers then gave up, and that a new group took over about 1702 when the navigation bridges were made, and once more failed. The explanation usually given for this failure is a flood, but if this had been so, one would have expected a mention of it from the deponents of 1737. It was probably just too difficult. This view is borne out by a petition of Salisbury to Parliament in 1772,[20] which asked for the relevant clauses of the 1664–5 Act to be repealed, so that the river might revert to Commissioners of Sewers, who could then remove obstructions dating from when it had been made partly navigable. The petition says that powers given by the Act

were partly carried into Execution, but the navigating the said River was soon found to be attended with so many Difficulties and Inconveniences, that it did not answer the Purposes intended, and is now wholly discontinued.

The corporation tried to revive it once more about 1730 and failed, for the rewards were less certain than, by then, the opposition of owners of water-meadows and mills. Horse towing paths were not built, and barges were at any rate sometimes sailed.

In September 1821 a short paragraph appeared that 'a navigable canal is about to be cut between Lymington, in Hampshire, and the city of Salisbury, which will form a junction with the Avon and Lymington rivers,'[21] but it seems not to have had any consequences in action.

In 1907 a small boat was refused the right to navigate on Winkton Water near Christchurch by the owner, in the interests of the river's fisheries. A protest meeting was held in the town, and a River Avon Public Rights Committee set up to raise money to take the case further, but it seems that this could not be done, for judgment was given by default against those who claimed that navigation rights still existed, since Christchurch defendants could not raise sufficient money for defence counsel. More recently, the matter has been discussed again.

Andover Canal

Brindley's presence in the south when he was surveying for the corporation of London in 1769, and his advocacy of the London Canal (see p. 191), and Whitworth's in the south-west, encouraged men to think about other possible canals. In 1770[22] Robert Whitworth made a survey for an Andover Canal, to run down the valleys of the Anton and Test to Redbridge at the mouth of the latter river not far from Southampton. Gilpin wrote of Redbridge in 1776:

> Ships of considerable burden come up as far as this bridge, where they take in timber from New-Forest, and other commodities.[23]

He estimated a narrow canal at £28,982,* and a bigger one at £31,654. Meetings in support were held at Andover, Stockbridge and Romsey, and in 1771 Parliament was petitioned for leave to bring in a Bill. This stated that the Act of 16 & 17 Charles II for making several rivers navigable† had included the Anton and Test rivers from Andover to Redbridge and Southampton River, but that nothing had resulted. Since then, 'the Country through which the said River runs is become much more populous, and greatly increased in Trade and Manufactures', and it now seemed more practicable to build a canal 'which will be of much more general Use.'[24] But no Bill followed,

> on account of some objections being made about the lands to be purchased, and the damages that might be sustained by particular persons, although the advantages that would accrue to this part of the country are very considerable: for it is a well-known fact, that before the navigation was made at Newbury,‡ the markets at Andover were very large, and a very great corn-trade was carried on there; but from that time it has declined, and is now in a manner lost, insomuch that the farmers carry their corn even from thence to Newbury: but when the pro-

---

* The figure may be £26,982. The type is indistinct.
† Such as the Hampshire Avon.
‡ The river Kennet.

posed canal from this place to Redbridge shall be made, the trade will of course return to its own channel.

This is the explanation given by Phillips,[25] but the newspaper notice of the revival in 1788 merely says that not enough money was subscribed.

In 1788 the project was revived because

several Gentlemen and Tradesmen, from their experience of the effects of navigable Cuts in other places, are of the opinion, that a navigable Cut from Andover to Redbridge, as before proposed, would be both advantageous to the proprietors and of great public utility to the places adjacent.[26]

They got the bailiff and corporation of Andover to call a meeting at the Star & Garter there on 4 August, at which the project was unanimously approved, a new survey commissioned, a committee appointed, and a subscription of £35,000 ordered.[27] By the middle of the month promises of over £19,000 had come in, and by September prospects were exciting enough for J. Rose of Chute to burst into a 10-verse *Ode on the intended Andover Canal Navigation*,[28] which began:

> *What joyful shouts shall rend the skies,*
> *When Anton* sees her treasures rise:*
> *Sees Quircus from his native sleep*
> *Descend, and travel to the deep;*
> *While awful Neptune greets new sails unfurled,*
> *To waft the riches of the western world.*

Robert Whitworth again did the survey, and in March 1789 the petition for a Bill was presented; £30,700 had been subscribed, on the hopeful estimate that 'the Income arising . . . will pay £7 per cent per annum and all expenses, and have an annual surplus of more than £700.'[29] There was some opposition from landowners, and from those who feared the Itchen's trade might be affected, but it received the royal assent on 13 July. The Act for the Andover Canal†[30] authorized a share capital of £35,000, and another £30,000 if necessary, £10,000 of which might be in shares. It granted a toll of 2d per ton per mile on all goods, and unusually among canal Acts, specified both the maximum size of barges (60 ft × 8 ft, to draw not more than 3 ft 6 in) and the hours the canal might be open (4 am to 10 pm). Special protection was given to the existing wharf near the canal's proposed entrance at Red-

---

* Andover lies on the river Anton, which joins the river Test at Fullerton below the town.

† Then officially spelt Andevor by the company.

bridge, whose tenant was a timber merchant, John Poore, and owner Sir Charles Mills, unless these failed to provide enough accommodation, when the company could build their own.

The canal began on the south side of the river Anton at Andover, which it followed downwards to its junction with the Test. At this point it crossed both rivers, and followed the east bank of the Test past Romsey to the tideway of Southampton Water at Redbridge. It was 22 miles long, with a fall to sea-level of 179 ft by 24 locks to take craft 65 ft × 8 ft 6 in. The deposited plan had provided for the canal to enter the Test on the foreshore in Redbridge village, but perhaps for lack of money, it in fact entered it just above the medieval bridge there.[31] The canal appears to have been completed about May 1794: a newspaper report of Monday 27 January reads:

A barge loaded with upwards of 20 tons burthen was on Wednesday navigated on the canal within two miles of Andover and the canal is now completed from Redbridge to Clatford.[32]

Rates of toll were settled by the company on 11 May.[33] The company's first engineer may have been Charles Roberts, who gave evidence before the Parliamentary committee on the Bill. If so, he had left by the summer of 1794, when he became engineer to the Manchester, Bolton & Bury Canal company. The cost had been £48,000, raised as to £35,000 by shares and £13,000 by loan.

There seem still to have been difficulties, perhaps from the Itchen or the Kennet proprietors, for Phillips, writing about this time, says:

No doubt can be entertained but this canal will answer the well-founded expectation of the subscribers and the public, unless the underhand proceedings of certain individuals should frustrate that hope; but this the spirit of the inhabitants of the country will prevent. Monopolies are always inimical to public interest.

The company had its own wharves at Andover, Stockbridge (where the coming of the waterway caused a market to be established in 1794) and Romsey, and the canal served a local purpose mainly in bringing coal and building materials upwards from Southampton Water to Romsey, Stockbridge, and Andover, and carrying down agricultural produce, but the trade was not enough to earn a dividend throughout its life for the proprietors. In July 1816 the tolls and wharfage were advertised to be let for one to three years,[34] in 1827 the company was eight years in arrears with its loan interest, and in 1838 the writer of a history of Hampshire remarks gloomily that:

ANDOVER CANA

T.	C.	Q.		£	s.	d.
6	0	0		1	10	0

No. 98 Loaded at *Redbridge Morestie*

Boat, No. *Messrs Heskerton* Owner of Cargo.

Glasspool Captain.

Iron to Clatford *[?]*

Collector.

THE ABOVE CONTENTS ARE TRUE.

17. An Andover Canal waybill of 1859

the traffic carried on by means of this canal is very trifling, and
must continue so, unless the state of the country shall undergo
some change of which there is at present no prospect.[35]
Later the position improved a little, for in 1851 when railway
competition began, the company was only one year in arrears with
its loan interest.

In 1845 the Manchester & Southampton Railway had agreed at
a meeting early in October to buy the Andover Canal for £30,000.
The Press observed that the agreement would be of advantage to
the canal shareholders 'as hitherto the original shares have been

considered of little value, but for which they will then realise nearly £40.'[36] A Bill was introduced, but between Commons and Lords the London & South Western Railway agreed to become part-owners, with the Manchester & Southampton, of the canal and the proposed railway from Andover to Redbridge. The Bill was lost on Great Western opposition. In 1847 the M & SR tried again and failed, but the L & SWR were authorized to make a railway from Basingstoke to Salisbury through Andover, and to buy the canal. This provided a roundabout but possible railway route from Andover to Southampton via Basingstoke. In 1849, the year work stopped on the line that had been begun from Basingstoke towards Andover, the canal company took over the responsibility for carrying on the canal themselves, and bought the sixteen 18-ton barges that were at work. They did this because the carriers had said that they could not continue without heavy toll reductions.

In 1850 the M & SR and the L & SWR agreed with the canal company that the canal should be closed when the purchase money had been paid over, and about £9,000 was actually found as an advance and distributed to the canal shareholders. The transaction was not completed, however, and in November 1851 a meeting of landowners at Andover formed the Basingstoke & Salisbury Railway to complete what the LSWR had left unfinished. Their prospectus showed the possibility of converting the canal to a broad-gauge line to link Southampton to the broad-gauge system.[37] When the railway reached Andover in 1854, price-cutting began, the railway carrying on its roundabout route to Southampton at rates which forced the canal company to make successive cuts to retain its traffic. The effect of the opening can be seen from the following figures. Tonnage carried was maintained, but the combined toll and carrying receipts fell, and little loan interest could be paid after 1854.

Year ending June	Receipts £	Year ending June	Receipts £
1852	3,276	1855	3,090
1853	3,751	1856	3,261
1854	3,623	1857	3,140

The interest of the L & SWR in the canal revived sharply after the GWR had promoted a company to make a Southampton to Bristol line via Salisbury, with which the canal company had late in 1856 made a provisional sale agreement and given notice of a Bill to close the navigation. The railway Bill was rejected, but the

L

following year the canal proprietors, apparently with GWR blessing, formed the Andover Canal Railway Company with a capital
of £130,000, later the Andover & Redbridge Railway, to convert
the canal to a broad-gauge line to Southampton, and possibly also
to build a link with the Devizes branch of the GWR at Pewsey. The
South Western unsuccessfully opposed it; then both that railway
and the Great Western tried to buy it; finally it was agreed between
them that the South Western should have it, and that it should be
laid on the narrow gauge.

The canal was stopped as from 19 September 1859, the Andover
& Redbridge Railway having agreed to pay £12,500 in cash and
1,250 £10 shares.* After cutting the first sod of the railway the
following day, Lord Palmerston said:

> All of us who live here know that the canal which connected
> Andover with Redbridge has not, from various causes, been
> attended with that public advantage which its projectors origi-
> nally contemplated.[38]

The railway, which Dendy Marshall tells us was known as the
sprat and winkle line, was opened on 6 March 1865, having used
about 14¼ miles of the canal.

One of the principal original promoters had been William
Steele Wakeford, the Andover banker. One of his shares was
transferred late in 1833 to Robert Tasker, the founder of the firm
that bears his name, and in the following year to his younger
brother William. Tasker's foundry iron came from south Wales
via Southampton and the canal, or else from the Forest of Dean.
In this case, along with Somerset coal, it came up the Kennet &
Avon to Burbage wharf and then by road waggon. Timber came
from Devizes or Honeystreet on the Kennet & Avon. Tasker's
used about 400 tons a year of south Wales and 100 tons of Forest
iron, and 200 tons of coal. A surviving waybill of the year the
canal was closed shows 6 tons of iron brought from Redbridge to
Tasker's wharf at Clatford by W. Glasspool & Mates. It took two
days.[39]

Proposed links between the Basingstoke Canal
and the Itchen or the Andover Canal

In 1783, in *An Address to the Public, on the Basingstoke Canal
Navigation*, the committee of that proposed waterway foresaw an
extension of it 'into the British Channel by Southampton or

---

* There must have been a small extra item, for the figure shown in the company's
account for 1861 is £25,357.

ANDOVER CANAL BILL.

(Transfer Discontinuance)

SIR,

I beg to inform you that application is intended to be made to Parliament in the next Session for leave to introduce a Bill to authorize the Company of Proprietors of the Andover Canal Navigation to transfer their undertaking to the Southampton, Bristol, and South Wales Railway Company; or to some other Company or persons.

The Canal Company intend also to seek power in the Bill to stop up, or discontinue for the purposes of Navigation, the whole or any part of the Andover Canal, and the Basins and other Works connected with it; and as I understand that you are interested (as Owner, Lessee, or Occupier) in certain Lands in which the Canal or Works so to be stopped or discontinued are situated, I think it right to apprise you of the intention to apply for the said Bill.

I am, SIR,

Your obdt. Servt.

THOS. LAMB,

Solicitor to the Andover
Canal Company

ANDOVER,.
NOVEMBER 26th, 1856.

To *The Surveyors of the Highways of Upper Clatford.*

18. The Andover Canal Company gives notice of proposed closure

Christchurch, with an Arm to Salisbury', and in August 1788, about six months after they had begun actively to build their canal, there was talk of an extension to the Itchen at Winchester,[40] and a line was surveyed, but interest then switched to another project.

At the end of 1789 the committee of the Basingstoke Canal, which was in touch with a group of promoters at Salisbury,* asked John Rennie to survey a possible extension to that city on the same scale as their own waterway, along a route that had already been looked over by Jessop. Rennie foresaw a difficult stretch through the high ground between Basingstoke and Polhampton near Overton, to which water would have to be pumped by steam engine, but 'after getting through the Hills there is no difficulty in continuing the Canal to Kitcomb Bridge, the place where the Andover Canal crosses the river Test.'[41] The Andover Canal, which had been authorized that same year, would then have to be built wider than planned to Kimbridge, whence a line could be carried to Salisbury, which would have 1,210 yd of tunnelling, and a summit fed by water from a waterwheel pump. This in turn, he thought, might be extended by Warminster to Bath and so to Bristol,† to give a through Bath–Bristol route superior to the Thames & Severn, just completed. His estimate to Salisbury was £135,770 for the cheapest of his alternatives, excluding the widening of the Andover Canal. Such a figure was too much for the Basingstoke committee to cope with at the time, and nothing further was then done, though a Parliamentary notice appeared in September 1790 for a canal from Basingstoke to Salisbury, to join the Andover Canal at Chilbolton and leave it again at Kimbridge,[42] and in 1793 there were Salisbury men who preferred a line from their city by Andover to the Basingstoke Canal to the Salisbury & Southampton Canal then being promoted.

At the time of the canal mania interest changed back to a Basingstoke–Itchen link, and a meeting was held in Southampton on 27 December 1792, with the mayor in the chair, and James d'Arcy the owner of the Itchen on the committee. The idea was soon afterwards incorporated in the plans that arose out of the mania scheme for a canal from Bristol to Salisbury, and men thought of a through line to London. While most of the other plans fell away, this did not, and in 1796–7 it was being seriously discussed under the name of the London & Southampton Ports Junction Canal. In 1796 two surveys of the line were made, one

* For what later became the Salisbury & Southampton Canal, see p. 178.
† For schemes for canals between Salisbury and Bristol, see p. 186

by Joseph Hill the engineer of the Salisbury & Southampton, quoting £127,000, and the other by George Smith, surveyor of the Basingstoke, at £157,566.*

Notwithstanding that the main arguments for the link were those of war, rising prices and canal difficulties elsewhere caused the plan to be laid aside till 1807, though in 1800 Ralph Dodd, in proposing his Grand Surrey Canal (see p. 102) from Rotherhithe to Kingston by the river Wey, said that it could be continued to the Itchen. It was then revived as the Portsmouth, Southampton & London Junction Canal, and re-surveyed by Michael Walker from the Itchen at Winchester by Alresford, Alton and Farnham either to the Basingstoke Canal near Aldershot or to the Wey (Godalming) Navigation at Godalming. The proposal was now for a barge canal about 35 miles long, which should at first have a 7-mile long railway incorporated in it at its highest point, later to be replaced by a 2-mile tunnel. The cost was now put at £140,000 with the railway or £200,000 with the tunnel, but the scheme's opponents claimed that it would cost £700,000, and even the Basingstoke Canal Committee, strong supporters of the plan, used figures of £300,000 with the railway and £400,000 with the tunnel and Rennie, early in 1809, estimated a tunnel line at £440,790. In favour, the argument was that

the great object will be obtained of a *safe and direct communication*, at all seasons of the year, (without regard to wind or weather, and without danger of capture by an enemy, in the most perilous times) *will be opened between the Dock Yards of Chatham and Sheerness, and the Depots at Woolwich and Deptford, and that of Portsmouth and Southampton Water*, (the grand rendezvous of all expeditions to the Westward).[43]

Against, it was alleged that it was a scheme to get more water into the summit level of the Basingstoke Canal, or to enrich George Hollis the sole owner of the Itchen. By early 1809, 1,244 shares of £100 had been subscribed, and deposits of 42s (£2.10) paid on each. Then, in January of that year, probably after Rennie's rather discouraging report, the proposal was abandoned after opposition from land and mill owners. The committee said in a circular:

Your Committee regret the Necessity which led to this Resolution, but the Obstacles were manifold, and at this period apparently insurmountable.

These obstacles were clearly the great expense, the probable lack of water, and the problematical amount of trade, especially when the war should be over.

* There seems to have been an earlier survey by John Chamberlain of Chester.

Finally, in 1810 Ralph Dodd put forward a scheme to link the Basingstoke Canal at Basingstoke directly with the Andover Canal by way of Overton, Whitchurch and the valley of the Test. This also raised opposition, and was quickly dropped.

These ideas were not seriously revived again, for their purpose was partially, at any rate, served when the London–Portsmouth route by the Wey & Arun and the Portsmouth & Arundel Canals was opened.

In 1902, as a result of experiments on the Wey between Guildford and Woodbridge with electric traction, a plan was produced for a Southampton Canal, 64 miles long from the Itchen through Alton, Godalming and Guildford to Ditton on the Thames, to take 250-ton barges electrically hauled from the towpath through overhead wires, a system already used in France. The project was similar to that of the Medway & Thames Canal (see p. 100) which was authorized in the same year. But nothing came of it.

Salisbury & Southampton Canal*

At the end of 1768 Liverpool papers carried the news that James Brindley had made a general survey for a canal from Salisbury to Redbridge on the estuary of the Test, where the city's imports by sea of groceries and other goods from London were landed. It was thought that about 12,000 tons of goods a year were then passing between the two points. Brindley estimated that a canal, about 24 miles long, would cost £38,230.[44]

Robert Whitworth having been engaged in 1770 by a group of Andover promoters to survey a canal thence to Redbridge, a Salisbury committee, headed by George Yalden Fort, tried to get Brindley again to do the same for a line from their city either to the proposed Andover Canal at Kimbridge, or direct to Redbridge or Eling, also on the estuary, as well as for the old Avon Navigation line to Christchurch. Brindley, when found, was now too busy to come himself, but he offered to send an assistant. Presumably another survey was made, for in September 1771 the promoters met to consider plans and estimates. But the Andover Bill of 1772 failed to materialize, and took this project with it, though in 1774 Christopher Gullet, who came from Tavistock, proposed a line from Salisbury direct to Eling, and presented a draft Bill to a public meeting.

The idea of a canal to replace land carriage was revived in 1789

* This is the name by which the canal is usually known, though on its seal it is given as the Southampton & Salisbury Canal.

when the Andover's Bill was in Parliament. On 28 March at Salisbury, merchants and others of Redbridge and Eling met those of Andover and Salisbury 'on the business of the proposed canal'. A cut from Kimbridge to Salisbury was accepted, but the meeting decided that a further survey was needed to see whether an extension to Southampton should leave the estuary at Redbridge or Eling. The newspaper reported that 'the whole money is already subscribed for the undertaking and £750 more.'[45] The promoters then seem to have got in touch with the Basingstoke Canal committee, who had just started construction, with the idea of seeking their help in building what would have become a London to Salisbury and Southampton waterway. These commissioned a survey and estimate from Rennie, but nothing followed the Parliamentary notice of September 1790 (see p. 176).

The idea remained alive, and during the canal mania it was raised again at a meeting at Southampton Guildhall on 27 September 1792, when subscriptions were taken.[46] Out of 89 who put their names down, 30 came from Southampton, 9 from elsewhere in Hampshire, mostly from places on the canal's proposed route, only 4 from Salisbury, and 40 from the Bristol district. The heavy Bristol subscription clearly links with the support given earlier by speculators there to a Bristol–Salisbury canal (see p. 186). After the meeting, sub-committees were set up at Southampton, Salisbury and Bristol, to raise money and supervise local business, seemingly meeting together as a promotion committee with a Southampton solicitor, Thomas Ridding, as their clerk. Arguments about the route then began.

The line proposed ran from Salisbury to join the Andover Canal at Kimbridge as the Basingstoke–Salisbury promoters of 1790 had suggested; it was then to leave it lower down and run to the sea at Godshouse Tower, Southampton, with a branch to the Itchen estuary by the Navigation wharves at Northam. The Salisbury–Kimbridge part of the line was generally accepted as a useful proposal, though some interests preferred a route from Salisbury direct to the Andover Canal near Andover and then on to the Basingstoke Canal, but much argument took place over the Redbridge–Southampton–Northam section. Some preferred a direct canal from Kimbridge to the Itchen. Others, like a pamphleteer of 1793,[47] pointed out that barges were already navigated from Redbridge to Southampton and Northam along the estuaries, and that ships drawing more water than was possible at Southampton Quay could come nearly to Redbridge, whence it was reasonable to suppose the trade to Salisbury would be carried on. He calls the

Northam branch absurd, and says that the whole Southampton part serves

the private ends of a few individuals who have been the principal managers in bringing forward this farcical exhibition.

The same writer was probably the author of the following lines on the subject:

> *Southampton's wise sons found their river so large,*
> *Tho' 'Twould carry a* Ship, *'twould not carry a* barge.
> *But soon this defect their sage noddles supply'd,*
> *For they cut a snug* ditch *to run close by its side.*
> *Like the man who, contriving a hole through his wall*
> *To admit his two cats, the one great, t'other small,*
> *Where a* great hole *was made for* great puss *to pass through,*
> *Had a* little hole *cut for his* little cat, *too.**

But there were good arguments for the cut: the extensive mud-lands made small boat navigation difficult between Redbridge and Southampton, and the only landing place between them was a hard at Millbrook; in any case, narrow canal boats were not suited to the sea, even if they could have been sailed. Otherwise goods would have had to be transhipped at Redbridge. The Bristol committee of the canal's promoters were clear:

your canal can never pay if it stops at Redbridge, because it will have to encounter uncertainty which . . . will render it unproductive.

The Redbridge–Northam section was also seen as a link in a possible canal system that would connect the Kennet & Avon at Pewsey with the Andover and Salisbury & Southampton Canals on the one side, and the Basingstoke and Itchen on the other.

A possible Kennet & Avon and Andover Canal link encouraged Salisbury: an undated MS letter of this time says:

The Corporation and principals of the City of Sarum are more anxious than ever for a Communication with the Sea, Because they consider it next to a certainty that the Kennett & Avon will Join Andover by which a very great junction will be formed, & Sarum cut out without a branch to the Andover Canal.

By then, however, there were other doubts, for when subscriptions were sought from the proprietors of the Andover Canal,

---

* I have not found the origin of this verse, but when an answering pamphleteer in 1793 (*Strictures upon Strictures*, etc) says the people 'have his ballad by heart' he is perhaps referring to it. It appeared in the *Gentleman's Magazine* for September 1800, and is attributed to Henry James Pye, Poet Laureate, by Davies in his *History of Southampton*.

who ought to have been anxious to support a project which, if
successful, would have increased their own revenues, their clerk
replied on 22 January 1794:

I this day communicated your Letter of the 10th Instant to a
Meeting of the Gentlemen of the Committee of the Andover
Canal; I am ordered by them to acquaint you, they are earnest
in their wishes for the Success of the proposed Canal and very
desirous to promote it, but that it is not convenient to them to
subscribe to it.

If I hear of any Gentlemen in this Country, willing to subscribe to your proposed Canal, I will inform you thereof
immediately.

However, the Andover Company had in November 1793 agreed
to reciprocal tolls, and this put an end to arguments about the
route. Joseph Hill of Romsey had surveyed a line, and estimated
it at £47,209, but by then it was too late for a Bill in that session.
Subscription lists were reopened and easily filled, support now
coming mainly from Salisbury and Southampton, while Bristol
had lost interest. Tensions between the two former were smoothed
away, and after Hill had revised his estimate to £48,930, the Act[48]
was obtained in 1795, authorizing a capital of £56,000 in shares
and an additional £30,000 if necessary, half in shares and half on
mortgage. There were 358 subscribers, very many of them for
only £100. Only one subscription, that of Admiral Alexander
Scott at £1,100, was for £1,000 or more. Among them was
Southampton Corporation, with £500, Denys Rolle, interested in
canals in Devon,[49] and John Poore, lessee of the private wharf at
Redbridge.

It was proposed that the canal should be 27 ft wide and 4 ft
deep, to take boats 60 ft × 8 ft. From Salisbury it was to climb by
5 locks up the Avon valley to the summit level, fed by two reservoirs, by Alderbury, passing a short tunnel, to be cut and covered,
and then a longer one of some 100 yd there before falling by
15 locks down the Dun (or Dean) valley and over the river Test
by a 4-arched aqueduct to join the Andover Canal at Kimbridge.
This section was to be 13¾ miles long. From Kimbridge boats
would use the Andover Canal for 9 miles to Redbridge, where
they would enter the second part of the canal, and pass for a
further 4¼ miles to Southampton. The line ran along the edge of
the river till near the old town; then it turned inland and entered
an 880-yd tunnel that ran under the present Civic Centre, dia-
gonally across the line of the railway tunnel. When it emerged it
took a straight line along the Town Ditches parallel to the street

now called Canal Walk, passing under the old gaol, to a sea-lock at Godshouse Tower. There was a lock at the gaol, and a branch ran thence for ¾-mile to a river-lock at Northam, a little below the end of the Itchen Navigation.

Under a committee of ten from Salisbury, ten from Southampton, and two from Bristol,* and with Hill as resident engineer, cutting began on both the Southampton and Salisbury sections, the latter upwards from Kimbridge. A contract for the Southampton tunnel was let to Thomas Jenkins,† who had been recommended by the Leominster Canal Company, a somewhat doubtful compliment in view of the state of their own tunnels.[50] There was trouble with water in the tunnel almost at once, and after three shafts had been sunk, it was decided to cut and cover most of it, and to reduce its length to some 580 yd. In January 1798 Rennie was asked to come over from the Kennet & Avon to look at it, after some 200 yd had been cut. He wrote that the work was 'by no means completed, those parts that are likely to stand are ill formed and seem to have been done with little care or Judgement.' He recommended the company to employ an experienced superintendent. On 28 March the committee commented:

> it appears . . . by Mr. Rennie's Report in his Survey of the Tunnel that the work has been injudiciously done and the Materials not of that Quality for such Work and that the Contractor has not gone on with the work in the way the Committee had a right to expect.[51]

The decision to cut and cover was soon afterwards reversed, and tunnelling went on to the reduced length, Jenkins being told to put defective work right at his own cost. Three months later Rennie inspected the whole line, and reported that the works 'are generally proceeding in a workmanlike manner'.

In May 1798 the last call was made, making the full £100 per share, though an extra one was asked for as 'the men have now nearly a month's wages due'. There had already been many defaulters, and the capital had been more than expended. Part of the tunnel had been cut, the canal from the tunnel mouth to Redbridge was nearly ready though there was trouble with the embankment between the canal and the estuary, much work had been done on the sea-lock and the cut to Northam, a good deal also on the Salisbury line to the summit, but no part was yet in use and floods had damaged the works in the Dun valley.

---

* These were presumably mainly interested in a canal link between Bristol and Salisbury.
† Or Jinkins.

Mortgages were now sought, and meanwhile Rennie was asked to survey the whole line and estimate the cost of finishing it. He put James Hollingworth to measuring up the work actually done in comparison with the money paid out. When he reported in May 1799[52] he was devastating both about Hill and the contractors. Apologizing for not having done the work more thoroughly, he said that

> the extra demands of the Contractors over or above their regular Contracts, which they could not be prevailed on to deliver till the 30th ult, are such that it is out of my power to ascertain them with any degree of accuracy, and your Engineer Mr Hill is unable to satisfy me on many of the Points, where charges beyond all reason and decency are made. I should have examined the different Charges on the Spot, when I went over the work in April last,

he went on,

> But this was impossible, the Contractors being confined to their Houses to avoid the Sheriff's Officers who were in search of them.

For the Southampton to Redbridge section there was

> the Largest extra Bill I ever beheld on so small a contract—and where so few difficulties existed,

and of the whole business he observed:

> I must say . . . that I never had through my hands a work where less attention seems to have been paid to the Proprietors' interest than has been here.

A committee was therefore set up to investigate the accounts. The resulting dispute with the contractors had to be arbitrated upon by Rennie and Jessop for the company and Dadford for them.

In addition to the £57,000 already spent, £30,000 more was needed to finish the canal and pay off debts, for raising which the atmosphere was now extraordinarily unpropitious. As a first instalment the company decided to finish the work on the Southampton part other than the tunnel, and to complete also from Kimbridge to the far end of the summit, where a temporary wharf would be built where road transport onwards to Salisbury would be reasonably convenient. It was probably the work on the Southampton section which in March 1799 caused the Oxford Canal company to consider whether coal from their canal could be sent to 'southern seaports' by way of the Thames, Kennet and, by road transport, onwards to the Andover Canal. Meanwhile an appeal was made to shareholders to allow calls on their shares up to £135, to be repaid with interest from the first proceeds of the canal, but it met with almost no response. A new Act[53] was obtained in 1800, the committee explaining that they had failed to raise £15,000 by offering additional shares, but that they were convinced they could raise £30,000 on mortgage. They might need more, however, because of rising wages and material prices.[54] The Act gave authority to raise the additional £30,000 granted in the first Act entirely by mortgage, and also another £10,000, also by mortgage. Some money now came in, including £2,000 from the Andover proprietors for the Salisbury part, and in September 1800 work began again, some of it on restoring damage that had occurred in the meantime. Joseph Hill had left the company, unpaid and disgruntled, and by 1802 was bankrupt. In his place was George Jones, a former Army engineer, who had been recommended by Rennie, now in charge of the work. The latter was also getting disgruntled, for on 3 February 1801 he wrote:

> When is Mr. Jessop and myself to look for payment of our Bill for the arbitration business on the Salisbury and Southampton Canal—besides the Arbitration there is a considerable sum due to me for the former Surveys and Reports.

New contractors had been appointed, who speedily went bankrupt, informing the clerk that 'wee are sorry to be under the Disagrable nessaty of leaving the Country', whereupon George Jones used direct labour. On 26 April 1802 the committee reported:

> the Canal being now navigable to West Dean All Sorts of Merchandize in proper Barges may be carried on it by paying the regular Tolls.

West Dean was about 5½ miles from the Andover Canal junction, and seven locks higher. On 8 December 1802 the section from the Andover Canal at Redbridge to the west end of the tunnel was reported open, and by January 1803 the canal was open to the fifteenth and summit lock at Alderbury Common, beyond which was the deep cutting leading to the 100 yd tunnel, not yet begun. It was proposed to make a wharf here, and a horse railway 629 yd long on wooden rails leading to the turnpike road on a higher level. It seems likely, however, that this was not done, and that instead a wharf was made about half a mile further back at West Grimstead above the thirteenth lock and 9 miles from Kimbridge. The reservoir at West Grimstead had been made, but not the other authorized, and some cutting continued the whole length of the summit and some little way down the other side towards Salisbury. Road carriage could be used onwards to Salisbury, and at the other end to the sea and the Itchen, but the canal was not yet attractive to carriers. The tolls of 2d per ton per mile, fixed in September 1802 for goods other than manures, were lowered to 1½d in March 1803 'to cause a greater Trade'. However, business had begun. Meanwhile, back in September 1802, the committee had decided 'That four Miners be procured from Newcastle as soon as possible to work on the Tunnel at Southampton.'

At this point Napoleon suddenly impinged, and the committee records that

Mr. Jones the Engineer to the Company having served under General Craddock on the Invasion of Ireland and having offered his services to conduct the Men working on the Canal as a Corps of Pioneers in Case of actual Invasion, Resolved, That the Thanks of the Canal Company be given to them, and that their Offer be immediately forwarded to the Lord Lieutenant of Hampshire.

The company was not far off success, but it had earned a bad name, and depression set in. Shareholders would not put up more money, or even attend the general meetings, creditors wanted payment, and a tontine plan to raise £15,000 was stillborn. In July 1803 Rennie estimated that £9,950 was needed for completion, and £2,000 to repair deterioration.

In Southampton work was still necessary on the sea branch, and the gaol lock was unfinished. The Northam line seems to have been completed, for in June 1804 the clerk wrote to the shareholders that

The Salisbury and Southampton Canal is now navigable from the West End of the Tunnel to the East End of Alderbury Common, and would be to Northam (the great Depot for Coals) but for an accidental Interruption in the Tunnel.

It is not clear whether the tunnel was ever navigable. The draft minutes for 31 October 1803 say that the tunnel was opened that day, and the accounts for January 1804 include two guineas for beer on that occasion. This may, however, mean that a heading was first opened on 31 October, not that a navigable tunnel was completed.

In June also George Jones issued a writ for his salary; by then he was working on the Royal Military Canal, and advertising for his 'navigators' to join him. It went by default, and sheriffs seized portions of the canal.

The shareholders would not move, and the towns of Salisbury and Southampton showed no official interest, one concludes because it had become obvious that the canal was unlikely to carry enough traffic to make it pay. After one further attempt to raise money the company, with debts of £25,000 and works decaying for lack of care, met for the last time on 18 March 1808. Traffic on the Redbridge-tunnel section had ceased by the end of 1806, and probably soon afterwards on the Kimbridge–Alderbury line.

In 1809 Rennie wrote to the clerk asking for his bill to be paid, and was told that there were two plans for the future of the canal, but that it was difficult to get the creditors together. The clerk ends: 'It is now running to ruin very fast.' On 1 December 1834, the clerk records that 'The Proprietors have mostly resumed their Lands, pulled down the Locks and filled it up.'

The canal was to reappear once more in history. When the railway tunnel was being built, the remains of the earlier work caused difficulties to the engineers. Before that, an application had had to be made to Chancery for leave to deal with the effects of the defunct company, so that the railway could be built over part of its line. The route of the old canal was followed in part by the railway line from Southampton to Redbridge, opened 1 June 1847, and in part by the Kimbridge Junction to Salisbury (Milford) line of the Bishopstoke & Salisbury Railway, opened 27 January 1847.

Schemes for canals from Bristol to Salisbury or the Andover Canal

Projects for such connections never took definite shape, yet for some years after the canal mania they remained as shadows in men's minds, to some extent influencing their actions.

The idea of a Bristol to Salisbury Canal seems to have arisen accidentally. As we shall find (see p. 236), during the canal mania a diversionary episode in the Kennet & Avon's promotion led to the ride to Devizes in December 1792. The would-be subscribers to the Kennet & Avon gathered there seem to have decided not to waste their fares, but to subscribe to a canal to Salisbury instead, and to have opened books on the spot. The following description by a historian of Devizes probably refers to it:

From the statements of the late Mr. Lucas of Devizes, it appears, that a day having been appointed in which the public were to be allowed the luxury of subscription, a tent was erected in the Market-place for the transaction of business, at one end of which the victims were permitted to enter, and to emerge at the other. Noone was to have more than five shares, but on each of these shares eight shillings deposit had to be paid for advertising and other preliminary expenses; so that the sum paid down was in most cases £2. As the crowd were sucked in at one end of the tent and discharged at the other, they were received at the door of exit by parties waiting, either to offer premiums, or to take possession of scrip of which they were the real though not the nominal owners. Hence many amusing scenes occurred. Some who bought for others, refused to surrender their shares. Many a common fellow having mustered £2 by loan or otherwise, found himself worth £5 or £10 soon after emerging from the tent: and this barter continued all through the day, even after the subscription books were closed.[55]

One result was the number of Bristol people who subscribed to the Salisbury & Southampton Canal as a stage in the projected through route. On the other hand, we must remember that in 1790 John Rennie, surveying for a Basingstoke–Andover Canal link with a branch to Salisbury, had envisaged the latter being extended to Bath and Bristol, and Rennie was of course also concerned with the Kennet & Avon and also with mania schemes for canals to the south-west, all of which had relevance to a possible Bristol–Salisbury line. The idea got so far as to crystallize into the most practicable route, that from Pewsey on the Kennet & Avon to the Andover Canal, with a possible branch from near Ludgershall to the Basingstoke Canal also.

In February 1794 a newspaper report said that Chamberlain had surveyed a line from the Kennet & Avon at Wilcot to Salisbury, 24 miles long and with 270 ft of lockage, and another from that canal at Wootton Rivers to Andover, 16 miles and 250 ft fall. The former was estimated at £65,000, the latter at £55,000.[56] From the latter a branch could be made to the Basingstoke Canal.

The last serious reference to this projected canal appears in the Kennet & Avon minute book for 6 December 1796, when it is recorded that the chairman and others, with Rennie the engineer, met the Salisbury & Southampton committee at Salisbury. At this meeting Rennie promised to survey a linking canal. Later, there are passing mentions of the desirability of such a canal or railway.

CHAPTER IX

The River Thames
and the Canals

✦✦✦✦✦✦✦✦✦✦✦✦✦✦✦✦✦✦✦✦✦✦✦✦✦✦✦✦✦✦◆✦✦✦✦✦✦✦✦✦✦✦✦✦✦✦✦✦✦✦✦✦✦✦✦✦✦✦✦✦

THE Thames[1] was never made navigable, for it had always been so; but its navigation has been many times improved. Fish-weirs were obstructions to navigation, and later the dams built by millers to hold back their water, in which flash-locks were built to allow the passage of barges. There appear to have been about seventy of these weirs and flash-locks between London and Oxford towards the end of Elizabeth I's reign.

By a charter of 1197 the care of the river was vested in the Mayor and Corporation of the City of London. It seems as if the whole river was meant, but in fact the City's jurisdiction, which it maintained till the middle of the nineteenth century, did not for practical purposes extend beyond Staines. The rest of the river was maintained by the local communities along its banks, while the Crown exercised general supervision.

In 1605 the river was considered navigable nearly to Oxford for barges, but needing improvement from Abingdon upwards. An Act of that year therefore set up a body of commissioners to improve the navigation of the upper part of the river. These commissioners improved the navigation from Oxford to Cricklade; in 1624 a further Act replaced them by the Oxford–Burcot Commission to improve that stretch, and so complete the navigation of the whole river. The commission built three of the earliest pound-locks on an English river, at Iffley, Sandford, and Swift Ditch (Abingdon); by 1635 the work was done. These locks, unlike those of 150 years later, were of masonry. The commission, later transformed into the Commission of Sewers at Oxford, lasted till 1790, when it sold its property to the Thames Commissioners for £600.

Apart from the Oxford–Burcot Commission and the City of

19. Seal of the Thames Commissioners

London, there was no general authority to control the charges made by the millers for passing through the flash-locks, the frequency of the flashes, or the general state of the navigation. In 1695 a commission was formed from the justices in the riparian counties. A more lasting arrangement was made in 1751, when all men with a certain property qualification from the seven upper riparian counties, and representatives of Oxford University and the riverside towns, in all some six hundred, were constituted commissioners, with powers, however, only to settle rates of charge for passage and to correct abuses.

At this time there was a considerable traffic on the river. In addition to barges loading up to 75 tons for Oxford and above* and up to 200 tons lower down, there were regular services to certain towns on certain days of the week. The following list, quoted by Thacker from a source of 1746, is interesting:

To Abingdon, Newbury and Reading—weekly
To Windsor—twice weekly
To Staines—twice weekly

* Their size being limited by that of the three existing locks.

M

To Shepperton, Sunbury and Hampton—thrice weekly in summer, twice weekly in winter

To Oxfordshire—(no day given)

To Chertsey and Weybridge—twice weekly

To Walton—thrice weekly in summer, twice weekly in winter

Guildford luggage boats—(no day given)

Trade was growing, and when the City of London early in 1770 called in James Brindley, the new age of navigation had begun.

Brindley was asked to suggest how best the navigation of the lower Thames could be improved, and came back in June to say that he proposed a canal taking 200-ton craft to bypass it between Monkey Island below Maidenhead and Isleworth, with branches to the river at Windsor and Staines, and perhaps to Shepperton for access to the Wey, at a cost of £47,885. He added:

> I am credibly informed that the Expence of taking a Vessel of 100 or 120 Tons, from Isleworth to Sunning, and back again to Isleworth, is £80 and sometimes more; which, by the Canal, at the Tonnage proposed, will be £16* and may easily be performed in fifteen Hours, consequently there will be a clear Saving to the Publick of £64 out of £80 upon every Voyage: Besides . . . in the present Navigation of the River, they are three weeks in going up, and near as long in coming down, often to the great Loss and Disappointment of the Proprietor in the Damage of his Goods.

Simultaneously, each influenced by the others, plans were being considered for a Monkey Island–Reading canal and for one from Monkey Island to Basingstoke.

The Common Council in July sent him back to study the river itself. He did not like that, and took a gloomy view when he reported again in December:

> it hath been found by Long Experience, to be impassable for Barges in Time of Flood, which in most Years continues several Months during the Winter, and is out of the power of Art to remedy.

The opposite trouble, drought, could be cured by building about twelve locks and weirs,

> But the Expence of improving so large a River in this Way, will be so great, that I suppose it will not be put in practice,

he added hopefully. A cheaper way would be to contract the channel: this would improve it for downward traffic, if that upwards could use a canal. On the lower river, he proposed a weir

---

* The toll he allowed, however, to arrive at this figure was only ½d per ton per mile, a very low one for canals.

To the Committee of the Common-Council of the City of L o n d o n.

GENTLEMEN,

PURSUANT to your Inftructions, dated 27 *July*, 1770, I have made a Survey of the River *Thames*, from *Boulter*'s Lock to *Mortlake*, in *Surry*, and have made a Plan and Profile of the fame, with a Level and Fall Line, remarking the different Falls from one Town to another; and likewife have examined the moft material Obftructions and Inconveniencies that attend the prefent Navigation, which are confiderable and many; for it hath been found by long Experience, to be impaffable for Barges in Time of Flood, which in moft Years continues feveral Months during the Winter, and is out of the Power of Art to remedy. It likewife is impaffable in Time of long Droughts, for want of a fufficient Depth of Water; but this Difficulty may be removed, and the moft effectual Way to do it, would be by making Dams and (Ciftern) Locks, the Dams to pound up one to another; the Number of which may be afcertained by the Profile, which, I fuppofe, will be about twelve, for if they be made to pound more than five or fix Feet, fome of the adjacent Lands will be laid under Water, or be fubject to be foon flooded, as may be feen by the Surface of it, which are reprefented by ☉ a, &c. in the Profile. But the Expence of improving fo large a River in this Way, will be fo great, that I fuppofe it will not be put in Practice.

It is impoffible for me to tell what the Expence would be, but dare make bold to fay, it will be five or fix times the Expence of making a Canal, and when done, will be far from being fo fafe and fpeedy a Conveyance; yet the River may be made better than it is, and that at no very extraordinary Expence. The Method that I would propofe is, to contract the Channel in the fhallow and broad Places, moft of which are marked in the Plan with ᵗᶜ, ᵗᶜ, &c. By this Means a fufficient Depth of Water, I fuppofe, may be obtained in all Places, or at leaft may be made much better than it is, but the Fall will remain the fame, and the Current increafe by the increafed Depth of Water, confequently will require more Strength of Men and Horfes to draw the Barges againft the Stream; yet by this Means it may be rendered much more certain than it is, and an eafy
Navigation

20. The firft page of James Brindley's report of 12 December 1770 on the lower Thames

with two locks between Mortlake and Kew; this would prevent vessels being delayed by low tides above it, and improve access to the canal. His plan of the river shows no horse towing paths, but those for men from Brentford to Petersham, a short section at Staines, and from Windsor bridge to Boveney. It also shows the projected canal from Monkey Island to Reading.[2] Barges were then bow-hauled by groups of men, who offered themselves for hire in the towns along the river.

The City of London supported Brindley's plan for what was now called the London Canal, and a petition for a Bill to build it with two branches, and also to improve the river between Boulter's lock and Mortlake, was presented, but the plan was taken no further. Three Bills did, however, come before Parliament in 1771: those for a canal from Basingstoke by Sonning to the Thames at Monkey Island below Bray (see p. 151); supported by the inhabitants of Reading, for a line from the mouth of the Kennet there by way of Sonning to Monkey Island, much of it on a similar route to the first; and by the Thames Commissioners to reorganize themselves and to raise money, one object being to build pound-locks on the same stretch of river. Evidence on the Bill for the Reading–Monkey Island canal gives us a picture of what the Thames navigation was like. Charles Truss, barge-owner, said that the usual time for taking a 120-ton barge downstream over the 26 miles between these points was 3 to 4 days, upstream 3 to 6 days, longer in summer and flood-time. He complained that the height of mill-weirs at the nine flash-locks (including that at Reading)* had recently been increased, presumably as mills became busier, thereby causing the river to run faster when they were opened and so scour deeper. More flash-locks were needed to increase navigation depth, or pound-locks, and also a horse towing path. If these were to be built, and could give 4 ft depth, the voyage time could be cut to 20 hours. The bigger barges, of 120 to 180 tons, were accompanied by lightening boats, into which part of their cargo could be unloaded if they went aground.

Robert Whitworth had surveyed the canal, and estimated it at £51,000. It was to be some 14 miles long, to have a stop-lock at the entrance, and seven other locks, and to take 120-ton barges, the intention being that barges should take the canal when going upwards, and the river downwards. Giving evidence in support, he thought it would carry a 120-ton barge from Reading to Monkey Island in 6 hours for a toll of $\frac{1}{2}$d per ton mile. He quoted cases where upward-going barges being winched through flash-

* There were none below Staines.

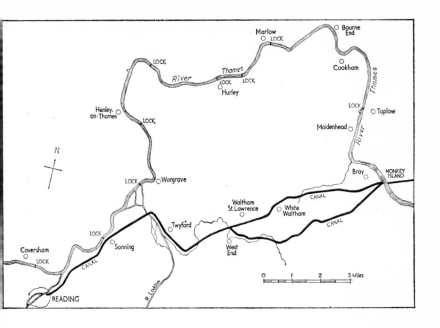

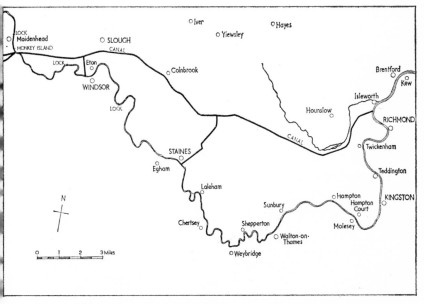

21. Routes of the Reading–Monkey Island–Isleworth canal schemes of 1770 and 1771

locks had taken three hours to pass, and had lowered the river level by 18 in to 2 ft over 3 miles in doing it. On the other hand, Joseph Nickalls, successfully opposing on behalf of the Thames Commissioners, emphasized the dangers of increased flooding at Bray, and said that were the canal to be built, the millers' income would fall so much that they would not be able to maintain the flash-locks, and that the river could be much improved by building eight pound-locks and a horse towing path between Reading and Monkey Island, though he admitted that under the Thames Commissioners' Bill the flash-lock owners would still get their tolls as well.[3] The Thames Bill was opposed by the City, which favoured the Reading–Monkey Island canal as a continuation of its own projected London Canal. However, the Reading–Monkey Island and the Basingstoke Bills failed, and that of the Thames Commissioners passed.

This enlarged their numbers by entitling all residents in the riparian counties who had £100 pa in real estate, or £3,000 in personal, to become commissioners, gave them powers to borrow, regulated charges, and divided the river into six districts: London to Staines, Staines to Boulter's Lock, Boulter's Lock to Mapledurham, Mapledurham to Shillingford, Shillingford to Oxford, and Oxford to Cricklade. However, in 1774 jurisdiction over the first district was conceded to the City of London with the same powers, except that they were not to collect tolls, but could spend £10,000 on improvements from their funds. An Act of 1777 enabled them to buy up tolls on their part of the river and substitute a single navigation toll, and this was done.

The commissioners were empowered to build and acquire towpaths (horse towing on the Thames dated from Elizabethan times, but useful paths only existed for part of the way), to acquire the old flash-locks, build pound-locks above Boulter's at Maidenhead, and make such regulations as that for the regular flash twice a week at all the mills between Oxford and Staines that was afterwards instituted.

Many hundreds of people were entitled to be Thames Commissioners by residence and property, or because of the offices they held. Above the limit of the City's jurisdiction at Staines, each of the five districts had its own committee and engineer, the latter often shared with others, and these were autonomous on ordinary matters of management. General meetings of the whole body took place as often as required: these dealt mainly with improvements, toll charges, legislation, and other matters of policy, and usually appointed sub-committees to see action through upon any decision taken. These policy meetings were regularly attended by a few active men such as William Vanderstegen, who for practical purposes were the commissioners. They had to watch for packed meetings, when supporters of a special interest tried to influence policy to suit themselves, but these were to some extent prevented by a rule that any proposed action had to be confirmed by the following meeting. On the other hand, the regulars were all active energetic men who, when they had decided upon a policy, could carry it out without worrying about shareholders or dividends, or being elected to a management committee, so long as they could raise loans and pay interest upon them.

Now and for some time afterwards the commissioners had a clerk, Henry Allnutt (later succeeded by the very competent Zachary Allnutt), but no single engineer. They supplemented the two who normally shared the work, with outside experts called in when an independent opinion was needed. It is in the light of this loose, but by no means inefficient, organization of the management of a great river that the details of the following years must be seen.

Eight new pound-locks,* all opened by 1773, were the first to be built on the river since those of the Oxford–Burcot Commission in the previous century. They were open-sided locks with timber framing to prevent barges grounding on the sloping grass banks. They were designed, and their erection supervised, by Humphrey Gainsborough, brother of the painter, who was pastor of the Congregational church at Henley, and who in 1773 was appointed Rate Collector of the locks from Hambleden to Sonning. The work does not seem to have been well done, for in 1780 the locks were reported as being in a state of decay and needing soon to be rebuilt. When the locks were finished, the bargemasters had to pay more toll, but their other expenses were so reduced that freight charges were lowered. At this time also, horse towing paths were extended, and the proportion of towing done by horses rather than men increased.

The Maidenhead–Kennet mouth stretch of river was now properly canalized, except for Cookham lock, added in 1830. Two further locks were then built upstream from Reading, Mapledurham in 1777 and Caversham in 1778.

The long pause thereafter was broken by the passing of the Thames & Severn Canal Act of 1783 (see Chapter XIV), which provided for a junction of that canal with the Thames at Inglesham a little above Lechlade, at a time when there were no locks on the

* Boulter's, Marlow, Temple, Hurley, Hambleden, Marsh, Shiplake, and Sonning.

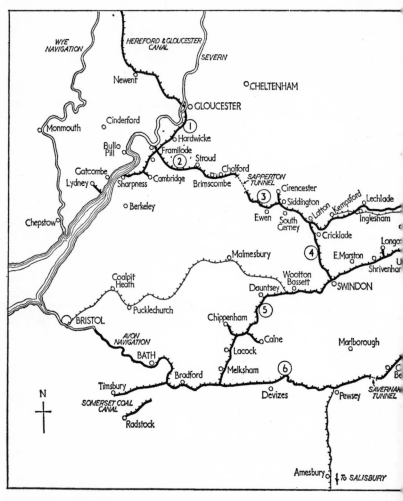

22. The Thames and its links with Severn and Avon: (1) Gloucester & Berkeley Canal; Canal; (6) Kennet & Avon Canal. The proposed routes shown are the Bristol Junction (Woot Marsworth, later Aylesbury); Hants & Berks Junction (Newbury–Old

er Navigation; (3) Thames & Severn Canal; (4) North Wilts Canal; (5) Wilts & Berks
tol); Pewsey–Salisbury; Lechlade (Kempsford)–Abingdon; Western Junction (Abingdon–
ing–Maidenhead–Isleworth, and Western Union (Maidenhead–Cowley)

Thames higher than Mapledurham except the three early seventeenth century specimens at Swift Ditch (Abingdon), Sandford and Iffley belonging to the Oxford Commission of Sewers. In the eyes of the canal company, the state of the upper Thames took on a new importance because of their hopes of creating a through water route from Staffordshire and also Bristol to Oxford, Abingdon, Reading and London.

The Thames Commissioners were ready to help within their resources. As soon as the Act passed, they sent a party to learn what the company proposed. These returned to recommend that

> should the tonage of Transportation on the Thames increase it would be but justice to render the passage of Barges up and down more safe commodious and certain.[4]

Above Oxford at that time 70-ton barges could navigate in winter, but in summer needed lightening boats because of the shoals. However, the arches of Folly, Godstow, Radcot and St John's (Lechlade) bridges were so low that with craft of this size cargo could not be piled higher than the barge sides. There was also no horse towing path.

In September of the same year Whitworth, the canal's consulting engineer, and Christopher Chambers, a shareholder in both the Thames & Severn and Stroudwater, and also a Thames Commissioner, called to enquire 'whether any and what Measures or Resolutions had been taken for amending the Navigation of the Thames from Pangbourn up to Letchlade.' What the commissioners did, they said, would influence decisions upon the size of their barges and tunnel, and

> unless great Amendments were speedily undertaken and made for facilitating the Navigation between Letchlade and Pangbourn the Utility of the Canal of Junction between the Rivers Thames and Severn would be greatly obstructed.[5]

The commissioners replied that they could not say what they could do until a survey had been carried out, but they appointed a sub-committee to take action and get a survey done.

However, they were distracted from this object by a proposal also made in 1783, seemingly by Abingdon interests with Thames & Severn support, to by-pass the upper Thames and also the three old locks above that town, which would only take 75-ton barges, by a canal from Lechlade. Robert Whitworth surveyed it in 1784, and proposed a line 22¾ miles long from Kempsford on the Thames & Severn above Lechlade to Abingdon, to avoid 45¾ miles of river. The route crossed the Thames above Inglesham by an aqueduct, and then followed the course of the river to

Fyfield, whence it swung away to Abingdon. A link with the river was proposed, from the canal near Fyfield to the Thames at Hart's Ferry between Newbridge and Appleton. The commissioners were not prepared to see this happen, and not until the Bill had been safely defeated did they again consider what ought to be done about the river above Mapledurham lock.

By this time they had a second incentive, for in 1786 the Oxford Canal Company began to extend their line southwards from Banbury to Oxford,[6] so promising the Thames a great deal of Midlands traffic. The connection was made via the Duke's Cut just above Oxford in 1790.[7] By building locks upwards from Mapledurham as far as Oxford, therefore, the commissioners would be serving the prospective trade of both canals, and at the same time increasing their own future revenue, since Thames tolls were charged not on a mileage basis but upon the number of locks passed. Whitchurch (designed by Jessop), Goring and Cleeve locks were opened in 1787, Benson in 1788, Day's in 1789, Abingdon,* Osney and Godstow in 1790, Iffley† in 1793 and Sandford† about 1795, so completing a reasonable navigation upwards from Boulter's to the Duke's Cut.

In June 1785, the threat of a possible Lechlade–Abingdon canal having receded, the commissioners sent an engineer, like a dove from the ark, to report whether the Thames & Severn, and especially its tunnel, was in fact proving practicable to build, and how long it was going to take. He returned to tell them that it was 'very practicable' and would be finished in four to seven years. Early in 1787, therefore, they asked William Jessop to survey the river from Oxford to Lechlade. He reported in March, and in its light they ordered Osney lock to be built and Radcot bridge to be enlarged. It was Josiah Clowes, resident engineer of the canal company, who advised the commissioners on Osney. Later Jessop did another survey, in which he said of the upper river:

> the great Evils that are complained of are—the want of Depth to enable Barges to carry their Burthen—the great loss of Time in waiting for flash Water; and the want of a convenient towing path for Horses.[8]

He recommended six locks above Oxford, a towing path, and improvements to the channel.

Then, at a Thames meeting on 7 February 1789, when the Thames & Severn was a year from completion, the canal company asked the commissioners to make a cut from the end of their

---

* Replacing the old Swift Ditch lock of the former Oxford–Burcot Commission.
† Replacing the older locks of the former Oxford–Burcot Commission.

waterway at Inglesham to below Buscot lock, and sent three of their shareholders led by Christopher Chambers to support their case. A second meeting in April agreed that a cut would be useful, but a third decided they had no power to make it, but that they would improve the river's course instead—a decision to which they were probably helped by friends of the powerful commissioner Edward Loveden Loveden of Buscot Park, who owned the private lock at Buscot which would have been by-passed.

The canal company, disappointed, then wrote the next day that their canal would be finished in six months, and that they 'expect and require that the Commissioners of the Rivers Thames and Isis' would improve their river 'in order that the public trade of the . . . Canal passing on the . . . Rivers may not be impeded.'[9] A sub-committee was then appointed to take charge of upper river improvements, a dredging programme above Oxford was put in hand, and, to show their willingness to co-operate, Clowes was commissioned to design pound locks at St John's (Lechlade) and Buscot, and John Nock of Daneway, a Thames & Severn mason, to build them. In July Clowes also reported on a survey he had done for the commissioners downwards from Lechlade to Old Nan's Weir just above Rushey, and his recommendations for action were preferred to Jessop's. They probably included Rushey lock, which was indeed in use before the end of the year, and Pinkhill in 1791. With St John's, Buscot, Godstow and Osney, six locks had been built above Oxford, four exclusively for the Thames & Severn. The commissioners, for all their unwieldy organization, had done well by the new canal, which had opened on 19 November 1789.

Early in 1791 the commissioners told the private weir owners between Lechlade and Oxford to put them in proper repair, and then, having authorized more expenditure on the upper river, called in Jessop to re-survey in the light of what had already been done. He was too busy, and the cantankerous, elderly Robert Mylne did the work, his temper not improved by being asked because Jessop, whom he disliked, had been too busy.

Mylne recommended the replacement of twenty-five weirs and flash-locks between Lechlade and Abingdon by a smaller number of pound-locks, the purchase of the old locks, a continuous towing path, and a deeper channel. He was downright in his opinions, saying of the upper district:

if Half a Dozen Boats were to trade constantly, from Lechlade to Oxford, and use the waters therein, in the present Way and Manner, formed and established for Trade, these Boats would all be fixed and stationary, in a short Time, for Want of Water. Any Acquisition of Trade and Motion on the River, would be the means of Stopping the Whole. It is the Height of Fallacy to say, that a Boat may now go that distance in two Days, and therefore it is a good Navigation. That may be true, in the Case of one Boat, or two Boats. But are these Boats to constitute the whole Navigation, and limit its extent?[10]

He says of navigation in the summer:

'On the Second Survey* all the Figures demonstrate such a low State of Water, that nothing could float in it above King's Wear. Barges, with very little Loading, were stuck fast on the Cills of several of the old Wears; and the Navigation Barge was often obliged to be lightened, by the Committee and the Attendants all going on shore.[11]

Finally, he says:

... I consider the Navigation, across the Island, is totally barred and locked up; unless, it is opened by the means herein recommended; or some other way, that may appear proper.[12]

Mylne's first report caused the commissioners to work upon a horse towing path. They also listened to complaints from bargemen of the tolls of 4d a ton return or 2d single for passing each of the new locks, and on 31 December 1791 cut the return toll to 2d for one year at all locks down to and including Abingdon for craft to or from the Thames & Severn, with an additional drawback of 2d a ton if the barge passed Boulter's, then the lowest lock on the river. The canal company, however, pressed for tolls to be levied on the cargo actually carried, an indication of light loadings, but this the commissioners refused as impracticable for them. But soon afterwards, as the drawback was being abused by bargemasters surreptiously changing cargoes that were ostensibly going through, they abolished it, and substituted a straight 2½d (raised to 3d in 1797) at all their locks for all trade off the Thames & Severn or the Oxford canals. They also told old lock owners to reduce their tolls where these were excessive, enquired of the City whether they in turn proposed to build locks on the river below Staines, and finished up by suggesting that the Thames & Severn should reduce its tolls as well.

The Thames & Severn Company, busily organizing its own carrying department, conscious of hope for more traffic from canals authorized to connect with the river Severn, the Worcester & Birmingham,[13] Herefordshire & Gloucestershire[14] and Leominster[15] in 1791, the Gloucester & Berkeley (see Chapter XV) in

* In July.

1793, not yet conscious of the deficiencies in their own line, still complained loudly of the commissioners. Their point of view was put to a House of Commons committee in 1793 by Christopher Chambers, a Stroudwater and Thames & Severn shareholder:

> the present State of the Navigation of the River Thames is injurious to the Thames and Severn Canal; that Applications have been made to the Commissioners to improve it, and he recollects the Improving of the River being objected to, until such Time as the Trade was brought thereon from the Canal, sufficient to satisfy the Expence; that if the Thames was put into as perfect as State as possible he thinks he should receive a fair Dividend for his Money, but now receives none; that the Canal was made in full confidence that the Commissioners of the Thames Navigation would complete their Navigation by the Time it was opened, but the Proprietors have been disappointed.[16]

The Commissioners' view was given by Vanderstegen in 1794:

> the tolls of the additional trade by that canal* did not appear, in the year 1792, to amount to more than 1000 tons: a small quantity to pay the interest of the £14,000 already expended above Oxford . . . nevertheless it merits and has received every attention of the commissioners to promote it.[17]

A bargemaster's view was that of Thomas Court before the House of Commons committee of 1793:

> That Part of the Navigation of the River from Lechlade is in a very bad Order, insomuch so, that supposing 70 Ton of Goods to be brought from Lechlade, they must have two Boats to bring them down to Brechen's weir;† another Boat is then wanting to lighten the others and bring the goods to Oxford, where one is sufficient to bring them to London . . . We have not brought any Coals down from the Severn Canal these two years; the Expences run so high we could not do it on the River . . . if the Improvements were made above Oxford, we . . . should be able to bring coal brought from the Thames and Severn Canal to Oxford, so as to be able to undersell the Coal brought to Oxford by the Banbury‡ Canal.

In 1796 the commissioners made their last concession to the Thames & Severn, when they agreed for an experimental period to charge half toll on barges going upwards empty to load at

---

* The Thames & Severn.
† Presumably Brookin's, a name used between 1789 and 1802 for Skinner's weir, 1½ miles below Bablock Hythe.
‡ Oxford Canal.

Brimscombe Port for a return voyage, and recommended private lock owners to do the same. By 1798, if not before, it was obvious that the canal was never going to bring the commissioners a return commensurate with what had already been spent in its interest on the upper river, let alone to justify more. Here are the tolls actually taken at the four uppermost locks for 1798:

	£		£
St John's	108	Rushey	98
Buscot	104	Pinkhill	88

Twelve years later, in 1810, just before the movement began to build the North Wilts Canal, the takings at St John's were only up to £154.

Below Boulter's at Maidenhead, there were no pound locks on the river. In 1789, the proposals for canals from Reading to Maidenhead, and from Maidenhead to Isleworth, were revived as part of the discussions on the state of the river, exemplified in a report of 1789 that although the channel should by law have a depth of 3 ft 10 in, yet

> great Obstructions for a considerable Time have in the Course of the last Summer and at other Times happened at Laleham and other Parts of the River to almost Richmond, by Barges laden to the Depth of 3 Feet 10 Inches, when the Water at those Places was not sufficient for such Barges to proceed.[18]

A joint inspection by the City authorities and the commissioners was made, and they agreed that the channel was reasonably clear, but that the towpaths needed improvement, and that the private sections where the farmers claimed the right to tow should be bought out. They found the worst obstructions in the lower part of the river, Laleham, Chertsey, Walton, and Sunbury being specially mentioned:

> the shallows we observed in this Part of the River, appear to us to be much more essential and difficult of Remedy than in the upper Part; and although the City have tried by Breakwaters, or Under-water Weirs, and by turning the Water of Side Channels into the navigable Stream, to remedy the Inconveniences (which have in many places had a good effect) yet there still remains many Places that are greatly obstructed by Shoals and Shallows at Low Water.[19]

In 1790 Charles Truss, clerk to the Navigation Committee of the City, published a pamphlet, *Considerations on the present State of the Navigation of the River Thames from Maidenhead to Isleworth*, which revived Brindley's 1770 proposal for a Maidenhead–Isleworth canal. The commissioners saw no advantage in a canal, but readily agreed that three locks were needed, and decided to promote the necessary bill. They decided, however, first to see how far the City would get with its canal. As no Bill was introduced in the 1792–93 session, they asked Robert Mylne to survey this part of the river. His report was made in August 1793, and came down in favour of a canal, though a shorter one from Boulter's to Eton, 4¾ miles long with three locks. Immediately afterwards, he was appointed joint engineer with Whitworth (who had worked with Brindley on the 1770 project) of the proposed London Canal.* A month later the canal promoters announced that they were preparing a Bill for Parliament, but nevertheless the commissioners decided to go ahead with one of their own for locks on the river. But then a meeting in February 1794, packed by canal supporters and with both Mylne and Whitworth present, reversed this decision, reaching the conclusion that

> pound Locks between Maidenhead and Staines would not be an effectual Remedy for the present Inconveniences of the Navigation . . . but would be attended with serious Injury to the Landowners, Inconveniences to the Country, and at an Expence which it is conceived the trade of the said River will not bear.[20]

The two sides then got together, perhaps encouraged to do so by the promoters of the new Kennet & Avon Canal from Bristol and Bath to Newbury and Reading (see Chapter X) who were talking of an extension canal from Reading by Windsor to London. As a result, the canal Bill already in Parliament was withdrawn and Rennie was called in to do another survey, this time of the whole river from Maidenhead downwards, including the City's section. It was expensive—Rennie charged the commissioners alone £478—but it was worth it. His report at the end of July 1794 encouraged them and discouraged the canal supporters, who thereupon dropped their scheme. In the autumn of 1795 an authorizing Act was passed, and in December, Romney lock near Windsor, the first below Boulter's, was ordered to be built. It was finished a year later. This Act, as well as enabling locks to be built below Boulter's, empowered the commissioners to buy private locks and weirs, take extra tolls arising from new trade through them, extend the horse towing path, and borrow more money.

Before this, canal schemes and actualities were coming to the commissioners from all directions. In 1790, when the Oxford

---

* This London Canal project is not to be confused with Brindley's 1770 scheme, or with the Regent's Canal, early plans for which went under this name.

Page 205 Stroudwater Navigation: (*above*) what is presumably the committee-boat passing Stonehouse church in 1781. Note that men are bow-hauling the following barge—a horse towing path was not built until much later; (*below*) a barge in Framilode basin c 1900. Beyond the lock lies the Severn

Page 206 (above) Stroudwater Navigation: *Gertrude* at Hilly Orchard bridge, Ebley, c 1900; (below) Thames & Severn Canal, South Cerney locks, c 1875

Canal joined the Thames by the Duke's Cut, a through route was created between such Midlands towns as Coventry, Birmingham and Manchester, and those of the river down to London. In March 1792 a proposal was made for a canal to leave the Oxford at Hampton Gay, six miles north of the city, and run to Isleworth, so that the Midlands traffic might avoid the river passage. This project, the London & Western[21] or Hampton Gay Canal, was supported by the Oxford Canal Company and also by the Thames & Severn as a means of bypassing the Thames. In July of the same year a rival group planned another such route, the Grand Junction, but this time leaving the Oxford Canal much higher up, at Braunston.[22] The latter did not much perturb the commissioners, for they had not realized what potential trade this route had: 'it does not appear that it would divert the Trade of the Thames unless such as might otherwise come thro' the Oxford Canal';[23] the former, much nearer the river, did, and they disliked both because they feared they might tap sources of Thames water. They opposed both, and were satisfied to see the Grand Junction prevail over its competitor. It was completed from Braunston to Brentford and Paddington in 1805, and diverted to itself almost all the trade between London and the Midlands. Indeed, the commissioners said in 1811 that traders at Oxford often preferred to send their goods to London by the Oxford and Grand Junction Canals, $157\frac{1}{2}$ miles, than by the Thames, 118 miles, and that goods from London had even been carried to Abingdon by way of Braunston.

At the time of the canal mania of late 1792, both schemes had found numerous supporters, and a problem had arisen, not for the last time. The commissioners had to minute:

It is highly improper . . . for a Subscriber to or person interested in any intended Canal which appears likely to deprive the Thames of its Trade or Water or otherwise injure that River to act or vote as a Thames Commissioner in any question that may be agitated relative to such Canals or the opposition to be made thereto.[24]

In 1794 the Kennet & Avon Canal was authorized, and in 1796 the Wilts & Berks (see Chapter XII) from the Kennet & Avon by way of the Vale of White Horse to Abingdon. There were also a number of projects, only one of which, the North Wilts, succeeded. Before we look at these, it may be useful to glance at the river generally as it was in the first few years of the nineteenth century.

Twenty-five pound-locks had been built, only one so far below

N

Boulter's, Romney near Windsor in 1797; those from Abingdon upwards being of stone and the rest of oak. The locks from St John's at Lechlade to Godstow were 110 ft long and 14 ft broad to take 70-ton barges, the rest 120 ft long and 18 ft broad to take 150-ton barges. In addition to the pound-locks, there were about nine flash-locks in use, and a number of disused flash-locks which had been replaced by pound-locks, but for which tolls were still payable. Twice a week a flash was organized from Lechlade downwards, the water travelling at 1 mph and taking three days to reach Sonning. In between flashes, if a barge were coming up, and especially below Windsor where there were no flash-locks, low water meant that

> the barge lies still, the bargemen are idle, or mischievous, through want of employment, the owner is delayed in his freight, and the freighter in his goods.[25]

The worst voyages were on this part of the river, yet the receipts of the City for the section from Teddington to Staines were not far short of those of the commissioners for the whole of the rest of the Thames.

In 1805 Jessop and Rennie surveyed the river from Kew to Boulter's lock for the City committee considering Thames improvements. They thought that the Kew–Staines section might be improved by contracting the channel to get more depth, so that 9 or 10 horses might replace 12 or 13, but that it would be more sensible to build a number of long cuts and five pound-locks. They thought the Staines–Boulter's section much worse than it had been in 1795, except for the one Romney lock. Yet it could be made a good navigation at reasonable cost. The proposal for long cuts was strongly opposed by landowners, and in 1809 Rennie suggested 9 pound-locks instead. The six in the City district were then built, Teddington at the tidal limit in 1811, Sunbury in 1812, Chertsey and Shepperton in 1813, Penton Hook and Molesey in 1815. These were followed, in the length between Staines and Windsor, by Bell Weir in 1817–18 and Old Windsor in 1822, and between Reading and Abingdon by Culham in 1809 and Clifton in 1822. Finally, Boveney and Bray above Staines in 1838 and 1845 respectively, and Cookham below Maidenhead in 1830, completed the tale of pound-locks in the canal age.

The biggest barges used to any extent were the same as those used on the Kennet, flat-bottomed craft carrying 128 tons and measuring 109 ft in length, and 17 ft in width. Barges from 90 to 128 tons were called Western or Westcountry barges; there were also smaller barges of 50 to 60 tons, and narrow canal boats which

The RIVERS THAMES and ISIS, Upper Districts.

THIS Ancient and important Navigation begins from the City's Jurisdiction, at the City Stone near Staines, and extends to Letchlade in Gloucestershire, being 109 miles in length, and is divided into 5 Districts; the 2nd is from Staines Stone (where the 1st or lowest ends by preceding Account) to Boulters Lock, and passes by *Windsor*, (population 4.993) and *Maidenhead*, (pop. 1.047) — The 3rd thence by *Marlow* (pop. 3.764) *Henley* (pop. 3.850) *near Reading* (pop. 9.742) to Mapledurham lock; — the 4th thence by *Wallingford* (pop. 2.900) to Shillingford Bridge; — the 5th thence by *Abingdon* (pop. 4.356) to *Oxford* (pop. 11.694) — and the 6th thence to *Letchlade* (pop. 1.200) —— By the Powers and Authorities in the Acts of Parliament of 24th Geo. 2nd and 11th 15th 28th and 35th Geo. 3rd the management of these Districts of the Thames and Isis, is placed in disinterested Commissioners, consisting of the Gentlemen residing in the Counties bordering the Rivers; the Commissioners thus authorised, have raised by several Loans 66.800£. and have expended the same, with the annual surplus of the Tolls, in making 27 Poundlocks, (being mostly 120 feet long and 18 feet wide) and nearly as many short side Cuts in which they are erected, in places where the Water has anciently been penn'd up, for the purpose of working Mills or for fishing: also great sums of Money have been expended, in making a convenient Horse-towingpath along the whole Navigation, and in ballasting the Channel of the Rivers, where necessary, and other Amendments, so as for Vessels to navigate without obstruction at 3 feet 10 inches depth at all Seasons: and the Commissioners have made Bye-laws and Regulations, to keep the navigable Channel always clear and open for Traders to navigate; and for the Water being let down in low water times by flashes, at stated periods: and have fixed Watermarks, to regulate the height the Water is to be kept for the Navigation : From the Effects of these extensive Amendments, and Regulations the Navigation is rendered safe, certain, and expeditious ; and the supply of Water is generally very abundant, from the many tributary Streams coming into the Thames : — Barges go downwards generally from 25 to 35 miles a day, and upwards from 20 to 30 miles a day; and the *Price of Carriage* has been reduced to only *Two-pence farthing per ton per mile*, which is much lower than Canals when compared, notwithstanding the circuity of the Rivers. —— The TOLLS are 3*d.* a ton each Voyage at each Poundlock, being only 6*s.* 9*d.* a ton for 218 miles of improved Navigation ; (besides a small Toll of about 2*s.* a ton throughout to the Weir Owners) and the great Trade on the Thames has been sufficient with this small Toll, to keep the Works in repair, to spend yearly a considerable Sum for New Works, and to lay bye a fund for Emergencies . — A Drawback of half these Tolls is allowed by the Commissioners on Barges going either way empty, or one Quarter of these Tolls, on Barges going either way only half laden.

	Per Ton.	Prices by Land Per Ton.
The PRICE of CARRIAGE of Goods from London to Windsor or Maidenhead by WATER, is	£.- 9s. 0d.	£.1 10s. 0d.
Do. —— Marlow or Henley - - - - - - -	12 0	2 5 0
Do. —— Reading or Caversham - - - - - -	15 0	2 10 0
Do. —— Wallingford or Bensington - - - - -	18 0	2 18 0
Do. —— Abingdon or Oxford - - - - - - -	1 2 0	3 5 0
Do. —— Faringdon or LETCHLADE - - - -	1 8 0	4 0 0

TABLE OF DISTANCES.

From London,

MILES.									
37	*to Staines,*								
45	8	*Windsor,*							
52	15	7	*Maidenhead,*						
60	23	15	8	*Marlow,*					
69	32	24	17	9	*Henley,*				
78	41	33	26	18	9	*Reading,*			
96	59	51	44	36	27	18	*Wallingford,*		
110	73	65	58	50	41	32	14	*Abingdon,*	
118	81	73	66	58	49	40	22	8	*Oxford,*
146	109	101	94	86	77	68	50	36	28 *LETCHLADE.*

23. The upper Thames—a page from Zachary Allnutt's *Useful and Correct Account of the Navigation,* 1810

usually travelled breasted-up* on the river. Of the Western barges Frederick Page wrote:

It is obvious . . . that vessels of this description do not easily obey the helm, and therefore the steersman is assisted by barge-men, who, with large ashen poles from 14 to 19 feet in length, with incredible dexterity, keep the barge in the proper navigable channel. The occupation of a bargeman requiring not only strength and activity but considerable experience and local knowledge, is very lucrative. The number of persons requisite to work the largest barges, is six men and one boy. One of the men, who has the care of the vessel, and who defrays the ton-nage, &c. is called cost-bearer, or captain. With the stream downwards, these barges of 128 tons require only one horse, with which they travel after the rate of three or three and one half miles in the hour; but against the stream in the upward passage, from 8 to 14 are necessary, according to circum-stances.[26]

The goods carried downwards on the Thames were in bulk more than twice those carried upwards. The downward cargoes were cheese from Lechlade and Abingdon; the products of corn ground at the riverside mills; wool; timber, mainly beech from Oxfordshire and Buckinghamshire; and paper from the mills on the river Wye, which flows into the Thames near Cookham. In, addition, there were goods brought onto the river by the canals mainly coal. This came from the Midlands on the Oxford Canal, from Somerset on the Kennet & Avon and the Wilts & Berks, and from Wales, Shropshire, Staffordshire, and the Forest of Dean on the Thames & Severn. It competed all along the river down to Reading with the Newcastle coal imported into London that was the main upwards traffic.

The average tonnage carried on the commissioners' part of the river for the seven years 1798 to 1804 was 655,303; the average receipts for that period were £8,398 and expenditure £7,234, in-terest on loans accounting for £3,040 of the latter sum, the balance being mainly for salaries and maintenance. The revenue obtained in proportion to tonnage is very much less than is usual in canal accounts—in its heyday the Kennet & Avon took about five times as much for carrying half the tonnage—and though the figures are partly accounted for by the predominance of short hauls below Reading, they also show the low maintenance costs of river navi-gation and explain to some extent the failure of canal schemes designed to compete with the Thames. On the other hand, the

* Lashed side by side.

Thames Commissioners had to borrow all their money and pay interest on it. They were not cushioned against adversity by being able to pass a dividend, and each improvement they made had to be judged by its ability to earn interest on its capital cost.

The tolls paid by the bargemasters to the commissioners (3d per ton per pound-lock) or to the City (4d per ton per voyage), were not the only payments they made; there were also tolls to the owners of the old locks and weirs. A load of five tons passing from Teddington to Lechlade would have paid 16s 5½d (82½p) to the City and the commissioners, and another 8s 9½d (44p) to the old owners. The freight cost would have been another £10 if the journey was upwards, or £7 10s (£7.50) downwards; the journey would have taken eight days on average upwards, and five down, and would have been interrupted for more than twenty days on an average each year on account of floods. These charges were much less than by road. In 1814, the cost of transport from London to Reading was said to be 2s 6d (12½p) per ton by road, and 11d by river. The intending consignor might have dispatched his goods after reading such an advertisement as this in his local newspaper, the wording of which remained much the same through the years:

All Gentlemen, Tradesmen, and others, who send Goods by Water to Lechlade, and Places adjacent, are hereby desired in future (if they expect quick Despatch) to order their Goods to the care of Mr. Rich. Day, Jno. Brook's Wharf, London, who will carefully expedite the Conveyance of all Goods committed to his Care with Punctuality to Wm. Prentice, Wharfinger, Lechlade.[27]

At this time the river was mainly used for carrying goods, and not for pleasure, but a local history[28] records that in 1806 the Reading Book Club invited 'a select party' of seventy-four to accompany them 'in a capacious barge, covered by an awning decorated with festoons', to Lord Malmesbury's seat at Park Place, Henley. The party danced home on the barge. 'It was universally agreed that twelve hours were never spent in more rational amusement or more engaging society.' Five years later a party of young men made an excursion to Sonning 'in a large boat towed by a horse'. Rowing at Reading began in the thirties, and the annual regatta in 1842. In that decade also water excursions and parties became more popular, and the change began in the use and appearance of the river with which we ourselves are so familiar.

On the lower river the difficulties of navigation had caused the

Basingstoke Company to become interested in a proposal of 1802 in connection with the Grand Surrey Canal to make a cut from Kingston to the river Wey. The Basingstoke Company said:

> there could be no doubt, but that the Thames, and Severn; the Kennett, Basingstoke, Weybridge Barges, and indeed, all the Barges going up the River, to Staines, Windsor, &c. would use it . . . it is highly the Interest of these several Companies to unite their Endeavours to get this Scheme effected; the Difficulty, Danger, and Expences, of haling the Barges up the Thames, proving a heavy Drawback from the Profits of the Navigation. To the Basingstoke Company, this Object is peculiarly interesting. As until a more safe and convenient Passage between London and Weybridge, shall be made, it will be vain to talk of any Extension, either to Newbury, Southampton or Portsmouth.[29]

The protests from the Basingstoke Company continued, but nothing more was heard of the project.

In 1811 a petition was presented for a Bill to authorize a canal from the river at Thames Ditton via Esher, Leatherhead and Dorking to Holmwood Common near Capel, but it did not conform to standing orders, and was dropped.[30]

Higher up, the shareholders of the Kennet & Avon, opened in 1810, with varying support elsewhere, put forward three plans for bypassing the Thames, the second and third with some persistence. The first was for a canal from the Kennet mouth to the Thames at Windsor, and from the river again at Datchet to Isleworth: this was a scheme contemporary with the Kennet & Avon's own Act, which was revived again in 1811, but became progressively less attractive as the Thames below Reading was improved.

The second was for a line from near Maidenhead to Cowley on the Grand Junction, usually called the Western Union,[31] which would have enabled Kennet & Avon traffic to bypass the river except for the Kennet–Maidenhead section. This was sometimes linked with a revival of old ideas for a Kennet-mouth to Maidenhead canal. Plans were deposited in 1795. It was raised again in 1810. In 1815 the Kennet & Avon Canal committee gave to its shareholders, as one of the three reasons for the low dividend of that year, 'the circuitous course of the River Thames, and the impediments on its navigation.'[32] The committee, after studying a report and plan by Francis Giles based on a survey by Rennie, recommended the Western Union idea as shortening the time to London and opening a communication to the north, but said that no estimates had been made. In July 1819 the committee reported that plans were in preparation, and that a meeting would be called before the application to Parliament. The canal, only 12 miles long, seemed a reasonably practicable proposition: it was finally estimated at £130,000, to be found by the Kennet & Avon and Grand Junction proprietors between them. After a brisk interchange of pamphlets between Zachary Allnutt, clerk to the Thames Commissioners and the canal proprietors, a Bill was introduced, but withdrawn in 1820 after passing its second reading. In the following year the Kennet & Avon told its shareholders that 'the depressed state of the Trade and Commerce of the Country forbids them, for the present, from holding out any prospect of carrying such a measure into effect.'[33] The idea remained alive till about 1828.

The third of the Kennet & Avon proposals, for a link between Newbury and Old Basing, the Hants & Berks Junction, probably dates back to 1778, for in 1810 it is said that

The Proprietors of the Basingstoke Canal will see in this the completion of their original design[34]

and in 1825

This measure is not new, but was in the year 1778 when the Basingstoke Canal Act passed in Contemplation and that great Undertaking would not have been compleated but under the full Expectation of this Extension to the Kennet which want of Capital alone prevented taking place long ago.[35]

Certainly it was suggested in a letter to a newspaper in 1793[36] and in the Basingstoke Canal report of 1802. In 1810 a notice stating that they proposed to apply for an Act was issued by the Basingstoke Company. The Kennet & Avon supported the idea;* but the times were unpropitious, and nothing further was done till 1824, when it was again revived, apparently by the Basingstoke Company. Francis Giles surveyed it, and the Basingstoke and Kennet & Avon Companies each subscribed £10,000 to the capital of the new concern. To pay the deposit, to advance money for the cost of the survey, and to prepare their canal for the expected increase of traffic, the former company had to suspend interest payments on its bond debt.

Giles proposed a canal 13 miles long with a ½-mile tunnel, an inclined plane, and a number of locks. A Bill was introduced in

* It was presumably as an extension of this project that in 1810 the Kennet & Avon was discussing a possible junction with the Grand Surrey, either by a direct line from Newbury to Vauxhall, or by leaving the Basingstoke Canal at Woking and extending thence to Vauxhall.

of a River are judiciously aided by artificial means, it has clearly the superiority over a common Canal; *a fortiori* over an uncommonly bad one: that the Basingstoke is about the worst possible Canal, and, from the want of water, is unsusceptible of improvement; while the Thames is of all the Rivers in the kingdom the first, as in all other respects, so also for the purposes of navigation: that to this end its natural advantages are great; that by art they have been made greater, and improved to a high state of perfection: that its preservation is of the very first importance to the Metropolis, and to the Country at large: that it is on behalf of the Nation that we claim for it protection at your hands: that it is the property of the Nation; a property of extreme value, and exposed to various injuries: that, as our Representatives therefore, you are called upon to guard it with a jealous vigilance, seeing that it is not more beautiful and magnificent than conducive to public utility: for, instead of resembling those mountain streams, which are mere brooks in summer, and absolute torrents in winter, the Thames merits to the very letter the well-known eulogium pronounced upon it nearly two centuries ago;

24. Counsel for the Thames Commissioners on the Hants & Berks Junction Canal Bill of 1825 praises the Thames

the session of 1824, was strongly opposed by the landowners and the Thames Commissioners, who were naturally anxious not to lose the traffic from the Kennet & Avon, and failed. The Bill was re-presented in 1826, again failed, and the idea was finally dropped in 1829.

Higher up the river, the Wilts & Berks was opened to Abingdon in 1810. Before that, however, the company had proposed to carry its canal over the Thames there, and on past Aylesbury to join the Grand Junction Canal at Marsworth near Tring. This proposed Western Junction Canal (see p. 281) was lost in Parliament in 1811, but was several times revived, sometimes as the Aylesbury & Abingdon Canal, and remained a threat to the Thames until about 1828.

Finally, a Bristol Junction Canal was proposed by the Wilts & Berks in 1810 to link their line to the Thames & Severn, so giving Gloucester and the latter an all-canal line, though a partially narrow-boat one, as far as Abingdon and, if the Western Junction were also to be built, to London. The commissioners naturally opposed it strongly, and were successful at first, but after a Parliamentary battle another Bill was passed in 1813, and what was now called the North Wilts Canal (see p. 283) was built from Latton on the Thames & Severn to Swindon on the Wilts & Berks, and opened in 1819.

E. L. Loveden, MP, the owner of Buscot Park and a prominent commissioner, in a report written to the commissioners in 1810,[37] took a gloomy view of the river's ability to compete with these canals if they were built. Of the North Wilts he writes:

The present trade from the Thames and Severn Canal, which pays 3d. per ton at 26 locks, is not inconsiderable; . . . We must, however, extend our view. The Thames and Severn trade is but beginning to show itself, and will in all probability increase in a tenfold ratio.

He says of the Marsworth proposal:

we may be satisfied the whole London trade will use the Marsworth line, if executed.

He also writes in general comment on these two proposals:

The Old Lock Owners will obviously be greatly injured if these cuts take place, and the Thames creditors also. The schemes, however, are brought forward with great arrogance; no permission asked, no compensation offered. Confiding in the supposed omnipotence of the Grand Junction Company, projectors think they can carry on their plans without any regard to public or private property, or rendering any satisfaction for

the loss it may sustain. That Company is certainly very powerful, much more so, perhaps, than Parliament should have suffered. The Commissioners are held in contempt: they are called
a rope of sand. It is to be hoped, however, they will act together,
and all the districts unite in resisting the confederacy and conspiracy against old Father Thames, and saving that royal river
from its meditated destruction.

In 1816 nine members of the City's committee for executing
Thames improvements made a round trip in their shallop: up the
river to Reading, through the Kennet & Avon, up the Severn to
Framilode, and back by the Stroudwater, Thames & Severn, and
the Thames. Their report commented upon the river navigation:

6th district (Oxford–Lechlade): This had been improved since
1811, especially its towpath, but there was much work to be
done in dredging, easing corners and improving the path if
traffic were not to go by the North Wilts;

5th district (Shillingford–Oxford): locks out of repair and inconvenient from the absence of lockkeepers, the number of
ferries,* and the aits between the channel and the towpath;

4th district (Mapledurham–Shillingford): the same comments, and
of the locks, the 'lock-keepers should reside at them, or be so
arranged as to assist effectively at the numerous Ferries';

3rd district (Boulter's–Mapledurham): lockkeepers' houses being
built; other comment as for the fifth district;

2nd district (Staines–Boulter's): the worst of all, the towpath 'extremely inconvenient', and new cuts and locks wanted.

Their conclusion was that the Thames was not good enough
for the trade the canals were bringing to it, and, as we saw earlier,
more locks were to be built.

By 1810 £66,800 had been borrowed by the commissioners; and
taking the average of the years 1816–20 receipts had risen to
£11,141 and expenses to £11,063, of which about £3,600 was for
interest. On the City part of the river the estimated annual income
was in 1812 given as £16,471, and the expenditure as £15,023. In
1825 the debt of the commissioners had reached £85,000, and in
1832 their receipts reached their highest point at £13,069. The
revenue collected above Reading, however, did not pay the cost
of maintenance, the balance arising from the Staines–Reading
portion. For the years 1829–32 the average receipts of the City for
the portion from Staines to Teddington were £14,375. In 1829 for
the first time, and for the moment temporarily, lockkeepers were
ordered to bring pleasure boat receipts into their accounts. Pre-

* To carry the horses over where the towpath changed sides.

viously they had been allowed to keep such receipts as there were from this source.

Lastly, a foretaste of new ways was given in 1818 when permission was given 'by way of experiment' to Marcus Parsons of Newbury to operate a vessel with a steam engine for towing boats, and a reminiscence of the old in 1832 when forty-three emigrants to America went by barge from Caversham on their way by river and canal to Liverpool.

From the early 1830s, the talk was not of building canals or improving the river navigation, however, but of railroads and locomotive engines. At the beginning of the railway age, the Thames below Reading was of great importance. Not only did London–Reading traffic and that to and from intermediate points pass along it, but it was part of the London–Bristol route by way of the Kennet & Avon. Higher up, there was a good deal of interchange traffic between that canal at Reading, the Wilts & Berks at Abingdon and the Oxford Canal at Oxford, as well as movement of cargoes to and from points on the stretch of river between Reading and Oxford. Above Oxford there was less traffic, for after the opening of the North Wilts most of the through trade from Gloucestershire used the Wilts & Berks route via Swindon and Abingdon, while the Thames carried only local trade from Lechlade down to Oxford.

Opposing the London and Reading 'Western Railway' Bill of January 1834, the commissioners said that the Thames, 'under the administration of a numerous body of Commissioners . . . acting gratuitously' had become 'one of the most perfect river navigations in the kingdom', on which over £250,000 had been spent. The commissioners' debt was then about £95,000, on which interest of £4,500 pa was being paid. The tolls were barely enough to cover this and to pay for repairs and management. Much of the revenue came from the section below Reading, due to the Kennet traffic, and any falling off would be hazardous. They had the 'assured conviction that so useless a scheme—useless as concerns the public—producing the most serious public and private injuries, without affording any real public benefit' should be dropped. But the Great Western was authorized, and opened to Reading in March 1840 and through to Bristol in June 1841. In 1841, also, the Oxford Railway was promoted from Didcot to Oxford. It was opposed by the Oxford Canal interest, headed by the Warden of Wadham as chairman of the canal company, but was carried. The line was opened in June 1844.

Competition with the river was now severe. The commissioners,

25. Shooting a weir (probably Hart's) on the Thames in 1868—if you were unlucky

who earlier had steadfastly refused to cut tolls to help the canals, themselves fell into similar difficulties. In 1844 they made a 20 per cent reduction, but in 1850 had to announce that owing to railway competition they could only pay 4 per cent on their 5 per cent bonds. Meanwhile, on the City's part of the river downwards from Staines, receipts had fallen from £16,000 in 1839 to less than £8,000 in 1849.

By 1865 the commissioners had no money available for maintenance. The Oxford Company, knowing this, themselves had a Thames Repair Fund for their engineer's use should any accident occur between Oxford and Wallingford to impede navigation. In the following year the commissioners' £90,000 of debt was quoted at 2s (10p) per £100 bond.

Since 1840 there had been legal arguments between the Crown and the City upon the ownership of the bed and soil of the river. The City was finally overborne and withdrew its claim, after which the Thames Conservancy was formed to take responsibility in 1857 for the river up to Staines. In 1866 an Act transferred the rest of the river up to Cricklade to the Conservancy. The preamble said that traffic and receipts had greatly diminished to the point where income was insufficient to defray expenses, but that were locks and weirs to be kept in good condition and moderate tolls levied, traffic, and so income, would increase. The Act therefore

26. Shooting Hart's weir about 1908—if you were lucky

took away the rights of old lock and weir owners to take tolls and provided no compensation, but relieved them of maintenance obligations. These old tolls were considerable. On the upper river, for instance, the following sums could be levied per loaded barge: Eynsham weir 2s 9d (13½p); Pinkhill weir, 1s 6d (7½p); Skinner's weir, 1s 6d (7½p); Ridge's weir 1s 6d (7½p); Rose's, Shifford, Duxford, Tenfoot and Tadpole weirs, 2s (10p) each.[38] All were abolished.

The Conservancy built a new lock at Osney, Oxford, in 1884, and proposed to close the river for two months to do it, much to the annoyance of the Oxford Canal Company. The former then agreed to provide means of transhipping cargoes while the work was done, and to give toll rebates. At the beginning of 1886, negotiated through tolls from the Birmingham area to London via the Oxford Canal were introduced, in an effort to compete with the Grand Junction's line. In the 1890s, at a time when there was hope that traffic by the Thames & Severn Canal could be revived, the Conservancy improved the upper river by four additional locks, at Radcot (1892), Grafton and Northmoor (1896) and Shifford (1898). Below Teddington also, the Richmond half-tide lock was opened in 1894.

The Conservancy now turned for their revenue more and more to the sale of water to the London water companies and to pleasure traffic. By the time of the Royal Commission of 1906 the commercial traffic had largely fallen back below Staines; it was as follows:

	tons
Traffic between Teddington and Staines	282,500
Traffic on the river above Staines	70,598
Traffic to and from the Wey Navigation	29,484
Traffic to and from the Kennet & Avon	3,974
Traffic to and from the Oxford Canal	19,610
Traffic to and from the Thames & Severn	425
Interchange traffic between these canals via the Thames	1,252

For the river above Staines the barge tolls, mainly from steam barges, were only £1,427 in 1906, against a revenue of £6,685 from pleasure traffic. In 1908 the Thames below Teddington was transferred to the Port of London Authority. Since then the pleasure traffic has enormously increased, and the commercial has fallen to some 50,000 tons, mainly below Shepperton.

CHAPTER X

The Kennet & Avon Canal

THE two river navigations of the Avon and the Kennet were built independently, and pursued their own lives until, three-quarters of a century after each had been completed, they were joined by the Kennet & Avon Canal[1] to make part of a through waterway from Bristol to the Thames at Reading, and so to London.

River Avon (Bristol)

From medieval times the tidal part of the river Avon from the Severn to Hanham Mills above Bristol, had been under the jurisdiction of the corporation of Bristol, and was greatly used by craft coming up to the town, then, after London, the greatest port in England.

Plans had been made since Elizabeth's reign for a canal to join Bristol and London by way of the Avon, and powers to make the river navigable were granted to Bath in 1619. It may have been as a step in such a scheme, as well as a project of local importance, that the corporation of Bath in the session of 1699–1700 petitioned Parliament for powers to make the Avon navigable from the tidal limit at Hanham Mills to Bath. Somerset Quarter Sessions opposed the project, and also many gentry, farmers, and traders who considered that they would be harmed by competition from goods carried cheaply by water. The Bill was therefore withdrawn. Some years later the corporation promoted a second Bill. Once more there was opposition, from land carriers, landed gentry who thought the import of food from Wales and other places where the value of land was low would render them unable to pay their taxes, and others. This time, in May 1712, the Bill was passed,[2] but nothing was done till 1724, when John Hobbs, a Bristol merchant, joined with thirty-one others, including such notabilities as Ralph Allen, to form a company, in which each held one share, to which the interest of the corporation of Bath was transferred. Six locks were built upon the 11½ miles of river (the engineer is said to have been John Hore, later of the Kennet), and on 15 December 1727 the first barge arrived at Bath, carrying 'Deal-Boards, Pig-Lead, and Meal'. Throughout the century there was no horse towing path, and the barges were hauled by men. The cost of making the navigation seems to have been about £12,000.

The purposes which had moved the corporation to apply for the Act of 1712 are reflected in the preamble:

Whereas the clearing, making and effecting a Passage for Boats, Lighters, and other Vessels upon the River Avon . . . will be very Beneficial to Trade, Commodious and Convenient for the Persons of Quality and Strangers (whose resort thither is the principal Support of the said City of Bath), advantagious to the Poor, and convenient for the carriage of Free-Stone, Wood, Timber, and other Goods and Merchandizes, to and from the said Cities and Parts adjacent . . . and be a means to preserve the high-ways near and leading to the said City of Bath, (which being formerly made ruinous and almost impassable, are now Repairing at a very great Charge).

To these commodities were later added others; for instance, copper to the brassworks on the river, and salt from Worcester. The need for water transport is reflected in the authorized toll of 5s (25p) a ton for goods from Hanham Mills to Bath, though in fact from the late 1720s only 2s (10p), or 1s 3d (6p) for coal, was charged.

In 1727 the prospects of success were better than they had been in 1712, and much better than in 1699. The great days of Bath were beginning, and with them the need for many things to be brought by water. In 1705, when Richard Nash was made master of ceremonies,

a somewhat primitive theatre had been built: within a few years an assembly room and pumproom were added, a London orchestra was installed, the lighting of the streets and the night watch were put in order, and a large sum of money raised at his instance to improve the Bath road, the wisest investment of all. Soon . . . remarkable changes for the better began to be made in the public buildings, and the accommodation for visitors.[3]

A second factor was the building between 1724 and 1731 of two horse railways to bring stone down to the river for loading into barges, that from Combe Down having been constructed by Ralph Allen.

On 9 May 1728, soon after the navigation had been opened,

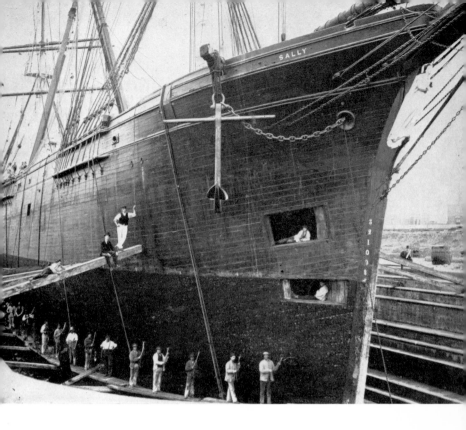

Page 223 (above) Sally, 1,367 tons, from Quebec, in dry-dock at Sharpness, August 1875. Note the ports at the bow for unloading timber; (*below*) Sharpness new docks under construction, 4 July 1872

Page 224 Towing on the Gloucester & Berkeley Canal in the 1930s: (*above*) narrow boats in Gloucester docks; (*below*) barges and a trow on the canal

Princess Amelia, who so disliked bad roads that she had travelled from London to Bath in a sedan chair, went thence to Bristol and back in a special decorated wherry, a visit which cost the corporation of Bristol £242 14s 11½d (£242.75). Even before the navigation had been fully opened, a passenger boat was running between Bristol and Twerton. By 1729, wherries were leaving Bath at ten every morning. It was presumably for the comfort of the passengers that certain lockkeepers began to sell liquor, a practice which the company prohibited in 1729, and then later in the year allowed in the case of ale

Provided they* Suffer no manner of Disorders nor any Injuries to ye Proprs of the Navigation.

Later, in 1740, Samuel Tonkins, who ran wherries, announced that he had added three new boats to his fleet, 'with a house on each, with sash windows'. At that time two boats ran daily, taking about four hours from Bath to Bristol, and charging a fare of 1s (5p).

Coal from the Somerset and Gloucestershire fields reached Bath by land carriage, but after the navigation was built it appears that some Shropshire coal was imported to Bath by way of the river, it being preferred to the local product for burning in grates. This seemed a threat either to the colliers or the road transport men. At the end of August 1731 the Avon proprietors advertised in the newspapers:

Whereas several ill designing disorderly Persons have Threatened to destroy the Navigation of the River Avon Between Bath and Bristol and by Letters dispers'd in the Neighbourhood of that River, have endeavour'd to draw great numbers of weak People into their wicked and dangerous purposes (out of Compassion to those unhappy People and that the principal Actors may see the misery they draw upon themselves, by endeavouring to destroy the just Possessions of their Peaceable and Innocent fellow subjects) it is thought necessary to give them Timely notice of the Shocking Consequence of so mischievous a design by printing the following Clause to Prevent the certain Ruin which upon the first Attempt of this Nature will Inevitably fall upon themselves and their familys, for in this Clause they will plainly see, that the Parliamt have been so sensible of the great Advantages which Navigable Rivers bring to this Kingdom that over and above the Common security of Private Property they have by this Act (as a new Encouragement to such laudable designs) made every attempt to destroy those works felony.[4]

* The lockkeepers.

O

There followed a quotation from the relevant Act.

There was evidently much local perturbation, for in a circular letter from the proprietors to the gentlemen of the neighbourhood, they say:

> I am farther to desire that it may be publickly known, yt the moment any attempt of this nature is begun, Application will be made to the government for a proper force to secure their Property till the Parliamt meets, who will then be mov'd for an Effectual redress that this part of the kingdom may no longer remain in a State of Insecurity, or continue under the daily Apprehension of the most Shocking Injuries and depredation from either weak, distracted or wicked people.[5]

The trouble died down, but apparently as a result of it, legislation of 1735 prescribed the death penalty for wilful damage to the works of a navigable river. In October 1738 the proprietors reissued their old warning with a reference added to the new penalty,

> But notwithstanding this, between the Hours of Eight o'Clock, on Thursday Night, and Four o'Clock on Friday morning, the 15th. and 16th. of November, 1738, the Lock at Solford* was almost destroyed by Persons unknown; who left two threatning Papers, which declared in Substance, That an Attempt was made only by Three Hundred Men, as the beginning of much greater Mischief that was intended against the Navigation, by as many Thousand, unless an immediate Stop was put to the sending of any more Coals by Water.[5]

A reward was offered by the proprietors for information, but it was not forthcoming, and the men were never caught.

As early as 1729 a proposal had been made to extend the Avon Navigation higher up the river, but the proprietors were not interested; in 1734 and 1735, however, they took part in talks upon an extension first to Lacock and then to Chippenham. Once more, in 1765, Fernando Stratford revived the idea of a Chippenham extension, which was for a time supported by the Bristol corporation until it, too, was dropped. This scheme later influenced the first-proposed course of the Kennet & Avon Canal.

By the end of the year 1730 the company was able to pay a maiden dividend of £10 per share upon its thirty-two shares of no par value, but which must have represented about £400 of capital spent by each co-partner. For the years 1730-7 inclusive the average receipts were £978, and the average dividend £14. From 1738 to 1754 no figures are available, after which we get the following averages:

* Saltford.

	Average receipts £	Average dividend £
1755–64	871	16·81*
1765–74†	1,149	25·89
1775–85‡	773	15·06

* Nine years 1756–64.
† Including two extra months owing to a change in the financial year.
‡ Eleven years.

The last period covers the War of American Independence, which hit trade generally, but seems to have affected the Avon heavily. A contributory factor is noted below.

From 1770 onwards more attention was given to seeking trade by varying tolls, and such commodities as lime and hay were encouraged in this way. From about this date also the old rule of one share to each proprietor appears to have been given up; in 1774, for instance, there were blocks of five, four, three, and two shares, the rest being held singly. In 1786 there was trouble of a kind that had similarities elsewhere. The joint treasurers had both died, and an investigation of the accounts showed that a large sum was owing to the navigation, the reason for low receipts and dividends for some years back. The money was recovered from the two estates, and a dividend of £47 per share was declared in celebration. Soon afterwards, the first proposals were made for what became the Kennet & Avon Canal, which was greatly to alter the fortunes of the navigation.

River Kennet

It is difficult to establish a criterion of efficiency for the management of an eighteenth-century navigation, for many of the problems raised by the necessity of controlling lock-keepers, labourers, and bargemasters spread out over a length of river had hardly been understood, much less solved. For their time rivers like the Medway and the Avon seem to have been well run, but the Kennet was a notable exception till in 1767 it passed under the control of Francis Page.

An Act of 1715 authorized seven undertakers to make the river navigable from Reading to Newbury. Six of them stood down after some work had been done, and the seventh, Henry Martyn, then took in new partners. These appear to have spent about £10,000 in building locks near the mill dams, but to have made no attempt to shorten the winding river. It then became clear that such a navigation would not compete successfully with land carriage, and in 1718 John Hore was engaged as engineer. He straightened the river by making a number of cuts, reducing its length to 18½ miles, of which 11½ miles were artificial cut, with 21 locks. The river would now take 80-ton barges, though because of shoals, second or lightening boats often had to be used with the barges to take off part of their cargo. The work was finished in 1723, except for the towing path, which took a year or two longer, at an expense of about £35,000 more.* Hore was a good engineer but no accountant; he failed utterly to render any statement of the money that had passed through his hands, and walked out when threats of legal action were made. In 1728 he produced some figures, and a committee of the proprietors was appointed to 'Meet & Examine what John Hore calls an Acco^t', but it was soon recorded that Unless John Hore can produce an Inteligable Acco^t Dr and Cr it is to no purpose to make any further proceeding therein.'[6]

The history of the first period of the river, from 1718 to 1734, is of a small group of undertakers in London, perpetually short of money, and forced to raise more from time to time to keep the navigation open, trying to run a business in the country with local superintendents who were either inefficient or fraudulent. It had been unfortunate that the construction work was being done during the South Sea crisis: here is a minute of the period:

The great scarcity of Money & ye necessity of a present supply being set forth the Proprietors backward in their Paymts were prest upon for Money, upon wch they declar'd they could not raise any Money at present, but was willing to Agree to any ways & means that could be thought of to do it, & was ready to give any settisfaction to such of ye Prop^{rs} as could advance upon which y^{ey} all declar'd they was out of Mony & could not.[7]

This shortage of money was chronic; fresh sums had to be raised somehow at high cost (in 1723 the proprietors had to pay 8 per cent pa to borrow £242 for two months), and because these were used to pay immediate expenses and losses, a number of bills for land and damage when the cuts or towing paths were being built remained unpaid for years. This annoyance with the navigation by landowners coalesced with the dislike of the millers, while the bargemen and people of Reading were irritated by a work which had removed part of their *entrepôt* trade to Newbury.

---

* A total of about £45,000 to this date is, I think, correct, though a minute of 1761 records that the total cost was 'not so little as £70,000', and Frederick Page supplied to Mavor's *A General View of the Agriculture of Berkshire*, 1809, the figure of £84,000.

THE
CASE
OF

Mr. John Hore *and Mr.* John Beale, *two of the Proprietors of the Navigation of the River* Kennet *in the County of* Berks.

THE Proprietors having wasted near 10,000 *l.* in their Undertaking, by employing an unskilful Person, occasioned their Application to Mr. *Hore*, to be their Surveyor and Engineer, to make the River *Kennett* Navigable : Accordingly, the Proprietors and Mr. *Hore* executed an Agreement in the Year 1718, That Mr. *Hore* should survey and make the River Navigable ; and for his Skill, Pains, and Trouble, should have only 60 *l. per Annum*. And when the Navigation was compleated, Mr. *Hore* should be Surveyor ot the Works for Life, at 60 *l. per Annum* ; and also have an additional Consideration for being Book-keeper, or Wharfinger at *Newbury*, for Life. And in regard Mr. *Hore* would necessarily be at great Expences in treating with Land Owners and others, during such an Undertaking, which could not be regularly accounted for, It was agreed, That it should be left to the Award of two Gentlemen of the County, to adjudge and determine what Mr. *Hore* should have on that Head : Whereupon, there hath been awarded him 840 *l.* and not one Shilling thereof paid.

Mr. *Hore* perfected the Navigation in a very skilful Manner, in the Year 1723. (And besides the 840 *l.*) expended in the Undertaking a very large Sum of Money of his own.

Mr. *Hore* hath applied to the governing Proprietors to be paid ; but instead of having Satisfaction, they immediately displaced him out of his two Offices for Life. And although Mr. *Hore* hath been for six Years endeavouring, by all possible Means, to obtain an amicable End with the acting, nay, governing Proprietors, yet as much as such governing Proprietors have declared against vexatious *Chancery Suits*, they have preferred two Bills in that Court against Mr. *Hore*. And it is notorious, they depend more on the low Circumstances Mr. *Hore* is reduced to in their Service, and the Tediousness of passing an Account in that Court of above 20,000 *l.* than the Justice of their Cause.

That Mr. *Hore* and Mr. *Beale* are entitled to Two Thirds of One Eighth of the Profits of the Navigation, clear of all Charges in making the River Navigable ; the governing Proprietors have not only received all the Profits of the River for six Years, but refuse to come to any Account, or pay Mr. *Hore* or Mr. *Beale* one Farthing.

That the governing Proprietors held all their Meetings at *London* (near 50 Miles from the River) and have all along acted there in an arbitrary Manner, exclusive of several other Proprietors ; and have done many Acts not only without, but expressly against the Consent of the other Proprietors, by placing in, and displacing Officers, receiving the Profits ; and even Leasing the Profits for three Years. And now they apply to the Legislature for an Act of Parliament; not only to justify their former unjustifiable Proceedings, but to continue them for the future : Whereby they will be the sole Managers of the Navigation, exclusive of other Proprietors.

If these governing Proprietors would act impartially and justly by their Fellow Proprietors, they would have no Occasion to apply to Parliament for the Purposes mentioned in their Petition and Case ; then, and not till Then, the Navigation will go on successfully.

ALL which is humbly submitted, &c.

27. John Hore's complaint against the Kennet proprietors

There were attacks on the navigation works in 1720 and again in 1725, the first apparently by the people of Reading, the second by a combination of elements, as well as threats to the barge-masters using the Kennet. All these and other troubles the proprietors tried to deal with by hurried trips down from London. An agreement was reached with Reading corporation in 1726, but there was a flare-up with the millers in 1727, and it was not till 1733 that the debts owing for land and damage were finally settled.

Meanwhile there had been difficulty in getting traders to work on the river. Back in 1723, when it was first opened, an extraordinary agreement had been made with Captain Orpwood, who had begun to trade with two barges, that if he would work as often as he could between London and Newbury for twelve months at agreed rates, the proprietors would at the end of the year

> make the said Cap. Orpwood a Gratuity as underneath, Viz.
> Fifty Pounds in Lawfull Money one Pipe of Good Port Wine to
> the Cap^{ts}. liking, and to make up the whole £100 in Plate for
> his Wife as he or she shall direct.[8]

Thenceforward there are many records of efforts to get more barges to work the river, to entice the Andover trade away from Reading, to persuade existing bargemasters to pay their accounts, and to compete with land carriage.

By 1734 it was quite clear that the river was being too inefficiently run ever to pay. In this year Lady Forbes, widow of one of the early undertakers, asserted herself, and got a relation of hers, Francis Forbes, made superintendent at Newbury. She was businesslike, and balances began to appear in the books. About 1748 a decision was taken to enter the carrying business, following out ideas that had been talked about, but not, I think, acted upon, since 1727. 'Foreign' barges, ie those not already working on the Kennet, were now forbidden. The carrying business lost money in most years, while the tolls remained steady at about their previous level of £2,000 a year, which probably represents a carriage of about 10,000 tons. The company also did a business in lending sacks to maltsters and others, but this again did not pay.

Then there were efforts to create a trade with Bristol which came to nothing, and endless appeals by the proprietors to their servants for economy. Still the carrying trade did not pay, and in the 1750s the shareholders tried to lease the concern, or to sell the barges to the bargemasters, but without success. In 1759 Francis Forbes, who left owing money, was replaced, and soon afterwards the Forbes interest seems to have given up any active effort, though in 1761 Francis Forbes offered to lease the river and drew an indignant letter from the proprietors:

> . . . man who offer'd them £600 a year clear profit upon a navigation which he had the entire management of 25 years & never clear'd one shilling for the prop^{rs} acount & for what little Interest have been paid of Debts formerly owing by the props & the amount of the Barges now on hand and about £500 paid to different people these together make the whole amount of all the profits arising.[9]

When he left, foreign barges were once more allowed on the river, which was now run by the one or two proprietors who bothered to attend meetings. A note of 1761 summarizes part of the trouble from which the river had suffered, seen from the proprietors' point of view; their servants might have thought differently:

> The undertaking has been ruin'd by Idle Servants Extravagant Wages Imbezelments & Loss of materials & by a superflous & unnecessary number of Hands all which Evils must be remedy'd by Industry, Frugality great care & application on your part & by laying it down as an invariable Rule that none of the props Servants shall eat the Bread of Idleness or Roguery.[10]

The name of Page occurs as far back in the records of the river as 1724. By 1760 Francis Page had built up a big coal trading business, and it is said of him that:

> Francis Page has always been a very Beneficial Customer to the Barge Trade & a well wisher & Friend to the Navigation.[10]

About 1767 he appears as a proprietor, and soon afterwards he seems to have become sole owner. The moment he took control he closed the London office, and had the books sent down to Newbury. He then advanced £1,581 to get repairs done and pay current expenses, and leased the river in 1770 to a former superintendent for £1,200, Page to do the repairs. Before long he seems to have resumed possession, and continued to do his own carrying, though other men's barges sometimes used the navigation. He gave the job care and attention, and built up a prosperous concern. He died in 1784, when Frederick and Francis Page, his sons, succeeded to the navigation. Soon afterwards the first meetings to advocate a junction between the rivers Kennet and Avon were held.

At some time during the century, but when I do not know, the original locks must have been enlarged to their later size of 122 ft by 19 ft, to take the big 128-ton Newbury barges. Three were of brick, the rest of timber with turf sides.

Kennet & Avon Canal

From the reign of Elizabeth I, men had been ambitious to join Thames to Avon. The idea seems to have started with Henry Briggs, who did a rough survey. He died before the Civil War, but the project was later revived by Francis Mathew, of Dorset, who had heard him speak of it. Writing about 1660, his scheme gained some support, but, according to John Aubrey, nothing happened for want of management and ability.[11]

In the remarkable burst of Parliamentary interest in waterways after the Restoration, four Bills were introduced for making a passage by water from London to Bristol, but none became law. A final Bill was introduced into the House of Lords by the Earl of Bridgewater in 1668,

> but some foolish Discourse at Coffee-houses laid asleep that great Design as being a thing impossible and impracticable.[12]

When the canal age came, the thing was done, though its beginnings were in a smaller scheme. On 10 March 1788 there was a

> Meeting of the Chief Inhabitants of the Borough of Hungerford . . . to consider the Utility of an Extension of the Navigable River from Newbury to Hungerford and as far further as shall hereafter be thought eligible.[13]

The meeting at Hungerford* supported the idea of what was then called the Western Canal, and referred it to a larger meeting of the gentlemen of Hungerford, Marlborough, and their neighbourhoods. It was at this meeting on 16 April 1788 that this resolution was passed:

> That it appears to this Meeting that a Canal from Newbury to Hungerford only would not be likely to meet with the general approbation and that nothing short of a Junction of the Kennett and Avon Rivers would answer, and be of material benefit to the Country at large.

The chair at this meeting was taken by Charles Dundas, who for over forty years was to be associated with the canal. A committee was appointed to collect information, and a pamphlet was published, which is remarkable among its fellows for its diffidence and lack of over-statement.[14] At the end of the year three engineers, Weston, Simcock and Barnes, were commissioned to make

---

* A suggestion by the Basingstoke Canal Committee in 1783, in *An Address to the Public, on the Basingstoke Canal Navigation*, for a junction between London and Bristol by means of their canal, does not seem to have been considered by those who met at Hungerford, even if it were known to them.

vent Iron coming to us; truly we fhould then be in a fine cafe! Therefore if the Iron Defign at *Chrift-Church* go on, it may do well; for Store will be no fore.

I hope now I have plainly made it appear, that by the two Manufactures of Iron and Linen, being incouraged as is fet down, all the poor People of *England* may be fet at work.

That nothing may be wanting that may conduce to the benefit and incouragement of things manufactured, as in cheap carriage to and fro over *England*, and to the Sea at eafie rates, I will in the next place fhew you how the great Rivers in *England* may be made Navigable, and thereby make the Commodities and Goods carried, efpecially in Winter time, for half the rate they now pay. Therefore you muft know that the *Thames* and *Severne* are the two great Mafter Rivers, that run fartheft into the Inlands of *England*, and fo into the Seas, and thefe Rivers are both of them already Navigable; *Thames* as far as *Oxford*, and *Severne* from the *welch* Pool (or within two Miles of it) to *Briftoll*: But one of thefe Rivers running directly South, the other Eaft, they are diftint in the neareft place forty Miles from each other, and fo there is no advantage made of thefe two eminent Rivers, in being helpful one to the other in point of Carriage. But it was about ten years fince projected (and a Bill brought into the Houfe) to make thefe two great Rivers communicable, by making a new Cut from *Lechlode* along near *Criclett* into *Avon*, and fo down *Avon* to *Bath*, and fo for *Briftoll*. And a Map was drawn for Mr. *Mathews* by Mr. *Moxon* to demonftrate the thing. Many Lords and Gentlemen were ingaged in it; amongft which were the Duke of *Albemarle* and the Earl of *Pembroke*. But fome foolifh Difcourfe at Coffee-houfes laid afleep that

28. A page from Andrew Yarranton's *England's Improvement by Sea and Land*, 1677, describing an early scheme for a Thames and Avon canal

WESTERN CANAL.

MARLBOROUGH, 29th July, 1788.

AT a Meeting of the Committee appointed to take the Opinion of the Public, refpecting an Extenfion of the Navigation of the Rivers Kennett and Avon, fo as to form a direct Inland Communication between *London* and *Briftol*, and the Weft of *England*, by a Canal from *Newbury* to *Bath*,

CHARLES DUNDAS, Efq. in the Chair,

RESOLVED, That a General Meeting be advertized to be held at the Caftle Inn, at Marlborough, Wilts, on *Tuefday* the 9th Day of *September* next, at Twelve o'Clock, at which Meeting the Landowners, and Parties interefted, are requefted to attend.

RESOLVED alfo, That the following Propofitions be fubmitted to the Opinion of that Meeting, *viz*.

1. That the Juction of the Kennett and Avon Rivers will be of Advantage to the Country.

2. That the under-named Gentlemen be propofed to the General Meeting as a Committee to regulate future Proceedings:

The Marquis of Lanfdown,	Matthew Humphries,	
The Earl of Ailefbury,	Andrew Bayntun,	
Lord Craven,	John Awdry,	
Lord Porchefter,	Paul Methuen,	
Sir Edward Bayntun, Bart.	Paul Cobb Methuen,	
John Archer,	James Montagu,	
William Brummelle,	James Montagu, jun.	
William Pulteney,	Samuel Cam,	Efquires;
John Walker Heneage,	Jofeph Mortimer,	
Lovelace Bigg,	—— Dickenfon,	
John Pearce,	Efquires;	Francis Page,
—— James,	John Baverftock,	
Charles Dundas,	John Ward,	
Arthur Jones,	R. H. Gaby,	
Ifaac Pickering,	—— Deane,	
John Hyde,	—— Vanderflighen,	

The Members for the Counties of Wilts, Berks, and Somerfet; the Members for the feveral Boroughs in the faid Counties; the Chief Magiftrates of the faid Boroughs; and fuch other Perfons as fhall be propofed and approved of at the General Meeting.

3. That fuch Committee be directed to employ Mr. Whitworth, or fome other experienced Surveyor, to examine the different Tracts by which the Navigation may be carried, and to make his Report to the faid Committee.

29. An advertisement for an early meeting of the Western Canal

a survey both for a narrow and a barge canal. These were experienced men: Samuel Weston had worked on the Chester and Oxford Canals and been a contractor on the Leeds & Liverpool; Samuel Simcock, one of Brindley's principal assistants, had built the Birmingham and part of the Oxford, while James Barnes was a surveyor on the Oxford, and was later to make his name as resident engineer of the Grand Junction.

In the middle of 1789 these surveys were sent to Robert Whitworth for his observations, and the committee busied themselves with collecting data upon possible traffic. In August 1789 Whitworth reported favourably upon a line via Hungerford, Marlborough and Calne, subject to the adequacy of water supply. Eventually in November 1790, when Rennie had reported that there would be no difficulty with water, a meeting

> Resolved Unanimously That a Junction of the Rivers Kennett and Avon, by a Canal Navigation from Newbury to Bath, by Hungerford, Ramsbury, Marlborough, and the Cherrill lower Level, under the White-Horse Hill, and through Calne, Chippenham, Laycock, Melksham, and Bradford, at the estimated Expence of 213,940£ is practicable, and will be highly useful and beneficial to the Subscribers, and to the Publick at large.

It was agreed that as soon as £75,000 had been subscribed, an Act should be sought. A prospectus was now issued, which again showed unusual and, as it turned out, unfortunate, modesty. One paragraph said:

> It has never been the Opinion of the Committee, that either the Computations of the Advantages, or Estimates of the Expences, of the Canal, that have yet been made, should be considered as all that is necessary to be done. If they should be sufficient to induce the Public to subscribe to the Amount of Sixty or Eighty Thousand Pounds, it is then intended to call the Subscribers together to deliberate upon the Scheme; if they think it worth pursuing, they will give Directions for more exact and authentic Information, than the Committee, for want of Money, have hitherto been able to obtain.[15]

A subscription list was opened and many took shares, among them Francis Page, part-owner of the Kennet. But only about £17,700 came in, and the project slumbered, though the committee remained in existence.

It is noticeable that up to this point no attempt seems to have been made to interest the Bristol merchants or corporate bodies, and the benefits described were all to the landowners and inhabitants of the intermediate towns. But in November 1792 Bristol was suddenly caught up in that nationwide wave of speculation that we call the canal mania. It began with the promotion of the Bristol & Severn Canal to Gloucester and beyond (see p. 320) and the Bristol & Western to Taunton,[16] and also with renewed interest in the dormant Western Canal. Rumours began to fly. It seems that a group in Bristol headed by Mr Bartley and Mr Daubeny proposed to create and monopolize the shares. They held an inconspicuous meeting at the White Lion on 10 December and subscribed £264,000, which sum included the original subscription of £17,700 raised by the previous and still existing committee, none of whom seem to have been present.

It seems likely that, fearing an outcry from a public deprived of the opportunity of subscribing for shares that they might turn to profit, the White Lion Junto, as they were called, had previously decided to provide a rival attraction. Certainly on the same day as their own meeting an anonymous advertisement appeared in a Salisbury paper calling a meeting at Devizes for Wednesday 12 December to consider the practicability of a canal from Bristol to the interior parts of Wiltshire. This ambiguous phrase was taken by the people of Bristol and Bath to refer to the Kennet & Avon, since they did not know the subscription had been filled the previous evening. The calling of this meeting in a half-secret fashion by means of the Salisbury paper caused the ride to Devizes. There was a rush from Bath and Bristol through the wintry lanes to that town, to the astonishment of the inhabitants; a frantic search for

The BUBBLE detected.

IN Consequence of a Paragraph having appeared in the *Salisbury Paper*, purporting that a Scheme was in contemplation to cut a *Canal* from *Bristol* through *Wiltshire*, by which it was universally understood to be intended to join the *Thames* at *Newbury*. A great number of the Inhabitants of the County of Wilts and City of Bristol are now collected together. A Subscription for that purpose was opened in *November*, 1790. but was never filled until Monday Evening last, when a private Party met at the *White Lion* in *Bristol*, and underhandedly compleated it.——This Junto in order to amuse the Publick and divert their Attention from their shameful Proceedings, are now about to bring forward a useless and unprofitable Canal through the interior Parts of this County to *Salisbury*.

The Publick will undoubtedly treat this Plan with the Contempt it deserves.

12th DECEMBER, 1792.

30. A broadsheet issued at the time of the ride to Devizes

T H E

M A D   G A L L O P;

O R,

A Trip to Devizes.

W HEN *trade* was brifk throughout the land

And men had money at command:

When enterprifing merchants chofe

To change their coafting barks for trows:

When far and near the topick all

Inclin'd to this or that *Canal*:

When high and low, rich, poor, good, bad,

Where juftly reckon'd *Canal mad*:

When

31a. Title-page from the time of the canal mania

beds; and in the morning another search for the meeting, during which the local magistrates, not knowing the cause of the invasion, nearly read the Riot Act. At last the town clerk was persuaded to take the chair at a meeting

and desired to know, for what purpose the Meeting was called, and declar'd, if no Gentleman came forward to avow the advertisement, he would adjourn the Meeting. After some time a proposal was made by some Person, to cut a Canal from Bristol by Devizes to Salisbury, but this was considered as a mere Pretence to amuse the Meeting, who considered themselves drawn together for no purpose, and there was a general cry of

CANALING:

A

POEM.

OH! for a muſe, to guide deſcriptive pen,
Peep at DEVIZES, and quick return again.

Inſpire me THALIA, SATIRE lift thy rod,
Help me gay MOMUS, laughter-loving GOD,
Aid me ye NAIADS, of CANALS to ſing,
(From whence, alas, BRISTOLIAN follies ſpring :)
Smooth flow my lines, as AVONS gentle ſtream,
Clear as its waters, mirthful, as my theme.

But though the POET, is to mirth inclin'd,
Againſt the choiceſt ear, there's nought deſign'd;
If a MAD GALLOP, does his pen employ,
No TH—RNE expreſſions, ſhall the ſenſe annoy :

31b. Title-page from the time of the canal mania

'Newbury, Newbury'.* Mr. N. Bartley of Bristol, one of the Subscribers at the White Lion, at length owned that he was the author of the Advertisement.[17]

The meeting eventually accepted this project for a canal to Salisbury (see p. 186).

This ride to Devizes was celebrated in two poems published soon afterwards, *The Mad Gallop*, by Romaine Joseph Thorne, which went through two editions in a fortnight, and *Canaling*, by Cornelius Vapid, Esq.

The quality of Thorne's verses, described by himself as Hudibrastic, can be judged from the opening lines:

> *When* trade *was brisk throughout the land*
> *And men had money at command:*
> *When enterprising merchants chose*
> *To change their coasting barks for trows:*
> *When far and near the topick all*
> *Incline'd to this or that* Canal:
> *When high and low, rich, poor, good, bad,*
> *Were justly reckon'd* Canal *mad:*
>
> *   *   *
>
> *When through the mountain's craggy side;*
> *Was doomed to flow commercial tide;*
> *A meeting (so report prevail'd)*
> *Was in* Wilt's *county to be held,*
> *At fair DEVIZES, pleasant town,*
> *An ancient borough of renown;*
> *Where all who wish'd to take a share*
> *In* Canal *plan must QUICK repair.*

Vapid, after a dig at the broadness of some of his fellow poet's expressions

> *If a MAD GALLOP, does his pen employ,*
> *No TH——NE expressions, shall the sense annoy:*

describes the mania:

> *The rage for CANALS so great thro' BRISTOL ran,*
> *(Like electricity from man to man),*
> *That every* coach *and* horse *throughout the place,*
> *Was hired, to go this* fortune-hunting chase;
> And many a horse was this day let for more
> Than would have purchas'd it a week before . . .

* Newbury was the eastern terminus of the proposed Kennet & Avon Canal

and the following morning in Devizes:

> *At length* Aurora *harbinger of day,*
> *Dispels the gloomy shades of night away;*
> *And early as the lark, soars toward the sky,*
> *Rose* Speculators, *from* bed, floor, *and* sty;
>
>   *   *   *
>
> *Forth rush'd the mob—but where alas! to go—*
> *They did not find, 'till now, they did not know.*
> *Where is the CANAL? each ask'd the other—where?*
> *Another cries, 'Tis doing at the* Bear;'
> *Swift as a hound, they run towards the place,*
> *But find, alas! it was a* bugbear *chace!*
> *Some scratch their heads, not knowing what to do:*
> *Whilst others raving, travel to and fro;*
> *CANALS were mention'd, but without a scheme,*
> *Nor where should* run, *or how* obtain, *the* stream;
> *And most of them, who to DEVIZES went,*
> *Knew but should* run *from* Wiltshire *into* Kent. . . .

Meanwhile, when the news of what had happened at the White Lion leaked out in Bristol and Bath on the following day, there was so much criticism of the Junto that the group had to give out that

they should consider themselves as holding the Shares for themselves and their fellow-citizens who might choose to become adventurers as well as other Gentlemen of the Country & especially the Land holders on the line; . . . and they declared their readiness to act entirely with the original Committee and Subscribers to the Western Canal.[18]

The original committee leapt smartly into action and themselves met at Hungerford on the 14th. Dundas was in the chair and took control of the situation. Meanwhile at Bristol the subscription of £264,000 made at the White Lion had been raised to £945,000. Dundas proposed a division of the shares between the old subscribers and the landowners on the line, the White Lion group, and the subsequent subscribers, and the addition to the old committee of ten men from Bath and Bristol representing the new blood. We may note that, in spite of the manœuvres of Mr Bartley of the White Lion group at Devizes, when ten days after the famous ride the committee of the proposed canal to Salisbury and Southampton wished to discuss a link with the Kennet and Avon, it was to 'the Committee of the Western Canal, subscribed for at the Celtic Inn, Marlborough on the 3rd. November, 1790', that they turned.[19] At the end of January 1793 it was agreed that the 3,500 shares should be divided into three equal parts as Dundas had proposed.

Action now began. Rennie was asked to make a new survey, and to communicate his results to Whitworth, who was to advise the committee. Approaches were made to the River Kennet and River Avon proprietors, and to the City of London as controlling the river below Staines. Dennis Edson, who had worked on the Chester and Stourbridge Canals, was taken on to survey a possible canal from Bath to Bristol to avoid the Avon, which is said to be 'subject to the Inconveniences of Floods and Shallows'. Both the River Kennet and River Avon proprietors promptly offered to sell their navigations at a fair valuation, which rather put the committee off; they decided to take no action with the Kennet, but to buy Avon shares individually. Rennie, who two years ago had recommended the Marlborough–Calne line, now turned against it, and the southern route by Devizes was chosen instead, with a branch, however, to Marlborough and another to Calne and Chippenham. It was now, in September 1793, that the name of the project was changed to the Kennet & Avon Canal.

The committee had interviews with a number of other committees who wished to join their canal: with the promoters of the Somersetshire Coal Canal, the Wilts & Berks, the Bristol & Salisbury, and the Boulter's Lock & Isleworth. In the case of the Wilts & Berks, they undertook to begin work at Bath so that the portion from Semington to Bath would be finished by the time the Wilts & Berks was built; they also agreed that the Wilts & Berks should serve Calne and Chippenham, unless that company failed to get its Act. The committee itself sent a deputation to the Thames Commissioners to press upon them the proposal that the commissioners should build a canal from Reading to Isleworth, because

> there at present exists great Inconvenience and delays in the Navigation of the said River owing to the great Circuity of its Course and other Causes.

Early in 1794 the estimate for the canal was £377,365 without the Marlborough branch, which had been dropped. The capital authorized by the Act[20] obtained in 1794 was £420,000 with power to raise an additional £120,000. As construction proceeded, a series of further authorizing Acts was passed, till by 1812 the total capital expenditure, including the cost of buying the Kennet Navigation and a controlling interest in the Avon, had reached £979,315.

P

The purpose of the canal was now described as to supply the country eastwards from Bath with Gloucestershire and Somerset coal, and maltsters with south Wales anthracite; to carry Bath stone and limestone for building and agriculture from near Bristol and Bath; gypsum from near Bristol and paving stones from the Marlborough Downs; iron, copper, and slates from Wales; and grain and timber back from Newbury.

. A committee of twenty-four was set up, ten from Bristol, seven from the Eastern (Hungerford) district, and seven from the Wiltshire (Marlborough) district to govern the concern. It was now, after the Act had been passed, that the vital decision was made to build a broad and not a narrow canal. The Kennet & Avon was finally built as a broad canal 40 ft (44 ft on the summit level) wide at top, to take barges 70 ft by 13 ft 6 in, carrying up to 60 tons. The line was 57 miles long from Bath by way of Devizes to Hungerford and Newbury, with 79 locks 80 ft long by 14 ft wide,* there being a rise of 404 ft 6 in from Bath to the summit and a fall of 210 ft to Newbury. The main feature was the great flight of 29 locks near Devizes, which ranks with that of 30 locks at Tardebigge on the Worcester & Birmingham Canal as the biggest in Britain.

One of the proprietors' first steps was to move towards control of the Avon Navigation. The Avon owners had changed their minds, and their clerk had said

that the proprietors had determined not to dispose of their Shares . . . but intend to improve the same so as to make it a complete navigation.[21]

There were possibilities of being held to ransom here, and the committee therefore decided to try to buy the thirty-two Avon shares by separate negotiation, on the basis of thirty years' purchase of the net annual value averaged over any ten successive years. They began with three for £2,700, which shows the net annual value to have been £30 at that time.† By the beginning of 1797 it seems that a nominal, though for some time not an effective, control had been obtained.

In 1795 there was still much talk of an extension from Bath to Bristol, but by 1796 the mania was over and troubles were setting in. Construction had begun in 1794. It was a time of rising prices and of a financial stringency that made it more and more difficult to get money for calls on shares, especially in face of mounting

---

* The locks on the Kennet were 122 ft by 19 ft, and those on the Avon 106 ft by 20 ft.

† Compare the dividend figures for earlier years given on p. 227.

costs. The committee was cheerful, but in July 1796 out of 3,500 shares, 822 were in arrear after six calls, and in September the first action against defaulters was authorized. The passing of an Act in 1796 for the Dorset & Somerset Canal, to run from the Kennet & Avon at Widbrook near Bradford on Avon towards Blandford[22] caused no interest. In 1797, 16 miles of the canal were building at the western end and 15 at the eastern, but the bank refused to advance money to push on the work faster than calls were made, 'on account of the pressure of the times'. The workmen were being paid with 21-day notes, and by June 1797 over 200 shares had been forfeited for non-payment of calls. Then a scandal occurred.

Francis Page, owner of the Kennet Navigation, was a committeeman of the canal and also one of those responsible for spending the company's money on construction. In July 1797 it was found that he owed the company over £10,000, which he could not pay, and he had to mortgage the Kennet to the canal company as security. In September Frederick Page, Francis's brother, offered to sell both their interests to the canal company, and one is surprised that the committee did not seize the opportunity. Money must have been too tight, but later, when the company had to pay £100,000 for the Kennet, they must have looked back with regret to the chance they had missed. Instead, Page was left at liberty to look out for a purchaser, and in March 1798 he was threatened that the company would sell the river, then valued at £27,055 and with the tolls let at £1,930 pa, to repay the debt due to them. In September an agreement for repayment was made with the Pages, and by September 1801 they had paid off the debt and resumed possession of the river, though in the process they had forfeited 47½ Kennet & Avon shares for non-payment of calls.

By July 1798 the full calls of £100 on each share had been made, and though the Newbury–Hungerford section was completed in this year, much had not yet been begun. The committee suspended all works not yet in hand, and reported ruefully to the proprietors:

From the very favourable reports, that the committee have for two years past submitted, . . . the Subscribers may reasonably be led to expect, that the Work is in a much more advanced state, than is the real fact.[23]

In March 1799 the committee received 'A Remonstrance from several of the Subscribers on the State and Management of the Company's Affairs', and this developed into an attack on the engineer, from which Rennie was later exonerated. In 1800 over

£50,000 worth of shares were forfeited for failure to pay calls, and found no purchasers at any price.

The section from Hungerford to Great Bedwyn was opened in 1799, and that from Foxhanger to Bath (but without the Bath locks to connect it to the Avon), was partially finished, though not completely till 1804. A double-track iron railway on wooden sleepers was laid down about the end of 1802 to join Foxhanger to Devizes, though in December 1803 the company was threatening to proceed against the contractor to enforce

> a complete Execution of the same unless the Contractors immediately proceed to the Repair of the Work and to remedy the Inconveniences that have arisen from the bad Execution of it.[24]

In 1803 the section from Devizes to Pewsey was being built, but that from Pewsey to Great Bedwyn had not yet been started. In the following year Rennie estimated that he would still need £415,100 more, and in 1805 it was

> Resolved that the Gentlemen of the Committee be requested to call personally on their friends and explain to them the State of the Subscription and to use their utmost Endeavours to prevail on Proprietors to cover their present Interest in the canal by subscribing for new Shares.[25]

Another attack on Rennie was fended off, and in 1807, after the Avon proprietors had refused to apply for an Act authorizing the building of a towing path, the canal company successfully did so, though the path was not built till 1813. In 1807, also, the Devizes–Pewsey section was open, and a passenger boat was running between Shrivenham on the Wilts & Berks and Bath. The Bath locks and the Devizes flight were not, however, completed till 1810, and the whole canal was open on 28 December of that year. On the last day of 1810 it was

> Ordered that the Treasurers Clerks be presented with Five Guineas as a Christmas present.

It must have been a joyful occasion to those who had struggled so long. Meanwhile an old proposal to build a floating harbour at Bristol had at last matured. A new cut for the Avon was begun in May 1804, and in January 1809 the water was diverted into it. The total cost of the scheme was some £600,000, double the estimate made by William Jessop.

The opening of the Kennet & Avon coincided with much enthusiasm for canals. With the encouragement of Welsh ironmasters who wanted an improved route to London, an Act[26] was passed in 1811 for a Bath & Bristol Canal ending at Old Market Street, Bristol, with a branch, 1½ miles long with 5 locks, from

Barton hill to the floating harbour. Calls were made, some land was bought at Temple Meads and Twerton, and Kennet & Avon representatives were appointed to the committee, which remained in existence for many years. Another Act was obtained in the same year for a canal from the river Avon near Bristol to Taunton[27] with a branch to the Nailsea collieries, which led the Kennet & Avon proprietors to envisage a through canal line to Exeter, and to take up privately 903 unappropriated shares in the Grand Western Canal,[27] planned from Taunton to near Exeter.

The energy of the proprietors, stimulated by the chairman, Charles Dundas, also showed itself by the purchase in 1812 of the Kennet Navigation for £100,000. Of this, £70,000 was paid in cash, the balance being left at a fee-farm rent of £1,500 a year. After this purchase various steps were taken to bring the Kennet into conformity with the standards of the canal. The committee had also for some years been buying shares in the Avon Navigation, in spite of the promotion of the rival canal. In 1812 they subscribed £7,000 towards the cost of a towpath on that navigation, and in 1816 they bought the effects of the Bath & Bristol company for £21,172, the main part of which was six shares in the Avon, bringing the Kennet & Avon holding to twenty-three shares out of thirty-two.

At the same time as these activities, plans were being discussed for linking the Kennet & Avon and its associated rivers with the Basingstoke and Grand Junction Canals in order to avoid the Thames Navigation. The state of the Thames was a constant worry, and the canal committee at one time even considered avoiding it by using land carriage. On 13 August 1817 it was referred to a sub-committee to discover

why so many heavy articles are sent by Waggons and particularly to observe that a Waggon has lately been set up to carry Goods from Bristol to London more regularly and expeditiously and at a lower rate than any others, and the said Committee are desired to consider whether the establishment of a Waggon upon a similar principle between London and Maidenhead or Reading to convey goods carried upon the Kennet and Avon Canal would be likely to be beneficial.

The through trade from Bristol past Reading towards London was energetically promoted. Nearly all of it passed by way of the Kennet & Avon, though in its early years the Wilts & Berks had tried to compete for the traffic. In the year both canals opened, 1810, the following prices per ton were quoted for carriage between London and Bath:

Kennet & Avon	£2	9s	6d	(£2.47½)
Wilts & Berks	£2	12s	6d	(£2.62½)
Land carriage*	£6	3s	0d	(£6.15)

* Land carriage greatly cheapened after the end of the war.

Many inducements were given to long hauls and full loads. For instance, in 1815 a list of goods was issued on which drawbacks would be given if carried the whole length of the canal in 40-ton lots; at the same time there were reductions in the combined charges for goods carried from the Kennet through the canal and on to the Avon, or vice versa. With all these efforts, however, the traffic passing on the Kennet & Avon and associated rivers between London and Bristol did not on the average exceed one-sixteenth of the total tonnage throughout the heyday of the canal.

The Kennet & Avon's main source of coal supplies was the Somersetshire Coal Canal (see Chapter XI), with which it linked at Limpley Stoke. This coal was carried to Bath, and also eastwards, both into the Wilts & Berks and onwards towards Reading. Here it was competing with other supplies, mainly with sea-coal brought up the Thames. We get an idea of the demarcation lines between the two from the drawbacks given by the company in 1832 upon coal that was meeting the competition: 1s (5p) a ton if landed at Reading, 2s 6d (12½p) between Marsh lock and Temple mills, 3s (15p) at Temple mills or down to Maidenhead, 3s 6d (17½p) at Maidenhead or down to Windsor.

There was, however, another source of supply, the south Gloucestershire coalfield to the north of the Avon and Bristol. From 1803 onwards suggestions had been made for a horse railway from these collieries to the river. In 1812, for instance, the Kennet & Avon's engineer made a survey, and in the next year there were efforts to raise money. In 1827 these proposals were revived, and when in December a plan for a railway from Coalpit Heath to Bristol with a branch to the Avon was produced to the Kennet & Avon committee, they saw the advantage of a link with the collieries and moved to express to the promoters their interest in the Avon branch. The two proposals were then separated, and in 1828 two Acts were passed, one for the Bristol & Gloucestershire Railway from the floating harbour at Bristol to Coalpit Heath, and one for the Avon & Gloucestershire Railway, to leave the main line at Rodway Hill and run to the Avon at Keynsham.[28] A special meeting of the canal company on 13 February 1828 agreed to subscribe £10,000 to the A & GR,

from the operation of which Works, your Committee confi-

Canal Office Sydney Garden
Bath 14 March 1822.

J Cole Esq.

Respected Friend

It is with due submission
I beg leave to address Thee as Chairman of the
Committee of the Kennet & Avon Canal Navigation,
in hopes that if thou should'st think proper to
enquire into my conduct, since the Committee
have been pleased to appoint me into this office,
it will be found that such unremitted attention
has been paid to the duties thereof, and the strickest
punctuality observed in handing my Accounts
and Cash transactions into the General Office as
will merit the approbation of the Committee.
and that it will not be thought presumptious
in me to hand thee the inclosed Paper contain:
particulars of an Increase in the Company's revenue
at this office since my commencing the System of
Guaging the Barges & Boats, amounting in the
space of little more than 5 Months to $383\frac{1}{2}$ Tons
and sum of £45 . 11 . 3, which according to the
mode of ascertaining the Tonnage by computation
as was previously practiced here, would be an
entire loss of so much to the concern.

p A.

32. Letter to Thomas Cole, chairman of the Kennet & Avon's committee, written in 1822 by a Quaker, M. Parry

dently anticipate a considerable accession of Tonnage, and a reduction of Price in the Articles of Coal, and Pennant Stone. In December of the same year the proprietors contracted for the remainder of the A & GR shares, in 1829 they were hopeful enough to agree that the bridges should be built wide so that the line could later be doubled, in 1830 they borrowed £20,000 on promissory notes for the railway, in 1831 another £10,000, and yet another £10,000 in 1832. The total cost was £52,710.

The Avon & Gloucestershire Railway, 5½ miles long, was reported complete in August 1831, but the connecting line from Rodway Hill to Coalpit Heath was not ready till July 1832. The opening of the railway was reported to have reduced the price of coal along the whole navigation by 3s (15p) to 4s (20p) a ton. The Bristol & Gloucestershire Railway was opened in 1835; steam traction and an extension to join the Cheltenham & Great Western Union Railway at Standish near Gloucester was authorized in 1839 and completed in 1844. The line was leased to the Midland Railway in 1845, and became their property in the following year.

Before we look at the later history of the Kennet & Avon, it may be useful to pause here to see a little of the effect such canals had upon the towns through which they passed. Reading, for instance, in 1811 a country town of 10,827 inhabitants, found itself able to import not only cheap coal, but cheap iron and hardware from Birmingham, stone from Bath, pottery from Staffordshire and groceries from London, and to send away timber and agricultural products in exchange. Indeed, it was said there were

> incalculable advantages which we derive from the navigable canal to Bristol, by which the produce of Ireland and our West India settlements, instead of coming round a dangerous coast to London, and from thence to this town, is now brought directly here through the country, and by our grocers distributed among the neighbouring towns and villages at a lower price than by the London merchants, thus causing an influx of wealth to our traders, which is felt through all the town.[29]

In 1835 it was thought that 50,000 tons of Reading's import and export trade moved by water, and a negligible amount by land.

The main events of this early period of the Kennet & Avon's life can be quickly told. In 1813 a steam barge passed through the canal from Bath to London. The first dividend, of 15s (75p) per £40 share free of property tax, was paid in 1814. In 1816 it is recorded that a French packet 'laden with linen drapery came up the river from London and cast anchor off High Bridge' at Reading; after a few weeks it left to 'go through the country to Bristol'.[30] By 1818 seventy 60-ton barges were working on the canal, as well as narrow boats, and it was stated that the average time taken for the 57 miles from Bath to Newbury was three days, nine hours. In this year also four Avon shares were bought at the greatly enhanced price of £2,625 each. In 1820 it was 'Ordered that no charge be made for the passage of a Boat which lately conveyed the Honourable Mrs. Curzon (in very ill health) along the Canal in her way from London to Clifton.'[31] In 1824 it was reported that barges between Bristol and London had almost superseded the land carriage because of their cheapness and speed, and that the carriers had undertaken to deliver goods in nine days, barring stoppages on the rivers or the canal. Another writer gives the time between London and Bristol for narrow fast boats as five days in summer and six in winter. Speed and regularity were now becoming more important, even at the expense of economy; in 1825 the clerk of the Wilts & Berks wrote to the Thames & Severn company:

The time is gone by for your large barges; even on the Kennet and Avon they are getting into the 30 Ton size.[32]

The income of the canal slowly increased, from £19,212 in 1815–16 to £48,694 in 1827, when the dividend reached 25s (£1.25) per £40 share. In this year four more Avon shares were bought for £20,000; this price of £5,000 a share, when compared with the £900 a share paid in 1798 for the 16½ shares that gained control, shows the improvement brought about by the canal in the value of the Avon navigation. The office management of the Avon was by now joined with that of the canal, but separate meetings of the proprietors were still held, to which the canal company sent a representative on behalf of its shareholding. In 1827 also some trade from Bristol by the canal, such as oats imported from Ireland, was diverted to Gloucester and the Thames & Severn by the opening of the Gloucester & Berkeley Canal.

A little earlier, in 1824 and 1825, there had been strenuous attempts to get an Act for the Newbury–Basingstoke link to avoid the Thames, given point by the projected London–Bristol railway which, if built, made good water communication with London more important than ever. The canal company eventually agreed to subscribe £25,000 and in 1826 an agreement was made with the Thames Commissioners that their opposition to the Bill would be withdrawn in consideration of compensation for loss of trade. After 1829, however, we hear no more of this plan; the initiative had passed to the new railways, except for a touch of the grandiose in 1830, when there was talk of a ship canal from London to Bristol, to take 400-ton vessels and cost £8m.

In 1829 the flight of locks at Devizes was lit by gas.

The Gas Works along the line of Locks at Devizes being now in operation—Resolved that no Barge or Boat be allowed to enter any one of the Devizes Locks after the Gas shall be lighted but on payment of one shilling for each Barge and six pence for each Boat which payment shall entitle the Owner to navigate his Barge or Boat through the said Locks so long as the Gas shall be lighted but no longer.[33]

In 1828 it was agreed that as convenient the grass-sided and timber-framed Kennet locks would be rebuilt in stone or brick to the smaller canal size, and a beginning was made in 1833. In the latter year the company contributed £50 towards experiments on the fast carriage of passengers and light goods on canals, on the lines that had been successful in Scotland.[34] They then bought the experimental boat, and she started running a passenger service between Bath and Bradford-on-Avon, always being called the Scotch boat.

Averaged toll, dividend and tonnage figures are given below. The Kennet is not included until 1815:

Years	Average toll receipts £	Average dividends per cent	Average tonnages tons
1809–11*	6,802	—	
8112–14	20,588	—	139,523
8115–17	28,092	1·5	
1818–20	33,569	2·125	182,739
1821–23	32,187	2·375	182,751
1824–26	39,416	2·958	
1827–29	46,326	3·125	
1830–32	44,789	3·125	
1833–35	45,060	2·58	
1836–38	46,061	3·292	
1839–41	50,629	3·125	
1842–44	33,142	0·9375	

* Year ending dates in May.

Charles Dundas, the chairman of the company, died in 1832, the year in which he had been created Lord Amesbury. He was eighty. The report of that year said:

> To his extensive acquaintance with influential persons, to his unwearied diligence, and to the respect in which his character was held, both in the Country and in Parliament, the obtaining of the first Act in 1794, was principally owing.

He died after having guided the affairs of the canal for nearly forty years. Although, because of its high cost of construction, dividends were still only 25s (£1.25) per annum on £40 shares, the canal was then carrying over 300,000 tons a year, and had a revenue of £47,000. It was the biggest waterway concern south of the Gloucester & Berkeley, and he left it at the peak of its prosperity, two years before a Bill was promoted to build the Great Western Railway. The canal age in the south had been short— shorter than in the north—and the death of Charles Dundas marked its real end.

There had been several proposals for a railway from London to Bristol, or for portions of such a line, before that which, strongly supported by the corporate bodies of Bristol, adopted on the 19 August 1833 the title of Great Western Railway. At the end of October the directors announced that they would seek powers in the next session of Parliament to build the line from London to Reading, with a branch to Windsor, and from Bath to Bristol, and in the following year those for the whole line. The proposal was supported in many of the towns to be served, while the waterways allied themselves with a number of opposing landowners, and those few independent people who did not believe in railways, like the correspondent of the *Reading Mercury* who considered that 'London and Bristol, as two places of import, could have neither community of trade nor reciprocity of interest', and thought the scheme would only fill the pockets of 'solicitors, surveyors, and contractors'.[35] The proposed line by way of Reading, Didcot, Swindon, and Bath would compete directly with the Thames to Reading, the Wilts & Berks to Swindon and beyond, and the Kennet & Avon between Bath and Bristol. Because this last waterway carried the bulk of the through London–Bristol traffic, however, it was likely to be hard hit.

On 19 February 1834, therefore, after having been told that the Thames Commissioners and some landowners were opposing the Great Western Bill, the committee of the Kennet & Avon decided also to oppose. The proceedings of the Parliamentary committee on the Bill took fifty-seven days, and were filled with misleading statements on both sides; then the Bill passed the Commons, and was thrown out in the Lords. The Kennet & Avon company realized, however, that the reprieve was temporary, for on 10 September 1834 they

> Resolved that a Special Committee . . . be appointed for the purpose of ascertaining whether any and what possible Reductions can be made in the expenses of the Company. Resolved that Mr. Blackwell and Mr. Brand be directed to visit every part of the Kennet and Avon Navigation and report for the information of the Committee in December what possible Reductions can be made and also what Improvements or Alterations in the Rates of Tonnage or in the mode of charging the same can be effected to promote the Trade of the Company.[36]

A Bill was reintroduced in the following year, but this time for the whole line of the railway. The landowners had given up their opposition, but the waterways were now joined by Eton College and the London & Southampton Railway Company, who were promoting a rival railway from their line to Bath, called the Basing & Bath Railway, by way of the Kennet & Avon route. The London & Southampton had approached the Kennet & Avon in March, and had

> submitted certain propositions for the cooperation of the

Kennet and Avon Co. with the promoters of the Basing and Bath Railway;[37]
but the canal directors had said that they were only disposed to co-operate with the Basing & Bath to the extent of opposing the Great Western. At this meeting the clerk had reported that the Thames Commissioners were willing to improve their navigation, but not to reduce their tolls, and also that an agreement had been reached for fast boats to run for five years between Bradford and Bath. Three days later a number of salaries were cut.

In June toll reductions were made while the Bill was being discussed, perhaps in order to make the railway look less attractive commercially, but the railway Act was finally passed on 31 August 1835. Before that the Great Western had agreed to pay £10,000 to the canal for land at Twerton needed for the railway, which belonged to the old Bath & Bristol Canal Company, the assets of which had been bought by the Kennet & Avon. Most of the money was used to replace six of the wooden locks on the Kennet. Later in the year the canal committee discerned another threat, for a sub-committee was formed to report upon the effect that steam road carriages might be expected to have upon their fortunes. In December the sub-committee reported that

the Establishment of Steam Carriages on the Turnpike Road between London and Bristol would be beneficial to the Kennet and Avon Company by discouraging Railways.[38]

In the following year of 1836 the canal's £40 shares, which in 1830 had stood at £27½, were steady at £22, and the committee could report that no boats belonging to traders were out of employment, and, in 1837, that in consequence of the increase of traffic, boats should be allowed to travel through the night without extra charge. The canal's total receipts rose as follows, partly, of course, because it was carrying material for the railway, till the opening of the whole Great Western line from London to Bristol on 30 June 1841, and then fell sharply away:

Year	£	Year	£
1836	44,631	1844	30,986
1837	45,915	1845	29,658
1838	47,938	1846	29,254
1839	48,365	1847	29,432
1840	52,348	1848	28,213
1841	51,174	1849	25,398
1842	36,395	1850	22,248
1843	32,045	1851	22,821

The competition with its local trade that the Kennet & Avon had so far avoided was not far off. The Berks & Hants Railway from Reading through Newbury to Hungerford was authorized in 1845 and opened in 1847. By that time, however, much had happened within the canal's committee room.

The Great Western was still building when in July 1838

> Mr. Robbins is directed to go to London in order to make Inquiries as to the Variations made in the Rates of Tonnage on the Grand Junction Canal in consequence of the opening of the London and Birmingham Railway.[39]

Thenceforward, in irritation at obstructions to the waterway caused by railway works, in talking of steam boats and discussing a proposed Bill to enable canal companies to become carriers, the committee waited for the railway to open, and even agreed with that company upon a junction between canal and rails at Reading, on the suggestion of Brunel. By September 1841, however, tolls on the canal had been reduced by 25 per cent, and the company were urging the Thames Commissioners to reduce theirs also. They were also writing to the Great Western itself, who had a credit account and were very short of ready money, to ask for a settlement of their bill, and to 'express the surprize of this Committee at not having hitherto received any communication from them on the subject.'[40] By June 1842 an economy drive was in full swing. Wages were cut, and employees reduced in number. The actual figures give an idea of the staff of a large canal at that time:

Lock-keepers reduced from	42 to 39
Carpenters reduced from	17 to 13
Blacksmiths remained at	2 2
Ballasters remained at	4 4
Puddlers reduced from	17 to 14
Labourers reduced from	26 to 20
Masons reduced from	14 to 8
	122 100

Even the mileage payment for the attendance of committeemen at meetings was reduced from 1s 6d (7½p) to 1s (5p) a mile. The report for 1841–2 said:

> The very great difference in the Receipts of the past year is to be attributed to the general depressed state of trade, and the absolute necessity of reducing the Tonnage duty, to compete with other means of Conveyance.

The Kennet & Avon Company was hampered in its competition

on the one hand by the refusal of the Thames Commissioners to co-operate in reducing tolls, and on the other by the attitude of the Somerset coalowners and the Coal Canal. The following letter, received in December 1842 from the Reading coal merchants, is an instance of the latter:

Gentlemen,

We the undersigned Coal Merchants respectfully call your attention to the prices at which the Great Western Railway Company are vending Newcastle, Welsh and Forest of Dean Coals, of which we enclose you their list. At such prices it will be impossible that we can compete with them & unless it is in your power to put us in a better position in the Market, we have no other alternative but to lose our Trade and you your Tonnage.

The committee

Resolved unanimously that this Company having reduced their Tolls to the lowest possible rate cannot in justice to themselves make any further concession whilst the Coal Canal Company are charging 2s 3d. per Ton for a distance of ten miles and the Kennet and Avon Canal Company only 5s. per Ton for a distance of 70 Miles.[41]

Somerset coalowners had often been accused of charging high prices, but when in 1847 they were asked by the Kennet & Avon to help them against railway competition, they also accused the Coal Canal:

before the Coal Masters could come to a decision as to any or what assistance they could grant it would be necessary for the Kennet & Avon and Somersetshire Coal Canal Companies to come to some definite arrangement as to what reductions they proposed to make on their Tolls for they felt assured from experience that whatever reductions or allowance they now made to the trade would only be taken of by the Somersetshire Coal Canal Company to maintain their present high rates of Toll as long as they could.[42]

Meanwhile the London trade in goods passing between the metropolis and the Kennet & Avon Canal had fallen from 54,000 tons in 1840 to 38,500 in 1843. In this year fly-boats which had hitherto only worked between Bath and Bradford were organized to run twice a week between London and Bristol in five days, the passage of the canal taking 36 hours. They were taken off in 1845. In other traffic the company was so far holding its own in tonnage carried, though not in tolls received.

There were now difficulties with the Avon & Gloucestershire

horse railway, which the company owned. It had never been a success, and in 1843 £45,000 of capital spent on it had to be written off. Then the Bristol & Gloucester Railway bought the Bristol & Gloucestershire horse railway, with which the A & GR connected, and converted it to the broad gauge and to locomotive operation, the narrow gauge being left in place for the part over which the A & GR ran to Coalpit Heath. It took an hour to pull an A & GR train over this section, and their trains were fitted in with the six steam trains a day of the Bristol & Gloucester. Somewhat naturally, the Kennet & Avon complained of the results of this system, and the Board of Trade stopped the working by horses when it came to their ears. Eventually after discussion the B & GR offered to haul two trains a day of A & GR waggons each way along the joint stretch with their locomotives at 6d (2½p) a ton including toll, and this offer was accepted.

The railway mania was now approaching, and Bills were promoted for many lines that affected the Kennet & Avon and its neighbours, and which it opposed. The pressure of these, and of further toll reductions made in June 1845 to meet reductions made by the Great Western, led the proprietors to wonder if there were not a way out of the net of railway competition. On 1 July 1845, at a meeting of proprietors in London, a resolution was unanimously passed:

> That the Committee of Management be requested by this Meeting of Proprietors to ascertain how far it may be practicable and desirable to convert the towing path of the Kennet and Avon Canal or the canal itself or any part thereof into a Railway.[43]

The Great Western, hearing of this plan, now seems to have done some brisk kite-flying. The two following newspaper extracts are interesting because they seem to bear evidence of that art, and because the meeting they refer to is not recorded in the Kennet & Avon books. The first is dated 23 July 1845, the second a week later.

> Great Western Railway. An arrangement is now in progress, and approaching completion, for the purpose of transferring the whole property of the Kennet and Avon Canal Company to the Great Western Railway Company.

> At a general meeting of the Kennet and Avon Canal on Tuesday, it was resolved unanimously that an offer of the canal be made to the railway company. There is no doubt whatever of the issue of this negociation, not only for what has already passed between the parties, but from the obvious interests of both.[44]

Meanwhile the committee appointed a sub-committee with powers to employ engineers and to report upon the best way of carrying out the suggestion made on 1 July. James Walker the engineer was engaged, his preliminary report was made in August, and the proprietors agreed to go ahead and apply for an Act on the basis that the canal company should pay one-third of the preliminary expenses, and the holders of the new shares to be issued the other two-thirds.

The engineer recommended that the canal should be retained, and the railway built alongside it. He said:

you have by rough walling the sides of the Canal, sufficient width generally for two lines of broad gauge and a better canal than the present, inasmuch as there is less friction in a walled canal than with sloping sides. I cannot help considering that your coming before the public with the Canal and Railway is very important both in obviating objections that may be made to the conversion of your Canal into a Railway by other Canal Companies or by canal carriers or the owners of warehouses and other property and by being practically useful afterwards—for canals may not always remain at their present discount and there must be a reluctance at resolving to destroy the substantial Locks Aqueducts and other Works which within 40 years have cost a Million of money.[45]

The estimated cost was £800,000, with a small additional sum for straightening out the curves and evening the gradients that would be met with if the canal line were strictly followed. Devizes was reported to be in favour of the plan, several new railway companies had made offers for the canal or for co-operation, extensions of the proposed canal railway were being thought of, and an enthusiastic report to the shareholders ends by saying:

Your Committee cannot conclude this Report without congratulating the Proprietors on the position of their Undertaking.[46]

Such was the effect of the railway mania. The Kennet & Avon's Bill, for the London, Newbury, and Bath Direct Railway from Newbury to Bath, was introduced in early 1846. It passed its second reading, whereas the rival Bill to extend the Great Western from Newbury to Hungerford was thrown out for non-compliance with standing orders. The committee was jubilant, and reported that theirs was:

now the only project before Parliament existing out of all the Lines proposed through the Vale of Pewsey towards Bath and Bristol in the autumn of last year.[47]

While the Kennet & Avon's Bill was before the House the canal's sub-committee was in touch with the Great Western, and

Q

when it was rejected in committee and the Hungerford extension, which had again been introduced, was authorized, the rejection was accompanied by an agreement between the canal company on the one hand and the Great Western and the Wilts, Somerset & Weymouth Railways on the other. The latter company had been authorized to build a line from Thingley Junction near Chippenham on the GWR main line to Weymouth. After many vicissitudes it reached Westbury from Thingley on 5 September 1848. I do not know the terms of this agreement, but it seems to have involved a payment to the canal company to drop their railway proposal, for on 9 September 1846 the minutes record that the first instalment of £5,000 payable under this agreement is now due.*

The proposed construction of the line from Thingley Junction was the cause of a newspaper paragraph which shows how absolutely the idea of railways had gripped the public imagination as the mania year began. A deputation of merchants and traders of Bristol had gone to the Great Western:

> The Deputation were unable to produce any favourable impression on the Board of Directors, but they did obtain that Board's direct admission . . . that it was neither expected or intended that the line to Thingley† was to be used as a Communication between Bath and Bradford, but that the intercourse between those two places, must be continued as heretofore by coaches and canal.

On which the paper comments:

> By coaches and canal!—by canal, especially, in these days of rapid intercommunication, when minutes, not miles, are the indications of distance. Surely the magnates of the Leviathan Company did not intend to insult the citizens of Bath and Bristol, and yet it looked very like it.[48]

The financial position of the Kennet & Avon was now thoroughly bad. The takings had fallen further, from £32,045 in 1842–3 to £25,398 in 1848–9. On the other hand, the tonnage carried in 1848–9 was higher than it had been ten years before, but it earned only a little over half the revenue, so strong was the competition. Dividends, which had been 30s (£1.50) on the £40 shares in 1840–1, were in 1848–9 only 7s 6d (37½p), or rather under 1 per cent.

---

* H. G. Lewin, in *The Railway Mania and its Aftermath*, 1936, says of the canal company: 'the Great Western bought off their opposition by an offer of shares and payment of their Parliamentary expenses.'

† In fact, the curve at Thingley Junction was specifically authorized (but not built) to give connection between Bath and Trowbridge. The direct line via Bradford was opened in 1857.

In 1848 the company made its last effort. On the one hand, a number of tolls were reduced, especially on coal; on the other, it entered the carrying trade. By the end of June, 33 boats had been bought, mostly bankrupt stock, Aurelius J. Drewe had been appointed traffic manager, and it was hoped that the London–Bristol trade would be revived, at least to 25,000 tons a year. By March 1849, £12,000 had been invested in the carrying business. Now, however, the committee's minds were turning to a possible arrangement with the Great Western for agreed charges by both companies, and an end to price-cutting. Mr Drewe called upon Mr Saunders, Secretary of the Great Western, to discuss the idea, but the absence of result led the canal company to approach the London & South Western and the South Eastern Railways to suggest that goods for London should be transferred to the LSWR at Reading, but 'the two Railway Companies were disputing so that for the present there was not much prospect of an arrangement.'[49]

There were now more cuts in tolls, and the carrying department, after a promising start, was losing money. The traffic manager resigned. The dividend for 1849–50, the last paid, was down to 4s (20p) per £40 share, and it was clear that the canal could not sustain the competition with the railway. In June 1851 the chairman and two members of the committee reported that they had been in touch with the Great Western, and had come to an agreement on the basis of an annual income to the shareholders of 6s (30p) a share, or £7,373 a year, the canal to be maintained in effective working condition. Meanwhile the canal committee was to manage the carrying business and the canal as trustees for the railway company. In August the proprietors ratified the agreement.

In this year of 1851 Admiral Dundas the chairman resigned, and the old name which had been with the canal from the beginning left it only as it ended its separate life. A junction cut was built at Aldermaston for the exchange of traffic with the railway, and, symbol of the new world of steam, the company's tug working on the Avon blew up, killing three men and a lad. On 20 July 1852 the committee heard of the

> serious illness of Mr. Matthews the Traffic Agent at Newbury occasioned by a Coup de Soleil and that he had been obliged to be removed to a Lunatic Asylum,

and on 29 July their last meeting was held.

The carrying business was continued by the railway till 1873, when it was closed down because of the losses that were being made. In December 1851 it was

Resolved that Mr. Chandler should be allowed to continue his packet boat between Wootton Rivers and Devizes at 2/6 per trip provided that the pace does not exceed four miles per hour,[50]

but I do not know what happened to this late example of passenger carrying under railway ownership. The Scotch boat between Bath and Bradford continued at least until the end of 1854.

The state of the Avon & Gloucestershire Railway is not easy to determine. In December 1849 there had been a complaint that the line was not open, and the committee had replied that they were ready to co-operate with the coalowners in 'endeavouring to get that portion of the Railway now under the management of the Midland Railway Company put into a proper state for the traffic.'[51] A year later no traffic was passing through from Coalpit Heath; elsewhere on the line economies were being made, and efforts to find someone who would lease it, but without success. In 1865 powers were obtained to close it, and after January 1867 it probably became disused, though sections were revived between 1881 and 1904 to serve first Warmley and later California colliery. On 9 July 1906 the general manager informed the traffic committee of the Great Western that 'all traffic on the Avon Tramway has now ceased'.

The River Avon, nominally independent to the end, remained to the end prosperous also. It will be remembered that these shares of no par value probably represented about £400 worth each of original capital, but from £900 to £5,000 each of Kennet & Avon shareholders' money. The dividends on these Avon shares for the last years of the canal were:

	£		£
1846	100	1849	64
1847	95	1850	55
1848	96	1851 (1st half)	34·17

Railway competition with the canal's trade increased after the opening of the Holt and Devizes line in 1857 and the Berks & Hants Extension from Hungerford to Devizes in 1862. After the Great Western took over the tonnage carried at first fell slowly, and then faster to the end of the century and beyond, while its condition slowly deteriorated. Representative figures are given in the table at the top of the next page.

The company's ownership was punctuated by complaints made by traders to them or to the Board of Trade. But witnesses of many opinions before the Royal Commission of 1906, from de Salis to

Date	Tonnage
1848 (canal management)	360,610
1858	261,822
1868	210,567
1878	132,654
1888	120,120
1898	83,373
1906	53,751

the representatives of the Great Western, saw little possibility of reviving through traffic, as much from sea as from railway competition. At this time there was practically no through traffic. Some moved between Reading and Newbury, but most of what remained arose from Bristol docks, and was carried to Bath or Devizes. About 12 per cent of this was coal.

Thereafter a general goods trade continued from Bristol to Devizes until about 1925, from Bristol or Bath to Semington mill until about 1931, and from Avonmouth to Honeystreet regularly until about 1929, and infrequently afterwards to 1937. On the Avon a daily tar barge ran until 1967. On the canal between Honeystreet and Newbury there was regular trade to about 1920, and an occasional barge to the early 1930s. Between Newbury and Reading general cargo was carried until about 1930, then occasionally to about 1934.

The rest of the period of railway ownership saw a continued worsening in the canal's condition and in its operating deficit, and in 1926 an unsuccessful attempt by the railway company to abandon it. By 1947 it was barely navigable. After its transfer to the British Transport Commission in 1948, increasing interest was taken in the canal's restoration as pleasure cruising on Britain's inland waterways increased, an interest that was fostered by the Kennet & Avon Canal Association (later Trust) and other concerned bodies. Legal actions and recriminations pursued the Commission, but after transfer to the British Waterways Board in 1962, hopes for eventual restoration grew. Work has since been done by volunteers and the Board, and as I write, a Government decision in favour of restoration seems likely.[52]

CHAPTER XI

The Somersetshire Coal Canal

✦✦✦✦✦✦✦✦✦✦✦✦✦✦✦✦✦✦✦✦✦✦✦✦✦✦✦✦✦✦✦✦✦✦✦✦✦✦◆✦✦✦✦✦✦✦✦✦✦✦✦✦✦✦✦✦✦✦✦✦✦✦✦✦✦✦✦✦✦✦✦✦✦✦✦✦✦✦

THE first proposal for a canal[1] to serve the thirty or so collieries
to the south of Bath seems to have been put to a public meeting
at the Old Down Inn on the last day of 1792, with John Billingsley,
a man much concerned with local improvements,[2] in the chair,
which decided to seek landowners' agreement to a canal to Bath.[3]
On 4 February 1793 another meeting at Old Down,
    of the several proprietors of certain collieries in the neighbour-
    hood of Dunkerton, Camerton, Timsbury, Paulton, and Rad-
    stock, denominated the Northern collieries, and also those in
    the neighbourhood of Kilmersdon and Holcombe, denominated
    the Southern collieries
agreed that a canal from the northern collieries
    to Bath, and to join any canal that may be cut by the river Avon
    to the city of Bath and its neighbourhood
would cheapen coal by reducing the cost of carriage. A committee
was set up, and instructed to engage an engineer to make plans
and estimates, who was also to survey and estimate for
    a branch from the proposed canal to Radstock; from Radstock
    to such place or places as may appear of general utility to the
    southern collieries.[4]
Rennie, who was then surveying for the future Kennet & Avon
Canal, was the obvious man to employ. Under him the survey was
done by William Smith, later the famous geologist, then a young
man of twenty-three whom Rennie had recommended to the committee, and Mr Haverfield, seemingly a member of the promotion
committee, was asked to advise on the plan and estimates when
they were made. William Jessop was also requested to make a
report independently of Rennie, being attended by Smith while he
did so: presumably his greater eminence netted him the £75 he
was paid, against £23 to Rennie.
    On 14 October the 'proprietors of several collieries in the vales

of Dunkerton and Radstock' met again to hear Rennie's report, which proposed a line from the Kennet & Avon at Limpley Stoke up the Dunkerton valley, with a branch along the Wellow valley, at a cost of £80,000. It was decided to seek a Bill, and to reserve 300 £100 shares for landowners on the line—a considerable sweetener at this time of the canal mania.[5] The deposited plans were prepared with Smith's help, and signed by Rennie.

A meeting on 1 February 1794 approved the Bill, which was passed on 17 April,[6] the same day as that for the Kennet & Avon. It authorized a canal 10½ miles long from the Kennet & Avon at Limpley Stoke to Gooseyard (Goodsard) Bridge, Paulton by way of Midford, Combe Hay, Dunkerton and Camerton, with a branch from Midford by Wellow and Writhington to Radstock,* 7¼ miles long. It was envisaged that each line would be joined by horse railways from the neighbouring collieries and quarries. The capital authorized was £80,000, with power to raise £40,000 more if necessary.

The first shareholders' meeting was held on 3 June 1794. The parliamentary line envisaged level canals except for two big alterations in height, one at Combe Hay on the Paulton line, and one at Midford on that to Radstock. There were to be tunnels at Combe Hay on the first, and Wellow on the second, though the former was greatly shortened by diversions approved under the 1796 Act. Two matters were quickly settled: the canal, unlike the Kennet & Avon, was to be built for narrow boats; and the water supply seemed ample: 'there should be a large surplus, even in . . . excessive droughts, to answer every purpose of the navigation.'

The problems lay in the hilly country to be traversed, the tunnels, and the best way to overcome the steep differences of level at Combe Hay and Midford. Whitworth and John Sutcliffe, a north-countryman, were now called in to do the detailed work, Sutcliffe in December being appointed chief engineer on a daily pay basis. Meanwhile two committeemen, Richard Perkins of Oakhill and Samborne Palmer, attended by William Smith, were despatched on a 900 mile tour to study canal and railway construction that took them as far as Newcastle. A meeting at Bath on 3 December heard the results of their explorations, 'a very elaborate, scientific and ingenious report' written by Perkins. It was the universal opinion, that by their researches, shares in this canal are rendered of more than double their former value;

---

* To Welton colliery a little beyond Radstock, though the canal as constructed ended in Radstock, the colliery extension being made by railway.

and that this city will experience, in a much shorter time than was before supposed, a most considerable reduction in the price of coal, through the means which the committee are now empowered to adopt.

At a committee meeting earlier, on 3 October, a letter was read from Dr James Anderson suggesting the use of his pattern of lift. Anderson was one of many who at this period invented ways of raising and lowering boats vertically. His lift[7] was similar to those later built on the Dorset & Somerset and Grand Western Canals,[8] two counterbalanced caissons being held by chains passing over pulleys between them, and being raised or lowered by subtracting water from the lower.

The snag about the system was that he described it as suitable for boats of up to 20 tons, and preferably of 10 or 15 tons, whereas the canal committee wanted to use narrow boats. But at the same meeting Mr Perkins read his report. The party's travels must have included visits to inclined planes and horse railroads, probably those in Shropshire, which attracted them as new developments, for the committee seem to have liked the idea of planes to overcome their differences of level. However, the party can have seen none able to take a narrow boat—those in existence were for craft of 5 to 8 tons—and so they thought of making them railroad planes and extending them as railroads along the upper lines to Paulton and Radstock, so that loads would only have to be transhipped once, at the bottom of each plane. In December, after the shareholders had heard the travellers' report, the committee were empowered to proceed either by canals with inclined planes, or by railroads, as they thought most expedient. By January 1795, however, they had decided that summit level canals were preferable to railroads.

William Bennet, then surveying for the Dorset & Somerset Canal promoters, was called in to help Smith in preparing plans, and tenders were sought, cutting to start between Paulton and Camerton and from Radstock towards Wellow. It did so about the middle of 1795. Early in 1796 a second Act allowed a number of variations in the original line. Bennet was now appointed engineer in place of Sutcliffe, Smith remaining as surveyor. Smith ceased to work for the company in the spring of 1799.

Meanwhile Robert Weldon had in the middle of 1794 put to the committee a proposal for a vertical lift, or hydrostatick lock as he called it. Later it was to be called a caisson lock. The idea attracted them strongly, presumably because it would take a full-length narrow boat, and in July 1795 they agreed to ask the Kennet &

Avon to join them in the cost of an experiment. The latter agreed to pay a quarter, up to £300, of the cost, assuming the lift worked. Weldon was thereupon ordered to build his lift on the Radstock line, altered soon afterwards to Combe Hay, he to have £200 for the use of his patent if it worked, nothing if it did not.

Weldon came from Lichfield, the home of the inventor-poet-doctor Erasmus Darwin. Darwin, who had been concerned in promoting the Trent & Mersey Canal in 1765[9] had entered in his commonplace book about 1779 a description of a canal lift identical in idea to Weldon's, except that Darwin's had two caissons and was counterbalanced.[10] It is likely, therefore, that Weldon had known Darwin. Weldon now had a model of his lift built at Oakengates in Shropshire, where it was

> exhibited to several persons of distinction, and others, conversant in that business, who expressed very great satisfaction at seeing so useful an invention brought to perfection.[11]

Demonstrations went on for six weeks in the hopes that other canal committees might be interested, but seemingly none were.

Weldon took some time to make his preparations, eventually starting work during the early months of 1796. In June the *Bath Chronicle* had said:

> We learn . . . with pleasure that in a few months this canal will be so far complete as to convey coal from Paulton to Dunkerton, and from Radstock to Wellow. The delay in completing the caisson-lock . . . will, it is hoped, be compensated by the advantages to be derived from it. Should this succeed, there will be two more caissons, and the saving by their adoption, instead of locks and reservoirs, will be at least £10,000, exclusive of the material advantage of supplying the upper canal with water from the lower level.[12]

From outside, prospects also looked good. In 1795 a pamphlet writer said:

> I believe it will generally be allowed that the supply of coal from the Somersetshire Coal Canal will be sufficient, of itself, to pay the subscribers to the Kennet and Avon an ample interest,[13]

while one of the declared purposes of the proposed Wilts & Berks Canal was to carry Somerset coal along the Vale of White Horse.

Weldon's lift consisted of a single watertight wooden caisson large enough to hold a narrow boat carrying 20 or 30 tons, which rose and fell within a chamber full of water in which the caisson was totally immersed. The water thus took the weight, and the caisson rose and fell as it was wound up and down by rack and

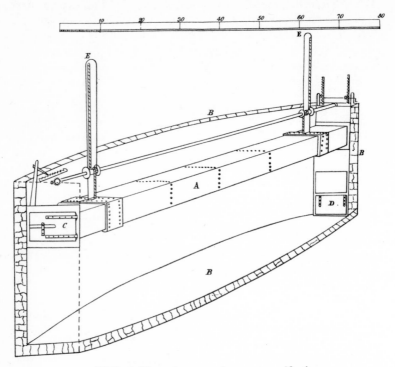

33. Weldon's lift, as shown on the patent specification

pinion gear,* the water finding its way round the caisson sides as this was done. Wheels, not shown on the patent drawing, kept the caisson equidistant from the sides of the structure. The dimensions of the chamber were: height from foundations to top, 88 ft, width in middle, 20 ft, width at each end, $11\frac{1}{2}$ ft, length 88 ft, lift obtained, 46 ft.[15] The lift was near Caisson House, used from about 1813 as the canal engineer's residence—but its exact site has not yet been established. It was built of brick, and for purposes of testing, a short length of approach tunnel was constructed below it. Weldon was at work on its construction in the autumn of 1796 and the whole of 1797.

In October 1797 tenders were sought to extend the Radstock branch from near Wellow to the top of the hill above Midford,

---

* As shown on the patent drawing. William Chapman, in his book of 1797,[14] describes an alternative, which is probably earlier, that of adding or removing water from the caisson: 'like an air balloon, it ascends or descends by a slight increase, or diminution, of the relative gravity; which, in this machine, is done by raising out, or admitting an inconsiderable quantity of water.'

and the main line from Midford to the Kennet & Avon at Limpley Stoke. The second was proceeded with, but no further work was then done on the Radstock branch, which remained completed from near Wellow to the basin, which lay just beyond the Walde-grave Arms in Radstock,[16] whence railways ran to the Welton and Middle Coal pits. On 30 September 1798 five boatloads of coal came down the Paulton branch from Camerton to Dunkerton to be taken onwards by road, and a regular service started, which was extended to the whole length from Paulton to Dunkerton in November 1799.[17]

By November 1797 the caisson at Combe Hay could be raised and lowered in the shaft. In February 1798, there was a full-dress test, during which part of the rack and pinion mechanism gave way, damaging the interior of the lift. Then in June

the Caisson Lock . . . underwent a compleat trial . . . when the principles of its action and utility were fully established. The descent of the Caisson from the upper to the lower level, the passage of the boat therefrom to the end of the tunnel, its return and admission into the Caisson and its subsequent ascent and discharge at the upper level, may be regarded as a compleat operation . . . After the experiment, several gentlemen, struck with the facility and safety of the operation, went down in the Caisson to a depth of more than sixty feet

though 'the working was retarded by a few obstructions altogether casual.'[18] However, Weldon undertook 'to pass through the cais-son-lock fifteen hundred ton of goods in 12 hours, with only one man to work the machinery, and the assistance of the boatmen.' The company then announced that they would build two more, another at Combe Hay and one at Midford, though later they deferred action pending a final trial of the lift they had.

By late 1798, however, the proprietors were in trouble over it. There was a report of 'repeated failures of the caisson',[19] and soon afterwards discussions began on 'some other mode of transferring boats from the upper to the lower level'.[20] However, the share-holders decided to keep trying.

We cannot but admire the persevering and liberal spirit of the Gentlemen who form the Committee of the Somersetshire Coal Canal respecting the Caisson Lock. The frequent disappoint-ments they met with, together with the occurring disagreeable accidents to the machine itself, were indeed almost enough for them to have abandoned the measure entirely; but happy for inland navigation they beheld these disappointments in a differ-ent view; convinced that they arose from the novelty of the undertaking *alone* and not from any *inherent* defect in the design they could not be diverted from this grand and important discovery by false arguments and sophistical conclusions.[21]

In spite of successful trials on 5, 17 and 27 April, at the last of which several brave spirits stayed with the boat: 'The time they first went into the boat to that of their coming out did not exceed 6 minutes and a half',[22] the great weight of water behind the lift walls made them bulge. In May, therefore, the company asked for tenders to rebuild the lift as well as to build others, 'it being probable that other cisterns of a similar or greater depth may be built on this line of Canal,'[23] but no satisfactory tender was received.

In their December 1799 report the committee, who had by then spent £4,582 on the caisson, justified it because it

has tended, at least, to prove the practicability of that machine in so full a degree, that the Scientific Gentlemen who were called in to decide on its merit, unanimously recommended it to be adopted.

The committee were now investigating the strength of the kind of stone (not brick this time), mortar and so on that would be necessary 'so as to satisfy their minds that the same can be rendered water-tight, and at a moderate expence.'

In the meantime, they wanted an immediate communication opened between the upper and lower canal levels on both lines, so that trade to the Kennet & Avon and the Wilts & Berks could start the following midsummer. So a long argument started upon how best this could be done. Messrs Whitmore & Norton of Birmingham* offered to build a balance lift† (they called it a geometrical lock) without payment, on condition that if successful they were to have £17,300 and a royalty of 4d per ton of goods passed. On this John Sutcliffe, called in, reported that he had seen a model in Birmingham, and that it was greatly preferable to the caisson lock, but he thought it would be better reduced in size to take 12-ton and not 24-ton boats, and in any case advised that the committee should wait to see whether Fussell's lift on the Dorset & Somerset worked properly before making up their minds.

Benjamin Outram, the engineer of the Peak Forest Canal and a plateway expert, whom William Smith had met on his tour, was called in and advocated rebuilding all the colliery railways as

---

* William Whitmore built weighing machines, and was later to work as engineer on the completion of the Stratford-upon-Avon Canal.

† This was of the type built on the Dorset & Somerset and the Grand Western Canal.

plateways to take 2-ton waggons instead of the existing 10-14 cwt trucks working on edge-rails. The trucks would then be run on to rafts* 90 ft long and 9 ft wide, each carrying twelve, which would be horse-towed to the tops of two inclined planes, one on each of the canal branches. The trucks would then be run on to plateways to take them down the planes and back on to rafts again or the coal unloaded into boats.

John Sutcliffe, who disliked both Outram and his plateways, criticized the plan by saying that the canal was too narrow for rafts, which would hit the banks when a wind was blowing and damage the puddling, and that there would be difficulty in getting the waggons on to them. Outram's plans for inclines, rafts and plateways to the mines was estimated at £22,035, including £3,500 for widening the canal, a figure Sutcliffe thought should be increased to at least £10,500. Instead, he advocated locks, at a cost of £16,692 on the Paulton branch and £18,981 on that to Radstock, which would cost less to maintain than Outram's rafts and inclines, and be more reliable. He also criticized the scheme of changing over from the present perfectly satisfactory small waggons working by gravity in gangs of six, with a boy to operate the brake, and a horse behind for the return journey. The small waggons caused fewer accidents, and gave cheaper discharge with less breakage of coal.[25]

Outram then changed his proposal, and suggested railways to join the levels, the coal to be carried in containers on the boats, and transferred to and from the railway by cranes. He had already successfully used containers for rail–canal transhipment on the Derby Canal at Little Eaton,[26] and was at that time just completing the plateway link at Marple between two levels of the Peak Forest Canal, upon which, again, containers were to be used.[27] The committee now took Outram's advice, and an inclined plane on the general lines he had recommended was built at Combe Hay for this method of working, which was described as 'letting down boxes full of coals, the descent of which, by means of ropes or wheels, drew up the boxes, either empty, or in part loaded with other goods.'[28] Below the plane, three locks were built to lower the canal fully to the Midford level.

The *Bath Chronicle* for 1 January 1801, commenting that the canal as far as Dunkerton, and the cart service, had brought the price of coal at Bath down from 1s 2d and 1s 3d (6p) a cwt a year before to 9d and 10d (4p), went on to say that the whole line via

---

* The idea of carrying trucks on rafts had a few years before been considered when the Charnwood Forest branch of the Leicester Navigation was being planned.[24]

the Kennet & Avon, including the inclined plane, would be open on 25 March. However, on 14 May it was still 'a few weeks' off completion. When it was brought into use, the plane was not a success. The Kennet & Avon Company said of it:

the Expence of Conveyance by the said Canal, as now executed, including the Injury done to the Coals, is nearly double what it would be by a Canal with Locks, and . . . it is not capable of conveying so much Coal, nor so expeditiously, as a Canal with Locks, and is attended with great Inconvenience to the Public,[29]

and complained that they had to charge less on their waterway than was reasonable, because the Coal Canal Company charged more. The Wilts & Berks, in a report of November 1802, referred to the plane 'where the Coal is shifted from the Upper to the Lower Level, occasioning much delay, labour, and injury, by breaking the Coal.'[30]

The Coal Canal Company therefore decided not to build a second plane on the Radstock line, but to replace both with flights of conventional locks, 19 on the Radstock branch, and 19 in addition to the existing three on the Paulton line. Calls of £150 per share had by April 1802 brought in about £106,000 of the £120,000 authorized, which had been spent along with £19,400 more which they still owed. An Act[31] of 1802 authorized the company to raise £20,000 over the £120,000 to pay its debts and finish its works. In addition, a unique arrangement was made in the form of a Lock Fund of £45,000 to build the two flights of locks, extend the Radstock line to Twinhoe, buy Dunkerton mill and build pumping engines. It had been agreed, and was set out in the Act, that willing subscribers from the Kennet & Avon and Wilts & Berks companies might join with the Coal Canal Company in subscribing £15,000 each. A joint committee, called 'The Deputies for managing the Lock Concerns of the Somersetshire Coal Canal' was set up and given powers to superintend the building of the locks and then to manage them; they were to charge 1s (5p) per ton for coal and ¾d per ton for other goods passing through the locks until the debt had been repaid. Thereupon the Combe Hay flight of locks was built, probably with William Bennet as engineer, and the water connection made on 5 April 1805, though it seems that trade down the locks did not begin until mid-January 1806. There was already a steam pumping engine at Dunkerton, and the Lock Fund deputies now provided another, from Boulton & Watt, to pump back up the locks at Combe Hay.

The money raised by the Lock Fund did not, however, run to

building a second flight of locks to the Radstock branch. Instead, a spur was constructed off the Midford line over the Cam Brook (the aqueduct is dated 1803) to basins on the south side. A mile-long tramroad was then built for £1,467 between Twinhoe, the end of the Radstock branch, and Midford, such coal as the Radstock pits produced being brought down the colliery railways to the basin there, along the canal to Twinhoe, and down the railway to the boats waiting at Midford.[32] The line was built by the Lock Fund, and then sold to the canal company.

The treble transhipment involved in this method of working was so obviously inefficient that, failing locks, it would be better to build a tramroad throughout from Midford to the pits. On 1 October 1814 a meeting was called

for the purpose of receiving and considering the report of Mr. John Hodgkinson as to the state of the Radstock Line of Canal; and proposals for making a Railway on the towing path of the said Line of Canal,[33]

and on 20 July 1815 the newspaper says:

We cheerfully avail ourselves of the opportunity now afforded us, of conveying to the Subscribers of the Canal and the Public the gratifying intelligence of the completion of the New Rail Road, from the village of Radstoke to the Canal near Mitford, a distance of upwards of seven miles; by which means a certain and regular communication is now opened to the several great collieries of Radstoke, Welton, Clandown and Smallcombe, from which works a constant supply of the very best Somersetshire coal may now be depended on to any extent.[34]

On this line three horses drew eight or nine waggons each holding 27 cwt.

By the end of 1810 the Kennet & Avon, the Wilts & Berks, the Thames & Severn and the Somersetshire Coal Canals were all open; together they had a considerable economic effect upon the area that lay between Salisbury Plain and the river Thames. The most important single result was the supply of coal to places along the lines of both the Kennet & Avon and the Wilts & Berks at prices considerably lower than previously by using land carriage. The main source of this coal was the Somerset field. The tonnage of coal leaving the Coal Canal rises steadily from this date, as can be seen from the figures* overleaf.

By 1828 the total tonnage on the canal, almost all of it coal, had reached 113,442, and in 1838 138,403. The carriage of this coal

* These figures are headed 'Coal and Stone' in the Kennet & Avon's reports, but it seems likely that the stone component can be ignored.

Year	Tonnage	Year	Tonnage
1811–12†	62,888½	1818	89,173
1812–13	66,741	1819	92,802
1813–14	77,737	1820	100,739
1814–15	81,751	1821	103,171
1816	76,079	1822	103,152
1817	74,115	1823	106,569

† Year 1 June–31 May.

brought a reasonable prosperity to the proprietors of the Coal Canal, in spite of their early troubles. In the year 1828 they distributed £11,114 in dividends on a capital of £140,000 and a similar sum in 1838, the total revenue being £14,809 in the former year and £17,010 in the latter. In addition, dividends were being paid by the Lock Fund to the three member canals, those going to the Coal Canal itself being included in the revenue figures given.

Coal was a highly competitive commodity. Newcastle coal came from London up the Thames towards Reading, in competition with that brought eastwards and southwards by the canals. From Somerset about one-third of the exports of the Coal Canal entered the Wilts & Berks and was distributed along its line, a quarter of this going as far as Abingdon for consumption in that town and for carriage upwards to Oxford and downwards towards Reading. A small quantity also passed through the North Wilts Canal into the Thames & Severn, for local use in Cirencester, Cricklade, and neighbouring places. Coal also came from the Midlands down the Oxford Canal to Oxford, whence it was carried upwards and downwards on the Thames to meet the other sources of supply. Lastly, the opening of the Thames & Severn had enabled coal from the Forest of Dean, Welsh, Shropshire, and Staffordshire mines to pass in varying proportions down the Thames and compete with Midlands coal. When the North Wilts was opened, coal from the Thames & Severn was expected to pass on to the Wilts & Berks to be distributed to Abingdon and the Thames, and also to Wootton Bassett and beyond.

This rivalry led on the one hand to competition in price between the coalowners of the various coalfields, and on the other to a system of drawbacks or subsidies to reduce the toll, given for the purpose of breaking into a new market or of holding an old one both by the coalowners and the canal companies. For instance, Forest of Dean coal coming down the Thames to Radcot wharf, and coal from Somerset coming to Longcot, were competing for the market in Faringdon, and in 1824 the clerk of the Wilts & Berks wrote to a coal merchant:

The Somersetshire Coal Canal Co. and the Coal Owners have agreed to allow a Drawback of 1s. 6d. per Ton on Coal carried through the Farringdon Gate* which is to be paid by our Wharfinger to the Consumer on taking away the Coal. I mean also to pay over 2s. in the same way . . . so that each person loading coal at Longcot will be entitled to 3s. 6d. per ton if they bring a certificate that the vehicle in which they load the Coal has passed through Farringdon Gate.

The merchant refused to reduce his prices also, and the clerk wrote again:

If you cannot reduce the price of Coal to assist us in drawing the Trade from Radcot I am sorry for it as I had hoped by this effort to have made a very considerable impression.[35]

Similarly, in order to compete with Midlands coal off the Oxford Canal, Mr Dunsford the clerk writes three days later to merchants at Reading:

Annexed I send you a Copy of the Coal Canal Co's resolution as to a further Drawback of 1s. per ton on Coal carried to Wallingford and Benson via Wilts and Berks Canal. You will please to inform me what your present selling price is and pledge yourself to reduce the shilling to your customers otherwise the additional Drawback will not be continued.[36]

The giving, changing, and withdrawing of these drawbacks to meet the constant changes brought about by every other interested party doing the same thing is bewildering now to anyone reading the minute books of the canal companies, and must have been confusing at the time to merchants and customers alike. To the poorer canal companies they were vital. The Wilts & Berks writes on 27 February 1838 to the Kennet & Avon when the latter was considering the abolition of a drawback:

You appear to consider Drawbacks in the light of a mere douceur or bonus to the Traders which may as well be saved by the company—I on the contrary deem them the means of inviting Trade which would not exist without them.

The competition for the coal trade was bitter. Mr Dunsford writes to a merchant:

I hope you do not meditate the introduction of the Staffordshire Coal at *our* Wharf at Wantage, as in that case I must candidly inform you that we shall expect a Wharfage to be paid equivalent to the difference of Tonnage† between it and the Coal

* Toll-gate. The stipulation was presumably to make sure the drawback was only given to coal going towards Faringdon, and not in the opposite direction.
† I.e. of toll.

R

brought from Semington . . . I consider the importation of Coal from the Oxford line to our very best Wharf, as a most unfair use of our Canal, and that we should combat such use with every weapon in our power. The Oxford Canal Company will not suffer the Somerset coal *to pass into their Canal*, and I cannot say I blame them. Of course they must expect equal obstructions as far as may be lawful.[37]

The Wilts & Berks was not always faithful to Somerset coal, for sometimes it considered that the coalowners and the Coal Canal were both charging too much, and at others it hoped that by encouraging Midlands coal it might obtain a back carriage of agricultural produce. In July 1828 it was sending Staffordshire coal imported via the North Wilts along its line to Abingdon, which annoyed the Oxford Company so much that their wharfinger at Abingdon

has orders to watch our price and always to undersell us. I have reason to believe that they would sacrifice half, or perhaps even two-thirds* rather than have their Thames trade interfered with.[38]

A few months later the chairman of the company writes to Mr Dunsford about the Somerset coalowners:

Staffordshire Coal owners are liberal in the measure they vend, having no inspectors to check the generosity or policy of each other. They neither dole out their commodity to the pound avoirdupois, nor have they, as I have heard, entered into any combination whatever against the interests of the public.[39]

For a time there was an outbreak of drawbacks to encourage Staffordshire and Forest of Dean coal, via the Thames & Severn, before the old arrangement, like an old marriage, settled down again.

A map of c. 1850[40] shows 31 pits then or previously connected to the Coal Canal system. On the Paulton line there were 7 pit tramroads totalling almost three track miles: on the Radstock tramroad line, another seven totalling 2⅝ miles. In September of this year the shareholders considered converting their property to a railway, but nothing came of it.[41]

Freedom from direct railway competition enabled the Coal Canal to maintain high tolls, and so to force the Kennet & Avon and the Wilts & Berks to bear the full weight of price-cutting. The opening of the Wilts, Somerset & Weymouth Railway's branch to Frome in 1854, enabling Radstock coal to be exported to Westbury and beyond, does not seem to have affected the tonnage they

* Of their tolls.

carried. Though the coalfield was a declining one, even in 1864 157,000 tons of coal passed over their line. Thereafter, however, Great Western ownership of the Kennet & Avon began to press upon them.

In 1871, rather surprisingly, the company sold the Radstock tramway to the Somerset & Dorset Railway for £20,000*. The railway company then used it for the extension of their line from Evercreech to Bath, which was opened in 1874. In the previous year the Bristol & North Somerset Railway had reached Radstock from Bristol. The combination of these events reduced the tonnage of coal carried on the Coal Canal to 24,581 in 1884. The purpose for which the canal existed had ended. The last fragmentary dividend was paid in 1889; in 1893, a year when 11,400 tons of coal were carried, the company went into liquidation; in 1898 pumping of water to the summit level ceased; and in 1902 a Board of Trade inquiry was held. The inspector reported that the canal was derelict, and was never likely to be reopened as a canal, because the collieries it served had been closed. The Great Western wished to buy the site, and an Act of 1904 authorized abandonment and enabled them to do so; they then built a railway from Limpley Stoke on the Bath–Bradford line to Camerton, which was opened in 1910.

The shareholders did badly in the final distribution. The former £150 shares had earlier been reduced in nominal value by the repayment of £25 2s 6d (£25.12½) a share, most of this probably coming from the sale of the Radstock tramway. The 800 shares only got a further 16s 3d (81p) each, in 1907. The 3,600 £12 10s (£12.50) Lock Fund shares got nothing. With the decline and closing of the Coal Canal went the last source of exclusive traffic the Kennet & Avon possessed.

* The prospectus for the extension of the Somerset & Dorset Railway (*Railway Times*, 13 January 1872) said: 'The Company have . . . purchased, on advantageous terms, the Somersetshire Coal Tramway, over which upwards of 100,000 tons a year are at present carried, which will connect the Line with all the principal pits in and near Radstock. . . .'

CHAPTER XII

The Wilts & Berks Canal

THE Wilts & Berks grew out of the 1784 proposal for a canal from the Thames & Severn near Lechlade to Abingdon (see p. 198), which had been promoted at a meeting called at Abingdon and supported by local landowners; a later proposal described by Frederick Page for a canal similar in dimensions to the Thames & Severn, and so able to take Thames barges, to run from Kempsford on that canal by way of Highworth and Longcot to near Wantage, where one branch would lead to Abingdon and another to Wallingford;[1] and the abandoned first route of the Kennet & Avon by way of Calne and Chippenham. A promotion meeting was held at Swindon on 12 November 1793, which decided that the scheme was not yet mature enough for the current session of Parliament, but, at the suggestion of James Black of the Thames & Severn, ordered their engineer William Whitworth to survey also for a junction with that canal.[2]

A revised plan, which included branches to Calne and Chippenham, was put by William Whitworth to a committee meeting at Swindon on 22 February 1794, with the Earl of Peterborough in the chair, and approved, together with an agreement made with the Kennet & Avon company. It was not until another meeting on 16 May, however, that the Abingdon termination was finally settled.[3]

A Bill was introduced, and opposed by the city of Oxford, which considered that the city and the Thames Navigation above Abingdon would be injured, inasmuch as the canal 'will considerably divert the Trade of the Navigation of those Rivers* . . . and from the . . . City of Oxford.'[4] Nevertheless, an Act[5] was passed in 1795 for a narrow canal to leave the Kennet & Avon near Trowbridge, and to run by Melksham, Dauntsey, Wootton Bassett, Swindon, Shrivenham and Challow to Abingdon. The main line was to be 55¼ miles long, but at the time the Kennet &

* The Thames and Isis.

Avon were proposing a deviation of their own route, and therefore the Act provided that, should this be authorized within three years and opened within seven, the Wilts & Berks should transfer their Semington–Trowbridge section to that company. In fact, after the deviation had been authorized, this section was made by the Kennet & Avon, thus reducing the Wilts & Berks's length to 51 miles of main line.[6] Three branches were also authorized, to Calne, Chippenham and Wantage. The canal's principal purposes were seen as carrying Somerset coal to the places along its line, and bringing away agricultural produce. Sea-coal interests had, however, inserted a ban on canal-borne coal carried on the Thames below Reading.

Robert and William Whitworth had signed the deposited plan, but William with John Ralph the estimate of £103,603 for the 55¼-mile main line, and £8,350 for the branches. Of this, £74,950 was subscribed at the time, £9,000 reserved for the Kennet & Avon's shareholders, and £28,003 for landowners. The authorized capital was £111,900 in £100 shares, with power to raise £150,000 more. The Act contained a curious provision for appointing the committee of fifteen, presumably to ensure continuity. Five were to be elected by Wiltshire and five by Berkshire shareholders, these ten then to nominate the remaining five: in subsequent years these five were to be chosen by the retiring committeemen. A Thames & Severn representative was also enabled to attend committee meetings.

Construction began under William Whitworth, though helped by Robert, whether senior or junior I do not know. Cutting started at the Semington end, for the company expected to get a coal trade started, and so revenue, on the line as soon as it had been finished as far as Melksham, Chippenham and Calne, and as soon as the Somersetshire Coal Canal and the western part of the Kennet & Avon had been built. By 1801, however, only £61,512 in cash had been raised from the shareholders. This, and more, had been spent, and £85,199 was now needed to complete the canal. As the company had no power to borrow until the original subscription had been filled, they had then to return to Parliament and get authority to raise £200,000 in shares of any denomination they thought fit, or in loan notes with the option of conversion, and also to cease paying interest on calls.

By the end of 1802 the line was open from Semington (whence there was access to Bath by the Kennet & Avon, except for the unfinished Bath locks, and to the coalfield by way of the Somersetshire Coal Canal) to Wootton Bassett, together with the Calne

Wilts and Berks Canal Navigation.

IN PURSUANCE of an Act of Parliament passed
in the 41st. Year of the Reign of his Majesty
King GEORGE the Third, intituled,

"An Act for enabling the Company of
"Proprietors of the Wilts and Berks Canal
"Navigation, to · raise money for complet-
"ing the said Canal ; and to alter explain
"and amend the Act, passed in the thirty-
"fifth year of the reign of his present
"Majesty for making the said Canal."

THIS TICKET certifies that *The Reverend I
Barrington of Buckland in the County of Berks*
is a Proprietor of this Undertaking and inti-
tled to a share therein numbered *1480*

IN TESTIMONY whereof the Common Seal of the Company is hereunto
affixed this *seventh* — day of
March -- in the Year of our Lord
One Thousand Eight Hundred and *six*.

34. Share certificate of the Wilts & Berks Canal

branch, and the committee could report that 'the demand for the
Somersetshire Coal is now become very great', and that 'the
Dorset and Somerset Canal, which will also communicate with
this, we are informed is taken up with spirit, and will produce an
additional supply of Lime, Stone, Coal, and other articles.'[7] Hopefully, they looked forward to finishing their canal by the middle
of 1805.[8] It was in fact opened to Swindon[9] in June 1804, South
Marston by July 1805, to near Longcot* in December 1805, and

* The Longcot branch was made about 1807, and was retrospectively authorized
by the company's Act of 1835.

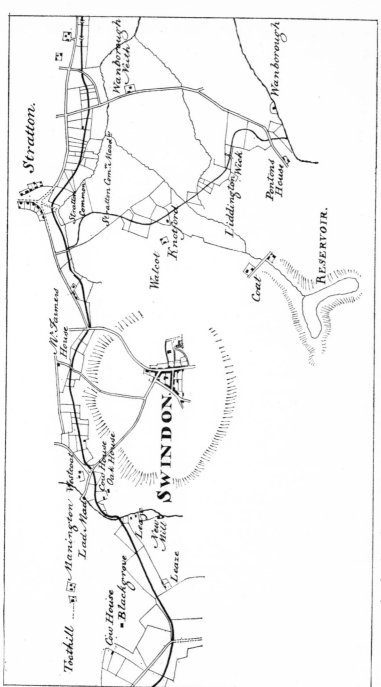

35. A redrawing of a part of the deposited plan to show the Swindon area at the time the Wilts & Berks was built

completely to Abingdon on 22 September 1810, when

> The opening of the Wilts and Berks Canal into the River
> Thames, at Abingdon, was celebrated there on Friday last with
> demonstrations of joy suitable to the completion of so impor-
> tant a part of inland navigation. At half past two o'clock a body
> of the proprietors in the Company's boat, with music playing
> and colours flying, passed the last lock into the river Thames
> amidst the loud huzzas of multitudes assembled to witness the
> spectacle. The party then left the boat and proceeded to the
> Council Chamber, where they were joined by a numerous as-
> semblage of gentlemen, including Members of Parliament for
> Cricklade, Abingdon, Oxford, Hereford, Ludgershall, &c. &c.
> and partook of a splendid dinner prepared for the occasion . . .
> The day was spent with great conviviality and harmony, en-
> livened by many appropriate toasts and songs; and the company,
> highly gratified, separated at a late hour.[10]

The conviviality was appropriate, for the proprietors had gone
through many financial troubles to finish their canal. It had cost
to this time £255,263. The 51-mile long main line rose 189 ft 3 in
by 24 locks from Semington to the summit level between Wootton
Bassett and South Marston, and then fell 163 ft 9 in by 18 locks
to Abingdon. The Calne branch was 3⅛ miles long with 3 locks,
that to Chippenham 2 miles, to Longcot (for Faringdon) ½-mile
and to Wantage ¾-mile. Water supply was at first from a deep well
near Swindon, which yielded insufficient, and was replaced in 1822
by Coate reservoir, and from another reservoir at Tockenham.

Most canals faced with the need to raise more money either
continued to make calls on the original shares, so increasing their
face value, or issued new shares of the usual nominal value of £100
or sometimes of £50. The Wilts & Berks proprietors, however,
made a number of share issues, each with shares of a lower value,
in the hope of attracting new classes of investor. The first issue
was of £100 shares, the next under the 1801 Act, at £65 and £60,
the next at £60 again, then at £40, at £25, and finally at £12 10s
(£12.50). Altogether 7,436 shares were issued, bringing in
£224,393; £22,200 was raised by optional notes, and the balance
was owed when the canal opened. By an Act of 1815, authority
was given to raise another £100,000, and further shares were
issued at low prices. It is interesting to see from the lists of subscribers to the optional notes that local financing is only just
holding its own against the influence of London. In 1802–3 money
was provided from the following places:

	£
Wiltshire	4,000
Berkshire	5,200
Bristol	4,000
Oxon	500
Notts	400
London	8,100
	22,200

An Act[11] of 1810, apart from its financial provisions, had repealed the ban on coal carried below Reading, and substituted Staines, the City coal limits[12] instead, in spite of opposition from Newcastle merchants and shipowners, and colliery proprietors there and in Co. Durham.[13]

The date of opening of the Wilts & Berks coincides with a number of schemes for its extension, towards London, Bristol, Stratford-upon-Avon and the Thames & Severn Canal.

In 1809 the company put forward the Western Junction extension of their line from Abingdon over the Thames by an aqueduct, and on for 36½ miles by way of Thame and Aylesbury to join the Grand Junction at Marsworth, so giving non-river communication from Framilode on the Severn to Brentford or Paddington. The Wilts & Berks and Grand Junction companies each agreed to subscribe £100,000 towards the cost, but the Bill was defeated on second reading by 10 votes on 25 February 1811 after opposition from the Thames Commissioners, and the Kennet & Avon, Oxford, and Warwick & Napton Canal companies. However, the project was the part cause of the building of the Aylesbury branch of the Grand Junction.[14]

In 1813 and again in 1817 an Aylesbury–Abingdon canal proposal was revived with Grand Junction support. In 1819 it was jointly surveyed at the expense of the two companies, and an estimate of just under £200,000 made for a line of 26 miles, to include a cast-iron aqueduct over the Thames. The cost was high, there were no estimates of revenue, and nothing more was done, though there was a revival of interest in 1828, and a new and lower estimate was made by W. A. Provis. Mr Dunsford, the clerk of the Wilts & Berks, in a letter of 1824, attributes the failure of the proposal to a demand by the Grand Junction for compensation payments for coal and iron passing onto their line —presumably in competition with that brought a longer distance on their own canal—and therefore to the unlikelihood of an Act being obtained, since 'clauses of this nature are objected to by Lord Shaftesbury in all Canal Bills.'

The proposed Bristol Junction Canal, to leave the Wilts & Berks near Wootton Bassett and pass by Malmesbury to the Gloucestershire coalfield near Pucklechurch and Coalpit Heath and on to Bristol, was put forward in 1810 after a preliminary survey by William Whitworth. Its supporters claimed that, together with the Abingdon–Marsworth cut, it would give an all-canal route of 154 miles from Bristol to London (much, of course, by narrow canal) against the 171 of the Kennet & Avon, and stated firmly that this line would ensure

A Punctuality in the Arrival and Delivery of Goods of the utmost Consequence in all commercial Transactions, which can never be attained where any Part of the Communication is *by a River*.[15]

It would also carry Forest of Dean coal to Abingdon and Oxford to compete with Midlands coal from the Oxford Canal. A Bill was introduced early in 1811, but was withdrawn before second reading after opposition from landowners, the Thames Commissioners because of feared water loss, and the Oxford Company.

A Central Junction Canal from Abingdon to the Stratford-upon-Avon Canal by way of Witney, Burford, Upper Swell, Batsford and Shipston-on-Stour, with a branch to the quarries at Lower Guiting, was also surveyed under Rennie's supervision. Estimated at £470,000 for the main line of 59⅝ miles, this unlikely route was immediately opposed by the Grand Junction, Oxford and Warwick & Napton companies, and did not get as far as a Bill.[16] As we have seen, a possible junction with the Thames & Severn was considered when the Wilts & Berks was first promoted. It was several times raised again before, in June 1810, the Thames & Severn Company received a letter from the Wilts & Berks saying that William Whitworth had surveyed a line to join the two canals from near Wootton Bassett on the Wilts & Berks to Yeoing* on the Thames & Severn, and asking for financial support for this proposed Severn Junction Canal.† The Thames & Severn committee did not like the line, but agreed to a meeting. This, on 14 July, 'Resolved that a Union of the two Canals will be of very great public Utility and of advantage to the Proprietors of both Canals,'[17] and decided on a line from Swindon to Latton. In December, the Kennet & Avon Company decided to oppose the

---

* This is Ewen, above Siddington, on the summit level.
† When the Wilts & Berks was planned, there had been proposals for a link with the Thames at Newbridge, and also for a Longcot–Kempsford connection with the Thames & Severn.

scheme as prejudicial to their interests. Early in 1811 a Bill for the Severn Junction Canal was introduced with Thames & Severn support because the Thames navigation between Lechlade and Abingdon was 'imperfect, precarious and dangerous'. It was met with a barrage of opposing petitions from Thames interests which seem to have taken the promoters by surprise, for support was lacking. The Bill had therefore to be withdrawn to avoid a defeat.

Though they had supported the Severn Junction Bill, in January 1812 the Thames & Severn proprietors resolved by the narrow majority of 572 shares to 401,

> That it is in the interest of the Thames and Severn Canal Proprietors to cooperate with the Commissioners of the river Thames in making every practical improvement in ye navigation thereof . . . and from reliance on the further assurances given by the Commissioners that the whole river within their jurisdiction should be forthwith made an effectual navigation, The Proprietors of the Thames and Severn Canal do not at present perceive any necessity for a junction with the Wilts and Berks at Latton & therefore judge it not now expedient to consent thereto.[18]

A conference was then held with the commissioners from which it emerged that they were not proposing to improve the upper river,* and in March the proprietors changed their minds and recorded that the proposed canal would be

> extremely useful when the natural river, from floods or other causes, may not be passable, and affording also a more extended Western navigation from Latton.[19]

Another meeting was held with the Wilts & Berks, and in June that company told their shareholders that the link might be built in two years at a cost of under £60,000:

> The measure promises a fair return for what it will cost, but at this time the Public can hardly be expected to raise the money, when the great advantages of it will be derived by the two existing Canal Companies . . . The manner in which the Wilts and Berks shares have once risen, by the prospect of the junction, and since sunk, by its supposed failure, so manifests the public opinion of its advantages.[20]

In September a promotion meeting for what was now called the North Wilts Canal was held at Cirencester, attended by shareholders of the Wilts & Berks and Thames & Severn and others

---

* A pamphlet of 1813, *Case of the Promoters of the Intended North Wilts Canal*, is stronger, and says: 'the Thames Commissioners acknowledged it to be wholly out of their power to improve that part of the Navigation.'

interested, at which it was agreed that the two groups of share-holders should each subscribe for a substantial block of the new company's capital, and that subscriptions should also be sought from the public. In October the two companies made an agreement, which incidentally protected the Wilts & Berks coal trade from possible competition from the north, to go back to Parliament, and soon afterwards the Thames & Severn agreed to subscribe for £5,000 worth of shares, reckoning that if it were built, their profits would rise by £2,000.

In 1813 the authorizing Act[21] was passed, the preamble stating that the canal would 'open a Communication between South Wales, the Counties of Hereford, Worcester and Gloucester, and His Majesty's Forest of Dean, and the City of London.' It allowed a capital of £60,000 in £25 shares, and £30,000 more if required, no work to be begun until £44,000 had been subscribed. Neither the Thames & Severn nor the Wilts & Berks were to lose water, but the new company was to pay the latter for such supplies as it wanted. The estimate, made by William Whitworth, was £52,000 and another £1,162 for the junction basin at Latton, and the private subscriptions were £26,525 at the time of the Bill. These included Wilts & Berks shareholders such as the Earl of Peterborough, William Hallett the chairman, Joseph Priestley jun the manager, and James Crowdy the solicitor. There were also Thames & Severn supporters like Lewis Disney-ffytche and E. J. Littleton, the Bullo Pill company, and Nathan Atherton, Benjamin Morland, Joseph Pitt and Richard Wootton, all of the Severn & Wye.[22] The North Wilts was therefore seen as an important means of extending the sale of Forest of Dean coal from Bullo Pill and Lydney.

The Bill was strongly contested, and both sides beat up for supporters. Fourteen towns petitioned in favour; against were Thames towns and interests, including the commissioners, the Oxford Canal Company, the Kennet & Avon and the City of London. Votes were taken on both second and third readings, the Bill being carried by 156 to 59, and then by 120 to 47. I do not know the actual cost of construction, but in addition to the Thames & Severn's £5,000 and the private subscriptions, the Wilts & Berks shareholders put up £15,000, and another £15,000 was borrowed from the Exchequer Bill Loan Commissioners. The North Wilts, 9 miles long, with 12 locks, a small aqueduct over the upper Thames, and a short tunnel near Cricklade, was opened on 2 April 1819,[23] so quietly that the Thames & Severn minute book does not record it, but only orders the selling price of coal at Lechlade, brought from the Severn, to be reduced.

In January 1821 a notice of the Wilts & Berks says:
The Managers of the North Wilts Canal having represented the impossibility of satisfying the demands of Government for the repayment of the Loan which they have contracted, are proposing an incorporation with this Canal; the Committee, considering the large stake which the Wilts and Berks Canal have in that Concern . . . are of opinion that the proposition should be acceded to.

An Act[24] of the same year replaced the two companies' legislation, North Wilts shareholders exchanging their shares for those of £100 in the united company, which also took over the Exchequer Bill Loan Commissioners' debt. Finally, in 1835 the £321,613 of capital was consolidated, the 20,000 shares in issue being reduced to 5,000.

The development of the Wilts & Berks after its opening in 1810 followed a quiet pattern. Apart from coal, the principal traffic was corn and agricultural products collected along the line and moved towards Semington on their way to Bath and Bristol. The tonnage of this trade in 1843 was 11,740 tons. There had been for a time at the beginning an attempt to work up a through traffic between Bristol and London, but the longer distance, together with the maximum toll charged by the Kennet & Avon for goods passing over their line to enter the Wilts & Berks, made it impossible for the company to compete successfully.

The takings from tolls rose slowly, from £5,523 in the first full year of the canal's operations to £6,254 in 1816,* £7,724 in 1822, £9,990 in 1823, £10,965 in 1826, £11,603 in 1830, and £12,877 in 1837, the last year before takings began to be affected by railway construction. The company paid its first dividend for the period mid-1811 to mid-1812, but soon afterwards the proprietors decided to deny themselves returns until improvements had been made to the line and wharves, the water supply increased by the purchase of new streams and the building of Coate reservoir, and the optional notes and other debts had been paid off. The rise in revenue that followed this policy enabled dividends to be resumed in 1831 with the following total sums:

	£		£
1831	4,000	1835	5,500
1832	5,000	1836	6,250
1833	5,000	1837	7,000
1834	5,000		

* These two figures are for the period 1 March to 28 February, the following ones for the calendar year.

Even the payment for 1837, however, represented only a little over 2 per cent on the capital. Throughout this period the loan from the Exchequer Bill Loan Commissioners for the building of the North Wilts was being liquidated; the final yearly instalment of £730 was paid in 1839.

About 1825 a fly or fast boat starting on the same days each week and running to a regular timetable, was put on between Bristol and Melksham. Later another ran from Abingdon to Melksham to connect with it, and by 1832 there were also boats from London via Abingdon to Gloucester by way of the North Wilts and the Thames & Severn.* These in 1825 took a week from London to Latton, of which five days were spent upon the Thames.

The company's 1835 Act, explaining that the through route to Gloucester was impeded by 'reason of the Inequality of the Locks, as well as great loss of Water arising in consequence thereof, upon the . . . Thames and Severn Canal Navigation,' empowered the Thames & Severn company, or themselves with T & S consent, to shorten such T & S locks as that company might think necessary. As a result, a number of T & S locks above Latton were in fact shortened. The Wilts & Berks, like most canal companies, were not normally carriers:

> I have found that it is better to hire freight than to have anything to do with Boats, and accordingly I have very few, just sufficient to keep me independent of the freighters in case of combination to raise prices.[25]

The company were traders in a small way in coal; they also owned quarries and dealt in Bath stone.

With its great neighbour the Kennet & Avon the smaller canal had little to do. They were hardly at all competitive, and most differences of opinion arose over the tolls charged on the portion of canal between the junctions of the Somersetshire Coal Canal and the Wilts & Berks. At one time, for instance, they complained that in spite of a tacit understanding by canal companies not to charge empty boats, those returning from the Wilts & Berks were being charged by the Kennet & Avon. Relations with the Thames & Severn were on more equal terms, and much brisk correspondence moved between the two offices. The attitude of the Wilts & Berks varied from raillery, as

> It therefore appears to me that your only hopes of a merchandize trade, must be by an amicable understanding with us, dismissing all jealousy of our interference with your 7 miles between Latton

* See the number of trips of these Gloucester–London boats given on p. 329ff.

and Inglesham, and in fact regarding your Canal as far as a
through Merchandize Trade is concerned as terminating at our
Junction,[26]

to querulousness, as in a letter to a brewer at Stroud, who had
said that he preferred the route to Abingdon by way of the Wilts
& Berks to that by the Thames:

> The anxiety of the manager of that concern* to cultivate their
> Coal Trade on the Wharfs on the line of the Thames, induces a
> disinclination to act with us in points where a mutual good
> understanding would redound to the advantage of both con-
> cerns.[27]

So to the last year of operation that was unaffected by railway
building. In 1837 the Wilts & Berks carried 66,751 tons of goods,
made up of:

	tons
Somerset coal	43,642
Other coal	965
Corn, stone, etc	14,884
Manure	1,578
Salt	1,550
Sundries	4,132

Because two-thirds of the traffic was in Somerset coal, well over
80 per cent of the total traffic moved from west to east, the boats
returning empty. In this year 2,475 boats passed the western end
of the summit at Wootton Bassett either going or returning, 2,674
passed the eastern end of the summit at South Marston, and 793
passed to or from the North Wilts branch.

The relative importance of the wharves on the line at this time
may be seen from the following list of the tonnages of Somerset
coal handled at each in this same year of 1837. It should be remembered that at this time Swindon was a village, not yet forced into
quick growth by the building of the railway works.

	tons		tons
Melksham	2,992	Stratton	774
Lacock	818	Marston	348
Chippenham & Stanley	4,709	Bourton	290
Calne & Foxham	3,695	Shrivenham	354
Dauntsey	2,270	Longcot (for Faringdon)	3,322
Wootton Bassett	3,141	Uffington	546
Wroughton	794	Challow	1,746
North Wilts branch	1,739	Wantage	2,120
Swindon	3,313	Abingdon	10,669

* Mr Denyer of the Thames & Severn.

There was a burst of interest in railways in 1824, and it is probable that the committee of the Wilts & Berks were startled to receive at their Swindon office a letter and copy of a minute dated 10 November 1824, from the Oxford Canal Company, of which the following are two paragraphs:

It appears to the Committee that these speculations will take from agriculture a very considerable quantity of land without a reasonable cause; and bring thro' arable and pasture, and parallel to, and across, public highways, a description of Engine and machinery which will terrify all sorts of cattle as well those drawing carriages on the roads, or ploughing in the fields, as those that are feeding in pastures.

As these schemes embrace not only the conveyance of the articles now carried by the Canals, but also of Passengers at an extraordinary speed, the locomotive Steam Engines will be passing without intermission, and the stationary Steam Engines incessantly at work, in districts of the Kingdom in which the inconvenience from Steam Engines is at present unknown.

Indeed, early in 1825 the Kennet & Avon Committee minuted:

In consequence of the numerous speculations entered into for making Rail Roads and in particular a Rail Road from London to Bristol and another from Bristol to Bath, it had been thought adviseable that Mr. Blackwell the Engineer of the Company should go into the North of England to see the operation of several Rail Roads and Locomotive Engines now in work and to report his opinion and observations thereon.[28]

This threat passed; not so that from the authorization of the Great Western Railway, whose proposed line ran near the Wilts & Berks from Abingdon through Swindon to Chippenham, where rail and waterway parted to take different routes to Bath.

In February 1835 the Kennet & Avon Company had written to ask whether the Wilts & Berks would help pay the cost of opposing the railway. Rather surprisingly, their clerk had replied off-handedly that 'there does not seem to be much dread of the Railroad'.[29] The opening of the railway, however affected almost all their traffic except that from the Coal Canal. The trade east of Swindon suffered most, being in more direct competition with the railway, and at the same time further away from the Somerset collieries.

While the railway was building, the canal's receipts benefited to an unusual extent from carrying construction material, to fall away heavily once it was opened. The following figures tell the story clearly enough.

Year	Net tolls* £	Year	Net tolls* £
1834	11,566	1842	9,395
1835	11,701	1843	8,477
1836	12,324	1844	8,458
1837	12,647	1845	8,746
1838	12,609	1846	8,374
1839	14,936	1847	8,415
1840	23,804	1848	7,657
1841	19,329	1849	6,487

* After deduction of drawbacks. The figures for 1834 and 1835 include about £150 worth of rents.

The company used their windfall income constructively, buying a wharf at Oxford, building houses, building a reservoir at Tocken-ham near Wootton Bassett, paying off Exchequer debt, and putting the rest to reserve.[30] The following figures show the total number of boats, loaded and empty, passing South Marston at the end of the summit level east of Swindon, and also those passing Seven Locks near Wootton Bassett west of Swindon, and illustrate both the short boost given by railway building and the following fall, and also the proportionately greater effect of railway competition upon the eastern traffic. The sum paid each year in dividends provides a check figure.

	Boats passing eastwards	Boats passing westwards	Total boats passing off the summit	Dividends paid £
1837	2,674	2,475	5,149	7,000
1838	2,468	2,347	4,815	7,500
1839	2,869	2,524	5,393	8,000
1840	4,180	3,257	7,437	9,000
1841	2,483	2,902	5,385	9,000
1842	1,923	2,447	4,370	6,000
1843	1,919	2,167	4,086	5,000
1844	1,884	2,208	4,092	5,000
1845	1,976	2,271	4,247	5,500
1846	1,563	2,210	3,773	5,500
1847	1,682	2,308	3,990	4,912

The quantity of coal and coke carried on the whole canal increased from 43,642 tons in 1837 to 47,470 tons in 1847, but that carried east of Swindon fell from 20,169 tons in 1837 to 18,278 tons in 1847.

It is curious that the Wilts & Berks Company does not appear to have foreseen the seriousness of railway competition, much

S

less its result. In the years 1836 to 1841 the company, like others from time to time, were investing surplus money in buying their own shares. The prices paid were as follows:

			Average price per share
1836	14½ shares for £305 10s	(£305.50)	£22 13s (£22.65)
1837	29½ shares for £648 0s		£21 19s (£21.95)
1840	14¾ shares for £428 10s	(£428.50)	£29 1s (£29.05)
1841	10¼ shares for £300 0s		£29 5s (£29.25)

In 1840 and 1841 the company would have been better advised to keep their money in the bank.

More competition arose at the western end when the Wilts, Somerset & Weymouth Railway was opened in 1848 from Thingley Junction near Chippenham to Westbury by way of Melksham. It was probably this competition that caused the number of boats passing Seven Locks at the western end of the summit level to fall from an average of 2,263 in the three years before 1848 to an average of 1,757 in the three years after it.

The railway pressure was such that trade was nearly driven off the section between Swindon and Abingdon. In 1863, for instance, only 964 boats passed the eastern end of the summit, compared with 2,674 in 1837. Westwards, however, trade stood up better, and in the same year of 1863, 1,289 boats passed the western end of the summit compared with 2,475 in 1837, a reduction of nearly one-half in the latter case and nearly two-thirds in the former. The trade on the North Wilts branch which joined the Wilts & Berks main line to the Thames & Severn and gave access to Gloucester was badly affected: only 332 boats passed in 1863, against 793 in 1837.

The staple commodity continued to be Somerset coal, wherever it could find a market without direct competition with that brought by rail. More was carried from the Coal Canal to wharves lying west of Swindon in 1862 than in 1837, 25,046 tons against 18,419, and more on the North Wilts branch, 2,156 tons against 1,739. For Swindon and wharves east, however, the tonnage had fallen heavily from 23,482 in 1837 to 10,690 in 1862. A large part of this drop, some 10,000 tons, was due to the loss of the trade at Abingdon itself and up and down river from the town. The rest of the reduction was distributed generally along the wharves except Stratton and Wantage, which showed increases. The other commodities carried on the canal, such as stone, manure, salt, corn, and groceries, did not fall greatly in tonnage (from 23,109 tons in 1837 to 18,374 tons in 1862), the main reduction being in corn, which itself reflected the decline in corn growing. The trouble was not in the tonnage carried, as we have seen before, but in the revenue obtained for it.

The years from 1861 to 1876 showed a sharp deterioration as maintenance on the canal got worse, mud deeper, weed thicker, and competition keener, while the closing of the Radstock tramway of the Somersetshire Coal Canal (see p. 275) affected coal supplies. Here are representative figures:

	1861 tons	1870 tons	1876 tons
Somerset coal	36,952	20,595	12,461
Other goods	18,374	14,284	14,970
	55,326	34,879	27,431

Dividends, which had reached a high point of £9,000 pa in 1840 and 1841 (2¾ per cent approximately on the capital of £321,613), fell away quickly to £5,000 in 1843, £2,456 in 1853, £1,128 in 1863 and a final £561 in 1870. On the other hand, the loan notes had all been paid off, and 511¼ of the 5,000 shares had either been forfeited or bought in. In the course of making economies lock-keepers and officers were reduced, their combined salaries falling from £1,841 in 1837 to £1,006 in 1873. Total takings dropped from £3,304 in 1869, showing a profit of £885, to £2,205 in 1873, with a loss of £255, there being by that time no trade at all east of Wantage. These necessary economies themselves contributed, of course, to the failure of this and other similarly-placed canals to hold their own.

The Great Western Railway competed all down the canal's line. Moreover, that company, owning the Kennet & Avon, charged heavily on it downwards from Semington, so making coal more expensive at the canal wharves, while offering low rail rates from Bristol and Radstock to towns on the Wilts & Berks. The canal committee, conscious that many shares were part-paid and carried a residual liability, and having failed to interest the railway in possible purchase, wanted closure. However, a group of share-holders and traders thought something could still be done, and tried to get a properly-attended shareholders' meeting together. For thirty years meetings had been called not by circular but only by advertisement, and they had to get a mandamus before they could obtain access to the shareholders' register. They did so, and the meeting was held on 4 September 1874, but after a long discussion closure was agreed upon,[31] and in November parliamentary notices were published, and a Bill drafted, to close or sell the canal.

Bristol Chamber of Commerce wrote to protest, and now a group of seven brick, stone or timber merchants already concerned with the canal formed the Wilts & Berks Canal Co Ltd[32] late in 1875 to buy it for £13,466. The opening in October 1875 of the Wantage Tramway, which connected the town with the Great Western main line and so competed with the canal branch, was not a good augury. The new purchasers seem to have intended to close the Longcot branch, but their Act[33] of June 1876 to incorporate themselves with a capital of £30,000, have the canal transferred, and dissolve the old company, bound them to keep the whole line open. Their working equipment was small: it was listed as including one steam dredger and four iron cranes, at Abingdon, Swindon, Lacock and Melksham wharves.

The new company took over in the spring of 1877, but in 1882 leased the canal to a group of Bristol merchants for £1,250 pa and so were enabled to pay a dividend of 4 per cent. The new group experimented with sectional boats 'with approved stem and stern, and body like a centipede, which could be cut asunder, and portions of the body about the length of a railway truck left at the wharves en route,'[34] but the result was too difficult to load, steer, break up and reassemble, and narrow boats continued to be used.

The Bristol adventurers in turn could not make the canal pay, and in 1887 forfeited £5,000 to be released from the lease. In this year 32,972 tons of traffic were carried. The 1876 company then worked the canal again until in 1891 another new concern was formed, the United Commercial Syndicate, which took over the canal and spent some £16,000 over the next five years in putting it in order. Its directors formed a separate carrying organization and operated a service of twelve regular fly-boats, upon which they lost £500 pa. They also participated in the Thames & Severn Canal Trust.

But the canal could not be made to pay, and in 1897 the syndicate tried to abandon it, supported by the Swindon Traders Association, who thought it a nuisance to the town, and resolved that:

the Canal as a Public Navigation is unnecessary to the trade of Swindon, the present traffic being insignificant in quantity and there being no prospect of any increase.'[35]

Their proposal applied to the whole canal, but after the notices had been issued the Thames & Severn agreed in case of abandonment to take over the North Wilts, so joining themselves to Swindon. The abandonment proposal was therefore changed

NORTH WILTS CANAL.

Contributed by Mr. Julius Auerbach.

The North Wilts Canal connects the Wilts and Berks Canal (p. 21) at Swindon, with the Thames and Severn Canal (p. 25) at Latton. It is 8¾ miles long, with 12 locks, all of which are (1893) in fair repair; and is worked by the proprietors of the Wilts and Berks, who charge a toll of 10s. for pleasure-boats, payable at the canal wharf, New Swindon. The canal is supplied with water from the Wilts and Berks, and falls the whole way from Swindon to Latton, the total fall being 59 ft. There is a lock-keeper at Morden, but a winch must be carried to open the other locks. The Wilts and Berks and Thames and Severn winches fit the locks. The entrance to the canal at Swindon is under an iron swing-bridge, too low to pass under. A handle for this can be obtained at the adjoining public-house. Just above this are the five Swindon locks, all close together; and for some distance the voyage is at times very disagreeable, owing to the foul stench of the mud stirred up by the oars. Apparently a good deal of sewage matter is somehow allowed to filter into the canal from Swindon. Above Morden Locks the scenery is rather pretty, and the smell diminishes. Several small swing-bridges similar to those on the Wilts and Berks have to be raised during the trip.

Miles		
	Swindon -	Junction with Wilts and Berks Canal (p 21).
¾	Swindon Locks -	5 locks in one mile.
2¾	Morden Locks -	Lock-keeper. 3 locks in half a mile. Near here on an aqueduct the canal crosses the Ray, one of the head-streams of the Thames.
4	Purton Priory or Pry Lock -	Purton, a pretty village, has Stat. G. W. R. (1 mile) and small inn near.
4⅝	Cross Lanes Lock	
5¼	Haynole Lock	
7⅛	Cricklade Wharf -	Stat. Mid. & S. W. Junct. R. Hotels, White Horse, White Hart. Land here if you intend to portage into Thames (¾ mile), p. 2.
7¼	Tunnel (100 yds.)	
8⅜	Aqueduct over Thames	
8¾	Latton Lock, and Junction with Thames & Severn Canal (p. 25) -	Close to the lock the canal crosses by an aqueduct the Churn, another head-stream of the Thames.

36. Pleasure cruising on the North Wilts Canal in 1893

without a change in the notices. On this technicality, and because of the opposition of landowners who valued the canal for its supply of water to their cattle, the abandonment failed. By 1898 only 8,168 tons were being carried.

The company again tried for a warrant of abandonment in 1900, arguing that the reconstruction of the upper Thames would provide a broad-lock waterway which would divert Thames & Severn traffic from their canal. They had already unsuccessfully offered it to both the Thames & Severn Trust, who were now in no position to take over the North Wilts, and the Sharpness New Docks Company, and had received no objections to closure from traders.[36] But after a Board of Trade enquiry at Swindon on 27 February, that proposal too was withdrawn.

Lord Wantage had provided most of the syndicate's share capital and had also lent it £10,000; after 1901 the interest on his loan could not be paid, probably because the Great Western no longer bought water from the company at Swindon. In 1904 Swindon corporation unsuccessfully introduced a Bill to cut off the water supply to Coate reservoir. Traffic ceased altogether in 1906, after which parts of the canal became unnavigable, and after a conference of interested parties in 1912, the corporation tried again, successfully this time. Their Act of 1914 closed the canal, and enabled the corporation to take over Coate Water, one of the two canal reservoirs, which had been a place of recreation since the 1870s, and some of the canal site, for public purposes. For these they paid £8,000 net. The canal company disposed of the rest to pay some of its debts.

CHAPTER XIII

The Stroudwater Navigation

✦✦✦

In the years 1697 to 1700, when many schemes to make rivers navigable were being proposed to Parliament, there were plans to make the Stroudwater, though it was hardly more than a brook, navigable from the tidal Severn to or near the town of Stroud, to serve the local woollen industry by bringing coal and carrying away cloth. But there was too much opposition from millowners on the lower river who depended upon it for water power.

About 1728 the idea was revived, and a plan prepared. John Hore, who had made the Kennet navigable, was called in and proposed a canal 8¼ miles long, 33 ft wide and 5 ft deep, with twelve locks, to take 60-ton barges at a cost of under £20,000.[1] The Act[2] that was passed in 1730, however, with the support of all the clothiers above Stroud, but against nine of the 19 millers below the town, was, in spite of Hore, 'to clear, scour, open and enlarge or straiten the . . . River . . . and to make . . . new Cuts.' It seems that flash-locks were envisaged. The Act contained two deterrents: between 14 August and 15 October craft could only pass by permission of a majority of millowners, a clause which in practice would be likely to close the navigation for two months each year, and the authorized tolls were high: 3s 6d (17½p) a ton on coal, grain and meal, 5s (25p) on other goods, about 5d and 7d per ton per mile respectively. It also appointed commissioners to deal with disputes, and to appoint others if the nine named undertakers had not finished the navigation by 24 June 1740. Nothing was done, and the feeling grew up that the mills made a navigation impracticable. John Dallaway, one of the commissioners, did not think so, and waited for a chance to revive it. This came in 1754, when 'a Spirit for such an Undertaking began to arise'. He got Thomas Yeoman the engineer and others to make a survey, and in 1755 published his scheme,[3] estimated at £8,145, for which he thought he could get finance at 5 per cent, and with a forecast revenue of £1,175 pa, £650 of which was to come from 7,000 tons

pa of coal. His argument was that the predominant Stroud trade
with Bristol cost £2 a ton by direct road transport, or £1 by
Gloucester and the Severn, whereas by a Stroudwater navigation
it could be carried for 10s (50p). He envisaged a navigation 9½
miles long from the Severn to Wallbridge just below Stroud, with
16 locks and four stanks,* taking barges 45 ft by 13 ft, but drawing
only 2 ft and carrying 30 to 40 tons. Water for working the locks
without affecting the millowners would be provided from a 2-acre
reservoir below Wallbridge, to be filled every Sunday when the
mills were not working. His proposed tolls were more attractive:
2s (10p) a ton upwards, 1s 6d (7½p) downwards.

He must have been supported, for in 1756 he got together a
meeting of the surviving commissioners. In March 1758 they approved Dallaway's plan, and by May £6,900 had been subscribed
out of £10,000 asked for. Then the millowners must have made
themselves heard against the scheme, for in August a new idea was
put to the commissioners by four other people, John Kemmett
being the leader. One was Thomas Bridge of Tewkesbury, who
had been one of those who had surveyed for Dallaway's plan of
1755; the others were Arthur Wynde and James Pynock.

They had a curious scheme which Bridge had thought of, to
make the river navigable without the locks to which the millowners objected, by means of cranes with two independently
operated jibs, mounted on walls 12 ft thick alongside the mill
weirs. The boats were to carry their cargoes in boxes of about
one ton capacity, which were to be interchanged at each weir by
means of the cranes.† The commissioners appointed them undertakers, and in 1759 an Act[5] authorized their effort, explaining that
'there are several Fulling and Corn Mills upon the . . . River, and
the making such River navigable, in the usual and accustomed
Method . . . might be prejudicial to the Working of the . . . Mills';
therefore no locks were to be built. In other respects the powers
of the 1730 Act were transferred, with a time limit of 29 September
1761, after which the commissioners could appoint other undertakers, unless lawsuits had delayed the work.

Kemmett and the others made a start, and by April 1761 'made
a considerable Progress therein, but by unforeseen Accidents and
other legal Impediments' were 'hindered or prevented from com-

---

* Presumably half-locks or staunches.

† Kemmett and his partners also put their ideas to the River Dun proprietors,
proposing to extend their navigation upwards from its head at Tinsley to Sheffield.
That businesslike company asked them to be more explicit, and they do not seem to
have responded.[4]

pleating.'[6] They were given a six years' extension, and their works were carried on

> for about half the way, but finding it unlikely to answer the Expence, as well from what was foreseen, a Want of Back Carriage, as the Costs of Banking and making Good the Damage of Leakage, they . . . deserted the Carrying the Navigation on any further, and left their Works in Ruins.[7]

They did in fact make nearly five miles of the river navigable, probably from Framilode to Chippenham Platt,* by making short cuts and building weirs and cranes. But their 10-ton boats were nevertheless too big for the tiny river, while at least 14 transfers of cargo were likely to be as expensive as they were damaging to the loads.[9] Yeoman in 1776 said that he had 'seen the Engines now remaining upon the River—that they are out of Repair not being used . . . most of the Iron work is lost.'[10]

The possibility of navigation was again raised in 1774, by which time much more was known about building and operating canals, such as the nearby Droitwich, and the growth of industry in the Stroud valley had greatly increased the demand for coal and corn, the latter being described as the most expensive in England. There were then 123 mills in or near the prosperous Stroud valley, 19 of them on the Stroudwater from Stroud to the Severn. A main incentive for canal building was the cost of road transport, and the state of the roads. Thomas Yeoman, giving evidence on the 1776 Bill, said 'he never saw worse Turnpike Roads'. A meeting held on 2 May at Stroud supported a plan to build a canal rather than make the river navigable. Those behind it, led by William Dallaway, the son of John, and himself a clothier, had approached the Staffordshire & Worcestershire Canal Company, from whose canal to Stourport, opened in 1772, coal supplies were likely to come, and invited them to a meeting on 26 May.[11] As a result, Thomas Dadford junior, the Staffs & Worcs's engineer, and John Priddey, who as resident engineer had built the Droitwich Canal and had then worked for a year as assistant clerk of works on the Oxford, surveyed the Stroudwater. Meanwhile the surviving commissioners were again gathered to appoint new members.

The engineer proposed a canal over most of the distance to avoid the mills, at an estimated cost of £16,750. The promoters raised £20,000 by July, and on 15 September the commissioners, who had got counsel's opinion that their powers under the 1730

---

* A map of 1776 shows 19 short cuts made between the Bristol–Gloucester road and Chippenham Platt.[8]

Act were still valid, and that the new plan was lawful under it,* cancelled the undertaking of Kemmett and his partners, and appointed nine new undertakers, among them William Dallaway, Thomas Baylis, Benjamin Grazebrook, George Hawker and Joseph Wathen. These were the leaders in a larger body of subscribers.

The veteran Thomas Yeoman re-surveyed the line, proposing a canal 42 ft wide and just under 8 miles long, with 12 locks, to take Severn craft, and offered practical advice. At the turn of the year Samuel Jones of Boston was appointed engineer with Benjamin Grazebrook as clerk and deputy, and work began upwards from Framilode after 14 barge-owners had agreed upon it as the best place for the entrance from the Severn. Within a month Jones had been discharged and Priddey engaged instead. On 23 January 1775, however, a threatening advertisement appeared in the local newspaper:

> The Subscribers to the Opposition against the Stroud-Water Navigation, and such other Persons as are likely to be injured by the said Navigation, are desired to meet . . . in order to consider of further Measures to be taken, and they are desired to bring with them the Names of such Persons as have already committed Trespasses on any of their Lands by Authority of the Commissioners at Stroud, or otherwise relating to the said Navigation.[12]

The objectors took the line that the 1730 Act did not authorize such a canal as the promoters were building. For some months, however, the latter went on with their work, and on 5 June 1775 it was recorded:[13]

> On Tuesday last the first stone was laid of the first lock upon the Stroud-Water river, by William Dallaway, Esq; and the name given the lock was the Framiload Lock . . . After dinner suitable healths were drank . . . The whole was conducted with great decency, accompanied with chearful shouts, and other acclamations of real joy, expressive of the satisfaction that was felt by those present, upon seeing so necessary a work, so long wished for, thus begun; and in so promising a way of being speedily completed; (*unless retarded by the malignant spirit of opposition*). A work of the utmost utility to the clothing trade of this county; and which will be a great relief to the poor in the

---

* There was a precedent. The Sankey Brook Navigation in Lancashire had been built as a canal without hindrance under the powers of an Act of 1755 which was granted to make the Sankey Brook itself navigable.

article of firing;* and likewise an ease to the neighbouring estates in the saving of the road. And it may with justice be added, *a work*, which begins an important aera of the British annals, and which will keep in view, 'till really accomplished, that great national object,

Of which the *bards* have sung, in visionary dreams,
The Union of *Sabrina's* floods with silver Thames.†

* When this navigation is completed to Wallbridge, the same coals, which now at the lowest rate are sold for 13d per hundred, will, on the same spot, be then sold for 8d per hundred, to the poor.

† It is proposed, when this navigation of the Stroud-Water is completed, to join it by a new canal to the Thames at Cricklade. This, upon a survey by an able Engineer, has not only been found to be practicable, but easy to be affected.

Meanwhile the malignant spirit of opposition, in the form of some local landowners and millowners, the former objecting to the severance of their lands and the latter fearing loss of water to their mills, had obtained counsel's opinion upon the legality of building a canal under powers for making the river navigable. The opinion advised that the matter be taken to the courts. The Court of Exchequer was therefore moved for an injunction to stop proceedings, while at the Gloucestershire Assizes it was held that the canal could not be made under existing powers.

With 1¼ miles of canal part-built, a half-finished entrance lock, and £25 per share called, cutting stopped as soon as the existing works had been made safe, and a new Act was applied for. Though strongly opposed, the need of the Stroud valley for cheaper coal and corn, and the great dependence of a much wider area, which included Cirencester and Tetbury, upon a prosperous woollen industry, ensured that it was passed on 25 March 1776,[14] authorizing a mainly canal navigation, with a capital of £20,000, including what had already been raised, and £10,000 more if necessary.

The passing of the Act excited no less than three poems. The first, from the objectors, was advertised as:

To the Proprietors of the Stroud Navigation. In a few Days will be published, The Retaliation; or the Lamentation of Haman, a Poem in Two Cantos.

Quid non mortalia pectora cogis
Auri sacra fames. Virg. Aen. Lib. 3.

This work, to be sold at 6d (2½p), was soon balanced by

The New Navigation; or Stroud Triumphant. A Poem in two cantos, Addressed to the Proprietors on their Success in obtaining a new Act to compleat the Canal.

> *Tacent; et ora pallor albus inficit;*
> *Mentisque perculsa stupent. Hor. Ep.* (2)

This capping of Virgil by Horace was concluded by a further announcement:

> This Day is published, in Quarto, Price 1s. A Prophecy of Merlin, an Heroic Poem, concerning the wonderful Success of a Project now on Foot, to make the River from the Severn to Stroud in Gloucestershire navigable. Translated from the original Latin, annexed, with Notes explanatory.*
>
> *Citizens of no mean City.*

Of the 200 shares, 144 were subscribed in or near Stroud, 15 in Bristol and 3 in Wiltshire, 76 of the 144 being in the textile business. Of the remainder, 29 were London based, of which 11 were in the name of Christopher Chambers of Mincing Lane, later to be a prominent supporter of the Thames & Severn Canal. Among the shareholders was John Billingsley of Shepton Mallet, who subscribed £200; he was afterwards to be much associated with Somerset canals.[15]

Work now restarted, with Priddey as engineer and Joseph Grazebrook as clerk, though Edmund Lingard, previously engineer on the Coventry Canal, soon replaced Priddey. Not enough canal cutters could be found locally, and Lingard was sent to Warwickshire and Leicestershire to find others. These, when recruited, seem to have been treated as a contracting unit, separate from the local contractors and their men. By December 1776 the canal was open to the Bristol road, where a coal wharf was established. Some profiteering began, for the company advertised:

> that all Coals sold to Waggons at a price not exceeding twelve Shillings and Sixpence per Ton shall be free of Wharffage, and all Sold above that Price Shall pay One Shilling per Ton Wharffage for the same.[16]

Work continued, the company's barge *Stroud* being used to fetch stone from quarries on the Bristol Avon, and bricks from Frampton. Lingard went in November 1777, and was succeeded by Benjamin Grazebrook, who with some professional help finished the job. The two Grazebrooks, Joseph and Benjamin, did much for the company in its early days. Joseph remained as clerk until 1788, when he resigned, having gone into banking, but became treasurer instead, a position he held until 1830. Benjamin, once the canal was built, started a carrying business on the canal to Bristol and Gloucester, which he continued until his death in 1810.

* The original Latin text had been written at the time of the first Act, in 1730.

By the end of 1777 the waterway was open to Chippenham Platt, by January 1779 to Ryeford, and on Wednesday 21 July to its terminus at Wallbridge just below Stroud, the committee having already ordered that 'the Company's Barge & Boats be Cleaned and fitted up ready for the Day of opening the Canal.'[17] Tolls were then settled as 3s (15p) a ton (about 4½d a mile) for coal up and most goods down, and 2s (10p) a ton (about 3d a mile) for corn up, and bricks, stone and some other traffic down. Coal taken on by road waggon to Cirencester, Tetbury or any place over 10 miles from a wharf earned 1s (5p) drawback. Pleasure craft were not welcomed: 'every Pleasure Boat Passing any of the Locks do Pay Twenty Shillings.'[18] Later coal, corn and most goods were moved to the full authorized 3s 6d (17½p) toll.

As completed, the canal was just under 8 miles long, with twelve broad locks, including the tide-lock at Framilode, able to take craft 72 ft × 15 ft 6 in, carrying about 60 tons. All were single except a staircase pair at Ryeford. It had cost £40,930, financed mainly by calling £150 on each of the 200 shares, and for the rest by loans from shareholders, tolls from the sections already opened, and running into debt. Very unusually on a canal, there was no horse towing path, craft being towed by men, or some-times sailed. At Framilode, a trow wishing to enter the canal sent its tow-boat ashore with a rope. This was attached to the capstan at the lock head, and the vessel was then hauled in. At night, cresset lights guided craft to the lock entrance.

The next few years were spent in building warehouses, improv-ing facilities for traders and staff, in paying off debts, and carrying about 16,000 tons in each, until for the year ending April 1786 a first dividend of £7 10s (£7.50) a share, or 5 per cent, could be declared. There were other preoccupations also. The most notable was with the possibility of an extension upwards to join the Thames near Lechlade, one that had long been thought a possi-bility, and had certainly been in mind when the 1774 plan had been made. The first step was taken at a Stroudwater shareholders' meeting in April 1781 (see Chapter XIV); a separate company was formed that included many Stroudwater shareholders; the two concerns agreed early in 1783 on terms, 'the Business being settled much to the satisfaction of the General Body of Proprietors'[19] and the Thames & Severn's Act was passed in the same year. That canal was opened to Brimscombe at the end of 1784, and through-out five years later. The Stroudwater then became part of a through route from Bristol or Staffordshire to the Thames, Oxford and London, and its takings benefited from both local and long-distance traffic brought it by the new canal. In the meantime, a substantial drawback of 2s 5d (12p) on 3s 6d (17½p) per ton was paid on coal from Dudbridge or Wallbridge carried by road transport to Lechlade 'upon the Halliers producing a Tickett from the Person receiving the said Coal at Leachlade.'[20]

In 1784, soon after the Thames & Severn had been authorized, Gloucester interests proposed a canal from that city to join the Stroudwater to avoid the river navigation down to Framilode. This the latter company opposed, presumably because they would lose tolls between Framilode and the proposed point of junction near Whitminster, though they minuted that they would be prepared to negotiate once the Thames & Severn had been opened. However, the project dropped for the time being. In the same year the Stroudwater Company learned that in dry seasons it was difficult to get coal down the Severn from 'northern collieries' and showed interest in Forest of Dean coal, to transport which, they said, a canal 3½ miles long to cost £14,000, with a 90 ft rise to the collieries, had been surveyed.* In 1785, at the request of Christopher Chambers, a large shareholder in the Thames & Severn Canal and their own, they petitioned to support the proposed Lechlade–Abingdon Canal (see p. 198), which could have much improved the prospects of a through trade to London.

In 1785 also a group of shareholders proposed to start trading in coal in order to encourage business. Though the company agreed to support them, nothing was done until 1788, when a coal committee was appointed; this began a profitable business that was continued until 1833, and eventually employed a working capital of £1,700. To begin with, most of the canal's coal supplies came from Shropshire collieries or down the Staffs & Worcs Canal[22] from Staffordshire, though by 1789 Kingswood coal from the south Gloucestershire field was being tried, and in 1791 some from the Forest.

In 1790 the company hopefully went into the fish business, the committee being told to

employ the Labourers in the Company's Service at proper times under the direction of the Clerk, in catching the Fish in the Canal, and dispose of the same for the Benefit of the Proprietors and report the Produce at the next General Meeting.[23]

---

* A line 3½ miles long from the head of Lydney pill near Lower Forge would take a canal to within half a mile of the collieries at Parkend. If this was the proposed line, the survey may have provided the basis for Pidcock's Canal, built a few years later.[21]

But the first half-year only produced £1 12s (£1.60), and presumably the labourers were put to harder work.

Late in 1792 the company was asked by the promoters of the Gloucester & Berkeley Canal (see Chapter XV) to subscribe. This was going too far, but the Stroudwater now had no objection in principle to a junction, and the two concerns came to an agreement on tolls, and on preventing water being lost to the Stroudwater. At the point near Saul where the two canals were to cross, this was to be prevented by building a new section of the Stroudwater from Whitminster lock (the next above the entrance lock at Framilode) to below the intersection, at a higher level and slightly to the

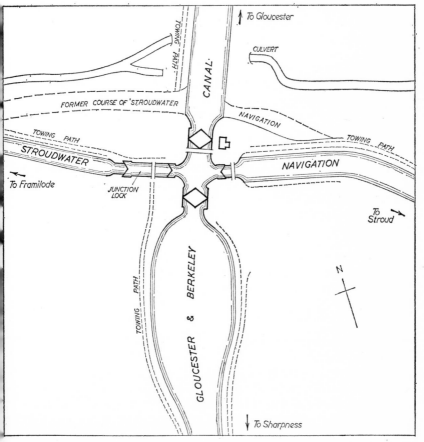

57. The Saul crossing soon after 1820, showing the original line of the Stroudwater Navigation

south, so that the two waterways would cross without loss of water to either. A new Stroudwater lock would be built at Gloucester & Berkeley expense just below the crossing. This new level meant the elimination of the fall at Whitminster lock. Later, craft could sometimes pass with all gates open, though a few inches difference of water level often made it necessary to use the lock. However, all this was in the future; it would be many years before the ship canal reached Saul.

The Thames & Severn Company had in 1794 pressed the Stroudwater to build a basin above Framilode lock for craft waiting for the tide, and had had their way. In 1799 they asked for a horse towing path, but this time were told that

although we are disposed to concur in every thing which may contribute to our mutual benefit, yet we cannot consent to the present proposed measure, not seeing a probability of its repaying so considerable an Expence.[24]

In 1812, the year after a horse path beside the Severn from Worcester to Gloucester had been authorized,[25] they tried again, to be told that it was a 'work attended with much expence without a prospect of any adequate advantage.'[26] It was not until October 1825, after the junction with the Gloucester & Berkeley had been made, and when a horse towing path existed over the whole length of waterway from Shrewsbury on the upper Severn to Teddington on the Thames except on their own canal and the Thames & Severn to Brimscombe, that they decided to build it. Even then, the estimate of £3,000 to construct a proper one seemed too much, and the company adapted the old bow-hauling path on the understanding that horse* traction was on a twelve months experimental basis. The path was finished in August 1827, a few months after the completion of the Gloucester & Berkeley, and no more was heard of experiments.

By 1803 coal from 'northern districts', that is, from Shropshire and Staffordshire, had become scarce and 'enormously dear'. Forest coal was not yet accessible, and therefore the company decided to import coal from Newport, and to build a 60-ton schooner to carry it. In February 1804 it brought its first cargo. Thereafter, Newport coal was regularly imported, though Shropshire and Staffordshire was still used, and Forest began to be sold from about 1810, after the local tramroads had made it more accessible, though for some time its sale had to be pushed. In

---

* In later years at any rate, donkeys did most of the towing on the Stroudwater and the Thames & Severn.

1816, for instance, these were the coal prices at Stroud and Dudbridge wharves:

		per ton
Bilston (Staffs)		24s (£1.20)
Newport		22s (£1.10)
Shropshire		21s 6d (£1.07½)
do	(slack)	19s (95p)
Forest of Dean		18s (90p)

Meanwhile, also in 1804, the company had loyally pledged the
use of its canal, vessels and servants to His Majesty in case of
invasion, but were justifiably annoyed when their own side and
not the enemy damaged their works:

> on Thursday Night . . . some of the Stanley Rifle Corps,
> wantonly fired Balls thro' the Gates at Chippenham Platt, Court
> Orchard, & Bristol Road locks, which has caused a Leakage in
> the respective Gates.[27]

One of the committee, also a captain in the Corps, was asked to
remonstrate.

In 1811 the company supported the North Wilts Canal* Bill,
for a connection between the Thames & Severn at Latton and the
Wilts & Berks at Swindon. This was opened in 1819, and, because
their locks would, fortunately, just take a narrow boat, immediately gave the Stroudwater line access to a better waterway route
to the lower Thames and London, which over the years greatly
helped merchandize traffic. In February 1820 the Gloucester &
Berkeley Canal reached the Stroudwater, so giving a canal link
from the Severn to Stroud that avoided the difficult navigation of
the Severn to Framilode, and in 1827 was completed to Sharpness,
to give improved access from Bristol, Wales and the lower river.
The Framilode entrance was now less used, though Forest coal
was imported there, especially from Bullo Pill, not only for the
Stroudwater, but to be taken by canal to Gloucester. Some
averaged figures are given in the table at the top of page 306. These
show how the canal's trade grew with that of the Stroud valley. It
was also benefited by the successive openings of the Thames &
Severn (1789), North Wilts (1819) and Gloucester & Berkeley to
Gloucester (1820), but adversely affected by the Kennet & Avon
(1810).

Traffic was mainly coal, a steadily increasing trade for domestic
use and to feed steam engines as the Stroud valley mills changed
from water power. Much of it came from the Forest of Dean, and
in the 1820s a number of Stroudwater shareholders also held

* Then called the Severn Junction.

T

Y.e. April	Average Receipts £	Average Tonnage tons	Dividends per cent*
1779–81	1,468†		
1782–84	1,804		
1785–87	1,601		3·75‡
1788–90	1,575		4·125
1791–93	2,062		5·33
1794–96	2,687		6·385
1797–99	2,767		9·5
1800–02	3,700		8·72
1803–05	3,726		8·66
1806–08	3,298		8·45
1809–11	3,799	50,434	9·22
1812–14	4,021	48,443	8·72
1815–17	4,940	56,200§	10·66
1818–20	5,490	63,078	13·55
1821–23	6,807	79,359‖	15·78

* These were in fact paid on the £150 shares, and have been converted to percentages.
† 1780 and 1781 only.
‡ 1786 and 1787; the first dividend was paid in 1786.
§ 1815 and 1816 only.
‖ 1821 and 1822 only.

shares in the Severn & Wye Company. Merchandize traffic was much less important. It fell when the Kennet & Avon Canal was opened late in 1810 and removed the Bristol–London trade, and did not recover until after the opening of the North Wilts Canal in 1819, which provided an all-canal route as far as Abingdon. Coal was carried to wharves up to Wallbridge, the most important being at Dudbridge, and was also transferred to the Thames & Severn. During the period covered by the following averaged figures, the Stroudwater's own tolls were high at 3s 6d (17½p), or about 4d a mile per ton, if going through to Wallbridge, but under the Thames & Severn Act of 1783 the Stroudwater company could charge 2s 3d (11p) for coal going to wharves between Wallbridge and Brimscombe, and only 1s (5p) on that to Brimscombe Port or beyond (plus, of course, T & S tolls in these cases), a drawback being allowed on the 1s (5p) charge for certain traffic going beyond the Thames & Severn. Coal, for instance, to Radcot or below on the Thames only paid 6s (30p).* These restrictions often made it cheaper to land coal at the T & S's wharf in Stroud than at Wallbridge a little lower down, and sometimes also to

* This was rescinded in 1819, in order to avoid having to give it also to traffic passing on to the North Wilts or Wilts & Berks Canals.

carry coal beyond Brimscombe to get the 1s (5p) rate, and then carry it back again by road. Here are the traffic figures. Merchandize going to the T & S cannot be distinguished from that on the Stroudwater only, but probably the greater part was local to the Stroud valley:

Y.e. April	Coal		Merchandize	Total
	Stroudwater	To T & S		
	tons	tons	tons	tons
1809–11	10,745	19,325	20,363	50,433
1812–14	12,305	20,524	15,615	48,444
1815–17	14,865*	24,796*	16,538*	56,200*
1818–20	16,431	30,205	16,442	63,078
1821–22	22,529	39,572	17,257	79,358

* 1815 and 1816 only.

In terms of tolls received, the figures come out as follows:

Y.e. April	Coal		Merchandize	Total
	Stroudwater	To T & S		
	£	£	£	£
1809–11	1,481	1,206	1,112	3,799
1812–14	1,713	1,270	942	3,925
1815–17	2,071	1,514	1,081	4,666
1818–20	2,260	1,851	1,002	5,113
1821–23	2,925	2,453	1,010	6,388†

† The figures in the last column are the gross tolls before drawbacks (negligible in this period), whereas those on p. 306 are total receipts. The difference is mainly accounted for by profits on coal trading and rents received.

As can be seen, the coal trade to the Stroudwater's own wharves produced more money than that to the Thames & Severn, though the latter accounted for nearly twice the tonnage.

The year ending April 1824 produced remarkable figures: total receipts were £8,193, and the dividend 21 per cent. They were too remarkable for some local coal users, who combined with outside railway promoters to suggest the Stroud & Severn Rail Road from Framilode Passage (a little south of the canal entrance) to Brimscombe Port, with a branch past Nailsworth towards Avening. The railway's committee were prepared to talk; the canal shareholders at once saw how dangerous the proposal could be, for the meeting which authorized their committee both to negotiate and to oppose the railway Bill also empowered them 'to vary and regulate the Tonnage rates on the Canal as they may think proper, and as circumstances may in their judgement require.'[28]

Within a fortnight they had agreed to reduce tolls to bring the full length charge down from 3s 6d (17½p) to 2s 9½d (14p). The

PROJECTED

Railway from the Severn to Brimscombe-Port.

Cainscross, January the 10th, 1825.

AT a MEETING of LANDOWNERS on the Line of this projected Railway, adjourned from the 27th of December last to this Day,

C. O. Cambridge, Esq. in the Chair,

READ—The Resolutions of the Meeting held on the 27th Day of December last, noticing a reduction already made by the Stroudwater Canal Company of One Shilling out of Three Shillings and Sixpence in their Tonnage Rates, and containing a recommendation to them to reduce those Rates Sixpence per Ton more on the whole Line of their Canal, and so in proportion to distance; and also containing a recommendation to the Tram-Road Projectors (on that reduction being acceded to) to abandon their projected Schemes;—

READ—The Reply of the Committee of the Stroudwater Canal Company; from which it appears, that the recommendation of the Landowners was acceded to, by an order to reduce the Tonnage Rates on the Canal Sixpence per Ton, in case the projected Railway be abandoned;—

AND READ—The Reply of the Committee of Subscribers to the Railway; from which it appears, that such Committee thought they had not the power to negociate; and that, if they had, they did not consider the suggested reduction of Tonnage on the Canal to be a sufficient inducement to them to enter into any negociation for abandoning the Railway.

The following Resolutions were then unanimously adopted:—

" That we will collectively and individually oppose the projected Railway, by every means in our power, and that we will unite in adopting such measures as may be necessary to effect our reasonable views, and the protection of our Property.

That, in order to strengthen our resistance, we will join the Stroudwater Canal Company, and other Parties disposed to unite with us, in such measures as may be recommended to give effect to our opposition."

That our reasons for this determination are—

FIRST.—" Because the projected Railway (parallel to and near the Canal) is unnecessary, and will be productive of serious injury to the Estates through which it will pass, and will destroy the personal comfort of many of the Owners and Inhabitants.

38. Part of the report of a meeting of landowners in 1825

railway promoters held out for more, and were offered another
6d (2½p) if they would drop their Bill. They did not. The canal
company then set about using its considerable influence to organize an opposition, so that in May 1825, after a further reduction
to 2s 6d (12½p), the Bill was defeated on second reading by 140 to
39 votes. Jubilantly they presented plate worth 100 guineas to
John Snowden of the committee, who had organized the victory,
tactfully reduced some more tolls, and abolished all charges for
wharfage, cranage and warehousing. Their solicitor's bill for the
costs of opposition was £1,285, but so pleased was the committee
that he was given £50 more. The reduction was not serious for
the Stroudwater's own trade, but because the Thames & Severn's
Act provided that any reduction must be given also to the trade
beyond Wallbridge and short of Brimscombe, the 2s 3d (11p) rate
was nearly halved to 1s 3d (6p). In 1828 the company cautiously
restored the full 3s 6d (17½p) rate for true merchandize, though
without changing that for coal and other bulk cargoes. They also
started to charge wharfage on coal again.

The effects were partly counteracted by benefits brought by the
opening of the Gloucester & Berkeley Canal throughout in 1827,
which the committee jubilantly celebrated by inviting the committees of the Gloucester & Berkeley and the Thames & Severn
to join them at dinner at the George Inn, Stroud, on 4 August
1828. Over the years from the toll reductions of 1824–5 to 1840,
the total coal trade increased from the 64,922 tons of 1822 to
76,191 in 1840. Within this total the share of the Stroudwater
wharves decreased from 25,239 to 17,796, but that of the T & S
increased from 39,683 to 47,040, about half of this being for the
section between Wallbridge and Brimscombe. In addition, a new
trade of 11,355 tons had arisen between Framilode and Gloucester
via the ship canal. Earnings from coal dropped sharply, however,
from £5,743 in 1822 to £4,357 in 1840. The T & S's share was
almost the same for the increased tonnage, the Stroudwater's own
income was down from £3,249 to £1,723, while the short-haul
ship canal traffic only earned £142. On the other hand, merchandize* carrying had much increased, short-distance in the Stroud
valley, and long-distance from Gloucester through the T & S to
the Wilts & Berks and London. It earned £1,844 against £1,021,
with a tonnage of 29,216 against 16,619. The total result was a
gross toll revenue of £6,201 (£6,185 net) and total canal revenue
of £6,427 against £6,764 (£6,733 net) and £7,380 in 1822, but a

* Merchandize includes everything except coal, e.g. stone, bricks and agricultural
produce.

tonnage of 105,407 against 81,541, and a dividend of 17·66 per cent in 1840 against 15·66 in 1822.

In 1831 the company introduced a drawback that was to encourage business and become important to them over the years: of half the toll on flour and other products of corn as back carriage if the corn itself had paid toll.* It was followed by the first of many long-distance drawbacks that were to be given in future years: on certain iron manufactures on the through voyage from Gloucester to London. Another of 1835, on salt to or beyond Pewsey on the Kennet & Avon, shows how far the canal boats went. Those were prosperous days, when plenty of good wine was offered to committeemen and shareholders at meetings: 'Ordered that Mr. Martin do supply to the Company Eight Dozen of Port Wine and Six dozen of Sherry.'[29]

In April 1842, shareholders were told that

The last two half yearly dividends were increased by the temporary transit of a large quantity of material, for the Great Western, Cirencester & Swindon Railway, which has now ceased; and the present Dividend is low in consequence of the very great falling off of Trade in general, and the consequent loss of Tonnage . . . the attention of the Committee is directed to the question whether any and what steps can be taken to preserve a fair share of trafic on this Navigation.[30]

The result was a number of new drawbacks, both to the Thames & Severn and beyond it. It was the end of an era, marked by the death of old George Hawker, still nominally clerk, who had been appointed in 1814 and had seen the company's best days. So pleased had they been with him that in 1822 his portrait was painted for the boardroom.

In February 1844, tolls on timber were cut, and in October merchandize charges were reduced to those on coal. These preceded the full opening of the Great Western line from Swindon past Stroud to Gloucester on 12 May 1845, which greatly affected the Thames & Severn, but the Stroudwater less. The latter's coal business went on increasing, both to its own wharves and for transfer to the Thames & Severn, and it held its own merchandize traffic at the lower rates, while the T & S quickly lost much of theirs.

A week after the railway had opened, the Thames & Severn's clerk came to a Stroudwater committee meeting 'to submit his Views with regard to an amalgamation of the two Canals'.[31] These

---

* In 1832 a drawback of the whole toll was offered, and in 1841 the corn toll itself was reduced for most voyages.

got no further, and the two companies began to drift apart. We now get Stroudwater drawbacks for combined canal–rail carriage that suited them but not the T & S, like that given to the carrier John George in October 1845 on coal and merchandize brought by canal from Gloucester to Wallbridge and taken thence by rail to Cirencester. There are also other types of rail–canal carriage, such as coal from Coalpit Heath in south Gloucestershire, carried by Midland Railway to Stonehouse station, and then put on canal for Dudbridge. We also get a series of small toll reductions.

By the end of 1852, railway competition for the Stroud valley trade was increasing, and the Stroudwater resolved in January that it was expedient

> to obtain a Lease of the Tolls on the Thames & Severn Canal in respect of Coals, Goods and Merchandise carried on to the Thames & Severn Canal and landed between Wallbridge and Brimscombe.[32]

This came to nothing, and major toll reductions were made: whole length on the Stroudwater, 1s 6d (7½p) against 2s 6d (12½p), and, in the case of coal, 9d on traffic up to Brimscombe on the T & S, and 6d (2½p) to and beyond it. The company were also feeling competition from rail-hauled coal from the Forest of Dean, carried at cheap rates that often undersold that brought by rail to Bullo for water carriage to the Stroud valley.

In 1859 Ford Bros were given permission to widen two locks so that the steam barge *Queen Esther* could reach their Ryeford mill. In July it got jammed in Framilode lock, but after that seems to have worked regularly on the canal.

The promotion by an independent company in 1862 of a railway from the Midland at Stonehouse up the valley to Dudbridge and then to Nailsworth was a serious threat, because the proposed line so closely paralleled the waterway. The Stroudwater opposed, but could get no concession except a free rail siding at Stonehouse wharf as compensation for the new railway passing through part of their property. The passing of the Stonehouse & Nailsworth Railway Act in 1863, continued pressure on rates for Forest coal, and serious losses of trade on the T & S line and beyond, caused the company in 1864, at the T & S's suggestion, to cut tolls further to 1s (5p) whole length and 6d (2½p) on traffic transferred to the T & S. Less than two years later, the Stroudwater were opposing a Bill promoted by the Thames & Severn to turn itself into a railway. Here are averaged figures for the period following those previously given, as set out in the table on page 312.

The S & NR did not build their bridge over the canal in the

Y.e. April	Average Receipts £	Average Tonnage tons	Dividends per cent
1824–26	7,350		16·33
1827–29	5,814		14
1830–32	6,244	72,754*	15·66
1833–35	6,596		26·33
1836–38	6,124	92,243†	17·11
1839–41	6,731	105,407‡	18·11
1842–44	6,132§	105,786	22·78
1845–47	6,301		17·30
1848–50	5,948	136,863‖	13·55
1851–53	6,064	141,251¶	16·11
1854–56	5,231		13
1857–59	4,452		11·11
1860–62	4,605		11·72
1863–65	4,796		11·66
1866–68	3,670		7·78
1869–71	2,974	100,204**	4·66
1872–74	2,585		5·05
1875–77	2,899		4·66
1878–80	3,396		5·28

* 1830 only.
† 1836 only.
‡ 1840 only.
§ 1842 and 1843 only.
‖ 1850 only.
¶ 1851 only.
** 1870 and 1871 only.

way their Act had provided, and in 1868 they agreed to pay the Stroudwater £1,060 damages and costs. The latter failed to get their money from the impecunious company until 1878, when it formed a useful fund to finance capital works.

In 1872 W. J. Snape was appointed clerk. He and his son, P. G. Snape, who succeeded him in 1915, managed the company until its liquidation eighty years later. In 1874 he helped some barge owners and traders to prepare a memorial on the state of the Thames & Severn which much annoyed the latter. Snape was backed by his committee, who told the T & S

not only do our Traders suffer, but . . . our Navigation also sustains great loss by reason of the very defective condition in which your Canal and works at present are . . . for years past my Company have ceased to derive any real benefit

from their connection with the T & S:

it seems obvious that your Co. should put their Canal into such order, as that heavy traffic in timber, corn and coal, can freely pass along all parts of it.[33]

Otherwise, they thought, they should be released from the very

low charges for traffic passing the Stroudwater and entering the
T & S imposed by the Act of 1783. They had justification. For the
thirteen years 1866–78 they passed on an average of 23,212 tons of
coal a year on to the T & S, most of which had almost certainly
travelled from Framilode or Saul on their canal. Their average
receipt was 4¾d a ton, or a little over ½d a mile. An average of
9,057 tons a year of merchandize also passed, most probably from
Saul, yielding about 6½d (2½p) a ton or 1d a mile. Back carriage,
however, was small, and therefore many boats returned empty,
passing the locks again toll-free. They followed their complaints
by getting Edward Leader Williams, the Severn Commission's
engineer, to survey the T & S. He justified them.

The Stroudwater company went on trying to get this clause
changed, and opposing the T & S's plans of becoming a railway.
In 1882 it joined a deputation to the President of the Board of
Trade 'from all the Canal Co's interested in keeping open the
water communication between the Thames and the Severn.'[34]
These companies then formed a joint committee with the idea of
working the T & S jointly, but their ideas got no further then (see
Chapter XIV).

The year 1879–80 was the last for which the Stroudwater paid
a dividend of 5 per cent. Thereafter payments dwindled, and
ceased after 1922. It is remarkable that in these circumstances the
company was carried on for some three-quarters of a century. One
motive was clearly the lower railway rates applicable to areas
where water transport was available.

In spite of their poor financial state, in 1888 the company discussed with the GWR, now controlling the T & S, buying that
canal, but their offer of £2,000 or £3,000 was rejected, the railway
company wanting more money, and also to exclude from the sale
property that the Stroudwater needed to finance necessary repairs
to the waterway. Soon afterwards the GWR sold some of the
property. Subsequently the Stroudwater Company contributed
£150 pa to the Thames & Severn Canal Trust and then to the
Gloucestershire County Council.

By 1902 traffic on the Framilode–Saul Junction section was
described as 'trifling'. The county council quickly found that the
difficulties of keeping the whole T & S open were too great, and
in 1910 told the Stroudwater that they thought of closing the
Chalford–Inglesham portion, seemingly in the hope of leasing
part or all. Talks were held, culminating in 1912 in the offer of the
Stroud–Chalford section on lease. It was refused because of the
state of the Stroudwater's finances.

The canal was still carrying some 30,000 tons of coal in 1916, most of it from south Wales and the Forest. In 1924 the county council again tried to sell or lease part of the T & S: having failed, it decided in principle to abandon. There were long discussions, which included the Ministry of Transport, and eventually the Stroudwater, local traders and local authorities between them promised to contribute some £700 pa to keep it open for two years from 25 March 1925. After that the Chalford–Inglesham portion was closed, the Stroudwater company and its supporters contributing diminishing sums on a yearly basis to keep open the remainder until 1933, when that also was abandoned.

By this time the Stroudwater had long been undredged, and could only take 30-ton craft. In 1936 the Severn & Canal Carrying Company experimented with a service on it, but found it too weedy and shallow, conditions the canal company had no money to remedy. The last commercial toll was paid in the spring of 1941, after which the company continued to supply water and manage property. It was finally abandoned by an Act of 1954, except for the short section between Saul junction and Walk bridge, Whitminster, which was transferred to British Waterways and is now used for pleasure craft moorings.

CHAPTER XIV

The Thames & Severn Canal

++++++++++++++++++++++++++++++++++++++◆++++++++++++++++++++++++++++++++++++++

THE idea of joining Thames and Severn[1] was probably in Lord Bathurst's mind at the time of the Stroudwater's 1730 Act. John Dallaway, in his pamphlet of 1755, suggested that his scheme would bring the two great rivers nearer, and so a 'Communication by Water between the Two chief Cities, London and Bristol'.[2] The Stroudwater Navigation having been opened in 1779, a shareholders' meeting of 12 April 1781 ordered that 'a Survey be made and a Levell taken for a Canal from Dudbridge to Cricklade' at a cost not to exceed £50. It was probably done by John Priddey, their former engineer. Sir Edward Littleton, who had been on the committee of the Staffs & Worcs Canal from its promotion, seems to have heard of the survey, and, thinking a new market might be opened for Staffordshire coal, to have written to ask whether such a canal were really practicable. The Stroudwater's clerk was ordered to tell him that it was. Priddey had done the job by August, having in the course of it decided that Wallbridge and Lechlade would be better terminals, and that plenty of water could be obtained at Cirencester. The Stroudwater company called a promotion meeting for 17 September at the King's Head in Cirencester, at which the idea took off independently of its parent, though a number of the promoters were committeemen and shareholders of the Stroudwater, notably Thomas Baylis, Christopher Chambers, John Colborne, John Hollings and Joseph Wathen. Christopher Chambers was a London merchant, who was to form the nucleus of the later strong London interest in the Thames & Severn.[3] Others joined in from the Staffs & Worcs Canal, notably Sir Edward Littleton, James Perry, John Jesson and Moreton Walhouse, together with Lord Dudley & Ward of the Dudley and Stourbridge Canals, John Lane of the Birmingham Canal, John Stevenson of Stafford, Edward Loveden Loveden of the Thames Commissioners, and Samuel Skey of Bewdley. The Thames & Severn was, then, a product of Staffordshire hopes for new markets for coal, Stroudwater hopes for new traffic and development of the Bristol trade, London hopes for profit from a trunk waterway, and local concern for local development. It may be that just because so much of the impetus came from a distance, and so many different interests were at work foreseeing benefit, two very obvious points were given insufficient attention: that without a good navigation of the upper Thames or canals to bypass it, the expected benefits would not accrue; and that water-supply was all important.

There were two possible routes, that proposed by the Stroudwater from their own canal up the Golden Valley and by way of Cirencester to the Thames, or from higher up the Severn to the Coln valley and so to the Thames at Lechlade. Robert Whitworth, asked to survey both, made it clear in his report that the line by the Golden Valley was cheaper, shorter and better supplied with water. The first two reasons were valid, but the last seems to have depended upon an enormous over-estimate of the yield of the little river Churn, which Robert Mylne in 1790 alleged he put at 21m cu ft per week, when the true yield was about 2m cu ft. In addition, he does not seem to have fully realized how much water would be lost by leakage off the summit level where it passed through the oolitic rock.

His estimate of £127,916 was based on a canal large enough to take Thames barges 12 ft wide, but not Severn trows 15 ft wide any higher than the proposed basin at Brimscombe, since these would not in any case be able to pass the Thames locks. A meeting of promoters on 17 January 1783 decided to go ahead on this basis with the Golden Valley line. Within three weeks almost 80 per cent of the capital had been promised, and on 17 April the Bill received the royal assent.[4] It authorized £130,000, and £60,000 more if necessary. Robert Whitworth and others laid out the line, Josiah Clowes, who had worked on the Chester Canal and the Trent & Mersey, was appointed 'Surveyor and Engineer and Head-Carpenter'—in other words, resident engineer—and James Perry acted as an active and efficient manager on behalf of the committee. The tunnel was a frightening difficulty. Harecastle on the Trent & Mersey was the only long canal tunnel so far built in England, and that was for narrow boats. In June, two months after the hurriedly-obtained Act, arguments over its dimensions were still going on, for a party of Thames Commissioners who visited the Stroudwater company to learn about the new canal reported back:

the Tunnel . . . is the greatest difficulty of the Navigation; If it is small, the Coals from the Severn or the Thames must unload at each end—If it is made large enough to pass Barges of 60 Tons, the size of the Tunnel and path for a length of two Miles will be extremely Expensive if not impracticable. It is therefore thought a narrow passage and small Boats must be adopted.[5] Then the great decision to build a broad tunnel was made, and by September advertisements for tunnellers were appearing.

The canal was to be 28¾ miles long, with a rise of 241 ft from Stroud to the summit level at the Sapperton tunnel by 28 locks, and a fall from the farther end of the summit at Siddington near Cirencester of 128 ft by 15 locks to the Thames at Inglesham near Lechlade. There was to be a 1½-mile long branch to Cirencester.

The passing of the Act, with its promise of through communication between the Midlands and London by way of the Severn and the Thames, led to a whole series of other moves. Round Birmingham the Stourbridge Canal Company, which had subscribed to the cost of Whitworth's survey, joined the Dudley, which also had, in proposals to the Birmingham Company for a junction with their canal; this was made when the Dudley tunnel was completed in 1792. They also encouraged a separate company to promote a Bill for a canal from near Stourbridge through Bromsgrove to Diglis below Worcester, which with the Dudley tunnel would have given them a route for Staffordshire coal independent of the Staffs & Worcs Canal.[6] The last-named itself sought but failed to get an Act in 1786 to improve the Severn below its exit at Stourport.[7] Lower down there was the Gloucester Canal scheme of 1784–5, to avoid the Severn between Gloucester and Framilode by building a direct Gloucester–Stroudwater canal (see p. 341), and on the Thames the Lechlade–Abingdon Canal Bill of 1784 (see p. 198) actively supported by the Thames & Severn.

In considering the subsequent history of the Thames & Severn, we must remember the time lag before such improvements as these were actually completed. The Worcester scheme, in another form as the Worcester & Birmingham Canal, was opened in 1815; the Lechlade–Abingdon proposal, as the North Wilts and Wilts & Berks Canals, in 1819; the Gloucester–Stroudwater connection in 1820; the improvement of the Severn not until the beginning of 1847.

By January 1785 the line was open to Chalford, and by the summer of 1786 the canal up the Golden Valley to the summit was finished and in use, and a wharf, warehouse, and coalyard had been provided at Daneway bridge. The contract for building the tunnel, 3,817 yd long with a bore 15 ft high and 15 ft wide,

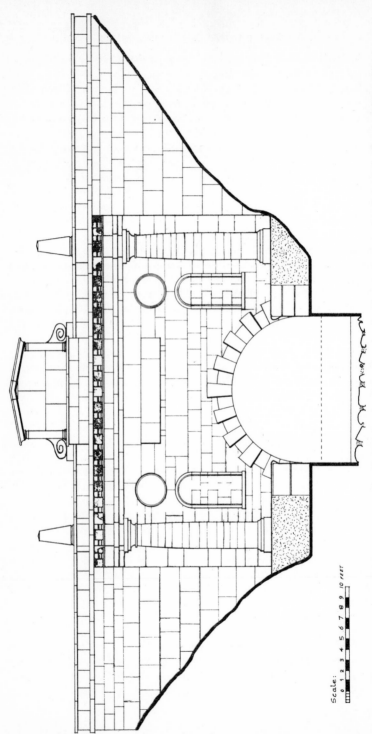

Scale: 0 1 2 3 4 5 6 7 8 9 10 FEET

39. The eastern (Coates) portion of Sapperton tunnel. The drawing is a reconstruction from measurements taken on the spot and from old prints

provided for construction in four years from the beginning of 1784. The original contractor, Charles Jones, fell into debt and completed only a little over one-third of it, and the tunnel was finished by a number of other contractors working each on a part. In addition to the work at each end, 25 working shafts were sunk, the deepest to 244 ft. The first boat passed through on 20 April 1789, the proprietors having pressed for its opening as soon as possible, but a year later it had to be closed for two and a half months for further work to be done on it. It was the longest and widest canal tunnel so far built in Britain, and remained the third longest, having been exceeded only by Standedge through the Pennines and Strood on the Thames & Medway Canal.

Meanwhile, the building of the remainder of the summit level had begun in June 1785, and was probably finished, including the branch to Cirencester and the basin there, by the end of 1787, and brought into use immediately the tunnel was open. The fall from the summit to Inglesham was then built, and the whole completed in November 1789, the first vessel passing through the canal and into the Thames on the 19th of that month.

The two and a half miles from Wallbridge to Brimscombe Port were built to take Severn trows, with locks as on the Stroudwater, 16 ft wide and rather over 70 ft long. At Brimscombe an interchange port was created, with wharves, warehouses, and the canal company's offices. Thence the size of locks changed to 12 ft 9 in wide and some 90 ft long, suitable for Thames barges. With the canal just opening and meetings frequent, members of the committee, many of whom came long distances, agreed to furnish their own rooms at the Brimscombe offices, Perry to provide servants and necessities.

On 19 November 1789, the Thames & Severn Canal was opened, and the *Annual Register* reported the event:

This day was effected the greatest object of internal navigation in this kingdom. The Severn was united to the Thames, by an intermediate canal ascending by Stroud, through the vale of Chalford, to the height of 343 feet, by 28 locks; there entering a tunnel through the hill of Saperton, for the length of two miles and three furlongs, and descending 134 feet by 14 locks, it joined the Thames near Lechlade.

With respect to the internal commerce of the kingdom, and the security of communication in time of war, this junction of the Thames and Severn must be attended with the most beneficial consequences, as even stores from the Baltic, and provisions from Ireland, may reach the capital, and the ports at the mouth of the Thames, in safety. And all the heavy articles from the mines and founderies in the heart of Wales, and the counties contiguous to the Severn, may find a secure and certain conveyance to the capital.

In short, this undertaking is worthy of a great commercial nation, and does great credit to the exertions of the individuals, who have promoted and completed a work of such magnitude, at an expence of near two hundred thousand pounds.

The arched tunnel, carried through the bowels of a mountain near two miles and a half long, and 15 feet wide, at a level 250 feet below its summit, is a work worthy admiration; and the locks ascending from Stroud, and descending from the summit, are executed in a manner deserving great commendation.

A through route between the rivers was at last in existence.

The Thames & Severn offered the first inland water communication between Staffordshire, places on the upper Severn, and London, and between Bristol and London. By the time it was effectively open, in 1792, the canal mania had arrived, and a number of linking schemes were projected.

Hopes of a Staffordshire–London trade quickly died away as a route from Birmingham to London via Oxford was opened in 1790, and a much better one via Warwick and Braunston between 1800 and 1805.[8] Nevertheless, the Midlands could hope for much new trade above Oxford, and in late 1792 a Worcester–Bristol canal was proposed in Birmingham, to carry on the canal line already authorized thence to Worcester in 1791 as the Worcester & Birmingham Canal. At Gloucester the first part of the Gloucester & Berkeley Canal, authorized in March 1793, promised to shorten the distance and improve the navigation between Gloucester and the Stroudwater.

Bristol was by now the point from which canal schemes ran south-west past Bridgwater and Taunton to Exeter.[9] From Bristol to Gloucester the Bristol & Severn barge canal was suggested. This dated from 20 November 1792, when an excited meeting at Bristol was

enthusiastically supported by influential persons, and a very large sum was subscribed by those present, who struggled violently with each other in their rush to the subscription book.[10]

This approved a canal line from Bristol to Gloucester 'or some other more convenient place' such as Worcester, and is said to have subscribed £700,000.[11] A canal that had to lock 160 ft up from Bristol and nearly the same down again to Berkeley was not attractive, and the project was wound up in 1797.[12]

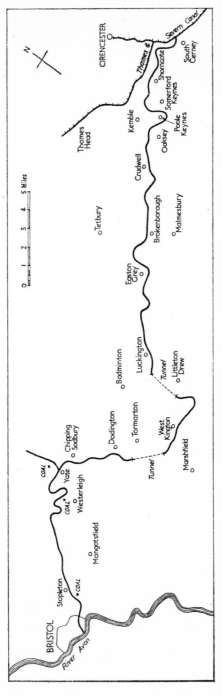

40. Route surveyed by Robert Mylne for the proposed Bristol–Cirencester canal of 1793

Even in 1792, however, it was obvious that a Bristol to Berkeley canal to link with the Gloucester & Berkeley, and so with the Stroudwater and the Thames & Severn, was a roundabout way to the upper Thames. The Thames & Severn company therefore got a survey started for a canal from Bristol by way of the south Gloucestershire coalfield direct to their own. This split into two, one with Bristol backing to join the Thames & Severn near Cirencester,[13] surveyed by Richard Hall and Robert Mylne, the other, planned by Robert Whitworth and locally supported, to Thames Head, where a better water supply could be anticipated.[14] Both were promoted during the first half of 1793. This second scheme had considerable local backing, but neither got started. These in turn were mentally linked with the London & Western project, encouraged by the T & S, for a canal from the Oxford Canal above Oxford to London,[15] and the Thames & Severn Company in May 1792 asked Robert Mylne to consider how best a canal might be built from the Thames above Oxford to join it.[16]

There was a moment when men actually envisaged a through canal route from Exeter to London by way of Taunton, Bristol, Cirencester, Lechlade, Oxford and the London & Western. But the obviously more efficient line from Bristol by way of Devizes and Hungerford to the Thames at Reading superseded these shadowy schemes as soon as the Kennet & Avon was authorized in 1794. Most were never heard of again, though the Bristol & Severn was revived at a meeting at Bristol on 5 June 1810, and seen as connecting Gloucester with the Kennet & Avon, Bristol & Taunton and Grand Western Canals to Exeter,[17] so 'opening a communication through the medium of this Port,* between the Northern, Western and Eastern parts of the kingdom,'[18] while the idea of a canal between Worcester and Gloucester reappeared in 1825 as the Worcester & Gloucester Union.[19]

The link between Thames and Severn was open, but both at Framilode and Inglesham the canal line of the Stroudwater and the Thames & Severn met unsatisfactory river navigations. The Severn situation was to be remedied by the Gloucester & Berkeley Canal, which from 1820 gave the canals an artificial channel to Gloucester, and from 1827 to Sharpness also. That on the Thames was more serious. It was tackled by the Thames & Severn in two ways: by encouraging bypass canals, and by putting pressure on the Thames Commissioners to improve the river.

We have noted the Lechlade–Abingdon project of 1783. After that failed, James Perry in 1788 proposed a cut, to be made by the

* Bristol.

Thames Commissioners, from Inglesham to Buscot. At first they were inclined to agree, but then changed their minds, so that the canal company felt it necessary to serve notice on them to improve their navigation by using the borrowing powers they had recently been given. The state of the Thames was a real deterrent to traffic, perhaps in reputation more than in actuality: John Rennie, for instance, surveying in 1790 for a curious London–Bristol route by way of Basingstoke and Salisbury, wrote that the Thames & Severn 'has so much of the bad navigation of the River Thames to encounter that no goods will ever be sent by thence that can go by this Canal.'[20]

As we have seen, the Thames Commissioners did much to improve the upper river in the ten years from 1786, but naturally not enough for the canal company, who were therefore driven back on cajoling or threatening them, and on encouraging bypasses. The most hopeful of these emerged as soon as the Wilts & Berks Canal had been promoted late in 1793. Two years before, the Thames & Severn had been thinking of a branch to Swindon to tap the Vale of White Horse trade, and now they sent a representative to urge the Wilts & Berks subscribers towards a connecting link. But these in turn were slow to respond, fearing to lose more by the competition of Staffordshire and Forest coal with their own Somerset supplies than they stood to gain from extra traffic, and it was not until 1813 that the North Wilts was authorized, or 1819 that it was opened, to give the Thames & Severn a bypass as far as Abingdon. But the final link that would have given an all-canal route to London, the Western Junction from Abingdon to the Grand Junction Canal, always eluded them.

As for water supplies, these do not seem to have troubled anybody until the summit had been completed. The committee presumably expected to rely on the Frome, the Golden Valley's other streams, the Churn (in spite of compensation payments to the millers), the Boxwell springs, the Coln, and a supply at Thames Head that was in April 1788 being obtained by a horse-operated pump. A little later they put in a windmill there, but it was not until Clowes tried to stop the summit leaking and failed, just before the whole canal was ready to open, that the seriousness of the situation broke upon them. In June 1790 they realized the Churn and the windmill would not give enough water, and invited James Watt down to advise on putting in a steam engine. They also had Mylne, notable for his gloom and his dislike of canal engineers. He was delighted to find the summit and tunnel leaking $1\frac{1}{4}$m cu ft a week, with the yield from the Churn, if all its water were taken, only 2m cu ft, with another ½m from Thames Head, whereas the canal, he reckoned, needed 5m per week.

It is inconceivable, how so great a Mistake should have crept into the Facts assumed, when the Canal was first projected, that the Churn alone, as stated from Mr. Whitworth's Figures produced no less than 20,805,120 Cubick Feet weekly 27th Octr 1782, or, that, *that essential Point*, of all others the most important, has not been duly investigated till the present day.[21]

As a result, a steam engine was immediately ordered from Boulton & Watt, and first put to work in September 1792, after which the Thames Head wells were extended to tap greater supplies. But leakage continued, and the canal was closed from August 1791 to early in the following year, to try to stop it, and to insert a shallow lock at Boxwell, South Cerney, and drop the canal level thence to the next lock, to get more Boxwell spring water into the canal. Mylne was back in 1793 to point out that the unequal falls of locks near the summit increased wastage. However, enough water could now be provided, though as much because the expected traffic failed to develop as that supplies were adequate.

It seems that only a moderate trade between Bristol and London was attracted from the sea route before the opening of the shorter and easier passage by the Kennet & Avon in 1810. Instead, the trade was mainly one of coal imported at Framilode, and distributed up the Stroud valley, at Cirencester, and down the Thames as far as Oxford and Abingdon. But the proprietors saw that even this trade would have to be created. Before the canal had opened, they had decided that craft should be acquired and worked, on the Severn and the Thames as well as on the canal, and coal bought and sold, by an autonomous trading committee 'to introduce the practicability of navigating the Canal'.[22] As the opening date approached, they went so far as to envisage carrying on all the coal trade, for they instructed the trading committee 'to provide such further number of Boats and quantity of Coal as they shall think sufficient for the consumption of the Country throughout the line of the Canal.'[23] With the aid of James Perry's firm, they bought supplies mainly in Staffordshire and Shropshire, but also from the Forest of Dean. This was sold at Brimscombe Port, Cirencester, South Cerney, Cricklade, Kempsford and Lechlade, and for a time at Abingdon. Apart from the coal trade, the company did their best to publicize the services available, by distributing rate cards, and advertising. In November 1792, also, they sent their agent into Shropshire, Worcestershire and Staffordshire

in order to acquaint the several Agents, Carriers & different

Manufacturers with whom he may be acquainted, that this Canal is now open for transacting business.[24]

In addition to the share capital of £130,000, the canal had in 1793 a mortgage and bond debt of £97,200, and owed another £28,600 for interest on shares entitled to such payment during the construction of the canal. At first, the interest on the debt was paid by creating more debt, but in 1796 all interest payments were stopped, it having been decided to use the money to buy boats and stock for trading, and an attempt was made to commute interest arrears for cash payments and new half-shares. The company struggled on, beset by the difficulty of navigating the Thames, 'the pressure of the times', 'the seizure of their vessels by the officers of the Customs on the River Severn, on doubtful and disputed grounds,'* and drought.

Shareholders' lists of the time show that the canal had been largely financed as a speculation from London, with support from those connected with the Staffs & Worcs Canal and the Staffordshire coal trade, and to a lesser extent by Bristol merchants. Local support was minimal. Here are figures for 1795:

	Shares
London area	841
Staffs & Worcs area	190
Bristol and Bath area	121
Thames & Severn area	32
Elsewhere and not known	116
	1,300

Those who held 50 or more shares were: John Chalié (London) 100; Sir Edward Littleton, Bt., (Staffs) 100; Robert Rolleston (London) 85; Matthew Chalié (London) 68; Lewis Disney-ffytche (Essex) 60; Christopher Chambers (London) 60; Lowbridge Bright (Bristol) 55; Mrs Frances Chambers (London) 50; the late Thomas Hayes (Bristol) 50; James Perry (Wolverhampton) 50.

By 1802 the company could look back upon the trading results that are set out in the table on page 326.

Though boats had been built by members of the committee and then sold to the company on hire purchase to save capital costs, and strenuous efforts had been made to develop the carrying trade, which had helped to push the toll receipts up for 1801 and 1802— and the distributable balance until costing was improved—the result had not been economic. For the year ending 1 April 1797

---

* Connected with the coastwise duties: the Customs then regarded the voyage from Newport to Framilode as a coastwise and not an inland one.

Year ending 1 April	Distributable balance £	Tonnage Receipts £
1794		4,288
1795		4,149
1796		5,153
1797	1,107	3,848
1798	3,527	5,749
1799	2,595	4,913
1800	6,035	7,275
1801	6,354	8,499
1802	2,926	5,618

only 3,030 tons had been carried in the company's boats to and from London, and £757 earned in tolls on their own canal, against which they had a net loss on the trade. Yet in 1798 the company possessed 30 Thames barges, 13 Severn trows of 56–90 tons, 2 frigates of 20–24 tons, 10 Staffs & Worcs narrow boats and 5 Thames & Severn barges, with two building, and in 1801 their stock of boats, coal and equipment was thought to be worth £10,000. The carrying trade was partly relinquished in 1802, and the following year it was recorded:

> that this General Assembly entirely approves of what the Committee have already done towards the relinquishment of the Carrying trade, and also of their declared intention of disposing of the remainder as soon as they shall find the same to be advisable and practicable.[25]

In June 1805 a newspaper advertisement offered the company's

> Severn Ketches and Trows, employed in the Coal Trade, in favour of Individuals wishing to enter into their Trade.[26]

In May 1806, four remained unsold.[27] The company kept some craft; they still had 25 Thames barges in 1812.

For the next six years the average annual disposable balance was £2,763, and this was clearly to be the level to which the future conduct of the company had to be assimilated. So finances were reorganized; the capital then raised by shares totalled £140,300, and in loans £117,125, upon which interest was long in arrears. These, like the shares, were largely held in London and Staffordshire, the biggest debtor being Lewis Disney-ffytche with £22,715. The resultant situation can be seen from a share sale of August 1805, when £100 shares sold for £3 to £4, and £250 mortgage bonds for £52 to £54. An Act of 1809 wiped out the debt, which with arrears of interest then stood at £193,892, and gave the company instead £115,000 of preference or 'red' shares to stand beside the original £130,000 of ordinary or 'black' shares. The company was now free of debt and in a position to pay dividends, and for the year 1809–10 a maiden dividend of 1½ per cent was distributed on both classes of share.

During 1810 both the Kennet & Avon and the Wilts & Berks opened, and competition developed in many ways. There was the ever-changing rivalry of the coal trade, and to a lesser extent those in iron, stone, and other goods from different sources, each helped by bounties or drawbacks. The search for lower prices also showed itself for instance in 1811, when the company agreed to reduce their tolls on a wide range of goods if certain carriers down the

Regular Inland Communication,

BY WAY OF

The THAMES & SEVERN CANAL.

THE BARGE OWNERS,

CONCERNED IN THE CARRYING-TRADE ON THE ABOVE NAVIGATION,

Respectfully inform the Public, that they have appointed

Wednesday in every Week for loading their Barges,

AT

HAMBRO' WHARF, THREE CRANES,

LONDON,

To such Depths only as they can proceed regularly with by which, they have no doubt of insuring that Preference it is their object to merit.

BY THE ABOVE CONVEYANCE

GOODS ARE REGULARLY FORWARDED

TO AND FROM THE UNDER-MENTIONED COUNTIES.

Oxfordshire	Somersetshire	Herefordshire
Berkshire	Glocestershire	Monmouthshire
Wiltshire	Worcestershire	Shropshire

AND SOUTH WALES.

On the following conditions which is always exposed to Public view at every Warehouse and Wharf where they receive and deliver Goods and Published in the Gazette in March 1811.

THE Several Proprietors hereby give public Notice that they hold themselves accountable to pay Ten per Cent and no more, on the amount of damage or loss on goods, properly packed and directed, if proved to have happened whilst in their possession; provided such per Centage does not exceed the value of the Vessel and Freight, and provided a printed Bill with this Notice inserted in it, is produced signed by the Wharfinger, or Warehouse keeper, acknowledging the receipt of the goods; but they will not hold themselves liable to any greater extent of loss or damage, nor will they be answerable for any loss or damage whatever, unless occasioned by want of ordinary care in the Master or Crew of the Vessel, nor for any loss or damage arising by Fire, nor for leakage, occasioned by unsound packages, nor for any loss or injury that the goods entrusted to their care may sustain by any accident whatever that may happen to any of their Barges.

ALL Goods which shall be delivered for the purpose of being carried, will be considered as subject to a general lien, not only the Money due for the Carriage of such particular Goods, but also for the general Balance due from the respective Owners to the Proprietor of the said Conveyance.

RICHARD MILLER, JOHN BAKER,	*Brimscombe-Port.*
I. & R. WYATTS, JOSEPH BROOKINGS,	*Oxford.*

41. Notice by the barge-owners working on the Thames & Severn Canal, about 1812

Thames and to the Severn and Wye reduced their freight charges, or in 1815 when an agreement was made with one large carrier for a single charge per ton that would include wharfage, warehousing, cranage, and weighing charges.

Meanwhile the Stroudwater Navigation naturally benefited by all traffic passing on or off the Thames & Severn westwards. When Zachary Allnutt wrote in 1810, he said that the Stroudwater was then taking 75-ton barges which passed to Brimscombe. Thence 56-ton barges and also 60-ton Severn trows were taking three days from Brimscombe to Lechlade, and eight to ten days from Lechlade to London.

Let us now look at the Thames & Severn as it was in 1817, two years before the North Wilts Canal joined it to the Wilts & Berks and altered the character of some of the trade. The main traffic on the canal was coal, entering the Stroudwater Navigation at Framilode. For the first six months of the year 9,481 tons of coal arrived at Brimscombe Port to be distributed in the neighbourhood and to points east. Of this total: 4,825 tons was Forest of Dean coal, 3,844½ of which was from Lydney, 52 tons from Gatcombe, and the rest from Bullo Pill; 2,357 tons was Staffordshire coal which had been brought by way of the Staffs & Worcs Canal to Stourport, and then down the Severn; 708 tons was Shropshire coal brought down the Severn; 1,631 tons was Welsh coal, the great bulk from Newport, a little from Tenby and Swansea.

In addition to coal the following tonnages of other goods were also imported to Brimscombe from the west. In some cases the merchandize was carried on coal boats, and probably would not have been brought if the coal boats had not been running: 178 tons from Framilode and places on the Thames & Severn and the Stroudwater below Brimscombe; 209 tons from Gloucester; 238 tons from Bristol; 105 tons from points on the Severn below Gloucester; 212½ tons of salt from Droitwich; 109 tons from Stourport (probably Birmingham goods); 34 tons from the Severn above Stourport; 48 tons from Newport.

To set against this tonnage of 10,615 tons of coal and other commodities imported from the west for distribution towards the east in the six months period, the following tonnages reached Brimscombe from the east: 332 tons from London; 208 tons from Abingdon; 124 tons from Lechlade and points on the canal east of Brimscombe; a total of 664 tons of back carriage.

In the year 1817 the following traffic passed Siddington toll, at the east end of the summit; in order to work it, and the empties, it was necessary in certain months both to use the steam engine at

Thames Head and to take water from the river Churn, for which payment had to be made to the millers.

Month	No of loaded boats	Av. depth of water on sill ft in	Av. hours water from Churn per day	Av. hours pumping by engine per day
January	32	5 2	—	—
February	35	5 0	—	—
March	34	5 0	—	—
April	24	4 2$\frac{3}{4}$	3$\frac{5}{8}$	1$\frac{1}{2}$
May	40	3 8	8$\frac{1}{2}$	10
June	27	3 4$\frac{3}{4}$	9$\frac{1}{2}$	3
July	27	4 7$\frac{1}{2}$	2	5
August	33	4 8	—	—
September	32	4 10	—	—
October	41	3 8	4	5$\frac{3}{4}$
November	72	3 8	8$\frac{1}{2}$	7
December	60	4 4$\frac{1}{4}$	3$\frac{3}{8}$	—

457

The traffic itself was as follows: 32 laden boats (7 per cent) passed Siddington going west, 21 to Brimscombe, 10 to Stroud, and 1 to the Severn; 176 laden boats (38½ per cent) were going east to Cirencester; 62 laden boats (13½ per cent) were passing east to points on the canal: of these, 31 were going to Cricklade, 15 to Latton, 14 to Kempsford, 1 to South Cerney, and 1 to Dudgrove; 169 laden boats (37 per cent) were passing east to Lechlade and the Thames. About half appear to be going to Lechlade itself to supply the coal business run there by the company till about 1824; 18 laden boats (4 per cent) were going to London.

In 1819 the North Wilts Canal was opened, and in 1827 the Gloucester & Berkeley. The opening of the North Wilts, and the additional traffic it offered, showed up the poor state of the Thames & Severn. Trying to borrow £10,000 from the Exchequer Bill Loan Commissioners in 1820, the committee wrote that their canal was in

> such a state of ill repair as to require immediate attention . . . the whole line . . . passes through a Country heavily burthened by Poor and where the rates are exceedingly high. The description of Work will occupy many hands with Spades.[28]

Let us therefore take the year 1834, and see what changes have taken place on the summit. There are now passing Siddington not only the older types of craft, but also narrow boats to and from the Wilts & Berks, and fly-boats running between Gloucester and London by way of the Wilts & Berks on regular schedules. The tonnage carried per boat has of course fallen, but the number of loaded boats to be passed, and so of empties, has greatly increased. The water supplies are therefore pressed hard, and it seems as if the canal is working almost to capacity. Indeed, in the following year and by agreement with the Wilts & Berks, the company was authorized to shorten its locks to save water, and later a number were so dealt with.

Month	No of loaded boats	Av. depth of water on sill ft in	Av. hours water from Churn per day	Av. hours pumping by engine per day*
January	134	5 0	—	—
February	119	5 0	—	—
March	176	4 7	1	—
April	76	3 8	$7\frac{1}{2}$	—
May	163	3 6	$6\frac{1}{2}$	$14\frac{1}{2}$
June	96	3 5	6	$15\frac{1}{2}$
July	126	3 $4\frac{1}{4}$	4	$14\frac{1}{4}$
August	110	4 $0\frac{1}{4}$	—	$23\frac{1}{2}$
September	147	3 10	1	$21\frac{3}{4}$
October	129	3 $9\frac{3}{4}$	$4\frac{1}{2}$	$20\frac{1}{4}$
November	156	3 $8\frac{1}{2}$	5	$19\frac{1}{2}$
December	186	3 7	5	19

1,618

* Thomas Toward, who had looked after the engine since it was first installed, retired in 1834. He had thought the work hard before the fly-boats started, and had said: 'I have often employed myself, both early and late, indeed sometimes for whole Nights, and even on Sundays when necessity required it, in consequence of the Engine being frequently at Work on those days, and also at Nights, for affording a bare sufficiency of Water for carrying on the proprietary concern in this Neighbourhood.'[29] It must have been still harder in 1834.

Of these boats, 392 were Thames & Severn barges, 297 were fly-boats, and 929 were other narrow boats. Because of the very different loadings of the three types of craft, any comparison with the destinations of traffic in 1817 had best be made in terms of the tonnage carried. If so, the following are the results: of the total traffic passing Siddington in the year of 37,894 tons, 3,316 tons (8 per cent) passed going west, including 1,582 tons to Birmingham;* 27 per cent went to Cirencester; 6 per cent passed east to

* The Birmingham loads seem to be part of a special order for stone, and are, I think, higher than would be normal.

EXPEDITIOUS WATER CONVEYANCE,

TO AND FROM

London to Glocester,

BY WAY OF ABINGDON, BRIMSCOMBE & STROUD.

⬦⬥⬧⬦⬥⬧

GEORGE FRANKLIN'S FLY BOATS

Leave Brooks' Wharf, Thames Street, London,	DELIVER GOODS AT	DELIVER GOODS AT	ARRIVE AT GLOCESTER,
	SWINDON, CRICKLADE, & CIRENCESTER,	CHALFORD, BRIMSCOMBE, STROUD, CAINSCROSS, EBLEY, & STONEHOUSE,	
TUESDAYS.	.... SATURDAYS.	.... MONDAYS. ...	..., MONDAYS. ...;
THURSDAYS.	Ditto......... TUESDAYS. ..	Ditto .... WEDNESDAYS	*Wednesday*
SATURDAYS.	Ditto......... THURSDAYS. .	Ditto .... FRIDAYS. ...	.... FRIDAYS. ...;

LEAVE GLOCESTER,	LEAVE BRIMSCOMBE,	Arrive at BROOKS' WHARF, THAMES ST. LONDON,	
.... MONDAY	.... MONDAY.	.... SATURDAYS.	
Wednesday.........	...... WEDNESDAY. ..;...	.... MONDAYS.	
....FRIDAY MORNINGS....	...... FRIDAY EVENINGS....	.... FRIDAYS.	

RATES FROM LONDON............ {		To Cirencester, and Thames Head.	To Brimscombe, Stroud, and Stroud Canal.	To Glocester.
Tallows......	Fuller's Earth ....|Patent Bricks	33s. per Ton.	33s. per Ton.	33s. per Ton.
Raw Sugars ..	Pipe Clay ....|Cement& Plaister.	ditto	ditto	ditto
Barilla	Dye Woods, uncut.|Block Tin	ditto	ditto	ditto
Soap	Pig & Bar Iron ..|Pig & Sheet Lead .	ditto	ditto	ditto
Lead	Rags ....|Red & White do ..	ditto	ditto	ditto
Pitch & Tar..	Deals & Timber ..|London Porter....	ditto	ditto	ditto
Woad	Pipe Staves ......|Oil & Vinegar....	ditto	ditto	ditto
Wool, Hops, & Tea		50s. per Ton.	60s. per Ton.	55s. per Ton.
Hemp, Flax, & Linen Drapery		45s. ditto	50s. ditto	45s. ditto
Household Furniture, 60 Cubit Feet to the Ton		35s. ditto	40s. ditto	40s. ditto
All other Articles		40s. ditto	45s. ditto	40s. ditto

RATES TO LONDON. .... {		From Glocester.	From Brimscombe, Stroud, & Stroud Canal.	From Cirencester & Thames Head.
Stone		21s. per Ton.	16s. per Ton.	
Pig & Bar Iron, Gross Iron Castings,..	Delivered	25s. ditto		
Tin & Tin Plates, Wire and Copper ..		30s. ditto		
Cider, in casks		30s. ditto		
Castings	to any part	30s. ditto		
Cheese		35s. ditto	40s. per Ton.	35s. per Ton.
Cloth	of London.	55s. ditto	55s. ditto	55s. ditto
Paper & Leather.......................		40s. ditto	45s. ditto	40s. ditto

GOODS CONVEYED BY THESE FLY BOATS, TO ALL PLACES ON THE BANKS OF THE THAMES; ALSO EXPEDITIOUSLY FORWARDED TO OXFORD; OR AS DIRECTED TO ANY PART OF THE KINGDOM.

42. Notice by an owner of fly-boats working between London and Gloucester by way of the Wilts & Berks Canal

points on the canal; 36 per cent to Lechlade and the Thames, including London; and 23 per cent to the Wilts & Berks. The figures for 1817 and 1834 cannot be directly compared without more details than are available, but some rough conclusions can be drawn. The traffic in 1834 is as one-way as before, for the percentage passing west is much the same. The percentage passing to Lechlade and the Thames is also much the same. Without being able to extract the figures for Lechlade only one cannot say how much went down the Thames, but it is clear that the opening of the North Wilts Canal had by no means ended the Thames traffic —probably mainly in coal — and the continuing complaints of the condition of the river support this view. Cirencester traffic is now a smaller proportion of the whole. As for the Wilts & Berks traffic, little off that canal moves west of Siddington; on the other hand, 244 boats (other than fly-boats) bound for it passed the summit.

If, however, we turn to the finances of the canal, we find that competition from the Wilts & Berks and probably from road carriage has kept the increase in takings far below the proportionate increase in boats passing. The following is the comparison, averaged over a seven-year period centred on the receipts for 1817 and 1834 in order to iron out single-year peculiarities; the toll figures follow.

		£
Period 1814–20		
	Distributable surplus per annum	2,212
	Total tonnage receipts per annum	4,477
Period 1831–37		
	Distributable surplus per annum	4,049
	Total tonnage receipts per annum	6,375

		Average dividends			
Years	Average tolls	(*new red*)		(*old black*)	
	£	s	d	s	d
1803–05	5,291				
1806–08	4,379				
1809–11	6,192	30	0 (£1.50)	30	0* (£1.50)
1812–14	4,417	28	2 (£1.41)	6	0 (30p)
1815–17	4,430	25	8 (£1.28½)	4	8 (23½p)
1818–20	4,518	30	0 (£1.50)	13	0 (65p)
1821–23	4,618	—		—	
1824–26	5,385	30	0 (£1.50)	21	0 (£1.05)
1827–29	5,442	30	0 (£1.50)	18	8 (93½p)
1830–32	5,776	30	0 (£1.50)	24	0 (£1.20)
1833–35	6,434	30	0 (£1.50)	30	0 (£1.50)
1836–38	6,465	34	6 (£1.72½)	34	6 (£1.72½)

* 1810 and 1811 only.

The committee met the Thames Commissioners and the City Navigation committee in 1827 about promoting trade between the Stroudwater and London. The Thames authorities agreed to tackle the private lock owners, to consider charging on actual tonnage and not on craft capacity, and to provide two flashes a week from Lechlade. One result was that the canal company sent a salesman round London architects and builders to promote the use of Painswick stone: it was an enterprising idea, but it failed. However, by 1829 the Thames down to Oxford had been dredged and the flash-locks were better worked, though the commissioners' locks needed repairs.

The fly-boats arose from a suggestion in 1828 that joint consultations should take place with the Stroudwater and the Gloucester & Berkeley companies upon the improvement of the route to London. In the following year it was decided that there should be a regular service between Gloucester and London, and this started in November. The boats were still running in 1835, and probably continued for some years after that.

In 1824 the Stroudwater Navigation had been threatened with railway competition from the proposed Stroud & Severn Rail Road (see p. 307), which however came to nothing. In 1835 a railway was proposed from Swindon to Cheltenham by way of Gloucester, and the Thames & Severn proprietors recorded that:

> A correspondence having taken place between Devereux Bowley Esqr. of Cheltenham and the Clerk of this Company on the subject of a projected Railway from Cheltenham by Stroud to Swindon the object of which was to suggest the purchase of this Canal by the proposed Company, Resolved that the Committee be empowered to enter immediately into a Negotiation for that purpose and ascertain what are the specific propositions of the said intended Company and report accordingly.[30]

The canal company had been too eager, for a few days later they tried a different approach:

> A communication having been received from Messrs. Laurence and Griffiths Solicitors to the Cheltenham and Great Western Railway Company . . . stating that the question of the purchase of the Thames and Severn Canal had never been brought before them, and it appearing highly desirable in order to prolong the time for negotiation that notices be given of the Intentions of this Company to convert the Canal into a Railway, in order either to enable the railway Company to take advantage of such Notices, or this Company to act upon them if upon mature Consideration of all the Circumstances of the Case it should ultimately be deemed expedient.[31]

A petition against the railway Bill was presented in March 1836, which stated firmly

> That the present means of Conveyance by the said Canal are sufficient for all agricultural, commercial and manufacturing purposes for the district through which it passes and that the amount of Tolls taken on the said Canal is so small as to shew the improbability of the Subscribers to the said Railway being ever remunerated for their outlay.

The petition went on to describe the engineering difficulties of the proposed tunnel, and remarked darkly that the 'plan of the said railway . . . is beset with these and many other engineering difficulties.'[32] The results of the petition and the threat to build a rival railway, for which plans were deposited, were meagre. The canal company spent £1,068 in opposing the Bill, and in exchange obtained the payment from the railway of £2,500 in cash and another £5,000 spread over 4½ years.

The Act for the Cheltenham & Great Western Union Railway was passed in 1836; after many troubles the line was opened to Kemble, together with the Cirencester branch, in May 1841. The canal had carried much railway construction material, and there were windfall profits. The ill wind blew good to some, for in 1840 it was

> Resolved that out of the Surplus in the hands of the Treasurer the sum of £122-10-0 be divided between Mr. Denyer, Mr. Jones and the two Clerks at Brimscombe in the Proportions of £50 to each of the two former and the sum of £11 5s to Mr Dicks and Mr Iles the two Clerks at Brimscombe.[33]

The present was repeated the following year.

In 1844 a barge weighing machine* was erected at Brimscombe Port. The company hopefully asked the Stroudwater to pay one-third of the cost, estimated at £1,100, but were disappointed.

The Cheltenham & Great Western Union was now bought by the Great Western, who cut a new Sapperton tunnel in less than two years and opened the line to Gloucester in May 1845. The Thames & Severn, who had jointly with the Stroudwater introduced in 1842 a number of drawbacks on various long-distance traffics, at once cut their tolls. There was now competition immediately between Swindon and Gloucester, and broadly over the whole London–Gloucester route. The effect can be judged from the figures of the number of boats, loaded and empty, passing in and out of the North Wilts branch from the main Wilts & Berks line at Swindon. They once more show a rise for the carriage of railway construction material, and then a fall as the competition takes effect.

1837	793	1843	545
1838	732	1844	445
1839	1,038	1845	616
1840	1,339	1846	373
1841	681	1847	389
1842	788		

Here again the carriage of Somerset coal into the North Wilts branch, probably mostly to Cricklade and Cirencester, was not

---

* There is a model in the Folk Museum at Gloucester. A similar machine, formerly on the Glamorganshire Canal at Cardiff, has been re-erected at the Waterways Museum at Stoke Bruerne.

affected, though the quantity was small; 1,739 tons in 1837 and 1,798 in 1847.

This Great Western competition from 1845 along almost its whole line was accompanied from 1851 by the ability of the South Wales Railway to divert supplies of Forest coal. Toll revenue fell heavily from some £11,000 in 1841 to £2,874 in 1855, in which year the Thames above Oxford became almost unnavigable due to the bad financial state of the Thames Commissioners. In 1865 the company proposed to turn itself into a railway, having the great asset of the Sapperton tunnel, and early in the following year their representatives had an interview with Daniel Gooch, the chairman of the Great Western, who asked what annual rental the company would want, on the one hand for the canal as it was, and on the other for any railway they might build. Their answer was £7,500 in the former case, and £27,500 in the latter. The Great Western did not follow up the inquiry, and the canal company went ahead with their Bill, which was thrown out in July 1866. In that year the Thames Conservancy took over the river above Staines from the old commissioners. The river navigation was then open to Inglesham except for the section between New-bridge and Radcot, 'navigable with some difficulty and by means of Flashes'.[34] They announced early in 1868 that they proposed to restore this section, and also that all old lock tolls above Oxford would be abolished, reducing the toll to 6d (2½p) per ton for that distance.

Here are toll and dividend figures:

Years	Average tolls				Average dividends			
				New			Old	
	£	s	d		s	d		
1839–41	8,368	53	6	(£2.67½)	53	6	(£2.67½)	
1842–44	6,798	36	10	(£1.84)	36	10	(£1.84)	
1845–47	6,232	33	0	(£1.65)	30	2	(£1.51)	
1848–50	5,443	30	0	(£1.50)	22	0	(£1.10)	
1851–53	4,521	30	0	(£1.50)	9	6	(47½p)	
1854–56	2,869	16	2	(81p)	—			
1857–59	2,817	18	0	(90p)	—			
1860–62	2,955	20	8	(£1.03½)	—			
1863–65	2,220	12	0	(60p)	—			

In 1874 the company received a memorial from traders and barge owners complaining of the canal's condition, which was supported later by the Stroudwater company itself. J. H. Taunton, the Thames & Severn's manager, wrote back asking where 'the works on the Thames and Severn Navigation are at present in a very defective condition as alleged by you.'[35] The Stroudwater accepted the challenge, employing Edward Leader Williams, engineer of the Severn Commission, to survey the T & S. He reported late in 1875, confirming that the canal was in poor shape. Still Taunton denied this, saying it was 'in an effective state of repair',[36] and that the company's own boats were using it regularly and uninterruptedly. A meeting between the companies was then arranged, but ended in disagreement, Taunton making no concessions, but asking for toll reductions that the Stroudwater thought uneconomic.

Taunton, an energetic man, tired of putting up a bold front to outsiders while trying to stir up his own committee, had been the probable cause of a new committee being formed early in 1875. Two of these new brooms are important to us, Richard Potter, timber merchant at Gloucester and former chairman of the Great Western Railway, and John Dorington, active in local and central government. The new committee started a carrying business, first with horse-drawn and then with steam craft, and got a tug working on the upper Thames. It soon proved unprofitable, just because their own boats could not use the canal regularly and uninterruptedly. It was in too bad a state, not only over the summit, but in the Stroud valley also. Beyond it, the Thames was also in bad condition, the Conservancy being unwilling to do much without knowing what the canal company were prepared to undertake.

Potter now sought to obtain a controlling interest by buying shares, did so, and proposed to form a new company to take over the canal. But a Bill for this purpose raised suspicions that his real motive was to turn the canal into a railway, and it was therefore opposed vigorously for different reasons by the Great Western Railway and the Sharpness New Docks Company, and dropped. A Bill was substituted to enable the old company to borrow up to £30,000.

If not earlier, then after spending some more money on repairs, Potter decided that the concern could not be made a success. He bought more shares, and at the beginning of 1882 prepared a Bill to close the whole canal, and build a 14¾-mile railway from Stroud to Siddington by way of Sapperton tunnel. At Stroud it would connect with the Midland's authorized Stroud branch, now to terminate on the T & S's Stroud wharf,* from the Stonehouse & Nailsworth line, which had access to Forest coal and south Wales traffic by way of the new Severn Bridge to Sharpness. At Siddington it would join the Swindon & Cheltenham Extension through

* This was later built, and opened on 1 July 1886.

Cirencester, which would connect at Swindon with the Swindon, Marlborough & Andover,* giving access to Southampton. The Midland, who would probably have worked the line, were active supporters behind the scenes.

A deputation of navigation companies went to Joseph Chamberlain, President of the Board of Trade, in February. They protested at the conversion proposal, and threw out the suggestion that they might be prepared jointly to take responsibility for keeping the canal open. Chamberlain seized on this point, and wrote asking if they meant it. At a meeting on the 27th of what became known as the Allied Navigations,† they agreed that they would be prepared to do so, managing it jointly, sharing its deficit of about £550 pa according to their respective traffic from it, maintaining it to a standard approved by the Board of Trade, paying interest on the debentures, 80 per cent of any surplus to the Thames & Severn's shareholders, and the balance to a reserve fund.

The conversion Bill was lost because of this intervention, and in November the Allied Navigations were considering a Bill to enable them to manage the T & S. But this was going too fast for the Severn Commission and the Staffs & Worcs. The idea of a Bill was dropped, and instead negotiations were opened in 1883 with the T & S company, only to be turned down flat, Holland, the chairman, saying the 1882 basis was

> objectionable, and that he declined to enter upon any discussion or in its present form place the same before his Committee or call a Meeting of Shareholders.[37]

This was not surprising, for by this time, unknown to the Allied Navigations, Potter had offered his shares to the Great Western Railway. They, afraid that the Midland might try again to get a competing line built, offered to buy his and anyone else's shares at £7 10s (£7.50) cash. Potter had bought his for much less. He made a profit of some £10,000 and left the scene; both the Allied Navigations and the president had been outmanœuvred, and the Thames & Severn company became a subsidiary of the Great Western Railway.

In June 1885, as a result of complaints by traders 'of the bad state of the Thames & Severn Canal above Chalford',[38] Snape of the Stroudwater was ordered to inspect it. He did so, and sent his report to the Sharpness New Docks Company, who proposed

---

* The two were amalgamated in 1884 as the Midland & South Western Junction Railway.

† They then consisted of the Sharpness, Stroudwater, Staffs & Worcs, Wilts & Berks, and Birmingham Canal Navigations companies, and the Severn Commission. Later the B.C.N. dropped out. The Thames Conservancy did not join.

x

another interview with the president. After a year of talking about 'the conduct of the Thames and Severn Canal persistently imped-ing by inattention the Navigation of their Canal,'[39] and after con-sulting counsel, they saw the president, Lord Stanley, at the end of 1886. He had the canal inspected, and was told that although it was in poor state above Brimscombe, deliberate neglect was not provable. As, however, the Great Western were unlikely to spend the necessary money on reinstatement, the inspector suggested that the Allied Navigations should negotiate with the railway company.

In 1888 the Stroudwater again inspected the T & S. Given its condition and that of the upper Thames, they did not think it worth much 'in view of the uncertainty of the outlay necessary for repairs, and of the traffic obtainable,'[40] but on their own offered the GWR £3,000. The railway stood out for more, and in the meantime sold off canal property which the Stroudwater hoped would finance the repairs they would have to make.

Then followed a lull until the end of 1893, when the T & S gave two days' warning of the closure of the canal between Chalford and the Thames until further notice. A hurriedly organized depu-tation, which now included not only the Allied Navigations but business men, local landowners and representatives of the Ciren-cester Local Board, saw the president, A. J. Mundella, in January 1894. He was most sympathetic, remarking 'there is no doubt, this is a bad case', and welcoming the news that the navigations would again consider taking over the canal.

This time they wanted it for nothing, and, having prevented the Great Western from getting higher tolls inserted in the revised schedules then being issued under the Railway & Canal Traffic Act,[41] the railway company gave way, on condition that the Thames & Severn would not be converted to a railway. An Act of 1895 thereupon authorized the Sharpness New Docks & Glou-cester & Birmingham, the Stroudwater, and the Staffs & Worcs Canal Companies, the Severn Commission, the county councils of Gloucestershire, Wiltshire and Berkshire, and the Urban District Councils of Stroud and Cirencester, to form a Trust to manage the canal, with power to raise £15,000. Under a representative com-mittee, management was by the Stroudwater's officers, and soon from that company's Wallbridge office.

Most of this was spent, while the Thames Conservancy ex-pended another £20,000 on new locks and weirs and in dredging the upper Thames; but it was not enough. The canal, reopened in March 1899, had to be closed again because of short water on the summit level, and now the Gloucestershire County Council agreed to take it over under powers contained in the Railway & Canal Traffic Act, 1888. It was Sir John Dorington, Potter's former partner and now county chairman, who at the end of 1899 circulated a paper saying that the canal was

> a valuable waterway connecting the Thames and the Severn, Gloucester and London, besides affording internal facilities for transport within the County,

that as a highway authority the council would find it useful for carrying road stone, that the recent improvement of the upper Thames had greatly changed the situation, that the liability of the council under the 1895 Act to pay £225 pa for another 27 years would be extinguished if the canal covered its costs, and that £3,000 more might complete the restoration.[42]

The Thames & Severn was transferred to the Gloucestershire

DISTANCES

Inglesham													
Kempsford	3¼	Kempsford											
Marston	5¼	2	Marston										
Cricklade	7¾	4	2	Cricklade									
Latton	8⅞	5⅝	3⅝	1⅛	Latton, Junction with North Wilts Canal								
South Cerney	12	8¾	6¾	4¼	3	South Cerney							
Cirencester	14⅞	11⅝	9⅝	7⅛	6⅜	2½	Cirencester						
Siddington	13½	10¼	8¼	5¾	5	1⅞	1⅜	Siddington, Branch to Cirencester					
Thames Head	17⅜	15⅛	12⅛	9⅝	8⅞	5⅜	5¼	3⅞	Thames Head				
Daneway Bridge	21⅝	18½	16⅜	13⅞	13⅛	9⅝	9	8⅛	4¼	Daneway Bridge			
Chalford	24¾	21⅜	19½	17	16¼	12¾	12⅝	11¼	7⅜	3⅛	Chalford		
Brimscombe Port	26¼	23	21	18	17¾	14¼	14⅛	12¾	8⅞	4⅝	1	Brimscombe Port	
Wallbridge	28¾	25	23	21	20¼	16¾	16⅝	15¼	11⅜	7⅛	4	2	Wallbridge

Forty-four Locks; width, 12 feet 6 inches.

Sapperton Tunnel, near Daneway, 2¼ miles long.

Tolls for Pleasure Boats and Steam Launches.

	£	s.	d.
Inglesham to Cricklade	0	10	0
,, to Daneway Basin, Sapperton, or any other place on Summit Level	1	0	0
,, to Wallbridge	1	10	0

Speed not to exceed four miles per hour.

The above tolls are for a voyage in one direction only. Return fare is a fare and a half if a return is made within seven days. Canoes and skiffs lifted at all the locks by the crews will be charged half the above rate.

43. Distances and pleasure-cruising tolls on the Thames & Severn Canal, 1908

County Council on 2 July 1901. The council then repaid the Trust's debts, but continued to collect the annual subscriptions of its surviving members.* Management was with the Stroudwater's officers.

By 1922 even the Wallbridge–Brimscombe section was difficult to navigate, though in reply to a Stroudwater protest, the council asserted that 'there is no difficulty in accommodating the Barges which generally use the Canal.'[43] As 1925 approached, the end of the 30 years from the 1895 Act during which money had been guaranteed by contributors, the council considered abandonment. The Stroudwater was now not financially able to consider a lease, even if it had wanted to, but after long negotiations between interested bodies, the Chalford–Inglesham portion was abandoned in 1927, while the Stroudwater organized a series of whip-rounds of local authorities, traders and navigation companies to keep the rest open. Then they, too, gave up, and this section also was abandoned in 1933, some of the council's stores of material being passed to the Stroudwater.

* The Wilts & Berks had dropped out.

CHAPTER XV

The Gloucester & Berkeley Canal

THE first idea of what was to become the Gloucester & Berkeley Canal was put forward about December 1783, when Thomas Baylis told the Stroudwater's shareholders that an application was to be made for an Act to build a canal from 'the Severn near Glocester to join the Stroudwater Canal'.[1] The scheme was linked with the Thames & Severn Canal, which had been authorized in 1783, in that it was an effort to improve the water line for traffic coming down the Severn and seeking to reach the Stroudwater on its way to the Thames.

The Stroudwater Company feared loss of tolls between Framilode and the point of junction near Whitminster, and decided to spend up to £1,000 in opposing it 'till they are fully satisfied of the necessity of such a scheme, and of the Stroudwater Canal being inadequate to the Business.' Robert Whitworth surveyed for the new line about April 1784, in November a promotion meeting was held, and in December Edward Elton, chairman of what was now called the Gloucester Canal committee, wrote to the Stroudwater Company to propose a toll agreement, but was told that it would injure the latter without compensating benefit, and that they could not agree, at any rate until the Thames & Severn had been finished. Meanwhile they put pressure on Gloucester corporation and local landowners to oppose the scheme. However, subscriptions were opened in January 1785, but then Sir George Paul (a member of the Stroudwater's board), decided that the new county gaol should be built on the site the committee had chosen for their basin at Gloucester. This seems to have killed the project.[2]

The Gloucester & Berkeley itself was quietly promoted by Gloucester and Upton-on-Severn interests during the summer of 1792, perhaps to exclude speculators, for the Parliamentary notice is its first mention in the *Gloucester Journal*. Nevertheless, a sub-

scribers' meeting in November, chaired by the Mayor, was told
that 'there was a redundancy of Subscriptions,' and it was agreed,
to prevent undesirable dealings, that no share should be trans-
ferable until 15 per cent had been paid up.[3] The arguments for the
idea were that the canal would shorten the navigation between
Gloucester and Berkeley from 35 to 16 miles; that ships of 500
tons could safely navigate to Berkeley, but no higher; and that the
port of Gloucester was already expanding rapidly. 'Hitherto', said
a newspaper account in the year the canal opened, 'access to the
port of Gloucester has only been practicable for a few days on
each spring-tide, and by vessels of small burthen, built purposely
for encountering the shallows and difficulties which beset the
upper part of the river Severn.'[4]

Though previous surveys had been made by Josiah Clowes
(who proposed a termination just south of Sharpness Point) and
Richard Hall, the Bill was so hurried through that Robert Mylne,
upon whose evidence before the Parliamentary committees the
promoters principally relied, was doing his first survey in January
1793, and preparing his estimates just before the Bill was taken.
Agreement on tolls and on possible water losses was reached with
the Stroudwater, there was little opposition, and the Act[5] was
passed in March, authorizing a capital of £140,000, and £60,000
more if necessary. It was the biggest canal so far planned in Britain.

The committee tried to get both Jessop and Whitworth to make
second surveys, but Jessop did not answer and Whitworth was
too busy; so Mylne was asked to re-survey, and was named 'Chief
and Principal Engineer'. He was then a man of 60, a good architect
and bridge-builder, engineer to the New River Company, and
often consulted on river and canal problems, especially on the
water supply side. He had, however, little actual construction
experience, and thought himself superior to 'common Canal Cutters', as he later called Jessop, the greatest of all the canal engineers.[6] It was the time of the mania, and while the committee were
still considering whether Mr Carne's cutting machine could be
used, and whether a steam engine should be ordered from Boulton
& Watt to pump water from the excavations, William Gibbons
was sent from Bristol corporation to ask whether the committee
would be interested in supporting the projected Bristol & Severn
barge canal to Gloucester and beyond. Talks and correspondence
went on for some time between the Gloucester & Berkeley Company and the committee and engineer of this project, but without
result.

Meanwhile Mylne had made his proposal for a canal 70 ft broad

at top, 18 ft deep, and 17¾ miles long, cutting across the Stroudwater Navigation at Saul, to admit ships of 300 tons, and with a
branch to Berkeley town, at a cost of £121,330. It was an underestimate only rivalled by one or two of Rennie's. He proposed to
cut from Gloucester to Saul first, and also to build a basin at
Gloucester and a lock to connect it with the river. The committee
agreed to his plan and to pay him £350 pa and travelling expenses,
with Dennis Edson as resident at £210. In September 1793 Mylne
was setting out the line, and in March 1794 prepared drawings for
an excavating machine. Instead, the committee tried one invented
by C. B. Trye, a director, and later another of Edward Haskew's,
but they did not prove worth while. Work started at Gloucester
basin and that end of the canal in October 1794. Soon afterwards
Robert Fulton asked for a contract to cut part of the canal and use
the digging machine he had invented, but was not employed,
though two contractors had died during the winter.

The next year of 1795 passed with putting out tenders for cutting to Whitminster near the Stroudwater, the dismissal of Edson,
and the engagement of James Dadford on Mylne's recommendation. Dadford, then aged 26, had only built a tramroad in Wales[7]
and done some carrying on the Glamorganshire Canal, though his
relations, the two Thomas Dadfords, were good canal engineers.
Already the proprietors were becoming nervous about the prospects of their canal, and in August Mylne himself was brought
down. Nervousness increased in 1796, as changes in the line to
save money were discussed. The company's solicitors were told to
proceed against defaulting shareholders, and Whitworth and
Jessop were brought in to report to a meeting that Mylne was
asked to attend.

In 1797, after the committee had in February announced itself
ready to receive proposals for cutting a further six miles of the
canal, the storm broke. It was started off by C. B. Trye of the
unsuccessful machine, who wrote to the committee to criticize
severely the small amount of time that Mylne gave to the canal,
and propose that henceforth he should be paid by the day, and
ended:

I postponed recommending this measure, because I firmly
expected that the influence of incontrovertible facts would have
produced his retirement or dismissal from the Company's service, and that the new mode of payment, might most con-
veniently begin with his successor. A small majority of Shares
resisting that influence, and great dissatisfaction consequently
prevailing among the Proprietors, I judged it right for some

time to suspend the execution of my purpose, in hopes of a time when a decision might be made with calmness and without personality.[8]

A copy of the letter was sent to Mylne for his observations. He came down in September and again in October, agreed to take four guineas a day and travelling expenses, and reported that it would cost more to cut the canal from Gloucester to the Stroudwater junction than remained uncalled from the share capital. In October Dadford and Mylne seem to have quarrelled. Mylne's diary reads

Oct 2. Mayor's feast—Dadford broke out. Home.

Oct 3. Home. Apology and pardon by Dadford.[9]

Soon afterwards Mylne ceased to be engineer, and forfeited the shares he had in the canal. Work went on under Dadford's supervision till mid-1799, when £112,000 had been spent and the canal had reached Hardwicke, rather more than half-way to the Stroudwater junction, and five and a half miles from Gloucester. Some traffic seems to have begun in this year.

Thenceforward all was discussion. Dadford was ordered to consider whether it was possible to bring the canal out to the Severn at Hock Crib, near Frampton on Severn, thus shortening its proposed length; an estimate was worked out for a narrow canal to join what had been done to the Stroudwater, completion being now referred to as 'keeping the grand Scheme in view'; and there were many efforts to raise money by mortgage, but unlike other canals in difficulties, one so little built as this had nothing to offer as security. In 1800 Dadford was given notice, and there was quiet.

In 1804 discussion began again, with a proposal to raise £110,000 by a lottery, and to end the canal at Hock Crib, some four miles further on. After six months' argument the shareholders agreed, and a Bill was drawn up. Unfortunately Pitt personally turned down the lottery idea, but on a proposal of Ralph Walker, the engineer, an Act was passed to extend the main line and then build a branch to Hock Crib. Authority was given to raise £80,000 in shares to do this, all of which had to be subscribed before work could begin, and in July subscriptions were sought for £60,000. By September 1810, only £50,000 had been promised. Meanwhile two horse railway lines had been proposed. In 1806 the Gloucester & Cheltenham inquired if its track could end at the canal basin at Gloucester, to which the company agreed; it was authorized in 1809 and opened in 1811. Meanwhile, in September 1810, the first coal arrived in Gloucester that had been carried from Cinderford on the Bullo Pill Railway and shipped from Bullo Pill nearly opposite Hock Crib. The line was reported to be of advantage to the canal.

In 1810 Hodgkinson and Jessop were asked to report on the canal and the proposed line to Hock Crib, and in 1811 Rennie also. Rennie put in a higher estimate—£128,656—to finish to Hock Crib than Walker, Hodgkinson or Jessop, and said that over £20,000 in addition must be spent on the existing portion. He finished his report with a slap at Mylne and Dadford:

> I have in my estimate gone on the supposition that all the new works are to be executed in a much more perfect and substantial manner that those already done on this Canal.[10]

There was now much enthusiasm. On the one hand a letter asking for subscriptions was drafted to the Dukes of Norfolk and Gloucester, Lords Somers, Sherborne and Beauchamp, and the Bishops of Gloucester and Bath & Wells, and on the other an effort was made to collect toll on the goods entering and leaving the basin by way of the Cheltenham Railway. This last was exuberance, for no legal claim existed, and after a few days a claim for rent of land was substituted, which was settled at £25 a year. The river-lock and basin were now opened to those who wished to use them to tranship goods from trows to up-river craft.

In 1813 John Upton had been appointed clerk. There was no engineer, and he seems to have assumed this office also, for he made the basin more usable, and then proceeded to survey the line, and write a pamphlet[11] which attacked the Hock Crib idea, and proposed a line to Sharpness Cove. His remarks annoyed the Hock Crib supporters on the committee, and at one point Mr Benjamin Hipwood, who had been forty-eight years in trows, was called in to demonstrate Upton's foolishness. However, the committee decided to get Benjamin Bevan the engineer to report, and he recommended Sharpness Point in preference both to Hock Crib and the original end at Berkeley Pill. The shareholders agreed, and resolved to complete to the Stroudwater without delay, and then continue 'with all reasonable and possible Dispatch'[12] to Sharpness.

Fortunately, when inability to raise money was again proving the worst obstacle, the Poor Employment Act was passed in 1817. This set up the Exchequer Bill Loan Commissioners, with power to lend money for public works which would employ unskilled labour to relieve unemployment. An application was at once made, and the commissioners agreed to lend half the cost of completing the canal to the junction with the Stroudwater. It was therefore

decided to raise money at once to take advantage of the commissioners' offer, and to promote a Bill to end the canal at Sharpness Point. Upton was sent to call personally upon proprietors
who lived in Worcestershire, Shropshire, and Warwickshire, but
returned to report no luck. When the Act was passed, however,
the commissioners increased their offer; money was raised by
shares; on 15 July 1818 the Duke of Gloucester laid the foundation
stone at Sharpness, and cutting was resumed early in the following
year, it being also decided to build a navigable water feeder to
Cambridge.

Upton now reverted to clerk, as a result apparently of selling
materials for building to himself as engineer, and he resigned
after a stiff letter from the commissioners and Telford their adviser.
John Woodhouse was then appointed engineer at 500 guineas a
year and expenses. Men were engaged, and by October 1819,
971 men were at work.

On Monday 29 February 1820 the junction was made with the
Stroudwater at Saul:

Upwards of twenty vessels passed the new line on Tuesday, and
ten vessels laden with coal, &c, entered the basin at Gloucester
the following day.[13]

At the same time the canal was opened beyond Saul to Cambridge
at the end of the Cam feeder, where a wharf was opened by Woodhouse's son and a partner to supply Dursley and other places near
with Staffordshire, Forest and south Wales coal and with roadstone and bricks.[14] The company now had another source of
income than Gloucester basin and the short length of canal from
it. At Saul two pairs of stop gates, each facing one way, were
installed on the ship canal on each side of the junction, with the
object of maintaining a constant level of water in the Stroudwater's pound. The latter canal only had ordinary stop gates.

The next trouble to come before the committee was a strong
letter from Telford saying that Woodhouse's son had been supplying stone of the wrong kinds to the works at Sharpness, and going
on:

I am of opinion that it is *absolutely necessary* to employ as Resident
Engineer a person wholly unconnected with Contractors for
Material or Labour in any shape.[15]

Woodhouse was therefore dismissed, and was succeeded by
Thomas Fletcher. Meanwhile the company had once again run out
of money, and at the end of the year the works came to a stop
after £268,000 had been spent, the company having to sell houses
and land to pay the interest and repayment of loan due to the

commissioners, who had announced that if payment were not made they would take over the canal. After eighteen months of threats by the commissioners, ending in their controlling the company's affairs jointly with the committee, and frantic efforts to raise money, the commissioners agreed to lend another £60,000, and rather more than this was raised by shares. Work began again early in June 1823, and by 1826 the commissioners were sufficiently optimistic to advance another £35,000, making a total of £160,000, and to authorize the building of two warehouses at Gloucester.

In 1826 the canal was nearly finished, and there was much practical activity, such as making joint arrangements with the Severn & Wye Railway & Canal Company for pilots to bring vessels from the Avon to Sharpness and Lydney. William Clegram was appointed harbour master, engineer, and general superintendent at £370 pa and a house, Fletcher to stay as resident engineer till the canal was opened. Clegram's son, W. B. Clegram, who was to stay some fifty years with the company, became clerk in 1829.

The year 1827 came, and after thirty-five years of waiting, the opening day drew near. A band was hired for ten guineas, two guineas (£2.10) were paid to the bellringers, and £2 3s (£2.15) for an awning for the committee's boat, though the commissioners would not allow a dinner. Then on 26 April,

at high water, about half past eight o'clock, the ship Anne, of three hundred tons, Philips, master, belonging to Mr. Irvine, Bristol, was hauled into the entrance lock, amidst the shouts and congratulations of the spectators, and the firing of guns. She was then admitted into the canal, when she hoisted all her colours, and manned her tops. The towing-horses were put to, and without any obstruction, the Anne, with the Meredith, another vessel, kept on their course to Glocester. Every yard in advance for the last few miles brought an increase to the number of spectators, till, on approaching the city, the crowd which lined the banks was almost too dense to move. The grand point of attraction was at the basin, which was surrounded by an immense mass of people of all classes; and the warehouses of the company, and every other spot which could afford a view of the scene, were filled with anxious spectators. The vessels entered the basin, about half past three o'clock, amid the firing of guns.[16]

The canal was open, but it was heavily mortgaged to the commissioners, who controlled its revenues. Ships at first were slow in coming, and a cut of one-third had to be made in tolls to attract trade. In 1828 the company had to borrow a further £12,000 from two banks on promissory notes to pay outstanding debts.

This canal, 16¼ miles long,* 86 ft 6 in wide and 18 ft deep, now taking craft of 600 tons, was the biggest in England. There were three locks at Sharpness, the ship lock of 163 ft × 38 ft which led into a basin from which a barge and a trow lock† gave on to the canal. At Gloucester there was a small barge basin as well as that intended for ships, and a lock out to the Severn. The waterway was crossed by fifteen double-leaved swing bridges, but none that were fixed, and therefore height was unrestricted. It had cost £444,000 by 1829, of which £160,000 had been lent by the commissioners; in addition, there were a few thousand pounds worth of debts and a large total of arrears of interest, both on the commissioners' and other loans.

Trade was slow to start, but it improved steadily as the years went by, for the new canal did away with much transhipment at Bristol, and with the Severn traders' former dependence on high tides in order to navigate the stretches below Gloucester. A few months after the opening, Pickfords advertised that they were using the 'Gloucester & Berkeley New Line of Canal', whether there were spring tides or not. In February 1828 the brig *Fortitude* sailed direct from Gloucester to London, the first ship to do so. In the same year timber from Newfoundland and Russia was being imported. Warehousing and wharfage facilities increased. It was reported that on one day in October 1829 10 large brigs, 4 schooners or galliots and 14 sloops were all moored in Gloucester basin.[17] Benefits spread up the Severn and to its connecting canals.

On 5 January 1830 the Worcester & Birmingham Company minuted that because of the ship canal 'the City of Gloucester is becoming a regular port, and is a steady and important depot for the shipment of Goods,' and remarked that the downriver coal and salt trades had improved. Receipts increased from £5,975 in 1828 to £9,777 in 1830 and £15,282 in 1832. It soon proved possible to pay the interest on all loans, and even to pay off some of the arrears, but repayment of the loans themselves and any dividend on the shares was still a long way off. In 1830, and again in subsequent years, the commissioners threatened to sell the canal unless arrangements were quickly made to repay their principal, but in fact, hard though the committee tried to raise the money, it was nearly twenty years before the government debt was paid off, partly by borrowing some £60,000 from the Pelican Life

* Shortened by ending at Sharpness instead of Berkeley Pill.
† These were 115 ft and 81 ft long.

Assurance Company at 4½ per cent, £2,000 to be repaid each year,
and partly by raising new share capital. One result of this freedom
was to enable the company to spend money on improvements;
under the commissioners' control all revenue except that for current expenses had had to be given to the repayment of debt. By
1852 the revenue had reached £29,436, and a small dividend was
being paid on the shares. Tonnage had increased from 321,854 in
1832 to 534,520 in 1852.

Meanwhile many happenings had been reflected in the broad
waters of the canal. At first the waters themselves had been in
short supply, being mainly derived from the river Cam by way of
the Cambridge branch, and long discussions went on with the
Stroudwater company and the millowners; some mills were
bought, an Act of 1834 reversed the old prohibition in the Act of
1793 against taking water from the Frome (Stroudwater river), so
enabling supplies to be obtained at Saul, and a steam engine was
built at Gloucester to pump water from the Severn.*

Market passenger and goods boats had been run from the time
the canal opened, and after a few years several were working,
owned by rival firms. It was therefore necessary that regulations
should be made to prevent them from racing or obstructing one
another. Such boats were still running ten years later; and in 1837
Mr Jones of Arlingham applied to run a passenger boat with
paddle wheels worked by men. The application was not granted.

In 1832 an agreement was made with the trackers or owners of
towing-horses that they should have the exclusive right of tracking
in exchange for keeping the towpath in repair and paying £20 pa.
This agreement lasted till 1837, when a single tracking contractor
took over, with whom the number of horses to be used for
different sizes of vessel, and the charges to be made, were agreed.
A steam boat was tried on the canal in 1833, and in 1836 it was
proposed to form a local company to tow by steam tug, but
Clegram advised against it on grounds of damage.

In 1836 a meeting took place to discuss the improvements of
the navigation of the Severn, a matter of much interest to the
company, since a good part of its trade came from craft which
used the canal from Sharpness not only to Gloucester, but as part
of a longer voyage to Worcester or Stourport, and more from
bigger vessels from which goods were transhipped at Gloucester
to move higher up the river. The Severn at that time had no locks,
nor any controlling authority, and its state was an expense and a
hindrance to waterborne traffic, and would make more difficult

---

* Electric pumps there still supply much of the canal's water.

the competition between canals and the new railways. From this year to 1842 plans were made and proposals canvassed.

The Gloucester & Berkeley opposed any change, fearing that the trade of Gloucester docks might be transferred to Worcester and that a toll on the river might discourage waterborne traffic, arguing also that a hitherto free navigation should not be controlled by a private company. They were eventually overborne, but had their way over the last point, for the Severn Commission, set up in 1842 to control the river between Stourport and Gloucester, was a public body representative of town and navigation interests. Being also frightened of silting, they made sure that the Act did not authorize a lock lower than Diglis, but only dredging to give a 6 ft depth.[18]

The year after the commission was set up, the Birmingham & Gloucester Railway were given permission by the company to lay their rails to the Gloucester docks, and in 1844 an agreement was made with the Great Western Railway who proposed to buy and enlarge the Gloucester & Cheltenham tramroad.[19] Unlike other canals, the ship canal welcomed railway connection in order to increase the hinterland it served, while it was too firmly placed to fear direct competition.

The South Wales Railway Bill of 1845 proposed to bridge the Severn south of Framilode. Because this would obstruct the river navigation, still of course used to some extent, especially by local traffic, the railway proposed to build a ship canal from Hock Crib to Framilode to cut off the horseshoe bend. This presented navigational difficulties of its own, and the idea was soon dropped, as was the bridge after the Admiralty had refused their consent.

The total income of the canal for the year 25 March 1852–3 was £24,583, of which £21,116 was derived from tonnage. This revenue was sufficient to pay the interest and instalment of principal to the Pelican, to pay 5 per cent on the preference capital of £105,600, and a small dividend of 15s (75p) per share to the shareholders, who participated to this extent in the profits now that the commissioners had been paid off.

Developments took place as the years went by. More railways were connected to the quays with the special hope that coal exports might be stimulated to correct the imbalance of a trade that was 90 per cent inwards; a new graving dock was opened; a telegraph line was set up between Gloucester and Sharpness; steam tugs were introduced; improvements were made at Gloucester docks; and there was talk of great changes at Sharpness.[20]

The tonnage on the canal had remained stationary for many

years; in 1842 it had been 496,251, in 1867 484,802. It had been clear for some time that Sharpness needed rail connection, especially to a coalfield, so that coal for bunkering and as return cargo could be supplied to ships that had unloaded there, and freight transported elsewhere than up the canal. The obvious move was a bridge over the Severn to the Forest of Dean and South Wales, and in 1865 Clegram, the company's engineer, commissioned a survey that found it practicable.

However, even without rail connection the basin needed to be bigger, though so far the money and the moment had been lacking. However, in 1869 Clegram was told to survey for such an enlargement. He reported:

> In the 36 days from the 18th. September to the 24th. October, 1868, so great was the crowding of vessels in the tidal basin at Sharpness, either too large to be passed through the lock into the Canal, or requiring to be lightened before this could be accomplished, that 136 vessels bound to Gloucester, sustained an aggregate detention in Kingroad of 699 days, & single vessels from 12 to 23 days each, waiting their turn to be admitted. The detention also of the outward bound vessels was nearly as great.

Clegram went on to point out that the canal had been built for sailing vessels, that size had increased with steam, and that steamer docks existed at Swansea, Cardiff, Newport, and Avonmouth. Finally he said:

> Gloucester is almost entirely shut out from a steam traffic, except in very small vessels: and as steamers are becoming more and more used for the conveyance of grain to England, unless Gloucester is provided with the means of admitting them, a very serious and direct blow will be struck at . . . the foreign trade of the port.

He suggested a new entrance, tidal basin, and docks below Sharpness at a cost of £150,000.

In September 1869 the General Meeting agreed to the plan at a cost not exceeding £200,000, to be raised partly by preference shares and partly by loan. The gross receipts had risen much since 1852; they were £37,617 for the year 25 March 1869–70, of which £34,141 was derived from tonnage, and the prospects were good, especially as in the middle of 1871 the final payment was to be made to the Pelican, and the concern would then be free of the old debt.

Work began. Meanwhile, in 1872 an Act was passed authorizing the Severn Bridge Company, whose chairman, W. C. Lucy, was also chairman of the canal company, and which had W. B. Clegram on its board, to build a railway bridge to cross the river above the new docks, and join the Severn & Wye.[21] In the following year when the bridge company ran short of money the canal directors were empowered to subscribe up to £50,000 towards its cost. The new docks were opened on 18 November 1874. There was now an entrance three-quarters of a mile lower down the river, with a lock 320 ft × 57 ft, a tidal basin 540 ft × 300 ft, and a floating dock 2,000 ft long and with an average width of 320 ft. Having bought the Worcester & Birmingham Canal[22] in 1873, and built the new docks, the company in 1874 changed its name to the Sharpness New Docks & Gloucester & Birmingham Navigation Company.

Revenue rose, and for the year 25 March 1877–8 it was £62,052 for the main undertaking, with another £23,550 for the Worcester & Birmingham Canal. The capital expended on the main undertaking now stood at £867,592, the new dock having cost nearly £400,000, with investments of £140,893 in the Worcester & Birmingham Canal, £50,000 in the Severn Bridge Company, and £9,972 lent to the Severn Commissioners, a total of £1,068,457. In the same year, another £25,000 had to be lent to the bridge company before the line was opened in October 1879. A swinging-span carried it over the canal to sidings alongside the wharves.

The outlook was not, however, now so good. Depression followed. There was intense competition with Avonmouth, and the bridge company, having amalgamated with the Severn & Wye Company in 1879, eventually sold its property to the Midland & Great Western Joint Railways in 1894 at a loss to the Sharpness Company of £53,573. There was talk of a ship canal to Birmingham, and of a still larger entrance at Sheperdine; there were reports for the first time of disputes between capital and labour at the port. A new dock and timber pond were built at Gloucester and the river lock there enlarged, while hydraulic machinery was installed at Sharpness to work the locks and capstans, the entrance was enlarged, and the dock deepened. Yet the century ended with the revenue for the year ending 25 March 1900 at £56,519 for the main undertaking and £13,035 for the Worcester & Birmingham, figures considerably less than those of 1878, though the tonnage carried on the ship canal had risen from 567,665 in 1870 and 687,490 in 1880 to 751,354 in 1900.

Prosperity then increased. Traffic passed the million ton mark in 1905, and a controlling interest was bought in the Severn & Canal Carrying Company in 1910. Receipts fell away during the first world war, rose after it, though not to the extent of the change in the value of money, kept steady for many years, and rose to record heights during the second world war. The following are representative figures; they include receipts from the steadily declining Worcester & Birmingham Canal.

Year ended 25 March	£
1914	80,761
1922	89,575
1939	98,712
1941	153,540

Then the canal came within the canals control scheme* till it was nationalized.

Throughout the twentieth century dividends had been erratic even on the preference shares, while the ordinary shares had received distributions only in very favourable years. The shareholders had done much for Gloucester, but less well for themselves.

In 1967, 135,744 tons were handled at Sharpness docks, where ships of up to 5,000 tons cargo capacity can be accommodated. The canal itself carried 547,686 tons. Small seagoing craft and those for Ireland of up to 750 tons capacity use the canal for merchandize, timber and container traffic, as do oil tanker barges. Timber wharfage at Gloucester has much increased in recent years.

Sharpness no longer has rail connection to the Forest: the Severn bridge was hit by two tankers in fog on 25 October 1960, and two spans were brought down. It was not repaired, but instead was dismantled in 1968.

* See *British Canals*, 4th ed., p. 265.

Y

AUTHOR'S NOTES & ACKNOWLEDGMENTS

I SHOULD like to thank the very many who have helped me: Mrs M. Course, Mr A. W. Picknell, Mr N. Pearce, Mr A. Greenfield and Mr Ian Dunkley for reading newspaper files; Messrs D. G. Kinnersley, F. G. B. Clayton and R. F. Hatton of the British Waterways Board; Mr A. M. Sowden of the British Railways Board, Southern Region; Mr A. G. Stirk and Mr Saint of the Kent River Authority; Mr K. P. Barrett of the Medway Lower Navigation Company; Mr H. S. Duck of the Dartford & Crayford Navigation Commissioners; Messrs Blake, Son & Williams Ltd and Marshall, Liddle & Downey of Croydon; Dr Edwin Course of Southampton University and Mr John Whyman of the University of Kent; Mr A. B. Fuller of Tasker's of Andover; Mr James Benson; Mr John Boyes; Mr Hugh Braun; Mr Lawrence Cameron; Mr K. R. Clew; Mr D. A. Cross; Mr J. H. Denton; Mr Donald Green; Mr Humphrey Household; Mr O. S. James; Mr D. G. King-Hele; Mr K. R. MacDonald; Mr N. W. Newcombe; Mr R. M. Penfold; Mr W. Vincent Rendel; Mr L. T. C. Rolt; Miss A. Roper; Mr P. A. L. Vine; Dr E. Welch and Mr R. A. Williams.

I should also like to thank the staffs of British Transport Historical Records, the House of Lords Record Office, the Public Record Office, the British Museum, the National Register of Archives, the Institution of Civil Engineers, the Goldsmiths' Library, the Port of London Authority, County Record offices and local libraries and museums for all their kindness and help.

My thanks are also due to the following for permission to reproduce photographs and other illustrations: Aerofilms Limited Plate on page 17 (above); Kent Archives Office, 17 (below), Fig 3; *Kent Messenger*, 18 (above); Sir Arthur Elton, Bt, 18 (below); Gravesend Public Library, 35 (above); British Museum, 35 (below); From the Collection of Hugh McKnight Photography, 36 (above), 69 (below), 88 (above), 88 (below), 121 (above), 121 (below), 122 (above); P. A. L. Vine, 36 (below), 69 (above), 70 (above), 70 (below); Winchester City Corporation and Dr E. Course, 87 (above); Andover Public Library, 87 (below); Wiltshire Newspapers, Swindon and Mr K. R. Clew, 122 (below); Mr K. E. Langley, 139 (above); The Ordnance Survey, 139 (below); Swindon Public Library, 140 (below); Gloucestershire Records Office, 205 (above), 205 (below), Figs 35, 36, 39, 40; Stroud Museum and Mr Lionel Walrond, 206 (above); South Cerney Trust, 206 (below); A. G. Simmonds, 223 (above), 223 (below); Walwins Limited, Gloucester, 224 (above), 224 (below); Woolwich Public Library, Fig 4; Corporation of London Record Office, Fig 11; British Transport Historical Records, Figs 12, 25, 27, 28; Blake, Son & Williams Limited, Croydon, Fig 13; Tasker's of Andover Limited, Figs 16 and 17; Bristol Public Library, Fig 29; Martin D. P. Hammond, Fig 37.

The painting reproduced on page 18 (below) is by J. B. Pyne and entitled *The South Eastern Railway: Thames and Medway Canal*; that on page 69 (above) is by W. H. Mason; and that on page 87 (below) is signed S.H.

NOTES

Notes to Chapter I

1. Figures taken from the three *County Reports*.
2. General preamble to *County Reports on Turnpike Trusts*, 1852.
3. *General Report on Turnpike Trusts for England and Wales*, 1857.

Notes to Chapter II

1. 47 Geo III c. 117.
2. Information from Mr P. A. L. Vine.
3. 6 Geo IV c. 164.
4. 38 Vic. c. 68.
5. In Ernest Straker's *Wealden Iron*, 1931.
6. 30 Geo III c. 52.
7. 3 Geo III c. 76.
8. Upper Ouse Navigation Minute Book, 12 April 1792.
9. Ibid., 4 April 1793.
10. Ibid., 18 September 1810.
11. I am grateful for the help of Mr W. Vincent Rendel and the clerk to the Kent River Authority in writing this account.
12. E. Austen, *Brede, the Story of a Sussex Parish*, 1946.
13. Plan in the East Sussex C.R.O.
14. Alexander Sutherland, *Reports . . . of the proposed Canal through the Weald of Kent*, 1802 (Goldsmiths' Library).
15. The Rennies' MS *Reports* (Institution of Civil Engineers Library).
16. *Maidstone Journal*, 30 December 1834.
17. G. G. Carter, *The Forgotten Ports of England*, 1951.
18. J. Holland Rose, *Dumouriez and the Defence of England against Napoleon*, 1909, p. 293n.
19. This account is taken from the MS letter-book of the Commander-in-Chief's correspondence.
20. *Account of Sums expended in the formation of the Royal Military Canal*, 1807, B.P.P. IV.
21. 47 Geo III c. 70.
22. P.R.O. T83.
23. Alexander Sutherland, *Reports . . . of the proposed Canal through the Weald of Kent*, 1802 (Goldsmith's Library).
24. See plan in Kent C.R.O.
25. 52 Geo III c. 70.
26. *Maidstone Journal*, 22 July 1823.
27. 6 Hen VIII c. 17.
28. Hasted, *History of Kent*, 1797–9.
29. Dorothy Gardiner, *Historic Haven: the Story of Sandwich*, 1954.
30. Hasted, *History of Kent, op. cit.*
31. For this and much early information, *see* C. E. Woodruff, *A History of the Town and Port of Fordwich*, 1895.

32. C. W. Chalklin, *Seventeenth Century Kent: a Social and Economic History*, 1965, p. 167.
33. D. Defoe, *Tour*, I, 119.
34. *Derby Mercury*, 17 May 1776.
35. Kent C.R.O., Sa/AH3.
36. *The Observer*, 10 September 1797.
37. Kent C.R.O., U1231.
38. Printed report of first general assembly, 25 June 1811 (Kent C.R.O., U1231).
39. 51 Geo III c. 144.
40. Newspaper cuttings in Kent C.R.O., U1231.
41. *The Practicability & Advantages of Navigating the River Stour through Canterbury & Sandwich Haven*, 1823 (Woolwich P.L.).
42. *Prospectus of an intended Navigation from the City of Canterbury to the Town and Port of Sandwich*, 1824 (Woolwich P.L.).
43. *Reports of the late John Smeaton*, 1812, III, p. 76.
44. *Stour Navigation and Sandwich Harbour, Report of Mr T. Telford* (Woolwich P.L.).
45. 6 Geo IV c. 166.
46. *Kentish Gazette*, 8 July 1825.
47. Ibid., 30 September 1825.
48. *A Short Exposition of the present state of the Canterbury Navigation and Sandwich Harbour Company*, 1826 (Author's collection).
49. See R. B. Fellows, *History of the Canterbury and Whitstable Railway*, 1930. I am indebted to this book for my quotations from the *Kent Herald* and *Kentish Gazette*.
50. Deal Junction Canal Minute Book, Kent C.R.O., De/AUc 1.
51. 27 & 28 Vic c. 112.
52. See S. Bagshaw, *History, Gazetteer and Directory of the County of Kent*, 1847, II, 264, and evidence before the SC of the H of C on the South Eastern branch to Deal and extension of the South Eastern, Canterbury, Ramsgate & Margate Railway Bill, 1845.
53. Woodruff, *Fordwich*, op. cit, pp. 63–4.
54. Canterbury Navigation Act, 1825, s. 97.
55. See map accompanying Benjamin Bevan's report of 1824 to the Stour Commission of Sewers.
56. 3 Vic c. 55.
57. J. Dunkin, *The History and Antiquities of Dartford*, 1894. S. K. Keyes, *Dartford. Some Historical Notes*, 1933. Dartford public library has a collection of papers relating to the ship canal project.

Notes to Chapter III

1. For the early history of the Medway Navigation, see also W. T. Jackman, *The Development of Transportation in Modern England*, I, pp. 169–71; T. S. Willan, *River Navigation in England, 1600–1750*, and C. W. Chalklin, 'Navigation Schemes on the Upper Medway, 1600–1665' in *The Journal of Transport History*, November 1961.
2. 17 Car II c. 6.
3. 14 Geo II c. 26.
4. 32 Geo III c. 105.
5. 42 Geo III c. 94.
6. *Maidstone Journal*, 7 October 1823, 10, 17 February 1824.
7. 5 Geo IV c. 148.
8. Hasted, *History of Kent*, 1798, IV, p. 263.
9. Upper Medway Navigation Minute Book, 5 June 1807.
10. *Maidstone Journal*, 30 September 1828.
11. *Maidstone Journal*, 18 May 1830.
12. Printed proceedings of the House of Commons Committee on the Upper Medway Bill, 1 June 1836.

13. *Maidstone Journal*, 15 September 1829, signed 'A Friend to Improvement'.
14. *Maidstone Journal*, 3 April 1832.
15. *Maidstone Journal*, 6 January 1835.
16. *Brighton Guardian*, 12 March 1834.
17. Upper Medway Navigation Minute Book, 4 June 1841.
18. Ibid., 15 August 1840.
19. Ibid., 12 February 1847.
20. Ibid., 14 June 1844.
21. South Eastern Railway Minute Book, 3 April 1845.
22. Upper Medway Navigation Minute Book, 12 February 1847.
23. P.R.O., BT 21/60415.
24. P.R.O., BT 21/87433.
25. Upper Medway Conservancy Minute Book, 16 January 1916 (Kent C.R.O.).

Notes to Chapter IV

1. R. Dodd, *Report on the proposed Canal Navigation forming a Junction of the Rivers Thames and Medway*, 1799.
2. For Dodd, see the *Dictionary of National Biography*, and D. Swann, 'The Engineers of English Port Improvements 1660–1830: Part II', *Transport History*, Vol I, p. 267.
3. J.H.C., 3 February 1800.
4. 39 & 40 Geo III c. 23.
5. Rennie's MS *Reports* (Institution of Civil Engineers Library).
6. J. Phillips, *A General History of Inland Navigation*, 1803 ed., p. 435.
7. 44 Geo III c. 46.
8. *The Times*, 1 December 1809.
9. Kent C.R.O., U888 E2.
10. Committee report to Special General Assembly, 25 November 1808 (Kent C.R.O., U888 E2).
11. 50 Geo III c. 76.
12. House of Lords Committee, 11 May 1810.
13. 58 Geo III c. 18.
14. *Maidstone Journal*, 2 March 1819.
15. Ibid., 21 November 1820.
16. Ibid., 1 May 1821.
17. Information from Mr H. G. W. Household.
18. F. W. Simms, *The Public Works of Great Britain*, 1838.
19. *Maidstone Journal*, 3 December 1822.
20. *Berrow's Worcester Journal*, 6 February 1823.
21. Telford MSS (I.C.E. Library).
22. *Maidstone Journal*, 22 July 1823.
23. J.H.C., 19 February 1824.
24. 5 Geo IV c. 119.
25. Telford MSS (I.C.E. Library).
26. Most of this information is from a paper sent to the City Corporation by John Pinkerton, engaged on the works under Pritchard & Hoof, about 1826 (Corporation of London R.O., Yantlet Creek papers).
27. For instance, 'over £350,000' in *A New Picturesque Steam-Boat Companion*, 2nd ed. (1835).
28. *Maidstone Journal*, 31 May 1826, and Simms, *Public Works, op. cit.*
29. Ibid., 6 June 1826.
30. See the relevant minutes of the Court of Aldermen, the supporting papers, and the records of the law cases, in the Corporation of London Record Office. Also a pamphlet, *Considerations on the Proposed Cut from the Medway to the Thames through Colemouth and Yantlet Creeks, and its probable effects on the Navigation of the Medway*, 1827 (Maidstone P.L.), which also fails to mention the canal.

31. *Maidstone Journal*, 23 January 1827.
32. Ibid., 30 January 1827.
33. Ibid., 6 February 1827.
34. Ibid., 13 March 1827.
35. Ibid., 28 August 1837.
36. See Frank C. Bowen, 'Gravesend to the Sea', *Gravesend & Dartford Reporter*, 9 November 1935.
37. Essex C.R.O., D/DE L C4.
38. Pasley's Report to the Board of Trade, 9 August 1845.
39. *Maidstone Journal*, 26 August 1828.
40. Ibid., 12 May, 25 August 1829.
41. F. A. Mansfield, *History of Gravesend*, 1922.
42. *A New Picturesque Steam-Boat Companion to . . . Gravesend . . . with a Trip up the River Medway*, 2nd ed. (1835). Maidstone P.L.
43. *Maidstone Journal*, 30 August 1831.
44. George Palmer before the H. of C. committee on the Medway Navigation Bill, 1 June 1836.
45. *Maidstone Journal*, 30 August 1831.
46. Ibid., 1 March 1842.
47. BTHR, HRP 6/16.
48. The *Railway Times*, 10 February 1844, says that interest was then 19 years in arrears on some £128,000 of loan notes.
49. Berkshire C.R.O., D/EPb C 21.
50. Report of the Select Committee on Railway Acts Enactments, 1846, App. p. 326.
51. *Railway Times*, 22 January 1842. This carries a report of the meeting and the prospectus.
52. *Maidstone Journal*, 3 January 1843.
53. Berkshire C.R.O., D/EPb C 21.
54. *Railway Times*, 30 March 1844.
55. See Major-General Pasley's reports of 9, 16, 27 August and 21 September 1844, and 4 January 1845.
56. *Maidstone Journal*, 28 January 1845.
57. 8 & 9 Vic c. 168.
58. *Railway Times*, 20 June 1846.
59. South Eastern Railway Minute Book, 28 May 1844.
60. Ibid., 1 October 1844.
61. *Maidstone Journal*, 13 January 1846.
62. 9 & 10 Vic c. 339.
63. For this period, see the articles by Frank C. Bowen, 'Gravesend and the Sea', LII et seq., *Gravesend & Dartford Reporter*, 9 November 1935 et seq.

Notes to Chapter V

1. 16 & 17 Car II c. 6 P.A.
2. N. Barton, *The Lost Rivers of London*, 1962, p. 79.
3. D. Swann, 'The Engineers of English Port Improvements 1660–1830: Part II', *Transport History*, I, p. 260.
4. 41 Geo III c. 31.
5. Grand Surrey Canal Minute Book, 15 October 1810.
6. Ibid., 31 May 1805.
7. *The Times*, 16 March 1807.
8. Grand Surrey Canal Committee Minute Book, 11 February 1836.
9. P.R.O., M.T. 19/41/157.
10. Procs Inst C.E., 1849–50, Paper No. 827.
11. J. Phillips, *A General History of Inland Navigation*, 1803 ed., p. 595.
12. For further information on these railways, see Charles E. Lee, *Early Railways in Surrey*, 1944.

13. 41 Geo III c. 127.
14. Quoted in W. C. Berwick Sayers, *The Old Croydon Tramroad, Canal and Railway* (typescript) (Croydon P.L.).
15. See my *The Canals of the West Midlands*.
16. *Report of Mr. Rennie on the intended Canal from Croydon to Rotherhithe*, 1800.
17. Estimate accompanying the deposited plan (H of L Record Office).
18. Evidence before H of L committee, 23 March 1808.
19. *The Times*, 27 October 1809.
20. Anderson, *Chronicle covering the Parish of Croydon*, 1880, p. 186, quo. Charles E. Lee, *Early Railways in Surrey*, p. 16.
21. Grand Surrey Canal Minute Book, 20 April 1813.
22. P.R.O., C103/104. Mr J. H. Boyes kindly told me of these.
23. See *Second Report from the Select Committee on Railways*, 1839, though the statement may not be reliable.
24. London & Croydon Railway Minute Book, 18 November 1834.
25. Ibid., 16 July 1835.
26. Ibid., 8 May 1837.
27. *The Times*, 27 January 1837. See also the following issue.
28. F. Slous, *Stray Leaves from the Scrapbook of an Awkward Man*, 1843: dialogue entitled 'A Dialogue between the Croydon Railroad and the Croydon Canal' (Croydon P.L.).
29. William Page, *My Recollections of Croydon Sixty Years Since, commenced on 12th August 1880*: in *The Reader's Index*, 1926 (Croydon P.L.).
30. See plans and committee proceedings in House of Lords Record Office, and plans in Merton Public Library.

Notes to Chapter VI

1. For a fuller account of the waterways described in this chapter, see P. A. L. Vine's *London's Lost Route to the Sea*, 1965.
2. This account of the early navigations is based upon information in Dr T. S. Willan's *River Navigation in England, 1600–1750*, 1936, and P. A. L. Vine's *London's Lost Route to the Sea*, 1965, Ch. II, 'The River Wey before 1789'. See also *The Origin of the River Wey Navigation, being an account of the canalization of the river from a manuscript written by Richard Scotcher in 1657*, 1895.
3. 22 & 23 Car II, P.A.
4. Daniel Defoe, *A Tour through England and Wales*, Everyman ed., I, p. 145.
5. W. Gilpin, *Observations on the Western Parts of England* (written 1776), 1798.
6. 33 Geo II c. 45.
7. 25 Geo III c. 100.
8. 31 Geo III c. 66.
9. J. Priestley, *An Account of the Navigable Rivers, Canals*, etc., 1831.
10. *Derby Mercury*, 24 March 1785.
11. *Report and Estimate of a Canal proposed to be made between Croydon and Portsmouth*, 1803.
12. R. Marshall, *An examination into the respective merits of the proposed Canal and the Iron Railway from London to Portsmouth*, 1803.
13. *Lewes Journal*, 5 March 1804.
14. John Rennie, *Report and Estimate of the Grand Southern Canal*, 1810.
15. Quoted in Charles E. Lee, *Early Railways in Surrey*, p. 12.
16. See my *The Canals of the East Midlands*.
17. John Rennie, *Report and Estimate of the Grand Southern Canal proposed to be made between Tonbridge and Portsmouth*, 1810 (Institution of Civil Engineers Library).
18. *The Times*, 26 July 1810.
19. *The Report of Edward Banks on . . . a Navigable Canal . . . between the Grand Southern Canal . . . to communicate with the River Thames at Wandsworth by means of the Surrey Iron Railway*, 1810 (I.C.E. Library).

20. 53 Geo III c. 19.
21. *Hampshire Chronicle & Courier*, 7 October 1816.
22. J. B. Dashwood, *The Thames to the Solent by Canal and Sea*, 1868.
23. The Rennies' MS *Reports* (I.C.E. Library).
24. 57 Geo III c. 63.
25. Lake Allen, *The History of Portsmouth*, 1817.
26. 59 Geo III c. 104.
27. J. Priestley, *Historical Account of the Navigable Rivers, Canals*, etc., 1831.
28. 2 Geo IV c. 62.
29. W. G. Gates, *History of Portsmouth*.
30. 9 Geo IV c. 57.
31. *The Times*, 19 September 1826.
32. See *Railway Magazine*, August 1938, p. 108. There is an illustration.
33. P.R.O., C26 507.
34. See my *The Canals of South West England*, chapter IV, 'English and Bristol Channel Schemes'. Cundy dedicated his reports to Alexander Baring, M.P. for Taunton, a supporter of the English & Bristol Channels Ship Canal.
35. *Aris's Birmingham Gazette*, 30 April 1827.
36. The Rennies' MS *Reports* (I.C.E. Library).
37. See N. W. Cundy, *Reports on the Grand Ship Canal*, 1827, and *Imperial Ship Canal . . . Mr Cundy's Reply*, 1828 (Goldsmiths' Library).
38. The Rennies' MS *Reports* (I.C.E. Library).

Notes to Chapter VII

1. For a full history of the Basingstoke Canal, see P. A. L. Vine, *London's Lost Route to Basingstoke*, 1969.
2. J.H.C., 21 February 1771.
3. J.H.C., 27 November 1770.
4. 18 Geo III c. 75.
5. J.H.C., 23 February 1778.
6. S. Shaw, *A Journey to the West of England in 1788*, 1789.
7. 33 Geo III c. 16.
8. Basingstoke Canal Report, 11 October 1822.
9. Quoted in C. F. Dendy Marshall, *History of the Southern Railway*, 1936.
10. *The Journey Book of England—Hampshire*, 1841, p. 6.
11. *Maidstone Journal*, 29 September 1835.
12. P.R.O., C.26/595 and B.T. 21/14039.
13. P.R.O., BT 21 3231/18917.
14. P.R.O., BT 21/135401.

Notes to Chapter VIII

1. For a fuller account, upon which I have drawn, see E. Course, 'The Itchen Navigation', *Procs* Hampshire Field Club, 1967, pp. 113–26.
2. *Victoria County History of Hampshire*, V, p. 451; *Hants Notes & Queries*, IX, 1898; Hilary M. Peel, 'A Bishop's Brain-child', *Country Life*, 29 September 1966.
3. Preamble to the Act of 1767, 7 Geo III c. 87.
4. 7 Geo III c. 87.
5. Preamble to the Act of 1795.
6. *Hampshire Chronicle & Portsmouth & Chichester Journal*, 6 September 1790.
7. 35 Geo III c. 86.
8. 42 Geo III c. 111.
9. The story can be read in full in Hollis's pamphlet of 1809: *An Answer to the Report of Benjamin Bevan and Richard Eyles, engineer and surveyor, respecting the Navigation of the River Itchin*.

10. 51 Geo III c. 202.
11. *Hampshire Chronicle & Courier*, 29 March 1819.
12. 1 Geo IV c. 75.
13. John Duthy, *Sketches of Hampshire*, 1839.
14. P.R.O., BT 21/109863.
15. For much new material in this account I am indebted to Mr D. A. E. Cross. See also Rev. E. Duke, *Prolusiones Historicae*, Salisbury, 1837, for much general information.
16. *Works of John Taylor the Water-Poet*, ed. C. Hindley, 1872.
17. 16 & 17 Car II P.A.
18. Wilts Record Office, MSS Radnor 490/1683, found by Mr A. C. East and made available to me by Mr D. A. E. Cross.
19. J.H.C., 12 December 1699, 17, 29, 31 January 1700.
20. J.H.C., 4 February 1772.
21. *The Times*, 18 September 1821.
22. For useful extracts from contemporary documents, see *Andover Documents No 1: The Andover Canal*, published by Andover Local Archives Committee, 1968.
23. W. Gilpin, *Observations on the Western Parts of England*, 1798.
24. J.H.C., 2 February 1771.
25. J. Phillips, *General History of Inland Navigation*, 1795 ed.
26. *Hampshire Chronicle & Portsmouth & Chichester Journal*, 21 July 1788.
27. Ibid., 25 August 1788.
28. Ibid., 29 September 1788.
29. Ibid., 16 March 1789.
30. 29 Geo III c. 72.
31. Inf. from Mr L. Cameron, based on the 1810 O.S. map and observations on the ground.
32. *Hampshire Chronicle*, 27 January 1794, quo. *Andover Documents No 1.*
33. *An Abstract of the Andover Canal Act*, 1792, Hants C.R.O., quo. *Andover Documents No 1.*
34. *Hampshire Chronicle & Courier*, 8 July 1816.
35. Robert Mudie, *Hampshire*, 1838, I, p. 228.
36. *Pictorial Times*, 11 October 1845.
37. R. A. Williams, *The London & South Western Railway*, 1968, I, 75.
38. *Railway Times*, 24 September 1859.
39. Inf. kindly provided by Mr L. T. C. Rolt.
40. *Hampshire Chronicle & Portsmouth & Chichester Journal*, 4 August 1788.
41. Rennie's MS *Reports* (I.C.E. Library).
42. *Hampshire Chronicle & Portsmouth & Chichester Journal*, 6 September 1790.
43. *Considerations on the intended Junction of the Ports of London, Southampton and Portsmouth by uniting the Basingstoke Canal, (or the River Wey, at Godalming) with the River Itchin.*
44. *Liverpool General Advertiser*, 29 January, *Williamson's Liverpool Advertiser*, 5 February 1768.
45. *Hampshire Chronicle & Portsmouth & Chichester Journal*, 6 April 1789.
46. Since my account of this canal was published in *The Canals of Southern England*, two detailed studies have appeared, those of Hugh Braun, 'The Salisbury Canal —a Georgian Misadventure' in *Wilts Arch & Nat Hist Mag*, Vol. 58, No 210, pp. 171–80, which is mainly concerned with the Salisbury section of the canal, and Edwin Welch's *The Bankrupt Canal*, Southampton Papers No 5, City of Southampton, 1966, which has more detail about the Southampton end. I have rewritten my account in the light of these and other new sources.
47. *Strictures & Observations on the intended canal from Salisbury to Southampton together with remarks on the general utility of canals.* By an Advocate of Canals.
48. 35 Geo III c. 51.
49. See my *The Canals of South West England.*
50. See my *The Canals of South Wales and the Border.*
51. See Rennie's MS report, 8 March 1798 (I.C.E. Library).
52. MS report, 6 May 1799 (I.C.E. Library).

53. 40 Geo III c. 108.
54. J.H.C., 12 February 1800.
55. James Waylen, *History of Devizes*, 1859.
56. *Hampshire Chronicle & Portsmouth & Chichester Journal*, 24 February 1794. See also abstract of *Report* of 13 September 1794 by Chamberlain and Thomas Morris (Wilts Arch. & Nat. Hist. Soc. Library, Devizes).

Notes to Chapter IX

1. For much information on the Thames navigation, see F. S. Thacker's two books, reprinted in 1968, *The Thames Highway: General History* and *The Thames Highway: Locks and Weirs*.
2. Manchester Central Library, ff 386 C9.
3. J.H.C., 21 February 1771.
4. Thames Commissioners' Minute Book, 14 June 1783.
5. Ibid., 27 September 1783.
6. See *The Canals of the East Midlands*.
7. This date, and not 1789 as given in *The Canals of the East Midlands*, 1st ed., seems to be the correct one.
8. *Reports of the Engineers appointed by the Commissioners of the Rivers Thames and Isis, to survey the State of the said Navigation, from Lechlade to Day's Lock*, 1791.
9. Thames Commissioners' Minute Book, 9 May 1789.
10. *Report the Second by Mr. Mylne . . . on the Navigation of the River Thames between Lechlade and Whitchurch*, 1791.
11. Ibid.
12. *A Report of the Committee of Commissioners . . . appointed to survey the Rivers from Lechlade to Whitchurch*, 1791.
13. See my *The Canals of the West Midlands*.
14. See my *The Canals of South Wales & the Border*.
15. See my *The Canals of South Wales & the Border*.
16. *Report from the Committee of the Hon. the House of Commons Appointed to enquire into the progress made towards the amendment and improvement of the Navigation of the Thames and Isis*, 28 June 1793.
17. W. Vanderstegen, *The Present State of the Thames considered*, 1794.
18. *Report of the Committee of the Thames Navigation Commissioners, of the State of the Navigation below Great Marlow*, 1789.
19. Ibid.
20. Thames Commissioners' Minute Book, 4 February 1794.
21. See my *The Canals of the East Midlands*.
22. See my *The Canals of the East Midlands*.
23. Thames Commissioners' Minute Book, 21 November 1792.
24. Ibid., 11 January 1793.
25. W. Mavor, *A General View of the Agriculture of Berkshire*, 1809.
26. Ibid.
27. *Gloucester Journal*, 19 December 1774.
28. W. M. Childs, *The Town of Reading during the Early Part of the Nineteenth Century*, 1910 (based on local newspapers).
29. Basingstoke Canal Report, 10 February 1803.
30. J.H.C., 1, 15 February 1811.
31. See my *The Canals of the East Midlands*, pp. 114–15.
32. Annual *Report* of the Kennet & Avon Canal, 15 August 1815.
33. Annual *Report* of the Kennet & Avon Canal, 25 July 1821.
34. Basingstoke Canal notice, 18 October 1810. For a full account of this project, see P. A. L. Vine, *London's Lost Route to Basingstoke*, 1969, ch. VI.
35. MS memorandum on Hants & Berks Junction Canal application to Parliament, c. 1825.
36. *Felix Farley's Bristol Journal*, 19 October 1793.

37. *Two Reports of the Commissioners of the Thames Navigation on the Objects and Consequences of the several projected Canals, which interfere with the interests of that River; and on the present sufficient and still improving State of its Navigation*, 1811.
38. Thames Conservancy advertisement in the London *Standard*, 24 January 1868.

Notes to Chapter X

1. For a fuller account of the river navigations and canal, see Kenneth R. Clew, *The Kennet & Avon Canal*, 1968.
2. For a short account of the history of the river before this Act was passed, see the article by Dr T. S. Willan, 'Bath and the Navigation of the Avon', in the *Proceedings* of the Bath & District branch, Somerset Archaeological & Natural History Society, 1936.
3. J. A. R. Pimlott, *The Englishman's Holiday*, 1947, p. 37.
4. Avon Navigation Minute Book, 24 August 1731.
5. Quoted in John Wood, *An Essay towards a Description of Bath*, Part Four, 2nd ed., 1749.
6. Kennet Navigation Minute Book, 27 September 1728.
7. Ibid., 4 July 1721.
8. Ibid., 16 October 1723.
9. Ibid., 3 June 1761.
10. Ibid., 20 May 1761.
11. John Aubrey, *Brief Lives*, ed. A. Powell, 1949, p. 134 (Henry Briggs) and Francis Mathew, *Of the Opening of Rivers*, pp. 7–9.
12. A. Yarranton, *England's Improvement*, etc., i, 64.
13. *Observations on a Scheme for extending the Navigation of the Rivers Kennett and Avon, so as to form a Direct Communication between London, Bristol and the West of England, by a Canal from Newbury to Bath*.
14. Ibid.
15. *Observations on the Advantages of the proposed Western Canal from Newbury to Bath*.
16. See my *The Canals of South West England*.
17. Account of the incident in the Minute Book of the Kennet & Avon Canal.
18. Ibid.
19. *Felix Farley's Bristol Journal*, 22 December 1792.
20. 34 Geo III c. 90.
21. Kennet & Avon Canal Minute Book, 4 September 1795.
22. See my *The Canals of South West England*, pp. 91–4.
23. Kennet & Avon Canal Report, 26 June 1798.
24. Kennet & Avon Canal Minute Book, 12 December 1803.
25. Ibid., 29 October 1805.
26. 51 Geo III c. 167.
27. See my *The Canals of South West England*.
28. For a fuller account of the Avon & Gloucestershire Railway, see Kenneth R. Clew, *The Kennet & Avon Canal*, ch. 7.
29. *Reading Seventy Years Ago*, 1887, quoted in W. M. Childs, *The Town of Reading during the Early Part of the Nineteenth Century*, 1910.
30. W. M. Childs, *The Town of Reading during the Early Part of the Nineteenth Century*, 1910.
31. Kennet & Avon Canal Committee Minute Book, 1 August 1820.
32. Letter-book of the Wilts & Berks Canal, 18 January 1825.
33. Kennet & Avon Canal Minute Book, 26 October 1829.
34. For passenger carrying on Scottish canals, see Jean Lindsay, *The Canals of Scotland*, 1968. Generally, see my *The Canal Age*, 1968.
35. Quoted in W. M. Childs, *The Town of Reading during the Early Part of the Nineteenth Century*, 1910.
36. Kennet & Avon Canal Minute Book, 10 September 1834.
37. Ibid., 17 March 1835.

38. For a history of steam carriages, see John Copeland, *Roads & their Traffic*, 1968, chapter 7.
39. Kennet & Avon Canal Committee Minute Book, 17 July 1838.
40. Ibid., 15 September 1841.
41. Ibid., 14 December 1842.
42. Ibid., 15 December 1847.
43. Kennet & Avon Canal Proprietors' Minute Book, 1 July 1845.
44. *Taunton Courier.*
45. Kennet & Avon Canal Committee Minute Book, 28 October 1845.
46. Ibid.
47. Ibid., 11 March 1846.
48. *Taunton Courier*, 8 January 1845, quoting *Felix Farley's Bristol Journal*.
49. Kennet & Avon Canal Committee Minute Book, 12 September 1849.
50. Ibid., 10 December 1851.
51. Ibid., 12 December 1849.
52. For a full account of the years since the railway purchase, see Kenneth R. Clew, *The Kennet & Avon Canal*, 1968.

Notes to Chapter XI

1. I should like to thank Kenneth R. Clew for his help. His book, *The Somersetshire Coal Canal*, which will appear soon after my own, gives a full account of this canal. Of especial value has been an article in the *Bath Chronicle* for 26 March 1874, found by Mr Clew, which quotes extracts from the company's lost minute books.
2. See R. A. Atthill, *Old Mendip*, 1964, Chapter 4, 'John Billingsley'.
3. *Bath Chronicle*, 10 January 1793.
4. Ibid., 7 February 1793.
5. *Bath Chronicle*, 24 October, 7 November 1793.
6. 34 Geo III c. 86.
7. Described in his *General View of the Agriculture of the County of Aberdeen*.
8. For these, see my book, *The Canals of South West England*.
9. See my *The Canals of the West Midlands*.
10. D. King-Hele, *Erasmus Darwin, 1731–1802*, 1963.
11. *Sherborne Mercury*, 13 October 1794.
12. *Bath Chronicle*, 15 June 1796.
13. *Enquiry into the Utility of a Canal from Bristol to Bath*, 1795.
14. William Chapman, *Observations on the various systems of Canal Navigation*, 1797, pp. 10–11.
15. For a description see Patent no. 1892 or the 1798 edition of J. Billingsley, *A General View of the Agriculture of Somerset*, Appendix, p. 317.
16. It is shown on an 1806 estate map of the Earl of Waldegrave in the Somerset Record Office.
17. *Bath Chronicle*, 14 November 1799.
18. *Bath Chronicle*, 7 June 1798.
19. Ibid., 5 December 1798.
20. Ibid., 17 January 1799.
21. Ibid., 11 April 1799.
22. Ibid., 2 May 1799.
23. Ibid., 23 May 1799.
24. For the Charnwood Forest branch, see my *The Canals of the East Midlands*.
25. *Report* from John Sutcliffe to Proprietors, 26 May 1800 (I.C.E. Library).
26. See my *The Canals of the East Midlands*.
27. See my and Gordon Biddle's forthcoming book, *The Canals of North West England*.
28. Rees' *Cyclopaedia*, article 'Canals', 1805.
29. J.H.C., 12 February 1802.

30. Goddard papers (Swindon P.L.).
31. 42 Geo III c. 35.
32. The existence of this tramroad, and the use of the Radstock branch canal, is now established from the report of the Lock Fund Committee for 20 May 1805, kindly shown to me by Mr K. R. Clew.
33. *Bath Chronicle*, 15 September 1814.
34. Ibid., 20 July 1815.
35. Letter-book of the Wilts & Berks Canal, 4 and 12 October.
36. Ibid., 15 October 1824.
37. Ibid., 9 August 1827.
38. Ibid., 23 July 1828.
39. Ibid., 10 October 1828.
40. Waterways Museum, Stoke Bruerne.
41. *Railway Times*, 6 September 1845.

Notes to Chapter XII

1. W. Mavor, *A General View of the Agriculture of Berkshire*, 1809.
2. Thames & Severn Canal Committee Minute Book, 22 November 1793.
3. *Gloucester Journal*, 17 March, 26 May 1794.
4. J.H.C., 23 February 1795.
5. 35 Geo III c. 52.
6. For the original line, see map of 1793, Berkshire C.R.O.
7. For the Dorset & Somerset Canal, see my *The Canals of South West England*.
8. Wilts & Berks Canal Report, 25 November 1802 (Goddard collection, Swindon P.L.).
9. For Swindon's relationship to the canal, *see* Martin Smith's thesis, 'Swindon and the Construction of the Wilts and Berks Canal', 1966 (Swindon P.L.).
10. Quoted from a newspaper account in J. Townsend (ed.), *News of a Country Town*, 1914.
11. 50 Geo III c. 148.
12. See my *The Canals of the East Midlands*.
13. J.H.C., 7 February, 6 March, 13 March 1810.
14. See also my *The Canals of the East Midlands*, pp. 115, 158.
15. *Proposed Canal from Bristol to the Wilts and Berks Canal*, 12 April 1810.
16. See Charles Hadfield and John Norris, *Waterways to Stratford*, 2nd ed., p. 85, and Rennie's MS *Reports* (I.C.E. Library), 29 and 30 October 1810.
17. MS minutes of the meeting.
18. Thames & Severn Canal Proprietors' Minute Book, 7 January 1812.
19. Ibid., 18 March 1812.
20. Printed notice of Wilts & Berks Canal, 28 July 1812.
21. 53 Geo III c. 182.
22. For the Severn & Wye, see my *The Canals of South Wales and the Border*.
23. *The Times*, 7 April 1819.
24. 1 & 2 Geo IV c. 97.
25. Letter-book of the Wilts & Berks Canal, 4 May 1829.
26. Ibid., 18 January 1825.
27. Ibid., 16 April 1827.
28. Kennet & Avon Canal Committee Minute Book, 19 January 1825.
29. Letter of 23 February 1835, Wilts & Berks Canal papers (Berkshire C.R.O.).
30. Wilts & Berks Canal papers (Berkshire C.R.O.).
31. *North Wilts Herald*, 5 September 1874. See also *Bristol Daily Post*, 23 November 1874 and *Wilts & Gloucestershire Standard*, 30 January 1875.
32. P.R.O., BT 21/10061.
33. 39 & 40 Vic c. 59.
34. *Devizes & Wiltshire Gazette*, 29 April 1897.
35. Glos C.R.O., D1180/5/34.
36. Ibid.

Notes to Chapter XIII

1. Information from Mr H. G. W. Household.
2. 3 Geo II c. 13.
3. John Dallaway, *A Scheme to make the River Stroudwater Navigable* . . ., 1755, Glos C.R.O., D1180/5/2.
4. Dun Navigation Minute Book, 10 August 1758.
5. 32 Geo II c. 47.
6. Commissioners' Minute Book, 8 April 1761.
7. *The Case of the Opposition for making a Navigable Canal from the River Severn up to Walbridge*, n.d. (Glos C.R.O., D1180/5/2).
8. Glos C.R.O., D1180/10/1.
9. Notes by William Dallaway for the bill of 1777. Glos C.R.O., D1180/5/1. On the scheme generally, see also J. Phillips, *A General History of Inland Navigation*, 2nd ed., 1795, pp. 213–16.
10. Glos C.R.O., D1180/5/1.
11. Staffs & Worcs Canal Minute Book, 19 May 1774.
12. *Gloucester Journal*, 23 January 1775.
13. Ibid., 5 June 1775.
14. 16 Geo III c. 21.
15. For John Billingsley and Somerset canals, see my *The Canals of South West England*.
16. Stroudwater Navigation Minute Book, 30 December 1776.
17. Ibid., 1 July 1779.
18. Ibid., 19 August 1779.
19. Ibid., 8 April 1783.
20. Ibid., 9 April 1782.
21. See my *The Canals of South Wales and the Border*, 2nd ed., p. 211.
22. For the Shropshire waterways and the Staffs & Worcs Canal, see my *The Canals of the West Midlands*.
23. Stroudwater Navigation Minute Book, 13 April 1790.
24. Ibid., 12 June 1799.
25. For the Gloucester & Worcester Horse Towing Path company, see my *The Canals of the West Midlands*.
26. Stroudwater Navigation Minute Book, 14 April 1812.
27. Ibid., 14 February 1804.
28. Ibid., 20 October 1824.
29. Ibid., 6 August 1833.
30. Ibid., 22 April 1842.
31. Ibid., 19 May 1845.
32. Ibid., 12 January 1853.
33. Ibid., 10 November 1874.
34. Ibid., 9 February 1882.

Notes to Chapter XIV

1. For a more detailed account of the Thames & Severn Canal, see Humphrey Household, *The Thames & Severn Canal*, 1969.
2. John Dallaway, *A Scheme to make the River Stroudwater Navigable*, 1755 (Glos C.R.O., D1180/5/2).
3. *Gloucester Journal*, 27 August, 22 October 1781.
4. 23 Geo III c. 38.
5. Thames Commissioners' Minute Book, 14 June 1783.
6. See my *The Canals of the West Midlands*, pp. 74–9.
7. See my *The Canals of the West Midlands*, pp. 53–4.

8. See my *The Canals of the East Midlands.*
9. See my *The Canals of South West England.*
10. J. Latimer, *Annals of Bristol in the Eighteenth Century.*
11. This may have been the same scheme as the Worcester–Bristol canal proposed in Birmingham.
12. For the Worcester–Bristol and Bristol & Severn projects, see *Gloucester Journal*, 3 December 1792, 13 February, 20 March, 17 April, 31 July 1797, and *Aris's Birmingham Gazette*, 26 November 1792, 13 February, 31 July 1797.
13. *Gloucester Journal*, 21, 28 January, 2 and 30 September, 25 October, 30 December 1793, 6 January, 25 February, 6 May, 2 June 1794, 29 January 1798, and Robert Mylne's report *To the Gentlemen of the Committee of Subscribers to the Proposed Canal from Bristol to Cirencester*, 1793 (Author's collection).
14. *Gloucester Journal*, 11 February, 11 March, 1 April, 1 July, 26 August, 7 October 1793.
15. Thames & Severn Canal Committee Minute Book, 25 February, 25 May 1792, and see my *The Canals of the East Midlands*, p. 109.
16. Thames & Severn Canal Committee Minute Book, 25 May 1792.
17. The Kennet & Avon was completed at the end of 1810. The Bristol & Taunton (as the Bridgewater & Taunton) and the Grand Western were each partly built. For these last, see my *The Canals of South West England.*
18. *Berrow's Worcester Journal*, 14 June 1810.
19. See my *The Canals of the West Midlands*, p. 118.
20. Rennie's MS *Reports*, 1 March 1790 (I.C.E. Library).
21. Thames & Severn Canal Committee Minute Book, 10 December 1790.
22. Thames & Severn Canal Proprietors' Minute Book, 7 April 1789.
23. Ibid., 6 October 1789.
24. Thames & Severn Canal Committee Minute Book, 13 November 1792.
25. Thames & Severn Proprietors' Minute Book, 14 June 1803.
26. *Berrow's Worcester Journal*, 20 June 1805.
27. Ibid., 8 May 1806.
28. Thames & Severn Canal Committee Minute Book, 29 June 1820.
29. Thames & Severn Canal Proprietors' Minute Book, 26 October 1824.
30. Ibid., 27 October 1835.
31. Ibid., 7 November 1835.
32. Ibid., 2 March 1836.
33. Ibid., 28 April 1840.
34. Letter from Conservancy to J. H. Taunton (Glos C.R.O., D1180/4/46).
35. Stroudwater Navigation Minute Book, 18 February 1875.
36. Ibid., 22 December 1875.
37. Ibid., 20 November 1883.
38. Ibid., 16 June 1885.
39. Ibid., 17 August 1886.
40. Ibid., 19 June 1888.
41. See my *British Canals*, 3rd ed., p. 246.
42. Dorington's paper of 28 December 1899, quo. Stroudwater Navigation Minute Book, 16 January 1900.
43. Stroudwater Navigation Minute Book, 16 May 1923.

Notes to Chapter XV

1. Stroudwater Navigation Minute Book, 8 January 1784.
2. *Gloucester Journal*, 18 October, 6 December 1784, 24 and 31 January 1785.
3. Ibid., 12 November 1792.
4. *Aris's Birmingham Gazette*, 9 July 1827.
5. 33 Geo III c. 97.
6. Letter to Wheeler, 1 February 1802 (Glos C.R.O., D2159).

7. For James Dadford's tramroad near Aberdare, see my *The Canals of South Wales and the Border*, 2nd ed., pp. 119–20.
8. Gloucester & Berkeley Canal Minute Book, 2 June 1797.
9. A. E. Richardson, *Robert Mylne, Architect and Engineer, 1733 to 1811*, 1955, p. 173.
10. Gloucester & Berkeley Canal Minute Book, 8 September 1811.
11. John Upton, *Observations on the Gloucester & Berkeley Canal*, 1815
12. *Aris's Birmingham Gazette*, 8 June 1816.
13. *Gloucester Journal*, 6 March 1820.
14. Ibid., 27 March, 3 April 1820.
15. Gloucester & Berkeley Canal Minute Book, 8 May 1820.
16. *Annual Register*, 1827.
17. *Hereford Journal*, 14 October 1829.
18. For a fuller account of the years 1836–42, see my *The Canals of the West Midlands*, pp. 118 et seq.
19. The tramroad had been bought in 1836 by the Birmingham & Gloucester and the Cheltenham & Great Western Union Railways jointly for £35,000. Though an abandonment Act was passed in 1859, it was used until 1861. For the line generally, and especially its connections to the canal, see D. E. Bick, *The Gloucester & Cheltenham Railway*, 1968.
20. The relations of the Gloucester & Berkeley company with the Severn Commissioners and the neighbouring waterways, and the company's purchase of the Worcester & Birmingham Canal, are described in my *The Canals of the West Midlands*.
21. For the Severn Bridge company, see H. W. Paar, *The Severn & Wye Railway*, 1963, Chapter 8.
22. For the Worcester & Birmingham Canal, see my *The Canals of the West Midlands*. The Droitwich and Droitwich Junction Canals, leased by the Worcester & Birmingham were also taken over.

APPENDIX I

Summary of Facts about South and South Eastern Canals and Navigations

A. *Rivers Successfully Made Navigable*

River	Date of Act under which Work was begun	Date Wholly Opened	Approx. Cost at Opening (£)	Terminal Points
Arun	1785	1790	16,000	Houghton Bridge–Newbridge
Avon (Bristol)	1712	1727	12,000	Hanham Mills–Bath
Avon (Hants)	1664–5	1684	3,500	Christchurch–Salisbury
Baybridge Canal (Adur River)	1825	Not known	c. 6,000	Bines bridge–Baybridge
Dartford & Crayford Navigation (Darenth River and Crayford Creek)	1840	1844	c. 12,000	Sea to Dartford Crayford Creek
Itchen	1664–5	c. 1710	[5]	Woodmill–Winchester
Kennet	1715	1723	c. 45,000	Reading–Newbury
Medway (Lower)	1792	[7]	28,000	Halling–Maidstone[8]
Medway (Upper)	1740	c. 1750	11,725	Maidstone–Tonbridge

[1] Some local traffic thereafter.
[2] These pound locks were probably built after 1693, as well as flash-locks.
[3] Size of locks.
[4] Little used after this date.
[5] Not known. The navigation was considered to be worth £12,000 in 1767.
[6] Later as for Kennet & Avon Canal.
[7] The river was navigable before the 1792 Act authorized improvements. Some were carried out under the 1792 and 1802 Acts, more under that of 1824.

Length	Greatest Number of Locks	Size of Boats Taken	Date of Disuse for Commercial Traffic	Date of Abandonment	Whether bought by Railway, and Present Ownership
13 miles	6	78 ft × 12 ft	1889[1]	1896	No
11½ miles	6	75 ft × 16 ft	1967		Yes. See Kennet & Avon Canal, British Waterways Board
c. 36 miles	3[2]		c. 1705		No
3¾ miles	2	75 ft × 12 ft 6 in[3]	c. 1861[4]	1875	No
2⅜ miles ⅝ miles	1	169 ft × 24½ ft[3]	Open	Open	Dartford & Crayford Navigation Commissioners
10¾ miles	15 and 2 half-locks	72 ft × 13 ft	1869		No
18½ miles	21	109 ft × 17 ft[6]	c. 1934	Open	Yes. See Kennet & Avon Canal, British Waterways Board
9 miles[9]	1	94 ft 8 in × 22 ft 8 in[10]	Open	Open	Medway Lower Navigation Co., Maidstone
16 miles	14[11]	73 ft 6 in × 13 ft[12]	1927[13]	Open	Kent River Authority

[8] 1792 Act, Aylesford–Maidstone; 1824 Act, Halling–Maidstone; 1888, Hawkwood–Maidstone.
[9] At greatest extent.
[10] Rebuilt to present lock size of 180 ft × 21 ft 6 in.
[11] Now reduced to 9.
[12] Later 80 ft × 18 ft 6 in.
[13] To Tonbridge; to Yalding and Brandbridges 1928. Still used to Tovil.

A. *Rivers Successfully Made Navigable*

River	Date of Act under which Work was begun	Date Wholly Opened	Approx. Cost at Opening (£)	Terminal Points
Ouse (Upper)	1790	c. 1812	30,000	Lewes–Upper Ryelands bridge branch to Shortbridge
Rother (Eastern)	None			Rye–Newenden[2]
Rother (Western)	1791	1794 1793	13,300 5,000	Stopham (Arun)–Midhurst branch to Petworth
Stour	1515	c. 1594[3]		Fordwich–Canterbury[4]
Thames	[5]			Teddington–Inglesham
Wey	1651	1653	c. 15,000	Weybridge–Guildford
Wey (Godalming)	1760	1763	6,450	Guildford–Godalming

[1] Upper part.
[2] Highest point of regular navigation. See text for information about branches.
[3] Became unnavigable again soon afterwards. Seemingly again made navigable c. 1695 and again ceased to be navigable soon afterwards.
[4] The river was a natural navigation up to Fordwich.

B. *Rivers with Uncompleted Navigation Works*

None.

Length	Greatest Number of Locks	Size of Boats Taken	Date of Disuse for Commercial Traffic	Date of Abandonment	Whether bought by Railway, and Present Ownership
22½ miles	18	48 ft × 13 ft 3 in	1861[1]		No
¾ mile			1868		
12¼ miles	1	45 ft × 12 ft	1909		No
11¼ miles	8	78 ft × 12 ft	1888	1936	No
1¼ miles	2		c. 1800		
2½ miles	2 flash-locks		c. 1877		
125½ miles	38 (1888)	120 ft × 17 ft[6]	Open	Open	Thames Conservancy
	43 (1954)	100 ft × 14 ft[7]			
15¼ miles	12	81 ft 6 in × 14 ft 3 in	1958[8]	Open	No. National Trust
4½ miles	4	84 ft × 14 ft 3 in	1946	Open	No. National Trust

[5] The Thames has always been navigable.
[6] Teddington–Oxford.
[7] Oxford–Lechlade.
[8] To Guildford.

C. *Canals, the Main Lines of which were Completed as Authorized*

Canal	Date of Act under which Work was begun	Date wholly Opened	Approx. Cost at Opening £	Terminal Points	Branches Built
Andover	1789	1794	48,000	Redbridge–Andover	
Basingstoke	1778	1794	190,000	R. Wey–Basingstoke	
Croydon	1801	1809	127,000	Grand Surrey Canal (New Cross) Croydon	
Gloucester & Berkeley	1793	1827	c. 440,000	Gloucester–Sharpness[2]	Cam
Kennet & Avon	1794	1810	c. 950,000	Newbury–Bath	
Portsmouth & Arundel	1817	1823	170,000	Ford–Portsmouth	
		1822			Chichester
		1831			Portsea Creek
Royal Military	None	1806	200,000	Shorncliffe–Cliff End, Winchelsea	
Stroudwater	1776[12]	1779	41,000	Framilode–Stroud	

[1] To Basingstoke.
[2] Sharpness was substituted for Berkeley pill as the terminal in 1818.
[3] Length as opened in 1827, 16⅜ miles. Extended to present Sharpness Docks, 1874.
[4] Ford–Salterns 12¾ miles, Salterns–Portsea 13 miles, Portsea Canal 2⅜ miles.
[5] Two at Ford, two at Chichester harbour, two at entrance of Portsea Canal.
[6] Ford–Hunston.

Length	Greatest Number of Locks	Size of Boats Taken	Date of Disuse for Commercial Traffic	Date of Abandonment	Whether bought by Railway and Present Ownership
22 miles	24	65 ft × 8 ft 6 in	1859	1858	Yes. Bought by Andover & Redbridge Rly for £25,357
37½ miles	29	82 ft 6 in × 14 ft 6 in	c. 1901[1]		No
9¼ miles	28	60 ft × 9 ft	1836	1836	Bought by London & Croydon Rly for £40,250
16¾ miles[3] 1 mile	None; tide and basin locks at Sharpness; river lock at Gloucester	190 ft × 29 ft	Open	Open	British Waterways Board
57 miles	79	70 ft × 13 ft 9 in	c. 1937 Not at present navigable throughout		Bought by GWR in 1852 for £210,415. British Waterways Board
27¾ miles[4]	6[5]	75 ft × 12 ft 6 in[6]	1830[8] 1847[6]	1896	No
1⅜ miles		90 ft × 18 ft 6 in[7]	c. 1906[7]	1928	West Sussex County Council
c. 1 mile					
30 miles[9]	1[10]	72 ft × 16 ft[11]	1909		No
8 miles	12 (13 from 1820)	72 ft × 15 ft 6 in	1941	1954	No

[7] Chichester–Salterns.
[8] Portsea Canal. The date of disuse may well be earlier.
[9] The full length, including the two canal sections, and enlarged portions of the rivers Rother and Brede.
[10] Iden lock at the junction with the Rother. There was a second lock, Scot's Float, on the Rother itself.
[11] The size of Iden lock.
[12] Construction begun under an earlier Act of 1730, found insufficient.

C. *Canals, the Main Lines of which were Completed as Authorized*

Canal	Date of Act under which Work was begun	Date wholly Opened	Approx. Cost at Opening £	Terminal Points	Branches Built
Thames & Medway	1800	1824	260,000	Gravesend–Frindsbury	
Thames & Severn	1783	1789	c. 220,000	Stroud–Inglesham	
		c. 1787			Cirencester
Wey & Arun	1813	1816	103,000	Shalford–Newbridge	
Wilts & Berks	1796	1810	255,000	Semington–Abingdon	
		1802			Calne
		c. 1803			Chippenham
		c. 1807			Longcot
		c. 1808			Wantage
	1813	1819	c. 60,000		Latton[7]

[1] Frindsbury–Higham. Rest of canal 1934. Two basins still open.
[2] Stroud—first lock above Brimscombe Port.
[3] Thence to Inglesham.

Length	Greatest Number of Locks	Size of Boats Taken	Date of Disuse for Commercial Traffic	Date of Abandonment	Whether bought by Railway and Present Ownership
7 miles	2	94 ft 8 in × 22 ft 8 in	1845[1]	1845	Turned into railway company, which was bought by the SER in 1846
28¾ miles 1½ miles	44	72 ft × 15 ft 6 in[2] 86 ft × 12 ft 3 in[3]	1911[4]	1927[5] 1933[6]	Under GWR control 1882–95
18½ miles	23	74 ft 9 in × 13 ft	1871	1868	No
51 miles 3⅛ miles 2 miles ½ mile ¾ mile 9 miles	42 3 12	74 ft × 7 ft 6 in	1906	1914	No

[4] Throughout.
[5] Inglesham–Chalford.
[6] Chalford–Stroud.
[7] North Wilts Canal.

D. *Canals, the Main Lines of which were not Completed*

Canal	Date of Act under which Work was Begun	Date Opened	Approx. Cost at Opening £	Authorized Terminal Points	Terminal Points as Built	Branches Built
Grand Surrey	1801	1810	c. 60,000[1]	Rotherhithe –Mitcham	Rother- hithe– Camber- well	
		1826				Peckham
Salisbury & Southampton	1795	1802–3	90,000	Salisbury– Kimbridge and Red- bridge– Southamp- ton Quay	Alderbury Common –Kim- bridge and Red- bridge– west end of South- ampton tunnel	Northam[3]
Somersetshire Coal	1794	1805	180,000[5]	Limpley Stoke– Radstock– Midford– Paulton[6]	All except Midford –Twin- hoe on Radstock line	

[1] Other than dock costs.
[2] About $\frac{1}{2}$ mile at the Camberwell end has been filled in.
[3] Finished, but unconnected to the rest of the canal.
[4] There is evidence only that the Salisbury & Southampton was a narrow canal, but one can, I think, assume that the boats using it would be the same size as those on the Andover.

E. *Canals Partly Built but not Opened*

None

Length	Greatest Number of Locks	Size of Boats Taken	Date of Disuse for Commercial Traffic	Date of Aban- donment	Whether bought by Railway and Present Ownership
3⅛ miles[2] ⅝ mile	2	109 ft × 18 ft	Open	Open	No. Owned by Port of London Authority
9½ miles plus 3½ miles	15	65 ft × 8 ft 6 in[4]	1806		No
17¾ miles[7]	23	70 ft × 7 ft	1898	1904	Former Radstock line (later tram-road) bought by s & dr in 1871 for conversion. Former Poulton line bought after abandonment in 1904 by gwr for conversion

[5] Including £45,000 for the Lock Fund.
[6] It is, I think, correct to regard this canal as having two main lines, to Radstock and Paulton from the intended junction at Midford.
[7] Reduced to 10½ miles when the Radstock line was converted to a tramroad, 1815.

F. Canals Authorized but not Begun

1811   Bath & Bristol Canal between those towns. The company bought some land and shares in the river Avon. The project was abandoned in 1814, and thereafter all shares and property were sold to the Kennet & Avon Canal Company.
1811   St Nicholas Bay Harbour & Canterbury Canal from St Nicholas Bay west of Margate to Canterbury.
1812   Weald of Kent Canal from the river Medway to the Royal Military Canal.
1825   Canterbury Navigation & Sandwich Harbour, to make a canal from near Sandown Castle to Sandwich, and the Stour navigable for 100-ton craft to Canterbury.
1864   Downs Dock, Act authorized a canal from the sea near Sandown Castle to Sandwich.
1902   Medway & Thames Canal, with electric traction, to avoid the coastal passage round the Isle of Grain.

APPENDIX II

Principal Engineering Works

A. *Inclined Planes*

Canal	Name of Plane	Vertical Rise	Dates Working	Notes
Somersetshire Coal	Combe Hay	129 ft	c. 1800–1802	Double track. Goods transhipped in boxes from boats to plane and back. Counterbalanced

B. *Lifts*

Canal	Name of Plane	Vertical Rise	Dates Working	Notes
Somersetshire Coal	Combe Hay	46 ft	1798	Single watertight caisson, which enclosed boat, itself totally immersed in water. Successfully tested, but water distorted shaft. Abandoned.

C. *Tunnels over 500 yards*

Thames & Medway Canal	Strood (Higham)	3,946 yd
Thames & Severn Canal	Sapperton	3,817 yd
Basingstoke Canal	Greywell	1,200 yd
Salisbury & Southampton Canal	Southampton	880 yd (unfinished)
Kennet & Avon Canal	Bruce (Savernake)	502 yd

D. *Outstanding Aqueducts*

Basingstoke Canal	Frimley (railway)
Kennet & Avon Canal	Avoncliff
	Dundas
Somersetshire Coal Canal	Dunkerton*
Thames & Severn Canal	Smerril (demolished)

* I refer to that beside the A367 road. There was another, now demolished.

INDEX

The principal references to canals and river navigations are indicated in bold type

Abingdon, 22–5, 188–9, 198–201, 207–8, 210, 215, 217, 272, 274, 276, 280–3, 286–8, 290, 292, 306, 323–4, 328
Abingdon–Lechlade canal project, *see* Lechlade
Admiralty, The, 135, 149–50, 350
Adur River, 15, 19, 22, **30–1,** 129–30, 132, 370–1
Agricultural produce, carried by coasting trade, 15, 20; on canals, etc, 19, 21, 24, 33, 46, 78, 100, 120, 125, 133, 147, 171, 221, 249, 274, 277, 285, 309n; on tramroads, 108; *see also* Beans, Butter, Cheese, Corn, Feeding stuffs, Fertilizers, Flour, Fruit, Hay, Hops, Linseed, Manure, Meal, Peas, Vegetables
Alderbury, 167, 181, 184–6
Aldermaston, 259
Aldershot, 157, 177
Allen, Ralph, undertaker, 221–2
Allied Navigations, The, 337–8
Allington, 64–5, 77, 80
Allnutt, Henry, clerk, 195
Allnutt, Zachary, clerk, 154, 195, 209, 213, 328
Alresford, 160, 177
Alton, 156, 177–8
Andover, 153, 160, 169–71, 173–4, 178–80, 187, 230
Andover Canal, 23–4, 27, 87, 128, 152, 165, **169–75,** 176, 178–81, 183–4, 187, 374–5
Andover Canal–Basingstoke Canal project, *see* Basingstoke Canal
Andover Canal–Kennet & Avon Canal project, 24, 160, 180, 186–7
Andover Canal Rly, 174
Andover & Redbridge Rly, 174
Anerley, 115–16
Anton River, 169–71
Appledore, 34, 37, 42, 46
Aqueducts, canal, 198; Abingdon (proposed), 215, 281; Avoncliff, 380; Dundas, 380; Dunkerton, 380; Frimley, 155, 380; Kimbridge, 181; Midford, 271; Orfold, 125; Smerril, 380; Thames, 284
Arun River, 15, 19, 22, 24–5, 34, 69, 71, 118, 123, **124–6,** 127, 129–30, 132, 134–8, 141, 143, 145, 148, 370–1

Arundel, 15, 25, 69, 123–6, 129–30, 132, 134–5, 147
Ash, 153, 156
Ashford (Kent), 46
Avon (Bristol) River, 15, 23–4, 29, 118, **221–2, 225–7,** 241–2, 244–6, 249–50, 259–62, 300, 347, 370–1
Avon (Hants) River, 22, **166–9,** 178, 181, 370–1
Avon & Gloucestershire Rly, *see* Tramroads
Avonmouth, 261, 351–2
Aylesbury, 215, 281
Aylesbury & Abingdon Canal project, 215
Aylesford, 62, 64, 95

Baker, Harry, owner, 163
Banbury, 23, 199
Banks, Sir Edward, engineer and contractor, 93, 130
Barcombe, 31–2
Barge weighing machine (Brimscombe Port), 334
Bark, carried on canals, etc, 119, 123
Barley, *see* Corn
Barnes, James, engineer, 232, 235
Bartley, N., speculator, 236, 239–40
Barton (Stour), 47–8
Basing, *see* Old Basing
Basing & Bath Rly project, 252–3
Basingstoke, 23, 151, 153–6, 158, 160, 173, 176, 178, 190, 192, 323
Basingstoke Canal, 23–5, 27, 70, 105, 107, 120, 123–4, 128, **151–9,** 163–4, 174, 176–80, 187, 190, 192, 194, 212–13, 232n, 245, 374–5, 380
Basingstoke Canal Syndicate Ltd, 158
Basingstoke Canal–Andover Canal projects, 24, 128, 152, 174–80, 187
Basingstoke Canal–Itchen Navigation projects, 24, 152, 163, 174–8, 180, 212
Basingstoke Canal–Kennet & Avon Canal project, *see* Hants & Berks Junction Canal project
Basingstoke & Salisbury Rly, 173
Bath, 15, 23–6, 155, 176, 187, 204, 221–2, 225, 235–6, 240–2, 244–6, 249, 251–3, 255, 257–8, 260–3, 269, 275, 277, 285–6, 288, 325

Bath & Bristol Canal project, 25, 241, 244–5, 253, 379
Baybridge Canal, **30**–1, 132, 370–1
Baylis, Thomas, shareholder, 298, 315, 341
Beans, carried on canals, etc, 67
Beckenham, 109, 111
Beer, carried on canals, etc, 123, 166
Bell Weir lock, 208
Bennet, William, engineer, 264, 270
Benson Lock, 199, 273
Berkeley, 320, 322, 342–3, 345
Berks & Hants Extension Rly, 254, 260
Berkshire County Council, 338
Bevan, Benjamin, engineer, 52, 345
Billingsley, John, shareholder, 262, 300
Bines bridge (Adur), 30–1
Birmingham, 23, 207, 220, 249, 268, 317, 320, 328, 330, 352
Birmingham Canal, 235, 315, 317
Birmingham Canal Navigations, 337
Birmingham & Gloucester Rly, 350
Bishopstoke & Salisbury Rly, 186
Blackwell, John, engineer, 252, 288
Board of Trade, 76, 97, 126, 256, 260, 275, 294, 313, 337–8
Bodiam, 34, 37–8
Bonnington, 37
Bottomley, Horatio, financier, 158
Boulter's lock, 23, 121, 192, 194, 195n, 199, 201, 203–4, 208, 216
Boulter's Lock & Isleworth Canal project, see Monkey Island
Boulton & Watt, engineers, 270, 324, 342
Boveney, 192, 208
Bow-hauling, see Towing
Boxwell springs, 323–4
Bradford-on-Avon, 235, 243, 251, 253, 255, 258, 260
Bramley, 135
Brandbridges, 42, 46, 74, 79n, 80
Brassworks, 222
Braunston, 207, 320
Bray, 151, 192, 194, 208
Brede, 37–8
Brede River, **37**–8, 41
Brentford, 192, 207, 281
Bricks, carried on canals, etc, 21, 42, 146, 158, 166, 292, 300–1, 309n, 346
Brickwood, John, shareholder, 111
Brickworks, 126
Bridge, Thomas, undertaker, 296
Bridges (opening), 34, 107, 145, 348, 352
Bridgewater, Earl of, promoter, 232
Bridgwater, 320
Briggs, Henry, projector, 232
Brighton, 33–4, 81, 146
Brighton Canal project, 33
Brimscombe Port, 202, 301, 304, 306–7,

309, 311, 316, 319, 324, 328–9, 334, 338, 340
Brindley, James, engineer, 23, 169, 178, 190, 192, 203–4, 235
Bristol, 15, 19–26, 28, 153, 155, 173, 176, 179–82, 186–7, 198, 204, 217, 221, 225–6, 230, 232, 235–7, 239–42, 244–6, 249–53, 255, 257–9, 261, 275, 281–2, 285–6, 288, 291–2, 296, 300–1, 305–6, 315–16, 320, 322–5, 328, 342, 347–8
Bristol–Cirencester canal project, 321–2
Bristol Junction Canal project, 215, 282
Bristol–Salisbury canal projects, 153, 176, 179, 182n, 186–7, 236–41
Bristol–Thames Head canal project, 322
Bristol & Gloucester Rly, 256
Bristol & Gloucestershire Rly, see Tramroads
Bristol & North Somerset Rly, 275
Bristol & Severn Canal project, 236, 320, 322, 342
Bristol & Taunton Canal project, 49, 245, 322
Bristol & Western Canal project, 236
British Transport Commission, 261
British Waterways Board, 261, 314
Brixton, 102, 104
Brockley, 109
Bromley, 111, 147
Brown, Lt-Col, Asst Quartermaster General, 39–41
Brunel, I. K., engineer, 254
Building materials carried by coasting trade, 15; on canals, etc, 21–2, 171, 242
Bullion, carried on canals, etc, 142
Bullo Pill, 284, 305, 311, 328, 345
Bullo Pill Rly, 284, 345
Bulpett, C. W. L., owner, 165
Bulpett, W. W., manager, 164–5
Burbage, 174
Buscot, 200, 203, 215, 323
Butter, carried on canals, etc, 19

Calne, 140, 235, 241, 276–7, 280, 287
Cambridge (Glos), 346, 349
Camberwell, 102–6
Camden, Lord, 39–40, 42
Camerton, 262–4, 267, 275
Canal cutting machines, 81, 342–3
Canal mania, 24–5, 176, 179, 186, 235–40, 242, 263, 320, 342
Canterbury, 22, 25–6, 46–9, 51–2, 54, 57
Canterbury Navigation & Sandwich Harbour, 17, 26, 47, 52, 54–6, 379
Canterbury & Whitstable Rly, 48, 56
Capital, of canals, etc, 29–30, 32, 46, 51, 54, 57, 61–2, 64, 67–8, 77–8, 82, 85, 89–90, 105, 110, 112, 133, 136, 141, 143, 148, 151, 153, 157–8, 170, 181,

184–7, 241, 263, 277, 280, 284–5, 296, 299–301, 316, 325–7, 342, 344–9, 351
Cardew, G. D., canal owner, 157
Cardiff, 334n, 351
Carne, John, inventor, 342
Carrying, by canal etc coys, 62, 66–7, 71, 74, 95, 112–14, 144, 153, 157–8, 160–4, 173, 201, 230–1, 254, 259, 286, 292, 324–6, 336
Carrying concerns, 61, 67, 77–8, 93, 96, 114, 143, 153, 156, 174, 192, 202, 230, 249, 253, 300, 311, 324, 327–8, 331, 335, 343, 348–9, 352
Carter, William, canal owner, 158
Carts, wooden parts for, carried on canals, etc, 123
Caversham, 195, 217
Cement, carried by coasting trade, 100; on canals, etc, 31, 100
Central Junction Canal project, 282
Chalford, 313–14, 317, 319, 337–8, 340
Chalié, John, shareholder, 325
Chalié, Matthew, shareholder, 325
Chalk, carried on canals, etc, 21, 31, 33, 46, 62, 82, 125, 129, 163; carried on tramroads, 108; (and see Lime)
Chalk, sold by canal etc coys, 62, 66–7, 81, 85, 89
Challow, 276, 287
Chamberlain, John, surveyor, 177, 187
Chambers, Christopher, shareholder, 198, 200, 202, 300, 302, 315, 325
Chapman, William, engineer, 54, 266n
Chatham, 15, 61, 65–6, 81–2, 84, 97, 99, 130, 146, 177
Cheese, carried on canals, etc, 19, 21, 210
Cheltenham, 81, 333
Cheltenham & G.W. Union Rly, 249, 333–4
Chertsey, 190, 203, 208
Chichester, 25, 129–30, 135–8, 145–7
Chichester Canal, 135–8, 143, 145–6
Chippenham, 226, 235, 241, 258, 276–7, 280, 287–8, 290
Chippenham Platt (Stroudwater), 297, 301, 305
Christchurch, 166–9, 176, 178
Christie, James, promoter, 67–8, 71–2, 74
Churn River, 316, 323–4, 329–30
Cider, carried on canals, etc, 21
Cirencester, 272, 283, 299, 301, 310–11, 315–17, 319, 322, 324, 329–31, 334, 337–8
Clapham, 102–3
Clark, Dudley, engineer, 110, 113
Clark, William Tierney, engineer, 85
Clarke, Turner P., manager, 165
Clatford, 171, 174

Cleeve, lock, 199
Clegram, William, sen, engineer, 347, 349
Clegram, W. B., jun, engineer, 347, 351–2
Cliff End (Winchelsea), 38, 40–1
Clifton lock, 208
Clowes, Josiah, engineer, 199–200, 316, 323, 342
Coal, carried by coasting trade, 15, 26, 92, 100, 136, 185, 210, 246, 277, 281, 304, 328; by road transport, 20, 300–2; on canals, etc, 19–21, 24, 31, 33–4, 37, 46, 48, 52, 57, 62, 65, 72, 74–5, 78, 80, 82, 100, 106, 111–12, 119–20, 123, 125, 127, 129, 133–4, 146, 152, 159, 161, 163–4, 166, 171, 174, 183, 202, 210, 222, 225–6, 242, 246, 248–9, 255, 259, 261–75, 277–8, 281–2, 284–5, 287–91, 295–7, 299–302, 304–7, 309–17, 324–5, 327–8, 331, 334–5, 346, 348, 350; on railways, 26, 75–7, 255, 290–1, 311, 336, 351; on tramroads, 108, 112, 246, 248, 260; sold by canal etc coys, 62, 65–6, 71–2, 74–7, 286, 302, 324, 326, 329
Coalpit Heath, 246, 248, 256, 260, 282, 311
Coasting trade, 15, 19, 26, 48, 52, 66–7, 93–4, 134–6, 141–4, 147, 154, 169, 261, 272, 324, 348, 353
Coastwise duties (coal), 325
Coate Water, 280, 285, 294
Colemouth Creek, 92
Combe Hay, 139, 263, 265, 267, 269–70, 380
Combe Hay tunnel, see Tunnels
Commercial Docks Co, 108
Commissioners appointed under canal etc Acts, 160–1, 163, 295–8
Containers, use of, 269, 296, 353
Cookham, 195, 208, 210
Copper ore, carried on canals, etc, 117, 222, 242
Corn, carried on canals, etc, 19, 21, 61, 67, 82, 90, 119–20, 123, 127, 130, 134, 142, 151–2, 164, 166, 169, 210, 242, 250, 285, 287, 290–1, 295, 297, 299, 301, 310, 312, 351; on tramroads, 130; by railway, 77
Cosham cut project, 135–7, 141
Coulsdon, 129
Crawley, 129, 132
Crawford Creek, 57, 370–1
Cricklade, 188, 194, 219, 272, 280, 284, 299, 315, 324, 329, 334
Crookham, 153
Crowdy, James, solicitor, 284
Croydon, 25, 102–3, 108–13, 115, 128–9, 147, 374–5

Croydon Canal, 20, 22, 25–6, 35, 81, 84, 102–4, 106–7, 109–16, 128–30
Croydon, Merstham & Godstone Rly, 108, 112, 129–30, 132, 146
Cubitt, William, engineer, 37
Cuckfield, 32
Cuckmere River, 34
Culham, 208
Cundy, N. W., engineer, 147–9

Dadford, James, engineer, 343–5
Dadford, Thos, jun, engineer, 183, 297, 343
Dallaway, John, promoter, 295–7, 315
Dallaway, William, promoter, 297–8
Daneway, 200, 317
D'Arcy, James, proprietor, 161, 163, 176
Darenth River, 57, 370–1
Dartford Creek, 57, 59
Dartford ship canal project, 57–8
Dartford & Crayford Navigation, 57–9, 370–1
Darwin, Dr Erasmus, inventor, 265
Dashwood, J. B., author, 135
Datchet, 107, 212
Dauntsey, 276, 287
D'Avigdor-Goldsmid, O. E., chairman, 78, 80
Davis, Benjamin, engineer, 23, 151
Day's lock, 199
Deal, 49n, 52, 56
Deal Junction Canal project, 56
Dean, Forest of, 19, 174, 210, 255, 272, 274, 282, 284, 302, 304–5, 311, 314, 323–4, 328, 335–6, 346, 351, 353
Dean River, see Dun (Hants) River
Dell Quay, 136
Denyer, John, official, 287, 334
Deptford, 81, 102–3, 105–7, 109–10, 112, 115, 147, 177
De Salis, H. R., 260
Devizes, 122, 155, 174, 186, 236–42, 244, 250, 257, 260–1, 322
Didcot, 217, 252
Disney-ffytche, Lewis, shareholder, 284, 325–6
Dividends, on canal etc shares, 29, 33, 62, 64, 66–8, 75, 77–8, 80, 96, 107, 112–13, 125–6, 134–5, 146, 153, 157, 165, 171, 202, 226–7, 249–51, 259–60, 272, 275, 285, 289, 291–2, 301, 306–7, 310, 312–13, 327, 332, 335, 349–50, 353
Dixon, canal owner, 157
Docks and harbours: Avonmouth, 261, 351–2; Bristol, 244–6; Commercial, 108; Deal, 49n, 56; Gloucester, 224, 343–8, 350, 352; Greenland, 108; Langstone (project), 150; London, 103, 108, 129; St Nicholas Bay (proposed), 49,

51; Sandown (proposed), 52, 54, 56; Sharpness, 223, 348, 351–3; Surrey, 103ff; Surrey Commercial, 108
Dodd, George, engineer, 103
Dodd, Ralph, engineer, 25, 81–2, 84, 102–3, 109, 177–8
Dodd, Robert, engineer, 103
Dorington, Sir John, 336, 339
Dorking, 147, 212
Dorset & Somerset Canal, 243, 264, 268, 278
Downs Dock Act, 1864, 56–7, 379
Drainage, land, 21, 23, 30–2, 38, 48, 52, 60, 79
Droitwich Canal, 297, 328
Drury, Henry, carrier, 93–5
Dudbridge, 302, 305–6, 311, 315
Dudgrove, 329
Dudley Canal, 315, 317
Duke's Cut, 23, 199, 207
Dulwich, 110
Dun (Hants) River, 181–2
Dundas, Admiral, shareholder, 259
Dundas, Charles (Lord Amesbury), promoter, 232, 240–1, 245, 251
Dunkerton, 262–3, 265, 267, 269–70
Dunsford, clerk, 273–4, 281
Dursley, 346

Earle, E. J. V., director, 78
East Farleigh, 78
East Grinstead, 34, 61
East Kent Rly, 100
East Peckham, 75
Eastern Rother River, see Rother
Eastney Lake, 135, 150
Edenbridge, 75–6, 130
Edgcumbe, Thomas and T. S., canal clerks, 145
Edson, Dennis, engineer, 241, 343
Effra River, 102
Egremont, Earl of, 125–7, 132–3, 136, 138, 142–3, 145, 149
Electric traction, see Towing
Eling, 178–9
Elliott, James, engineer, 37
Elmes, James, engineer, 147–8
Elton, Edward, promoter, 341
Emsworth, 129–30, 135, 147
English & Bristol Channels Ship Canal project, 147
Epsom, 102, 147
Erith, 26, 117
Esher, 212
Etchingham, 34
Eton, 204, 252
Ewell, 102, 147
Exchequer Bill Loan Commissioners, 51, 89, 138, 143, 284–6, 289, 329, 345–9

Exeter, 245, 320, 322
Exports, carried on canals, etc, 129
Eynsham, 220

Falmouth, 136, 142
Faringdon, 272–3, 280, 287
Farnborough, 156
Farnham, 119, 153–4, 156, 177
Faversham, 46, 51, 84, 99
Feeding stuffs, carried on canals, etc, 78
Fertilizers, carried on canals, etc, 21, 95;
    see also Manure
Fish, sale by canal etc coys, 302–3
Fishing, in canals, etc, 106, 112, 116, 188
Flash-locks, 31, 47, 88, 125, 167, 188–9,
    192, 194, 199, 208, 295, 332, 335
Fletcher, Thomas, engineer, 346–7
Flint-stones, carried on canals, etc, 89; on
    tramroads, 108
Flour, carried on canals, etc, 21, 66, 82,
    119, 123, 151–2, 210, 310
Fly-boats, 156, 249, 253, 255, 286, 330–3
Folly bridge (Oxford), 198
Forbes, Francis, official, 230–1
Ford, 124–5, 135, 138
Fordingbridge, 167n
Fordwich, 47–8, 51–2, 54, 57
Forest Hill, 110, 116
Forest Row, 61, 71, 74
Fort, George Y., promoter, 178
Fortrey, Samuel, engineer, 166
Fox, Henderson & Co, contractors, 96, 99
Framilode, 205, 216, 281, 297–8, 301–5,
    307, 309, 311, 313, 317, 322, 324, 325n,
    328, 341, 350
Frampton-on-Severn, 300, 344
Freshfield bridge (Ouse), 32–3
Frimley, 151, 153, 155
Frindsbury, 84–5, 89–90, 92, 95–7, 99–
    100
Frindsbury tunnel, see Tunnels
Frome, 274
Frome River, 323, 349; see also Stroud-
    water
Fruit, carried on canals, etc, 22, 94; by
    railway, 77
Fuller's earth, carried on canals, 112; on
    tramroads, 108, 112
Fulton, Hamilton H., engineer, 117
Fulton, Robert, contractor, 343

Gainsborough, Humphrey, official, 195
Gason, John, undertaker, 47
Gasworks, at locks, 250
Gasworks, water transport to, 20, 80,
    106, 117, 146, 159
Gatcombe, 328
Geary, Sir William, promoter, 42, 46, 82
Gibbs, Joseph, engineer, 113

Giles, Francis, surveyor and engineer, 46,
    132, 135, 148, 155, 212–13
Giles, Netlam, surveyor, 38, 46, 132, 135
Gloucester, 24–6, 28, 215, 224, 236, 248,
    250, 286, 290, 296, 300, 302, 304–5,
    309–11, 317, 320, 322, 328, 330–1,
    333–4, 336, 339, 341–53
Gloucester canal project, 302, 317, 341
Gloucester & Berkeley Canal, 22, 24,
    26–8, 201, 223–4, 250–1, 303–5, 309,
    320, 322, 329, 332–3, 341–53, 374–5
Gloucester & Cheltenham Rly, 344–5,
    350
Gloucestershire County Council, 27, 78,
    313–14, 338–40
Godalming, 23, 118–20, 123–4, 132–3,
    145, 177–8
Godstone, 75, 108
Godstow, 198–200, 208
Goring, 199
Goudhurst, 46
Grafton lock, 220
Grain, see Corn
Grain, Isle of, 82, 92, 101
Grand Imperial Ship Canal project, 149
Grand Junction Canal, 24–5, 107, 129,
    207, 212–13, 215–16, 220, 235, 245,
    254, 281–2, 323
Grand Southern Canal project, 25, 46, 68,
    130–2, 135
Grand Surrey Canal, 25, 27, 28n, 49, 81,
    102–8, 110, 112–13, 129n, 146, 177,
    212, 213n, 378–9
Grand Surrey Dock, Canal & Junction
    Rly project, 106
Grand Surrey Docks & Canal Co, 108
Grand Western Canal, 49, 245, 264, 268n,
    322
Grant, B. A., canal owner, 157
Gravel, sales by canal etc coys, 79
Gravesend, 25, 35, 81–2, 84–5, 89–90,
    92–3, 95–7, 99–100
Gravesend & Rochester Canal, see
    Thames & Medway Canal
Gravesend & Rochester Rly, 96–100
Grazebrook, Benjamin, shareholder, etc,
    298, 300
Grazebrook, Joseph, clerk, 300
Great Bedwyn, 244
Great Western Rly, 27, 173–4, 217, 250–
    61, 275, 288, 291–2, 294, 310, 313,
    334–8, 350, 352
Greenwich, 117
Greywell Tunnel, see Tunnels
Groceries, carried by coasting trade, 178;
    on canals, etc, 22, 37, 48, 67, 120, 123,
    134, 142, 249, 290; see also Wines
Guildford, 22, 25, 118–20, 123–4, 127,
    132–4, 147–8, 156, 178, 190

2A

Guildford Junction Rly, 123
Gunpowder, carried on canals, etc, 123

Halkett, Admiral Sir Peter, shareholder, 144
Hall, Edward, engineer, 57
Hall, John, shipowner, 103, 105
Hall, Richard, surveyor, 322, 342
Hallett, William, shareholder, 284
Halling (Medway), 64
Hambleden, 195
Hammer bridge (Ouse), 32
Hampton, 190
Hampton Gay Canal project, see London & Western
Hanham mills, 221-2
Hants & Berks Junction Canal project, 25, 155, 212-15, 250
Hardham, 24, 125-6, 134
Hardwicke, 344
Harmsworth, A. J., owner, 158
Hart's Ferry (Thames), 199
Haskew, Edward, inventor, 343
Hastings, 34
Havant, 129-30, 135
Hawker, George, clerk, 310
Hawkhurst, 34
Hawkwood, 80
Hay, carried on canals, etc, 61, 227
Hayling Island, 135, 138
Haystack Hole (Medway), 65
Haywards Heath, 34
Headcorn, 42
Henley-on-Thames, 121, 195, 211
Herefordshire & Gloucestershire Canal, 201
Herne, 48
Heygates, the, bankers and promoters, 49, 105
Higham, 82, 94, 96-7, 99-100
Higham tunnel, see Tunnels
Highworth, 276
Hill, Joseph, engineer, 177, 181-4
Hobbs, John, undertaker, 221
Hock Crib (Severn), 344-5, 350
Hodges, T. L., MP, 72
Hodgkinson, John, engineer, 271, 345
Hodskinson, Joseph, engineer, 48, 52
Holcombe, 262
Holland, Col T. J., promoter, 100
Holland, Thomas, chairman, 337
Hollinsworth, James, engineer, 138, 183
Hollis, F. J., manager, 164-5
Hollis, George, owner, 163-4, 177
Honeystreet, 174, 261
Hoops, carried on canals, etc, 119, 123, 134
Hops, carried on canals, etc, 19, 47, 61, 67, 93, 95-6, 156; on railways, 77

Hore, John, engineer, 222, 228-9, 295
Horsell, 153
Horsham, 30-1, 125, 127-30, 132, 147
Horsham & Guildford Direct Rly, 135
Houghton (Arun), 125-6
Hungerford, 155, 232, 235, 240, 242-4, 254, 257-8, 260, 322
Hunston, 135, 138
Hunt, Sir Frederick, owner, 158
Hurley lock, 195n
Hythe, 39, 42

Ickham Navigation, 57
Iden lock, 37, 41-2, 46-7
Iffley, 188, 198-9
Imports, carried on canals, etc, 48, 62, 66, 128, 249, 319, 348, 351
Inclined planes, 104, 109-10, 130, 213, 264; Combe Hay, 269-70, 380
Inglesham, 195, 198, 200, 287, 313-14, 317, 319, 322-3, 335, 340
Iron, carried on canals, etc, 34, 60-2, 82, 119, 174, 242, 249, 281, 327; on tramroads, 108; sold by canal etc coys, 62, 66
Iron manufactures, carried on canals, etc, 61, 249, 310
Iron ore, carried on canals, etc, 37, 166
Ironworks, 19, 31, 34, 37, 60-1, 108, 244, 320
Isleworth, 23, 151, 190, 203, 207, 212, 241
Itchen Navigation Ltd, 165
Itchen Navigation–Basingstoke Canal links, see Basingstoke Canal
Itchen River, 15, 22, 24, 87, 152, 156, 160-6, 170-1, 174, 176-80, 182, 184, 370-1
Itchenor, 136

James, William, railway promoter, 56, 146
Jessop, Josias, engineer, 132
Jessop, William, engineer, 31-3, 102-3, 108, 126-9, 132, 152, 176, 183-4, 199-200, 208, 244, 262, 342-3, 345
Joint Stock Trust & Finance Corporation, 158
Joliffe & Banks, contractors, 130n
Jones, Charles, contractor, 319
Jones, George, engineer, 184-5
Jones, Samuel, engineer, 49, 51
Jones, Samuel (of Boston), engineer, 298

Kemmett, John, undertaker, 296, 298
Kempsford, 23, 198, 276, 282, 324, 329
Kempsford–Abingdon Canal project, see Lechlade
Kennet River, 19, 22, 24, 29, 169, 171, 183, 192, 195, 208, 212-13, 221-2,

227–31, 235, 241, 242n, 243, 245–6, 250–1, 253, 295, 370–1
Kennet & Avon Canal, 22, 24–9, 105, 107, 122, 155, 160, 166, 174, 180, 182, 186, 204, 207, 210, 212–13, 215–17, 220, **221–2**, **225–61**, 262–5, 267–8, 270–1, 273–7, 281–2, 284–6, 288, 291, 305–6, 310, 322, 324, 327, 374–5, 380
Kennet & Avon Canal Trust, 261
Kennington, 103–4, 106
Kent County Council, 27, 78
Kent River Authority, 38, 42, 80
Kent & Sussex Junction Canal project, 42–3
Keppel, Zachariah, contractor, 133
Kew, 192, 208
Keynsham, 246
Kilmersdon, 262
Kimbridge, 176, 178–9, 181–4, 186
Kingston-on-Thames, 102–3, 105, 177, 212
Kingston–River Way canal project, 177, 212
Knapp, Edward, lessee, 162

Lacock, 226, 235, 287, 292
Laleham, 203
Lamberhurst, 42, 46
Lambeth, 102
Land carriage, *see* Road transport
Langstone Docks & Ship Canal project, 150
Langstone harbour, 135, 141, 145, 147, 150
Latton, 215, 282–4, 286, 305, 329
Lead, carried on canals, etc, 222
Leather, carried on canals, etc, 61, 160
Leatherhead, 147, 212
Lechlade, 195, 198–200, 202–3, 208, 210–11, 216–17, 283–4, 301–2, 315–17, 319, 322, 324, 328–9, 331–2
Lechlade–Abingdon canal project, 23, 198–9, 276, 302, 317, 322
Leeming, William, canal owner, 157
Le Marchant, Harold, director, 78, 100
Leominster Canal, 182, 201
Lewes, 15, 24, 31–4
Lewisham, 109
Lifts, canal; Combe Hay, 264–8, 380; Dorset & Somerset Canal, 264, 268; Grand Western Canal, 264
Lime, carried on canals, etc, 21, 46, 112, 125, 146, 227, 278; on tramroads, 108, 112; (*and see* Chalk)
Limekilns, 21, 62, 117
Limestone, carried on canals, etc, 21, 61
Limeworks, 108
Limpley Stoke, 246, 263, 267, 275
Lindfield, 31, 33–4

Lingard, Edmund, engineer, 300
Linseed, carried on canals, etc, 67
Little Stour Navigation, 57
Littlehampton, 25, 118, 125, 132
Littleton, E. J., shareholder, 284
Littleton, Sir Edward, promoter, 315, 325
Lock Fund (scc), 270–2, 275
Locke, Joseph, engineer, 96, 155
London, Brighton & South Coast Rly, 31, 107, 135, 145
London Canal project, *see* Monkey Island
London, Chatham & Dover Rly, 100, 149
London, City of, 92, 105, 169, 188–90, 192, 194, 201, 203–4, 208, 211, 216, 219, 241, 281, 284, 332
London, Newbury & Bath Direct Rly project, 257–8
London–Portsmouth barge canal schemes, 25, 38, 111, 118–20, 123–38, 141–6
London–Portsmouth ship canal schemes, 26, 118, 143, 146–9
London Rly project, 129
London & Brighton Rly, 33–4, 108, 145–6
London & Croydon Rly, 26, 106, 113–16
London & Greenwich Rly, 106–7
London & Hampshire Canal & Water Co Ltd, 157
London & Portsmouth Canal project, 128–30
London & South Western Canal Co, 158
London & South Western Rly, 146, 155n, 156, 173–4, 259
London & Southampton Rly, 106–7, 145, 155–6, 164, 252
London & Southampton Ports Junction Canal project, 176
London & Western Canal project, 207, 322
Longcot, 272–3, 276, 278, 280, 282n, 287, 292
Loveden, E. L., Thames Commissioner, 200, 215, 315
Loxwood, 123, 148
Ludgershall, 187, 280
Lydney, 284, 302n, 328, 347
Lymington, 168
Lympne, 39–40

MacMurray's Canal, 117
Maidenhead, 23, 107, 190, 194–5, 203–4, 208, 212, 245–6
Maidenhead–Isleworth canal project, *see* Monkey Island
Maidstone, 18, 22, 27, 60, 62, 64–7, 72, 75, 77–80, 84, 93, 95–6, 99, 156

Maidstone, Rochester & Gravesend Rly project, 96
Malmesbury, 282
Malt, *see* Corn
Maltsters, 230, 242
Manchester & Southampton Rly, 172–3
Manure, carried on canals, etc, 20, 37, 41, 78, 82, 100, 111, 287, 290
Mapledurham, 194–5, 198–9, 216
Maresfield forge, 31
Margate, 49, 51
Marlborough, 232, 235, 241–2
Marlow, 195n
Marsh lock, 195n, 246
Marsham, Charles, promoter, 82; (*and see* Romney, Lord)
Marsham, Lord, shareholder, 85
Marsworth, 215, 281–2
Martin, John, promoter, 107
Martineau & Co, cement manufacturers, 100
Martyn, Henry, undertaker, 227
Mathew, Francis, projector, 166, 232
Maytham (Eastern Rother), 37–8
Meal, carried on canals, etc, 66, 222, 295
Medway Catchment Board, River, 80
Medway Conservancy, 80
Medway, Lower, Navigation, 62, 64–6, 77, 80, 370–1
Medway River, 15, 22–3, 25, 27, 38, 42, 60–8, 71–82, 84, 90, 92, 95, 100, 129–30
Medway, Upper, Navigation, 18, 27, 29, 60–8, 71–80, 95, 100, 161, 227, 370–1
Medway & Thames Canal project, 27, 100–1, 178, 379
Melksham, 235, 276–7, 286–7, 290, 292
Merstham, 108, 129–30, 132
Midford, 139, 263, 266–7, 269, 271
Midhurst, 126–7
Mid-Sussex Rly, 125, 128
Midland Rly, 248, 260, 311, 336–7, 352
Midland & swj Rly, 337n
Mills, on rivers, 31–3, 36, 47–8, 52, 57, 61–2, 66–8, 71, 102, 119, 123, 126, 160, 163, 167–8, 177, 188–9, 192, 194, 210, 227–8, 230, 246, 261, 270, 295–7, 299, 305, 311, 323, 329, 349
Mills, Sir Charles, wharf owner, 171
Millhall (Medway), 64–5, 72
Milton (Portsmouth), 138
Mitcham, 25, 102–4, 108, 129
Mole River, 22, 132
Molesey, 208
Monkey Island–Isleworth canal project, 23, 151, 169, 190–2, 194, 203–4, 241
Monkey Island–Reading canal project, *see* Reading
Morgan, James, engineer, 52, 56
Mortlake, 107, 192

Mudeford, 168
Mylne, Robert, engineer, 200–1, 204, 316, 321–4, 342–5

Nagden Creek (Faversham), 51
Nailsworth, 307, 311
Nash, Richard, of Bath, 222
Nately Scures, 158
National Trust, 124
Naval stores, carried on canals, etc, 25, 60–1, 65–6, 120, 128–30, 137, 147, 151–2
Navvies, 67–8, 86, 97, 127, 152, 185, 243, 300
New Basingstoke Canal Co Ltd, 159
New Cross, 103, 109–10, 112
New Hythe (Medway), 64–5
Newbridge (Arun), 24, 118, 125–7, 130, 132, 141, 147
Newbridge (Thames), 199, 282n, 335
Newbury, 22, 24, 122, 155, 169, 189, 204, 212–13, 217, 227–8, 230–2, 235, 239, 242–3, 249, 254, 257, 259, 261
Newenden, 34, 37–8
Newhaven, 15, 32
Newmill channel (Rother), 37, 42
Newport (Mon), 304–5, 325n, 328, 351
Nickalls, Joseph, engineer, 194
Nicolay, Lt-Col., engineer, 41
Nock, John, mason, 200
Norfolk, Duke of, 111, 345
Northam, 162, 164, 179–80, 182, 185
North Wilts Canal, 25, 203, 207, 215–17, 272, 274, 282–7, 290, 292–4, 305–6, 317, 323, 328–9, 331, 334, 376–7
Northmoor lock, 220
Norton, engineer, 268
Norwood, 110, 116

Oats, *see* Corn
O'Carroll, Patrick, promoter, 165
Odiham, 151–3
Oil, carried on canals, etc, 78, 353
Old Basing, 153, 155, 213
Old Windsor lock, 208
Osiers, sale of, by canal coys, 112
Osney lock, 199, 200, 220
Ouse (Sussex) River, 15, 23–4, 31–4, 129–30, 372–3
Outram, Benjamin, engineer, 268–9
Overton, 176, 178
Oxford, 22–4, 26, 188–9, 194, 198–200, 202, 216–17, 219–20, 272, 276, 280, 282, 289, 301, 320, 322, 324, 332, 335
Oxford–Burcot Commission, 22–3, 188, 195, 199n
Oxford Canal, 22–4, 183, 199, 201–2, 204, 207, 210, 217, 219–20, 235, 272–4, 281–2, 284, 288, 297, 322
Oxford Rly, 217

Paddington, 129, 207, 281
Paddock Wood, 75–7, 96
Page, Francis I, owner, 227, 231
Page, Francis II, owner, 231, 235, 243
Page, Frederick, owner, 210, 228n, 231, 243, 276
Painswick, 332
Pallingham Quay, 22, 125–6
Pangbourne, 198
Paper, carried by coasting trade, 100–1; on canals, etc, 66, 95, 100–1, 117, 119, 210
Pares & Heygate, bankers, 49
Parker, Joseph, surveyor, 151
Pasley, Major-Gen, railway inspector, 94n, 97
Passenger-carrying, on canals, etc, 82, 95, 118, 225, 244, 249–51, 260, 349
Paul, Sir George, committeeman, 341
Paulton, 262–5, 267, 269, 274
Peas, carried on canals, etc, 67
Peckham, 103, 106
Penge, 109, 111
Penshurst, 60–1, 67–8, 71, 75, 79
Penshurst Canal company, 67
Penton Hook lock, 208
Perkins, Richard, committeeman, 263–4
Perry, James, shareholder, 315–16, 319, 322, 324–5
Peterborough, Earl of, promoter, 276, 284
Petersham, 192
Petworth, 125–6, 128
Petworth Canal, 126–7
Petworth marble, carried on canals, etc, 127
Pewsey, 24, 160, 174, 180, 187, 244, 310
Phillips, John, author, 82, 108, 170–1
Pickfords, carriers, 348
Pidcock's Canal, 302n
Piddinghoe, 31–2
Pilstye bridge (Ouse), 31
Pinkertons, contractors, 32, 92, 94n, 152
Pinkhill lock, 200, 203, 220
Pleasure boating, 27, 42, 67, 79–80, 95, 100, 112, 116, 121, 124, 135, 146, 211, 216, 220, 261, 301, 339
Plumstead, 117
Plymouth, 136, 142
Poole, 136
Poor Employment Act, 1817, 345
Poore, John, merchant, 171, 181
Port of London Authority, 108, 220
Portsbridge cut, 141, 145
Portsea Canal, 69, 135, 137–8, 141–3, 145
Portsmouth, 15, 25, 38, 68, 102, 111, 118, 120, 125, 128–30, 132, 135–8, 141–2, 144–8, 150, 165, 177, 212
Portsmouth Ship Canal project, 148–9

Portsmouth, Southampton & London Junction Canal project, 177
Portsmouth & Arundel Canal, 25, 69, 71, 118, 127, 130, 135–8, 141–6, 149, 178, 374–5
Potter, Richard, shareholder, 336–7, 339
Pottery, carried on canals, etc, 123, 249
Press-gangs, 65–6
Price, Henry H., engineer, 106
Priddey, John, engineer, 297–8, 300, 315
Priestley, Joseph, jun, official, 284
Pritchard & Hoof, contractors, 85
Provis, W. A., engineer, 281
Pucklechurch, 282
Pulborough, 125, 128–30, 147
Pynock, James, undertaker, 296
Pyott, Edward, proprietor, 160–1, 165

Quarries, 21, 263, 282, 286, 300

Radcot, 198–9, 220, 272–3, 306, 335
Radstock, 262–7, 269–71, 274–5, 291
Radstock tramway, 271, 274–5, 291
Rafts, coal waggons carried on, 269
Railway-canal interchange facilities, 75, 106, 254, 259, 311
Railway Commissioners, 107
Railway construction material, carried on canals, etc, 156, 253, 288–9, 310, 334
Railway & Canal Traffic Act, 1888, 338–9
Railways, horse, see Tramroads
Ralph, John, engineer, 277
Rastrick, J. U., engineer, 96–7
Reading, 19, 23–4, 26, 107, 128, 151, 189, 192, 194–5, 198, 203–4, 208, 210–12, 216–17, 221, 227–8, 230, 241, 245–6, 249, 252, 254–5, 259, 261, 272–3, 277, 281, 322
Reading–Monkey Island canal project, 23, 151, 190, 192, 194, 203, 212, 241
Reading–Windsor–Isleworth canal project, 212
Reculver, 49
Redbridge, 169–71, 173–4, 178–84, 186
Regent's Canal, 52, 107, 129, 204n
Reigate, 108, 129, 147
Rennie, John, engineer, 25, 37–8, 40, 46, 49, 51, 68, 82, 102–3, 109–10, 125, 128–30, 132, 135, 176–7, 179, 182–4, 186–7, 204, 208, 212, 235, 241, 243–4, 262–3, 282, 323, 343, 345
Rennie, Sir John, engineer, 149–50
Rennie, George and John, jun (Sir John), engineers, 37, 138, 141–2, 145, 147–9
Reservoirs, 46, 72, 74, 110, 296; Coate Water, 280, 285, 294; Norwood, 110, 113; Sydenham, 110, 113; Tockenham, 280, 289; West Grimstead, 184
Richborough, 48

Richmond, 107, 203, 220
Ridding, Thomas, clerk, 179
Road carriages, steam, 253
Road transport, 16, 19–20, 26, 48–9, 51,
  60–1, 66, 76, 95, 110, 119–20, 136–7,
  153, 155–6, 174, 178, 183–4, 209, 211,
  221, 225, 228, 230, 245–6, 249, 267,
  269, 271, 273, 296–7, 302, 332
Roads, 15–16, 19, 21, 26, 39, 41–2, 49,
  60–1, 66, 78, 89, 103, 106, 112, 117–18,
  127, 222, 225, 299, 339
Roadstone, see Stone
Roberts, Charles, engineer, 171
Robertsbridge, 34, 38
Rochester, 15, 25, 66, 80, 82, 84, 89, 92–4,
  96–7, 99, 146
Rolle, Denys, shareholder, 181
Rolvenden, 37
Romney lock, 204, 208
Romney, Lord, promoter, 42, 46, 64, 82,
  85; (and see Marsham, Charles)
Romney Marsh, 38–40
Romsey, 153, 169–71, 181
Rother (Eastern) River, 15, 25, 34, 37–8,
  39–42, 46–7, 130, 372–3
Rother Levels, 37–8
Rother (Western) River, 24, 118, 126–8,
  372–3
Rotherhithe, 25, 102–3, 109–10, 112, 147,
  177
Rowe, John, engineer, 103
Royal Clarence Ship Canal project, 26,
  117
Royal Commission on Canals & Water-
  ways, 220, 260
Royal Engineers, 39, 149
Royal Military Canal, 17, 25, 37, 38–42,
  46–7, 185, 374–5
Rushey Green, 104
Rushey (Thames), 200, 203
Rye, 15, 25, 34, 37–8, 40–2, 46
Rye & Robertsbridge Canal project, 38
Ryeford, 301, 311
Ryelands, Upper, bridge (Ouse), 33

Sacks, hiring of, by canal etc coys, 230
St Aubyn, William, canal owner, 157
St Nicholas Bay Harbour & Canterbury
  Canal project, 25, 46, 49–52, 379
Salisbury, 22–4, 26, 153, 160, 166–8, 173,
  176, 178–87, 236–7, 239–40, 323
Salisbury, Lord, projector, 166
Salisbury–Lymington canal project, 168
Salisbury & Southampton Canal, 22–4,
  163, 166, 176–7, 178–86, 187, 378–80
Salt, carried on canals, etc, 22, 163, 222,
  287, 290, 310, 328, 348
Salterns, 135, 138, 146
Saltford (Bristol Avon), 226

Saltpetre, carried on canals, etc, 95
Sand, carried on canals, etc, 42, 82, 146
Sandford, 188, 198–9
Sandown Castle, 49, 52, 56
Sandwich, 15, 47–9, 51–2, 54, 56–7
Sapperton tunnel, see Tunnels
Saul junction, 303–4, 313–14, 343, 346,
  349
Scot's Float sluice (lock), 37–8
Seaton Navigation, 57
Selhurst, 110
Selsey, Lord, promoter, 30
Semington, 241, 261, 274, 277, 280, 285,
  291
Severn Bridge (rly), 336, 350–3
Severn Commission, 313, 336–8, 350, 352
Severn Junction Canal project, 282–3,
  305n; see also North Wilts Canal
Severn River, 22–4, 201, 212, 216, 221,
  281, 284, 295–8, 301, 304–5, 315–17,
  319–20, 322, 325–9, 339, 341–2, 344,
  348–51
Severn & Canal Carrying Co, 314, 352
Severn & Wye Rly & Canal, 284, 306,
  347, 352
Sewers, Commissions of, (Brede & Pett),
  38; (Hants Avon), 166, 168; (Itchen),
  160; (Medway), 60–1; (Oxford), 188,
  198; (Rape of Bramber), 30; (Stour),
  47, 52, 54
Shaftesbury, Lord, 282
Shalford, 123, 132–3
Sharpness, 223, 305, 322, 336, 342, 345–
  53
Sharpness New Docks etc Company,
  294, 336–8, 352
Sheerness, 65, 95, 177
Sheffield bridge (Ouse), 32–3
Sheffield, Lord, shareholder, 33
Sheperdine, 352
Shepperton, 190, 208, 220
Shifford lock, 220
Shillingford, 194, 216
Shiplake, 195n
Shoreham, 15, 30–1, 146
Shorncliffe, 38–41
Shortbridge, 31, 33
Shrivenham, 244, 276, 287
Siddington, 282, 317, 328–31, 336
Simcock, Samuel, engineer, 232, 235
Simmonds, Henry, carrier, 93
Simmonds & Jackson, carriers, 77
Simmonds & Masters, carriers, 95
Slates, carried on canals, etc, 21, 82, 242
Small Hythe (Eastern Rother), 37
Smeaton, John, engineer, 23, 31, 52, 102,
  119
Smith, Edward, shareholder, 84, 111
Smith, George, surveyor, 177

Smith, J. B., canal owner, 157
Smith, William, engineer, 32, 262–4, 268
Snape, P. G., clerk, 312
Snape, W. J., clerk, 312, 337
Somerset & Dorset Rly, 275
Somersetshire Coal Canal, 24, 27–9, 32, 100n, 139, 241, 246, 255, **262–75**, 277, 286, 288, 290–1, 378–80
Sonning, 151, 190, 192, 195, 208, 211
South Cerney, 324, 329
South Eastern Railway, 75–8, 96–7, 99–100, 259
South London Union Rly project, 107
South Marston, 278, 280, 287, 289
South Wales Rly, 335, 350
Southampton, 15, 24, 26–7, 128, 153–6, 160, 163–5, 169, 173–4, 176–7, 179–83, 185–6, 212, 240, 337
Southampton Canal project, 27, 178
Southampton & Salisbury Canal, see Salisbury & Southampton Canal
Southern Railway, 100
Southsea, 150, 165
Sowerby, William, engineer, 107
Staffs & Worcs Canal, 297, 302, 315, 317, 325–6, 328, 337–8
Staines, 107, 188–90, 192, 194, 201, 204, 208, 212, 216, 219–20, 241, 281, 335
Steam-engines, 90, 110, 113, 138, 141, 176, 253, 270, 275, 288, 305, 323, 328–30, 342, 349
Steamboats and tugs, 52, 76–80, 94–7, 101, 107, 138, 142, 144–5, 148, 217, 220, 249, 254, 259, 311, 336, 339, 349–51
Stevens family, navigation owners and carriers, 36, 124
Stockbridge, 169, 171
Stonar Cut (Stour), 48
Stone, carried on canals, etc, 21, 33–4, 37, 42, 78, 82, 112, 222, 242, 249, 278, 287, 290, 292, 300–1, 309n, 327, 330, 332, 339, 346; on tramroads, 112, 248; sold by canal etc coys, 62, 66, 72, 286; see also Limestone, Petworth marble
Stonehouse, 205, 311
Stonehouse & Nailsworth Rly, 311–12, 336
Stopham, 127, 134
Stour (Kent) River, 15, 22, **47–57**, 372–3
Stour, Little, Navigation, 57
Stourbridge Canal, 241, 315, 317
Stourport, 297, 317, 328, 349–50
Stratford, Fernando, projector, 226
Stratford-upon-Avon, 281
Stratford-upon-Avon Canal, 25, 268n, 282
Stratton, 287, 290
Streatham, 110

Strood, 81, 84, 89, 92–3, 95, 97, 99–100
Strood tunnel, see Tunnels
Stroud, 23, 287, 295–8, 300–1, 305–7, 309–11, 313, 317, 319–20, 324, 329, 333, 336, 338
Stroud & Severn Rail Road project, 307–9, 333
Stroudwater, 295, 297–8; see also Frome River
Stroudwater Navigation, 22–4, 27–9, 198, 202, 205–6, 216, **295–314**, 315–17, 319–20, 322, 328, 332–6, 337n, 338, 340–6, 349, 374–5
Sturry, 47, 49, 52
Sunbury-on-Thames, 190, 203, 208
Surrey & Hampshire Canal Corporation Ltd, 157
Surrey & Hants Canal Company, 157
Surrey & Kent Canal, 102
Surrey Iron Rly, 102, 108–9, 112–13, 116, 128–30, 146
Surrey, Sussex & Hants Railroad project, 146
Sussex Ouse River, see Ouse
Sutcliffe, John, engineer, 263–4, 268–9
Sutherland, Alexander, engineer, 25, 42–3, 46
Swansea, 328, 351
Swindon, 140, 215, 217, 252, 276, 278–80, 282, 287–90, 292, 294, 305, 310, 323, 333–4, 337
Swindon, Marlborough & Andover Rly, 337
Swindon & Cheltenham Extension Rly, 336
Swift Ditch, 188, 198, 199n
Sydenham, 109–10, 112

Tar, gas, carried on canals, etc, 261
Taskers of Andover, 174
Taunton, 236, 245, 320, 322
Taunton, J. H., official, 335–6
Taylor, John, poet, 166
Teddington, 27, 103, 208, 211, 216, 220, 304
Teise River, 42
Telford, Thomas, engineer, 21, 48, 51–4, 89, 346
Temple lock and mills, 195n, 246
Tenterden, 37, 42
Test River, 169–70, 176, 178, 181
Tetbury, 299, 301
Tewkesbury, 296
Textiles, carried on canals, etc, 249
Thame, 281
Thames Conservancy, 23, 219–20, 335–6, 337n, 338
Thames Ditton, 178, 212
Thames Head, 322–4, 329

Thames Navigation, 188–204, 207–20, and *passim*
Thames & Medway Canal, 18, 25–7, 35, 42, 46–7, 51, 64–5, 81–6, 89–101, 102, 141, 319, 376–7, 380
Thames & Severn Canal, 23–8, 78, 100, 176, 195, 198–203, 206–7, 210, 215–16, 220, 249–50, 271–2, 274, 276–7, 281–4, 286, 287n, 290, 292, 294, 299n, 300–2, 304–7, 309–12, 315–40, 341, 376–7, 380
Thames & Severn Canal Trust, 292, 294, 313, 338, 340
Thorney Island, 135, 138
Tiles, carried on canals, etc, 21
Tillingham River, 38
Timber, carried by coasting trade, 15, 169; on canals, etc, 19, 21–2, 31, 34, 42, 46, 48, 57, 60–2, 65–6, 78, 82, 106, 110, 112, 119–20, 123, 125, 127, 129, 134, 151–2, 158, 166, 174, 210, 222, 242, 249, 292, 310, 312, 348, 352–3; on tramroads, 112; sold by canal etc coys, 62, 66–7, 72; *see also* Bark, Cart-parts, Hoops
Timsbury, 262
Tockenham, 289
Tonbridge, 23, 60–2, 66–8, 71–2, 74–6, 79–80, 130
Tooting, 103–4
Tovil, 27, 80
Towing, Towing Paths, 30, 32, 37, 48, 61–2, 64, 71–2, 74, 82, 84, 86, 94, 97, 112, 116, 148, 160, 168, 178, 192, 194–5, 198–201, 203–4, 208, 211–12, 216, 222, 228, 244–5, 301, 304, 347, 349; electric, 27, 101
Townshend, Hook & Co, papermakers, 100
Tramroads, 46, 177, 264; Alderbury (projected), 184; Avon & Gloucestershire, 246, 248, 255–6, 260; Bristol & Gloucestershire, 246, 248, 256; Bullo Pill, 284, 304, 345; Combe Down, 222; Croydon Canal, 112; Croydon, Merstham & Godstone, 108, 112, 129–30, 132, 146; Foxhanger–Devizes, 244; Gloucester & Cheltenham, 344–5, 350; London projected, 129; London–Portsmouth projected, 102, 128; Radstock, 271, 274–5, 291; SCC, 263, 268–9, 271, 274; Severn & Wye, 284, 304, 347; Stroud & Severn projected, 307–9, 333; Surrey Iron, 102, 108–9, 112–13, 116, 128–30, 146; Tonbridge wharf & SER, 75; Wantage, 292
Transport, Ministry of, 314
Trowbridge, 24, 258n, 276–7
Trows, 301, 316, 319, 326, 328, 345, 348
Truss, Charles, carrier, 192

Truss, Charles, clerk, 203
Trye, C. B., committeeman, 343
Tugs, *see* Steamboats
Tunbridge Wells, 75–6
Tunnels, canal, 22, 33, 100, 130, 176–7, 213, 235; Alderbury (projected), 176, 181, 184; Bruce (Savernake), 380; Combe Hay, 100n, 263; Cricklade, 284; Frindsbury (*see* Strood); Greywell, 152–3, 158, 380; Hardham, 24, 125–6, 134, 142, 144; Higham (*see* Strood); Merstham (projected), 129–30; Sapperton, 100, 199, 316–20, 335–6, 380; Southampton, 181–6, 380; Strood, 18, 82, 85–6, 89–90, 92, 94–100, 319, 380; Wellow, 263
Turgis Green, 151–2
Turnpike Trusts, 16, 26, 136, 156, 273, 297; *see also* Roads
Twerton, 225, 245, 253
Twinhoe, 270–1

Uckfield, 33–4
Udiam, 34
Uffington, 287
United Commercial Syndicates, 292
Up Nately, 158
Upper Medway Navigation & Conservancy, 78–80
Upstreet, 49, 51
Upton, John, clerk, 345–6
Upton, May, engineer, 31, 133

Vanderstegen, William, Thames Commissioner, 195, 202
Vauxhall, 25, 102–3, 106–7, 213n

Walker, James, engineer, 68, 71, 257
Walker, Michael, surveyor, 177
Walker, Ralph, engineer, 82, 84–5, 344–5
Wallbridge (Stroud), 296, 299, 301–2, 306, 309, 311, 315, 319, 338, 340
Wallingford, 219, 273, 276
Walton-on-Thames, 190, 203
Wandle River, 102–3, 117, 130
Wandsworth, 102, 107, 117, 129
Wandsworth Creek, 108
Wandsworth–Croydon Canal project, 102
Wantage, 273, 276–7, 280, 287, 290–1
Wantage, Lord, 294
Wantage Tramway, 292
Ward, canal owner, 157
Warwick & Napton Canal, 281, 282
Water, sales of, 157, 159, 314; sale by canal etc coys, 105, 107, 110, 220; supplies to canals etc, 62, 71–2, 90, 92, 102, 109, 134, 138, 176–7, 235, 263, 270, 275, 280, 284–6, 294–6, 303, 315–16,

322–4, 330, 332, 338, 342, 346, 349; *see also* Reservoirs, Steam Engines
Waterloo bridge, 103, 129, 146
Wathen, Joseph, shareholder, 298, 315
Watt, James, engineer, 323
Weald of Kent Canal project, 25, 38, **42–3, 46–7**, 49, 130, 379
Weldon, Robert, inventor, 264–7
Wellow, 263–7
Wells, Dymoke, contractor, 32–3
Welton colliery, 263n, 267, 271
West Grimstead, 184
West Grinstead, 30, 132
West Sussex County Council, 146
Westbury, 258, 274, 290
Western Canal, *see* Kennet & Avon Canal
Western Junction Canal project, 215, 281–2, 323
Western Union Canal project, 25, 212–13
Weston, Samuel, engineer, 232, 235
Weston, Sir Richard, undertaker, 118
Wey (including Wey (Godalming)) Navigation, 22–3, 25, 27, 29, 36, **118–20, 123**–4, 127, 130, 132, 134, 141, 143, 147, 151, 153, 156, 177–8, 190, 212, 220, 372–3
Wey & Arun Junction Canal, 22, 25, 118, 120, 123–5, 127, **130, 132–5**, 136–8, 141, 143–4, 178, 376–7
Weybridge, 36, 118, 124, 151, 153, 190, 212
Weybridge, Woking & Aldershot Canal Co, 158
Weymouth (Melcombe Regis), 160, 258
Wheat, *see* Corn
Whitchurch (Thames), 199
White Lion Junto, 236, 239–40
Whitminster, 302–4, 314, 341, 343
Whitmore, William, engineer, 268
Whitstable, 48, 51, 56
Whitworth, Robert, jun, engineer, 49, 51
Whitworth, Robert, senr, engineer, 23, 169–70, 178, 192, 198, 204, 235, 241, 263, 277, 316–17, 322, 324, 341–3
Whitworth, William, engineer, 276–7, 282, 284
Wilcot, 187
Williams, Edward Leader, engineer, 313, 336
Williams, J., promoter, 138
Wilson, J. W., engineer, 117

Wilts & Berks Canal, 24–5, 27–8, 140, 207, 210, 215, 217, 241, 244–6, 249, 252, 265, 268, 270–4, **276–94**, 305, 306n, 309, 317, 323, 327–8, 330–2, 334, 337n, 340n, 376–7
Wilts & Berks Canal Co Ltd, 292
Wilts, Somerset & Weymouth Rly, 258, 274, 290
Wiltshire County Council, 338
Wimbledon, 117
Wimbledon & Wandsworth Canal project, 116–17
Winchelsea, 38, 41
Winchester, 22, 24, 87, 153, 155–6, 160–1, 164, 176–7
Winchfield, 153
Windsor, 189–90, 192, 204, 208, 212, 246, 252
Wines, carried on canals, etc, 22, 48
Winkton, 167n, 168
Woking, 70, 123, 151, 155, 158–9, 213n
Woking, Aldershot & Basingstoke Canal & Navigation Co Ltd, 158
Woodhouse, John, engineer, 346
Woodmill, 162, 164
Wool, carried on canals, etc, 21, 61, 160, 210
Woollen goods, carried on canals, etc, 67, 295
Woollen industry, 19, 295–300, 305
Woolwich, 26, 117, 177
Wootton Bassett, 272, 276–7, 280, 282, 287, 289
Wootton Rivers, 187, 260
Worcester, 89, 222, 304, 317, 320, 322, 349–50
Worcester & Birmingham Canal, 201, 242, 317, 320, 348, 352–3
Worcester & Gloucester Union Canal project, 320, 322
Writhington, 263
Wroughton, 287
Wylye River, 166
Wynde, Arthur, undertaker, 296

Yalding, 42, 60–1, 80
Yantlet Creek, 92
Yantlet Creek–Colemouth Creek canal, 92–3
Yarranton, Andrew, engineer, 166, 233
Yeoman, Thomas, engineer, 295, 297–8